LORD LYONS

LORD LYONS

A DIPLOMAT IN AN AGE OF

NATIONALISM AND WAR

BRIAN JENKINS

McGill-Queen's University Press
Montreal & Kingston • London • Ithaca

ISBN 978-0-7735-4409-3 (cloth)
ISBN 978-0-7735-9635-1 (ePDF)
ISBN 978-0-7735-9636-8 (ePUB)

Legal deposit third quarter 2014
Bibliothèque nationale du Québec

Printed in Canada on acid-free paper that is 100% ancient forest free (100% post-consumer recycled), processed chlorine free

This book has been published with the help of a grant from the Research Office of Bishop's University.

McGill-Queen's University Press acknowledges the support of the Canada Council for the Arts for our publishing program. We also acknowledge the financial support of the Government of Canada through the Canada Book Fund for our publishing activities.

Library and Archives Canada Cataloguing in Publication

Jenkins, Brian, 1939–, author
    Lord Lyons : a diplomat in an age of nationalism and war / Brian Jenkins.

Includes bibliographical references and index.
Issued in print and electronic formats.
ISBN 978-0-7735-4409-3 (bound). – ISBN 978-0-7735-9635-1 (ePDF). – ISBN 978-0-7735-9636-8 (ePUB)

1. Lyons, Richard Bickerton Pemell Lyons, Earl, 1817–1887.
2. Diplomats – Great Britain – Biography. 3. Diplomatic and consular service, British – History – 19th century. 4. Great Britain – Foreign relations – 1837–1901. 5. United States – Foreign relations – 1861–1865. 6. Franco-Prussian War, 1870–1871 – Diplomatic history. I. Title.

DA565.L86J45 2014   327.42092   C2014-902386-3
                                               C2014-902387-1

Typeset by James Leahy in 11/14 Minion Pro

Contents

Preface

Richard Bickerton Pemell Lyons believed that an extensive private correspondence with the foreign secretary of the day was essential for effective diplomacy. The papers of the second Lord Lyons, together with those of his father, are on deposit at the West Sussex Record Office, Chichester. There are some 300 boxes, many of them catalogued in only a rudimentary way, and that number does not do justice to the collection's extent. Lyons's correspondence was carefully copied into thick, hard-backed notebooks. Many boxes contain several of these. The papers of both lords are held by the Record Office for the Trustees of Arundel Castle on behalf of His Grace the Duke of Norfolk, whom I thank for permission to quote extensively from them. Of Lyons's private correspondence with foreign secretaries, that with Malmesbury, Clarendon, Russell, and Derby (Stanley) proved especially useful and revealing. I thank the Earl of Malmesbury for permission to quote from the papers of the 3rd Earl, which are available for research at the Hampshire Record Office. Those of the 14th and 15th Earls of Derby were consulted by courtesy of the Liverpool Record Office, Liverpool libraries. The Bulwer Collection, held by the Norfolk Record Office, was another very useful source, and I thank the Record Office for permission to quote from it. The papers of Sir Edward Malet, held by the Duke University Library, North Carolina, are equally important. I wish to express my appreciation for the unfailing helpfulness of the staff of the Duke Library and of the staffs of the several Record Offices. Alan Readman, then the county archivist, and the search room staff in Chichester merit special praise. They were kindness itself, ever ready to help guide me through the Lyons papers.

That my many visits to Chichester became a pleasure was due to the hospitality, generosity, and friendship of my hosts, Lynne Amon and her husband Jim. She made sure I saw the surrounding countryside, and he gained me temporary admission to the local tennis club. Never has a researcher had it so good.

No thanks would be complete without acknowledging the two women who read the entire manuscript and were constant in their encouragement. My wife Jean was one and the other was, after her, my best friend and most loyal supporter, the late Josephine Langham Brown, to whose memory this book is dedicated.

Brian Jenkins

Bickerton Lyons on his mission
to Naples. Lyons Papers.

Lyons on the eve of going to
Washington. Lyons Papers.

Lyons in Washington. Photograph by Matthew Brady, ca 1860–65, Library
of Congress Prints and Photographs Division, Brady-Handy Collection,
LC-BH824-5129.

Lyons and Henri Mercier, *Harper's Weekly*, February 1862.

Lyons with family of his sister Anne, Ems, September 1877. Lyons Papers.

Lyons as ambassador to France. Lyons Papers.

LORD LYONS

Introduction

Richard Bickerton Pemell Lyons's entire adult life was one of diplomacy. He entered the service on coming down from university and died fifty years later shortly after his retirement. By then he was considered Britain's most successful diplomat. His influence lived on long after his death thanks to the "Lyons school" of British diplomacy, whose pupils have been somewhat condescendingly termed the "new bureaucrats" of professional diplomacy. Two contemporaries, Charles Sumner, the chairman of the United States Senate Foreign Relations Committee, and Austen Henry Layard, a minor Liberal minister put out to graze in diplomatic pastures, claimed that the Foreign Office was Lyons's absolute guide, that he slavishly followed the instructions he received via the telegraph. But a historian of his service in Washington, from where he had no rapid line of communication with London, described him admiringly as a "man of sense, of industry, of honesty and of great dignity and one earnestly devoted to his country and his profession." It was a profession, however, derided by a Tory foreign secretary as the grave of genius and the paradise of the dull. Had that been the case, Lyons's success would require little explanation. But it was not. He was never merely the messenger of the instructions he received from home.[1]

Since he was not born into that rarefied segment of British society from which members were traditionally recruited, why had he chosen this profession and how had he entered it? While he was still an adolescent friends suggested that the Foreign Office might be the place for him, and his education at a public school had instructed him in the values of a "Foreign Office mind," which considered character more important than intellect and gave precedence to public service over self-advancement. It was his father's transition from ambitious naval officer to diplomat, one he reversed on the eve of the Crimean War, that opened this door for his son. Sir Edmund Lyons was rewarded for his performance as British minister to the fledgling nation of Greece with Bickerton's appointment as an unpaid attaché. He brought with him the emotional baggage of his intense relationship with his mother and the dismal failure of his undergraduate career at Oxford.

He was always looking forward to living with her, talking with her, and loving her, he wrote. Whenever in difficulty or doubt, he asked himself what she would advise him to do because he was sure he would then act "right." This "mother complex" did not escape his father, who described his elder son's love of his mother as "excessive." It certainly shaped his character and influenced his behaviour as a senior diplomat. Without being a misogynist, for he developed friendships with married and mature women, he considered women a disruptive influence in a diplomatic mission. This was one of the lessons he chose to learn when his father was succeeded as minister in Athens by Thomas Wyse. Lyons eventually became notorious for always seeking to exclude married men from any legation or embassy of which he was the chief. Young men, whose company he preferred, felt it necessary to apologize when they decided to marry. Yet his bachelorhood was often in conflict with his intense ambition. Having disappointed his parents academically while at Oxford, he remained true to his commitment never again to disappoint them. He promised to succeed professionally. Marriage might have eased his progress as it did that of Odo Russell, the only contemporary who came to rival him in reputation. Ironically, in light of his aversion to wedlock, it was the brilliant marriage of his younger sister Minna to the future 14th Duke of Norfolk that did so much to elevate the social standing of the Lyons family and provide father and son with influential connections in their common relentless pursuit of promotion.

Bickerton Lyons began his career in Athens and for almost fifteen years lay becalmed in the diplomatic doldrums. His advance in the profession was slowed by a chronic problem with his eyes, which caused him to take frequent medical leaves, and by an extended leave to care for his brother. The policy which he helped first his father and then his father's successor to implement was that of creating in Greece a stable, relatively liberal constitutional monarchy which would cease undermining an Ottoman Empire that Britain had long sought to prop up as a bulwark against Russian penetration of the Mediterranean. The construction of the Suez Canal was to reinforce Britain's strategic resolve. Yet during his years in Athens, especially the last handful which he served under Thomas Wyse, Lyons developed a framework of diplomatic conduct. It was a foolish junior, he quickly realized, who was disagreeable to a head of mission no matter how much the fault lay on the senior man's side. On the other hand, it was a wise chief who won the loyalty of his juniors with hospitality, courtesy, consultation on matters of business, and a little formality. Herein lay the origins of Lyons's conduct as a chief of mission. He cultivated a family atmosphere, dining with his juniors several times a week, was solicitous of their welfare, and keen to ease whenever possible the burden of work. In return, they gave him their personal devotion and loyalty. It was in Athens that he decided that British legations and embassies should always be symbols of the nation's wealth and power, and national pride rather than creature comfort explained this almost obsessive concern. But he also grasped the importance of being personally liked by fellow members of the diplomatic corps, seeing in personal affability and excellent dinners the obvious means to this end. Before leaving Athens, Lyons played an important role in the settlement of the notorious Don Pacifico affair, and those privy to the negotiations credited him with the lion's share of the credit. Unfortunately for him, his contribution went largely unrecognized in London.

Foreign Office recognition finally came when he served as Britain's unofficial representative to the Papal States, an anomalous post which he probably owed to his family connection to the Catholic Norfolks. British policy sought stability lest Italian turmoil led to a general European conflict. Lyons was expected to urge reform of the unrepresentative and unpopular papal government, and this he did but without success. In Britain's opinion, the French and Austrian troops who guaranteed the pope's survival as a temporal sovereign, by propping up the regime over a large area of the peninsula, were preventing the development of constitutional freedom throughout Italy. However, Lyons's analyses of the problems, the clarity of his dispatches, and the solid good sense of his recommendations won him admirers at the Foreign Office. He excelled in his performance of the diplomat's fundamental duty to keep his masters in London fully informed of the state of affairs in Rome and the true feelings of its citizens. Lord John Russell, who had appointed Lyons to Rome, greatly admired his achievement in regaining for Protestant Britain a measure of influence with the papal authorities. He dissuaded the Vatican from establishing a Catholic hierarchy in Scotland, which might have ignited another explosion of anti-Catholicism, an accomplishment made possible by his repudiation of expressions of impotent discontent and ill will and his commonsensical rule of not interfering in matters over which his government could not exercise effective control. So impressed was Russell that on taking charge of the Foreign Office in 1859 he urged his nephew Odo, who had succeeded Lyons in Rome, to make as much of the position as his predecessor had done.

Lyons was a man who considered quiet a luxury for which one ought to be willing to pay. He deliberately avoided publicity even though he craved promotion. As his career prospered he made discreet use of the press to advance policies but only rarely had personal dealings with journalists and never played to the press as Odo Russell was frequently accused of doing. This helps to account for the curious criticism of Lyons in the present-minded research and analytical paper published on the Internet by the Foreign and Commonwealth Office. His concept of ambassadorial duties, it sniffs, "would be unacceptable by today's standards." But his postings took him to the heart of four of the great international issues and crises of the second half of the nineteenth century: Italian unification, the American Civil War, the decline of the Ottoman Empire, and France's replacement by the newly unified Germany as the dominant Continental power. At the time of his appointments to the United States and to France profound crises were not imminent. He went to Washington to maintain amicable relations so far as was possible with a Republic which the Foreign Office considered expansionist and aggressive. Soon he was obliged to explain the Union's disintegration and collapse into civil war. In his response to this profound domestic crisis, which had very serious international consequences, Lyons reached the peak of his diplomatic effectiveness and developed the diplomatic formula to which he was to remain true following his return to the European scene.

He foresaw a brutal and bloody conflict from which he expected the Union ultimately to emerge victorious, but for the triumph to be pyrrhic. After massive bloodletting, he could not conceive of a Union cordial enough to function after being reconstructed. Hence his assumption that a more prudent policy than that pursued by President Lincoln during the spring of 1861 might have led to peaceful separation and then to peaceful reunion. This dubious notion was a product of his dismay at the terrible loss of life inevitable in war, although lurking in the background was the fear of a suspension of cotton cultivation in the South and the disruption of its trade, which might do irreparable damage to that flywheel of Britain's economy, the textile industry. Nevertheless, his private sympathies were with the Union and were generated by a loathing of slavery, a respect for law, and a greater social affinity for the North than for the South.

Once the fighting began he held fast to the position that the war's outcome should be decided by the belligerents themselves. He counselled non-intervention, concluding that interference without the backing of force would do more harm than good and might lead to war with the Union. He had dedicated himself to averting an Anglo-American confrontation. How different the modern world would have been had Britain accepted any of the French invitations to joint intervention, thereby sealing the division of the United States. To discourage the Union from adopting policies that would harm British interests, Lyons was prepared to keep it off balance on possible British recognition of Confederate independence. He did not invite quarrels, however. His humble role, as he described it, was by watchfulness and minute attention to detail to forestall differences, and when disagreeable questions did inevitably arise to prevent them from descending into serious disputes. As an element of this strategy, he worked hard and successfully to establish a fruitful relationship with the secretary of state, William Seward, and eventually had great influence with him. By sidestepping questions of principle, he avoided a collision and reached an understanding with Seward not to kick up a row over the treatment of British subjects. He was determined to keep open to the very last minute the door to "spontaneous" Union action to resolve problems, constructing what he called a golden bridge across which the Union might retreat from national vanity with its dignity intact.

Americans did not care "at all for words," Lyons advised his government, so to restrain them when they appeared likely to act rashly he improvised a "strict concert" with his French counterpart in Washington. The Union, already at war with the Confederacy, had every reason to avoid alienating both European powers. But in moments of genuine crisis, such as that sparked by the removal of Confederate diplomats from a British vessel on the high seas, Lyons recommended military preparedness. The Americans had to be disabused of the notion that there was no limit to his nation's forbearance. The Palmerston Cabinet had decided on a firm response before Lyons's recommendations reached London, but they arrived in time to confirm its necessity. He then played a vital role in the peaceful resolution of the *Trent* affair. He had an equally important and constructive role in the successful negotiation of a treaty to suppress the slave trade and was proud that it carried his name. When he returned to Washington in the fall of 1862, having been home on leave, where he tirelessly counselled against meddling in the conflict, the Chairman of the Foreign Relations Committee welcomed him back to his great duty of maintaining peace between the two nations. He had earned American respect by his straightforwardness and honesty in all his dealings. His conduct certainly influenced William Seward's notion that an Anglo-American special relationship was possible, while at the Foreign Office he was now recognized as one of Britain's most intelligent and skilful diplomats.

"Sick headaches" caused by stress led to Lyons's resignation as minister to the United States, but he had every expectation of receiving an appointment that was even more prestigious if not quite so taxing. He was named ambassador to the Ottoman Empire and went to Constantinople carrying the traditional British policy of defending the empire's territorial integrity, but not to the extent of war. Hence he quietly modified the policy. He strove to prop up the empire long enough so that the collapse when it came would cause few international ripples. As in Rome, he struggled again with scant success to persuade the regime to implement reforms that would by easing discontent extend its life. He had more success in his efforts to persuade the Porte to withhold concessions to France which might give it absolute control of the Suez Canal, a strategic lifeline to the Indian Empire. His diplomatic effectiveness was hampered, however, by the blow Bismarck had delivered to Britain's credibility during the recent crisis over Schleswig-Holstein. Lyons responded by drawing the French ambassador into an effective partnership. This made possible a settlement of the issue of the Danubian Principalities that did not, at least on the surface, further erode the empire's territorial integrity. Indeed, he recovered much of the influence which his predecessor had lost. This was enough to win him the most senior post in the diplomatic service, that of ambassador to France, despite his lack of a wife.

In France, Lyons was a witness to two decades of profound domestic change and a far-reaching loss of French international influence. When he arrived in 1867, at the height of the Paris Exhibition, the Second Empire appeared to be secure, the emperor appeared to be Europe's most influential figure, and France appeared to be the Continent's most powerful state. He reported extensively on Napoleon's efforts to ensure the survival of his dynasty, on the folly of his war with Prussia which destroyed the empire, on the siege of Paris, on the insurgency of the Commune, on the shift eastwards of the centre of European power from the French capital to the German, and on the long domestic struggle to develop a generally acceptable form of government. The options were a restoration of the monarchy, a third Bonapartist empire, or the creation of a Third Republic. Eventually, the Republic was established and was to survive until the Second World War. Lyons welcomed the revival of French military strength in the belief that it would correct the imbalance of power on the Continent. For him the primary object of diplomacy was its peaceful re-establishment. He worked hard to revive the rapprochement with France, a task complicated by the state of French public opinion, anglophobia, the chronic instability of French governments, and by the seemingly instinctive and certainly traditional Foreign Office distrust of their cross-Channel neighbour. Indeed, as retirement approached, the francophile Lyons became disenchanted with the French.

Confident that he would never be instructed to do anything that was morally wrong, Lyons did not spend time fretting whether the policies he had, with his reports, helped shape were ethical. Nor did he slavishly follow his own instructions. Instead, he interpreted and modified them and was in this sense a very modern diplomatist. An ideal ambassador, he believed, possessed the confidence of his government and shared its sentiments but was not a political partisan. Lyons was proud of his non-involvement in British politics, and his promotion to the highest ambassadorial rank by the Tories has seen him identified as the first diplomat to be advanced for professional not political considerations. Yet he was faced on several occasions with the sensitive issue of the relationship between professional diplomat and party politics. Clarendon, a foreign secretary who had been a diplomat, admitted the advantage to the foreign service if men in important posts were not partisans, for if they were the result would be an upheaval whenever there was a change of government. This was not the position of Gladstone, the self-confessed political moralist at the head of Liberal governments, or of Granville, the son of a former ambassador to France. Both paid lip service to the notion that it was not right to ask a man to vote against his political opinions, having mistakenly identified Lyons as a Tory, yet both insisted that it was a very dangerous doctrine that a peer should refuse to take a political position on account of personal convenience. Gladstone later refined his argument. So long as some Tories intended to vote for a measure, he saw no good reason why a diplomat of "no party" should not do the same. Lyons did obey the Cabinet summons to return to London to vote for the disestablishment of the Church of Ireland, fearful that if he did not he might well lose the Paris embassy, but on later occasions he dug in his heels.[2]

Lyons believed that an ambassador should not be an aspiring politician and thus always thinking of his position and image at home. His task was to ensure that he understood fully the wishes and views of the government he served; hence an extensive private correspondence was essential. Equally, he should be acquainted with diplomatic business and transact it accurately and diligently. In other words, diplomacy was a profession. An ambassador should desire to remain long at his post, form friendships with the statesmen of the nation to which he was accredited, be able to take part in society, and seek to improve relations and smooth difficulties by personal influence. He should avoid as far as possible expressing an opinion to a foreign government on any political matter which was likely to excite domestic controversy, and avoid meddling in matters with which properly he had little if any concern.

A signal achievement of his in the fractured United States was to be hailed as a model ambassador. In Rome, Washington, Constantinople, and Paris he protected his reputation by refusing to engage in covert activities. Espionage would violate the straightforwardness which was for him the essence of British diplomacy. He ensured that any such activities were conducted without the involvement, indeed without the knowledge, of any legation or embassy of which he was chief.

Lyons was equally careful to maintain excellent relations with the permanent staff of the Foreign Office, especially the undersecretaries. Henry Addington became something of a mentor to him during his early career, and in his successor, Edmund Hammond, he had a family friend. Housed until 1861 in a dilapidated and cramped building in Downing Street, then moved for seven years to neighbouring houses in Whitehall Gardens before returning to the new building on the original site, the overworked staff was employed on menial tasks not policy formulation. The absence of consistency on promotions, governed as they frequently were by personal connections or political affiliation, rather than seniority or proven ability, created from time to time a poisonous atmosphere in which animosity thrived. On occasion the two undersecretaries, the parliamentary and the permanent, so disliked each other that they engaged in mutual frustration instead of co-operation. When Tenterden succeeded Hammond as permanent undersecretary he failed to inspire the loyalty of his staff, and whenever the foreign secretary was a poor manager, and Granville was a case in point, confusion reigned. Evidence that the staff was "downcast, disgusted, [and] dismayed" brought appeals for a thorough reorganization of the office from top to bottom. This was not the most sound bureaucratic base for the development of a coherent foreign policy.[3]

The sesquicentennial of the American Civil War has led to a revival of historical interest in the second Lord Lyons. This is not inappropriate, for his years in Washington were the most important of his career. His appointment as ambassador to France placed him at the pinnacle of his profession, but the Franco-Prussian War greatly reduced the diplomatic significance of the post. Between 1861 and 1864, however, he held the future of Anglo-American relations in his hands, and given this daunting responsibility it was little wonder that the resultant stress took its toll. Appropriately, three volumes of his Civil War dispatches have been published (2005). Somewhat earlier (1993) selections from his confidential correspondence appeared in *Private and Confidential Letters from British Ministers in Washington to the Foreign Secretaries in London, 1844–67*. In his two volumes on *Lord Lyons*, which he subtitled *A Record of British Diplomacy* (1913), Lord Newton had very little to say of his years in Rome and sped through his service in the United States. Yet these two postings effectively defined Lyons's career. Half of Newton's first volume and the entire second are devoted to Paris, yet momentous as they were, these twenty years did not test Lyons to the same extent as had the five he spent in Washington. However, Newton's assessment of Lyons, from the point of view of someone who had worked closely with him, has been influential. But he joined the Paris embassy late in Lyons's tenure and at a time when he was in decline physically and of reduced importance diplomatically.

The Lyons known to Newton was painfully shy, an impression supported with an imaginative story that over the course of a week at Woburn Abbey he never left the gardens "because he was so much embarrassed by the salutations of an adjacent lodge keeper." Edward Malet told a similar tale of an ambassador who did not look his house servants in the eyes but distinguished them on the shape of their calves. Of course, he may in this instance have been checking whether the footmen had taken advantage of his dispensation permitting trousers instead of formal attire. Lyons's natural shyness prevented him, Newton wrote, from deriving much enjoyment from society. He was a "total abstainer" who claimed that during his five years in Washington he never took a drink. He boasted that the chief entry in his Paris police dossier was of his absence of vice. "He had never been in debt, never gambled, never quarrelled, never as far as was known, ever been in love," and Newton attributed his failure to marry to his devotion to his younger sister, the Duchess of Norfolk and her family. He never took the slightest exercise, Newton added, detested outdoor life, and never cared for sport. He was, however, a large eater and gave excellent dinners, and nothing could "exceed the dignity and faultless taste of the Embassy arrangements." Little wonder he was a "heavily built man" who resembled the cartoonist's depiction of the "conventional British squire."

His diplomatic assets as listed by Newton included a command of several languages, acute perception, a peculiarly retentive memory, and a love of work. He was so industrious that it was a disadvantage to his subordinates, leaving them little responsible work to do. His industry, Newton wrote, was matched by "an almost preternatural caution." He never volunteered advice to a foreign secretary, and the opinions he expressed were always based on "conscientious investigation." He began the day studying the French newspapers but kept the press at arm's length. The only possible criticism of his conduct was his narrow life, moving in too restricted a circle. "He was essentially a diplomatist of the old type, consorting entirely in Paris with the official classes." Nevertheless, he achieved an unparalleled position in British diplomacy even though some colleagues were perhaps more brilliant. This is the image of Lyons that has endured, for as the only detailed account of his career it has naturally influenced historians.

Beckles Willson in *Friendly Relations: A Narrative of Britain's Ministers and Ambassadors to America* (1934) borrows heavily from Newton. Daniel Carroll in *Henri Mercier and the American Civil War* (1971) summarizes Lyons as a professional diplomat of long training, fairly young for his position, the host of stiff, formal dinners, solid, prudent, and reserved, a complement to the French minister's "chancy flamboyance." D.P. Crook's Lyons in *The North, the South and the Powers, 1861–1865* (1974) was a fussy, shy, and earnest bachelor, a perceptive, temperamentally cautious, and dutiful defender of British interests. In Philip E. Myers's *Caution and Cooperation: The American Civil War in British-American Relations* (2008) Lyons remains something of an enigma because the author sees in British conduct during the war a continuation of the rapprochement which he believes the two nations had reached over the preceding half-century. Had that been the case Lord Napier would surely have been retained as British minister to the United States and Lyons would in all likelihood never have gone there.

Raymond Jones's *The British Diplomatic Service, 1815–1914* (1983) acknowledges Lyons's diplomatic ability and skill but develops an interpretation which Newton merely implied. By 1860, Jones wrote, the future of British diplomacy "belonged to the new bureaucrats, Lyons, Malet and Monson – self-effacing, subordinate, and anonymous – fit persons to execute the policy of the foreign secretary at the behest of the electric telegraph." Of course, Lyons was not at the end of a telegraph line during the American Civil War. However, he had trained both Malet and Monson. While he describes Lyons as painfully shy, T.G. Otte, *The Foreign Office Mind: The Making of British Foreign Policy, 1865–1914* (2011), credits him with significant posthumous influence through the graduates of the "Lyons school" of diplomacy. Amanda Foreman, in her magisterial *A World on Fire: An Epic History of Two Nations Divided* (2010), approaches Lyons with the eye of the skilled biographer. He was an eccentric character, uncomfortable with displays of emotion, was reluctant to look people in the eye, never developed a taste for alcohol and smoking, was "witty and erudite" in conversation, "tactful and discreet to the point of parody," had few interests outside work, and his most regular female correspondent was his younger sister, the Duchess of Norfolk. More recently still, Walter Stahr in his *Seward: Lincoln's Indispensable Man* (2012) describes Lyons as "something of a prig" who neither drank nor smoked, never relaxed in Washington, was prejudiced against Americans in general and against Seward in particular, yet was diligent, careful, and calm.

Since so much of what has been written about Lyons is based upon his last few declining years in Paris, it is at odds with his earlier life. He was reserved but had cured his shyness by acting in amateur theatricals at Woburn Abbey. He was cautious but not preternaturally so. He was industrious but rarely if ever to the disadvantage of his subordinates. He did make use of the press in Washington, Constantinople, and Paris, and in both the American and French capitals did on occasion deal directly with journalists. He was not prejudiced against Americans, and he developed a friendly relationship with Seward, as he had with Cardinal Antonelli in Rome and with Fuad in Constantinople and a succession of French foreign ministers. He enjoyed society and developed a wide circle of friends; only in later life did he resolve to drink only water with his meals, and took exercise in the form of walking. More importantly, his non-partisanship, his sterling reputation for integrity, and confidence in his ability led the Queen to recommend him first to Gladstone and then to Disraeli as a suitable foreign secretary; in the latter instance she had the support of a senior Tory cabinet minister. Almost a decade later a Tory prime minister, Lord Salisbury, offered him the portfolio. But cursed with chronic ill health, most evident in a persistent and violent cough which caused a very painful sore throat, weary, if not physically exhausted, and never having sought personal popularity or dramatized himself or his achievements, he had no wish to be on his feet in the House of Lords explaining and defending the nation's foreign policy.

CHAPTER ONE

Beginnings

Richard Bickerton Pemell Lyons was born on 26 April 1817, the second child and first son of Edmund Lyons, a "sea officer." The Royal Navy had been famously described the previous year as the "means of bringing persons of obscure birth into undue distinction, and raising them to honours which their fathers and grandfathers never dreamt of." Thanks to skill in the marriage mart which tied it, at least in Ireland, to the aristocracy, the Lyons family would have escaped this snobbish censure. One branch of the family migrated to the sugar island of Antigua, where a useful connection to the deputy governor guaranteed access to land; the Lyons plantation eventually totalled some 560 acres worked by 250 black slaves. Sugar planting rivalled naval service as a means of rising above one's station at birth, while preferential tariffs and the popularity of the product virtually guaranteed wealth. The ultimate aim of many British planters was to return "home" once a fortune had been made, and this was the path trodden by the Lyons family during the second half of the eighteenth century. John Lyons, the eldest of eleven children, returned to the island to manage his inheritance and married a cousin, Catherine, the daughter of the fifth Marquis of Vallado; with their surviving child they quit this unhealthy environment following the death of the second born. In England, another dozen children were born and Catherine died shortly after delivering the last of these. The widower soon remarried, taking Elizabeth Robbins as his wife in 1804, and she quickly presented him with three additional children.[1]

John Lyons settled his large family in the New Forest of Hampshire, leasing a property close to the little town of Lymington. St Austens was a manor house of simple design and elegance, and with the estate of 190 acres it befitted a country gentleman. As a man of some wealth and social standing, he made appropriate provision for his numerous progeny, eleven of them young men. Five entered the service of the East India Company, he purchased a military commission for a sixth, and three others joined the Royal Navy. As elsewhere in British life, connections were helpful if not essential. Edmund, the fourth-born son, was especially fortunate to have as his godparents Captain Sir Richard Hussey Bickerton and Lady Bickerton, she being a distant relation of the Lyons family. Bickerton secured the boy's underage admission to the Navy and arranged for his own cousin, Richard Hussey Moubray, to accept him aboard his frigate. Keen to learn and eager to please, young Lyons attended well to his lessons, steered clear of the "evil" members of the ship's company, and was rewarded with the rating of a midshipman in 1805. As a lieutenant he later distinguished himself while serving in the Dutch East Indies, and his return home in December 1811 brought him back within the comfortable and beneficial reach of his godfather. Admiral Bickerton soon signed Lyons's commission as a commander, and three years later, as commander-in-chief of the Portsmouth naval base during the allies' somewhat premature celebrations of the final defeat of Bonaparte, the admiral assigned him to ceremonial duties that brought promotion to the vital rank of post captain.[2]

Although with peace Edmund Lyons faced an uncertain period ashore on half pay, he decided to marry the woman to whom he was devoted. Augusta Louisa Rogers, aged twenty-three, thus a year younger than the bridegroom, was the second of the two daughters of the late Captain Josias Rogers, from whose executors John Lyons had leased St Austens. With the outbreak of war with Revolutionary France in 1793, the Rogers men, three brothers and a nephew, had joined the fleet dispatched to the West Indies to dispossess the French of their islands. Only one of them, Thomas, returned safely from the notoriously unhealthy Caribbean and became a surrogate father to his nieces. The young couple married on

18 July 1814, and Augusta came with a respectable dowry. She had inherited a moiety of her father's estate, which twenty-one years earlier he had valued at £18,556, and she and her sister were joint heirs of their uncle Thomas's estate. The newlyweds appear to have set off on a tour of newly restored Bourbon France, for the honeymoon was emerging as an element of British popular culture, and met with Thomas Rogers in Tours only for him to die literally in his niece's arms. Over the next seven years four children were born to the couple: Anne Theresa Bickerton on 26 August 1815, Richard Bickerton Pemell on 26 April 1817, Edmund Moubray on 27 June 1819, and Augusta Mary Minna on 1 August 1821. Three of them thus bore the names of their father's naval patrons. As the family grew in number, so its finances became a problem, one that was to leave an indelible imprint on its members. A captain on half pay, which was less than £200 a year, needed to live economically if he lacked a substantial private income. Edmund Lyons's hopes of receiving a small fortune in prize money as a result of his conspicuous role in the capture of the Dutch spice islands were dashed first by the Treasury, which was committed to paying down the massive war debt, and then by the grasping directors of the East India Company, who had been the principal beneficiaries of the rich haul of spices. Hence he was dependent on his share of the profits of the sugar plantation, which averaged £240 a year. The shares became a source of acute sibling tensions, largely because of the irresponsibility of several of Edmund's brothers, who revealingly turned to him for advice. "I look to you as the person who has supplied the place of my poor father in the world," one wrote, for "I conceive that you act in everything as he would have done." When two brothers sailed for India with commissions in the East India Company's service they carried Edmund's strictures that gambling was the parent of ruination and debt the root of perdition. They had before them the sad example of their elder brother Theodore, who had disgraced himself and in his brothers' eyes shamed the family before his early death.[3]

Edmund's realization that he was living beyond his means saw him, as had Jane Austen's fictional half-pay captain in *Persuasion*, seek a "residence unexpensive by the sea" where he could indulge his passion for sailing. This quest finally brought the Lyons family to St Peter Port, Guernsey. The island had much to recommend it. The chief administrative officer, Sir John Colborne, was another New Forest man and a hero of Waterloo, where he had led the charge that finally broke Napoleon's Imperial Guard. On Guernsey, he had launched an ambitious program of improvements that promised a healthy, interesting, exciting, and educational environment for the Lyons children. A product of one of England's great public schools, Winchester, he reformed and provided for the expansion of the failed Elizabeth College, where parents were assured that their sons would receive a "complete classical education" together with instruction in English, French, "commercial arithmetic," writing, and the "history of revealed religion." Here was a curriculum to equip them for "future situations in adult life, independently of the learned professions." Edmund and Augusta Lyons were two of the many parents who responded. Their elder son, known always as Bickerton to family and friends, entered the school with a guide to personal conduct compiled by his parents. Envy, anger, avarice, ingratitude, indolence, and pride were all to be repudiated, but ambition, industry, liberality, wisdom, and patience were to be embraced. True wisdom consisted of the fear and love of God, while study of the word of God was man's noblest employment. Without God's merciful assistance, his mother warned Bickerton, he would be unable to resist the "temptation to do wrong by which even at your age you are surrounded." His father also laid stress on academic distinction, and Bickerton's winning of a Latin prize in 1828 prompted the excessively proud parent to fund an annual Lyons prize at the school. He also anticipated that his clever son would have a brilliant university career.[4]

Edmund Lyons remained desperate to return to sea duty, and the death of his young brother Maine Walrond Lyons, who was serving as a lieutenant in the Aegean, opened the door. Hearing of the loss, the Duke of Clarence, heir presumptive to the throne, Lord High Admiral and Edmund's former commander, appointed him to the command of a forty-six-gun frigate. When the *Blonde* anchored at the Crown Colony of Malta on 20 May 1828, Lyons came highly recommended. Both Admiral Bickerton and Admiral Saumarez, Guernsey's favourite naval son, hailed him in letters to the commander of the fleet as a man of intelligence and great ability. Lyons was "blessed" domestically as well as professionally. He was accompanied by the wife he "perfectly adored" and their four "amiable, clever and perfectly healthy" children. They were at last living in relative comfort, having rented the most expensive house in Valetta, and Lyons organized the home schooling of his children. He sought to provide his sons with a sound grounding in grammar and style, and his choice of a work by a central figure of the Scottish Enlightenment, William Robertson, suggests he accepted the contention that home education ensured a "close relationship between children and parents so that the latter could best guide the youthful passions into polite channels." But Bickerton was soon fretting that this informal regime was not enhancing his prospects of achieving the academic distinction his parents were anticipating. Fear of failure, of disappointing his father and his mother, but especially the latter, was making its insidious way into his mind.[5]

Assessing her brood, Augusta credited Moubray with "great impetuosity and love of every description of amusement"; thought Anne had many "little disagreeable habits" and needed a "little animation"; and considered Minna the "sweetest child in the world." But Bickerton was her favourite for already at the age of eleven he was exhibiting good sense and steadiness. She brought his trifling faults to his attention and urged him always to speak the truth, to avoid the appearance of equivocation, which she knew he did not "really possess," to keep up the religious duties that bring "internal peace," to never allow himself to be mastered by difficulty, and to cultivate the habit of constant employment. A great mass of information might be absorbed in moments otherwise passed in "listless activity," she repeatedly reminded him. This rigorous schedule was one to which he adhered throughout his life.[6]

Their father's patrol duties in the Eastern Mediterranean naturally encouraged the boys to take an interest in a region where the contemporary decline of the Ottoman Empire was a source of British concern. Russia's territorial encroachments in the north appeared inexorable, and its suspected encouragement of the rebellion by fellow Orthodox Christians, the Greeks, was presumed to be acquisitive. Further to the south, Ottoman control of Egypt was crumbling. A ruthless ethnic Albanian, Mehemet Ali, not only had made himself a virtually independent ruler of the viceroyalty but plainly had imperial ambitions. Confusion characterized British policy even though Ottoman territorial integrity had long been considered essential to the balance of power, the protection of the Indian Empire, and prevention of Russian penetration of the Mediterranean. Although the Greek rebellion enjoyed considerable popular as well as poetic support in Britain, the governing Tories disparaged the rebels as ignorant, depraved, and unfit for full independence. However, the Sultan resisted Anglo-Austrian pressure to accept their mediation as a means of checking further Russian encroachment of the region. Instead, he ordered his forces, reinforced as they had been by the troops of Mehemet Ali to whom he promised territorial gains, to intensify the campaign against the rebels. Disaster followed, for the combined Turkish and Egyptian fleets were destroyed in Navarino Bay by a British force, and Russia declared war.[7]

After his initial and successful tour of duty in these treacherous political waters, Edmund Lyons returned to Malta for a refit of the *Blonde*, and when it sailed again for the Aegean on 30 January 1829 both his sons were aboard. The voyage would expose them to the wider world, would test Moubray's affinity for a life at sea, would familiarize Bickerton with the classical world, and would introduce them to influential men who might one day be useful patrons. Lyons appointed as his ship's chaplain a young man with considerable teaching experience gained at his father's school in Greenwich, the site of the magnificent Royal Hospital for Seamen. Unfortunately, in his first sermon to his captive congregation he assured them that on the Day of Judgment all true believers would rise from their graves with their flesh intact. He failed to make clear whether they would have the appearance of youth and beauty or of age and decrepitude. Lyons, a devout Anglican, scorned the sermon as the most "abominable," "absurd," and "disgusting" ever preached. However, he and the chaplain/schoolmaster devised a Spartan educational regime for the boys which began with gymnastics at 5:30 a.m. followed by hours of schooling. When the *Blonde* reached the Aegean there were excursions to islands redolent of Greek mythology. All the while Bickerton and his mother were corresponding with astonishing frequency, her gentle corrections of syntax and grammar contributing to his development as a writer of admirable clarity. She strove to reassure him that he was witnessing "many uncommon, interesting and important events" while boys of his age at school in England were confined to the playground. His opportunities for improvement and the accumulation of information would be useful in later life, she promised. Her disappointment would be bitter, she added, were he to fail either to improve in every branch of education or to develop his abilities to the utmost. This did little to still his fear of failure. He would never neglect any of her advice, he replied. "I love you too well for the very idea of giving you pain not to make me miserable."[8]

The British embassy at Constantinople lacked an ambassador. The incumbent, Stratford Canning, resigned when the Tory prime minister, the Duke of Wellington, rejected his advice to create a Greek state that had generous boundaries and acknowledged Ottoman suzerainty. He was replaced by Sir Robert Gordon, younger brother and principal confidant of the foreign secretary, Lord Aberdeen. His demanding assignment was to end the Greek rebellion and the Russo-Turkish War. Lyons, who had joined the British squadron at Besika Bay outside the Dardanelles, was chosen to transport the new ambassador to the Ottoman capital and instantly won Gordon's appreciation by ensuring that he beat the French ambassador there. Bickerton and his brother as fellow passengers suddenly found themselves travelling in elite company and arriving at Constantinople at another crucial moment in the empire's modern history. One consequence of the Russian advance on the capital was the "seduction of the subjects of Turkey from their allegiance." Five centuries of Ottoman rule had not extinguished ethnic identities in the Balkans. Desperate to halt the disintegration of their empire, riddled as it was with administrative inefficiency and corruption, several sultans had attempted reform. Mahmud, the current ruler, had eliminated or emasculated those elements of Turkish society that "from entrenched positions of ancient and accepted privilege" might challenge his will. He had ordered ministers and military officers to shave their beards and discard their traditional and distinctive attire. Not that any of this impressed George Finlay, the Philhellene historian, who mocked the "Royal Spirit of Tailoring." Tight pants and shaven chins, he observed, would not "renovate the rotten fabric of civil society." However, as an amused Bickerton wrote to his mother, corsets were now to grace the "capacious waists" of Turkish women.[9]

Bickerton was impressed with the mosques and the minarets from which the *muezzin* called the faithful to prayer five times a day, and the city was full of reminders of a past glory which ought to have inspired him as a young classical scholar. Instead, he was soon heartily sick of the capital and horrified by the retributive justice, decapitation, meted out on its streets. He longed to return to Malta and to his mother, and not even a visit to the seraglio excited his interest. His father, on the other hand, thinking as ever of career advancement and the future of his boys, relished mixing with the "best society." Lord Yarmouth, later the Marquess of Hertford, a member of the ambassador's retinue, was the heir to an immense fortune and was reputed to control as many as eleven parliamentary seats. Lyons was already thinking of the foreign service as a suitable profession for his older son and so pushed him into the society of men "in that line." His homesickness eased by the news that his mother and sisters would be visiting the following spring, Bickerton happily kept company with the diplomats. He was amused by the news that Gordon's ceremonial audience awaited the identification of a propitious day by the Sultan's soothsayer, and when it finally arrived he and his brother were minor participants in the exotic event. Although barely twelve, Bickerton was not overawed. He described the Sultan, who sat on a silver divan, as "rather a short man with a long black beard and a very expressive countenance," and Mahmud's request several days later that the boy visit him "created an *extraordinary* sensation." The Sultan gave him a handful of gold pieces, which he generously shared with his family, and he jokingly informed his mother that Mahmud had proposed that his elder sister Anne be given to him in marriage.[10]

All the while the rumble of Russian artillery was growing louder, and Lyons began to fear for the survival of the empire and the dynasty. But the triumphant czar had compelling reasons to accept terms, not the least of which was the inevitable scramble among the Great Powers to share in the spoils were he effectively to expel Turkey from Europe. A provisional peace was negotiated, although it was 1833 before the final terms were signed. Mahmud, to secure a reduction in the war indemnity, made additional territorial concessions to an independent Greece, having been assured of Britain's anxiety to ensure he retain his remaining dominions. Throughout this delicate period Bickerton had been fully integrated into the select company. He took meals with the diplomats, had the freedom of the library, and was taught card tricks by Yarmouth.

When the entourage moved to the ambassador's summer residence at Therapia on the Bosporus, a place of "surpassing beauty and novelty" where the villas appeared to overhang the water, he and his father were reunited with Moubray, who for the past two months had been living aboard a French frigate improving his language skills. Soon, an ambitious thought took shape in the mind of the *Blonde*'s restless captain. Why not chart the Bosporus and cruise the Black Sea noting Russia's forts, defences, and naval strength? In the event of another crisis this would be valuable intelligence. Under the guise of a training session for his long-inactive men, Lyons set sail with both sons aboard. This proved to be no pleasure cruise. Gales, heavy seas, heavy rains, blizzards, thick fog, and arctic cold made for a miserable experience and were agony for a violently seasick Bickerton. The naval intelligence collected was more widely disseminated than Lyons had intended. The copies of his reports mysteriously went astray, having probably been stolen by servants in the pay of the French and the Russians.[11]

"Nothing interrupts Bickerton's studies," his father assured his mother. He did have time to relax, taking afternoon walks, riding with Gordon and playing cricket, while his detailed record of his correspondence suggested a well-organized and orderly young man. Nevertheless, it was a disconsolate youth who waved goodbye in the spring of 1830 first to his mother and sisters and then to his father and brother. He broke down and kept to his room for an entire day following the latter departures, but the decision to leave him behind was a calculated one. Gordon was plainly fond of him, and as a family friend observed, should Bickerton's "mind and talents continue to expand as they hitherto have done, the secretary of states [*sic*] office is the place for him." Lyons had employed three tutors for his son, and they were supplemented on an informal basis by Edward Villiers. More academic than diplomat, he was the younger brother of the future Earl of Clarendon. Villiers had described Bickerton to Augusta Lyons as a prodigy, astonishing the company "by construing Livy on sight, doing it perfectly." Yet he and Gordon strongly recommended that Bickerton be sent to England to complete his education. They agreed that time at public school would be more profitably spent than continued residence at Constantinople. The departure of Villiers to secure his fellowship at Merton College, Oxford, and Gordon's certain replacement as ambassador by the new Whig government back home, settled the matter. Bickerton sailed for Malta in the spring of 1831, but his extended residence in the Ottoman capital had served his father's purpose. Gordon promised always to befriend him to the extent of his ability. The adolescent of fourteen was more mature, more socially assured, and more self-reliant than the youth who had sailed from Malta two years earlier.[12]

Edmund Lyons was transferred from the *Blonde* to the command of a more modern frigate, the *Madagascar*, when its captain dropped dead of a stroke. In late October, he sailed from Malta to Spithead, where the ship was to be paid off. On board was his entire family. Once home he had a friendly audience with the "Sailor King," who had read his report of the Black Sea cruise, and received a "wonderful reception" at the Admiralty. He had also developed excellent political connections via a correspondence with the son and private secretary of the new Whig prime minister, Earl Grey. Lyons had in his letters shown such an impressive grasp of the situation in the Eastern Mediterranean that Charles Grey drew him to the attention of his father. Lyons was invited to call on the prime minister, and the few minutes assigned to the meeting extended to an hour, at the end of which he was asked to return the following day to meet with the new foreign secretary, Viscount Palmerston. The pair "sucked [my] brains well," Lyons informed Augusta. They then insisted that the Admiralty waive the regulations which would have prevented him from resuming command of the *Madagascar*. He was to sail it back to the Eastern Mediterranean, where Mehemet Ali's designs on Syria threatened to spark another Eastern crisis. The Whigs were also sending Stratford Canning back to the region as ambassador to the Porte. In line with his earlier proposals, he was to secure a more generous and defensible Greek frontier with the Ottoman Empire. This, together with a substantial Greek loan guaranteed by the Great Powers, was expected to simplify the search for a European prince to accept a Greek throne. The British assumed he would behave as a constitutional monarch.[13]

What have you done with Bickerton? a friend asked Lyons. The immediate answer was that he had been sent to the village of Elm in Somerset for intense tutoring in the classics, which dominated the public school curriculum. His tutor was Dr William Bayly, the stipendiary curate, who had undoubtedly been suggested by the Reverend John Coles, the husband of the other Rogers daughter and thus Bickerton's aunt. A recent companion of aristocratic diplomats, he was dismissive of Mrs Bayly, with her "small vulgarities" and "rather low origin," and was condescending towards the couple's two children. He quickly revised his opinion of the household. He admired his tutor's erudition and became fond of Mrs Bayly, who proved to be good-hearted and generous. The Baylys, he recognized, were very nice people "in their way." He had been taught a useful lesson. It was unwise to form an opinion of anyone in a hurry. In future he would invariably wait "for the test of time."[14]

Bickerton's uncharitable initial response to his tutor's wife may have been influenced by his unhappiness on again being separated from his mother. Their relationship remained extraordinarily intense. "You cannot imagine how I long to see you if it were only for a moment," he wrote shortly after his arrival in Elm and her return to Malta. "I can hardly write anything but my grief at not being with you, and to write to you is the only consolation I have." He wished to be with her selecting colours for the house, talking about alterations, and taking long walks. "Indeed I do not know that I was ever so happy as that last time at Malta, when we were quite alone. While we were in England we were never quite so, and I used to think even my Aunt [Coles] and Cousin an interruption to my happiness with my dearest Mama."[15]

Sensing Bayly's reservations about his mastery of composition, which the tutor drew to the attention of his father, Bickerton was haunted by the fear that he would disappoint his parents. When he entered Winchester, the chosen public school, would he suffer the humiliation of being placed lower than boys his own age? The arrival in Elm of cousin John Coles, who was already attending the school, did at least ease his worries about its social life. He now knew how to behave in order to gain acceptance by his peers.[16]

That seven expensive, exclusive boarding schools were called public schools was not more British drollery but the expression of their supposed "openness to all comers." They were the most characteristic of all the national institutions, a Tory periodical averred, for within their walls a young man was taught to keep his honour inviolate, to earn the esteem of his fellow citizens, to suffer evil with stoicism, and to be faithful to the truth. In short, he was prepared for the life of a gentleman. Whether he was prepared for a truly useful life was a bone of contention. A curriculum dominated by classics might, in the words of a down-to-earth fictional mother of a manufacturer, "do well for men who loiter away their lives in the country or in colleges" but not for men who "ought to have their thoughts and powers in the world of today." In a modern, rapidly changing age what young gentlemen required was knowledge of history, the "higher branches of arithmetic," and modern languages. And the narrow curriculum was not the only target of the schools' critics. They were assailed as citadels of "vices and immoralities" where those who believed that "manliness consisted in premature vice" would find every opportunity for "the indulgence of every sensual inclination." Augusta Lyons was aware of some of this criticism, but her concerns may have been eased by a family friend, Captain William Clarke, whose son Tom was at Winchester. In a public letter, Clarke extolled the school's strict discipline, sound system of instruction, and its "inculcation of moral and religious scruples." In reality, as John Coles told Bickerton, the faculty had a cavalier attitude towards teaching. The religious instruction was no better and thus did little to fortify boys against "moral temptations." Nevertheless, his mother was confident that Bickerton's "good feeling, strong principles and just sense of that which is for his future advantage" would guide him safely around the pitfalls. School life would acquaint him, she believed, with the "rubs he must expect to meet in the world." He was entering a society in which the manners of all were "moulded to one stamp of vulgarity, mingled however with a great deal of gentlemanly feeling." He was advanced the means to ensure that he was always dressed in clean, well-tailored clothes, which protected him from the most despised reputation, that of being "niggardly and stingy in the extreme."[17]

The school's headmaster, David Williams, was a man of taste and scholarship, "handsome, dignified, courteous, a good Christian and Churchman, and a thorough gentleman." Unfortunately, his attempts at reform were frustrated by the hidebound conservatism of governors dominated by the master and fellows of New College, Oxford. To his credit, Edmund Lyons made sure that his son broadened his fields of study beyond the classics to include more history, geography, divinity, and some astronomy. Before long Williams was writing to assure him that his son was adding to his character for ability and diligence.

Bickerton did well in prize competitions, and his appointment as one of the school prefects, who were charged with the discipline of the boys, made for an easier life and quiet study. Sir Robert Gordon's report to the boy's parents, following a visit to Winchester, that Bickerton's manner was "strikingly good" and that he had been given a very high character by his masters, produced "tears of joy." Mother and father were now certain of his future academic fame, and their confidence increased the pressure on him to shine.[18]

Extravagant professions of love continued to be the dominant feature of the adolescent Bickerton's letters to his mother. He declared himself always looking forward to living with her, talking with her, and "oh how more than loving her." In "every grief, every difficulty," he wrote, "it is to my mother's love I turn for comfort, and when in doubt I think of what she would advise me to do and I am sure I shall act right." This was not the only evidence of a "mother complex." He took his school holidays at the Silchester parsonage of the Reverend John Coles because his aunt was so like his mother. When she died he rarely returned there. Edmund Lyons was not blind to his elder son's *excessive* love" of his mother, but the relationship of father and son was not distant, nor was it distorted by Oedipal envy. Yet Bickerton's sexuality was tied to his mother. He never appears even to have experienced sexual desire for another woman, and he never married. His close and intense friendships were with men.[19]

While kicking his heels in England waiting for a new assignment, and having completed the plum one of ferrying to Greece the young Bavarian prince, Otho, who was to assume the throne, Edmund Lyons spent a great deal of time with his son. They attended court, a royal ball at the exotic Brighton Pavilion, and dined with William Clarke, who was now chairman of the East India Company. He offered Bickerton a writership which would have taken him to India but was believed to be a passport to wealth. Father and son consulted friends before giving a definite reply. Lady Bickerton, who thought of herself as a proxy grandmother to "dearest Edmund's" children, warned that acceptance would break Augusta's heart. Dr Williams insisted that Bickerton was one of the few young men who could do better. He had been singled out, the headmaster revealed, by one of the dons who had come down from Oxford to examine the boys on the verge of leaving school. He had been heard to say that "Lyons of Winchester is an unusually clever fellow." But the decision to refuse the writership was increasing the pressure on Bickerton to perform brilliantly at university. However, he was able to relax during a summer in Athens, for on 3 July 1835 his father had been appointed minister plenipotentiary to Greece by Palmerston largely on the strength of their "personal compatibility."[20]

On his autumn journey to Oxford Bickerton was accompanied as far as Paris by his mother, and his nervousness increased as he approached the university. As he passed beneath the famous tower of Christ Church in mid-October 1835, his fear of disappointing his parents and especially his mother intensified. He was filled with a "kind of dread" that generated excuses for his possible failure to earn a first-class degree. Bayly's tutoring had prepared him for school but not for university. At Winchester he had acquired a dislike for studying alone, had developed "bad habits," and had not been instructed adequately in "things" highly valued at Oxford. His plan to devote his evenings to study was abruptly discarded when he encountered several short-sighted scholars, concluding that this was the inevitable fate of those who read long by candlelight. Then to homesickness was added the painful misery of an infected molar, which caused his face to swell up so much that he could barely see. The failure of the expensive remedies of local apothecaries to provide relief sufficient to allow him to eat sent him hurrying to London to have the tooth extracted. At the end of his troubled first year he secured permission to stay down during the Michaelmas term of 1836, a request inspired by his mother's desire to have him close and by his cold feet about the upcoming "little go" examination. Yet he passed it with little difficulty when he returned in January 1837, though the modest success brought a renewal of parental pressure. He would achieve distinction, his mother wrote. When have "you ever disappointed me or caused me to experience any feelings but those of pride, joy, and love, dear, dear child," she gushed, "how I doat [sic] upon you. How fondly my heart clings to you." Everyone attached the highest importance to his coming down with a first-class degree, she added. Little wonder he despaired. Friends suggested he study with a private tutor, and while the prospect had little appeal for him the decision was taken by his father, who cheerfully agreed to the expense. Edward Villiers did his best to bolster Bickerton's confidence, praising his "steadiness of purpose," which was the "one great and supreme element of success with every man in every undertaking." So he began reading with a celebrated tutor, Richard Michell of Lincoln College, but his heart was never in it, and he was dismayed when his mother urged him to remain in Britain to study during the long summer vacation. "I never felt so conscious before that all my affection and all my happiness centred in you alone as I do now," he replied, "but I will not dwell upon my bitter disappointment nor the entire destruction of all pleasure in looking forward to the future, which I feel so overwhelmingly at present."[21]

Since undergraduates were not permitted to remain in Oxford out of their colleges, and Christ Church was one of the number that prohibited residence during the vacation, Michell found a spot where his students could study in peace and free of distractions. It was the remote Welsh fishing village of Aberdyfi, which was admired for the "poetry of [its] pastoral life, sequestered, uninterrupted, safe and happy." Bickerton and Tom Clarke travelled there together, by road and then by ferry. They and the other students took one of the houses overlooking the broad estuary of the Dyfi, where they ate and slept for a mere £2 a week. Bickerton's expenses, including tuition, was no more than £100. Although he assured his parents that there were no inducements to make excursions at the expense of study, he took the ferry to the nearby town of Aberystwyth to attend horse races and watch cricket matches. As the summer drew to a close he claimed he had done all that he could by "moderate reading" and the hour-long daily tutorials to improve his prospects of a good degree. But on his return to Oxford he discovered that Michell doubted that he would graduate well. He was mired in despondency, and his mother's twenty-first birthday greeting the following spring only deepened his depression. His father, she wrote, was proudly describing him as one of the very few sons who had reached his majority without causing his parents a single uneasy moment. His plea that he had attempted too much, and that his eyes and general health had suffered as a result of intense study, won him little sympathy from Michell. Lyons, he observed, had never possessed the stamina for hard reading.[22]

He deferred his viva voce until Michaelmas 1838, his anxiety briefly eased by his mother, who assured him that she would not be

disappointed whatever the class of his degree. His father belatedly recognized the strain his son was under. "If you study to the last moment
to the utmost, which I am sure you will do," he wrote, "I shall be satisfied whatever may be the result, but if you give up in despair I shall not
be contented." Bickerton listed the fewest and simplest books on which
to be examined and was placed in the fourth class. This, he sought to
convince his parents, was an achievement of sorts. It "is the only honour
given to those who only attempt the pass examination," he informed
them, "and is considered a great compliment if only the common books
are brought up and is one that has rarely been paid to any one who offered such very easy books as I did." The irony was unintentional, and
he immediately fled Oxford. His undergraduate experience had fed his
chronic fear of failure but conversely had nourished a consuming ambition to make his parents proud of him. He promised never to disappoint
them again. But what would be his profession? He had no interest in
the church as a vocation, while diffidence was no asset in a barrister.
The Foreign Office had frequently been mentioned as a possibility, and
his interest in diplomacy had been stirred in his youth and had grown
with his father's appointment. His reservation was the knowledge that
for young entrants the diplomatic service was at first both expensive
and unprofitable, "whatever it may be afterwards." They could talk of his
future when he reached Athens, his father wrote, and "it is just possible
that I might get you in diplomacy if you wish it."[23]

Lord Stanley, later the 15th Earl of Derby and twice foreign secretary,
sought to dissuade friends from placing a son in the service, declaring it the "Sepulchre of genius and the Paradise of industrial dulness
[sic]." John Bright, the influential Radical politician, mocked it as a form
of aristocratic outdoor relief. Of course, men of this rarefied class possessed the best available education. Like Bickerton, they were, almost
without exception, products of public schools where "good manners,
rigid conventions, and minute conventions" replicated the society beyond the gates. He had at Winchester been taught British diplomacy's
value system, the "Foreign Office mind." Character was more important than intellect and service took precedence over self-advancement.
The British diplomat was a gentleman who behaved honourably in
his dealings, had a command of French, still the principal language of

diplomacy, and possessed the social polish and self-confidence to move at ease in foreign aristocratic circles.[24]

Lord Palmerston informed Sir Edmund in February 1839 that his son had been appointed an unpaid attaché in the Athens mission. Lyons boasted to friends that it was unusual for a young man to enter the service so soon after coming down from university, but he was improvising. Two months shy of his twenty-second birthday, Bickerton was the average age of entrants and shared the belief of many of them that Britons were a "chosen people of history." They as agents of liberty were destined to do great work for mankind. On the other hand, he did not have a high opinion of the Greeks, who according to his mother were a violent people with a propensity for brigandage and rebellion. Britain's policy was crafted by Palmerston, now in his second occupation of the dilapidated and cramped building in Downing Street. There was a gulf in status between secretary of state and permanent staff, and Palmerston's "barbarous manner" of conducting business was bitterly resented by the toilers, who considered themselves gentlemen, and it may account for their naming the house dog "Pam." Palmerston would invariably arrive in the early evening when they had been at their desks all day, and behaved as if it were midday. He expected them to work on at the menial tasks of copying, docketing, and duplicating, occasionally at ciphering and deciphering, infuriated them with criticism of their handwriting, and promoted favourites over more senior staff. What was worse, he sought in the words of one of them "to cut our Emoluments & injure our prospects; and this for a cheese-paring saving, which even the ultra Radicals do not call for to the injury of hard working publick [sic] servants." There had been a three-fold increase in business since Palmerston first took possession of the building but very little increase in staff. He did not extend to senior staff an advisory role especially when in his third term he inherited Henry Unwin Addington as the permanent undersecretary. Palmerston had removed him from the diplomatic service some years earlier on the grounds that he was "too reactionary and stupid." He worked extremely hard himself, reading everything that came through the office, and later explained to his physician that he did so standing up so that when he fell asleep the fall woke him up.[25]

Britain, France, and Russia had been signatories of the protocols that in 1830 recognized the independence and sovereignty of Greece, but a traditional distrust of France and Russia and long-standing support of the Ottoman Empire were the general outlines of Palmerston's response to Eastern crises. Political stability was what he sought in Greece. Greeks fixed on domestic development might be diverted from the ethnic nationalism which made those of them who remained subjects of the Sultan a dangerous destabilizing element with his empire. But British expectations that their contributions to Greek independence would give them greater influence than any other foreign power were never fully realized. The "English interest" was countered by a "Russian interest" and a "French interest." British doubts grew that Greece would prove a useful and trustworthy ally in blocking Russian access to the Mediterranean, while the Tories charged that the Whigs were laying the "keys of the Dardanelles, [and] the throne of Constantine" at the feet of the czar. Palmerston's response was to recommit Britain to the maintenance of the Ottoman Empire's territorial integrity.[26]

In his quest for Greek political stability, Palmerston strove to mould the young Bavarian he had placed on the throne into a constitutional monarch. The establishment of representative government was therefore an "absolute necessity." The Greeks' habits and history, both ancient and modern, their fight to escape the Sultan's autocracy, and their national assemblies during the conflict rendered "utterly impossible" their contentment under an absolute monarchy, the foreign secretary believed. To Britons, principally Tories, who insisted that the Greeks lacked the education in civil liberty necessary for a complex and advanced system of government, Palmerston replied that no set of men were "too ignorant to understand their own interests," for the knowledge "requisite for political affairs" was in his opinion "speedily acquired by the very act in taking part in them." This admirably liberal position was not one he adopted in Britain. The need to establish a liberal government swiftly and securely became an even greater concern when Otho selected as his consort the Grand Duchess Amalia of Oldenburg, a young woman notoriously and excessively proud of her blood connection to the autocratic Romanovs of Russia. Her choice convinced some observers that the young monarch was an "imbecile." And there was no comfort in the diagnosis of the three physicians who were consulted on his mental condition. This being the age of phrenology, they identified a "malformation" of the head as a source of Otho's "absolute want of positive

knowledge," "invincible distraction," "incapacity to read and comprehend," "absolute want of activity," and "extraordinary pretensions." A
long reign was a fearful prospect, Palmerston groaned. Moreover, the
once excellent relationship between king and British minister, developed during Otho's original journey to his kingdom, had soured. Lyons's following of his instructions to advise and promote constitutional
government had alienated a monarch who had set his heart on personal
government. Immature and frustrated, he publicly humiliated Lyons.
Several envoys immediately formed a choir of the British minister's critics in which the French voice was the most "vile." This was the poisoned
atmosphere in which the new, unpaid attaché embarked on his career.[27]

The year 1839 proved to be momentous for the Lyons family. Both
sons had entered professions, Moubray receiving a naval commission,
and both daughters married. Among the constant file of British visitors
to Athens was Lord Fitzalan. He was in the direct line of succession
to the dukedom of Norfolk and had been packed off to the Levant by
his father, the Earl of Surrey, to sever an unwelcome romantic attachment. But on calling at the legation in mid-October 1838, he was smitten
with Minna Lyons. She was "attractive, natural, modest, unaffected, very
clever and cheerful" if, in the opinion of her father, not "very pretty."
Lyons was naturally protective of his daughter and feared she might not
prove any more acceptable to the mighty Howards than the other young
lady. She was Protestant and they were Britain's premier Roman Catholics and surely expected a future Duke of Norfolk to form "the *highest*
and *richest* alliance in the kingdom." But Fitzalan assured him that his
mind was "irrevocably fixed." After he had sailed early in the new year
to inform his parents of the engagement, the Lyons family spent an anxious seven weeks before word arrived that it had been confirmed. The
wedding was speedily arranged and took place in England. The social
benefits of "so mighty a connection" were immediately evident. All the
world, Augusta reported to her husband and son, both of whom had remained in Athens because of the ongoing regional political crisis, seems
to "think us such rising stars, that those who scarcely acknowledged
us as acquaintances now court us." The bride was given away by Edward Villiers, and her attending uncle John Lyons gushed that her sister
Anne's "delight and animation on the happy events will show her natural

character to advantage and this will trap some good hearted fellow like Fitzalan." The elder Miss Lyons had already formed an attachment but feared her parents would not approve of her choice. He was neither English nor Protestant. Phillipe de Wurtzburg, a younger son of a Baron, was an aide-de-camp to his childhood friend Otho. Edmund and Augusta Lyons agreed to the union, if a trifle reluctantly, but Bickerton was far more enthusiastic. He liked Wurtzburg "excessively."[28]

Throughout this exciting year Bickerton was getting on "famously" as an apprentice diplomat. His command of French and growing mastery of modern Greek made him of "infinite" use at the legation, while his copies of dispatches in a large and bold script were enthusiastically welcomed by Palmerston at a Foreign Office ill lit by candles and oil lamps. The foreign secretary demanded "large, round, legible hands" and the use of the darkest black ink. The son was emerging as the father's mainstay, someone in whom he felt able to confide "unreservedly." Bickerton did not always agree with British policy, the rebellion in Crete being a case in point. His response to reports of Turkish atrocities was a credit to his humanity. Such "perfidy and cruelty ought no longer to be endured," he fumed. And while the insurgency and the enthusiastic support of it by the mainland Greeks did improve his opinion of them, his confidence in their capacity for improvement quickly faded. They were pretending that the revolt was still viable, he believed, in order to collect monies from European sympathizers which they would then divide among themselves. The only consolation for him was the likelihood that the revolt would do Otho harm. Resentment of the king's conduct towards his father, and his sarcastic comment on being shown a portrait of Minna, that it was by no means a true likeness, was only a partial explanation of Bickerton's deepening personal dislike of the monarch. Otho's ignoring of the widespread distress of his subjects, and his apparent blindness to their anger over his efforts to increase revenues "most cruelly," inspired Bickerton's contempt. The king had in his opinion gone "stark, staring mad" and seemed oblivious to the looming crisis, which barely a week later, on 15 September 1843, erupted as revolution in the form of a military coup.[29]

It had been precipitated by the financial chaos which saw the swollen military budget slashed. Angry troops surrounded the royal palace on the night of 14 September, and Lyons, now Sir Edmund, appears to have known what was being planned. Wurtzburg slept that night at the legation for the first time since the marriage. Lyons took the lead in impressing on the terrified Otho the necessity for him to approve the decrees drafted by a hastily assembled Council of Ministers. They summoned a constituent assembly to write a constitution, established an interim provisional government, awarded decorations to the soldiers of the revolution, and excluded foreigners from state service. This had been a moderate and orderly revolution, Lyons assured the Foreign Office, now occupied again by Aberdeen, and it had cleared the path to a form of representative government. Sir Edmund was a familiar figure in the "smoky, confined and impure air" of the constituent assembly, where he worked effectively with the slippery French minister, Theobald Piscatory. What emerged was a bicameral legislature, a bill of rights, and the naming of the Orthodox Church as the established religion but with assurances of toleration of other creeds so long as they did not proselytize. Yet this constitution was no jewel of liberalism. The monarch retained extraordinary powers on legislation; the appointment of ministers, senators, and judges; the negotiations of alliances and treaties; and the declaration of war. The document, however, did not banish factional politics. The "French interest" quickly gained control of the government, and it was liberal only in its resort to torture and other horrors.[30]

Bickerton continued to labour away, and in the "dull, monotonous, desponding" capital he welcomed the opening of an attractive theatre where operas were performed on four nights of every winter week. The prima donna was a pretty young Italian whose weak voice escaped censure. The report that her father had been beheaded for his involvement in an Italian rebellion had the hint of a libretto and created a well of romantic sympathy deep enough to drown criticism of her vocal deficiencies. When the theatre did not divert him, Bickerton played whist with his mother and Philip Griffith, a senior attaché, with either his father or Wurtzburg making up the four. As summer approached he complained so often of the heat, of the sand flies and various other insects, and of his inability to sleep at night that his mother began to fear he was thinking of leaving Athens for good. Ambition explained his decision to soldier on. He feared his career would be blighted by too swift a departure from

Greece, and the decision to remain was eased by the "mania" he developed for exploration. "Bickerton is so enchanted with travelling in Greece," his relieved mother observed, "that he thinks, talks and dreams of nothing else."[31]

His constant companion was a Greek guide, Yani. He was quite dull without him, he told his family, and the ability to practise his modern Greek with him explained his seeing so much of him even in Athens. The pair were "inseparable," Minna understood, and her brother "quite devoted" to his "beloved Yani." No member of the family betrayed a hint of concern or surprise over his relationship with a Greek who had no interest in either the classics or ancient history. Male romantic friendships were not considered unusual and were rarely distorted into "consummated sexual activity." If it fell short by only one degree of "the sweetest sentiments entertained between the sexes," the American author Herman Melville wrote, an intense male relationship was "considered perfectly acceptable and even admirable." In most cases marriage was its end, but Bickerton never married. Without being a misogynist, he appears to have been one of those persons "primarily or exclusively attracted to people of their own sex." He may have been "non-heterosexual rather than positively homosexual" or may have suppressed his sexual inclinations or even been unaware of them. His relationship with Yani and later with other young men may have been "homosexual in attitudes if not in practice."[32]

Bickerton's wanderlust sustained his interest in Greek antiquity, and the exercise of writing up what he saw developed and refined his powers of description and analysis. However, shortly after his second trip to the Ottoman frontier in 1843, and the revolution, his parents packed him off to Patras. A painful eye complaint attributed to excessive reading and writing had not been cured by either the poultices or the caustic administered by local physicians. They had discovered small pimples under the eyelid but his mother was unable to find them. The following spring he sailed for home to consult a leading London ophthalmologist and celebrated his twenty-seventh birthday at Malta. He reached London on 16 May 1844, where he lodged with the Fitzalans in fashionable Belgrave Square. As had his mother before him, he made the discovery that the Norfolk connection opened every society door. "I have been plunging into the vortex of dissipation in a manner you would entirely approve," he assured her. He attended late evening balls, accepted invitations to early morning breakfasts, and sampled London's cultural pleasures such as opera. He went to the Lyceum for a discussion of "Polka mania," the belligerent expansionism of James K. Polk, the presidential nominee of the American Democrats. He read *Martin Chuzzlewit*, to which Charles Dickens, who had visited the United States two years earlier, added a savagely satirical portrait of aspects of the Republic in an effort to boost the disappointing English sales of the novel. He revisited old haunts, such as Winchester, the Clarkes' mansion in Leatherhead, called at the ancestral home of the Howards, Arundel Castle, then set off for Bath to see the widowed Lady Bickerton. He took the opportunity to travel via Bristol to see for himself the commissions of the engineer Isambard Kingdom Brunel. He found that work had been delayed on the Clifton Suspension Bridge but was almost complete on the iron-hulled *Great Britain*, the world's largest steamship.[33]

Good news awaited him in London. His father had been awarded a Knight Grand Cross of the Order of the Bath (GCB), and with this honour safely in the bag Lyons lobbied Aberdeen on behalf of his son, who had contributed significantly to the smooth running of the legation. He drew the foreign secretary's attention to his financial sacrifices as a chief of mission who lacked a private fortune. The advancement of sons, he reminded Aberdeen, was the "recompense which public servants not unreasonably look to for a life and fortune spent in service of their country." Bickerton was lifted into the ranks of paid attachés at a salary of £250 a year, which was considerably more than he had expected. His career had been truly launched.[34]

CHAPTER TWO

Rome

Bickerton was in the public gallery at the opening of the new session of Parliament in February 1845 and was struck by the "beauty and distinctiveness" of the Queen's reading of the throne speech. The Conservative government's attempt to conciliate Ireland's politically active Catholic priesthood by funding more generously the poorly maintained and overcrowded seminary at Maynooth infuriated Evangelical Protestants, who suspected a plot to effect the concurrent endowment of the Roman Catholic Church. Bickerton deplored sectarianism. His own tendencies were liberal if not ecumenical. When in Arundel he worshipped in both the parish church and the Fitzalan Chapel, and suffered none of the spiritual anguish of his parents on Minna's inevitable conversion. The startling number of High Anglicans who also converted to Catholicism was mainly attributable, he believed, "to the revulsion of feeling which naturally arises on comparing the Roman Catholic religion such as it really is, with the preposterous notions of it, in which most English Protestants have been brought up."[1]

Bickerton's eyes were still painful. He had consulted several British specialists, among them Henry Alexander, surgeon-occulist to the Queen, but neither belladona pills nor steaming eased the painful complaint, while talk of experimental therapies alarmed him as did the expense of "all the Doctoring." That concern did not prevent him from embarking on a European medical odyssey. He twice visited Aix-la-Chapelle, which boasted that its springs were the hottest north of the Alps, and, accompanied by his mother, sampled the waters of the more fashionable Bad Kissingen. When she left for Athens he went on to Dresden, whose specialist came highly recommended, but the solution he put into Bickerton's eyes so inflamed them that they could not be opened for a week and had to be bandaged far longer. They would soon be at least as well as when he arrived, he quipped. Spring of 1847 found him in Paris consulting yet another prominent occulist, then he returned to London to see John Dalrymple, who had published *The Anatomy of the Human Eye* the previous decade and was currently a surgeon at the Royal Ophthalmic Hospital. He recommended absolute rest and a course of waters that had "steel in them," so Bickerton set off again to Germany. He went first to Homburg, which at least provided entertainment in the form of an "excellent band," and then to Dusseldorf, where a local physician had established a reputation as a healer of eyes. However, Bickerton was finally reduced to hoping that his problem would "some day go away of itself."[2]

Not all of this largely wasted professional time proved a career liability. He was making social connections that promised to be helpful. He accepted the repeated invitations of the Duke and Duchess of Bedford to join gatherings at their ancestral home, Woburn Abbey. There he made the acquaintance of Lord John Russell, the duke's younger brother, who headed the Whig government formed when Robert Peel's remedial measures proved too indigestible for a large element of his fellow Conservatives. Guests were served afternoon tea, the duchess's contribution to English civilization, and were obliged to participate in the amateur theatricals staged each evening. Bickerton, determined to please, threw himself with gusto into the performances and by so doing overcame a problem that might otherwise have damaged his career. "I have had a good lesson in getting over shyness having come out in tragedy, comedy, opera, and ballet at once," he assured his parents. "The fun of getting up the things is so great as almost to compensate for the horrible fright one gets into when one has to appear in them."[3]

Astonishing news from across the Channel in February 1848 was of revolution in France and the flight into English exile of King Louis

Phillipe travelling under the traditional pseudonym of "Mr Smith." The spread of revolution across Europe drew Bickerton to the newspaper accounts as a moth to light. Wearily, he resolved to do the best he could with his eyes as they were and informed the Foreign Office of his intention to return to Athens during the autumn. The European turmoil had brought excitement to the Greek capital, where the royal couple panicked and an attempt was made to assassinate the Ottoman minister plenipotentiary. With Whig policy under parliamentary and press fire, Palmerston as foreign secretary asked Stratford Canning, who was on his way back to Constantinople as ambassador, to assess the Greek situation. His rudeness and his interference in the country's internal affairs by advising Otho on ministerial appointments angered Sir Edmund. Canning had "offended almost the whole of the Corps Diplomatique" and had driven Greek constitutionalists to "despair and almost to doubt the faith of England," he fumed. He welcomed the return of a "fat and well" Bickerton in September, having ensured that he was well briefed on the situation by forwarding to him in England copies of his dispatches to the foreign secretary. Bickerton was a great "comfort and pleasure" to his criticized father, for many in Britain blamed him for its strained relations with Otho, yet the Lyonses were entirely unprepared for Palmerston's decision at the end of January 1849 to recall Sir Edmund. He delivered the bombshell in a characteristically jaunty way, informing Lyons that he had been rescued from the fringes of civilization. He was the new British minister to Switzerland, a diplomatic backwater. What made the decision harder to bear was the discovery that Otho had been informed of the transfer before Lyons himself.[4]

Knowing that he was being held responsible for the failure to create a constitutional monarchy and a stable state, Lyons was determined to erase the stain on his reputation. Otherwise, his career prospects and those of his son would in all probability be blighted. He asked Palmerston for a letter of approbation only for their meeting in April to end in acrimony. Eventually, when threatened by Fitzalan with a debate in the Commons, the foreign secretary wrote to express his entire approbation of Lyons's conduct. Nevertheless, Sir Edmund was still on his way back to Berne, and his son remained a paid attaché in Athens, where on 6 June 1849 the new minister arrived. An Irishman and a Whiggish supporter of Ireland's union with Britain, Thomas Wyse had been rewarded with a minor office only then to find himself put out to diplomatic pasture when Russell needed the position for another. Initially, Bickerton considered Wyse and his accompanying niece "kind, considerate and agreeable," but the minister's evident shortage of funds soon led to a reassessment. Wyse failed to settle speedily the account for the furniture he had purchased from Sir Edmund, did not furnish fully many of the legation's rooms (their wretched appearance offended Bickerton's national pride), and at receptions and diplomatic dinners was unable to serve wines either properly or of reasonable quality. Champagne was on occasion not chilled or the bottles too few in number, but worse still was the "Hibernian impudence" of serving inexpensive *vins ordinaire* as good wines to which they bore not the slightest resemblance. People resented "the attempt at imposture," and this "shabby means of going on" was contributing, Bickerton believed, to his nation's "contemptible" image locally.[5]

Bickerton's relationship with the Wyse women – for the minister's sister-in-law, mother of the niece, soon joined the household – did not prosper. He came to loathe Mrs Wyse, whom he considered "dangerous, intriguing, foolish," her head filled with trash about "spies concealed in neighbouring houses, and what not." Unavoidably, he saw a great deal of them when the senior attaché, Philip Griffith, took leave. Occasionally Bickerton accompanied Miss Wyse on her daily rides. When Minna suggested, perhaps jokingly, that the Wyses were setting their sights on him as a prospective suitor of the young lady, he avowed absolute immunity to feminine charms. But another source of his uneasiness was the direction of British policy, for Wyse failed to take him into his confidence. What was clear was the dreadful blow British influence had suffered as the result of the brutal suppression of a rebellion on one of the Ionian Islands. Although Britain had retained the island, the dissidents sought union with the mainland. Relations with Greece worsened when Palmerston threatened to end by force a dispute over two islets and demanded that British subjects be compensated for a variety of injuries inflicted by Greeks. One of the claimants was a Don Pacifico, whose house in Athens had been invaded and set ablaze by an anti-Semitic mob, his family assaulted, and his wife's jewels stolen. He had also lost, he claimed, documents that would have ensured his recovery of £26,000 from the Portuguese government. Bickerton dismissed as absurd Don Pacifico's request that Britain resort to gunboat diplomacy, hence his surprise when in mid-January 1850 a naval force arrived to exert pressure on the Greek government.[6]

Admiral Sir William Parker, the squadron's commander, dined at the legation, was presented at court, and warned the Greeks that there would be serious consequences over a refusal to pay compensation. With the expiration of his deadline for an agreement, Greek ports were blockaded and several Greek merchant vessels were seized. At home, meanwhile, the pressure was mounting on Palmerston to accept some form of arbitration. "The whole press of England and France is against Lord Palmerston," Augusta Lyons noted in mid-February, "and so is the universal feeling in England." He agreed to the dispatch of a French intermediary to Greece, Jean-Baptiste Gros, who reached Athens on 5 March. Yet there was an ambiguity in his role which did not escape a keen-eyed Bickerton. Was he merely to use his "good offices" in the pursuit of a settlement, or was he to arbitrate the claims? Gros earned credit with Bickerton and his colleagues by working very hard, by scorning the Greek ministers as corrupt and iniquitous, and by concluding that most of the British claims were "just in principle" and their "amount indisputable." However, the Frenchman questioned the nationality of Don Pacifico, for he had been born in Gibraltar, and considered the man's estimate of his losses "grossly exaggerated." When Gros announced the suspension "momentarily" of his mission, and the British warships ostentatiously prepared for a resumption of coercive activities, the intimidated Greek government capitulated. Wyse was asked what terms he would accept. They resembled the recommendations of Gros. The Greeks agreed to pay compensation and to apologize to Britain for a number of incidents, but the question of Don Pacifico's documents was referred to a mixed commission, which subsequently awarded him the derisory sum of £150. Seeking this cloud's silver lining, Bickerton commented: "The award is not so unsatisfactory to us, as it appears at first sight, for our principle is in some measure established by his getting anything."[7]

Of far greater concern to Bickerton, Griffith, and Walker was the conduct of Wyse. His indolence, indecisiveness, and ineffectiveness throughout the negotiations had proven a sore trial. Parker had found it impossible even to go through the form of consulting the minister. The three of them and John Green, the British consul, had made all the important decisions and Bickerton had composed the majority of notes sent to the other ministers. Wyse "did not even inquire before they were written as to the nature of them, not even if replies, whether they were to be in the affirmative or negative," Bickerton scornfully recalled. With the exception of the "long despatches" which he sent home, and for which he properly received the credit, Wyse's contributions had been at most clumsy insertions which simply obscured the note's meaning. "This is far from his greatest deficiency as a Diplomatist," he moaned, and "it is hopeless to suppose any Mission can get on with such a Chief."[8]

Lyons deserved the lion's share of the credit for the settlement, Parker and Griffith agreed. The former admired his "quickness and intelligence," while the latter wrote to the Foreign Office to declare the paid attaché the "soul of the Mission." At last, Sir Edmund believed, his son's "wonderful discretion" was about to be recognized with a promotion. He hurried home from Switzerland in March 1850 on learning of the death of Lady Bickerton. Her dog had chewed to pieces her original will and her dementia had raised questions about the validity of the replacement. That problem was settled without difficulty, her godson inheriting a small fortune and his children, with the exception of the well-married Minna, receiving bequests of £1,000 each. But the real purpose of Edmund Lyons's visit was to lobby for promotion for himself and his diplomat son. Thinking Bickerton's presence in the capital would be helpful, he approached Palmerston with a request that he be granted leave, which was quickly granted. Lyons misinterpreted the decision as proof that something was to be "done for one or other of us."[9]

Bickerton arrived in London on 11 June and was immediately invited by the Palmerstons to a reception, where he was taken aside by the foreign secretary to discuss an upcoming parliamentary debate on foreign policy. He was in the gallery of the House of Lords two evenings later to hear a scorching attack on the Russell ministry by the Earl of Derby, the leader of the Protectionist Tories who had broken with Robert Peel four years earlier over the repeal of the Corn Laws. The debate ended in a vote of censure, prompting Lord John Russell to seek a vote of confidence in the Commons. Edmund Lyons and his son were two of the team that scoured the Foreign Office's haphazardly shelved volumes of manuscripts, perhaps 3,000 in number and with only a rudimentary index adopted forty years earlier, for material helpful to Palmerston's defence. They were hoping to benefit from his reputation as a politician who took good care of those who had rendered him valuable service. "We have been doing what we can to help Lord Palmerston through," Bickerton wrote to his mother in Switzerland. "I hope he will be grateful if he weathers the storm." Weather it he did after four stormy days of debate.[10]

An invitation to Palmerston's Hampshire retreat, Broadlands, and a request that they extend their stay, appeared to signal "some good intention to us." But they rarely saw their host, and when they did he spoke only of Greece. They left empty-handed, and the disappointed Bickerton joined his mother on an autumn tour of Germany, returning to London in late November. He celebrated Christmas and the New Year with the Bedfords at Woburn Abbey, and on 6 January 1851 learned that his father had been appointed minister plenipotentiary to Sweden. There was nothing for him. With a mind full of "sad thoughts" about his career prospects, he set off in the spring for Athens, which he reached on 28 April, having marked his thirty-fourth birthday quietly at sea. He found the Greeks in a state of despair and Wyse as lethargic as ever. The loss of British influence alarmed him. No one, he moaned, "could wish for more easy convenient opponents, or could find more indolent, useless friends." Depressed, he was laid lower by "sick headaches" but in December escaped from this toxic mix of boredom, frustration, and disappointed ambition. His brother Moubray had been hospitalized in Malta to halt his "melancholy and despairing" slide into a deep depression, and Admiral Parker had written to Wyse to suggest that Bickerton be given leave to be with his brother. The minister readily agreed, keen as he was to see the back of him. Moubray had begun to improve even before they sailed for home on 9 January 1852, the voyage reminding Bickerton of why he avoided the sea whenever possible. They booked into Fenton's Hotel, London, which was only a short walk from Norfolk House, and Moubray was examined by Dr Alexander John Sutherland. He prescribed residence in an airy area of the capital, the keeping of regular hours, a strict and generous diet, and the exclusion of agitation and nervousness. Bickerton rented a comfortable house with a large garden in St John's Wood, a leafy suburb that had undergone gentrification, and employed an experienced manservant.[11]

Besides taking long walks daily with Moubray, weather permitting, Bickerton dined frequently with Minna and Fitz at their new home in Carlton Terrace. He always seemed to have a beneficial effect on Fitzalan's health and spirits, cursed as his brother-in-law was by chronic "bilious colds." Another source of anxiety within the Lyons family was the health of Augusta. "Anything that sets her heart beating [fast] even for a few minutes," Bickerton had warned his sister during their mother's most recent visit to England, "does mischief which it is difficult to estimate." She must never be either hurried or given cause to be agitated. But he half-dreaded letters from Stockholm, fearful of their contents. "We are very well," his mother wrote on 24 February, a local physician having assured her she was in no danger despite the shortness of breath and "very weak" general condition. Her death soon afterwards, probably from congestive heart failure, was a heavy blow to the son to whom she had been almost suffocatingly close. He found some solace in his faith and its promise of resurrection, writing to his grieving father: "Mine is a peaceful, painless sorrow."[12]

While in the capital Bickerton made sure he was seen as often as possible by all those who might aid his quest for promotion. He consulted Henry Addington, the permanent undersecretary at the Foreign Office, who encouraged him to take his case directly to the new Tory foreign secretary. Palmerston had been dismissed by Russell for seemingly endorsing a coup d'état in France by Louis Napoleon, who had been elected president of the Second Republic despite his questionable commitment to constitutional government. Palmerston in a "tit for tat" then helped to bring down his former colleagues, and Derby formed a minority government. Since Aberdeen, the experienced former Tory foreign secretary, was leading the Peelite Tories, Peel having died two years earlier, Derby named the Earl of Malmesbury as foreign secretary. The choice of this friend and shooting companion raised eyebrows, but Malmesbury was not as ignorant of foreign affairs as some observers fancied. He later recalled that the Foreign Office staff expected him to give them trouble with requests for their advice but was confident that his editing of the papers and correspondence of his grandfather, a career diplomat, had provided him with a grasp of the language and routine work of the office. He had travelled widely in Europe and had forged a friendship with Louis Napoleon which might reinvigorate the entente with France that Aberdeen had promoted under Peel. He and Derby were keen to remain on good terms with Russia, Austria, and Prussia. Both were opposed to "Palmerstonian meddling" in the internal affairs of other nations, and neither favoured the exportation of liberal ideas. Very few foreigners were in their opinion capable of mastering the "civic duty necessary to the blessings of British parliamentary government, rule of law, religious freedom, and liberty of the press." Their evidence of this was the coup d'état in France and the personal rule of Emperor Napoleon III.[13]

All that Malmesbury could offer Bickerton was a transfer to Dresden, and so desperate was he to avoid returning to Athens that he accepted this lateral move with fawning thanks. Yet his long service in Greece had amounted to a primer on diplomatic conduct. Only a foolish junior was disagreeable to a head of mission "however much the fault may have been on the Chief's side." This helped to explain his failure to receive, outside of a small circle of intimates, the credit he deserved for his contribution to the solution of the Don Pacifico affair. Another lesson taught by Wyse's mistakes was that a wise chief won the loyalty of his juniors with hospitality, great courtesy, a little formality, and by taking them into his confidence on business. His residence should be a fitting symbol of Britain's wealth and power; he should scorn stinginess at receptions, offering champagne at least five times an evening unless a great variety of wines was available, and should entertain the diplomatic corps. "It is evidently of the greatest use to a Diplomatist to be really personally liked by his colleagues," Bickerton accepted, and the traditional method of winning favour was to put on excellent dinners. Dining, Palmerston was to remark, "is the soul of diplomacy." However, only two years earlier, one senior diplomat had been subjected to much ridicule following his statement to a Commons committee that he had "no idea of a man being a good diplomat" who did not give good dinners. Finally, Otho notwithstanding, Bickerton remained an advocate of constitutional monarchy. It enjoyed prestige, was an assurance of political stability, was a visible sign of national unity and independence, and inspired respect abroad.[14]

Moubray accompanied him to the capital of Saxony before going on to their father in the Swedish capital. The British minister in Dresden, Francis Forbes, a younger son of the late Lord Granard, had been very kind to Bickerton when he called at the city on his medical odyssey. The legation was something of a menagerie, housing two of the minister's sisters, his nephew the young Lord Granard, a large pack of lap dogs, and a virtual aviary of twittering birds. Bickerton declined gracefully the invitation to join them, preferring the nearby and aptly named Hotel Victoria. His duties far from demanding, he used his time to acquire some German and to enjoy a city many Britons considered a German Florence. The king had one of the finest art collections in Europe, which he opened to the public, and his capital had been dubbed the mecca of the musician perhaps because of its immense opera house that could seat 2,000. To the large helping of high culture was added the sauce of high society. He was presented at court and invited to the New Year's reception at which the royal family sponsored state card playing. Whist was the game of choice, and it was one at which he excelled. With the arrival of warm weather he went boating on the Elbe with the French minister, Henri Mercier, whose friendship was to serve Bickerton well a decade later.[15]

At home, the Tory minority government had fallen in December and a coalition of Whigs and Peelites headed by Aberdeen took office. For a brief period Lord John Russell occupied the Foreign Office, keeping the seat warm for the Earl of Clarendon. Little wonder Bickerton hoped for promotion, having made Russell's acquaintance at Woburn Abbey while Clarendon was the elder brother of Edward Villiers. Bickerton learned that Russell had appointed him Britain's unofficial representative to the Papal States. The man he was replacing, William Petre, a Roman Catholic, had in the opinion of Malmesbury been "only fit to be used at the old ladies tea tables." However, it was obvious that so long as Britain was represented by a "clandestine agent" only, it would not exercise significant political influence. When prime minister, Russell had sought to establish formal relations only for the necessary legislation to be amended in a way that made it unacceptable to the Holy See. Next he proposed the sending of a special agent to counsel the pontiff on his dealings with Britain only for his intended nominee, Fitzalan, to be attacked as "weak-minded and in the hands of the Jesuits." His support of ultramontanism had angered even his father, who considered it incompatible with allegiance to the Crown and the constitution. Now, as temporary foreign secretary, Russell appointed Fitzalan's Protestant brother-in-law to replace Petre. He had a "very high opinion" of Bickerton's diplomatic ability: his family connection would make him acceptable to the Holy See; he had a command of Italian, the language of Tuscany and Rome; while his Greek experience would stand him in good stead in the ill-governed Papal States.[16]

The attractions of the post were manifold. Italy's natural beauty, its identification with Roman civilization, with the Renaissance, and with high culture gave the name "a kind of magic sound." The struggle of Italian nationalists had captivated Britons, many of whom admired and even revered Giuseppe Mazzini and Giuseppe Garibaldi. The pope's flight from Rome during the revolutions of 1848, the establishment of a Roman Republic, the invasion of the Papal States by Austria from its province of Lombardy-Venetia, the expulsion of the Republicans, and the restoration of the pope by a French expeditionary force had been followed closely in Britain. There Italy was "metaphorically recast as a woman in distress, a tragic figure in need of being rescued" from herself and an assortment of tyrants – the pope, the Austrians, and the French. Bickerton relished finding himself at the centre of British and European interest, while a salary that was higher than that of an ordinary attaché not only was welcome financially but created an appearance of "more apparent importance." Although the position lacked substance, character, and name, he recognized that with "activity and discretion" it might very well serve as an "excellent stepping-stone" to higher office. With that ambitious objective in mind, he needed to impress his masters in London. Direct communication with them was essential, but he found no Petre dispatches in the Foreign Office archives. They had been sent to Florence, for the unofficial representative in Rome was officially a member of that legation, and there Petre's dispatches had remained. But Edmund Hammond, the head of the Foreign Office's Italian section who was soon to be promoted to permanent undersecretary, promised to arrange for Bickerton's dispatches to be sent on from Florence as written.[17]

Among the documents that Bickerton read most closely was an analysis of the Papal States by the controversial and assertive minister to Tuscany, Sir Henry Bulwer. Bulwer had estimated the population at 3 million, described the economy as stagnant, and reported a chronic operating deficit. Pope Pius IX was in his judgment weak and irresolute, dependent on the French and Austrian troops to keep his discontented subjects under control, and was a pawn of the violent clerical party hostile to England. The ambition of the Vatican, Bulwer warned, was to "extend the power of the Church over the State, it matters not whether in Protestant or Catholic countries." That the papal regime was the root of the Italian problem was something on which Whigs and Tories agreed, and they considered its reform essential for the peace of the peninsula and Europe. Tories, in the interests of order, were willing for the Austrians to remain in Lombardy-Venetia, whereas Whigs sought to limit French and Austrian influence and promote constitutional government by encouraging much of the peninsula to unite around its most developed state, the kingdom of Sardinia-Piedmont. The "temporality of Popedom" was anathema to British Liberals following Pius's repudiation of his early liberalism on being restored to his throne by French arms. Palmerston had expected President Louis Napoleon to oblige a grateful pope to maintain a parliamentary system of government, but Bonaparte was more interested in attracting and retaining the political support of France's ultramontane clergy first for his coup d'état and then for the creation of the Second Empire. Hence he made no challenge to the pontiff's repudiation of liberalism and constitutionalism. The result was a papal regime riddled with the "most crying abuses" which, thanks to the presence of the French and the Austrians, prevented the "spread of constitutional freedom to the whole of Italy." What sense was there in a system of government, Palmerston asked, which saw an elderly priest chosen as the temporal sovereign of several millions of people by thirty or forty other elderly priests, few if any of whom had any natural or national link to the people concerned?[18]

Bulwer, home on medical leave, met with Bickerton and warned him: "Those who know little of Rome (which is a place by itself), fancy honestly things can be done there, simply because they are reasonable, which cannot be done." The warning revived Bickerton's fear of failure which this appointment had promised to lay to rest. "I am afraid there is no chance of my doing so well as to be promoted as a reward," he glumly observed, "and I hope not much of my doing so badly as to be promoted to be got rid of." In addition to reform of the papal government, he was expected also to persuade the pope to discourage the activities of Irish priests engaged in the political campaign to repeal the Act of Union. The pope's naming of Paul Cullen to head the Irish branch of the Roman Catholic Church had infuriated Clarendon, then lord lieutenant of Ireland, who considered the former rector of the Irish College in Rome a bitter sectarian enemy of the Protestant state. To avoid another such "outrage," and to steer the papal government towards constitutionalism, formal diplomatic relations were essential. With these objectives in mind, Foreign Secretary Clarendon instructed Bickerton to disabuse the papal authorities of the notion that Protestant Britain was hostile to Rome. He should avoid involvement in intrigues and be "scrupulously straightforward" in all his dealings. He had learned in Greece, Bickerton replied, the wisdom of this code of conduct.[19]

He volunteered to carry dispatches to Turin and Florence, thereby charging to the Foreign Office his expenses as far as the Tuscan capital. He reached Turin at midnight on 10 April after a hair-raising passage through the high Mount Cenis Pass. He had an interesting and useful discussion with the minister, James Hudson. He agreed with Bulwer that the Vatican would never be persuaded to accept a British minister in Rome without Britain's acceptance of a priest as papal nuncio, but Parliament required the pope to have a lay representative in London. When Bickerton reached Florence, which he dismissed as "mean and ugly," his reading of Petre's dispatches filled him anew with dread that he would fail to detect the real wishes and sentiments of the papal authorities. He thought it unlikely that they would speak frankly to a Protestant, even one who came armed with letters of introduction written by such prominent English Catholics as his brother-in-law. Nor was he willing to resort to covert activities or "corruption in high quarters," for he abhorred them. He would adhere to the "regular straightforward course."[20]

It was Sunday, 17 April, when Bickerton reached Rome. He went to an English church in the morning and to St Peter's in the evening, and was disappointed by the great edifice of Roman Catholicism. The interior was imposing but not splendid, he commented, while the exterior struck him, as had Florence, as "mean and ugly." He met with Petre, who warned him that he would be under surveillance by agents of the government and should therefore keep his distance from John Freeborn, the British consular agent. Freeborn had earned the displeasure of the papal authorities and had given his name an eponymous ring by his generous distribution of passports to the political refugees fleeing Rome after the collapse of the Republic. Matching activity with discretion, Bickerton sent off twenty dispatches during his first six weeks of residence. Welcome as they were at the legation in Florence, Peter Scarlett, the chargé d'affaires in Bulwer's absence, observed that he appeared to be reluctant to become better acquainted with the cardinal secretary of state. Instead, Bickerton's caution was a response to the gossip about Giocomo Antonelli. A cardinal deacon not a priest, he was reputedly sensual, slippery, and venal yet had a seemingly iron grip on the office. His loyalty to the pope, his constant trimming of his own views to match those of his inconsistent master, and his intelligence, administrative ability, and ingratiating manner explained his retention. At his meeting with Bickerton on 23 April he gave no ground on the question of formal diplomatic relations between the two states. The British requirement that the pope appoint a layman as his representative in London might be matched by the pontiff's insistence that a Catholic bishop be the British minister to the Papal States, Antonelli tartly observed. As for papal restraint of politically active Irish priests, he was unable to resist the temptation to give the British liberal state a gentle, ironic poke. He did not approve of the priests' language or behaviour, he admitted, but understood that "great license" was allowed them as British citizens.[21]

Bickerton's first audience with the pope a fortnight later went well. He kissed the hand of the pontiff, who inquired after Minna and Fitz, spoke to Bickerton "almost familiarly," and laughed pleasantly at the wild ideas British Protestants entertained about his objective in reviving the Catholic hierarchy of England and Wales. Bickerton delivered the little speech he had prepared avowing his government's friendly feelings towards the papacy, and the audience concluded with a papal blessing and an assurance of Pius's willingness to meet with him whenever he wished. "He is unquestionably the most agreeable sovereign I have ever seen," Bickerton informed Minna, but he found even greater difficulty than he had anticipated in gaining "correct intelligence" on the "peculiar and complex" papal government. However, his father's return to naval duty in the Mediterranean with flag rank, as tension mounted between France and Britain on one side and Russia on the other, promised to help solve the problem. He expected members of the diplomatic corps to come to his door for information on the deepening international crisis, and he might exchange it for what they knew of papal affairs. All is "give and take in diplomacy," he reminded his father. One nagging concern was that Bulwer would steal the credit for whatever he managed to achieve. Then there was his salary. Should he seek an increase to lessen the likelihood that when promotion came it was not to the rank of a mere secretary of legation? A larger salary would permit him to "assume a little more position." "A man living in a lodging with a single servant must if he send the servant out open the door himself," he grumbled, "which is not a dignified way of receiving an ambassador, or a man high in the Pope's household, and would probably disincline such persons to repeat their visit."[22]

Bickerton had a quick and modest measure of diplomatic success. He persuaded Antonelli that it would be unwise at this time to establish a Catholic hierarchy in Scotland. The sectarian fire lit in 1850 by the re-establishment of a hierarchy in England and Wales was still smouldering, he warned the cardinal, and any fresh breeze from Rome would fan it back into flame. He negotiated an informal reciprocal commercial agreement which was welcomed as a "great step on the high road to a friendly intercourse," and secured the release of a British Evangelical Protestant detained for proselytizing. He forwarded to the Foreign Office a careful analysis of the political situation. Disaffection was "so great and universal," he reported in the summer of 1853, that any scarcity of food would lead to "very serious troubles and disorders." Dissidents had not been pacified by a promise of consultative provincial and municipal councils, very few of which were to be elective. What was more, there were to be no popular contests for another three years. He dismissed as myopic the policy of the papal authorities. They considered hopeless any genuine reconciliation of people and government, being content to "ward off, as much as possible, troubles and inconveniences, for the moment, and leave the future to take care of itself." Had they been impressed with the wisdom of the Frenchman who observed that the most dangerous moment for a government such as theirs was when it decided to reform?[23]

The "bad" government of the Papal States was able to survive because of the divisions within the "Revolutionary Party" of nationalists, and these Bickerton analyzed in some detail. Mazzini sought a single, indivisible Italian Republic, but most of his followers were believed to come from the lower classes infected with "Communist principles." Federalists sought urban republics bound loosely together. Fusionists sought a greater measure of national unity as a means to end foreign domination of the peninsula. Constitutionalists, with whom Bickerton identified, deprecated revolution, had the support of men of education and the middle classes, but unfortunately were not of one mind. Some wished Sardinia-Piedmont to extend a single constitutional monarchy throughout Italy, whereas others favoured constitutional governments in each of the existing states. That these revolutionaries were able to operate under a system of police that was considered absolute, repressive, and unscrupulous led Bickerton to the conclusion that the organs of law and order were corrupt as well as inefficient, and their denunciations of individuals were governed by "interest, vindictiveness and other passions not zeal in the service of their employers."[24]

Bickerton had taken up an excellent position in Rome, undersecretary Addington complimented him. Continue as you have so successfully begun, he wrote, "doing everything openly, without disguise or intrigue, and as becomes a straight forward English diplomatist and Gentleman." Although these words represented the Foreign Office mind, they echoed the comment of the French statesman Talleyrand, who was considered the very model of cynicism: "If straightforwardness is of prime value anywhere it is in political transactions" he advised, "for it is that which renders them solid and durable." "Straightforwardness is incompatible with ruse," he added. Bickerton was still adhering to the guide to personal conduct drafted for him by his parents a quarter of a century earlier. But he had difficulty reconciling its first and last watchwords:

ambition and patience. Yet, at the age of thirty-six, he was beginning to hope that he was finally set fair to acquire "esteem and reputation" for himself while securing for his nation the "honour and influence" it desired to wield in Rome.[25]

"Many English people are announced," Bickerton noted in early November 1853. So many Britons visited the Eternal City each year, perhaps 1,500, temporarily swelling the more permanent community of painters, sculptors, architects, and authors, such that there was a thriving English subculture. The Hotel d'Angleterre, English pensiones, an English Church, an English club, an English reading room, English physicians, an English chemist, an English grocer who sold English tea, even an English tailor, all catered to English needs. Hence "the chill of English manners," the "sibilance of English speech," and the "fastidiousness of English hygiene," which was well advised since the streets were infamous for their filth and stench and a *mal aria* rose from the Pontine Marshes. The social season traditionally ran from the carnival to celebrate the New Year until Easter, when the approach of the months of "unendurable heat" and greater danger of epidemics of disease led to an annual exodus. Bickerton took advantage of the resultant availability of rental accommodation to take a well-furnished apartment only to quit it on discovering that his resident landlord was Freeborn's *cancelliere* and thus probably under constant surveillance. He moved a short distance to the house of an English Catholic widow on the Via Gregoriana, which meant that he was only a short distance from the Spanish Steps, the Piazza below where the expatriate community often gathered, and the Office of Antonelli. He was thus saved the expense of a private carriage whenever he called there, considering it inappropriate and unbecoming for a "British Ambassador" to arrive in a "numbered hackney carriage."[26]

His acceptance by the diplomatic community, despite his anomalous position, was swift thanks to an unfortunate incident. A sergeant of the French occupying force arrested two English Catholics, one of them a chamberlain to the pope, whom he mistook for revolutionaries. The deeply embarrassed French ambassador, Comte Alphonse de Rayneval, apologized profusely to both pontiff and Lyons. Here was evidence, Bickerton privately chortled, that he was considered a figure of consequence. The Prussian minister and his English wife took him under their wing, and he established an enduring friendship with the Austrian chargé d'affaires, Lucas Count Gozze. They often hiked together along the banks of the Tiber, but Bickerton considered the city too "close and ugly" to make the exercise truly pleasurable. Unlike the great majority of his countrymen who visited Rome, its "treasures of art and records of antiquity" did not inspire him, having been taught in Greece that Roman was a term of reproach for relics of the classical past. Modern culture was another matter entirely, and he welcomed enthusiastically the opening of a new opera season at the Apollo Theatre, where he and Gozze shared a box. With the arrival of the British in large number, the pace of his social life accelerated. "I am wearied out by all these gaieties," he assured Henry Addington a little unconvincingly, "but it is so evidently desirable that I should make acquaintances, and be seen and heard in society, that I have made it a point to accept all invitations." Keen to be briefed for encounters with visiting prelates, he secured from his sister a copy of the "Catholic Register and Almanac," took a subscription to one Catholic newspaper, *The Tablet*, and read another, the *Catholic Standard*. An early arrival was Cardinal Nicholas Wiseman, with whom he had become acquainted through the Norfolks. Uneasy over his inability to learn the cardinal's purpose in Rome and plainly suspecting it was to press for some further enlargement of the Catholic Church in Britain, he reminded Antonelli of Wiseman's unreliability as an interpreter of British public opinion.[27]

Bickerton continued to forward to London "very able" analyses of the papal government's failings, its inefficiency and corruption, the favouritism and nepotism, the deplorable state of its finances, and the "great and almost universal disaffection." The arbitrary arrests of dissidents, their long confinement without trial, and the appalling prison conditions were, by creating a sense of insecurity, alienating those who desired only quiet. Meanwhile, the huge disbursements for police, spies, and prisons were magnifying the chronic operating deficit. The public disclosure in May of its staggering size convinced Lyons that bankruptcy beckoned unless there was genuine fiscal reform. Instead, there was further resort to "temporary expedients for getting on from day to day," beyond which the administration never seemed to look. Eventually, the pope so distrusted the finance department that he began taking revenues "into his own keeping" to ensure that they were "exclusively applied" to the purpose for which they had been collected. While highly critical of Antonelli's handling of chronic domestic problems, Lyons admired his independence internationally despite the intimidating presence of French and Austrian troops, and his seeming freedom from sectarian suspicion when dealing with him as a representative of Protestant Britain. No other secretary of state, he believed, could have kept relations on so secure a footing. Equally welcome was the papal government's surprising response to the deteriorating crisis in the Levant. There was in Rome a strong feeling against Russia and a warm sympathy for Turkey, and this apparent preference for Muslims over Orthodox Christians was rooted, Bickerton believed, in the Ottoman Empire's tolerance of its Roman Catholic minority and the deliberate injury done to the Roman Catholic Church by Russian governments.[28]

Foreign Secretary Clarendon was pleased by the unexpected influence Britain's unofficial representative had gained in Rome. Bickerton attributed it to his commonsensical rule of not interfering in matters over which his government could not exercise effective control. But praise was no substitute for promotion, and his spirits sank every time he learned of a younger man leapfrogging him. The announcement of his commission as attaché "to Our Legation in Florence, to reside in Rome" was some consolation for it was highly unusual in itself and had been granted "in consideration of the exceptional position in which you are placed, and of the diligence which you have displayed in performing the duties which devolve upon you in Rome." This "entirely new step" would permit him to count the entire length of his service in Rome towards the twelve years required to earn a pension. There was reason to celebrate, then, the fifteenth anniversary of his admission to the profession. "For in point of interest and responsibility, and, I hope, claim of promotion," he observed, "I think the permanent quasi-independence of the Attaché here is at least an equivalent for the temporary position of Chargé d'Affaires in which the Secretary of an ordinary Legation is occasionally placed."[29]

The news that Henry Addington, a mentor, was retiring from the Foreign Office would have dismayed Lyons had not his successor as permanent undersecretary been Edmund Hammond, who had already

been helpful and was a close friend of one of his aunts. Thoughts of promotion were forced back to the front of his mind on his thirty-seventh
birthday, 26 April 1854, for Bulwer's imminent return to Florence re-
awakened the fear that by insisting they conduct an exclusively private
correspondence the minister would ensure all dispatches to the Foreign
Office went over his name. But Bulwer was no thief of credit, and he and
Bickerton proved to be of one mind on the question of a formal British
diplomatic relationship with the Papal States. So long as a ban on a papal
nuncio in London remained on the statute book, they agreed it was useless to return to the subject. Indeed, Bickerton suspected that Pius and
Antonelli welcomed the current impasse following the purchase by the
Prussians of a palace on the Capitol with the apparent intent to build a
Protestant chapel on this commanding site. Pope and secretary of state,
he surmised, did not want yet another conspicuous Protestant legation.[30]

Bickerton especially regretted, with the approach of another summer, the departure of Edward and Adelaide Sartoris, who had become
close friends. She was a member of a great British thespian family, the
Kembles. She had a famous sister, Fanny, who styled herself Mrs Kemble
following her divorce from her American slave-owning husband. She
and Bickerton were introduced on 8 May 1854 and then were together almost daily until she left the city at month's end. She was no conventional
beauty, her face marked by smallpox and her build short and stocky,
but her personality was compelling. Bickerton enjoyed her company,
as she was high-spirited, ever willing to express emotion, often "cruelly
and wittily outspoken," and her conversation was "rich in anecdote." Her
disastrous marriage had given her an aversion to wedlock that matched
his own, for he had recently declared that a person should marry before
thirty-five or not at all. Perhaps because his only profound emotional
relationship had been with his mother, he did have friendships with
mature and usually married women. That with Fanny Kemble was to
be lifelong. Together with the Sartorises they explored the area around
Rome, picnicking on the Campagna. We used to leave the carriages,
Fanny later recalled, "stray and wander and sit on the turf, and take our
luncheon in the midst of all that was lovely in nature and picturesque in
the ruined remains of Roman power and the immortal memories of Roman history. They were hours in such fellowship never to be forgotten."[31]

Lyons spent a second summer in Rome carefully recording the daily temperature readings in his rooms. Happily, they rarely rose above 80 degrees, though heavy rainfall produced conditions reminiscent of a Turkish bath. The conditions explained the small quantity and poor quality of the information he forwarded to Bulwer, for the flight of all who could escape the city much diminished his chances of gathering interesting material. Winter brought the British flocking back much like swallows returning to Capistrano. He saw a great deal of the Sartorises, and his invitations to the French embassy increased now that Britain and the Second Empire were allies in the Crimean War, whose progress he watched closely. His father assumed command of the Black Sea fleet following the dismissal of Admiral Dundas, who was made the scapegoat of Britain's failures, and was joined by Moubray, who commanded one of the Royal Navy's first wooden screw ships. Bickerton immediately wrote to him for information on naval and military operations. Their father's intelligence had been "both interesting and useful," he told his brother, and the more he received the greater his bargaining power with diplomatic colleagues.[32]

Bickerton was present in St Peter's on 8 December 1854 at the Mass to celebrate the promulgation of the decree of the Immaculate Conception. Casting his eyes over the fifty-four cardinals, one patriarch, forty-three archbishops, and ninety-seven bishops, fifteen from Britain and its dominions, he judged the gathering a "very remarkable manifestation of the increase of the influence of the Popedom in the Roman Catholic Church." The new article of faith, that The Virgin had been conceived in her mother's womb free of the taint of original sin, had been objected to by several American and German bishops. They warned it would further alienate Protestants. Equally, Bickerton believed that many ordinary Catholics wished the Church to concentrate on the eradication of evils and abuses and especially on the "lamentable condition of its temporal authority." Instead, the pope appeared to be laying the groundwork for a declaration of his "infallibility in matters of Faith." Ultramontanes were certainly extolling the "sublime spectacle" of the Vicar of Christ undisturbed by either temporal difficulties or international affairs, "calmly occupying himself with the sacred mission of ascertaining and declaring Heavenly Truths." So impressed was he by Bickerton's commentary that

Bulwer sent it on in its entirety to the Foreign Office, where Clarendon was another who read it with great interest as well as admiration of the author.[33]

The presence in Rome of six members of the Irish Catholic hierarchy led by its dominant figures, Archbishops Cullen and MacHale, the latter a strident political nationalist, turned the Foreign Office mind to the unresolved problem of politically active Irish priests. Clarendon sought a plain expression of the pope's disapproval of the violent language of priests and their participation in political strife. Yet he realized such an expression would be ignored if the priests suspected it had been prompted by the British government. Bickerton had little hope of making ground on this issue, Antonelli explaining that the pontiff had neither the "canonical right to prohibit" the behaviour nor the "means of enforcing obedience to His exhortations." Furthermore, the likes of MacHale claimed that the Vatican did not understand the true state of Ireland, did not appreciate that the behaviour was vital to the clergy's popular influence, or realize that an attempt to interfere "authoritatively" would imperil the attachment of priests and people to the Holy See. This was not a threat to be taken lightly, and the Vatican could claim the cover of the British liberal state. The law in Ireland, Antonelli reminded Lyons, appeared to permit the strong language and proceedings of some priests. Moreover, even undeniably moderate clergy believed they had a legitimate interest in election results. His failure to persuade the Vatican to rein in politically active priests, or to establish formal diplomatic relations with Britain, did not damage Bickerton's burgeoning reputation. "I cannot help stating," Bulwer wrote to Clarendon, "how very much I agree in the substance of all communications I receive from Mr. Lyons, and how satisfied I feel as to the judgment and ability which dictate them."[34]

When in January 1855 Bulwer, worn down by ill health and an unhappy marriage, announced his resignation, he placed on the official record his admiration of Lyons's "zeal, intelligence and discretion." He had shown that he was as "capable of comprehending great questions as of getting through small ones" and recognized the usefulness of Catholicism as an antidote to communism. The mind of the masses "must be occupied with something," Bulwer observed, "and when it is not so

by religion it is always by some substitute for it." Here was an alternative concept of religion as the opiate of the masses. By the end of the
month the Aberdeen coalition had been forced to resign as a result of
its inept conduct of the Crimean War, and Bickerton was relieved to
hear that there would be no change at the Foreign Office. Palmerston
became prime minister and retained Clarendon as foreign secretary, but
a more aggressive war strategy seemed certain until the death of the czar
less than a month later dramatically improved the prospects of peace.
Bickerton, as a matter of national pride, did not welcome a swift end to
the hostilities. "The incapacity of the English Generals and of the Admirals (except one) has lowered the prestige and power of England," he
moaned, "and one cannot wish for peace until it is raised again" by the
capture of the Russian fortress and naval base at Sevastopol. However,
on 27 June he received a telegram over the recently opened telegraph
line to Rome informing him of his brother's death and granting him
leave. On 7 July, accompanied by his faithful personal servant Giuseppe
Cartelucci, he sailed for Marseilles, where he boarded the first of two
trains for the journey through France. He reached London, perhaps appropriately under the circumstances, on Friday, 13 July.[35]

His brother had won a Queen's commendation for the highly successful campaign of destruction he had led in the Sea of Azov which,
by denying Sevastopol essential supplies, had in his father's judgment
been the turning point in the capture of the fortress. But Moubray's
courage was on occasion reckless and his taking of his vessel very close
to Sevastopol to maximize the effectiveness of his guns resulted in a
wound which quickly became infected. He died at the age of thirty-five
on the night of 23 June while being cared for in the naval base hospital
at Therapia. There he was buried with full naval honours three evenings
later. Bickerton was lost for words. "I say little," he wrote to his father,
"because I feel so much about you and so hopeless of comforting you."
He did ensure that the memorial tablet prepared and paid for by Moubray's officers and crew was erected in St Paul's Cathedral as part of the
Crimean Memorial.[36]

Pausing in London only long enough to meet with Clarendon and
the senior Foreign Office staff and to dine at Norfolk House, Bickerton went down to Donnington Priory in Newbury to stay with Minna

and family. December brought another invitation to Woburn Abbey, where the party included Palmerston and several prominent Whigs, but a heavy snowfall caused it to break up early and Bickerton enjoyed a quiet Christmas at the Priory. He and Fitz travelled to Folkestone on the second day of the New Year to greet Sir Edmund, who was to participate in the war council summoned by the French. To prepare for it, he sat with the Cabinet on 5 and 6 January to settle the British position at the upcoming allied conference. Bickerton then joined him when a select group set off for Paris on 9 January. Sir Edmund participated in the conferences at the Tuileries Palace and the Ministry of Marine but they did not produce an agreement on strategy. Napoleon, acutely sensitive to a pacific drift in French public opinion, had welcomed the Russians' acceptance six days earlier of an Austrian ultimatum to negotiate peace. Father and son returned to London on 22 January, where Sir Edmund did not hesitate to capitalize on the sympathy aroused by the death of his younger son to further the career of the elder.[37]

Lyons reminded Clarendon of his son's widely praised conduct and prolonged residence in Rome, where Asiatic cholera had recently taken the lives of several diplomats. Privately, Bickerton disdained a "second rate Secretary of Legationship," but Peter Scarlett's appointment as minister to Brazil brought a rethink. The vacant post in Florence was offered to him, and while he considered it about the most insignificant in the profession and craved something more, to hold it while retaining his half-independent post in Rome would bring general recognition that he held "one of the *best* Secretaryships." So he accepted the position. "They have done enough to make it impossible to look upon any Secretary of Legationship as promotion from Rome," he consoled himself, "and not made Rome so good a thing, as to excuse their delaying me real promotion, which is what I want."[38]

Palmerston, impressed with Sir Edmund's commentaries on the conduct of the war, suggested he be sent back to Paris to lay down Britain's tough terms of peace at the congress set to meet there. Clarendon objected. Lyons, he argued, had little understanding of the political issues, was "singularly deficient in judgment," and was "irritable" and peculiarly vain. He had cultivated an image of a latter-day Nelson, which did not endear him to many of his senior colleagues. So he went to Paris in a humbler role. There too, as ordered by the Foreign Office, went Bickerton, who had been enjoying in London the company of Fanny Kemble. To keep *au courant* with the latest news and opinions while in the French capital he took *Galignani's Messenger*, a highly respected English-language daily whose declared mission was to promote an entente cordiale, and *L'Univers*, an organ of ultramontane propaganda. He gleaned additional information from a dinner at the British embassy and from his meeting with Lord Normanby, the new minister to Tuscany, who had once escaped from the Cabinet to the premier diplomatic posting of Paris but had resigned it in 1852. His selection as Bulwer's successor was a surprise since as ambassador to France he had provided information which had led to Palmerston's removal as foreign secretary in 1851. For Bickerton, his time in Paris had otherwise been uninteresting. "I have literally nothing to do, and do not see anyone on matters of business," he complained, "but it will be satisfactory to go back [to Rome] with Lord Clarendon's last instructions."[39]

He was being held in Paris at the request of Count Cavour, the prime minister of Sardinia-Piedmont, who more by crook than hook was endeavouring to place the Italian question on the Peace Congress's agenda. It was a question the French emperor believed would be solved by force alone. Neither Rome nor Austria would implement or agree to reforms without coercion, the emperor argued, and he had no intention of bullying the pope. Clarendon had intended to call for the withdrawal of the French and Austrian troops but did not do so for fear this would embarrass the emperor's relations with the French clergy and might, should the troops leave hastily, be followed by mass "throat-cutting" in the Papal States. Bickerton met separately with Cavour and Clarendon on his last full day in the French capital, 15 April. The Sardinian made plain his agreement with the French emperor that the Austrian obstacle on the road to Italian unity could only be removed by a "coup de canons." He credited Napoleon, a potential ally, with a sincere interest in Italy and a genuine desire to withdraw his troops. For the time being, however, he intended to pursue Italian unity by diplomacy alone and suggested Bickerton further the cause by intimating to Antonelli that Britain would wash its hands of responsibility for the consequences if political reform continued to be delayed. Clarendon covered much the same ground.

The pope needed to address the "evil" of the military occupation, he emphasized, perhaps by raising a reliable military force that would enable him to dispense with the unpopular Austrian troops. The French would have to remain for a time because Napoleon could not afford to risk allowing a hair of the pope's head to be touched. During his meetings with Antonelli Bickerton was to stress the power and independence the pontiff would enjoy at the head of an effective and efficient administration with certain and sufficient revenues. Yet the case of reform was to be made "very milk and water." If Britain adopted too strong a line, the foreign secretary cautioned, it would quarrel not only with Austria but also with France, which was the only power capable of doing anything.[40]

Leaving Paris the following day, Bickerton followed the unnerving route through the Mount Cernis Pass to call on James Hudson in the Piedmont capital. After a restful weekend there he travelled via Genoa and Leghorn to Florence, arriving in the early afternoon of 22 April. Now secretary of legation, he remained for almost a fortnight, conferring and dining with Normanby, getting up to date on developments during his long absence, taking long walks, and attending the theatre and the opera. "I like this place very much," he informed Minna, revealing a dramatic change of heart, "but I shall be glad to get to Rome and settle myself and set to work." All the while his temper was being frayed by the government's failure to honour his father with a peerage for his distinguished war service. To the entire family's relief, Sir Edmund was created Baron Lyons of Christchurch in the County of Southampton. But Bickerton could not forget that it had been grudgingly awarded after persistent lobbying by Fitzalan, now the Duke of Norfolk, and several other friends and political allies.[41]

Bickerton finally reached Rome three weeks to the day after leaving Paris, but he was not hopeful of making diplomatic progress. In the pope's mind his coronation oath to preserve the ecclesiastical government prevented him from agreeing to its secularization. According to Antonelli less than a score of priests were holding office, but that was as hard to believe as his claim that papal prisons held no more than fifty political offenders and that they had all been condemned by regular judicial tribunals. There was popular discontent, the secretary of state admitted, but he planned to introduce ambitious public works that would provide jobs and thus divert minds from politics. One of his projects was a rail connection to Bologna, but the opening of the line to Frascati had proven something of a disaster, for frequent accidents often obliged passengers to complete the journey on foot. Genuine quiet in the Papal States depended, Antonelli insisted, on the removal from Mazzini's home town, Genoa, of the "Revolutionary Committee," and a cease to Cavour's "active connivance" with nationalist revolutionaries. On the subject of reform, the French and Austrian ambassadors proved as uncooperative as Bickerton had expected, with Rayneval insisting that the "weaknesses and imperfections" of the papal government were no different nor were they greater than those of all governments. So at his audience with Pius on 17 May 1856, Bickerton delivered the message of reform in a manner designed to excite little resentment. Irritated by what he described as "excessive" caution, Clarendon instructed him "to return to the charge and endeavour to affect a breach" in the system of papal resistance. This he did, but again in a manner calculated to avoid raising papal hackles. For this Antonelli was grateful. Bickerton was learning to interpret his instructions rather than act merely as a messenger. He suspected, however, that his dispatches were no longer pleasing to the foreign secretary. Yet his latest commentary, Normanby observed, "must convince everyone who reads it that the British cannot do any good at the present."[42]

Continued pressure for reform might work to the advantage of the occupying powers and further erode British influence by reinforcing the papal government's belief that Protestant Britain was its natural enemy. Hence Bickerton welcomed a sudden Foreign Office silence, concluding that the Palmerston Cabinet was finding so much difficulty in deciding what to do that they thought it safer to remain silent. But the publication in France of a Rayneval dispatch threatened to ignite a parliamentary explosion. The French ambassador claimed that the papal government was "clement" towards rebels, constant in the pursuit of useful reforms, and overwhelmingly secular in administration, while constitutional government on the English model was inapplicable. Then came reports from the British consul at Ancona, George Moore, whose watching brief included the territories occupied by the Austrians, of street violence by members of an anti-wine-drinking league. Their targets were consumers. Were they seeking by limiting demand to drive down prices?

Were they agents of the government anxious to retain Austrian troops as suppressors of dissent? More alarming still was a dramatic surge in murders, which were eventually judged sectarian crimes, providing further evidence of the inability of the papal authorities to maintain order. Even the Swiss mercenaries were reported to be deserting in large numbers. Expecting the Italian policy of indecision to be assailed by the opposition when Parliament met in February, Clarendon asked Bickerton for a publishable report of some recent improvement in papal governance such as the pardoning of political prisoners. His dispatch mentioned "embryo reforms" but with a nod to honesty allowed that needed improvements in the judicial system were "not yet in shape to be mentioned."[43]

Bickerton had his annual audience with the avuncular Pius on 9 January 1857 and met monthly with Antonelli even though they rarely had business to discuss, understanding as he did that his influence "must always be more personal than official." Although he was continuing to take long walks for exercise, he was gaining weight and fretted that he was becoming "indolent in mind as well as in body." Normanby's decision in late May to undertake a tour of northern Italy obliged Bickerton as secretary of legation to take charge of the mission during the minister's absence. On the way he dallied in Siena to admire the cathedral and Galgano Saracini's gallery with its priceless collections of paintings, porcelain, ceramics, and jewellery. In Pisa he considered the illuminated leaning tower at night the most beautiful thing of its kind he had ever seen. Once safely established in the Tuscan capital, he welcomed his father, who brought the fleet to the Leghorn on 27 June, impressing the locals with Britain's naval might. Before leaving, the admiral entertained Florentine society on his gaily decorated flagship. There being little business to transact, Bickerton settled down to a comfortable existence only for a Normanby family crisis to prompt the minister's departure home on leave. Bickerton now became chargé d'affaires, which brought him a welcome additional two pounds a day, and the Normanbys generously allowed him to make use of their city residence. His duties did not become any more demanding, and he wrote little to the Foreign Office on Tuscan affairs. Instead, he corresponded fully with the minister so as to avoid the risk of sending home dispatches that were not consistent with his views. What he did send to the Foreign Office were reports on developments in the Papal States.[44]

The decision of the Austrians to relieve the pope of the cost of their troops promised to benefit papal finances to the tune of £50,000 a year, but one likely result, Bickerton fancied, would be the papal government's relaxation of its "endeavours to maintain itself by its own means." Recent French proposals for the reform of that government he treated with skepticism, regarding them as a ploy by the emperor to recover the ground he had lost with Italian liberals when he permitted Rayneval to return to Rome as ambassador. This coquetting with liberals would never be ardent, Lyons reminded Clarendon, lest it damage Napoleon's relations with the ultramontane clergy. As for the apparently popular response to the pope during his summer tour of his territories, the vast numbers who turned out in Austrian-occupied territory had been encouraged to do so by the troops. Elsewhere, the crowds had been too "quiet and decorous" to indicate "great devotion or enthusiasm." The pope's progress had in Bickerton's opinion been much like that of a "good-natured proprietor on a first visit to his estates, receiving compliments and congratulations, and in return granting small favours, and directing small local improvements, without much reflection or system." Nevertheless, were Protestant Britain to intervene in Rome in order to promote the reform that was necessary the Vatican would "immediately cry out that the Father of the Faithful cannot even allow it to be supposed that he [was] influenced by the council of Heretics."[45]

Lyons returned to Rome on 23 November, his mind as ever fixed on promotion. He continued to receive plaudits, James Hudson declaring that after twenty-six years in the service he could not recall a man of Bickerton's relative youth "whose mind was so evenly balanced – whose opinions were expressed more clearly and with as much consciousness, and was more thoroughly master of his business, or who in speaking carried more strongly conviction with him." Normanby was similarly complimentary, while Clarendon praised his "excellent despatches" and described him as "one of our most rising Diplomatists." Palmerston was another admirer of the content, clarity, and conciseness of his reports. "These things, if taken seriously," Bickerton brooded, "only serve to raise unreasonable expectations." But he was irritated at the age of forty by the frequent references to him as a promising young man. His analyses of the twenty-four men who held the rank of secretary of legation placed him very low on the list and this at a time when seniority was finally emerging as an important factor in promotions. Then came the news in February 1858 of the toppling of the Palmerston ministry, a scant ten months after its dramatic and convincing victory in a general election. Derby formed a second minority government and Malmesbury returned to the Foreign Office. Given the long connection of the Lyons family to the ousted Whigs, would Bickerton be overlooked by the Tories? Were her brother to be slighted, their father confided to Minna, it "would almost break my heart."[46]

CHAPTER THREE

Envoy Extraordinary and Minister Plenipotentiary

The arrival in Rome of the Duc de Gramont, the new French ambassador, late in 1857 raised Bickerton's hopes of French co-operation in his struggle to persuade Pius and Antonelli to reform the papal government. The fact that the Frenchman's previous posting had been the capital of Sardinia-Piedmont made James Hudson, the minister at Turin, the obvious source of information on Gramont. He was a political weathercock, Hudson replied. Raised with the family of the last Bourbon monarch, Charles X, he had in 1830 supported the Orléanist revolution. Eighteen years later he backed the revolution which gave France a Second Republic and a President Bonaparte. Now he was a loyal servant of the Second Empire. Personally vain but no fool, he was amiable and generously endowed with "French vivacity and acuteness." Unfortunately, his view of the problems of the Papal States could in Hudson's opinion only be described as "supremely ludicrous." Furthermore, the news of mass arrests of innocent French Republicans following the attempted assassination of Napoleon on 14 January 1858 made it unlikely that Gramont would be receiving imperial instructions to promote liberal reform in the Papal States.[1]

Palmerston's attempt to appease the French, who were infuriated by evidence that the plot had been hatched by political refugees granted asylum in Britain, contributed to the fall of his government on 20 February.

A fortnight later Bickerton received a telegram from Foreign Secretary Malmesbury instructing him to be ready to travel to Naples. He welcomed a change of air and climate for he was suffering chest pains and was plagued by a persistent cough much aggravated by the length of time he was spending at his writing desk. There was something so elastic in the air of Naples, one Briton wrote, that he had never been anywhere else where he felt he could "make exertions so easily." It was certainly a place of awe-inspiring natural beauty. Vesuvius had been especially active the past six months and so many people bearing torches were hiking up it at night that the slopes appeared to be "glittering with glow worms." The ruins of Pompeii and Herculaneum inspired awe of a different kind, while the city's century-old museum was a depository of ancient treasures, sculptures, mosaics, and bronzes.[2]

Bickerton's assignment was to ascertain the views of the Neapolitan government with respect to a pair of British engineers imprisoned and awaiting trial for their alleged involvement in another of Mazzini's nationalist conspiracies. Their plight was developing into a *cause célèbre* in Britain, despite the distraction of the Indian mutiny, for William Gladstone had exposed the appalling injustice of the legal system and the deplorable treatment of prisoners. They were an "outrage upon religion, upon civilisation, upon humanity, and upon decency," he had charged. The *Glasgow Examiner* described a reign of terror in which the innocent and the guilty had their nails torn out, boiling water poured over them, and iron caps screwed on them. It was widely reported that a special device consisting of iron bars and wires was used to deaden the screams of the tortured by forcing their jaws closed. The Neapolitan government, which "martyrizes with a smile and exposes you to torture with the most refined courtesy," a correspondent of *The Times* wrote, was laughing at the British government. The new Conservative ministry, whose leader had been accused during the recent general election of a willingness to stand by as "any despotic ruler so act towards his people as to dishonour Christendom and outrage humanity" and of approving the policy of the Neapolitan government, could ill-afford to ignore the plight of the engineers reportedly being "Driven Mad by the Neapolitan Police." "If you get these men out," Malmesbury wrote to Bickerton, "you will be adored in this country."[3]

Derby and Malmesbury were convinced that problems such as this would never have arisen had there been a resident British minister at Naples. He had been withdrawn in 1856, as had his French counterpart, following the unsuccessful attempt by their two nations to force King "Bomba" – a derisive appellation following the bombardment of Palermo on his orders – to moderate the harsh suppression of liberal critics of his rule. Gladstone from his own pocket and Palmerston from the secret service account had helped to fund one rescue project. "If we rescued a Prisoner for every 100 pounds we contributed it would not be bad Employment for the Money," Palmerston casually observed to Clarendon; £600 had been advanced. Unfortunately, the vessel purchased to carry to safety prisoners being held on the island of Santo Stephano sank before the operation was launched. Britain did secure the dismissal of the brutal Neapolitan state police minister, who stood accused by the then British minister, Palmerston's brother, of terrorizing liberals. Further to humiliate the monarch, Ferdinand II, who had been sympathetic to Russia during the Crimean War, Britain and France had dispatched fleets to Naples confident the display of force would frighten him into granting not only an "ample" amnesty to political prisoners, but also the reform of the legal system which Gladstone had insisted was essential if an amnesty was to be more than a single act of mercy. Unexpectedly, this gunboat diplomacy proved an embarrassing failure. The French withdrew their fleet on discovering that the French claimant to the throne in the event of Ferdinand being deposed would never win popular acceptance. The British fleet followed it, and in a vain effort to save face both nations broke off diplomatic relations with the Neapolitan regime. The "ground of the rupture," Derby observed, was "absolutely indefensible."[4]

Mazzini, learning of the covert British funding of the ill-fated Santo Stephano rescue, may have expected the Palmerston ministry to be similarly well disposed to the venture he was organizing. In late June 1857 he met in his home city of Genoa with Jessie Meriton White, famous as a feminist, an unsuccessful applicant for admission to an English medical school with the intention of specializing in midwifery and the diseases of women and children, and an ardent advocate of the Risorgimento. Mazzini met also with Carlo Pisacane, an impoverished Neapolitan nobleman who had served in the Neapolitan and French armies before his involvement in the short-lived Roman republic. As reported by James Hudson, who had excellent nationalist sources, the rescuers planned to seize as many steamers as possible in Genoa harbour, rifle the local arsenals, and then descend in force on Naples and Sicily. He thus paid little attention to the seizure by twenty-five well-armed men of a mail steamer running between Genoa, Sardinia, and Tunis – the *Cagliari*, which had a complement of thirty-two crew and passengers. It first put in at the island prison of Ponza, claiming to be in urgent need of repair, where its small force led by Pisacane overran the puny garrison, liberated the prisoners, and loaded the vessel with weaponry. The *Cagliari* then steamed to the Gulf of Policastro in Calabria, landing Pisacane and his men at Sapri, where they were swiftly rounded up by Neapolitan troops and Pisacane killed. The ship had already sailed for Naples, where its captain, according to his later testimony, intended to report the incident only to be intercepted by two Neapolitan warships. When a boarding party found a small quantity of arms, it was detained and its captain and crew arrested, among them two British steam engineers.[5]

Palmerston's reputation as the most robust defender of British subjects abroad, to which Bickerton had made a significant but largely unrecognized contribution in the Don Pacifico affair; the near-universal British contempt for King "Bomba" and interest in the plight of his thousands of political prisoners; and the certainty of an ever more excited public concern for the welfare of the engineers ensured a government response. The families of the two engineers, Henry Watt and Charles Park, appealed to it. Watt's health, in particular, had reportedly deteriorated "in a foul, small, fetid, verminous, damp" cell during the three hottest months of the year. "I thought at one time, my Lord," his brother wrote to Clarendon, "that a British subject could not be insulted, far less imprisoned with impunity in almost any part of the world, and I am sorry that this impression must be relinquished." Requests for access to the men by the British acting vice-consul – acting because the consul had been stricken by a stroke following the departure of the minister – had been rejected by the Neapolitans, who no doubt saw an opportunity of inducing Britain to re-establish full diplomatic relations. The sense of crisis deepened with the news that Park had attempted suicide by cutting his throat with a razor. Palmerston, ever sensitive to the drift of public opinion, immediately took a personal interest in the case. He sent word that the government had its eye on the engineers and would do everything possible to ensure they suffered no injustice. To that end, he ordered the employment of the best local lawyer as defence counsel in the event the pair were brought to trial.[6]

News that the engineers had been moved from Naples to Salerno in preparation for their day in court brought a swift Palmerstonian response in the form of demands for fair and public trials, for the naming of the defence counsel by the acting vice-consul, Lewis Barbar, and the forwarding to him of a copy of the indictment and his free access to the pair. The king initially ignored the demands, and Palmerston found himself under public pressure to do more. So Clarendon took the highly unusual step, given the absence of formal diplomatic relations, of writing to his Neapolitan counterpart Ferdinand Carafa. Carried to Naples by a member of the Foreign Office staff, the letter repeated the demand for consular and family access to the prisoners and repeated the earlier warning that a refusal to comply would be interpreted in Britain as "a deliberate act of hostility." News that Watt had also attempted suicide was the key that now unlocked the cell doors. Both Barbar and the father of Park were allowed to visit the pair, who described to them their ill treatment. The resultant public pressure in Britain for decisive action increased when a group of released crewmen exonerated the Britons of involvement in the attempted insurgency.[7]

On reading the indictment, Barbar ridiculed the charges as "too absurd to require any observation," while the report that a special high-ranking Neapolitan mission had left for France to congratulate the emperor on his escape from assassination excited the suspicion that "Bomba" was seeking a "separate reconciliation with the French Court." That at this juncture Palmerston and his colleagues were forced from office, and the part played in their defeat by the Conspiracy to Murder Bill, which had been introduced to appease the French, was an irony that did not escape Malmesbury. "I am in a singular position on this question," he dryly remarked. "I am made minister on purpose to resist interference on the part of France with our laws, and am also expected to keep up a quarrel with Naples in support of our interference with her institutions. What a set we are."[8]

Non-intervention in the domestic affairs of other nations and friendly relations with other Great Powers remained fundamental to the foreign policy of the Tories. They considered the entente cordiale with France vital to European civilization and moved quickly to repair the strained relationship. The Queen and the Prince Consort were sent to tour the worryingly enlarged French naval base of Cherbourg, where Napoleon acted as their guide. A close watch was kept on French "refugees" in Britain, and while their inflammatory republican publications were not suppressed, French customs officials were alerted of imminent ship-ments. In their response to the problem with the Neapolitans, Derby and Malmesbury resolved to adhere to the Paris Protocol of 1856, which sought to promote the peaceful resolution of international differences through mediation and arbitration. "We did so," Malmesbury later re-marked, "to show a respect for the principle and a good example." He might have added that "minor national disputes" were inconvenient at a time when British forces were heavily engaged in India suppressing the Sepoy mutiny. Hence the decision was made to send Bickerton Lyons to observe the trials of the engineers, give "a fair and complete report of their state," and not remain a day after the business had been settled. The emissary, Malmesbury assured the French, would not strive to re-establish diplomatic relations. Britain had no ulterior motive, he wrote, taking some licence with the truth, for Bickerton was to investigate dis-creetly the possibility of a resumption of formal diplomatic relations.[9]

A weary Lyons reached Naples late in the evening of Wednesday, 10 March, his carriage having been "upset" during the crossing of the Pontine Marshes. He would have little opportunity to relax and see the sights, he quickly realized. The trials had formally opened on 29 Jan-uary, though Watt had refused to attend court. Diagnosed by several physicians as "labouring under a mental aberration," he had been ef-fectively bailed into the care of the acting vice-consul and had the com-panionship of his brother, whose expenses were being defrayed by the Foreign Office. However, newspaper reports of Watt's "insanity" contin-ued to roil the political waters at home, and Benjamin Disraeli, the Tory leader in the Commons, was mocked for his "timid, tentative, feeble &

deprecatory" replies to questions. The belligerent sentiment on display in the lower house reminded Malmesbury of the need to secure quickly the freedom of the two men. In Naples Bickerton lost no time checking on Watt, attending court, and discussing with Carafa both the situation and the threatening mood in Britain. Watt was speedily liberated and was accompanied on the trip home by a Foreign Office courier as his escort. On arrival, at the suggestion of Lyons, he was placed in the care of a "doctor of mental disorders."[10]

The credit for this success was Lyons's, foreign secretary and press agreed. As for Park, Malmesbury had no intention of issuing threats "without a certainty of action if those threats are despised." Instead, Bickerton was authorized to dangle before Ferdinand II the carrot of a possible resumption of full diplomatic relations should Park be freed and sent home before Parliament resumed sitting after the Easter recess. As a first step Bickerton negotiated the release on bail of the "nice, intelligent lad." Brought to Naples from Salerno, he was lodged in the British infirmary, where he swiftly recovered his health while Bickerton secured his unconditional discharge. He sailed on 10 April for Genoa, where he was reunited with his waiting parents. There was a postscript. Twenty years later, having fallen on hard times, Park made an unsuccessful application to Lyons for appointment as a Queen's messenger.[11]

"Mr Lyons" was an agent fully worthy of the foreign secretary's confidence, Carafa informed Malmesbury, for the sincerity of his character guaranteed that the British government received "the most correct information." Malmesbury agreed and warmly applauded his exceptional judgment and discretion. "I am very much pleased myself with what I have done here," Bickerton informed Minna, "not that I feel very sure it will be thought well of in England, but that I am rejoiced at having done so much good to the two poor engineers themselves." Some Britons regretted Park's liberation, Lyons knew, arguing that his continued imprisonment and his trial would have improved the chances of both men winning handsome financial compensation for their suffering. If these comments irritated Bickerton, for the prison cells had been visited by a particularly malignant strain of typhus, so did newspaper reports written by journalist friends of the acting vice-consul that depicted him as the true hero of the hour. Barbar would do a better job of feathering his nest if his friends praised Lyons and Malmesbury "instead of going on as they do," a mordant Foreign Office official remarked. Bickerton, having whispered a word of friendly caution into Barbar's ear, sought to dampen Foreign Office suspicions of him. The Neapolitans, not Barbar, had been the source of the information used by one of the journalists, he wrote, and he did not expect the scribe in question to be any less indiscreet in future. He was an honest man who wrote what he thought, endeavoured to be accurate as to facts, and, like many other Britons, wanted "matters brought to extremities between England and Naples."[12]

The others in this category, Lyons reminded the Foreign Office, were "Revolutionary Italian partisans" and the government of Sardinia-Piedmont. The latter's legation in London had leaked to the press the report of the distinguished international lawyer Robert Phillimore, who accused the Neapolitans of seeking to import the "extraordinary rights" of belligerents into pacific relations. Consequently, Phillimore was not at all surprised by the demand of the Sardinians for the restitution of ship, cargo, and crew in order to "resist this unjustifiable infringement of the rights of nations." If Cavour went to war he ought to be shot, an agitated Malmesbury commented, "because no one knows better than he does the consequences which may follow – We and France ought to prevent it and not allow a man to move and disturb the Peace of Europe." To forestall a Sardinian resort to force, he handed to Lyons the delicate diplomatic task of persuading the Neapolitans to release the *Cagliari* and its crew.[13]

Derby plotted the government's revised course. He instructed Malmesbury to be effusive in his thanks to Ferdinand II for the release of the men and for waiving criminal proceedings against them, but to make plain Britain's requirement that they be indemnified for their long confinement in appalling conditions on charges unsupported by the prima facie evidence. Since the engineers had suffered "mental malady" and "broken health," which in men of their class was tantamount to "starvation," Lyons was advised that payments of £1,000 each would be acceptable. Less clear was international law with respect to Sardinia's demands for compensation. The Neapolitans had been legally justified in boarding a vessel notoriously involved in a "piratical attack" on their territory, Britain's law officers had concluded, but it and the crew should then have been handed over to Sardinia. So Derby cautioned Malmesbury against going too far with the Sardinians on this aspect of the affair. They should advise the Neapolitans that the return of the *Cagliari* would be an act of courtesy agreeable to Britain, who would use its good offices to persuade Sardinia to accept it in the same spirit. Then, on some "plausible pretext," Britain and France might reward Ferdinand with a resumption of diplomatic relations.[14]

The "somewhat unfriendly zeal" of the Sardinians, who were again playing with British public opinion and might push matters to extremes, led Malmesbury to look to France for help in restraining them. When the French declined to come to his aid he promised the Sardinians "moral support" only for the recovery of vessel and crew. Britain gave no assurances on the subject of their claim for compensation. There was always a danger, however, of being outmanoeuvred by the wily Cavour, who proposed that in the event of a Neapolitan refusal to compensate the two Britons the two nations should jointly propose either mediation or arbitration of their respective claims. Since Britain had urged this peaceful course it could not in honour flatly reject the Sardinian's artful proposal. Nothing, Malmesbury suspected, would satisfy Sardinia-Piedmont "but our sending Lord Lyons' ships to help her to eat macaroni at Naples, in which process I confess I see neither glory to my own country nor benefit to mankind."[15]

Much depended, therefore, on the diplomatic skill of the admiral's son. There was little likelihood of him failing to act "with the greatest judgment and tact." The "most valuable function of diplomatists consists in the tact and temper with which they generally settle trifling difficulties, which might be exasperated into serious quarrels," Bickerton believed. His primary task was to obtain the compensation for the engineers that would save his government from the embarrassment of going to mediation or arbitration as a co-plaintiff with Sardinia. It would also relieve the pressure being exerted by the *Morning Post*, Palmerston's mouthpiece, for military reprisals in the event that compensation was withheld. A refusal to compensate the men would in all probability oblige Britain to act with Sardinia, Bickerton was to inform Carafa, and rejection of their joint proposal of mediation would lead to reprisals. "I shall seize a ship or two full of macaroni," Malmesbury half-jokingly remarked, "sell it, pay Park and Watt, and give Naples the change if there is any." Should it become apparent that the obstacle to a settlement was Ferdinand II's fear that he would then be obligated to make similar provision for the crew of the *Cagliari*, Malmesbury suggested Bickerton offer the king an escape from this predicament. He might bill Sardinia for the loss of life and damage to property at Ponza and Sapri, and the cost of the pensions paid to the families of the Neapolitans killed. Of course, this tidy solution should not be traced to the British government.[16]

In "minor disputes prudence is more indispensable than zeal," Bickerton believed, echoing the French diplomatic cynic Talleyrand, so he kept to himself the idea of a Neapolitan counterclaim against Sardinia and made no mention to Carafa of possible reprisals if the engineers were denied compensation. Instead, he astutely presented to the foreign minister the letter in which Malmesbury, who privately moaned that the Sardinians were a "cannonball attached to our leg," demanded compensation and called for a response within seven days. Ferdinand blinked in the face of the implied ultimatum. He agreed on 11 June to pay £3,000 in compensation to the engineers – it was divided between them, though Watt's share was given to the care of trustees – and to place the *Cagliari* and the remainder of its crew at the disposal of the British government. The settlement "is indeed a triumphant termination of English interference in a matter so closely touching our honour," the British press crowed. Ten days later the vessel sailed in the charge of Barbar but under the command of its captain, who with many of his crew had been imprisoned for almost a year. The Tories appeared to be enjoying one of those runs of luck that turn the heads of gamblers, *The Times* commented, though it recognized that "in the presence of more urgent anxieties politicians will soon forget the past perversity of Naples."[17]

The government had already turned its attention to the uncooperative French, who were reportedly purchasing immense quantities of saltpetre, an ingredient of explosives, although sulphur was used in the treatment of "wine disease" and phylloxera may already have been detected. The reported hostility to Britain of members of the emperor's household, blaming it as they did for the attempted assassination, was another source of concern. Did the staff speak for the emperor? Ambassador Cowley's belief that the ill will was confined to senior officers of the army and the navy was not particularly reassuring since the emperor was "proportionately in their hands." A recall of the Mediterranean fleet to home waters was rejected for fear of fostering a sense of crisis, but Admiral Lyons was instructed to keep an eye on French naval activity and match any movement to the Channel. To calm the British, Napoleon confidentially advised them that his military preparations related to the Italian question, but the Foreign Office suspected him of planning an intervention in Mexico. The "alarmists" were dismissed by Disraeli as dupes of a Russian agent whose task was to sow distrust between Britain and France. The pigeonholes at the French foreign ministry, he told Derby, were jammed tight with schemes to invade every country of Europe, Africa, Asia, and America, and he claimed personally to have seen one which envisaged a Franco-Spanish assault of Mexico. This did not calm Malmesbury, who argued that with such a reckless neighbour Britain's command of the Channel was vital and that the Royal Navy should therefore be strengthened. Derby, however, had concluded that Napoleon was indeed planning to expel Austria from Italy.[18]

Bickerton could stake a claim as Britain's most careful analyst of the Italian problem, and his performance in Naples had strengthened his growing reputation as a deft negotiator. Unaware of Malmesbury's private boast that he had named only men of the "right colour" to vacant positions in the diplomatic service, Lyons was looking for promotion. He did not wish to go elsewhere as a secretary of legation, nor did he desire "one of the horrible Chargé d'Affaireships in South America," regarding both as a "terrible blow" to ambition. He was probably heartened by the fresh cries in Britain for reform of the service in order to end the tradition of "providing for aristocratic partisans at the public expense." The call by *The Times* for the promotion of "rising talent and those tyros of diplomacy who, though long since turned 40, are still with cruel sarcasm called 'young men'" must have resonated with him. A month shy of his forty-first birthday, he fell into that category. What he feared was that the Tories would lose office before he was rewarded, for if the friendly Clarendon returned to the Foreign Office he fancied he would be kept in Rome. Any other Whig might not even give him a thought.[19]

Bickerton first fixed his eye on Naples, where he knew the government was thinking seriously of reopening the legation, but the removal of Normanby from Tuscany opened another possibility. The minister railed against his cavalier treatment by the Tories. They had embarked on a ridiculous policy of removing peers not decked in their political colours, he protested, describing it inaccurately as "Quite a new doctrine." After all, fellow Whigs dominated as chiefs of mission, and his successor, the Honourable Henry George Howard, the secretary of legation at Paris, was a member of a distinguished Whig family. Arriving in Florence on Saturday, 22 May, he left two days later, telling staff he was too ill to remain. Claiming to be a victim of St Anthony's fire, he announced he was returning immediately to Paris to consult a physician in whom he had confidence. Howard's family attempted to salvage his career, urging Malmesbury to reappoint him as minister, but the foreign secretary declined to rescue a man of the wrong "colour" who had "brought contempt on himself and the Queen by his eccentric conduct." He understood that this was a "woman's story," that Howard, a widower, had become involved with a married woman or a widow and she had written to say "*she* was miserable." Learning of this "marvelous escapade," Bickerton hurriedly consulted his father on what to do.[20]

The Tuscan mission was not a great prize, being rated a third-class post and carrying a modest salary of £2,000 per annum. Nevertheless, as an envoy extraordinary and minister plenipotentiary Bickerton would have a better chance of securing a far more important posting. Moreover, for the time being there would be no one of rank in either Rome or Naples. The admiral entered the lobbying stakes, although his son's political bloodline was unlikely to impress Derby, the nation's foremost owner of racing horse flesh. Nor could Bickerton claim the seniority that had recently emerged as an important if far from exclusive factor in promotions as the choice of Howard had demonstrated. Yet he considered himself superior in intelligence, wisdom, and ability to most of the men who outranked him in years of service. His performance in Rome merited recognition. He had gained a presence there, something Petre had lacked, and despite his awkwardly unrepresentative post had established considerable personal influence. His dispatches were informative, insightful, and admirably clear, which accounts for his irritation with the heavily edited versions published in the Blue Books. He had never shared Normanby's confidence that the Vatican could be persuaded to introduce liberal reforms. It understood, he recognized, that the great mass of Italians had an aversion to the constitution of the papal government "quite independent of the goodness or badness of its administration." Change, it reasoned, could "only weaken its position." The people of the Papal States would never be satisfied unless "the essential principles of temporal Ecclesiastical Sovereignty" were abandoned. Bickerton had supplemented his analyses of the regime's structural deficiencies and the seething popular discontent with insightful commentaries on the French and Austrian occupations, on papal relations with other nations, and on the issues of peculiar interest to his own government, such as the political activism of Irish Catholic priests. He had certainly more than met the fundamental responsibilities of the diplomat, those of providing the foreign secretary with "up-to-date information about the state of affairs in the country" to which he was posted and "the true state of feeling in the country." As a result he bequeathed to his successor a well-organized archive rich in content. "I had the pleasure of digging up B. Lyons from Dresden, and giving him the mission in Rome," Lord John Russell was to write to his nephew Odo. "I hope you may do as well and get on as quickly." Odo Russell was to help himself by his advantageous marriage to the daughter of another foreign secretary, Clarendon.[21]

Bickerton heard during the second week of June that he was to replace the "run away" from Florence. The decision may have been influenced by a Commons debate six weeks earlier during which critics of the traditions of the diplomatic service drew attention to the continuing domination of the most senior positions by peers or their near relations and the rarity with which long-service professionals made it to the loftiest heights. Bickerton had impressed Malmesbury with his cool-headedness, reliability, adaptability, judgment, and discretion, and although connected to one of the nation's most illustrious dukedoms was a professional diplomat. Officially gazetted minister plenipotentiary on 18 June while still in Naples, he took his leave of Carafa on 1 July and in Rome made a round of farewell calls; in a valedictory dispatch he dwelt upon the latest follies of the commander of the French troops. The general had been dissuaded only with great difficulty from fortifying St Peter's Square on the day of the festival of Corpus Domini and from declaring a state of siege following an incident between papal soldiers and several of his men. "His proceedings are so ill judged as certainly tend both to bring the Papal Government into contempt and to make himself and the troops he commands ridiculous," Bickerton reported. He then set off for Florence, accompanied as far as Empoli by his friend Gozze, and reached the Tuscan capital on Sunday, 11 July. Five days later he journeyed to beautiful Lucca to present his letters of credence to the grand duke.[22]

As a chief of mission Lyons was carrying in his baggage significant additions to those personal rules of diplomatic conduct drafted as a result of his trying experience in Athens. He understood that it was unwise to interfere in matters in which his government could not exercise effective control, and that his dealings with foreign governments should be governed by straightforwardness and honesty, which also excluded involvement in covert activities. There were other means to gain intelligence without compromising his personal honour, such as an exchange of information. In diplomacy all was give and take, he accepted. He had learned that prudence was more indispensable than zeal when minor disputes arose. Tact and temper were two of the most valuable qualities of the diplomat when he sought to solve trifling difficulties which might otherwise escalate into serious quarrels. Bickerton Lyons was committed to easing tensions and avoiding confrontations; hence he was increasingly willing to adapt his instructions to changing local circumstances and not simply deliver them.

He assured the Normanbys, with a certain economy of truth, that his appointment had been spontaneously made by the foreign secretary. This exercise in personal diplomacy did not go unrewarded. Although smarting over his removal and the refusal of the Tories even to permit him to "resign," Normanby still rejoiced "at the hands into which the business of this Mission is about to pass." The couple gave Lyons the warmest of welcomes. He dined and spent most evenings with them while they lingered in the city, and when they retreated from it for the summer he rented their residence, the Palazzo San Clemente. He now belonged, after twenty years of service, to the second level of diplomatic agents. Only ambassadors stood above him. His duties on first reading were a little intimidating. He was expected to determine how best to approach the state to which he was accredited in order to secure or amend an alliance; to maintain good correspondence with the diplomatic representatives of friendly states in order to discover the private views of their governments and procure early information of any discussions those ministers were having with the host nation; to give "constant attention" to Britain's commercial interests; to provide assistance to British traders and in the event they became embroiled in disputes to do his best to ensure they received "good and speedy justice"; to obtain the "most accurate information" on the fortifications of the host nation, its armed forces and the means of their augmentation; to submit detailed economic analyses which included the host government's expenses, revenues, means of levying extraordinary supplies, extent and nature of its commerce and "manufactories," and the size of its population; to forward intelligence which might be of advantage to British dominions; to correspond with British ministers at other foreign courts, but never to communicate with private friends on public business or allow members of his staff to do so; to ensure the security of ciphers and deciphers, and the accuracy of secret communications; to receive from his predecessor and deliver to his successor the "official" correspondence; and on quitting his post to write a final comprehensive report. To this daunting statement of duties the retired Henry Addington added a piece of sound advice. Send dispatches only when you have something of interest to say, he wrote, for "unnecessary writing" was not welcomed by an already overburdened Foreign Office staff.[23]

Bickerton had little reason to pester London, for a postal convention was the only item of business on his agenda. He corresponded with Hudson in Turin, who had written to congratulate him on his promotion. Sir James revealed that Cavour had been much impressed with Bickerton's "intimate knowledge" of Italy when they met in Paris, and reported the talk in the Piedmont capital that Napoleon III was planning war against Austria. Grateful for this intelligence, Lyons promised to forward to Hudson any that came his way. Turin, he wrote, was "the real centre of Italian politics." But money often rivalled promotion as a Lyons obsession. He moaned that he was poorer in Florence than he had been in Rome and had "barely suffice to keep up a decent appearance." He declined his father's offer of assistance and resolved to live within his income. Consequently, when Normanby reclaimed his Palazzo, Bickerton regarded with "horror" the expense of setting up his own establishment. He opened negotiations for the lease of a fully equipped residence, laboured over the design of the liveries of servants down to the shape of their buttons, approached the best cook in Florence, and wrote to Moët et Chandon for a supply of champagne. These preparations were brought to a halt on 5 October. "Your father is seriously ill," Malmesbury telegraphed, "and it is desirable you should come to England immediately."[24]

The admiral's health had long been a source of anxiety. He had lost a great deal of weight, which was not surprising given the pain he suffered when he ate and drank. Even eggs beaten up with sherry could only be swallowed with great discomfort. He had declared himself well enough to command the squadron which escorted the Queen and Prince Consort across the Channel to meet with the Emperor at Cherbourg but was unable to participate fully in the festivities. On his return to Spithead, he hauled down his flag and retired to Arundel. There he continued to decline and by early October could only sleep with the aid of "Morphia." Bickerton had convinced himself that convalescence in the Sussex countryside would restore his father's strength but left Florence as soon as possible after reading Malmesbury's telegram. He reached Arundel in the early afternoon of Sunday, 10 October, and was soon joined by sister Annie and her eldest son. Although suffering himself from a throat infection, Bickerton went up to London on 11 November to meet with Malmesbury and senior Foreign Office staff. He may have entered the building nervously for it was "tumbling down," one end heavily shored up, and the foreign secretary was fearful of being "smothered" in the ruins of his "shop." Malmesbury balked at the estimated cost of the proposed new building, £230,000, which he considered triple a reasonable sum. The new theatre at Covent Garden, the new hotel at Paddington, even the new Westminster Hotel, which was reminiscent architecturally of the Tuileries Palace, had all been built for far less. Nor did he approve of the proposed neo-Gothic design, for in 1856 it had been decided "to bring together in one great edifice, the Home, Foreign, Colonial, India and Local Government Offices." He welcomed an engineer's assurance that the building would be safe for at least another two or three years, and three years later the Foreign Office was temporarily relocated while a new building was raised on the site of the old. Palmerston, as prime minister, shared Malmesbury's dislike of the neo-Gothic design, which was revised to give the offices an "Italian character."[25]

Bickerton returned to Arundel on 12 November and one week later accepted the post of British minister to the United States. The news cheered his father, who died peacefully of "general debility" on 23 November, having celebrated his sixty-eighth birthday two days earlier. He was interred in the family vault in the Fitzalan Chapel, and *The Times* offered the ultimate tribute by dubbing him a latter-day Nelson. If Bickerton's relations with his father had never been as intense or as intimate as those with his mother, he had been proud of the admiral, and pride caused him to deny Alexander Kinglake access to his father's papers for his eight-volume work on the *Invasion of Crimea*. Kinglake had in his opinion written disparagingly of the admiral. Bickerton's promotion to ministerial rank by the Tories first in Tuscany and now in the United States was a measure of the respect he had won by his professionalism. His "detachment, coolness, and foresight" would be assets in dealings with the difficult Americans. Yet his sudden rise owed something to plain good fortune. Henry Howard's bizarre flight from Florence was one stroke of luck, opening as it did the door to the Tuscan mission. Similarly, the transfer to the Hague of the Whig heading Britain's legation in Washington and the refusal of his intended successor to cross the Atlantic were additional pieces of good fortune.[26]

Francis, Lord Napier, had entered the profession at much the same time as Bickerton, serving in Vienna, Naples, and Constantinople before Washington. Just as Lyons had enhanced his reputation in Naples so had Napier made his name and earned Palmerston's respect while serving there as secretary of legation during the Sicilian revolution of 1848. In Washington, he sought and found a house in a good area of the American capital. He leased it from Hamilton Fish, a former congressman, a former governor of New York, and a former senator who was to return to Washington in 1869 as secretary of state. Napier followed to the letter his instructions to entertain on a lavish scale, his "hospitable and generous manner of life" winning him friends and influence, but his salary of £4,500 proved "scarcely commensurate to the expenditure."

Lacking a large private income, he saw financial ruin looming on his horizon. He knew, however, that an increase of his salary would excite the parliamentary critics of the diplomatic service. They would point out, he glumly predicted, that he was already being paid almost as much as the president of the United States. The comparison would be invalid, he argued, since the president's living expenses were paid from the public purse and several recent tenants of the executive mansion had by living "meanly" banked half their incomes. To ease the financial strain, Napier was permitted to dip into the secret service fund and was granted a modest addition to his house allowance. Nevertheless, he was still "considerably in debt" at the opening of the 1858 social season. Should he make "a sudden and indecent alteration in his social conduct" by attempting to live within his income, he asked Malmesbury, or should he persist with his "previous indulgent habits"?[27]

"I live in the midst of a shifting, miscellaneous society altogether given up to dining, drinking, and dancing, primitive and coarse in some respects, but jolly and prodigal and all pressing towards the house of the 'British Minister,'" he wrote. "I therefore think I have some claim on the public purse." His persistent pleas for additional funds may have irritated the overworked and underpaid staff of the Foreign Office but it was his undiplomatic opinions that led the Tories to doubt this Whig's suitability for this post. Elements of the Northern press accused him of being a pro-slavery partisan. A prominent member of the newly formed Republican Party, which opposed any expansion of slavery, claimed he talked as glibly as President Buchanan on the right of settlers of a territory "to establish Slavery if they see fit." Napier had "allowed himself to be crammed with all the subtleties & apologies by which the Administration [had] surrounded its course" in the territory of Kansas, wrote Senator Charles Sumner of Massachusetts to his influential British friends and admirers. More damaging still in the eyes of his own government was the perception that he was "Yankee bitten." During a widely reported speech to the St George Society of New York he declared that the "peaceful and legitimate expansion of the United States forms a matter of satisfaction and pride for every reasonable Englishman." This was likely to be interpreted by Americans as an assurance of the British government's intention "to withdraw all pretensions to Central America, and allow the United States Government to rule and reign there as they please." Britain should tolerate American "filibustering" in the Americas, the American press observed, because its conquests in Asia were the British version of it. The analogy was false, Britain's most popular newspaper indignantly replied, for Britain had "never had recourse to the system of covertly aiding and abetting a piratical horde in its descent upon a neighbouring Power, already torn asunder by internal quarrels."[28]

Napier had made a "mess" not only by his public statements but also by "confidential conversations uncovered by official documents and the Yankees have taken advantage of it," Malmesbury informed Prime Minister Derby. To resolve the problems in Central America, Napier advocated British acceptance of the American interpretation of the Clayton-Bulwer Treaty of 1850, whose opaque meaning had become a fresh source of Anglo-American friction. American possession of Mexico together with broad swathes of Central America would in his opinion be advantageous to Britain while their annexation of Cuba would facilitate suppression of the slave trade. He had welcomed Malmesbury's return to the Foreign Office in the belief that he was a Tory who did not "view the expansion of the United States southwards with any jealousy." However, the foreign secretary had been dismayed by Napier's conversation with Lewis Cass, the American secretary of state, during which he had said "we recognize the Monroe Doctrine which all our Governments have ever repudiated." President James Monroe, its author, had in 1823 effectively declared the Western hemisphere an exclusively American sphere of influence.[29]

One of Napier's fiercest critics was Sir William Gore Ouseley, a veteran diplomat who had begun his career as an attaché in Washington, had a "charming American wife," and had been appointed by Clarendon to seek a solution to several Central American problems. When he arrived in Washington to seek recognition as the British negotiator, tension quickly developed between the two. Ouseley ridiculed Napier's "apparent anxiety to yield anything and everything" to the Americans, describing his attitude as fit only for a debating society of "Little Englanders." The minister was "positively dangerous," he warned the Tory government. "Napier's own policy seems to be that of giving up everything the United States can wish for, even before they ask it," commented a

prime minister who flattered himself that he understood Americans because he had once toured a large section of their country. In its dealings
with them, Britain must always employ very temperate but firm language and be willing if necessary to fight for its rights "rather than yield
to a spirit of democratic encroachments, which, if not steadily resisted,
will have no limits to its demands." They should, Derby declared, be
"very civil, very firm" and go their own way. "It is the only way to deal
with them, and in spite of all their bluster, they will think twice before
they quarrel with us."[30]

Derby proposed to finesse the problem by moving Napier to Madrid.
His recall from the United States serves to cast doubt on the recent contention that the two nations had developed such a rapprochement over
the previous half-century that conflict was almost impossible. Derby
planned to send the current minister to Spain, Sir Andrew Buchanan, an old hand and a Tory, in the opposite direction. He had briefly
served in Washington as a much younger man, and being "a downright
sort of man, without Conceit" was in Malmesbury's opinion ideal for
the American post. Benjamin Disraeli, on the other hand, considered
him "perfectly useless," and it was fortunate that Buchanan declined
the transfer. He pleaded advanced years and poor health. Approaching
fifty-two, he needed a "dry warm climate" and was not fit enough to endure the heat and humidity of the American capital, which was built on
marshland. Not even the tempting bait of a KCB (Knight Commander of
the Order of the Bath) could hook him. In truth, few British diplomats
of aristocratic birth or pretensions, and Buchanan was the only son of
the eldest daughter of an earl, welcomed transatlantic "exile." The vast
distance from home and Continental Europe, the lack of amenities, the
reportedly rough and rude society, and the notoriously unpleasant and
unhealthy climate were reasons enough to decline a posting there.[31]

Lyons had been informally approached by Malmesbury on 8 November, when Buchanan had stated emphatically his unwillingness to
cross the Atlantic. Asked if in the event of a vacancy he would accept
the American mission, the chronically ambitious Bickerton, perhaps
confident that summers in Rome had conditioned him physically for
Washington, replied by return mail. Six days later Malmesbury dou-
ble-checked to ensure he was of the same mind, as indeed he was. Regarded within the profession as "the most important mission next to the

Embassies," it had been the only one outside of Europe to which several years earlier he would have gone as secretary of legation. His interest in the United States may also have been sparked by the long residence there of his Uncle William, whom the family had been modestly supporting for many years, and by the experience in Washington of his old Athens friend Philip Griffith. He admitted that the summer heat was "stewing," but relief came with the onset of the "most lovely weather imaginable," Indian summer. House rents were excessive, servants' wages "ultra extravagant," and a decent horse expensive, yet the politics were in many respects challenging and fascinating. No country was so weak for "war purposes," Griffith wrote, yet some "rash act of her turbulent and unruly people" might at any moment plunge the Republic into a general war. In that event, unless the result of some unjustifiable aggression, the conflict would cause the Union to "fall to pieces of itself." Nevertheless, legions of visitors, among them political philosophers and literary giants, and a host of diplomatic scrapes, had constantly drawn the attention of the British public to this burgeoning political and economic giant.[32]

Malmesbury asked Lyons to keep mum on the appointment until he had an opportunity to inform Napier that he was being transferred to the Dutch capital. That the Napiers' departure from Washington was deeply regretted by so many of the capital's influential residents surely confirmed in Derby's mind the wisdom of the decision. The old bachelor in possession of the executive mansion had been charmed by Lady Napier and avowed that no lady had ever made a more favourable impression on local society. The immense gathering in the vast ballroom of Willard's Hotel on 17 February 1858 to bid them farewell was proof of their popularity. The breadth of the Napiers' appeal was illustrated by the event's joint sponsors: James Murray Mason, a senator from the slave state of Virginia and chairman of the Foreign Relations Committee; Senator William Henry Seward of New York, the odds-on favourite to secure the presidential nomination of the Republican Party; and Senator John J. Crittenden of Kentucky, one of the border states where Unionism and slavery coexisted uneasily. Bickerton Lyons faced an uphill task in gaining the same measure of American respect and affection.[33]

"Your mission here ought always to be filled by a first rate man whose character is known in this country and whose acts and opinions will command respect and influence in England," Buchanan wrote somewhat reproachfully to a British acquaintance. His countrymen knew little of Lyons, he pointed out to Lord Clarendon. George Dallas, a former senator, a former vice-president, and the current American minister in London, had known the first Lord Lyons, and this disposed him to be "partially inclined" towards his son. The new minister was quite "unexceptionable," he advised the State Department, though he lacked what Napier had possessed, the "immense advantage" of a wife. "A Legation without a lady is but half composed," Dallas observed, "a column sans capital, a piano sans pedal, coiffure sans curls." Not that this necessarily doomed the mission. Lyons impressed the assistant secretary of the American legation, Benjamin Moran, as "a sensible man, calculated to be popular at home [United States]. He is about 40 years of age, short, thick set, of dark complexion, and is an unobtrusive man." That popular voice of respectable and informed middle-class English opinion, the *Illustrated London News*, had urged the government to name "the very best man at their disposal," a man of high rank as well as of recognized ability, a "clever" man in both the British and American sense of that word. Such an appointment would gratify Americans by making plain the value Britain placed on their nation's friendliness. With their choice of Lyons, Malmesbury believed that he and Derby had done exactly this. Lyons was a "very intelligent and promising public servant," and the Queen concurred. What the new minister possessed in abundance, according to William Schaw Lindsay, a shipping magnate and member of Parliament, was admirable tact, prudence, judgment, politeness, and great common sense.[34]

Bickerton was granted two months' leave to wind up his father's affairs, he and Fitz being the executors. It proved a time-consuming business. The admiral had invested heavily in railroads, principally at home but also in Canada, where he owned stock in the Grand Trunk. His net worth amounted to some £34,000, of which £6,000 went to Annie and her family, and another £3,500 to the far more comfortably situated Minna. Bickerton inherited the balance along with the house in Bath, which had been part of Lady Bickerton's bequest. This he sold for £2,000. More of a problem was what use to make of the seven chests of plate and the 2,315 bottles of wine, among them first-rate sherry, claret, sauternes, and champagne, being held in a Plymouth bonded warehouse. Other useful items included table linen, dinner service, dessert sets, and lamps, many of which would be worth taking to the United States. The captain of the screw frigate HMS *Curacao*, which was to carry Lyons in appropriate style across the Atlantic, had several large, temporary cabins constructed on the main deck which added usable storage space and provided excellent accommodation for the passengers. Lyons was given a berth on the starboard side adjoining the captain's fore cabin and with easy access to a WC, a doubly fortunate arrangement given his suffering whenever obliged to travel by sea. Into two vacant cabins went the plate, wines, three cases of china from the Bath house, and luggage. Those household items for which he had no use were then auctioned off and the money raised applied to the cost of transporting his effects to the ship and their insurance against damage or loss during the voyage.[35]

The captain, no doubt after consultation with his sea-averse passenger, decided on a southern ocean crossing, which promised to be far calmer than the traditional more northerly and shorter route. They were to call at Madeira to take on coal, for the ship could carry only enough for four days under full steam, and then seek the trade winds to make full use of the vessel's sails. Having weighed anchor, appropriately enough under the circumstances on George Washington's birthday, 22 February, passengers and crew enjoyed a "smooth good passage" to Madeira, where they tied up on 1 March, St David's Day. Although frequently seasick Lyons had been well enough to sit up during the day, walk the deck, and eat. His two accompanying staff members, E. Douglas Irvine and Edmund Monson, the latter his private secretary, proved pleasant companions. He went ashore at Madeira, where not even "oppressive heat" detracted from the charm of trees in full leaf and geraniums and roses in bloom or deterred him from riding to the island's highest peak. The *Curacao* set sail on 3 March, but failed to find the trade winds. Although three weeks passed before they sighted Bermuda, the slow passage had its compensations. Lyons observed the constellation of the Southern Cross, was entertained by "coveys of flying fish," and had an opportunity truly to get to know Irvine and Monson. Leaving Bermuda, a "barren, ugly collection of islands," on the last day of the month, the *Curacao* immediately ran into "extremely rough weather," which thankfully did not persist. It entered Chesapeake Bay on 5 April and moved up the following day to Annapolis, the state capital of Maryland, where Lyons found the entire Napier family. They had kindly come down by train to escort him back to the nation's capital.[36]

On 12 April, a fortnight short of his forty-second birthday, the second Lord Lyons presented his letters of credence to President Buchanan and delivered the customary remarks. He expressed his monarch's esteem and regard for the president, her interest in the welfare of the American nation, and her government's desire for friendship and good understanding with the United States. Malmesbury had undoubtedly recited Derby's simple rule for dealing with Americans: "be very civil, very firm, and go our own way." Napier's error of assuming that American politicians would behave like English gentlemen was similarly instructive and cautionary, as was the foreign secretary's criticism of Ouseley. "I am only afraid of his stupidity increased by large quantities of brandy and water to which he is addicted," Malmesbury had remarked. In his briefing of his successor, Napier suggested that Ouseley had seen himself leading a Central American resistance to American "filibustering." He had misconceived his mission, converting a "sedative remedy into an irritant," and, his American wife notwithstanding, had exhibited a prejudice against Americans that "rendered him ill-adapted to his functions."[37]

Napier's assessments of the president and the secretary of state were similarly severe. Buchanan was sly and chronically indecisive, while the more "hearty and open" General Cass was old, forgetful, irresolute, false, weak, and devoid of any "real influence on the solution of affairs." Both men were in his opinion trimmers and cowards who flinched in the face of a discontented public. As a result Buchanan had been reduced to a virtual political non-entity. His plan to purchase Cuba and his request for extraordinary executive powers with respect to the problems of Latin America had been either resisted or ignored by Congress. His position would be even weaker when a new Congress met following an election in which the administration and the Democratic Party had been held to account for a misbegotten attempt to secure Congressional approval of the pro-slavery constitution fraudulently drafted and adopted as the basis of statehood in the territory of Kansas. On a more personal note, Napier recommended that Lyons communicate officially and in writing with the administration and be equally wary of the American press. As a reader of *Martin Chuzzlewit*, Bickerton was alive to that danger and deplored "violent" newspaper articles asserting American pretensions to control the Western hemisphere. These articles' excitement of popular passion promised to make difficult the maintenance of cordial relations with the United States. Recalling his own time in the American capital, Philip Griffith wrote that he had been forced to "eat dirt" and to read in the press constant abuse of Britain. The time had come to abandon the policy of giving way to the Americans.[38]

Lyons took the advice to heart. The outbreak of war between France and Austria over the Italian question brought from Malmesbury a request for his assessment of the likely American response should Britain become involved in the conflict. Ever cautious, Lyons forwarded the "crude ideas" developed after a mere two months in a small town that was nominally the nation's capital but virtually deserted at this particular time of the year. "The admiration of bullying and violent proceedings on their side, which appears to be universal among the population here, and the want of firmness on the part of the Government in withstanding it," he observed, "seem to me to constitute some of the greatest difficulties we should have to contend with in keeping at peace with America when we were at war with other Powers." The people would demand the grabbing of Cuba and Mexico even though wiser heads recognized the danger of a territorial expansion that would introduce both Spanish and "mixed races" into American society and excite fresh and bitter debate over the expansion of slavery. For Britain there was some comfort in the knowledge that territorial acquisitiveness was directed southwards. Only the "most rancorous Irish," Lyons believed, exhibited a wish to excite disturbances in Canada or other British colonies. But a Britain at war would find a neutral United States "punctilious, exacting and quarrelsome" in its defence of American rights at sea. The commanders of American men of war, whenever a superior force, would resort to violence to prevent American merchantmen being interfered with. However outrageous such conduct, and however serious the violations of international law, popular applause and the desire to profit from neutrality would discourage any disavowal of high-handed actions. What was more, the "irritable and excitable" populace had a "great longing to play the part of a first rate power" and the government would in all likelihood follow its lead and become "exacting, captious and 'bumptious' to a very irritating extent." Clearly, Lyons shared the belief, held by many Britons, that a democratic Republic was a dangerously volatile and aggressive force in international relations. This made his task all the more demanding for it seemed obvious that "a powerful prejudice prevails against [England] in the minds of all the transatlantic republicans."[39]

Turning to popular attitudes and the soundest policy for controlling them, Lyons detected in the Republic's upper classes strong sympathy for Britain, pride in its position in the world, an anxious desire for its good opinion, and an admiration of its political institutions. Unfortunately, he added, these were the very people who stood aloof from political life and thus had scant influence on public affairs. The mass of the people, always excepting the anglophobic Irish immigrants, while not chronically hostile to the "old Country," would enjoy seeing it in difficulties. Even those among them more inclined to be friendly would, he suspected, still wish to find some means of gratifying their pride at Britain's expense. The recipe for smooth relations which he proposed and planned to follow was similar to that sketched by Derby. Britain should gratify the Americans' vanity "by treating them in matters of form as a great people." He would communicate with them respecting Britain's views and intentions as if they were "really a considerable military force," and would avoid interfering in matters in which Britain was not "sufficiently interested to make it worthwhile to raise serious questions." Here was a rational and pragmatic approach to issues that might merely touch upon British national pride, such as those in Central America. Whenever and wherever the interests and rights of Britons were clearly involved, however, they needed to be "clear and distinct" in their language and "firm and decided" in their conduct. The Americans had to understand, Lyons forcefully argued, that when "in the right and earnest" Britain would be more unyielding, not less, in dealing with them. In short, the best policy was "to avoid as much as possible raising questions with them, but not to give way on those we raise."[40]

CHAPTER FOUR

The United States

Defeated in the House of Commons on April Fool's Day, Derby and his colleagues followed through on their threat to appeal to the electorate. The Whigs astutely fought the election on the foreign problem of Italy not the domestic issue of parliamentary reform, and while the Tories emerged as still the single largest party in the Commons they remained a minority and surrendered office. The Queen tried unsuccessfully to avoid another Palmerston ministry, but it was soon apparent that he alone could command a coalition of anti-Conservatives. Despite his age – he had been born in 1784 – he exhibited the vigour and breezy self-confidence of a much younger man. He "is as young in mind & spirits as ever," Malmesbury admiringly admitted, and "shews age in nothing but his face. He must be the hardest-fellow in Europe." Of fifteen chairs at the Cabinet table, eight were filled by Whig-Liberals, five by Peelites, among them William Gladstone, and two by Radicals. Although the Prince Consort thought the Cabinet at sixes and sevens on foreign relations, foreign policy was an adhesive of sorts even though one of the most prominent Radicals, Richard Cobden, declined the presidency of the Board of Trade because he considered Palmerston quarrelsome, a meddler in other nations, and belligerent. The Foreign Office was Lord John Russell's price for entering the government, and its payment so annoyed Clarendon that he refused office. He, the Queen, and several members of the Cabinet considered Russell little more than Palmerston's understudy, but he had held the office briefly a few years earlier, was the author of a book and several pamphlets on international problems, had frequently acted as a spokesman on foreign affairs, and was not wanting in self-confidence. He considered himself a "heaven-born foreign minister designed to settle the affairs of the whole world," an ironic critic mocked.[1]

The fate of Italy, which the war between France and Austria was currently promising to settle, drew Russell to the Foreign Office. The French had defeated the Austrians at Magenta barely a week before he moved into Downing Street, and won a second and even more sanguinary victory at Solferino a week after his arrival there. The carnage shook Napoleon's resolve and he reached a quick settlement with the Austrians. They handed Lombardy to him and he handed it on to Sardinia-Piedmont, but Austria's retention of Venetia was a betrayal of the secret understanding Cavour had reached with Napoleon under which France was to receive Savoy and Nice. These territorial spoils were soon secured, however, by France's support of the plebiscites which delivered Parma, Modena, and Tuscany to Sardinia-Piedmont. Inevitably the acquisitions gave new life to British suspicion of the emperor's ambition and it grew with his construction of an ironclad navy which threatened Britain's naval supremacy. Palmerston's instinctive and costly response – a matching naval program, the improvement of defensive fortifications, and the raising of a volunteer force to help repel any French invaders – dismayed his Peelite chancellor of the exchequer, Gladstone. This was the unstable European backdrop to the framing of an American policy.[2]

A Foreign Office analysis circulated within the Derby Cabinet had described relations with the United States as "satisfactory." Its author, Edmund Hammond, was the son of the first British envoy sent to the United States following the American Revolution. The permanent undersecretary was a physically imposing figure whose "colossal industry and retentive memory enabled him to direct single-handed, the whole current work of the department." He revisited the Anglo-American relationship at the close of the Tory government. President Buchanan, he noted, had expressed a desire for the United States to be on good terms with Britain and had denounced in "unqualified terms of reprobation, the attempts made by freebooters [filibusters] ... to disturb the peace of Nicaragua and Costa Rica." Nevertheless, Hammond admitted to a "certain anxiety" given the inherent difficulty of dealing with a nation whose powers of government were "much more restricted than in other countries" and whose executive, from motives of "self-preservation," was frequently obliged to yield to "external pressure." Hence its constant temptation to raise a cry against Britain, and in particular to divert public attention from domestic problems. Buchanan had lost the confidence of Congress and might therefore seek popular favour "by avowing, at whatever cost, the jealous feelings" towards Britain which seemed to lurk forever in American minds. The most recent presidential message to Congress envisaged territorial expansion, which would materially impinge on British interests and if resisted "would probably bring the two nations into collision." Another source of the tension was the slave trade conducted in the Caribbean by vessels flying the American flag. "The Government of the United States will neither exert itself to put down the abuse of its flag," Hammond reminded ministers, "nor admit of our cooperation for that purpose."[3]

The United States was in the opinion of the Foreign Office staff an aggressive nation, an opinion Palmerston shared. Its plundering of Mexico a decade earlier and the freebooting in the Caribbean and Central America were merely the most recent evidence of belligerence. Indeed, many Britons were beginning to suspect that the filibusters were unacknowledged agents of national policy because their "incessant" activities left Britain with few good policy options. The Reciprocity Treaty in 1854, which permitted freer trade between Canada and the Republic, had been promoted in the Union as a step towards the integration of British North America into the economy and culture of the United States. But the colonials' disinclination to exchange monarchism for republicanism posed the question of whether filibusters would be sent north. Britain had no wish for a confrontation. The Crimean War, the Indian mutiny, the conflict between France and Austria over Italy, Napoleon III's supposed ambition to rearrange the map of Europe as drawn with the final defeat of the first French Empire in 1815, the maintenance of the free flow of cotton from the southern States to the textile industries of Lancashire and Cheshire, the fact that British bankers were the Union's largest creditors, and the vulnerability of British North America, all dictated caution.[4]

In Central America, Britain's "interests" were the colony of British Honduras, or Belize, its protectorate of the Miskito Indians living along the coasts of Nicaragua and Honduras, its claim to have established a colony in the Bay Islands off the latter country's coast, and the control of the ports which would command both ends of any Nicaraguan interoceanic canal. John Crampton, when the British minister in Washington, had pragmatically recommended their withdrawal from those areas where there was no prospect of a canal being constructed. Similarly, he considered unwise any attempt to defend Britain's position in Belize with its interpretation of the ambiguously worded Clayton-Bulwer Treaty. The American signatory, John Clayton, asserted that Britain was obligated under its provisions not only to refrain from acquiring additional territory in the region but also to relinquish existing possessions. Specious though this interpretation was, Crampton warned that the Americans would stick to it with pertinacity. Hammond agreed. The Americans, he believed, considered the treaty "a sure and never failing resource" of anglophobia.[5]

One revolution in communications, the Atlantic telegraph, had briefly promised to have a profound effect on Anglo-American relations, but its failure in water too deep to permit repair only weeks before Lyons accepted the position of minister to the United States meant that he retained a degree of autonomy denied British diplomats in Europe. The prime minister, Palmerston, to whom he would be reporting via the Foreign Office, had celebrated his seventy-fifth birthday on 20 October 1859. He spoke on occasion of Anglo-American cousinhood, of the bonds of blood, language, law, and literature, but his public life had begun at a time when British popular opinion was bitter against the Americans. Their declaration of war in 1812 had been considered a stab in the back at a moment when Britain stood face to face with its most dangerous adversary, Emperor Napoleon. Peace in 1814 had not led to reconciliation but rather to resentment of the Americans' success and insolence. Palmerston had a jaundiced opinion of the Union. He considered it a threat to British North America and a potential source of European republicanism. The Americans' boast that their slaveholding nation was "the last best hope of earth" excited his scorn. In his opinion his own nation was the true international missionary. Britain was the agent of constitutionalism and liberalism and its parliamentary system was a more effective protector of freedoms. The Americans were saddled with a president for four years whereas a prime minister whose policy became "pusillanimous or perilous" was, as Palmerston knew to his cost, ejected from office. The mistake was not one likely to be repeated. He saw in national pride and honour the means with the help of the press of attracting and retaining the political support of an educated middle class. Pride had been affronted only three years earlier by the Americans' expulsion of John Crampton for his involvement in a scheme to raise mercenaries in the Republic to fight in the Crimea. Even the normally amiable Clarendon had responded with a "sweeping and merciless" attack on the United States and its legal system. All judges were "under executive or party control," he railed, all citizens, if witnesses, "corrupt and perjured," and all juries "unworthy of confidence." Palmerston acknowledged the difficulty of dealing with the Yankees on American problems, proof of which he found in the drawing of the border from Maine to Oregon. The settlements often had a strong odour of appeasement, for Britain's middle classes appeared indifferent to most American questions with the exception of commerce and finance. This had been a factor in Britain's irresolute policy in Central America. The less the British had to do with those "moribund republics," one organ of middle-class opinion trumpeted, the better "for their repose, for their pockets, and for the peace of the world." More arguable is the recent contention that the rational reluctance to allow differences to end in conflict amounted to a determination to avoid war at all costs. The key to Anglo-American peace, Palmerston believed, was for both peoples to be satisfied that the desire to remain on good terms was mutual. There was the rub, the Foreign Office establishment argued. The American people were anglophobes; hence disputes were likely always to be "subservient to Party Purpose."[6]

Wariness of the United States was bipartisan. Lord Stanley, heir to the Derby title and to the Foreign Office, although he had to wait seven years to inherit the portfolio, considered American pandering to popular anglophobia unbecoming of statesmen and "hardly within the limits even of international courtesy." Yet, on the eve of being sworn into office, President-elect Buchanan had declared that Americans and Britons owed it to "their own dearest principles and interests to cultivate the most friendly relations with one another." Doubts of his sincerity immediately surfaced with his nomination of a notorious anglophobe, General Lewis Cass, as secretary of state. Cass had been the unsuccessful Democratic nominee for the presidency in 1848 and was the author of the contentious and ambiguous doctrine of popular sovereignty which had intensified the sectional dispute over the extension of slavery to the nation's territories. Punished in 1856 with the loss of his Senate seat, Cass was awarded the State Department for his energetic campaigning at the age of seventy-five on behalf of Buchanan. "His age, his patriotism, his long and able public services, his unsullied private character, and the almost universal feeling in his favor rendered his appointment peculiarly appropriate," Buchanan explained to disappointed Britons. In any event, as a former tenant of the State Department himself, Buchanan intended to direct foreign policy, and it was to his annual messages to Congress that Britain looked for clues to the Union's intentions.[7]

Transatlantic developments were reported in some detail by the British press, which was critical of the Union's perceived ambition to bring Mexico, Central America, and Cuba under American sway. Would the expansion southwards extend and perpetuate slavery? they asked. The conduct of the most successful filibuster, William Walker, who seized control of Nicaragua, suggested it would, while Buchanan was chided for his willingness to allow the domestic slave trade to continue in the southern States. British admirers of the Union, on the other hand, such as John Bright, hailed its absence of a hereditary aristocracy and its progressive adoption of universal (white) manhood suffrage. Conservatives, in reply, warned that democracy led to political corruption and territorial expansion by driving the "wise and the good" from public life. These worthies declined to stoop to the "compliances, the corruptions, [and] the intrigues" through which alone "a candidate for Congress [was able to] worm his way to a seat on the benches of the Capitol." Here was an explanation of the Republic's lawless society, one in which legislators carried deadly weapons into their chambers. Nevertheless, the Union's material progress, its energy, the constant movement of its people, its advances in the arts, the diffusion of education, and the rapid absorption of hordes of immigrants became familiar to literate Britons thanks to the legion of literary tourists of the Republic. If it continued to double its population every twenty-five years its people would soon be as numerous as those of China, *The Times* calculated, making that nation more powerful than the combined nations of Europe. This rendered even more reprehensible, in the newspaper's judgment, the "piratical" inroads on neighbouring nations that jeopardized national unity by exacerbating sectional tensions over the extension of slavery. The decision of the Supreme Court in the case of Dred Scott, which coincided with the inauguration of Buchanan, had draped in the sanctity of constitutionalism the right of slaveholders to carry all their property into all the territories. The attempt by a radical abolitionist, John Brown, to excite and equip an emancipation crusade by raiding the Federal arsenal at Harper's Ferry, Virginia, was an ominous development. So also was his elevation to martyrdom following his execution, which had taken placed shortly before Lyons set out for Washington.[8]

"Crude at the surface, rotten at the core" had been Charles Dickens's caustic assessment of the slave Republic. Slavery was the root problem of American society, but the formidable obstacles to its speedy eradication were recognized by British periodicals. The slave states dominated the executive branch even when the president was a northerner, Buchanan being the proof, and they had the numbers in Congress either to control vital committees or to block legislation. The broad agreement that the Federal government lacked the constitutional authority to interfere with slavery in those states where it already existed explained the tactics of the anti-slavery proponents. They focused on its removal from the capital, its exclusion from the territories, and a ban on the domestic trade depicted heart-wrenchingly by Harriet Beecher Stowe in *Uncle Tom's Cabin*. John Brown was a timely and violent reminder that the movement in the north had become "too highly wrought to be quelled either by constitutional fictions or by acts of the Constitution itself." However, George Dallas, the American minister in London, was confident that the Sepoy mutiny in India and the disillusionment with the economic consequences of West Indian emancipation in 1833 had eroded British support of abolitionism. Certainly this was the contention of American slaveholders, and it impelled Senator Charles Sumner, an abolitionist, to plead with his British friends for a parliamentary vindication of the "grand and Beneficent Act" of West Indian emancipation. The "moral elevation of the African race through the influence of Freedom can be displayed beyond all doubt," he insisted, and "this alone would be enough, even if coffee & sugar did fail." Less obvious was the moral ambiguity in British attitudes. The persistent and at times aggressive effort to suppress the international slave trade was accompanied by consumption of slave-grown cotton on such a scale that it strengthened the commitment of plantation owners of the southern states to the institution. As an advocate of East Indian cotton sarcastically observed, had abolition in those states depended on the willingness of Britons to pay a small amount more for their cloth the institution would have gone on forever. Their trade should not be dependent on the abolition of slavery in other lands, one of the two Radicals in the Palmerston Cabinet declared. Indeed, Britons made huge commercial investments in the slave economies of Latin America.[9]

Lyons discovered in the French minister, whom he had known in Athens, an object lesson in how to alienate one's hosts. Eugène de Sartiges had failed to hide his disdain for the American people and their nation, an attitude that was doubly inadvisable given his easily ridiculed pigeon English. Even his marriage to a singularly attractive American had failed to rescue his reputation. Instead, she was abused by her fellow countrymen for her "condescension to a depraved Count" whose amours were "notorious from Persia to Peru." As doyen of the diplomatic corps, Sartiges gave a grand and exclusively male dinner for the new British minister which was attended by four members of the Buchanan Cabinet. They and the other Americans he met were "unpolished" in the European sense, Lyons allowed, but had good manners and were uniformly kind, proper, and correct. A week later he was one of a large party that dined at the White House, which was only a short walk from his own residence. He had taken over the Napiers' lease, even though he considered the rent excessive, but it at least saved him the anguish of house hunting and it rescued his predecessor from a heavy financial penalty. The house, which was on H Street just west of Lafayette Park, struck him as vaguely Italianate in design. Not that he thought it either nice or convenient despite its proximity to the executive mansion and the State Department. Black walls and black shutters not only gave it a sombre appearance but also absorbed heat, which with poor insulation guaranteed uncomfortable summers. He made a number of improvements to the interior. The modest dining room was converted into a waiting room and the ballroom into a spacious dining room. He furnished it with items bought from the Napiers, others picked up at the auction of the household effects of the departing Sartiges, and pieces shipped from Florence and London. Unfortunately, many of his fine wines had not survived the Atlantic crossing, but his shipping of them in large quantity and his earlier criticism of Wyse suggest that at this point in his life he was no abstainer from alcohol. He employed a local "fair cook" but planned to import a French culinary expert.[10]

Lyons resumed the social diplomacy conducted so successfully and expensively by Napier. Among the distinguished British visitors to whom he was especially attentive was Richard Cobden, a Radical member of Parliament, who leapt to the conclusion that Lyons was too inexperienced for his post and too recent an aristocrat to impress the Americans. He was, he sneered, a lord without antecedents. Another of Bickerton's early visitors was his Uncle William, whom he took to the White House to be introduced to the president, thereby providing him with a story to impress his neighbours on his return home to Ohio. Having long made a very modest living from private tutoring and portrait painting, William saw his income greatly reduced by the development of public schools and photography. Although convinced that his uncle would fritter away any substantial sum of cash in rash speculations, Lyons eventually forwarded to him a very modest ten guineas every quarter. His own monetary concerns led him to wheedle an additional £300 out of the Treasury to complete his "outfit" and to curtail expenditures. However, the success of the large dinner he hosted for the Sartiges caused him to abandon the idea of deferring this form of social diplomacy. He invited American politicians and members of the diplomatic corps. One of the latter, Eduard de Stoeckl, the Russian minister, who like many other "Dips" had taken an American wife, proved "jovial" and a "good companion." He it was who encouraged Lyons to persist with his dinners. At a second gathering of prominent politicians Senator Stephen Douglas was the centre of attention. Although the author of a despised piece of legislation that would open to slavery territories from which under an earlier compromise it had been excluded, he remained the front-runner for the Democratic presidential nomination in 1860.[11]

Lyons remained in Washington throughout the summer, having heard that the available accommodation at even the most fashionable watering places was of poor quality and the crowds so dense that it was impossible to be "quiet or alone a moment except when literally in bed." Moreover, thinking it unwise to be absent from the legation for more than a few days at a time, he had no desire as a reader of Dickens's *Martin Chuzzlewit*, and perhaps the same author's *American Notes*, to travel frequently on trains reputedly "entirely destitute of comfort." Instead, he explored Washington, which was not as yet an impressive national capital. "We are still at the soup and fish, and have not got to the first *entree*," one British wag remarked. There were handsome public buildings of granite and marble which Lyons considered "magnificent in proportions and design," and a good number of attractive red brick private residences, but far more numerous were "very mean houses and absolute huts and hovels dotted about, with waste spaces between much frequented by pigs." Indeed, large sections of the city were a "rambling mass of streets without houses, and houses without streets." The thoroughfares within the city and the roads leading out of it were "bad beyond belief, mere tracks of mud and dust, in the best places something like a ploughed field." A scarcity of riding horses obliged him to hire a light, high, four-wheeled American buggy in which he made short forays into the countryside. Unfortunately, these bumpy, dusty, and painful expeditions made worse the medical problems for which he had consulted physicians before leaving home. The pain in his chest and the need to clear his throat had become so much more constant that he envisaged the possibility of resignation before the year was out.[12]

The news that Lord John Russell had accepted the Foreign Office did not disturb Lyons one jot. He was confident the man who had rescued him from the diplomatic obscurity of Dresden was still "favourably disposed" towards him, and they were soon communicating in the "most confidential manner." Lyons did not expect the calm of his first few months in Washington to survive the meeting of Congress in December.

Quietly he set about the task of convincing the Buchanan administration of his nation's anxiety "to cultivate friendly relations." A measure
of his success was the word Buchanan sent to London of the favourable
impression Lyons had made. Central America loomed as a diplomatic
problem. Buchanan predicted a "devil of a row" if the Mosquito Protectorate and the Bay Islands were still in British hands when Congress
met. Earlier British assurances should now be honoured, Lyons advised
Russell, who in the past had spoken of the two nations reaching a real
family compact. But at this particular moment the Americans needed
to understand, the foreign secretary responded, that "a little place called
Europe" was giving Britain "a great deal of trouble." He wanted no rep-
etition of Napier's error of yielding too much for that would merely encourage the Americans to make "other and more awkward demands."
Their contention that in signing the Clayton-Bulwer Treaty Britain had
abandoned its protection of the Indians was dismissed by Russell as
"sheer fudge," yet he coveted neither the Bay Islands nor the Mosquito
Protectorate. His replacing of the feckless Ouseley with Charles Lennox
Wyke, and his authorizing Lyons to reveal to the Americans the new
agent's instructions, did serve a conciliatory purpose. Wyke had considerable experience of Central American affairs and was convinced that
a settlement of the issues in dispute would "tend greatly to bring about
that feeling of cordial good will and sympathy which ought ever to ex-
ist" between the British and American governments. The upshot was a
series of bilateral agreements. The claims of Honduras and Nicaragua
to the Mosquito Coast were recognized, while the Indians of the former
protectorate were now penned in a "narrow and precise reservation"
and offered only "nominal" British protection. The Bay Islands were
surrendered to Honduras, and Guatemala secured a favourable frontier
with Belize.[13]

While Wyke was extracting Britain, with "credit and honour," from
the Central American imbroglio, Lyons was preparing for any other
challenges to good relations with the United States. In a nation of so
vast a geographical extent, one in which as he somewhat simplistically
expressed it "each separate State is in most respects independent of the
Federal Government," he had in British consuls a potentially valuable
source of intelligence. The consuls' primary duty was the promotion of

their nation's commercial interests or, as one of them put it, to act "as a kind of dry-nurse to the seafaring population." All but two of them were permitted to supplement their small salaries with private trading, and this often led to their deep involvement in the local community. This gave them insights into both local concerns and local responses to national issues, but the relationship between consulates and legation was "very undefined and somewhat anomalous." Theoretically they came under the orders of the minister, but difficulties of communication, the cost of postage, and the social gulf between consuls and diplomats meant that in practice there was little direct contact. To rectify this, Lyons instructed consuls to send all reports and confidential comments on political developments to him. Vital and urgent intelligence might in exceptional circumstances be sent directly to the Foreign Office, but in those instances copies had to be forwarded simultaneously to him. He soon discovered that some had sent political dispatches to the foreign secretary of which he knew nothing, and it was to fill this hole in his system that in May 1861 the Foreign Office issued a circular which established the subordination of the consular to the diplomatic service.[14]

Two consulates, New York and Charleston, were especially important and their consuls were forbidden to trade privately. New York was the centre of much of the nation's commercial activity, the principal hub of transatlantic travel, and a prime destination of immigrants. Yet the office, because of parsimonious allowances, was up three flights of stairs "in a back street." Since 1857, the post had been occupied by a Nova Scotian, Edward Mortimer Archibald. A lawyer, a former chief clerk and registrar of the Supreme Court of Newfoundland, a former attorney general of the colony, a member of the commission that in 1854 negotiated the Reciprocity Treaty with the United States, Archibald was urbane, conciliatory, and a man of good judgment and address. He rapidly gained the confidence of Lyons, who engaged him in a far more regular political correspondence than was customary. "I attach very great value to your private letters," he wrote. Important telegraphic communications were to be in cipher, but the copying of just one of the Foreign Office ciphers was a task "simply too great" for the understaffed legation. So he forwarded to Archibald a simpler version which would not be too difficult to break but would do until they devised one that was more secure.[15]

Robert Bunch, a veteran of the service, had held the Charleston consulate since 1853, and during a brief visit to Washington he impressed
Lyons as "very clever, agreeable and gentlemanlike." The importance
of his post was Charleston's role as an entrepôt of the cotton trade so
vital to Britain's textile industries and the city's reputation as the hive
of the most aggressive secessionist bees. In the absence of a promotion
ladder, Lyons supported the applications both men made for increased
allowances. The industrious Archibald had risked his health to gather
intelligence of the highest quality and merited an upgrading to consul
general. This he eventually received. Bunch was another official of superior ability who was deserving of a more generous stipend. The straits
to which consuls without private means were reduced – and Lyons cited
as an example the man at Mobile who had literally been obliged to pawn
or sell his silverware in order to make ends meet – brought "serious discredit on England." The allowances of Archibald and Bunch were soon
substantially increased.[16]

The want of sufficient junior staff to ensure the efficient and smooth
operation of the legation was another of Lyons's concerns. "All kinds
of people write to me on all kinds of subjects [and] all Americans are
excessively susceptible," Lyons informed the Foreign Office, "and great
numbers of them have the means of doing mischief, and are sure to
use them if they think themselves slighted or neglected." Foreign Office
complaints of illegible dispatches provided him with the opportunity to
unburden himself on the subject of chronic understaffing. He had immediately lost E. Douglas Irvine, who on learning that his father was seriously ill returned home on the *Curacao* with the Napiers. Inferior ink,
a "treacherous composition" which ate through paper, and poor handwriting explained the illegibility of the dispatches. He replaced the ink
and requested a good, young, unpaid attaché who wrote a "thoroughly
good hand" and was "really industrious and desirous to learn." The ability to spell would be another distinct advantage, he added mordantly,
but that "seems almost too much to expect in these days." A truly ambitious young man who was punctual and had a "good hand" should in
his opinion welcome a posting to Washington, where he would receive
excellent training. This was no empty promise, for several of the young
men who served under Lyons went on to highly successful careers. He

created a family atmosphere, dining with his staff three or four times a week and celebrating every Christmas with them and with any stray English gentlemen who happened to be in town. Nevertheless, as he admitted to Minna, the "worst of the Mission" was the desire of every subordinate to secure a post in Europe, or if granted leave to avoid ever returning. Edmund Monson was a case in point.[17]

A younger son of a member of the lesser nobility, Monson had come down from Oxford with a first in law and history. He had graduated in 1856 to the diplomatic service, passing the new entrance examination at the age of twenty-two, and had arrived at Florence as Howard's private secretary. Abandoned in Florence by Howard, he volunteered to serve Lyons in the same capacity on the understanding that he would at some point be permitted to return briefly to England to retain his fellowship at All Souls, Oxford. Paid £100 per annum plus bed and board, he was considered a member of Lyons's own family, and the minister covered all his expenses. Lyons quickly became so dependent upon him that he would not travel when Monson returned to Oxford. He considered all the other juniors unsuitable companions. Irvine's return, after an absence of six months, eased the problem. He was agreeable and accompanied his chief on his daily walks and rides around Washington. The arrival of another attaché gave Lyons hope that when Monson returned he would have him entirely to himself. Hence his anxiety on hearing that Monson had developed a "dreadful cough," a persistent chest pain, and difficulty with breathing. The patient dosed himself with cod liver oil, understanding that it would do "wonderful things," only to develop an abscess in his side for which surgery was required. A post-operative infection then laid him up for several additional weeks. Although Lyons encouraged Monson to remain away until he had fully recovered, he looked to his return as the "epoch of all good things" and by the spring of 1860 wanted him more than ever. To speed his return he promised him full relief from the drudgery of the chancery, temporary relief from Washington summers, and appointment as the second attaché. He admitted: "I have felt quite widowed without him."[18]

Even as he wrote of his sense of widowhood, Lyons was denying reports of his impending marriage. Washington was all agog with the story that he had been transported across the ocean in a personally chartered vessel and that among its passengers had been the "personages comprising his household," "domestics and skilful gardeners, and even growing plants for his conservatory." Other whispers had him using a solid gold dinner service when hosting ladies while producing the "costliest silver plate" for gentleman guests. Before long gossips were predicting his imminent capitulation "to the charms of some American woman, and speculation was rife as to who would be the probable bride." The *Washington Court Circular* speculated that he would "lead to the Hymeneal Altar" either Miss Harriet Lane, the president's niece and hostess, or the widow of a late foreign minister. Miss Lane was considered the most likely bride since her colour and physique were considered more English than American, in that she was "handsome and healthful and good to look upon." Lyons gallantly described American women as very pretty but insisted to a friend that his heart was "too old and too callous to be wounded by their charms." He was not going to marry anyone he vowed. He admired Harriet Lane but exclusively for her skill and charm as a hostess. She made visits to the White House exceptionally pleasant by raising its functions to their "highest degree," and she was the guest of honour at his first large dinner held in the impressive new dining room. He also sent her three of the pheasants shipped from Arundel by his sister, dryly remarking that they were not a "very sentimental present."[19]

His "unconstrained and easy" manner did embolden one of his female guests, the wife of Senator Clay of Alabama, to suggest "the possibility of some lovely American consenting to become 'Lyonised.'" He responded good-humouredly with a quotation from *Tristram Shandy*, that once married "you will never sleep slantindicularly in your bed." Yet he evidently felt a need to provide friends with some more conventional explanation of his aversion to matrimony. Marriage was "better never than late," he asserted, and was provided with timely proof of the wisdom of this contention. John Crampton, following his expulsion from the United States, had been rewarded with the ambassadorship to the Russian court. While there he married a young opera singer, which drew from Lyons the comment: "poor Sir John Crampton – what a dreadful warning to old bachelors." Lyons did not doubt that the bride was charming and virtuous, "but no one who has been on the stage can live without excitement, and how is a man of 53 to find continual excitement for a girl of 18." In fact, Victoire Balfe was a little more mature and was the daughter of Michael Balfe, an Irish musician and composer whose most enduring work was the perennial music hall favourite "Come into the Garden Maud." The union proved the disaster Lyons had predicted. In 1863, after only three years of wedlock, Lady Crampton secured an annulment through court order and papal decree on the grounds of Crampton's impotence. This was not to be his only embarrassment. When transferred from St Petersburg to Madrid, Crampton discovered that his ex-wife, now the Duchess of Frias, lived almost directly opposite the legation.[20]

The marital gossip may not have been unhelpful to Lyons as he campaigned to cultivate the capital's influential figures. He flattered himself that he did not arouse in Americans what some British lords certainly did, that is the suspicion that he was privately mocking their language and manners. There was no looking down the lordly nose, and he continued to give a great dinner every week of the season. One problem was his failure to find a really good "cook," but no one who came to these dinners knew, or so he believed, whether the cooking was good or bad. More discriminating were the guests at his more intimate small dinners, so he commissioned Monson, who had made his way to Paris in search of health and strength, to find him a French cook. This he eventually did. In March 1860, the "Black Republicans" came to dine. They included the recently elected Speaker of the House of Representatives, whose chair it had taken congressmen almost four months to fill, and two of the most prominent Northern senators, William Seward and Charles Sumner. The latter, who had spent time in Britain recuperating from the brutal assault by a slave state representative almost four years earlier, returned to dine alone with Lyons three weeks later. He then undoubtedly expressed the opinion that Seward was the favourite to capture the Republican nomination for the presidency. Lyons viewed the coming congressional and presidential elections with apprehension, fearful for the survival of his good work. He suspected that the goodwill he had won with good dinners and personal amiability would not survive, that during the elections candidates would find irresistible the temptation to appeal to popular anglophobia. He was also beginning to fret that he was spending too lavishly on large dinners and he was finding their management increasingly difficult in a polarized and bitterly partisan society. Pro-slaveryites refused to speak to anti-slaveryites, while the latter disliked being asked to dine only with one another. Many of the neutrals, such as his fellow diplomats, had so poor a command of English that they were of little use as conversationalists. Lyons did not withdraw from society. He attended dinners and balls, as many as three a week, but was thankful that he was able to escape early from those held in the afternoon with the house shutters down and the gas lit. American society remained amusing, he assured Minna, before adding that he had as yet not made any particular friendships. That soon changed. He made friends of Eduard de Stoeckl and his American wife, and an old acquaintance was on his way to the American capital. Henri Mercier had been appointed French minister.[21]

The basic Lyons rule of diplomatic conduct was ostensibly simple. He placed before his superiors the material with which to formulate policy and then implemented it without reference to his personal opinion. But he had already demonstrated in Rome and Naples his willingness to interpret instructions. The oft-quoted remark of a Jacobean diplomat – that an ambassador was "an honest man sent to lie abroad for the good of his country" – was written as a witticism not as a truth. In any event, confident that he would never be asked to lie or do anything else that was morally or religiously wrong, Lyons saw no necessity to engage in "casuistical questions of Diplomatic ethics." A careful and cautious man, he did not plan, given his distance from home, to chart an impulsively independent course. He had ample reason to be doubly cautious in his dealings with the Americans. "The Country is governed by lawyers," he observed, and "it periodically suits one party or the other to make a show of quarrelling with England." Hence his pessimism that there would ever come a time when there were "no serious questions between the two countries." The laxity of American discipline threatened to permit petty subordinate officials to get up serious disputes along the immense border with British North America. As seemingly "numberless questions" cropped up, the Foreign Office relied on him to manage them and maintain a measure of cordiality while doing so. Straighforwardness and honesty were two of his rules for dealing with foreign governments, as were tact and temper in the handling of trifling questions.

He continued to see no point to British interference in problems, even in those instances where their interest "lay that way," unless it could be effective. "There is nothing," he cautioned, "which has so bad an effect upon our relations with this Country as making remonstrances which we do not enforce and showing what the Papers civilly call 'impotent discontent and ill will.'"[22]

His hopes for a comparatively quiet life were raised by the evidence that American questions did not top Lord John Russell's agenda. The foreign secretary's eyes were fixed on Europe. Supposed French territorial ambitions in the Rhineland, the suspicion they were seeking an alliance with Russia to complete the destabilization of the Ottoman Empire which might in turn open the door to French dominance of the Mediterranean, and French control of the Suez Canal project that the Sultan was currently obstructing were Russell's more pressing concerns. The questions put to him in the Commons in 1859 concerned Italy and France, especially after the French annexations of Savoy and Nice. An Anglo-French Commercial Treaty, which Richard Cobden helped to negotiate, and which its free-trade enthusiasts believed would promote international peace and prosperity, did dampen popular unease. Malmesbury muttered his objections to the treaty only to Derby. It would encourage a taste for claret among the middle and lower classes he grumbled, and as beer consumption declined so would the Treasury's revenues from the malt tax. Moreover, Napoleon would secure the cheap coal and iron with which to enlarge his steam and commercial navies and improve his artillery. This had long been the emperor's ambition, the former friend of Bonaparte observed, but he had been forced to wait for the winegrowers' lobby to counteract protection-minded French iron masters. Despite these misgivings, the treaty's general popularity convinced Malmesbury that it would be folly to seek its defeat in the Lords.[23]

Preoccupied with Europe, Russell preferred a quiescent relationship with the United States. He instructed the circumspect Lyons to assure the Americans of his commitment to deal with them in "the most candid, open and friendly spirit." As proof of this he indicated that it was his intention to make no objection if the Americans assumed some form of protectorate over strife-torn Mexico. Although this would amount in his opinion to a violation of the terms of the Clayton-Bulwer Treaty, he would not protest so long as Britain's transit rights were respected along with the security of its subjects and their property. "If we can get these things under the shield of the United States, I shall not complain of the change," he informed Lyons. "But I do not see reason for saying anything, either officially or privately, till we are obliged to speak." Britain hoped that the liberal Mexican government of Benito Juárez would win international recognition, and Lyons was instructed to caution Secretary Cass against insisting on terms humiliating to the "Spanish pride" of the Mexicans. To do so would only weaken the liberal faction the United States ought to support. "We do not interfere with American policy in Mexico," Russell continued, "but for ourselves we shall require less and take care not to make demands any Mexican Government would find offensive to their pride." As for the Union's own deepening domestic crisis, Russell doubted that abolitionists were "doing any good to the negroes by making [John] Brown a martyr and inciting insurrection." Slave owners who were trembling with rage and fear might embark on a brutal campaign of white terror.[24]

That Lyons would continue to interpret his instructions broadly was evident in his response to Russell's resolve to try before American courts the plight of detained free black British seamen. From time to time six of the slave states had enacted legislation providing for the incarceration of these men on entering their ports. They were considered potential threats to the stability of the institution. Under intense British consular lobbying these laws had been modified and Robert Bunch in Charleston had secured the exemption of the British seamen so long as they did not leave their vessels. But in March 1859 Louisiana revived its lapsed legislation and black British seamen faced temporary imprisonment at New Orleans. Lyons instructed the consul there not to take legal action without first consulting him. He feared a court challenge would galvanize the pro-slaveryites and the advocates of states' rights throughout the South, and if a case went to appeal he saw no prospect of the Supreme Court striking the law down as unconstitutional. The Dred Scott decision had shown that the court was *Pro-Slavery*," Lyons warned Russell, and "even if we get a good case of an imprisonment of a British Subject of Colour before it, it would be much inclined, if it could not decently decide against us, either to get rid of the question upon some technical ground or to postpone indefinitely giving its decision." In the improbable event of the court invalidating the Louisiana law, he predicted the state would defy the decision while the Federal government would have "neither the will nor the power" to compel its submission. Britain's only gain would be a "good *casus belli* against the United States," and for this she had no use. Happily, the issue was quietly resolved through an informal agreement between the consul and the chief of the New Orleans police. Free British blacks were to be released on the consul's assurance that they would remain on board their vessels.[25]

On 15 June 1859, three days before Russell took possession of the Foreign Office, there was a minor incident on the island of San Juan off the Pacific northwest coast of British North America. Possession of the island was in dispute, and it was one of the small band of American settlers who precipitated the crisis by killing a pig that was the property of the Hudson's Bay Company. Fearing arrest, for a British magistrate was known to be on his way to the island, the American appealed for American military protection. The area commander, General William Selby Harney, was impetuous, notoriously ill-tempered, and brutal. Dubbed "the butcher" by the Sioux, he had once beaten a female slave to death. Nor did he inspire loyalty in his officers. He was one of those subordinates of the American government whom Lyons had identified as capable of getting up a serious border dispute. Harney ordered sixty-six men to the island under the command of a Captain George E. Pickett, who had overcome his dismal performance at the West Point Military Academy, where he had ranked dead last in his graduating class, with a display of remarkable if foolhardy courage during the Mexican War. Nevertheless, his military limitations, which were to have tragic consequences in the American Civil War, were evident in his initial choice of a camp site on the island. It would have been exposed to devastating fire from any passing British warship. Ironically, the one-eyed British magistrate, Major John De Courcy, a Crimean War veteran, whose imminent arrival set in train the American military occupation of the island, was eventually to serve in the Union Army during the Civil War while at its end Pickett, a Confederate general, was to flee to Canada.[26]

Harney's conduct in reinforcing the American force on the disputed island angered Russell. It was the nature of Americans to push themselves where they had no right to go, he fumed, just as it was the nature of their government "not to venture to disavow acts they cannot have the face to oppose." He was half-inclined to retaliate by ordering occupation of some other island to which Britain's claim was, in his opinion, as poor as that of the Americans to San Juan. But discretion remained the better part of impulsiveness, and several of his Cabinet colleagues were by no means sure of Britain's title. So Russell waited to hear from Lyons and to learn how the colonial governor of Vancouver Island, James Douglas, had reacted to Harney's provocative behaviour. The foreign secretary gave some thought to a possible temporary arrangement under which the two nations would alternate occupation of the island until its owner-ship was settled but accepted as more practical Palmerston's proposal of joint occupation along the current line of demarcation until the interna-tional boundary was definitively drawn.[27]

Lyons worked to prevent a deterioration in relations. He impressed upon Rear Admiral Robert Baynes, the British naval commander on the Pacific coast, a "noble old fellow," and a veteran of the Napoleonic Wars and of the Battle of Navarino Bay in 1827, the need to ensure there was no "unfortunate collision." The home government would be furious, he wrote, should the current "particularly good understanding" with the United States be jeopardized. He informed Baynes of Buchanan's deci-sion to order to the scene the Republic's most senior military officer, Winfield Scott, a journey which took weeks to complete, and of the gen-eral's "most conciliatory" instructions. They included a temporary con-tinuation of joint occupation. Similarly, Lyons urged Governor Douglas to receive this distinguished emissary courteously, yet he was privately pessimistic of a satisfactory and honourable outcome. The attention of the American press had been drawn to the incident, which was likely to become an issue in the upcoming American elections. Anglophobia, Lyons brooded, was already popular with the "rabble who alone take part" in elections. The people, "spoiled by constant success in their grasping attempts," set up an outcry whenever a claim to territory, how-ever unjust, was abandoned, and Buchanan lacked the backbone to face it down. Only the conviction that Britain would go to war rather than surrender the island would induce the Senate to advise the president to accept Britain's terms. The idea "that happen what may England will never really declare war with this Country has become so deeply rooted that I am afraid nothing short of actual hostilities would eradicate it," a gloomy Lyons reported.[28]

Baynes, although resentful of the "tissue of falsehoods" uttered by Buchanan and Cass, restrained Governor Douglas from sending a military force to the island without explicit instructions to do so from home. In that event, he convinced Douglas to give the American commander prior notice of the dispatch of the British force and of its commander's orders to establish a "perfect understanding" with him. On the last day of February in this leap year, Baynes learned of Russell's acceptance of Scott's proposal that he station on the island marines equal in number to the American troops. The admiral was careful to ensure that the marines kept a good distance from the American camp, and he had the new American commander, the amiable Captain Lewis Cass Hunt, to dine on his flagship. Harney continued to make trouble, and this so angered Scott that he had him reassigned to distant St Louis. In Parliament, Russell had little difficulty depicting joint occupation as something of a British diplomatic success, for the 800 men Harney had ultimately ordered to the island had been reduced to 100 and were now matched by the British force. The modest Lyons disclaimed credit for the avoidance of a confrontation. He and Dallas in London had been mere mailmen forwarding the exchanges between Russell and Cass, he informed Baynes. Secretary Cass did propose arbitration as the basis of a permanent solution, but past British experience made Russell wary of this process. The Americans had a history of rejecting unfavourable decisions as partial and unfair. A mordant Lyons jested that possession be decided by a coin toss, for Buchanan no longer had the power to win Senate ratification of any agreement acceptable to Britain. Thirteen years were to pass before Britain finally recognized exclusive American possession of the island.[29]

As for the Mexican crisis, Russell continued to hope for the triumph of the liberal faction led by Benito Juárez. It was centred on the port of Vera Cruz and promised to "democratize and secularize the country, stimulate capitalist ventures, protect human rights and private property, guarantee equality under the law, and forge a new nation out of all the disparate regions." But it could not be formally recognized while the Conservatives led by Miguel Miramón remained in possession of the national capital. He was strongly supported by a Catholic Church which had been deprived of its special privileges by Juárez when he was acting as minister of justice in an earlier, short-lived Liberal government. Russell was keen to know what the Americans had in mind and as he suspected Buchanan's acquisitive eyes had settled on the northern provinces of Chihuahua and Sonora. However, Congress denied him the authority he sought, for territorial expansion southwards was resisted by those Americans, principally Republicans, determined to halt the expansion of slavery.[30]

Buchanan and his Cabinet were "at their wit's end about Mexico," Lyons informed Russell. Their weakness in Congress even prevented them from responding vigorously to Mexican border provocations. Lyons had thoughtfully organized for himself a supply of "political" intelligence. His source was the senior British naval officer in Mexican waters whose personal belief it was that in a Liberal victory lay the best hope of bringing to an end the anarchy in the Central American state. After all, Juárez and his followers were at least striving to do good with principles that were based on justice and moderation. They were hampered, however, by a deficiency of funds, by the want of leaders of energy and integrity, and by the lack of competent generals. Lyons now believed that the Americanization of a portion of Mexico was both natural and inevitable. If that happened, he relied on the Southern slave states to stymie any move in the annexed territories towards economic protectionism harmful to British commercial interests. The British consul in Mexico City, on the other hand, suggested that Britain would recover lost prestige by "taking some decided part with the United States in the pacification of the country." Lyons doubted that the Palmerston government had troops to spare for a Mexican adventure. Similarly, he doubted the desire of the United States to send a large force into Mexico, and was certain that neither his nation nor the United States "would acquiesce in an exclusively French occupation" of the country. Indeed, in the name of the Monroe Doctrine, he expected the Americans to oppose any European intervention. Moreover, memories of Greece were sufficient to discourage any thought in his own mind of a tri-nation protectorate. As for formal British recognition of the Juárez regime, he noted that its behaviour towards British subjects had been far better than that of Miramón, whose agents had entered the British legation and confiscated the interest payments due to British creditors. Yet the behaviour of the Liberals might have been influenced by the fact that their stronghold of Vera Cruz was within range of British naval guns. Furthermore, the Liberals' prospects were still "far from good."[31]

Russell, seeking at least a suspension of violence, instructed the British agents in Mexico to press for a temporary armistice. But as Miramón was already besieging Vera Cruz and lacked secure communications with Mexico City, for the capital was surrounded by guerillas, the instructions did not reach the British consul there. The "Mexican Question seems as far from a solution as ever," Lyons wearily reported in May 1860. The flight of Miramón, and evidence that the whole country with the exception of the clergy was sick of war, revived his hope of an end to the violence. If the triumphant Juárez and his colleagues were careful not to repeat the mistake of the previous Liberal government, and squabble among themselves, there seemed at last a real possibility of political stability and repayment of European debts. Church reforms – the nationalization of church property, the closing of monasteries, a ban on the recruitment of novices for nunneries, the prohibition of religious ceremonies outside church buildings, the denial to clergy of the right to wear religious dress beyond their churches, assurances of religious toleration – and a commitment to freedom of the press were encouragingly progressive measures. But by the time the new British minister, Charles Wyke, reached the capital in May, he found little grounds for optimism. The Liberal party, he informed Lyons, "have managed to disband the army, squander the church property and disgust everybody connected with them." Its expulsion of the Spanish and Guatemalan ministers, and of the papal nuncio, had made enemies of those states, and their number almost doubled following the proclamation of a decree suspending debt repayments for at least twelve months. Foreign remonstrances are ignored, Wyke reported, and a people "spoilt by our former leniency and indulgence think they can do anything they like with impunity." He did not expect American help in fending off foreign intervention. His American counterpart was obsessed with the danger of Mexico falling into the hands or the embrace of the newly organized Confederate States of America.[32]

CHAPTER FIVE

The Disunited States

Southerners had reacted hysterically to the incident at Harper's Ferry, but George Moore, the British consul at Richmond, Virginia, who was well known to Lyons as the former consul at Ancona in the Papal States, expected the execution of John Brown on 2 December 1859 to calm them. However, he admitted that disunion was not impossible should the public excitement remain at a high pitch. A Southern Rights Association was aggressively campaigning for a boycott of Northern-produced goods and wares, and to that end a group of merchants announced the launch of the Virginia and Liverpool Packet Company. But Robert Bunch doubted that Southerners possessed the energy needed to make a success of direct trade. He expected them to focus instead on a revival of the slave trade, given the current dramatic rise in the price of slaves. The refusal of Southern juries, both grand and petty, either to return true bills of indictment against suspected slave traders, or to convict those brought to trial, encouraged violations of the existing ban on the trade. That it was continuing was confirmed by the consuls at Galveston and Mobile, who reported the landing of "African negroes."[1]

Lyons instructed Southern consuls in their intelligence-gathering responsibilities. "All matters bearing upon the dispute between the North and the South are particularly interesting and important," he impressed upon them, "and the more information you give me about them, the greater will be the obligation to you." He wanted to know whether the direct trade movement was likely to divert commerce from Northern ports; whether the Southern Rights Association was curtailing consumption of Northern products; whether a trade boycott could endure; whether local opinion was supportive of slavery and secession; whether hostility to the Union was stronger than ever before; and whether there was any abuse of British subjects by the Southern vigilantes currently terrorizing residents and visitors suspected of anti-slavery sentiments. Who in the United States, he asked himself, was a British subject? Britain's commitment to indefeasible allegiance meant that the number was approximately 2 million, but a great many of them, and Irish immigrants in particular, had become naturalized Americans. Those British subjects who had completed the process of naturalization and were living in the Republic had no claim to his protection, he decided.[2]

Seeking a clearer understanding of American opinion, Lyons packed Irvine off on a tour of the West. Visits to Cincinnati and St Louis convinced him that local hostility to slavery was by no means moral. Westerners considered the institution unprofitable because of the relative ease with which slaves might escape to the free states, he reported, but they also disliked it because it discouraged white immigration. Lyons, for whom slavery was the root cause of the sectional tensions, considered the violent response of Southerners to the "foolish affair" at Harper's Ferry "not very confirmatory of the confidence which the Planters profess to feel in the 'happy and attached peasantry' by which euphonious appellation they designate their Slaves." On the other hand, the lack of Northern interest in British proposals for the "efficient" suppression of the international slave trade he blamed on the "professed Abolitionists" who were making handsome profits out of it. In New York City, the United States marshal appointed by the Buchanan administration had permitted the trade to operate out of the port. But Lyons's zeal for freedom, at least "in the abstract," his ridicule of the Southerners' contention that slavery was a "divine institution," and his private sympathy with the Republican party's "anti-slavery principles," did not blind him to his nation's material interests. Britain's important textile industries needed to secure a reliable alternative supply of cotton before any "tricks were played with the 'systematized labour' of the South." Nor was he free of racism, describing fugitive slaves as "nigger deserters" and mocking "negresses" for their style of dress and attempts to part and comb their "wool."[3]

Lyons was surprisingly confident at the opening of 1860 that the year would not end with disunion. While North and South had "never before been so near a breach," he expected the free states again to "avoid proceeding to extremities" by not venturing to elect an "Anti-Slavery President." Nor could he believe that the Southern states would be so "mad" as to push matters to extremes. They surely recognized the protection slavery enjoyed within the Union, where the eighteen free states were held in check by the Constitution. Were the fifteen slave states to secede this would no longer be the case, and in the past they had always gotten their way by simply threatening to do so. But Lyons did recognize the danger that a North, tired of yielding, might finally "put the Southern resolution to the proof."[4]

"I go often to the 'Capitol' (as it is absurdly termed) to hear the debates," Lyons informed Minna, and "have never heard a speech upon any other subject than Slavery, but then I believe they never do speak upon any other subject." He made the acquaintance of Senator James Murray Mason of Virginia, a grandson of a hero of the Revolution who nevertheless entertained visiting Englishmen with mildly mocking stories of the demigods of the Revolutionary era. He was an "agreeable man, extremely well informed on his own subjects, and possessing that ready flow of language by which well-educated Americans are in general distinguished." An attorney by profession and a politician by vocation, the Virginian was an aggressive defender of slavery. To Britons, in particular, he described it as patriarchal, "such as is described in the Old Testament," an institution which rested on a "sense of mutual dependence." He admitted that the separation of families did occur but only when a plantation or estate was sold and thus was, happily, a rare event. But he contradicted himself with his authorship of the hated Fugitive Slave Law. However, it was his chairing of the Senate's Foreign Relations Committee which attracted Lyons to him and perhaps explained his losses to him at whist. "After a night of disaster, I am impressed with the promptness of your memory, & its accuracy to a shilling," the Virginian wrote with all the bonhomie of the winner. A month later, while sitting on a sofa with the Senate's leading Republican, William Seward, Lyons was suddenly dragged into the bitter sectional controversy. They were spotted by Louis T. Wigfall, a radical "state's righter" and recent arrival from Texas. Wigfall yelled: "There is the Republican platform. It is talking to Lord Lyons. There it is sitting by the British Minister." Democrats had long libelled Republicans as the servants of British abolitionism, thereby doubly damning them in the eyes of anglophobic Americans. In drawing attention to the British minister, who swiftly slipped away, the Texan had committed a serious breach of Senate decorum. "There has never before been offered such an insult to a foreign minister," one Republican newspaper thundered, before asking how long it would take for Southern gentlemen to open their eyes "to the fact that slavery engenders this barbarous and disgraceful conduct." Wigfall immediately wrote a letter of apology which Mason may have dictated and certainly hand delivered to the British legation. In it, the Texan protested that his allusion had been to the Republicans' support of a Homestead Bill not their position on slavery. Fig leaf that it was, Lyons graciously acknowledged the "promptness and courtesy of the explanation" and returned to the chamber the very next day to demonstrate his acceptance of it.[5]

The arrival of spring, normally a season of renewed hope, was this year marred for Lyons by family and diplomatic anxieties. The health of his brother-in-law, Fitz, which had never been robust, was causing grave concern. He was no longer recovering swiftly from the bilious attacks that had long plagued him, and month by month his strength was ebbing away. On the diplomatic front, Lyons watched uneasily the progress of the campaign for a protective American tariff. Aware of the Canadians' fear that its passage would spell the end of reciprocity, he decided, while discreetly maintaining contact with its American friends, to steer clear of the subject at least until after the presidential and congressional elections. He also met with Canada's most influential newspaper publisher and a leader of the opposition in the Canadian legislature, George Brown, to impress upon him the difficulty of defending the commercial pact when Canadian politicians "unpatriotically" implied that the Americans had good reason to violate it. An even greater worry was the talk of the United States looking for a foreign crisis as a "desperate remedy for the distracted state of the Country." Britain, he assumed, "would be the country selected for the experiment if it were made." He expected, at the very least, a cynical bid in the approaching elections for the Irish vote via some "violent anti-English proceeding." To counter this danger, he urged the Palmerston government to deny American "braggarts" the irresistible temptation of British entanglement in a European crisis, and if still provoked to "put forth [the nation's] whole strength at the outset and give [the Americans] a sharp lesson, before they have time to get up an Army or Navy."[6]

The presidential nominating conventions in late spring dampened hopes that political strife would not be pushed to "extremities." Delegates from a majority of the slave states bolted the Democratic convention in Charleston when it failed to adopt a platform that demanded Federal promotion of slavery in the territories. The only truly national political party had now divided along sectional lines. The current vice-president, John Breckinridge, was nominated by Southern Democrats, while their Northern and Western counterparts chose Stephen Douglas to run on the discredited platform of "popular sovereignty." Robert Bunch, who had witnessed the divisive events in Charleston, concluded that the Republican candidate, whose party was exclusively Northern and Western, was now assured of victory. William Seward, to the surprise of many observers, failed to win the nomination. The New Yorker's reputation as a radical opponent of slavery, which he had striven to shed, had become a political millstone, and on the convention's third ballot Abraham Lincoln was nominated. Lyons knew little of the Illinois lawyer, for not one of the leading Republicans whom he had consulted had even mentioned him as a likely nominee. He was "a rough Westerner, of the lowest origin and little education," Lyons was told, who had begun life as a farm labourer and who had "got on by a talent for stump speaking." What could not be mistaken was the candidate's opposition to the institution of slavery. He had spelled it out during his narrowly unsuccessful campaign two years earlier to deny Stephen Douglas another term in the Senate. If the Democrats' schism had shortened the odds on the election of an anti-slavery president, there was a possibility that no candidate would win the required absolute majority in the Electoral College. The respected John Bell of Tennessee, who had left the Senate the previous year, now returned to the political fray as the nominee of the newly formed Constitutional Union Party. It was the "Neutral or respectable Party," Lyons submitted. With a platform that called for the preservation of the Union, it was seeking to deny any candidate the necessary majority of the Electoral College. The contest would then be thrown into the House of Representatives as it had been in 1824, where each state irrespective of its population cast a single vote. That ballot, his sums told Lyons, would deliver the presidency to Breckinridge.[7]

The hot and humid summer, which saw the political temperature rising apace, brought the arrival of the new French minister, Henri Mercier. By coincidence or design, he presented his letters of credence on 4 July 1860. Bickerton was very happy to see him. July also brought a welcome escape from Washington with its "hovels and swamps." After fifteen months, he was finally going to travel more than six miles from the capital and see something of the country and of the continent's natural wonders. He was to accompany the heir apparent to the British throne, Edward Prince of Wales, on his royal tour of Canada and parts of the United States. What made Lyons uneasy was the timing of the tour, taking place as it would during the crucial American elections. Would the Irish of New York and other cities stage demonstrations against the "Saxon" visitor? Would the Americans, invariably hypersensitive where Britain was concerned, take umbrage at the seclusion essential to princely comfort and dignity? Any dispute over etiquette would be "destructive and harmful" as well as incompatible with royal dignity. Would the Prince be presented with controversial addresses that would inflame either the South, the North, or home opinion? One task was to "keep the Americans in a good humour," while another was to keep the Prince safe. Would he be exposed to physical danger by travelling extensively on American trains and river steamers? Lyons had read the alarming statistics which indicated that the risk of disaster was much higher than at home. Hence his insistence on a pilot train to ensure track safety and his wish to confine the American excursion to New England. This proved impossible when the city of New York extended an invitation to the Prince, and the President of the United States invited him to the White House.[8]

Lyons set out for Canada on 28 July, travelling at a gentle pace. He stopped briefly in Baltimore and Philadelphia, dismissing both as "ugly and uninteresting like all American towns." Approaching New York City by water, he considered the bay "rather pretty" but on landing was disappointed to find so few public buildings and such uninteresting church architecture. The massive Trinity Church at the head of Wall Street, locally known as the "Cathedral of the city," did not inspire him with awe. He did admire the shops, though more for their appearance than their merchandise. They were, he admitted, "magnificent far beyond anything in London or Paris." A.T. Stewart's giant dry goods store had been the first to be built on Broadway, but other palaces of consumption were now joining it. Continuing his journey by river boat and in easy stages, he called at Saratoga the site of the first truly humiliating British defeat during the Revolutionary War but now a summer "watering place" where visitors seeking health drank its "putrid-tasting" water. On reaching Montreal he steamed down the St Lawrence to Quebec, whose setting he considered one of the most beautiful he had ever seen. This was high praise from a former resident of Athens, Rome, and more briefly Naples. Lyons was given rooms in Parliament House, where his fellow guests included Sir Fenwick Williams, the British military commander, and Rear-Admiral Sir Alexander Milne. On 18 August he went aboard HMS *Hero* to meet the royal visitor. Not yet twenty, the Prince was short and slight of stature, "boyish," "remarkably courteous and self-possessed," "remarkably kind and considerate to all about him, very agreeable, fond of jokes and easily amused." To the immense relief of Lyons, the young man seemed fully capable of playing "extremely well" the role of the appreciative tourist.[9]

The *Hero*'s deep draught prevented it from going beyond Quebec, so a private steamer was chartered to carry the royal party to Montreal. During the trip Lyons settled the Prince's itinerary with his political guardian, the hirsute Duke of Newcastle. Edward was to travel at his own expense, stay at hotels and pay for accommodation at the "proper price," decline all invitations to dine, with the exception of the president's, make no speeches, pay only limited attention to the Republic's British residents, and "studiously avoid showing any preference for any political party." Peculiarly unwelcome was the invitation issued by a group of Southern gentlemen who urged the Prince to visit the slave states in order to judge for himself their social condition and "overthrow

the barriers which prejudice or misguided philanthropy seek to erect."
Buchanan endorsed it as the means of enabling the future monarch
to form a "correct opinion of *the Institution*," for a tour of a plantation
would convince him "that no labouring population was so happy and
contented as the negro slaves of the South." Backed by the president,
the invitation could not be bluntly declined. Newcastle and Lyons fi-
nessed this potential public relations disaster by limiting the Southern
tour to Richmond. An unfortunate shortage of time and the unhealthy
season of the year would prevent the Prince from remaining longer in
the South, they explained.[10]

In Montreal a severe rainstorm wrought havoc with the flimsy triumphal arches erected in the Prince's honour, so he and his party remained on board the steamer for an extra day while they were repaired.
On 25 August, in much improved weather, he dedicated the Victoria
tubular bridge across the St Lawrence. In Ottawa he laid the corner-
stone of the new Canadian Parliament building, but his intended calls at
Kingston and Belleville were cancelled to avoid receptions organized or
dominated by the controversial and sectarian Orange Order. The royal
party sailed on to Toronto, with Lyons suffering acute discomfort from
a bout of diarrhea and a very nasty boil. Then it was on to Niagara Falls,
where the nighttime illumination was "extremely beautiful." Tiring of
"illuminations, triumphal arches, processions and addresses," the royal
party welcomed the thought of a more subdued reception in the United
States.[11]

Instead, 30,000 people were on hand at Detroit on 20 September to
greet Edward when he crossed the river separating Province and Republic. The next day he took the train to Chicago and from there to the prai-
rie village of Dwight for some shooting. The brisk pace resumed with
stops at St Louis, Cincinnati, Harrisburg, Pittsburgh, and Baltimore en
route to Washington, where Edward was a guest of the president. Buchanan gave an official banquet in his honour, and Lyons hosted a legation dinner to which the diplomatic corps was invited. There followed
the traditional round of sightseeing, with obligatory visits to the unfinished Capitol, to the unfinished Washington Monument, and to George
Washington's nearby home of Mount Vernon, where the Prince planted
an acorn on a little hillock close to the tomb. Following the flying visit

to Richmond, the party swiftly retraced its steps through Washington, Baltimore, and Philadelphia en route to New York. There followed another round of receptions, but the ball proved to be particularly lively. The false floor collapsed under the weight of the assembled guests, and more excitement ensued with the discovery that a carpenter had been "inadvertently nailed down" beneath the rapidly repaired floor. What amazed Lyons was the size and friendliness of the crowds. "The reception of the Prince was astounding," especially in New York, he informed Minna, where "there were at least half a million people in the streets – the enthusiasm and the perfect order were marvellous." The last round of royal stops took him to the West Point Military Academy, to Albany, the state capital, and to Boston, the heart of the American Revolution. There, ever game, Edward hiked up Bunker Hill to see the recently completed monument commemorating that conflict's first serious military engagement. He sailed from Portland for home on 22 October.[12]

The tour had been hard work for Lyons. His "incessant attention" had been necessary "to keep matters straight with the Americans." He had obtained from consuls in those cities the Prince was to visit lists of the prominent citizens who might expect to be introduced to the heir to the throne. It was Lyons who declined as graciously as possible unwelcome invitations, and refused as gently as possible gifts. Yet he had relished this extended association with fellow countrymen, and there was no disputing the visit's success despite the refusal of Irish militia companies to parade in honour of the "Saxon oppressor." "The unanimity of the feeling is wonderful," a member of the New York reception committee recorded, and the "old anti-British patriotism of twenty years ago is nearly extinct." General Winfield Scott declared that the "transit of the Young heir apparent to a mighty empire ... has obliterated the remaining war prejudices, among us, against the country of our forefathers." Charles Sumner, who in a few short months was to find himself chairing the Senate Foreign Relations Committee, was similarly confident of the diplomatic benefit. The Duke of Newcastle was "carrying home an unwritten Treaty of Alliance & Amity between two great nations," the senator advised British friends. Would this good feeling last? Ever the realist, Lyons was far from sure. They would soon face the labour of beginning all over again with a new president leading a new administration, he reminded Russell, and Abraham Lincoln's victory seemed assured by the time Lyons returned to Washington on 27 October. Almost three weeks earlier, the Republicans had carried Pennsylvania by an unexpectedly large majority. "So the question is settled," one intelligent observer concluded, "and Honest Abe will be our next President. Amen. We may as well ask the question at once whether the existence of the Union depends on the submission to the South." In the event of "extremities," Lyons would face a delicate and difficult situation. That the South was "mad enough" to dissolve the Union he still had difficulty believing, sharing as he appears to have done the opinion expressed in the border states that disunion would be an act of suicide motivated by the fear of dying. But Lyons suspected the Republicans of planning "to divert men's minds from disunion" by engaging in a little bullying of Britain.[13]

November brought the beginning of winter and the end of a life. Fitz died. "My heart is always with you, but I have no words that can be written to you," Bickerton wrote Minna. "I feel I am not wronging his poor Mother and sisters," she replied, "when I say that I do not think that *any* one will feel it as you will or will know so well what it is to me." He sought to lift her spirits with the news that his reward for his skilful piloting of the Prince through the potentially treacherous waters of the United States was his decoration as a Civil Knight Commander of the Bath. This was an honour rarely bestowed on someone not already in possession of a C.B. He offered to return to Britain to be by her side, but she did not wish him to jeopardize the extended regular leave to which he would soon be entitled. Anyway, as he admitted, the Palmerston government "would probably have made great difficulties about my coming home, in the extraordinary condition of this country." The Union's crisis now fully occupied him.[14]

Lyons continued to be puzzled by the response of the slave states to Lincoln's election, and it is unlikely that he would have understood it any better had he known that "by a wide margin slaves were the most valuable investment in the country." The Republican president would, after all, have "small" constitutional means of either interfering with the institution of slavery in the South or of otherwise injuring Southern interests. Similarly, the "Anti-Slavery Party" would not control Congress unless Southern senators and congressmen abandoned their seats. Why would the South cut off its nose to spite its face? Lyons asked himself. Furthermore, he expected the president-elect to "endeavour to conciliate the South by forming a reassuringly conservative administration." Nevertheless, the possibility of irrational behaviour could not be excluded. The "prosperous, contented and calm" country they had so recently travelled together now appeared to be travelling the road to ruin with characteristically American "speed and energy," Lyons wrote to Newcastle. He instructed the consuls in the South to do nothing that might "embarrass Her Majesty's Government in determining eventually the policy to be pursued" or might provide the Republicans with an excuse to spark a foreign crisis. William Seward spoke ominously in December of its domestic usefulness during a speech at the Astor House. From Virginia, where there were few if any Republicans, Moore also reported wild talk of rescuing the Union by starting a "rattling war with Great Britain." The new era of good feelings, the rapprochement, excited by the Prince's visit was proving as transitory as Lyons had feared it would.[15]

He vetoed Bunch's request for the stationing of a British warship off of Charleston for fear its appearance would "give rise to all sorts of conjectures and interpretations." Reading the consul's reports from the "very dunghill of the Confederate game-cock," Lyons became progressively more uneasy as the man he had named Britain's primary source of Southern intelligence betrayed undiplomatic sympathies. "Just now [the Southerners] promise us everything – free trade amongst the rest," Bunch wrote, "and it seems to me quite on the cards that a Southern Confederacy (if such a thing can be reached without a bloody civil war) may be a powerful addition to the list of nations." Lyons immediately issued a supplementary set of explicit instructions. Should South Carolina declare itself an independent state, Bunch was to make no move to recognize it as such. He was a British consul "in a part of the United States by virtue of an exequatur from the Federal Government." As such, he was not to communicate with any "independent" government but might remain on good personal terms with its members. He was not to provide any South Carolinian commissioner with a letter of introduction to Lord John Russell, for that would be tantamount to recognizing the state's right to appoint a diplomatic representative to Britain. Bunch

hurriedly assured Lyons of his "hatred and detestation" of slavery. Determined to control the flow of information to London on which policy
would be based, Lyons reminded all consuls that all their reports on
political developments forwarded directly to the Foreign Office must
be copied immediately to him. This was to ensure that the latest information was incorporated in his dispatches and that they arrived in
good time at the Foreign Office. This would prevent misunderstanding
and promote unity of action. Indeed, with these objectives in mind, he
asked the consuls to send to him far more detailed accounts of political
developments than they forwarded to a foreign secretary burdened with
global issues.[16]

The Southern states, Britons admitted, possessed not only a favourable climate and soil for the production of cotton but also "capital, labour,
skill, and above all, a comprehensive organization of resources resulting
from years of commercial experience and success." Other regions of the
world had the climate and the soil but not these other essentials. Of
course, Lyons resented the talk of "King Cotton," which in his opinion
amounted to an arrogant assumption by Southerners that Britain was at
their beck and call. What they failed to grasp, he remarked, was that it
was more necessary for them to sell than it was for Britain to buy cotton.
That these "exaggerated and false ideas about cotton" were likely to produce "foolish conduct" received a timely illustration. One of the most
rabid secessionists, Robert Barnwell Rhett, casually informed Bunch
that an independent South would reopen the international slave trade.
Slavery was a bitter enough pill for Britons to swallow, Lyons angrily
observed, but if the slave trade were added to the dosage even the "least
squeamish British stomach" would reject it. And while he professed a
total ignorance of commercial matters, Lyons was confident he understood the basic laws of supply and demand. There were other places
in the world where cotton could and would be grown if its price rose
too steeply, while Southern talk of coercing Britain by withholding the
staple from the market would surely have the same result – its growth
elsewhere or the development of a substitute.[17]

The Buchanan administration's vacillation in the face of the ever-
deepening crisis, which was not entirely surprising since the Cabinet
was in a geographical sense a microcosm of the nation, aroused in Lyons

a mixture of disbelief and scorn. In his final message to Congress, on 3 December 1860, Buchanan held Northerners responsible for the crisis. Their denunciation of slavery had caused it, he asserted; consequently it would be solved if they halted their attacks. No state had the right to secede without the consent of the other members of the Union, the hapless president declared; nor had the Union the right to hold them by force. Buchanan had shown, Seward mockingly observed, that it was the president's duty to execute the laws unless somebody opposed him, while no state had the right to leave the Union unless it wanted to. But a public abandonment of leadership by a president who still had three full months of his term to complete was no laughing matter. Although Buchanan called on Congress to enact pro-slavery and pro-Southern legislation, he made the situation worse by guaranteeing that few if any Republicans would respond positively. The resignations of the Cabinet's two most senior members, Lewis Cass and Howell Cobb, the latter the secretary of the Treasury, merely compounded the confusion. Cass left because of the failure to re-provision and reinforce the Federal forts built to protect Charleston. His departure was much regretted by Lyons. The old general had overcome his reputation as an anglophobe, whereas his successor Jeremiah Black, the former attorney general, was entirely ignorant of foreign relations and an inept administrator. Cobb, meanwhile, on his return to his home state of Georgia, had urged its citizens to secede, and Southern extremists were encouraged to act by Buchanan's profession of powerlessness. At 9 p.m. on 20 December, with Robert Bunch discreetly positioned behind a pillar in Charleston's "Secession Hall," the president of the specially summoned state convention declared South Carolina "a sovereign and independent Commonwealth." The declaration set off a "hideous" round of celebrations, dominated appropriately as time was to tell by the boom of cannons and the explosions of fireworks. "I am somehow sorry for the old Union, altho' he was a braggart," Bunch sighed. "We have yet to see whether he will find any friends at the North to avenge his death."[18]

Georgia, with "more people, more voters, more slaves, and more slaveholders than any other Lower South state," briefly rallied hopes that Southern Unionism would as in the past reassert itself. If the Northern states repealed legislation obnoxious to the slave South, such as the personal liberty laws designed to frustrate enforcement of the Federal Fugitive Slave Law, secessionist sentiment would be dampened down, the British consul at Savannah believed. Instead, a combination of Unionist overconfidence, secessionist zeal, and political chicanery saw a state convention pass an ordinance of secession on 19 January 1861. Meanwhile, from Richmond, George Moore had forwarded to Lyons an account of one of the largest political meetings he had ever witnessed there. Ominously, it had concluded with the humiliation of a lone Unionist, who had courageously spoken up, and with the passage of a resolution calling for secession. "This is the strongest manifestation of disunion spirit that I have yet seen," the consul admitted. Within days it was certain that the seven slave states of the lower South would have seceded before Lincoln took the oath of office in March. Delegates from six of the seven assembled in Montgomery, Alabama, a city with few new public buildings and a population of 9,000 split almost evenly, ironically, between whites and blacks. It was in this "odious hole," as Bunch described it, that the Confederate States of America was born early in February. Two questions immediately sprang to mind. Would the Confederacy be joined by Virginia and the other slave states? Would the Republicans endeavour to tempt the dissident states back into the Union with large political concessions? An affirmative answer to the second question appeared unlikely. There was less not more "disposition towards concession" in New York, Archibald informed Lyons, for the "relief of the money market has imparted to people a stronger feeling of *independence.*" Lincoln's election in accordance with both the Constitution and the law, as Senator Stephen Douglas pointed out, gave neither just cause nor reasonable ground for secession.[19]

Yet Lincoln's victory had been sectional. His name had not been on the ballot in ten Southern states, while in the few where he was listed he had received a derisory percentage of the votes. In the North, on the other hand, he had carried every state bar one, but nationally he had received less than 40 per cent of the total ballots. He did not respond to those who urged him to offer a nervous public some insight into his views and intentions, preferring to honour the tradition of pre-inaugural discretion. Like many Republicans he may initially have considered talk of secession an election ploy of the Democrats. Perhaps he still underestimated the extremists' resolve and believed they would soon be squashed by Southern Unionists because he failed to grasp "that the overwhelming majority of southern whites were committed to their slave society." He feared emboldening disunionists by being too concili-atory and feared alienating the rank and file of his own party. Hence he declared "inflexible" his adherence to the central plank of the Republi-can platform: opposition to the extension of slavery to the territories. He concentrated on constructing a representative Cabinet and filling a mul-titude of lesser public offices, observing that while 30,000 partisans were seeking the latter 30,000,000 Americans were not. Meanwhile, abhor-ring the policy vacuum created by Buchanan's indecision and Lincoln's silence, Congress naturally sought to fill it. The House of Representa-tives struck a Committee of Thirty Three and the Senate a Commit-tee of Thirteen to seek a Union-saving political compromise. Another forum was the peace conference summoned by Virginia and attended by representatives from twenty-one states who gathered in Washington in early February. Tellingly, the seven seceded states and three free states declined to attend. Several weeks earlier, William Seward had delivered a conciliatory speech in the Senate. He spoke with the authority of a man who was widely expected to be appointed secretary of state and who assumed he would be the incoming administration's controlling figure. His proposals included repeal of state legislation that negated the Federal Fugitive Slave Law and a constitutional amendment denying Congress the authority to tamper with slavery in those states where it already existed. Lincoln ignored these suggested measures, determined as he was never to accept any arrangement that opened the door to an extension of slavery. As put more starkly by Charles Sumner, a civil war must be avoided if possible but there must be no abandonment of the founding principle of the Republican party.[20]

Lyons had kept the Foreign Office well briefed on the astonishing events. Federal forts and arsenals, he reported, were being seized even in states which had not as yet seceded. The conduct of the governors amounted to treason. The South Carolinians, who had seceded, had fired on the national flag when the Buchanan administration made a pathetic attempt to re-provision Fort Sumter in Charleston harbour where over Christmas local Federal garrisons had been concentrated.

As for the peace convention, it could only claim to have postponed the shedding of blood. The policy with which Seward was increasingly identified, of avoiding at almost any cost a violent confrontation with the South, in the belief that passivity would ultimately lead to peaceful reunion, was not one Lyons expected Lincoln to adopt. The New Yorker's confidence that the politically inexperienced chief executive would "leave the whole management of affairs to him" was misplaced. The senator "has little or no personal acquaintance with the President Elect, and very little knowledge of his views or intentions, or means of judging of the amount of influence he himself will have with the new chief magistrate," Lyons astutely noted. Lincoln's more resolute views finally became clearer during his long, meandering rail journey from his home town of Springfield, Illinois, to the capital. The trip, it was thought, would allow Lincoln to consult other Republican leaders along the way, bolster his image as a popular figure, and divert attention from the problem of secession. At Indianapolis he made plain his determination to resist secession, although at other places he dismissed the crisis as artificial and urged his fellow countrymen to remain cool. Anxious not to alienate the slave states still within the Union, he avoided the subject of slavery in speeches and statements along the route and denied the existence of a genuine national crisis. But at Trenton, New Jersey, the single Northern state he had failed to capture, and again the following day at Philadelphia, he affirmed his intention to meet force with force should there be another attack on the Federal government as had happened the previous month in Charleston harbour.[21]

The Confederacy had formed a provisional government led by the respected former Mississippi senator and experienced administrator Jefferson Davis, described by perhaps the most famous Texan, Sam Houston, as "Ambitious as Lucifer and cold as a lizard." In his inaugural address on 18 February, Davis rooted the Confederacy in the Declaration of Independence, which was Lincoln's ideological source. There was no British observer in Montgomery because Lyons suspected that the appearance there of a member of the legation would be misconstrued. King Cotton's courtiers would boast that Britain was behaving as they had long predicted, for Davis had invited Tennessee to secede with the promise that cotton would finance war. Another Lyons concern was that the presence in Montgomery of a British diplomat would stir up the political quacks keen to prescribe a foreign concoction for the domestic malady. But he cautioned the Foreign Office against being impressed, as Bunch had been, with the Confederacy's "bid for European support." How long, he asked, would its ban on the Atlantic slave trade, and its promise of virtual free trade, survive in the event the Confederacy became independent? The ban was designed with the slave states of the upper South in mind, he argued, for they were heavily involved in the profitable domestic slave trade and would value this promise of protection from less expensive imports. A clearer clue to the real sentiment of the South was, he believed, the call in the Confederate Congress for an export duty on all raw cotton being sent to non-Confederate ports for shipment overseas. This was another of the levers, he observed, with which Southern slaveowners expected to move Britain in their direction.[22]

Distant American turmoil had difficulty rivalling close European instability for the attention of the Palmerston government. Napier, shortly after arriving in the Hague, had informed Lyons of disturbing developments in Germany and Central Europe. Public opinion in their countries was so anti-French, German diplomats informed him, that at any moment there might be a march across the Rhine. Russian intentions were another source of concern. They were suspected of planning revenge for Austria's conduct during the Crimean conflict by playing the old game of fomenting revolt in the Ottoman Empire. So when a despondent Edward Everett, a former congressman, a former governor, a former minister to the United Kingdom, a former secretary of state, a former senator, and a former nominee for the vice-presidency, suggested to Lyons that Britain, France, and Russia jointly offer to mediate between North and South, he forwarded the proposal to the Foreign Office with a strong recommendation that it not be pursued. The Americans had always haughtily repudiated European intervention in the Americas let alone in the Union, he reminded Russell. Nor did he forget British public opinion. "It would, I should think, be difficult for England to be a party to an arrangement for securing and perpetuating Slavery anywhere," he added, "and the Northern States are quite ready to yield on everything except the *extension* of slavery." Britain would do better to act in concert with France, since if William Seward took the State Department he would be unlikely to "adopt an intolerable tone of bullying towards England and France united."[23]

Lyons's advice encouraged Russell to decline that offered by Thomas Baring. The influential banker, a strong supporter of the Union, with the security of the bank's American investments very much in mind, was another who favoured British mediation of the American crisis. But the foreign secretary thought the slave states had a "good ground" for separation. The American Constitution, specifically Article IV, provided for the recovery of fugitive slaves, although its drafters had preferred the euphemism of persons "held to Service or Labour." The effective frustration by free states of the enforcement legislation amounted in Russell's opinion to a violation of the constitutional "bargain." By implication, he was accepting the "breach of compact" argument advanced by secessionists and in support of which they cited the writings of James Madison, a founding father of the Constitution who had gone on to become the nation's fourth president. Russell could not see how the Union could be "cobbled together again by any compromise" since the Republicans considered secession "high treason" and demanded its suppression. The breakup of the Union was therefore "inevitable," and it was his hope that Northerners would come to their senses and acknowledge the right of secession. Perhaps he had in mind, as Confederates certainly did, his earlier declaration that Britain would not recognize an Italian regime imposed by force contrary to "the national wishes." What he envisaged across the Atlantic was two American Republics, one constituted on the principles of freedom and personal liberty, and the other on slavery and the mutual surrender of fugitives. He wished the division to be settled peacefully. Furthermore, he could afford to wait to see how the crisis developed, for he was not under parliamentary or popular pressure to interfere. The dependence of the textile industries on American cotton, industries which *The Economist* calculated "directly and indirectly sustained one-fifth of the population of Britain," had not as yet excited great anxiety. The Union's troubles received scant attention in Parliament, which reopened early in February, although Charles Buxton, a younger son of a famous anti-slavery father, expressed the hope that any recognition of the Confederate flag would be conditional on the non-revival of the Atlantic slave trade. No such recognition was being contemplated by the government. Russell was content to instruct Lyons to preach against civil war and above "all things" endeavour to prevent any blockade of the South for it would almost certainly bring "misery, discord, & enmity incalculable" to the textile districts.[24]

Few who heard him speak, or read newspaper accounts of his speeches, could doubt Lincoln's resolve when he declared the Union "perpetual." More questionable was his fitness for the daunting task that confronted him. Richard Cobden, a reputed British friend of the United States, admitted to serious doubts. He had met the Springfield lawyer during his visit to the Republic less than two years earlier, when Lincoln had been representing the Illinois Central in which so many Britons had invested. Lincoln, Cobden informed his friend John Bright, was "a backwoodsman of good sturdy commonsense but plainly unequal to the occasion." Lyons, as one of the company who sat down to dinner with the president-elect two days before his inauguration, assessed him as "a little uncouth but mild and quiet," a "good natured and pleasant" man. His height and his large feet and hands struck most observers, as did his unusual features. The long "dark face, strongly marked, tanned and crowsfooted, and fringed with coarse and tangled hair, is so uncouth and so rugged," one careful observer later wrote, "that it narrowly escapes being either terrible or grotesque." That impression was countered, he added, "by a peculiar soft, almost feminine, expression of melancholy."[25]

As he rose on 4 March to have the oath of office administered by Chief Justice Taney, the author of the despised *Dred Scott* decision, and to deliver his inaugural address, Lincoln was cheered by the large crowd "but not very loudly." The new president sought to reassure Southerners. Sitting to the left of the canopy, in the area reserved for diplomats and other dignitaries, Lyons admired his delivery, remarking: "I heard every syllable of it distinctly." He grasped the subtlety of Lincoln's remarks, observing that almost "anything *may* or *may not* be done without contradiction by the new Administration." There was a soothing emphasis on "forbearance and the rule of law" but no retreat from his firm position on the Union. He intended to execute the laws faithfully in all the states, Lincoln announced, but would not interfere with slavery in states where it already existed. He would not initiate conflict but would not tolerate aggression. "You have no oath registered in Heaven to destroy the government," he informed secessionists, "while I shall have the most solemn one to 'preserve, protect and defend' it." "We are not enemies," he concluded, "but friends. We must not be enemies."[26]

Lincoln's "pacific intentions" briefly gave "great satisfaction" in New York, where Southern sympathizers applauded the speech but its more careful readers detected, as had the careful listener Lyons, the "clank of metal." Stocks soon tumbled, and an apprehensive Archibald wrote to the minister: "I trust we may not be miscalculating the chances of a bloodless termination of the national troubles." The president's moderate tone was dictated, in part, by his efforts to hold onto the slave states of the upper South and the border. If they all remained loyal the disaffected states might abandon the quest for independence, but George Moore's reports from the capital of the most important of these states were far from encouraging. Richmond was in a political ferment. Every day there were secessionist speeches to vast crowds from hotel balconies and from the windows of private homes, while displays of the Confederacy's "handsome flag" invariably produced a "great sensation." Unionists were not despairing, Moore admitted, and disunionists remained a "decided minority," but sentiment in favour of secession was steadily increasing.[27]

At the very moment when the Union most wanted European goodwill, and needed to enlist commercial interests in its favour, the Republicans pushed through Congress, thanks to the departure of so many Southerners, "a nearly prohibitive tariff bill." Protectionists had blamed the financial panic of 1857 on the "heresy of free trade" and the Republicans had made a protective tariff a campaign issue in the recent elections. The bill convinced Lyons that they were "demented," while the Governor General of Canada, Sir Edmund Head, was moved to sarcasm. The Americans, he wrote, were offering "a bribe to Europe to acknowledge & support the Southern States." Although the tariff deepened Canadian uneasiness over the future of reciprocity, Lyons continued silent on that subject. He decided not to raise the matter for fear of an unwelcome response and counselled agitated Canadians to behave as if nothing had changed. Of course, the more immediate British commercial concern, given Lincoln's promise "to collect the duties and imposts" in all the states, was the possibility that the shipments of cotton would be disrupted. A Union blockade of the Confederate ports would cause difficulties as Russell had warned, but Britain's interests as the world's foremost naval power had also to be borne in mind. Initially, Russell had intended to stand behind the long-standing American doctrine, which the Congress of Paris had endorsed in 1856, that to be binding a blockade had to be established for a military purpose and be "effective." Before long, however, he was to loosen the test of effectiveness. What Britain required was "an actual blockade kept up by an efficient force." An unacceptable alternative was Federal legislation declaring the Confederacy's ports closed. This would bring to the fore, the foreign secretary informed Lyons, recognition of the Confederacy. From Charleston a somewhat chastened Bunch expressed the hope that the three Confederate diplomatic commissioners, who were about to be sent to Britain and Europe, would not receive too friendly a welcome. "They go," he observed, "believing in their inmost hearts that we cannot do without their confounded cotton – and that we will do anything or yield anything to get it. This is not a flattering estimate." That assumption explained the selection of William Yancey to lead the commission, for while his choice made domestic political sense it was diplomatically inept. His reputation as a rabid secessionist, a pro-slavery extremist, and an advocate of the slave trade guaranteed him a frosty welcome in Britain.[28]

Yancey and Pierre Rost, another of the commissioners, were in Havana when Edmund Monson landed there on 5 April. His health restored, he was returning to Washington. With Foreign Office approval he had elected to take the southern route across the Atlantic, calling at Cuba before travelling on to New Orleans. This would allow him to cross the Confederacy, a prospect that appealed to Russell, keen as he was to learn all he could of what was happening in the South. At the residence of the British consul general in Havana, Monson was introduced to the Confederates, who had already been received with formality by the colony's governor. He had even assured them that the new Republic would be recognized by Europe's Great Powers. Monson was far more circumspect. In Britain, he informed them, they would be received by the prime minister and the foreign secretary as private individuals only and there would be no hope of recognition without the South's adoption of "a systematic policy of discouragement and suppression" of the slave trade currently flourishing around Cuba. For their part, Yancey and Rost urged him to visit Montgomery and provided him with letters of introduction to leading members of the Confederate government. He accepted them, he wrote to Lyons, in the belief that his chief would welcome the information he gathered. But on his arrival in the temporary Confederate capital Monson found a telegram awaiting him in which Lyons expressed alarm at the possibility of the attaché being regarded as "some official emissary or messenger." This would be deeply embarrassing given Unionist talk of reuniting the nation through a foreign crisis. Consequently, when "President" Davis sent a message of welcome and offered assistance, Monson replied through an intermediary that as a member of the British legation he could not meet with any member of the Confederate government nor "hold any intercourse as a private individual with officials whom his Government did not recognize."[29]

The uneasiness of Lyons was a response to the calculated unpredictability of the new secretary of state. Seward had once described himself as an enigma and claimed to unite in his person the two streams of the mysterious Celts. Small of stature, slight of build, he had a somewhat predatory appearance. A receding chin accentuated a beak-like nose that was flanked by a pair of dark, alert eyes often unreadable beneath bushy eyebrows. He was clever, calculating, manipulative, devious, and gregarious. "He talks a great deal & is very much given to raconter & badiner," Britain's most famous newspaper reporter noted, "a subtle quick man not quite indifferent to kudos." He affected a republican's disdain for aristocracy yet boasted of his intimacy with Britain's nobility, who had feted him, thinking him the next president, during his visit there in 1859. Ambition for power, personal and national, had been the driving force of his long and successful political career; hence the crushing disappointment of his failure to capture the Republican nomination in 1860. Napier had recommended him to his successor as "truly benevolent," "sincere," and "full of political craft and management," and Lyons had speedily made his acquaintance. Their common passion for whist provided him with the opportunity, and at the close of the Senate session in June 1860 he had invited Seward to dine privately with him and had made a refusal difficult by leaving entirely to him the choice of day and time. Although initially disconcerted by Seward's tendency to be somewhat peremptory in his comments, Lyons grew to respect him and eventually came to look upon him as a friend. "He is not at bottom a quarrelsome or an unfriendly man," he was later to observe, "and apart from the occasional ebullitions of a rude overbearing spirit, has a desire to be esteemed a courteous man of the world." To his credit, Seward did not take offence if his own rudeness was matched and he was not a man to bear malice. The way to deal with him, Lyons came to realize, was to treat all attempts at bullying as non-avenues of discussion and when the volcanic verbal eruption subsided calmly return to the business at hand.[30]

Lyons did not expect the president to play a large role in the conduct of foreign policy and did not see him often. As late as 1863, following a rare interview, he reported that Lincoln did not pay a great deal of attention to foreign affairs. More accurate was his assumption that the president declined to discuss them in the absence of the secretary of state. Lincoln was clearly more familiar than Lyons realized with Britain's culture and institutions. Equally, he and Seward had quickly settled on the Union's essential foreign policy objectives – the prevention of foreign recognition of Confederate independence, the curtailing of European support of the Confederacy, and the avoidance, if possible, of a foreign war with a Great Power. Hence the premium they placed on peaceful relations with Britain.[31]

Seward's attitude towards Britain was an unstable compound of admiration, envy, and challenge. Britain, he wrote in a carefully constructed aphoristic sentence, was "the wisest of nations, though not the most learned, the strongest of nations, though not the most valorous, and the freest of nations, though not the most chivalrous." On occasion, he referred to Britain as a "fraternal state" and in private spoke lyrically of a possible "rapport between the English-speaking countries," but wary of being dubbed an anglophile, he was careful publicly to label it "the greatest, most grasping and rapacious power in the world." This was music to the ears of anglophobes, not the least of whom were the Irish Catholic refugees from the great famine, many of whom had settled in Seward's home state. Similarly, he voiced sympathy for those Irish patriots either incarcerated or transported to the other side of the world for endeavouring "to restore their native land to liberty and independence." His identification of Britain as the principal obstacle to the Republic's domination of the Western hemisphere, and to American global commercial supremacy, had obvious appeal for much of the electorate, as did his talk of the inevitable annexation of Canada. By extending American influence in the province, the Reciprocity Treaty had been portrayed as the essential first step. However, the enthusiastic reception the Canadians had given their future monarch knocked firmly on the head the notion that they wished to join the Republic. Hence American annexationists welcomed Seward's promise that any conflict with Britain would be fought on the soil of British North America.[32]

During its first few weeks in office the new administration wrestled with the problem of the isolated and desperately under-provisioned Fort Sumter in Charleston harbour. Its plight had been revealed to Lincoln shortly after his inauguration, and Confederate commissioners were soon in Washington seeking peaceful relations and the surrender of all Federal installations in the new nation. Seward, who judged Lincoln a novice more likely to sink than swim in Washington's deep and treacherous political waters, continued to assume that he would be the administration's leader in all but name. He was surprisingly slow to recognize Lincoln's ability. While still president-elect Lincoln had rebuffed Seward's attempt to control the selection of Cabinet officers and had deftly outmanoeuvred the New Yorker when, in the belief he could panic the novice into acknowledging his leadership, Seward withdrew his acceptance of the State Department two days before the inauguration. Instead, Seward received a request that he withdraw his letter but was given the name of his replacement should he choose not to do so. As it happened, he and Lincoln were of the same mind. Both regarded slavery as immoral and neither advocated racial equality. Both, as practical politicians in a land of white manhood suffrage, shaped their anti-slavery positions according to their understanding of what that electorate would accept. Both insisted that the Union was permanent, and both were committed to its preservation by force if necessary. Seward, when consulted, had strengthened the conciliatory passages of the inaugural address, sure as he was that the avoidance of bloodshed would lead to peaceful reunion. This was an illusion, as the Fort Sumter problem quickly revealed, and the crisis extinguished any lingering doubts of Lincoln's determination to lead the administration.

Sumter was the "critical question," Lyons realized. Was it to be abandoned or re-provisioned and reinforced? Evacuation would indicate the administration's intention "to withdraw their troops from such of the remaining fortresses in the South as cannot be held without the risk of fighting." No doubt influenced by Seward, who believed that yielding the fort would strengthen Unionism in the border states, Lyons thought that Sumter would be evacuated and more defensible forts reinforced. They would thus stand as symbols of a Federal presence in the South and perhaps calm Northern anger over the surrender of Sumter. This argument did not impress Lyons. In his opinion, and it was one Lincoln appears to have held, this response was more likely "to prevent the evacuation producing any conciliatory effect in the South, while the blow to the pugnacious North and Northwest of striking the national flag at Sumter will hardly be weakened." It could not be denied that it would represent a humiliating retreat by the president from his commitment "to hold, occupy and possess the Property and Places belonging to the Government." Then again, Lyons surmised, if Lincoln was willing to risk civil war "by launching the militia and volunteers of the North into the South," he would need to induce in them "the feeling of bitterness and animosity." A Confederate attack on Fort Sumter to prevent its re-provisioning might well serve this purpose.[33]

Lyons was approached on 20 March by an apprehensive secretary of state. Hearing of the gossip in the diplomatic community that Britain and France were inching towards recognition of the Confederacy, Seward asked how the two Great Powers would respond should Brazil and Peru, as were rumoured, take this step. No European power was "likely to quit 'an attitude of expectation' provided that in practice its commerce was not interfered with," Lyons answered. He was aware of the unresolved struggle over policy within the administration. Lincoln had two days earlier polled several of his Cabinet on "a forcible collection of the duties in Southern Ports" or proclaiming a blockade. Lyons warned Seward that the first option might create irresistible pressure in Britain for recognition of the Confederacy and would be inconsistent with the recent position of the United States in a similar situation in

Peru. Five days later, following dinner at the British legation, an animated secretary of state sought from Lyons and Mercier copies of the
instructions they had given their respective consuls in the South. Both
ministers, considering the request a diplomatic impertinence, replied
that the consuls were under orders to do their best to protect their nations' commerce. They and Stoeckl, another guest, warned Seward that
the course the administration appeared to contemplate would be tantamount to an unacceptable "paper blockade" of the Confederacy. This,
they added menacingly, would oblige foreign powers either to submit to
a form of coercion they had outlawed in 1856 or recognize the Confederacy. Seward, perhaps by this time under the influence of Lyons's fine
wines, responded with a "tirade" against "Foreign relations." Lyons and
his two colleagues concluded that the "more violent party in the Cabinet
had prevailed" and that interference with foreign trade was imminent.[34]

His uncertainty on how the domestic crisis would develop, and how
the Lincoln administration would behave internationally, led Lyons to
enlarge on his policy recommendations to Russell. He had advised his
government to avoid entanglement in a European crisis, for that might
tempt the Americans to disregard the concerns of foreign nations. If
provoked by them, he had urged a Palmerstonian response. Britain
should put forth its "whole strength" to teach them a lesson. He had
discouraged any diplomatic intervention in the American crisis unless it
was invited by the United States, had advised "caution and Watchfulness
to avoid giving offence to either party," and had stressed the wisdom of
a concert with France as a means of checking any American inclination
to go beyond talk of creating a foreign crisis. Now he recommended the
exploitation of Seward's evident concern over possible European recognition of the Confederacy. This should be utilized as a weapon to discourage the Union from interfering with foreign trade especially that in
cotton. For example, the Southern commissioners dispatched to Europe
should "not meet with too strong a rebuff in England and France," and
"nothing should be done to give colour to the assertions so boldly made
that England and France would under no circumstances recognize the
southern confederacy." On the other hand, he rejected the impulsive
Mercier's proposal that they obtain from their respective governments
discretionary authority to recognize the Confederacy should civil war

appear imminent. This would bring only embarrassment, Lyons argued. Both of their governments would presumably wish them to remain in place after recognition, but this would be difficult if they had taken "an ostensible part in effecting it." The Union would not want them. Far better to refer home such an important and potentially dangerous decision.[35]

Russell favoured caution. The instability of Europe and a healthy respect for the "subtlety" of the American cousins convinced him to leave the American problem in the capable hands of the sensible Lyons. "I rely on your wisdom, patience & prudence to steer us through the dangers of this crisis," he wrote. "If it can possibly be helped Mr. Seward must not be allowed to get us into a quarrel." As Lyons advised, the foreign secretary declined to give an assurance that Britain would never recognize the Confederacy, and agreed to "see the Southerners when they come but not officially, & keep them at a proper distance." Across the Atlantic, Seward had made another attempt to gain control of administration policy. He forwarded to the White House "some thoughts for the President's consideration." After a month in office the Cabinet had yet to formulate a clear policy, he wrote. Lincoln had been busily engaged instead in the distribution of patronage. He "ought to be meditating the condition of the country & his great public duties," Charles Sumner agreed, "instead of listening to the tales of office seekers." Not that he as chairman of the Foreign Relations Committee had a good word to say for the secretary of state. Privately, he accused Seward of exciting the distrust of all of the foreign ministers in Washington at the very moment when the United States required "the confidence and goodwill of other Powers." [36]

Seward remained committed, his unfortunately dated memorandum of 1 April implied, to the "foreign war panacea." News of Spain's reoccupation and annexation of Santo Domingo, and talk of a possible French intervention in Mexico, provided the excuse to demand "satisfactory explanations" from both nations. Should they fail to do so, war would follow. Explanations of their policies should also be sought from Great Britain and Russia, and agents dispatched to Canada, Mexico and Central America "to rouse a vigorous continental *spirit of independence*." Domestically, Seward would evacuate Sumter, reinforce and defend the forts in the Gulf of Mexico, and recall the Navy from overseas to blockade the Confederacy. Evidently, his private talk with Lyons and heated discussion with the three ministers had convinced him that simply to declare or legislate the Southern ports closed would result in European recognition of the Confederacy. He expected to administer the policy he outlined and had arranged with Henry Raymond of the *New York Times*, and Thurlow Weed of the Albany *Evening Journal*, to publish his proposals along with Lincoln's anticipated acceptance of them. Instead, Lincoln let Seward know that he was committed to the policy he had announced in the inaugural address. He intended to hold the places and property of the United States government, which included Sumter, and "to collect the duties and imposts." The absurdity of inviting a foreign war at this perilous domestic moment – though Seward was probably still thinking of a foreign crisis rather than hostilities – was too obvious to merit discussion.[37]

On that same April Fool's Day Lyons informed Russell that Lincoln had taken so great a personal part in the distribution of patronage that he had not as yet found the time "to come to any conclusion as to his own policy." Seward may well have been his source, and Lyons was at pains to ensure that the Foreign Office kept within its walls his confidential dispatches lest any disclosure of their contents checked the apparent freedom with which the secretary of state was talking to him. Hence his assumption that Fort Sumter was about to be evacuated. Little more than a week later Edward Archibald reported from New York that stocks had slumped with the discovery that an expedition was being organized in the Brooklyn Navy Yard to go to the aid of the beleaguered Federal garrison. Thoughtfully, Lincoln dispatched a messenger to South Carolina to inform the governor of the imminent attempt to supply Sumter with provisions only. If there was no resistance to the mission, no effort would be made "to throw in men, arms, or ammunition," he promised. Whether or not Lincoln was artfully seeking to provoke a Confederate attack on Sumter has remained in historical dispute, but the likelihood of the resupply expedition having this effect could not have escaped so subtle a mind. Certainly, it had not escaped that of Lyons, who concluded that the president was ensuring that the Confederacy would bear the responsibility for a descent into the hell of civil war. Confederate artillery began a bombardment of the fort in the early morning of 12 April, witnessed by Robert Bunch, who sailed out into the harbour in a small boat. More than thirty hours later, and without suffering a single fatal casualty, the garrison surrendered on the unluckiest day of any calendar month, Friday the thirteenth.[38]

The patriotic fervour of the North's response to the attack on Sumter, and to Lincoln's call for 75,000 militia to suppress the "combinations" opposing and obstructing the execution of Federal laws, vindicated his management of the situation. "Great enthusiasm and unanimity prevails here (now that the contest has begun) in sustaining the U.S. Government," Archibald informed Lyons, adding that money and means were being liberally contributed by public bodies and private individuals. "The day of insincerity & duplicity is now passed," a relieved Sumner assured a fellow Republican senator, and "*all* the cabinet is united in energetic action. It will be needed for the Slave States will be united." The governor of Virginia had defiantly refused to answer the call for militia, and in the opinion of George Moore the state was for all intents and purposes out of the Union by 18 April. The secession flag was flying over the state capitol, the United States customs house had been seized, and its name board was lying smashed on the pavement. He evidently saw this as a symbol of the shattered Union. The previous evening the state convention in secret session had resolved to secede, a decision which caused several western members to bolt and return home in protest. Within months, fifty western counties were on the road to a form of secession, which ultimately saw them admitted to the Union in 1863 as the state of West Virginia. Nevertheless, Virginia was soon followed out of the Union and into the Confederacy by Arkansas, Tennessee, and North Carolina. But the slave states of Delaware, Kentucky, Missouri, and Maryland remained within it, though in the case of the last three not without internal strife. Indeed, rioting secessionists in Baltimore were to sever communications temporarily between Washington and the Northern states, leaving the national capital briefly isolated and vulnerable.[39]

Lyons was no admirer of the way Lincoln had played a difficult hand. The administration "is now it seems bent upon war to the knife, or is at all events taking a line which is sure to produce such a war," he commented. A prudent policy consistently pursued, on the other hand, might have led to a peaceful separation and possibly to a peaceful reconstruction of the Union. This had been Seward's line of argument. Sumter's loss, however, was "calculated to arouse feelings of resentment and humiliation in the North, which will overwhelm the party of Peace, and throw the people with bitter eagerness into war." Or as Lyons wrote to Bunch, the "Administration have set fire to the train, and the war feeling of the North has exploded tremendously. I suppose we can hardly hope now to avoid a fierce civil war." That American nationalists declined to opt for "peaceful separation" was evidently difficult for this dispassionate foreign observer to understand. Yet Lyons's preference for peace ought not to be confused with animus to the United States. He was dismayed by the thought of the terrible human cost of the conflict now begun. "I am really grieved to see these people bent upon cutting each other's throats," he privately observed. He could see no good coming from it. Of course, he was also aware of the probability that war would injure his own nation economically. The Union was certain to exploit its one great immediate belligerent advantage, the Navy. Jefferson Davis's sanctioning of privateering, which had been outlawed at the Congress of Paris five years before the birth of the Confederacy, brought an immediate response from Lincoln in the form of a Proclamation of Blockade. Unwelcome as any disruption of trade was, Lyons and Mercier regarded this form of economic coercion preferable to legislation declaring the Southern ports closed. A seizure of a British ship found in American waters "on the plea that by going to a Southern port she had violated United States Customs Laws" would, Lyons brooded, see British commerce "exposed to vexations beyond bearing." It would amount to "a paper blockade of the worst kind" and would justify both recognition of the Confederacy and action to compel the United States to treat British and French vessels as neutrals.[40]

Another of Lyons's worries was the story that members of the administration were again thinking of making up for the loss of the South by adding Canada to the "remnant of the Union." The persistent floating of this idea throughout the secession crisis by the *New York Herald*, and the quality of his informant in this instance, prevented Lyons from dismissing it out of hand. The news that Seward was sending a personal friend, George Ashmun, on a mission to Canada, lent it credibility. A former Whig congressman from Massachusetts who had chaired the Republican convention in Chicago, he was likened by a prominent Irishman to "an Englishman of the best type," sagacious, pleasant, and fond of sport. Lyons immediately advised the governor general to be on his guard. In thanking him, Sir Edmund Head forwarded an account of a conversation between Ashmun and the colony's finance minister when they happened to be fellow passengers on a steamer. Recognition of the Confederacy would be regarded by the Union as a cause of war, this influential Republican had warned. The Lincoln administration's "arrogant spirit and disregard of the rights and feelings of Foreign Nations" was again displayed with its demand that a Canadian steamer, the *Peerless*, purportedly purchased by the Confederates, be seized by the British authorities. When Lyons explained that proof of sale was essential before seizure, Seward announced that orders had been issued to take it whatever its papers and flag. An unusually angry Lyons reminded the American of how sensitive the United States was to any foreign interference with vessels flying its flag. Happily, the storm was confined to the proverbial teacup with the news that the buyer was a Northerner. Nevertheless, this unpleasant little episode convinced Lyons of the folly of permitting the Union to purchase arms from arsenals in British North America. The conduct of the United States did not show "that scrupulous regard for the rights of neutrals which should incline us to disarm in order to transfer our rifles to American hands," he sarcastically observed. Hence his sharp criticism of Archibald's telegram to the lieutenant-governor of Nova Scotia asking whether weapons could be released from the local "Queen's stores" and sold to under-equipped Union militiamen. Archibald had made the additional mistake of betraying his Union sympathies too clearly. "We are not to be led away by our sympathies," Lyons admonished the consul, "but to obey orders, and carry out the policy of Her Majesty's Government," which, his own private sympathies notwithstanding, he anticipated would be one of strict neutrality. To protect this valued information asset, however, Lyons urged the lieutenant-governor not draw Archibald's indiscretion to the attention of the Foreign Office.[41]

CHAPTER SIX

The American Civil War

Six weeks before the surrender of Fort Sumter, Lyons' had received a note from Earl Granville introducing William H. Russell, the well-known war and foreign correspondent of *The Times*. "He will tell you that which will interest and amuse you," the Cabinet minister wrote, and he would be a good means of enlightening the British public on the American crisis. Russell needed no introduction, having written so well of Admiral Lyons in his reporting of the Crimean War. He and Lyons, who was to celebrate his forty-fourth birthday on 26 April, were similar in age and build though the Irishman was naturally more congenial. A frequent guest at the British legation, he quickly judged Lyons a strong supporter of the Union. The correspondent dined with both Lincoln and Seward yet was no clearer on the Union's intentions. Equally un-enlightening was his meeting over dinner with the Southern commis-sioners who had arrived on the fool's errand of negotiating a peaceful separation and the surrender of the Federal forts in the Confederacy. So on 12 April Russell set off for Charleston, the likeliest flashpoint. It was while waiting for a steamer in Baltimore that he learned of the attack on Fort Sumter.[1]

The man from *The Times* was no Southern sympathizer. Lyons in a letter to Bunch described him as "very agreeable and not at all prying or indiscreetly inquisitive," and primed the consul on the line to take in his conversations with the correspondent. He was to mention the home government's hope that trade would not be disrupted for uninterrupted commerce would enable it to maintain an "expective attitude" towards the looming conflict. Lyons saw in William Russell and the press a useful diplomatic instrument if utilized with subtlety. His reports, which would almost certainly be reprinted and widely read in the United States, might serve to discourage the Union from severing trade with the cotton-producing South if they implied that any such action would precipitate British recognition of the Confederacy. However, in this instance, the decision to blockade the Confederacy was taken before Russell's reports could discourage it.[2]

Bunch promised to give the journalist every assistance. Influential locals, he reported, were "perfectly wild" to make a favourable impression on him, and the group of distinguished South Carolinians he invited to dine with the visitor on 18 April stayed for seven hours. Russell was quietly amused by the conversation, several of the Southerners voicing a "general desire" for the "rule of a Prince of England," but he took far more seriously their assurances that they would never return to the Union. "This is going to be a terrible war if it be fought out," he realized, for the Confederates had an exaggerated idea not only of their military strength but also of their importance as the world's principal producers of cotton. But he considered their cause doomed because of the Union's crucial advantages of numbers and resources and his assessment that Southerners lacked the necessary fitness for a "defensive & protracted contest." They would lose heart, Russell predicted, when their "sheet anchor," cotton, failed them.[3]

Lyons was no less aware that a civil war would be brutal and bloody. He also believed that the Union would eventually emerge victorious and had no doubt that an Englishman's sympathies ought to be with the free states. "Abhorrence of slavery, respect for law and a more complete community of race and language" explained his attitude. Perhaps, subconsciously, he was influenced by his former posting at the focal point of a unifying nationalism, the Risorgimento. Yet military victory would in his opinion almost certainly be pyrrhic. A Union cordial enough to function peacefully could not be reconstructed after a massive bloodletting that left the North crippled by depopulation and debt and the

South devastated. Lurking behind this pessimism was the fear that the war would cause a "calamitous" suspension of cotton cultivation. Could he prevent a prolonged interruption of the supply? He did not place a great deal of stock in Seward's assurances that the rules of blockade would give "liberal consideration" to the interests of neutrals. Hence he continued to identify the implied threat of recognition of the Confederacy as his one trump card. This might induce Union caution. Henri Mercier wanted, as ever, to go further. He suggested they each advise their governments to notify the administration that they intended to break the blockade "as soon as it seriously interfered with commerce." Lyons saw little point to, and less national honour in, such a declaration. Why give arrogant Southerners who boasted of cotton's absolute rule over European policy "a moral encouragement hardly consistent with neutrality"? he asked. Would the president's "violent counsellors" create such a commotion in protest that the North might be tempted to engage in some "violent proceeding with regard to England and France"? Lyons remained committed to denying wilder Unionists an excuse to quarrel with Britain and advised Sir Alexander Milne to keep his vessels clear of places they did not normally visit and to instruct his commanders not to interfere with a blockade should one be proclaimed.[4]

Richard Cobden, who with John Bright was sarcastically dubbed a member of Parliament for the United States, was another pessimist. "I cannot see how the North and South are ever to live together again in harmony," he wrote to his friend, "or how they are to arrange their present disputes without bringing the coloured population into the arena as parties to the settlement." He was haunted by a black spectre. He feared the "fanatical anti-slavery party" would gain control of the Federal government and then promote a slave revolt. After all, only the abolition of slavery could morally justify the waging of a tragic civil war. Therefore, the only hope of avoiding the ultimate horror of servile war was an "immediate accommodation." A blockade was another of Cobden's despairs, and he urged Bright to advise the Union's leadership to abandon any thought of employing it. Why risk trouble with Britain and Europe? he asked. The son of a cotton manufacturer, Bright understood the alarm of the textile districts as the price of the staple rose on the fear of a blockade. His own answer to a possible cotton shortage was half-time work. The wages of operatives were in his opinion high enough "that the bulk of them could live moderately well on half their present incomes, and they and their employers might learn something useful by a little suffering." As the price of cotton continued to climb during the summer Bright's faith in the moral value of suffering strengthened. "Nations learn little except thro' great calamities," he preached, and in the current one he saw the means of teaching the British public and government "some regard for reason and morality in public affairs." Only pain, he insisted, "will teach wisdom."[5]

The operatives did not share Bright's moral enthusiasm for short time and they failed to find the moral therapy in the loss of wages. Their response to the American conflict was likely to be heavily influenced by concern for a living wage, or as *Punch* put it in one of its doggerels, with the North they might sympathize but with the South they had stronger ties. Elements of the British press, led by *The Times*, did speculate on the benefits to Britain of the Union's division. A divided and thus weakened America would surely be less aggressive, less insolent, and less irritable. Yet, as Lyons had anticipated, British opinion was also divided. Britons sympathetic to the Confederacy and its right of self-determination had conveniently forgotten their government's intolerance of the recent Irish effort to secede from the United Kingdom. Those Britons who understood the Union's refusal to allow the slave South to secede still questioned, as did Lyons, whether there was a reasonable prospect of reuniting the nation by force of arms. A partisan fault line was soon apparent. Many Conservatives, impressed with literary depictions of the South as aristocratic, genteel, and effectively a separate nation, were inclined to regard secession as constitutional and the inevitable consequence of democracy. They declined, as did the Whig prime minister, to wring their hands in despair over the fracturing of the Republic. Opposed to slavery, they were of a mind to acknowledge that its practice in the Southern states was more paternal than critics allowed. Even heartier British sympathizers with the American abolition movement doubted that war was the best means of furthering the cause and feared it would degenerate into a horrifying servile rebellion. Others, among them the foreign secretary, believed that the departure of the slave South would in freeing the Union of complicity with slavery happily leave the "disastrous institution" without hope and means of expansion and survival. An "enormously powerful" United States might have carried it to Central America but a comparatively weak Confederacy would be held permanently in check by its mightier neighbour.[6]

Although the governor of South Carolina understood an indiscreet Robert Bunch to say that the Palmerston government would recognize Confederate independence in the event of a blockade, there was never any likelihood of precipitate British action. Union nationalism, which claimed to balance the liberal freedoms of person, speech, and the press "with more conservative ideals of order and authority," had an instinctual appeal for large segments of Britain's political classes. With the "Southern cauldron" boiling over, Lord John Russell assumed that Seward would not risk British intervention by indulging "the insolence of his nature." For its part, Britain had good reason to remain on good terms with the Union, which had influential friends in financial circles. Thomas Baring, head of the bank and a member of Parliament, was advancing funds to the agents purchasing arms for the Union. August Belmont, the American agent of the Rothschilds, soon arrived in England, where he hinted that interference in the conflict or the adoption of a neutrality favourable to the South might lead to a ruinous Anglo-American collision. *The Economist* warned that the costs of the resultant injury to British shipping, investments, and trade – for the United States was Britain's largest market – would be far higher than those of a cotton famine.[7]

In the House of Commons on 2 May, the foreign secretary spoke briefly of the American crisis and declared: "For God's sake, let us if possible keep out of it." The Crown's law officers judged it a *justum bellum* and counselled the government to apply to it all the rules respecting a blockade and to seek from the belligerents their agreement to respect two provisions of the Declaration of Paris: namely, the protection an enemy's goods, except contraband, enjoyed when being shipped under a neutral's flag and the renunciation of privateering. With these objectives in mind, the naval force operating in North American waters was strengthened, and captains were instructed to abide by the rules governing blockades. Four days later Russell sent Lyons "timely notice" of the imminent recognition of Confederate belligerency. Reports that

Confederate agents, as well as Union, were in Britain seeking the means to wage war on sea as well as on land helped to stir the government to action. It signalled its intention to issue a proclamation based on the Foreign Enlistment Act, and in the House of Lords on 10 May Granville emphasized that it would be "as plain and emphatic as possible." Dated 13 May, printed 14 May, and forwarded to Lyons on 15 May, the Proclamation of Neutrality prohibited both British military enlistments and the fitting out and "equipment" of ships of war for either belligerent. The action was generally welcomed, and the newspaper widely considered a Palmerston mouthpiece warned those who planned to ignore it that they would do so at their peril. The leader of the opposition, Derby, agreed that Northerners were not entitled on the one hand to claim the rights of belligerents for themselves with the blockade while on the other treating Confederates as rebels. Personally, he hoped for a prolonged conflict in the belief that it would humble both belligerents. The party's spokesman in the Commons, Benjamin Disraeli, a somewhat paradoxically cynical romantic, expected the South to triumph and thought the collapse of the American Republic would deliver a blow "in favour of aristocracy."[8]

That the Union intended to treat Confederates as rebels and would resent Britain's recognition of Confederate belligerency was confirmed by the new American minister to Britain. Charles Francis Adams was a member of one of the nation's most illustrious families for whom diplomacy was a genetic inheritance. He arrived in London just as the Proclamation of Neutrality was being printed for publication, having delayed his departure from the United States to attend the wedding of his elder son. When he met with the foreign secretary on 18 May he was in possession of a note in which Seward gave vent to "no little indignation" provoked, at least in part, by the deliberately ambiguous behaviour of Lyons on the subject of recognition. The secretary of state appeared to be seeking from Britain a "perpetual pledge" never to recognize the seceded states. Such a pledge, Russell observed, would be entirely at odds with the Republic's own past conduct. The immense size and large population of the South, Britain's commercial interests, and its wish to live on amicable terms with both North and South had been, he declared, the deciding factors in Britain's recognition of Confederate belligerency. He might have added that the Confederacy possessed "all the necessary apparatus of government," but contented himself with an allusion to the Union's effective recognition of belligerency with the announcement of a blockade. Russell did promise Adams that he would be given sufficient notice of any contemplated recognition of Confederate independence to enable him to contest it.[9]

Russell sent Lyons an unusually detailed account of his meeting with the American minister and authorized him to make use of his remarks in his encounters with Seward. This, he emphasized, did not imply waning confidence in Lyons's skill and "good judgment and sound sense," or in his ability to perform his "grave duties." On the contrary, the Cabinet had "perfect reliance" on his "discretion and firmness." Should any British vessel be seized by the blockading force without sufficient grounds the government would insist on ample reparation, Russell wrote, but Milne's "powers of argument" were not to be utilized without "absolute necessity." Furthermore, the government's decision not to admit prizes into British ports, which evidently worked in the Union's favour since its ports were open, had been taken in the belief that it would gain Britain credit in the North. However, the Union reacted with the fury Adams predicted to the news of British recognition of Confederate belligerency. The Union, Lyons later recalled, had expected a benevolent British neutrality since their cause was "pre-eminently just, noble, and advantageous to humanity." Instead, the recognition of Confederate belligerency was interpreted as a neutrality benevolent to the South.[10]

"In the present temper of the public mind here," an anxious Archibald informed Lyons, "a *casus belli* seems a question only of time." The Union, he tartly observed, merely wished "all the established precedents of bye-gone times to be overruled in order to procure a 'neutrality' on our part which would be more potent in effect than an alliance." Henry Halleck, soon to be a senior Union general, had, in his influential treatise on *International Law*, drawn a sharp distinction between the "rebellion" of the slave states and a true civil war "fully equivalent to an interstate war – with the laws of war and neutrality fully applicable." Consequently, a "ruling government" had the legal right to apply "*only* its own national laws and not the international law relating to war." Thus the ports of the rebellious states might be closed as ports of entry by Federal legislation, thereby avoiding a blockade with its implied admission of Confederate belligerency. The Confederacy controlled a huge territory, governed it effectively, and commanded very large, organized armed forces, but as there was no settled law and practice concerning this limited form of recognition, foreign nations were under no obligation to extend it. "I appreciate completely the embarrassments of England," Charles Sumner assured one British friend before insisting that foreign sympathy alone would protract the crisis. Recognition of their belligerency, he protested, would fill Southerners with hope that recognition of their independence would soon follow. An angry Seward agreed, though Russell rejected as "silly" his proposals for the withdrawal of recognition. The American conflict was no local riot, he observed.[11]

The possibility of a confrontation with the United States had been a source of worry for Lyons even before the explosion of public rage against Britain. Bellicose articles in newspapers regarded as organs of the Lincoln administration, and the publication of Seward's strongly worded dispatches, deepened his unease. The Americans' arrogance was in his opinion nourished by their conviction that Britain would swallow almost any provocation. Fear for the safety of Canada, the distraction of European political tensions, and the traditional and chronic distrust of France had plainly persuaded Seward and his colleagues that Britain was hamstrung. The danger was that this would tempt them into conduct that was reckless and certain to end badly. Lyons found in Seward's unfulfilled presidential ambition an explanation of his behaviour. He was planning to organize a new Union party that would attract a great many Northern Democrats by "advocating the maintenance of the Union at any price" and would court the Irish vote with an attitude of hostility towards Britain. This analysis did the secretary of state an injustice. He may have been reacting instead to a sense that the governing British aristocracy was more concerned with securing cotton than with ending slavery, a priority that was likely to steer Britain towards the South. Seward was in this instance doing Britain's aristocracy an injustice, though his suspicion was inadvertently nourished by a Lord Lyons committed to keeping him off balance on possible British recognition of Confederate independence.[12]

The Lincoln administration had "lost sight of the essential feature of the situation," Lyons complained, which was the existence of a recognized and obeyed de facto Confederate government. If they were to protect their subjects in the South, foreign powers had to accept this fact. Indeed, Union anger over the recognition of Confederate belligerency was even alienating its British well-wishers. Seward's aggressiveness, the protective American tariff, and the abuse of Britain by the Northern press were making Britons more critical of the Union without necessarily making them more sympathetic to the Confederacy. George Moore, home on a leave, informed Lyons of a significant shift in public sentiment. Charles Dickens, the nation's most popular and successful novelist and editor of *All the Year Round*, reflected it. Dickens denied that slavery was at the heart of the conflict. The struggle over the territories was driven by political power not morality, he insisted. North and South had each been striving to advance or defend their distinct sectional interests. The author joined the ranks of those Britons who believed that the Union's division into two adjacent Republics, one free and the other slave-holding, would benefit the cause of freedom. No longer would the Union "as a whole" support the evil that afflicted the South; hence it was not immoral to favour Confederate independence.[13]

Americans cared not at all for words, and to keep them "quiet" Britain had to make sure they understood that it had both the will and power to defend its North American colonies, Lyons impressed upon the foreign secretary. They had to be disabused of the absurd notion that with threats and boasts they could carry any point with Britain. That in the midst of a profound domestic crisis the Union would contemplate war with a Great Power seemed preposterous, but it was a possibility to which Lyons could not shut his eyes. "To avert it is the main object of all I do here," he informed Edmund Head, for even those members of the Lincoln Cabinet who had advocated moderation were now "out-heroding the wildest Herod in Violence." He decided to chart a course which by steering him clear of the shoals of dangerous topics would deny Seward and his colleagues the excuse to use language it would be inconvenient for him to hear. Not that he expected to be able to fend off problems indefinitely by such "small means." He sought help from the government at home, which must make no concession to the Union's "haughty tone or overbearing conduct" and back its stand with a display of force. "The best safeguard against being driven into war, in this perhaps even more than in ordinary cases, will no doubt be found in being manifestly prepared for it," he forcefully argued. Britain's territories should be equipped with the means to resist attack and compel respect of its neutrality.[14]

In calling on the imperial government to put Canada in a "complete state" of defence, Lyons denied suffering from "visionary apprehensions." His knowledge of "men and things" in Washington, their anger over Britain's refusal to occupy the "untenable position" of benevolent neutrality, had convinced him that Seward and the Lincoln Cabinet "would see with pleasure disturbances in Canada." On this point he and the governor general were in full agreement. Convinced that the crisis had driven Americans "quite crazy," Head required no encouragement to prepare for trouble. He asked Lyons to given him fair warning by telegram of an impending invasion and proposed a simple sentence that would indicate the point of attack. About to retire, he advised the Colonial Office to appoint a senior general as his successor. He forwarded to London the dimensions and depths of the locks, forty-seven in number, on the canal system that provided a secure inland supply route from Montreal to Kingston. This would enable its use by the gunboats excluded by treaty from the Great Lakes but which might be held in readiness in the St Lawrence. He requested military and naval reinforcements from Britain and learned that on the advice of Lyons the Palmerston government had already decided to increase the imperial garrison and to dispatch weapons and equipment for the Canadian militia. Furthermore, instead of sending the regulars and supplies "without parade," which had been the original intention, the government in a dramatic gesture leased as a transport the world's largest ship.[15]

Another of Lyons's devices for keeping relations with the Union on a more or less even keel was the "concert with France." He was fortunate to have as his French colleague an old friend who proved very important to him politically. Personally "very agreeable and satisfactory," although his extraordinary whiskers gave him a faintly comic appearance, Henri Mercier was always more impulsive than his phlegmatic friend. He was far more sympathetic than Lyons to the South and was more obsessive about cotton. The French textile industry, although dwarfed by Britain's, was more dependent on Southern cotton. That dependence prompted policy proposals that Lyons successfully opposed with the indirect assistance of the French emperor. Keen to secure British co-operation for his major foreign policy initiatives, Napoleon III was willing at this point to follow Britain's lead in the American crisis. A month-long French delay before formally recognizing Confederate belligerency had already fed the Foreign Office suspicion of the old enemy. In fact, foreign minister Thouvenel had instructed Mercier to inform Seward that France had come to the same decision as Britain but the minister had chosen to put off informing him for fear of provoking another temper tantrum. The secretary of state did know of the decision but in the absence of a formal notification saw an opportunity to drive a wedge between the two ministers. He quickly discovered that the Frenchman had no intention of obliging him.[16]

Lyons and Mercier received identical instructions to approach Seward jointly with a proposal for the Union's limited adherence to the Declaration of Paris. The American had announced several weeks earlier a willingness to abide by all four of the Declaration's provisions, believing this would win the sympathy of both powers and oblige them to enforce the ban on privateering. Hence his dismay when Russell announced that Britain would not treat Confederate privateers as pirates because to do so would be "unneutral." Lyons did not hurry to the State Department with the formal notice of this decision, nor did he and Mercier hasten there with the proposal for limited Union adherence to the Declaration. Fearing another Seward eruption, they decided to take "a few days for reflection."[17]

Lyons was relieved to learn, probably from Charles Sumner, that the Lincoln Cabinet was finally restraining the secretary of state. Another of the secretary's intemperate dispatches had been approved and sent but on the understanding that it was seen by Charles Francis Adams only. Not that Lyons was able to relax, for "men of influence" were talking again of legislation to empower the president to declare Confederate ports closed and to seize and confiscate any vessel suspected of intending to enter them. Lyons warned, seemingly without effect, that this would still amount to an unacceptable paper blockade. He read Seward's reluctance to receive formal notification of French recognition of Confederate belligerency as an attempt to leave open the door to the legislation and to close that on the Franco-British concert. The American's complaint that the joint communications were disagreeable to the Union, his charge that it was "an offence for foreign powers even to communicate with each other on American questions," and his refusal to receive any communication founded on the notion that the "Rebels" were belligerents, strengthened the suspicion that he was striving to disrupt the concert. Yet Lyons was confident that several important points had at least been made. The "intimate union" of Britain and France had been established, as had the Union's readiness to adhere to the principles of the Declaration "with regard to the treatment of Neutral merchant vessels." Finally, Seward had been notified that so long as the personal safety and interests of British and French subjects in the South were dependent on the Confederate government, both nations would communicate with it "more or less formally" but "without in the slightest degree" recognizing it diplomatically.[18]

His irritation with the Federal government for its "exaggerated susceptibility" on foreign dealings with the South saw Lyons readily fall in with Mercier's suggestion that they initiate, at arm's length, discussions with the Confederacy. Lyons named Robert Bunch as his agent and Mercier selected the British consul's French counterpart in Charleston. The pair approached William Henry Trescot, a former United States assistant secretary of state but now a well-connected Confederate citizen, to be their intermediary with the Confederate government. The upshot was a reaffirmation by the Confederate Congress of privateering, but its acceptance of the Declaration's three other articles. In return, the Confederacy expected the two powers to apply to the Union blockade the test of effectiveness agreed to in 1856. Bunch had told them, Southerners claimed, that he had already reported its utter ineffectiveness to London. Lyons may not, therefore, have been surprised to learn that Bunch was considered a Confederate sympathizer. What did startle him was the police report handed to him by Seward in which the consul was charged with transmitting treasonable correspondence to Britain. Lyons immediately instructed all consuls to issue passports only with extreme caution and never to forward private letters that commented on military and political developments. Foolishly, Bunch had issued a passport to a Robert Mure and employed him as a courier despite his naturalization as an American citizen and his holding of a colonel's commission in the

South Carolina militia. Mure was arrested in New York, perhaps on a trumped-up charge of seeking to purchase arms for the Confederacy, and the consular bag he was carrying was forwarded unopened to London but all the private correspondence was read. What the examiners found was a reference to a comment attributed to Bunch. He was alleged to have remarked that the discussion of the Declaration of Paris with the Confederacy was the first step towards "direct treating."

Seward demanded the consul's recall, and when the demand was ignored he revoked Bunch's exequatur. That he took no action against the French consul involved was interpreted by Lyons as fresh evidence of his intent to disrupt the Anglo-French concert. The immediate publication of Bunch's alleged remarks in the New York press reinforced this belief. No one who read the consul's reports, Lyons reminded the Foreign Office, could consider him a Confederate sympathizer. Bunch was a "little lively & indiscreet" on occasion, William Russell privately admitted, but he was also "able indefatigable & thoro'ly British." This was not an opinion Edmund Hammond shared. He considered Bunch perverse or stupid and unfit for his post. Another critic was Milne, who forwarded to Lyons a letter Bunch had sent to one of his naval officers in which the consul appeared to favour the use of force to deter Union vessels from preventing a pair of British merchantmen from leaving the small South Carolina port of Beaufort. The letter's tone, the angry admiral complained, flatly contradicted his instructions to captains to avoid any act "which might involve the two countries in war." Although Lyons reprimanded the consul, he begged Milne not to draw this latest indiscretion to the attention of Hammond at the Foreign Office. Lyons's protection of the consul was a measure of his respect for a man who at great personal risk, and at the cost of forfeiting his life insurance policy, had remained at his post throughout the unhealthy season. Both as a public servant and the source of "much valuable information," he was too useful to lose. Although subsequently relieved of his consular functions, Bunch remained in Charleston as an observer.[19]

"Things are not going on by any means satisfactory here," Lyons acknowledged in early June, "but there is nothing that worries me personally." He attended the president's first dinner for the diplomatic corps on 4 June, and the "new people" in the White House were particularly civil to him even though they and he "had not had time to become well acquainted." As he looked around, his aesthetic sense was offended by the state of the executive mansion's public salons, which had "a bare and uncomfortable look, something between that of the waiting-room at a railway terminus, the drawing room at an hotel, and the *foyer* of an opera-house." Nor was he truly impressed when the president declared that the United States had little reason to complain of the conduct of any European power. The comment failed to allay Lyons's fear that grave difficulties with the Union were possible so long as Canada appeared vulnerable to attack, and he advised Milne to be on his guard.[20]

All the while Lyons was conducting an immense correspondence. He opened all letters, indicated in pencil the tenor of the reply, reviewed and invariably amended the draft prepared by his staff, and checked the final copy before signing it. This painstaking procedure made for a hard legation life. The attachés reported for work at nine o'clock each morning, ate sandwiches washed down with lemonade at their desks during the normal lunch break, walked to Willard's for an early evening cocktail, went back to the house to dine with Lyons, and then often returned to the chancery and worked on into the early hours of the morning. Plainly, the legation was understaffed, and Lyons requested at least two additional attachés. Of the current complement William Brodie was of little use. He was chronically unwell, derelict in his duties, deeply in debt, and "guilty of graver private delinquencies." He had conducted a pair of "infamous liaisons" with local women and had been dishonest in his personal dealings with colleagues. An acute embarrassment, he was packed off home. His replacement, Lyons informed the Foreign Office, should be a good, steady, and industrious copier and "well conducted in private life." One junior who did labour heroically in the heat of this "abominable place" was Monson, but he was another who lacked an iron constitution. Lyons's own "proper duties" prevented him from easing the burden on his young staff. "Indeed, I shall soon break down," he warned the Foreign Office.[21]

By mid-June the diplomatic tension had thankfully begun to ease. The closing of British ports to Confederate prizes played its part, Seward trumpeting it as the death blow to Southern privateering. Another factor, Lyons surmised, was the state of the Federal government's finances.

European investment was vital because of the politicians' reluctance to finance the war with ever-heavier taxation, so it was essential to give a "satisfactory appearance" to foreign relations. Yet Lyons was not in the visitor's gallery when the Senate opened on 4 July. The reason was his strained personal relationship with Seward, which was also keeping him away from the State Department. Were he to be insulted by Seward, difficulties might follow. His hope was that a strong performance by the Confederacy in the approaching major battle south of Washington would discourage further diplomatic provocation. But a Confederate victory would be "little consonant" with his personal "feelings and sympathies." He recognized the serious deficiencies of the large military force assembled by the Union. It lacked "instructed officers," system, adequate training, discipline, and experience acting in large numbers. He assumed that the Confederate army would be no better prepared for a large-scale battle. When the two armies collided at Bull Run on 21 July, fighting which began well for the Union ended disastrously. Federal troops fled in panic back to Washington. Defeat made "matters here more interesting and exciting," Lyons coolly observed, but he took no pleasure in the Union's reversal and he continued to credit it with the moral and physical materials necessary "for a great nation."[22]

The Union army had been "completely routed," Lyons informed Russell. Presumably, he sarcastically added, Seward would now admit "the Confederates had belligerent powers if they had not belligerent rights." He attributed the defeat to poor morale, lack of discipline, and the tactical superiority of the Confederate commanders, all of whom were ante-bellum Union officers of considerable merit. Equally apparent was the battle's political meaning. The war was going to be long, and this was likely to cause additional domestic strains given its unpopularity in the northwest and the uncertain allegiance of the border states. Kentucky had declared itself neutral, Missouri had descended into a vicious if "petty civil war," while Maryland was being held in the Union by a large body of Federal troops and a series of other coercive measures including the suspension of habeas corpus. With Congress now in session, Lyons expected the politicians to behave in a "violent and childish" manner. They will, he predicted, vote "men and money on paper by millions," attack Southerners with treason bills, attempt to "ruin them by confiscation acts," even "decree the immediate and unconditional abolition of slavery in the Southern states" and declare the ports closed. He anticipated a very testing time for the "humble" role he intended to play in the American tragedy, that of "endeavouring by watchfulness and minute attention to details to prevent causes of difference growing up." Edmund Head approved his choice of parts. Large views and distant objects were likely to lead to "mischief," the governor general wrote, citing Klaus von Metternich as his authority. "All that can be done is to work on from day to day as you are doing," he encouraged Lyons. "Time is everything."[23]

"I am getting a longing for home, which it will be difficult to gratify, for I don't see how can I well get out of the scrape of happening to be the Minister here just now," Lyons wrote to an anxious Minna in August. "I don't want the Americans to quarrel with us, and would rather not be removed in consequence of making some blunder, and I see no other means of getting away." His pragmatic policy of dealing with the Union by concentrating exclusively on immediate problems depended for its effectiveness on his "intimate union" with Mercier. Hence his hosting of a dinner despite the intense heat for the visiting Prince Napoleon, a cousin of the emperor, to which he invited Seward, Chairman Summer of the Foreign Relations Committee, and the Union's new military star, General George McClellan. Mercier's subsequent lengthy absence from Washington as he escorted his visitor on a tour of the West and Canada excited fresh Foreign Office suspicion of the French. Distrust of Napoleon III, whom Palmerston described as the "crafty spider of the Tuileries," had led to the earlier acceptance of Lyons's recommendation of close co-operation with France. With Europe apparently on the verge of a political upheaval, and convinced that the emperor would happily see Britain embroiled in the American crisis, thereby gaining a freer hand for himself on the Continent, Palmerston and Russell saw in the concert a means of preventing him from spinning fresh webs. Lord Cowley, the British ambassador in Paris, was convinced that French proposals of some form of Anglo-French diplomatic intervention in the American conflict were mischievous. The emperor would "get us into hot water with the North" and then "look on" when Britain found itself defending Canada, he warned. Edmund Hammond was similarly suspicious of

Mercier, but Lyons assured him that the French minister had shown no sign of leaving him in the lurch. The Frenchman had expressed an interest in Anglo-French recognition of Confederate independence, Lyons admitted, without alarm. To his mind this was but another example of diplomatic vanity. Mercier wished in characteristic French fashion "to give éclat to his mission by a policy which would make a noise in the world."[24]

Lyons and Mercier watched with dismay as Congress passed on 12 July the legislation declaring the ports of the Confederacy closed. This would authorize patrolling Union vessels to seize the merchant ships of neutrals suspected of planning to enter Southern ports or of having just left them. The bill's supporters fancied that they were not only freeing the Union of the "necessity of maintaining at all points an effective blockade" but also reversing "the quasi-recognition" of Confederate belligerency implied in Lincoln's Proclamation. For Lyons, this was one more "alarming symptom of the reckless temper of the Legislature and Country." Palmerston had already decreed that Britain could not submit to such a violation of the international rights of neutrals, though in fairness to themselves and to the Union he thought they should make this clear to the Americans. Charles Francis Adams was duly informed but prime minister and Cabinet had no wish for war with the Union. They had a natural aversion "to take part apparently with the party of Slavery extension," a reluctance "to expose Canada to invasion," and a disinclination "to enter into a mighty contest with 20 millions of free Americans of our own race." As Russell wrote to Lyons, "It is of course desirable not to get into a quarrel sooner than we can help, nor at all if we can help it." Mercier, he added, would be receiving nearly identical instructions. In "every case of difficulty" Lyons was to refrain from action without previous instructions from home. He and Mercier continued to coordinate their tactics. They met separately with Seward but delivered the same ominous message: their nations' rejection of the ports' bill. The news that Milne's command was being reinforced served to emphasize the point, and on 16 August Seward advised Lyons that there would be no resort to the bill's provisions. Unknown to Lyons, his warnings had hit a mark in the White House. Lincoln, who was aware of the Union navy's current inability to blockade all the Southern ports, had thought to use the bill to close those that could not as yet be blockaded effectively. But he now gathered that if enforced "it would result in a foreign war." Ever pragmatic, he decided to expedite naval construction and "blockade such ports as our force would enable us to, and say nothing about the rest." Seward's assurance to this effect, and Mercier's temporary absence from the capital, gave Lyons an excuse to pocket a final stern British note on the subject. The issue quietly faded away.[25]

Britain's complex American interests – fiscal, commercial, and political – the vast number of her subjects domiciled in the United States, the tortured state of that nation, and the heightened susceptibility of its people to anything that could be represented as British arrogance, tested to the full Lyons's ability to prevent difficulties developing. The arrest of British subjects and their detention in appalling conditions became a chronic problem. He deplored the "tacit acquiescence of the Courts and people in the daily violation of the law and Constitution by the Executive and Military Authorities." Lincoln's suspensions of habeas corpus resulted in "arrests and imprisonments *ad libitum*." The liberties of the people were being destroyed and with it their greatness and prosperity, Lyons grieved. He likened the many "petty vexations" to those commonly associated with the "absolute governments of Europe," and privately applauded Chief Justice Taney's "clarion call for the president, and the military authorities under his command, to respect the civil liberties of American citizens." Lincoln was merely exploiting the Constitution's failure to specify the branch of government that had the power to suspend the writ. He claimed it as chief executive whose highest priority was to preserve the government and the Union. The British law officers, on the other hand, endorsed the chief justice's opinion that the right to suspend belonged to Congress. Lyons therefore informed Seward, in what for him was an unusually sharp note, that the arrest and imprisonment of British subjects on the reports of informers represented a "despotic and arbitrary" power inconsistent with the American Constitution and with the treaties of amity between the two nations. However, he did not follow his instructions and notify the secretary of state that he was contemplating testing the legality of the arrests before the courts. This was another wise decision, for Seward skilfully enlisted "popular passions" in support of the writ's suspension. He framed the issue publicly as a problem with a foreign power and waspishly remarked that the American government did not look to Britain for its interpretation of the American Constitution.[26]

By handling the cases individually, by resisting the "natural temptation" to write "spirited Notes," and by sidestepping questions of principle, Lyons avoided a serious confrontation. He and Seward quietly came to an understanding not "to kick up rows about British subjects." Of course, they were simply postponing the problem. Similarly deferred was the matter of resuming the cotton trade. If Britain and France could get through the coming winter and spring without cotton, and if they could keep the peace, they would have attained a great object, Lyons argued. If the Northern war effort still had not made real progress by the summer of 1862 it would be obvious to all, he added, that the task of reuniting the nation was hopeless and foreign powers might act accordingly. Conversely, should real military progress have been made then the cotton trade would almost certainly be "greatly freed from impediment." Neither patience nor stoicism appealed to the more mercurial Mercier. He had been influenced by a pair of British Southern sympathizers: Sir James Ferguson, a senior Tory member of Parliament, and the Hon. Robert Bourke, a younger son of the Earl of Mayo. They arrived in Washington fresh from a flying visit to the Confederacy. Ferguson described a South absolutely united in support of independence and willing to suffer "extremities" rather than allow the exportation of cotton without European recognition of Confederate independence. Derby, to whom Ferguson sent this report, sent it on to Palmerston, who had already been advised by Lyons that it was too partisan to be trusted. At the same time Seward sought to head off trouble by assuring Lyons and Mercier that a major Southern port would soon be opened by the Union navy, making cotton available.[27]

Action against an ineffective blockade and diplomatic recognition of the Confederacy "were somewhat illogically joined" in his French colleague's mind, Lyons concluded. Indeed, Mercier was coming to the conclusion that travelling in tandem with Britain guaranteed late arrival at the desired destination. He read to Lyons on 19 October a dispatch he had that day received from Édouard Thouvenel, whom Lyons knew well from Athens, in which the foreign minister authorized Mercier to

approach Seward with a proposal that the Union permit limited European trade with the "insurrectionary States." Mercier was convinced,
thanks in part to Ferguson and Bourke, that recognition of the Confederacy was the sole means of obtaining cotton in quantity and he recommended to Lyons that they prepare the Union for its inevitability
by routing the delusive idea that the European powers would continue
patiently to tolerate disruption of the trade. Lyons, who did not believe
that his nation was as yet in desperate need of cotton, that the blockade
would ever be really effective, that the South had yet done enough to
make diplomatic recognition either proper or desirable, or that recognition would bring the American conflict to an end, chose not to discourage Mercier from forwarding Thouvenel's proposal to Seward. It would,
he calculated, serve the useful purpose of checking the Union's assumption that in a conflict with Britain it could count on the neutrality if
not the assistance of France. He also had not modified his opinion that
recognition of the Confederacy would be followed by a suspension of
diplomatic relations and perhaps war with the Union. Of course, he fancied the hostilities might be "nominal." Current war expenditures were
already running at the breakneck and ruinous pace of $1,200,000 a day,
so to inflate them further would be financially disastrous. Then again,
a foreign crisis might see power transferred to a party willing to recognize the Confederacy and make peace with the world. But that, Lyons
stressed, was far from certain.[28]

The likelihood of a difficult winter in the textile counties brought to
Palmerston's mind the adage that it was wise "to put one's house in wind
and water tight condition against the time when foul weather comes on."
He asked what steps had been taken to lessen dependence on American
cotton and received a less than reassuring answer. The Cotton Supply
Association was about to investigate Egypt and India as possible alternative large-scale producers, but the recent increase in Indian shipments
was merely a drop in the ocean of need. Meanwhile, the Queen's Advocate, the "clever but flighty and intractable" Sir John Harding, was
surprisingly uncritical of the Union blockade's effectiveness. Perhaps in
response to his opinion, the Foreign Office rebuked two naval officers
who had lodged a complaint of its ineffectiveness with the Americans.
Why, Hammond asked, "should we urge them to make the blockade

more effective?" In addition, there was no enthusiasm in the government or the public at large for recognition of the Confederacy. To one of the handful of parliamentarians keen to raise the question Richard Cobden remarked that recognition would be so premature and unprecedented that it would constitute an act of hostility. Equally unpleasant was the possibility that a Union driven to extremities by foreign interference would "let loose the blacks against their masters," transforming the conflict into a crusade of black against white. The South, he grimly predicted, would become "a vast St. Domingo with all its horrors." Like so many others who raised the spectre of Santo Domingo he failed to note that the revolt there had been provoked by an attempt to re-enslave the island's blacks.[29]

Lord John Russell, betraying mildly pro-Southern sympathies, was willing to contemplate extending recognition at the first good opportunity. Speaking in the northern industrial city of Newcastle, he reduced the civil war to a struggle between empire and power. Lincoln's nullifying of a proclamation issued by the commander of military operations in Missouri, which had placed the state under martial law and declared free the slaves of rebels, encouraged the belief that reunion would cripple American abolitionism. This was the reason Russell gave Lyons for wishing for disunion. Anti-slavery policy was a "Separation policy," he insisted. If the Union was restored the agitation for a "limited expansion" of slavery would "revive and gain fresh force" and might result in the spread of slavery all over the New World. He envisaged joint action by Britain and France early in the New Year, perhaps in the form of "terms of pacification" backed by an ultimatum. Rejection of the terms would see the obdurate belligerent, undoubtedly the Union, listed as an enemy of the two powers. But Palmerston still opposed intervention. Lyons's assessment that only an overwhelming British naval force in North American waters would deter the Union from going to war rather than submit to foreign interference had made an impression on the prime minister. He had noted the ease with which the blockade was run, was only too aware of Canada's vulnerability, and harboured a deep-dyed suspicion of Napoleon III. He was sure the emperor would, as Cowley had warned, play Britain false in the event of war. He would leave Britain to face the Union alone and seize the opportunity to redraw the map of Europe. They should lie on their oars and thus deny the Union any pretext for a quarrel, Palmerston told Russell, now an earl. He in turn instructed Lyons on 2 November that Britain's conduct must remain "strictly neutral."[30]

Another reason to avoid trouble with the United States was the decision to join with France and Spain in a punitive expedition against Mexico. The stated purpose was to compel it to honour its debts to European creditors. If the divided Union had little option other than acceptance of the Europeans' intervention in the Central American Republic, Palmerston and Russell knew that this thumbing of a nose at the Monroe Doctrine would be bitterly resented and remembered. Charles Wyke, the sympathetic British minister to Mexico, had advised Lyons that without some form of limited foreign action the Mexican confederation would disintegrate. As an interim measure designed to avoid physical intervention, Wyke arranged with his American counterpart, Thomas Corwin, to have the monies raised by the Mexican government from the sale of "waste lands" applied to the payment of the interest on foreign loans. Corwin went a step further and agreed to arrange for Mexico to raise American loans secured by its public lands and mineral rights. This arrangement would amount to its purchase of a mortgage on which the United States would soon foreclose, a sardonic Palmerston remarked. Instead, the United States Senate rejected the agreement, which left the door open to the European intervention. Napoleon III was its driving force. He had secretly promised a Mexican throne to an Austrian archduke in the belief that this would improve his relations with the Austrian Empire and perhaps secure its withdrawal from Venetia.[31]

Rumours of a French plan to establish a Mexican monarchy reached London shortly before the three powers signed a convention there on 31 October in which they disclaimed any intention to violate the sovereignty, independence, or integrity of the Mexican Republic. Yet Palmerston was convinced of the superiority of constitutional monarchy as a form of government. The sorry example of Spanish-American republics, and of the "disunited States," should have cured reasoning men of Republicanism, he mused. "The day on which a monarchy on substantial foundations and on Constitutional Principles was established in Mexico, would be for the People of that country the happiest and most fortunate of their existence." However, he recognized that to succeed it had to be the work of a "considerable Party in Mexico" to whom the Europeans might lend moral support and "countenance." Britain was not seeking to establish a government, Lyons was assured, for one created by foreigners was doomed. Charles Wyke, meanwhile, rather than present the Liberal government of Benito Juárez with an ultimatum on the debts, as he was instructed to do, negotiated a convention on their repayment, which he hoped would satisfy London. Unfortunately, the Mexican Congress rejected it, leaving him with no alternative but to deliver the ultimatum and demand his passports. His French colleague followed suit.[32]

Palmerston's attention had already turned back north. Britain's standing as a world power would be grievously damaged were it to lose its North American provinces to the Americans after the "Bulls Run Races," he growled. He and Russell therefore sought to increase significantly Britain's naval and military forces in North America. They encountered dogged resistance from the four ministers most deeply involved, those responsible for the War Office, the Admiralty, the Colonial Office, and the Exchequer. But there seemed ample reason to be concerned about Canada's security. American talk of annexation and biting press criticism of Britain were taking a toll on colonial morale. The lieutenant-governor of Nova Scotia informed Lyons that popular sympathies there and in Canada had become decidedly pro-Southern, and on 17 October Seward issued a startling circular to the governors of seaboard and Great Lakes states, instructing them to put their harbours and ports in a condition of complete defence as precaution to avert "the evils of foreign war." Although something of a domestic disaster, for the "stock market plunged and subscriptions to a pending federal loan dried up," the circular revived, as was perhaps the intention, the fear that Seward was returning to his panacea of "making the severed States reunite by war with England." An "entirely reliable" source had informed Archibald, and he forwarded the information to Lyons, that Seward already had agents in Canada making drawings of defensive fortifications. Indeed, they were believed also to be seeking copies of the colony's military preparations and even of the next governor general's instructions. The Lincoln administration, Lyons reported in early November, was accumulating "political capital" by its "spirited conduct" towards Britain, which it was confident would remain passive.[33]

Lyons was beginning to despair of "getting on at all" with the Lincoln administration unless Britain and France reached an understanding with it "on the nature and extent of the communication which they mean to hold with the *de facto* Government of the Confederates States." What he had in mind was an Anglo-French agreement and its announcement in Washington. Britain had, its senior law officer declared, a perfect right to communicate with the South when British persons and property were in question. Lyons had not changed his mind that the preservation of peace depended on the "unmistakable" unity and determination of Britain and France. Russell agreed to a joint approach to the Confederacy, but almost as an afterthought added the important words "with Lincoln's permission." His note was dated 16 November, a day on which the news broke in North America of a dramatic incident on the high seas which threatened to sink all of Lyons's hard work in the cause of peace.[34]

CHAPTER SEVEN

Crisis

"If Americans were not so offensive to England we might go on very different terms at present," William Russell noted on 4 November 1861. Ten days later he dined with Seward, whom he found surprisingly "civil" though the food was "bad" and the wine "poisonous." More appetizing was the evidence that the secretary of state had realized that his "startling manifestoes" and menaces were alienating without intimidating foreign powers. He had the previous month dispatched a "collateral" mission to Britain and France to disabuse their citizens of "misunderstandings." The members were Charles McIlvaine, the Episcopal Bishop of Ohio, a well-known and respected figure among members of Britain's Established Church which was one of the "sub-structures of Anglo-American diplomacy"; John Hughes, the Irish-born Catholic Archbishop of New York; and Thurlow Weed, the secretary's arch political "fixer." Weed's assignment, Lyons understood, was to rally British anti-slavery feeling behind the Union. The archbishop's mission was more general. He and Lyons had first become acquainted in Rome. The fact that they were on excellent personal terms was a tribute to Lyons's good sense and interpersonal skills, for Hughes had a well-deserved reputation as an anglophobe. Nevertheless, he had done his best to discourage the Irish of New York from raining on Prince Edward's parade.[1]

The Union trio were expected to "counteract the proceedings" of a Confederate duo. They were James Murray Mason and John Slidell. The latter, a former senator from Louisiana, appeared well equipped to operate successfully at the heart of the Second Empire. Conspiratorial, crafty, persevering, he also spoke excellent French. His diplomatic partner was the more imposing figure physically. Mason's red face, bluff manner, Taurean appearance, aristocratic lineage, and reputation for being "manly," "straightforward," "truthful and bold," fostered the illusion that he would be embraced by English society. In short, both men seemed capable of exploiting to the full the Confederacy's improved prospects following the military victory at Bull Run. The Union's defeat would surely dampen European interest in its bonds; Seward's offer to adhere to the Declaration of Paris had failed to cripple Confederate commerce raiding; the Federal government had not dared to enforce the legislation declaring the Southern ports closed; and the blockade was still far from effective. Hence Southerners had little difficulty believing the report in the *Richmond Dispatch* that the English newspaper most closely identified with Palmerston, the *Morning Post*, had accepted that the Confederate states had "achieved their independence."[2]

Recognition as a legitimate nation was for many Southerners a "psychological desire" as well as a diplomatic imperative. Mason was expected to impress upon the British that they had a moral responsibility to bring the bloodshed to an early end, and that this was one of those rare instances in which the interests of humanity were entirely consistent with more mundane concerns such as political advantage and commercial profit. Confederate independence would create a genuine balance of power on the continent from which British North America would benefit; it would check the growing American challenge to Britain's commercial and industrial supremacy; and it would see cotton flow freely across the Atlantic. The Confederate government had left the enforcement of a cotton embargo to state and local agencies, which allowed it to deny responsibility for the consequent hardship in Britain and France. But in commenting on the blockade's ineffectiveness, Britain's most influential newspaper, *The Times*, reminded its readers that the Southern embargo was primarily responsible for the dearth of cotton.[3]

Mason and Slidell and their entourages slipped out of Charleston and through the blockade on the night of 12 October. Missing a connection with a transatlantic steamer at Nassau, they sailed on to Cuba. As the remainder of their journey would be aboard neutral British vessels, they assumed they were safe from Union "molestation." Instead, their seizure was being planned by the American consul general in Cuba, Robert Shufeldt, and Captain Charles Wilkes of the USS *San Jacinto*. Wilkes was a zealous, impulsive, vain officer who craved fame and promotion and was confident that the capture of the Confederate commissioners would bring him both. He had little difficulty persuading himself following a scan of the consul general's law texts that the Confederates' seizure would be legal. He waited in the narrow Bahamas Channel for the British mail steamer, the *Trent*, on which the Confederates had taken passage. He obliged the vessel to heave to with a shot across its bows on 8 November and sent over a boarding party which removed the commissioners and their secretaries.[4]

By the time he delivered his prisoners to Fort Warren, Boston, on 23 November, Wilkes was being hailed the national hero he had long considered himself to be. The Northern press exulted in his exploit, which prompted the British novelist Anthony Trollope, who was on a visit to the United States, to ridicule the public adulation of a naval officer who had merely tapped "a merchantman on the shoulder in the high seas, and told him his passengers were wanted." Lyons was far less sanguine. The power of popular opinion in the United States, and its influence on policy, left him in little doubt that he was facing a very serious diplomatic crisis especially when the chairman of the Senate Foreign Relations Committee, who made no secret of his resentment of Britain's response to the Civil War, endorsed the seizures. When Wilkes returned to his Washington home, which was a mere stone's throw from the British legation, Lyons had noisy evidence of the captain's popularity. One ray of hope was the president's silence on the incident in his annual message to Congress at the beginning of December, but among the documents accompanying it was the report of the secretary of the navy, Gideon Welles. He declared his unqualified approval of Wilkes's action and Congress immediately voted the captain a national hero.[5]

No one at the legation doubted that there would be "great irritation" at home over the incident. How could Britain permit political offenders to be seized from one of its vessels, a neutral sailing between neutral ports, without sinking "low in the scale of nations"? The young attachés did not mask their indignation, and a parade of ministers, led by Mercier and Stoeckl, called to express sympathy without giving "official counsel." Lyons appeared "quite out of sorts[,] uneasy & perplexed," but wisely instructed his staff to make no comment. "Lord Lyons is a very odd sort of man & not quite the person to deal with this crisis tho' he is most diligent, clear headed & straight viewed," William Russell eventually concluded. "He is nervous & afraid of responsibility – & has no personal influence in Washington because he never goes into American society tho' he gives dinners very frequently." This criticism was both unfair and inaccurate and may have been produced by the journalist's pique at failing to receive an invitation to a dinner Lyons hosted for "diplomats and swells." "These men like Lord Lyons who have not a little of my real influence," the resentful scribe scribbled in his diary, "think they do me honour by asking me now & then to a scratch dinner – a collection of the polloi or the trial of a cook." In fact, he dined at the legation at least once a week.[6]

Lyons was briefly hamstrung by the report making the rounds in Washington that "Bull Run" Russell's editor, John Delane, had informed him that in the opinion of the British law officers a Union naval commander might remove the Confederate diplomats from a British mail steamer. Delane's information had come from the prime minister himself on 11 November. He had been assured by Charles Francis Adams, Palmerston told the editor, that the Federal cruiser, whose appearance in British waters had given rise to the suspicion that it was planning to waylay the West India Packet on which Mason and Slidell were believed to be passengers, was "not to meddle with any ship under a foreign flag." Palmerston, his hearing deteriorating with his advancing years, then misunderstood a verbal briefing by the Crown's law officers. The written opinion they delivered that same day to the Foreign Office was unambiguous. Outside British territorial waters, the American cruiser was legally entitled to stop, board, and search the packet, put a prize crew aboard, and send it for adjudication in a Union prize court. The cruiser had no right to remove Mason and Slidell and carry them off as prisoners while permitting the packet to complete its voyage. This was the opinion Palmerston gave to the Queen on 13 November. Yet in writing to Lyons three days later, Edmund Hammond, for Earl Russell was at home unwell, added to the confusion by advising him that nothing could be done to prevent interference with the packet outside the three-mile limit of Britain's national waters. A full month passed before he amended this statement and declared mere removal of the Confederates illegal. Lyons had pressed William Russell to treat Delane's information as confidential only then to make the mistake of mentioning it himself to the voluble Mercier. The Frenchman informed Lincoln, who on 10 December assured a senator friend that Britain's legal officers had concluded that the Union was "justifiable by the law of Nations in the arrest of Mason & Slidell, and that there would probly [sic] be no trouble about it." Within three days the first reports of British outrage appeared in the New York press.[7]

Wisely, Lyons chose to keep his counsel until he received crystal clear instructions from home. He wryly remarked that he was perhaps the only man in America who had not expressed an opinion on either the legality of the arrests or the likely response of the British government. He received early in December of a copy of the law officers' opinion but could not find in it a "firm" statement on the legality of the Confederates' seizure because it had been hurriedly copied by the overworked Foreign Office staff. So he maintained his sphinx-like pose only to learn over dinner with the Canadian finance minister, Alexander Galt, a "man of much vigour of intellect," of the province's utterly inadequate defences. Here was another reason to act cautiously and for the Canadians to behave discreetly. This was the message he sent to the new governor general, Viscount Monck, who was an Irish Whig politician not a military man.[8]

Lyons copied to Monck what he had written to the foreign secretary. He could not believe the accounts of the incident found in the American press; he dared not risk compromising national honour and the inviolability of the British flag by asking for a reparation that might prove inadequate, and conversely had no desire to prejudice a final settlement by making a demand that proved excessive; he realized that the Lincoln administration would not accede to any demand made by him until it knew how the British government had reacted to the incident; and any demand made by him would lessen the admittedly slim chance that reparation would be spontaneously offered. He had worried almost from the outset that to admit the legality of the seizures would provide short-term relief but do long-term injury to Anglo-American relations by strengthening the Yankees' belief that Britain could be insulted with impunity. It would be far better to declare the captures unjustifiable, demand the release of Mason and Slidell, and be prepared to act imme-diately if it was refused, he had written to Earl Russell on 22 November. The time had come to leave the Americans in no doubt that there were limits to Britain's forbearance; of its resolve to make no further conces-sions to bullying language and conduct; and of its readiness if necessary to go to war. Putting Canada in a "complete state of defence" was one way to impress the Lincoln administration with Britain's grim resolve, and the mother country should take the lead by dramatically dispatch-ing thousands of troops across the Atlantic. This, he was sure, would have a "manifestly sedative effect." For his part, Monck quietly bolstered the province's active militia only to watch in dismay as General Fen-wick Williams, the commander of the 5,000 British regulars, proved too highly strung an old warhorse to be held on a tight rein. His urgent defensive preparations to resist a possible American attack attracted at-tention and comment on both sides of the long border.[9]

The Palmerston government acted with the forcefulness that Lyons considered essential if peace was to be preserved. The prime minister summoned an eyewitness of the incident to the capital, recalled Cabinet ministers who were off in the country, and obtained an updated legal opinion from the law officers. He informed his assembled colleagues on 29 November that he would not stand for the American action, and understanding that Wilkes had broken international law the Cabinet agreed to demand both the return of the Confederates and an apology by the United States. The following day Russell presented to his col-leagues his instructions to Lyons only for their "meagre" wording to excite considerable debate. When forwarded to the Queen they were embellished and the tone softened by a mortally ill Prince Consort, but there was no retreat from the demands. In an accompanying note Rus-sell instructed Lyons to give the Lincoln administration seven days to make a satisfactory reply. If it failed to do so he was to request his pass-port and return home. This would sever diplomatic relations but not amount to an immediate declaration of war.[10]

The Cabinet initially balked when Palmerston and Russell proposed a ban on the export of munitions and military stores to the lucrative American market. The resistance faded with the news of the ecstatic American applause of Wilkes, the arrival of Lyons's first reports including his recommendations of 22 November, and Palmerston's threat not to defend inaction when the opposition pounced on it in Parliament. Lord Derby had told one minister that the only way to deal with the Americans was to make it perfectly clear that Britain would not stand for any "nonsense," and another senior Tory had warned William Gladstone that he and his colleagues would be driven from office if they failed to defend the nation's honour. This certainly impressed the chancellor of the exchequer, and a string of measures followed which the Cabinet evidently hoped would secure the surrender of Mason and Slidell. Troops, beginning on 6 December, were shipped out from Britain and eventually totalled 12,000; 30,000 stands of arms were sent to equip the Canadian militia; Milne's command was strengthened and several ships of the first division of the Steam Reserve were urgently readied for commissioning. Britain's diplomatic hand was further strengthened by a promise of French moral support. The French ambassador read to Russell the dispatch Thouvenel was sending to Mercier which condemned Wilkes's conduct as a violation of international law and asked what gain was worth the risk of a rupture with Britain. A paraphrase was immediately sent off to Lyons, but it failed to represent the French position accurately and the Foreign Office was obliged to forward an amended version eight days later. Circulated among the European powers, Thouvenel's comments were warmly applauded by them all except Russia. Little wonder gloom shrouded the American legation in London.[11]

In Washington, the Lincoln Cabinet was betraying a nervousness for which Lyons could claim some credit, having maintained his unnerving silence. With the diplomatic corps wearing its sympathies on its sleeve, Seward instructed Adams to inform the British that the arrests had been made without the Federal government's knowledge and were therefore "free of embarrassment." Before long he was aware, thanks to his own sources and the British press, of Britain's likely demands, and when he discussed them with the president on 15 December Lincoln revealed his apprehension in a characteristically anecdotal way. He recounted the story of a ferocious bulldog and the probability of its biting its owner's neighbours. The following evening found Seward barking loudly at the Portuguese legation. An Anglo-American war would wrap the entire world in flames, he declared, perhaps in hope of prompting France to urge Britain to temper its demands. However, both he and the president received disquieting letters from Thurlow Weed warning that Britain was in earnest, was on a war footing, and that the Confederates had to be surrendered. In the event of war Britain would surely recognize the Confederacy and just as surely France would do the same; the blockade would be broken, much of the Union navy captured or destroyed, and a British blockade of the Union mounted; the American mercantile marine would be driven from the high seas; and an independent Confederacy would enter into a free trade agreement with Britain, which would be followed by the massive smuggling of British goods into the Union. In short, the entire North American continent would become a "manufacturing dependency of England." These were the dismal prospects that Chairman Sumner, who had reconsidered his approval of Wilkes's action, spelled out to the president.[12]

Lyons received Russell's instructions late in the evening of Friday, 18 December, the Queen's messenger having hired a special train for the last leg of the journey from Baltimore. Still convinced that Mason and Slidell would only be given up by the Lincoln Cabinet if it understood that war was "really the only alternative," Lyons set himself the task of making them aware of this without resorting to menaces which would make the concession "too great for them to bear." This subtle strategy he implemented with skill and finesse. He called at the State Department the following afternoon, where he exercised his own "excellent judgment" instead of following the line recommended by the foreign secretary. At Seward's request, he provided him with a copy of the demands on the understanding they would be seen only by him and the president. He disclosed, again confidentially and informally, that an answer would be required within seven days of the formal delivery of the demands and quietly stressed that only the return of the Confederates to British protection would suffice to end the crisis. Yet now placing the secretary on "the peace side" of the Cabinet, he granted him a little extra time to influence his colleagues and the president. A brief delay would also allow

Britain's war preparations to be fully reported and understood, and for France's strong moral support of Britain to be known. Thouvenel's dispatch still not having arrived, Lyons sent Mercier to the State Department to ensure that Seward understood the strength both of Britain's determination and of the "strict concert."[13]

Lyons agreed at Seward's request to postpone until Monday the formal presentation of the demands, but he advised the secretary that his report on the American response was going to be sent by the packet scheduled to depart New York on New Year's Day. Here was a reminder of the time limit without a resort to menace. On Sunday he wrote to the governor of Jamaica to inform him that in the event of the demands not being met by 30 December he would be requesting his passport and quitting the Union. He urged Milne to ensure that his captains did not behave provocatively yet were prepared to counter any unauthorized action by the notoriously ill-disciplined American subordinate officers. At the State Department on Monday morning Lyons read Russell's dispatch to the secretary, left a copy, and agreed not to make the seven-day period of grace "part of the official communication." The mere appearance of an ultimatum would, he realized, make more difficult Seward's task of persuading his colleagues to agree to the surrender of the Confederates. There should be no allusion to an ultimatum in the edited dispatches selected for publication in the Blue Book, he immediately advised the Foreign Office. He was keen, in fairness to a co-operative Seward and with the future of Anglo-American relations in mind, to ease the Lincoln administration's path to concession by ensuring it had "as much as possible the air of having been done spontaneously." On the other hand this was the moment to give the Americans "a good lesson" if Britain was to avoid having "the same trouble with them again very soon, under less advantageous circumstances."[14]

The crisis was soon over. Lincoln and his Cabinet met on a Christmas Day that was eerily reminiscent of Indian summer, the sun bright, the temperature mild, the streets thronged with people on their way to or from church, and children letting off firecrackers. There was little light-heartedness in the Cabinet room. Senator Browning, who had been all for defying the British only ten days earlier, was now just as insistent that a rupture be avoided "if it could be done without humiliation or dishonour." This was the president's position also, so when Sumner, who also attended the meeting, read from the letters of Bright and Cobden in which both Radicals exhorted the administration to propose arbitration, Lincoln was briefly taken with the idea. "The President is naturally and instinctively for Peace," Sumner later assured Cobden, and "covets kindly relations with all the world especially with England." But arbitration was not an option as Seward well knew, and the timely arrival of Thouvenel's dispatch, which Mercier immediately sent into the meeting, extinguished any lingering hope of French assistance. No definitive decision was taken, but there was no serious dissent on Boxing Day when Seward read the draft of a very long note returning Mason and Slidell to British protection. He had written it in a style designed to make the decision "most acceptable to the American people." Wilkes was defended; his only mistake, itself the result of his gentlemanly concern for the comfort of the innocent passengers, was his failure to take the vessel in for prize adjudication. The Confederates were dismissed as unimportant figures and their surrender trumpeted as a triumph of the American concept of neutral rights. The world's mightiest naval power, frequently accused in the past of abusing the rights of neutrals, would now be obliged to respect the liberal American definition of them.[15]

Seward's publication of his note served both him and the administration well in the important urban centres of the North, where the press assured its readers that the Union had been neither humiliated nor disgraced. Ex-president Buchanan and ex-senator Hamilton Fish, Lyons's landlord, were privately critical, however, of Seward's "pettyfogging." Fish grumbled that it was less the surrender of which Americans should be ashamed and more the manner in which it was done. Undeterred by the secretary's playing to the gallery, Lyons continued to do "everything to make the pill as easy to swallow as possible." He had no desire to rub American noses in the dirt by insisting on a "distinct apology," and hoped, as he wrote to Russell, that the unconditional return of Mason and Slidell would be considered sufficient. Moreover, he ensured that the Confederates were taken aboard a British warship with as little fanfare as possible. Seward did his part by arranging for the transfer to be made at Provincetown on the tip of Cape Cod. There HMS *Rinaldo* was waiting for them, and perhaps Lyons remembered that this had been

the name of his father's first important independent command. He issued instructions to her captain in cipher. The Confederates were to be
collected as discreetly as possible, and the transfer was to be made with
"good taste," "good feeling," and without any hint of triumph. Aware of
the anti-Union sentiment of the Nova Scotians, the captain made for
Bermuda not Halifax. Little wonder Seward expressed his appreciation
of the "great kindness and consideration" with which Lyons had negotiated the *Trent* affair.[16]

His handling of the crisis enhanced Lyons's growing reputation as
one of the nation's most intelligent and skilful diplomats. Earl Russell,
long an admirer, wrote: "Your silence, forbearance, & friendly discretion
have gone far to secure this favourable result." Edmund Hammond, the
permanent undersecretary, wholeheartedly agreed. You "probably have
saved us from immediate war by making it impossible for the United
States government to pick a quarrel with you and us in consequence
of the manner in which you executed your instructions." When Parliament opened early in February both Palmerston and Britain's foremost
friend of the United States, John Bright, paid handsome tribute to Lyons's judgment, delicacy, and "courteous manner." A proud Minna was
delighted that her brother "should have been the means of saving a war
and all its miseries," her only regret the fact that their parents had not
lived to enjoy his success. It was a regret he shared, for much of his ambition to excel had been driven by a determination to achieve what they
had expected of him. No one, he assured his sister, had ever taken more
pains to prevent a war. Writing to Milne, he modestly stated that his
diplomacy would not have settled the crisis without the military preparations, but he might have claimed a large share of the credit for them.
Both before and during the *Trent* affair he had recommended demonstrations of Britain's will and ability to defend her national interests.[17]

Lyons was not expecting a quieter and a simpler diplomatic life. He
didn't expect ever to be free of "disagreeables," nor did he expect them
all to end as well as the *Trent* crisis. Therefore, escape from his current
post would be welcome but not if the price were a loss either of credit or
of rank. There were two reasons for him not to solicit a transfer. First,
the unsolicited award of the Grand Cross of the Order of the Bath meant
that he was honour bound to remain in Washington for as long as the

Foreign Office wished him to do so. Second, he did "not want to go to a lower post, even though a pleasant one." For him, a promotion was essential.[18]

The Americans were "horribly out of humour," Lyons soon realized, and he suspected them of looking for some means of annoying Britain "without danger to themselves." There was talk of imposing discriminatory duties on British goods, of passage of a non-intercourse act, and of the immediate repeal of the Reciprocity Treaty, though he considered this the least likely retaliatory measure since it would be a serious breach of the agreement and "an indisputable *casus belli*." But he continued to urge Canadian preparedness to repel regular American invaders or filibusters, for the great bulk of the British military reinforcements had yet to arrive. When later in January they landed in the Maritime provinces, Monck believed their arrival had finally put paid to the popular notion that it was impossible to aid Canada militarily during the long winter. Neither Seward's act of "bravado" in announcing that British troops, horses, and munitions would be permitted to land on American territory, nor the evident reluctance of the Lincoln administration to give Britain "anything like a *casus belli*," persuaded Lyons to modify his stance. Britain's military preparations, he continued to believe, had produced the improved relations with the United States.[19]

During the brief diplomatic lull that followed the settlement of the *Trent* affair Lyons attended to the welfare of his overworked staff, which had been joined in November by William Stuart. The brother of the 12th Lord Blantyre, one of Scotland's representative peers in Parliament, he came highly recommended by Lord Normanby and was an experienced diplomat. He and Lyons were able to reminisce about diplomatic life in Athens, but it was the life of his junior staff that concerned the minister. Washington was a "terrible place" for them, he fretted, for it was not well provided with such diversions as theatres and clubs. They were effectively confined to the house during the winter because of the capital's impassable streets. When the weather improved he wished to keep them away from the bar at Willard's Hotel. Recalling his visits to Woburn Abbey years earlier, he encouraged them to erect a stage in the large dining room and put on popular plays. Such was the success of the amateur theatricals that when large dinners were resumed distinguished guests found themselves seated in the temporary theatre's pit. Little wonder the attachés' admiration of their genial chief grew exponentially, and legation life became even more diverting with the arrival from Canada of a number of British military officers.[20]

Several of the arrivals were on an intelligence mission, seeking working drawings of the rifled and breech-loading artillery being used in the Civil War. Lyons refused to engage in what he called "underhand activities." Espionage was contrary to the straightforwardness and truthfulness which he considered the essence of British diplomacy. "I consider it to be of the utmost importance," he informed Russell, that such practices "should be conducted not only without the instrumentality, but absolutely and *bona fide* without the knowledge of myself or of any member of this Legation." He had no intention of jeopardizing the sterling reputation he had gained in the United States. He was, in the opinion of the *New York Tribune*, "a MODEL Embassador [*sic*]," as courteous and as inoffensive as his duties allowed, faithful to his instructions but no meddler in matters with which properly he had no concern. The news that the Union intended to sink stone-laden vessels in the channels of Southern harbours in an effort to improve the blockade's effectiveness was a matter of concern to him. His complaint was brushed aside by Seward, who noted with irony and asperity the arrival in Charleston, where a channel had already been blocked, of a British blockade runner loaded with contraband. Indeed, blockade runners were arriving and departing daily, and so regular was the service that a recent Confederate order for medicines and quinine had been sent to New York via Nassau and filled within three weeks. The sinking of stone-laden vessels was soon halted, however, and in rejecting the French proposal of limited European trade with the Confederacy the secretary of state announced that Southern ports would soon be reopened by Union forces.[21]

The transfer of the power to make arrests from the State Department to the War Department briefly gave Lyons hope that the British subjects who had been imprisoned without legal process would quickly be freed and that only "spies and other depraved persons" who threatened the success of military operations would be detained. Seward, he believed, had taken too much pleasure in the power. The new secretary of war, Edward Stanton, a "vigorous ill tempered dyspeptic," was even more uncompromising than the secretary of state. Legal niceties, as Lyons quickly discovered, were unlikely to restrain him, and arrested Britons were not swiftly released. The situation made Lyons despair of constitutional government in the United States. Consent of the governed was receiving a "rude shaking," he lamented. Elections were supposed to manifest the will of the nation, but how long would respect for their results survive when state legislatures were dispersed by military force and voters adverse to the government were arrested or "driven from the roll"? Unfortunately, if not surprisingly, three-quarters of a century earlier the authors of the Constitution had failed to anticipate immense debt, heavy taxes, a huge standing army, and a disaffected population millions strong. It was the Union's added misfortune, Lyons concluded, that at this moment of profound crisis democracy had placed mere party politicians in positions of leadership.[22]

The picture Lyons painted of the Union at the beginning of 1862 was not an attractive one. Congress had pledged itself to raise the equivalent of 50 millions sterling to support a huge armed force that was estimated at 660,000, and this from a people "unaccustomed to pay any apparent taxes at all for Federal purposes." Expecting the return from Britain of American securities, bankers had suspended specie payments. To fiscal worries had been added fresh political problems with the opening of a schism in the ranks of the Republicans in Congress. Lyons identified a "Revolutionary Party" of Radical Republicans, dedicated to fighting the war to a bitter end by prosecuting it "at all hazards and by all means." They would, he informed Russell, willingly turn out the Cabinet and the president, keep Congress in permanent session, maintain a paper currency, pursue a foreign policy reckless in conduct and language, abolish slavery in the South, and even promote a slave rebellion. "The question is rapidly leaning towards the issue of either peace and recognition of the separation, or a Proclamation of Emancipation and the raising of a servile insurrection," he suggested. The fear of racial violence was not unique to him. Were a proclamation to be followed by anarchy which threatened cotton production, foreign powers would rally to the Confederacy, Seward suspected, making reunion even more difficult.[23]

Opposed to Radicals was a "moderate reasonable party" which Lyons believed would be willing to end the war just as soon as the people tired of the suffering and sacrifices currently demanded of them. This was the faction he was sure Seward aspired to lead. Another Union military reverse might bring to the fore the question of peace and with it danger to Britain. The "violent party" would respond recklessly while the moderates might provoke a foreign conflict to provide themselves with an excuse to abandon the struggle or to divert an angry people from that decision. Meanwhile, the administration was overwhelming Britain and France with "demonstrations of friendship and confidence" in an effort to ease the money market and deny them a pretext to recognize the Confederacy and break up the blockade. "Too much love is almost more inconvenient to a Diplomatist than hatred," an unusually sardonic Lyons observed. Military gains in the west and a minor success on the eastern seaboard were certainly boosting the confidence of troops and civilians alike, but he dismissed as hollow the boasts of Charles Sumner and others that within weeks New Orleans, Mobile, and Savannah would be in Federal hands, and that within months Union troops would control Missouri, Kentucky, Tennessee, Virginia, and the entire Atlantic seaboard.[24]

Seward's argument that Union successes merited withdrawal by Britain and France of their recognition of Confederate belligerency was not treated seriously by Lyons and Mercier or their governments. Palmerston mockingly remarked that the two nations might as well declare that the sun did not shine at midday. The "great question" which Lyons asked was whether the Southerners would in the face of defeat "hold to their determination to bear suffering and privation to the last extremity." A senior member of the French legation reported on his return from Richmond that the reverses had strengthened Confederate resolve. If this was indeed the case they might well wear out the North, Lyons admitted, and "then the separation may be effected, which would have saved all the evils to both sides, if it had been consented to at once." In short, his discreet Union sympathies notwithstanding, he remained skeptical of its ability to govern a defeated South.[25]

Across the Atlantic, the public and private British reaction to the surrender of Mason and Slidell had smacked of relief mixed with self-congratulation. Lord Derby declared with aristocratic hauteur that it was as well that such "scum" as Seward and his colleagues understood how unsafe "blustering" was in their dealings with the United Kingdom, and Palmerston quietly enjoyed the "humiliation" of John Bright's "favourite North American Republic." However, he and Russell drew to the attention of their Cabinet colleagues the dangerous implications of accepting Seward's claim that Wilkes's only serious error had been the failure to take the *Trent* in as prize. This interpretation of international law, Palmerston growled, would allow other American "heroes" to take liberties with British merchantmen. Or as a minister friendly to the Union put it, any cross-Channel ferry found to be carrying a Confederate emissary might be seized and taken to a New York prize court. To discourage Union vessels from hovering in the waters around Britain, the government severely restricted the belligerents' use of Britain's ports.[26]

That the American war was responsible for the depression in the textile districts of Lancashire and Cheshire was the assumption of the general public, but the presidents of the Board of Trade and the Poor Law Board, the two Radical members of the Cabinet, did not agree. Cotton stocks at the end of 1861 were higher than they had been a year earlier; consequently the slump in employment was laid at the door of depressed markets. Chancellor of the Exchequer Gladstone assured the public that losses in American trade were being offset by the increasing trade with France thanks to the Commercial Treaty of 1860. In the opinion of the law officers, there was no strong legal argument for British intervention. They were unimpressed by the evidence of the blockade's ineffectiveness. All they required to judge it effective was sufficient vessels off a port to pose an evident danger to blockade runners. Here was an opinion attuned to Britain's future interest as the world's greatest naval power. Palmerston and his colleagues had no desire to interfere "materially" with the rights of a belligerent, and they could not overcome their distrust of France. It was French policy, Russell advised the Queen, to undermine governments in trouble and then use the chaos as the excuse for interference.

In the absence of any opposition pressure for a change of policy, Russell fended off without difficulty the attacks in Parliament by the Confederacy's sympathizers. They seized upon the Union's mistreatment of British subjects, the ineffectiveness of the blockade, and Lincoln's suspension of habeas corpus. The foreign secretary reminded the Union's

critics of Britain's suspensions of the writ during the French Revolutionary Wars but overlooked its swift suspension in Ireland during the insignificant rebellion of 1848 by the government he then led. Privately, he
agreed with Lyons that the most expedient policy was one of patience.
This was his refrain when the friends of the Confederacy launched a debate on the blockade on 7 March. Why act if the blockade was so ineffective? Paraphrasing Lyons, he warned that to challenge the blockade was
to challenge the Union and this was no time to invite trouble when there
were troubles enough in Europe. There, Prussia and Denmark were disputing possession of Schleswig-Holstein and the Poles were becoming
ever more restive under their Russian masters.[27]

As spring approached, Lyons's assurance that relations with the Union had at last "got into a very smooth groove" was greeted with relief
by Russell. However, the evidence that Secretary of the Treasury Chase
planned to finance the war essentially with loans and paper currency,
the "greenbacks," did not improve the chances of large-scale British purchases of American securities, which might have given Britain a vested
long-term interest in the Union's survival. But Thurlow Weed's success
in persuading the American expatriate banker George Peabody publicly
to uphold the Union cause did give it a boost in Britain when the philan-
thropic banker announced a very generous donation to help build housing for London's poor. Peabody was the first American to be buried, if
briefly, in Westminster Abbey. Equally helpful to the Union's image was
its acceptance of the anti-slave trade treaty Britain had long sought. Lyons knew how large an obstacle the Americans had been to the success
of his nation's mission to stamp out the international trade in slaves. Not
only had they refused to permit the searching of vessels flying their flag
even when they were evidently engaged in the "immoral commerce," but
their own law banning the trade was sadly deficient. The few cruisers
which the United States stationed off the African coast were restricted
to seizing vessels flying the American flag and found loaded with slaves.
Similarly restrictive were the orders of American captains operating
off the coast of Cuba, where the trade was flourishing. Whereas British
commanders investigated and seized vessels operating without a flag,
their American counterparts were not even permitted to interfere with
vessels whose captains destroyed both flag and papers. Joint cruising

had been rejected by the Buchanan administration, and with the opening of the Civil War the American cruisers assigned to the suppression of the slave trade were recalled for blockade duty.[28]

Questioned by Lyons on the recall of the anti-slave trade cruisers and whether additional measures were likely to be adopted to prevent slavers from avoiding capture by flying American colours, Seward made the startling reply that he was not as squeamish about searches of suspect vessels as his predecessors at the State Department had been. The Republicans intended to be far more flexible with respect to Britain's efforts to suppress the trade off the coast of Africa so long as there were reasonable grounds of suspicion and searches were conducted in the proper manner. Seward even signed a "secret" memorandum to this effect with Lyons. But could he as something of a weather vane of public opinion be trusted not to excite a crisis, as the Buchanan administration had done, over British searches of vessels flying the American flag in the neighbourhood of Cuba? So Palmerston encouraged Russell to seek a formal agreement with the Union. The "Informal Memorandum" of 12 November 1861 fell far short of the agreement Russell was seeking, and further discussions were blocked by the *Trent* crisis. Then, on 20 February 1862, the day on which the Lincolns suffered the tragic death of a young son, and on the eve of the first and only execution of an American international slave trader, Seward suddenly revived the issue. His hope, he later wrote, was to cultivate the friendship of Britain, thereby lessening the danger of its diplomatic intervention in the Civil War.[29]

Lyons eagerly grasped this opportunity to "effect something practical as regards the Slave *Trade*." His first thought was to revive an earlier proposal for Congressional legislation modelled on the British provision that permitted seizure and condemnation of any vessel found to be equipped for the transport slaves. What he received from Russell early in March was a draft treaty, the foreign secretary having taken to heart his caution against entering into anything less than a formal agreement. It provided for the ships of one signatory to stop and search suspect ships of the other and created mixed courts to adjudicate cases. Lyons presented the draft treaty to Seward on 15 March, and the chances of its being accepted improved nine days later when Lincoln sent to Congress a message recommending Federal "pecuniary aid" to any state that agreed to abolish slavery gradually and implied that in the event of a protracted war compulsory emancipation might become "indispensable" to its efficient and successful prosecution. The importance of the message, Lyons acutely observed, was its declaration of the government's commitment to emancipation as the "ultimate object of its policy." The ending of slavery had been made a national goal, and this the president confirmed by signing a bill which prohibited Union officers from using their forces to return fugitive slaves. The administration also took the practical and symbolic step of recognizing the two states populated by former slaves, Haiti and Liberia.[30]

Lyons contributed to the treaty's successful negotiation by readily agreeing that it should be represented as an American initiative, and he hastily wrote home to ensure that no public mention was made of the truth. When Seward returned the draft as his own, having added a provision limiting the initial term to ten years, but renewable, Lyons made a pretence of resisting in order to maintain that illusion. They signed the treaty on 7 April 1862, and Lyons considered it a fitting way to mark the third anniversary of his arrival in Washington. His flexibility had greatly increased the prospects of ratification. The Senate vote of approval, just two days before his forty-fifth birthday, was unanimous. As the manager of the treaty in the Senate, Sumner predictably credited the success to his own "special pertinacity." Seward, on hearing the vote, reportedly leapt from a sofa in excitement. Even the usually restrained Lyons "overflowed with gratitude & delight," declaring to a tearful Sumner his joy that a treaty of "such importance" carried his name. It quickly reduced the flow of slaves into Cuba from a torrent to a trickle.[31]

The introduction of legislation to provide for the voluntary compensated emancipation of the slaves of Unionists was hailed by Lyons "a great measure as a beginning." Although not one of the border slave states took advantage of the scheme, the 3,000 slaves in the District of Columbia were freed. That a president keenly aware of American racial conservatism justified compensated emancipation as a means of shortening the war and thus of economy, and "not as an act of humanity to the slaves," explains Lyons's cynical analysis of his motive. The anti-slavery measures were designed, he assumed, to save the credit of Lincoln with fellow Republicans in the event that he decided to make concessions to

the South with respect to slavery in order to speed the Union's reconstruction. Another reading of the measures, which Seward implied and
Sumner expressed, was that they and the Lyons-Seward Treaty were a
pledge of Anglo-American goodwill and friendship. But Union hopes of
a more benevolent British neutrality were doomed to disappointment.

The British press responded with skepticism to the proposed scheme
of compensated emancipation, asking where the money was to come
from to free 4 million slaves. It amounted to an admission by the Union
that its cause was lost, Russell concluded, for if fully restored its "old disgrace & its old danger" would remain in place. This reading sustained
him in the belief that separation would be the conflict's "fair solution."
He had seen no evidence of a Southern majority genuinely favourable
to reunion, while the Southern climate and Southern spirit were in his
opinion "invincible." Aware how unwelcome this opinion would be in
Washington, he remained publicly committed to non-interference. The
claim of one amateur diplomat and Confederate sympathizer following
his return from Paris that the emperor favoured a joint Anglo-French
recognition of Confederate independence served only to increase Foreign Office wariness of Napoleon III.[32]

Lyons would not have been surprised by Mercier's news that he had
received instructions to recommend to Seward that the North come to
favourable terms with an independent Confederacy and thus avoid the
"complications" which would inevitably result from an extended conflict causing such distress in Europe. When he met with the secretary on
10 April Mercier expressed instead a desire to see for himself how matters stood in Richmond. Seward, with Lincoln's consent, sanctioned his
visit to the Confederate capital perhaps in the hope the French minister
would return convinced that the time had come to withdraw the recognition of Confederate belligerency. No doubt Seward also saw the trip as
a possible wedge with which to ease the two ministers apart. That was
certainly how Lyons read the secretary's consent, and it fed his anger
over Mercier's failure to discuss the matter with him before speaking
to the secretary of state. He was not reassured by the Frenchman's vow
to advise the Confederate leaders that their cause was doomed, that it
was time to make some arrangement with the Union, and that it was
"useless to expect countenance from the European Powers." Diplomats,

even those whose relations were confidential and intimate, were, as Lyons admitted, prone to suspect one another. "I suppose no Frenchman could resist the temptation to make something like a Diplomatic coup, if it were presented," he remarked. But things had gone too far to be reversed, so he acquiesced in the visit while conspicuously withholding full approval of it.[33]

The conviction that the "strict concert" remained vital to the maintenance of a stable relationship with the Union explained Lyons's exasperation with Mercier and his concern when Seward raised with him Napoleon III's transformation of the allied expedition to collect Mexican debts into a military campaign to establish a monarchy. The assurance Lyons had given the American only a month earlier, that the British government had no intention of imposing on the Mexicans a form of government not of their choice, had plainly encouraged him to seek to exploit another Anglo-French disagreement. The battalion of marines that had been Britain's military contribution to the original expedition was withdrawn early in March even as the ambitious French objective became evident. This was creating "bad feelings" between Britain and France, Seward happily informed Lyons. In early April, having negotiated a scheme for debt repayment with the Juárez government, Britain and Spain formally withdrew from the Mexican expedition. Charles Wyke and Russell agreed that the French project was doomed, the foreign secretary writing to Lyons: "I fear the French will make a mess of it." Of course, from Britain's standpoint, this was not an entirely unwelcome prospect. An emperor embroiled in distant Mexico would have a diminished capacity for mischief in an unstable Europe.[34]

Mercier returned to Washington on 24 April, the day the Senate approved the Slave Trade Treaty. Lyons had suspected from the outset that his partner in the "strict concert" had gone to Richmond expecting to be confirmed in his Southern sympathies; consequently Mercier's comments did not surprise him. Hostility to the Union was universal, secession was a "thoroughly national movement," and there was "no disposition to listen to any terms of accommodation" short of "absolute independence," the Frenchman announced. The Union would never negotiate on this basis, Lyons knew, but he found some comfort in Mercier's admission that the present moment would be "particularly unfavourable" to a move to recognize Confederate independence. To preserve the concert he dissuaded the Foreign Office from lodging a protest at the French Foreign Ministry over Mercier's behaviour. Meanwhile, to dampen American hopes of a breach, Lyons went out of his way to parade his intimacy with the Frenchman. "Never were two diplomatists better friends or more cordial in their relations with each other," Sumner wrote to a British acquaintance. "They are together daily, I often see them together, & often hear them speak of each other."[35]

By mid-May Lyons had detected mounting Union uneasiness over talk in Britain and France of intervention. American nervousness had one advantage, which was a more amiable Seward. On the other hand Lyons had to hold in check his impatient French colleague, who wished to advise his government to bring the conflict to an end by intervening at the first good opportunity. Intervention at this moment meant recognition of the Confederacy, Lyons explained to Russell, something he considered neither useful nor effectual until "one or other of the parties was willing to make peace *at any price*." Privately, he agreed with the Frenchman that the South would not abandon the struggle until the entire country had been laid waste but declined to debate the matter with him. He regarded it as too dangerous a subject, for intervention would in his opinion lead to war with the Union. The autumn, he suggested, would be a far more sensible time to re-examine policy. If the current Federal military campaigns were repulsed, the people might become disillusioned, the troops demoralized, and recruiting and credit falter. If a peace party then emerged, Britain and France might give it support. There were, however, three facts to which the Palmerston government should not shut its eyes: the unlikelihood of cotton soon flowing across the Atlantic; the absence of Union feeling in the South as the residents of the recently captured port of New Orleans were proving; and the transformation of the conflict from one of separation to one of subjugation. These were Lyons's final thoughts before setting off home on a well-deserved leave.[36]

Mid-May was "dreadfully hot" in Washington and Lyons had never tolerated heat well. A sojourn at a watering place was still not an option since he knew of no truly cool place within twenty-four hours of the capital and "a journey in the heat and in American railway carriages" would "knock him up" for a month. The great increase in the expense of the legation caused him to doubt that he could afford to live for an extended period at a summer retreat in a manner that befitted his official position. In more than three years, he reminded Russell, and with the exception of the royal tour, he had never spent more than four nights out of the capital. He complained of a recurrence of a throat condition, probably an infection, of a chest condition, and of severe, incapacitating headaches undoubtedly the result of stress. He needed a leave to recover his health and strength and to keep in closer touch with thinking at home. He would be able to leave the legation safely in the hands of the experienced William Stuart because there appeared little likelihood of serious developments during his absence. Even the capture of Confederate ports and the Confederate capital by the Union would not in his opinion make much of an impression on the South. International problems would develop once the Union's internal troubles subsided, he admitted, but that was a remote prospect.[37]

The autumn being the time to reconsider American policy, it would be simple good sense for him to be on hand in London. He would be able to speak to Cabinet ministers and hear their views. What would he tell them? First, that Northerners were united by an "ardent desire to recover lost territory" and were unique in their identification of their nation's greatness with the extent of its dominion. Second, that military victory would not reconcile Americans to the loss of territory, and at a moment of success they would not agree to the permanent separation of any part of the South. Third, that separation might be the result of the conflict if the South found the means and will to struggle on until the North wearied of the contest. Fourth, that Lincoln's annulling of the order by the commander of the Federal forces at Hilton Head, South Carolina, declaring free the slaves of that state and those of Georgia and Florida, was evidence of the strength of Northern Conservatives as opposed to Abolitionists, and nothing so strengthened the Southerners' grim resolve to fight on as fear that capitulation would be followed immediately by emancipation. Fifth, that despite the current "smooth" relations he was by no means confident that Britain was safely out of the woods. The pragmatic president's remark that one war at a time was enough did not inoculate the two nations against an unwanted war. His own principal objective remained what it had always been: the maintenance of peaceful relations with the Union. Unfortunately, the American animosity towards Britain might lead to serious consequences should a "favourable moment" arrive for its indulgence. Hence safeguards against hostilities should not be weakened. British regulars must remain in force in British North America.[38]

Lyons called on the president before leaving the capital. They had "quite an affectionate parting," Lincoln putting Lyons at ease, as was his wont, with stories "more or less decorous." He asked Lyons to assure his countrymen that he meant them no harm. For his part, Lyons gave careful instructions to Stuart. He was to keep things smooth, prevent issues from arising if possible, refer home all doubtful matters, and make no great difficulty out of a small matter even when the case was clear. On 17 June, Lyons took his leave of Seward in New York City. The American was reluctant to see him go, appreciative as he was of the Englishman's just and friendly conduct, which had helped to strengthen their personal relationship and to stabilize that of their two nations. His final words were an expression of hope that Lyons would explain to his government the true state of American affairs and perhaps recommend withdrawal of the recognition of Confederate belligerency.[39]

CHAPTER EIGHT

Intervention?

The *Persia* with Lyons aboard called at Queenstown on 27 June before tying up at Liverpool the following morning; from there he took the train to London, where his rooms at Norfolk House in St James's Square had been prepared for him. In the hope that Lyons would reach the capital on Saturday, the foreign secretary had waited for him until the early evening before going off to Pembroke Lodge, his retreat in Richmond Park. And it was there that Lyons went on Sunday for a long talk with Russell. That conversation and his reading of the press convinced Lyons, in a little more than a week, that public opinion would "not allow the Government to do more for the North than maintain strict neutrality." Moreover, even that might not be possible if the Union engaged in "further strong provocations." The "unreasonable American bitterness against England" had alienated many Britons, and the balance of popular sympathy appeared to be tipping against the Union. Richard Cobden had reached the same conclusion. There was an almost unanimous belief, he wrote to Charles Sumner, that the North could not subject the South. The *Trent* affair, the North's failure to declare a crusade against slavery, the military reverses, and the lack of respect for civil liberties explained the erosion of support. Lincoln's progressive suspensions of habeas corpus, the muzzling of the press on his "fiat," and the arrest of those who protested his conduct shocked British liberals. Their more radical colleagues complained that the president was giving advanced British liberalism a "very bad odour" and aiding Tory "false reasoners" who insisted that slavery should have little bearing on Britain's attitude. It was, after all, friendly with Spain and Brazil, both slave societies, and had recently fought a costly war to uphold an Ottoman Empire suspected of involvement in the white slave trade.[1]

Several periodicals and newspapers did still support the Union, and a number of the nation's intellectuals argued strongly that in progressively emancipating itself from its founding compromise with slavery the Union had conclusively established its moral superiority over the Confederacy. Harriet Martineau, Britain's first female writer of newspaper editorials, hailed the abolition of slavery in the District of Columbia as a momentous event which had terminated a period of guilt and danger. Her philosopher friend John Stuart Mill defended the right of Unionists to fight the dismemberment of their nation. British governments, after all, had suppressed Irish separatism. Professor John Elliot Cairnes, who looked to Mill as his mentor, published *The Slave Power* in which he argued that the North's right to subjugate the South and hold it by force if necessary was as clear as any state's right to suppress murder and piracy. The Union's supporters had expected the capture of New Orleans to swell their ranks for there was an assumption that the Confederate planters of the Mississippi Valley would now trade their raw cotton through the port. Instead, New Orleans became for the Union something of a temporary public relations disaster when the commander of the occupying force reportedly threatened to treat as prostitutes women who abused his troops. Russell sensibly gave the order the least offensive meaning, but in the Commons the former "Prince Cupid" heading the government expressed Victorian outrage and much of the press followed his lead. Furthermore, the episode was trumpeted as proof of the absence of Union sentiment in the South and evidence that the disaffected states could never be successfully governed following a Northern military victory. The deepening distress in the mill towns of Lancashire and Cheshire, where cotton stocks were being rapidly depleted and perhaps half the operatives were unemployed and in need of relief, represented another challenge for the Union's friends. "Cotton, Cotton, Cotton. This is the cry of the day," one Radical MP entered in his diary on 19 June.

Richard Cobden, who continued to believe that nothing but harm could possibly be done "by interference of any kind," acknowledged that where the welfare and lives of millions of persons were at stake "you cannot present the alternative of a greater possible evil to deter a government from attempting to remedy so vast a present danger."[2]

To ease the pressure for cotton, Cobden recommended that the Union avert trouble with Europe by permitting merchants to ship goods, except contraband, to New Orleans and exchange them freely for cotton in the Confederate interior. Russell had through Lyons made a similar suggestion to Seward weeks earlier but there was little Union interest in an arrangement which would bolster the fiscal resources of the Confederate government and would be deeply unpopular in the North. Although Lyons later recalled that the blockade kept relations in "perpetual hot water and within an inch of war with the United States," and that the labour of avoiding a rupture was almost the death of him, there was by 1862 little likelihood of its denunciation by the British government. Russell had publicly accepted its effectiveness, a decision he and Palmerston defended as one that preserved the right of blockade for Britain in any future conflict. Nevertheless, the cotton shortage and the attendant suffering of the operatives was grist for the mills of Confederate propagandists. James Spence's *American Union*, which had appeared late in 1861, was proving more popular than *The Slave Power*. Spence was another who assured Britons that slavery was not the root of the conflict, and that secession had been the natural result of a misguided attempt to maintain unity within a nation whose dramatic and swift expansion had created an enormous, complex, and diverse land. Henry Hotze, Swiss by birth and Confederate by adoption, who had arrived recently in Britain, immediately put his journalistic experience to good use. His letters calling for recognition of the Confederacy were sent to the editor of the Palmerstonian *Morning Post*, and he soon launched the *Index*, a newspaper in which, as a translator of Arthur de Gobineau's *Essai sur l'inégalité des races humaines*, he constructed a racial hierarchy and provided its "scientific" justification which was consistent with popular Anglo-Saxonism.[3]

Hotze had been heartened by rumours of Anglo-French mediation, but Russell informed Parliament on 13 June that the government had "at the present moment" no intention of mediating the American war. Palmerston dismissed mediation as a waste of time, but there were more substantive restraints on British policy. The American conflict remained for many Radicals proof of war's insanity and a government dependent on them for its survival in the Commons would be doubly ill-advised to risk a collision with the Union those self-same Radicals admired. Moreover, the government had enough foreign concerns already. A contest was developing between Austria and Prussia for supremacy in Germany, and the appointment of Otto von Bismarck as the Prussian ambassador to France suggested a willingness in Berlin to seek the favour of the Foreign Office's *bête noire*. Napoleon's construction of a formidable navy made Britain more vulnerable to invasion, and the high cost of defensive fortifications and matching naval construction produced additional tensions within Cabinet and among parliamentary Radicals. There was a crisis developing in Greece, where Otho seemed certain to be deposed and thus a successor had to be found. There were strains in Italy, where the struggle to deprive the pope of his temporal power was continuing. Tension was building between Denmark and the Germans, between the Poles and the Russians, and yet again in the Balkans. He could "hardly imagine a more unpleasant state of affairs," the Tory leader remarked. Not surprisingly, Palmerston opted for "Home Intervention" in the cotton crisis. Severely distressed poor law unions were permitted to secure aid from wealthier unions in their counties and even to borrow to fund relief. The government had, in the opinion of a Radical sitting in the House of Commons, "been driven to act ag[ains]t the dictates of its intellect, whether fortunately or otherwise I will not venture to say."[4]

The "gloomy prospects" of the industry that had served as the flywheel of the entire economy worried Lyons. He persuaded himself that cotton in quantity could be supplied by India and that woollens would be accepted as substitutes yet asked himself how the public would react if the Union failed to evince a desire to enable Britain to obtain cotton in quantity. Would the government be able to resist popular pressure for action? Then there was the possibility of policy being modified by military developments, and of these Stuart was keeping him informed. He wrote on 30 June of another Union reverse but, fearful of committing a career-blighting blunder, urged the minister's early return to Washington. In the meantime he appeared to be willing to be guided by the experienced Mercier, news that neither Lyons nor Russell welcomed. The French minister had been quick, following Lyons's departure, to discuss with Stuart an offer of mediation whenever it could be made "without too great a risk of war." It might succeed now if made energetically, Mercier had confidently asserted. Much to Russell's relief, Stuart had sense enough not to agree. It would be "too great a risk at present" he admitted, recommending they wait for a Union military disaster. That calamity he reported on, of all days, 4 July. General McClellan's advance on Richmond had been halted, his command was in disarray, his troops demoralized, and some senior officers were "openly saying that the Confederacy must now be recognized." Stuart admitted that the Union army was recovering from "despondency," but he was more impressed by the claim of Frank Vizetelly of the *Illustrated London News* that he had failed during a visit to the South to detect even a shred of Union sentiment.[5]

The Union was in a "panic," Stuart bluntly stated. Lincoln had called for 300,000 volunteers, and "extraordinary bounties" were being offered as inducements to enlist. Seward had warned that "unless volunteering went on rapidly, and our army was greatly increased" there was a danger of Anglo-French intervention. The War Department had called "into immediate service a draft of three hundred thousand men, to serve for nine months, unless sooner discharged." They were in addition to the volunteers, Stuart noted, and frantic British subjects were seeking his protection from a War Department aggressively pursuing persons suspected of fleeing, or evading, military service. He improvised a form of legal documentation for those British subjects who had never applied for American naturalization. Against this background, Congress having abolished slavery in the territories the previous month, a renewed Union attack on the institution was always likely to be interpreted as an act of desperation. Now, a month later, the president sought Congressional authority to compensate any border state that adopted "gradual abolition," and Congress passed a Confiscation Bill which declared free the slaves of "rebels." After some hesitation, for a number of Republicans doubted its constitutionality, Lincoln signed the bill into law. Sumner, over dinner with Stuart at the legation, declared it the "death blow of slavery." This measure was soon followed by an address "from a portion of the Republican members of Congress to the 'loyal people of the United States'" which advocated the arming of former slaves and breathed "defiance of foreign powers."[6]

Abolitionists were "getting ahead" and servile war was increasingly regarded as the only means of preventing the South's separation, Stuart advised Lyons, yet so far as he could tell the slaves were not exhibiting much desire for freedom or much resentment of bondage. He understood from Mercier that in Paris there was mounting impatience with the war and surmised that the French minister might soon be ordered to intimate to Seward that recognition of the Confederacy would be "taken into consideration" unless an end to the conflict was in sight. Mercier favoured an Anglo-French proposal of mediation and suggested that it be made in October. Influenced by a conversation with Stoeckl, Stuart maintained that if mediation were then offered and declined Britain and France might recognize the Confederacy without finding themselves at war with the Union. He was convinced that the old Union could never be restored and suspected that there was "no measure, however strong, which would be found too strong" by a desperate North. In his opinion, the demands for a more energetic war policy meant a resort to "Confiscation, Emancipation and the arming of slaves." Lincoln had "resisted the extreme pressures," he acknowledged, but if emancipation were proclaimed it would "endanger discipline" among troops who had enlisted to restore the Union not to effect a social revolution. But given the "general hatred of England" it would be a mistake for Britain to remonstrate against "vindictive measures." British protests, as the New Orleans episode had illustrated, simply made such measures more attractive and their sponsors more popular.[7]

For Stuart, who was still thinking of Anglo-French-Russian mediation, and knew that his chief's principal concern was to avoid conflict with the Union, any diplomatic intervention should be conditional on there being no risk of hostilities. The question of what Britain should do was very much on Lyons's mind as he made the rounds in London. He made a courtesy call on Charles Francis Adams, whom he judged "frank and sensible," and dined with him at the American mission. At the French embassy he spoke with the visiting Thouvenel, to whom he lauded Mercier as an excellent colleague and was relieved to hear the foreign minister admit that for the present nothing could be done to bring the war to an end. American policy was the topic of conversation during his frequent meetings with Russell at Pembroke Lodge on three of Lyons's first four weekends home. He also had a long talk with Palmerston and a "sufficiently long conversation" with Lord Derby, who was his near neighbour in St James's Square. He went out to Watford, north of the capital, to visit the Clarendons. And the American war was undoubtedly the major topic of conversation over lunch with the Prince of Wales at Buckingham Palace. In early August he was a member of a house party at Lady Marian Alford's, the art patron. Hearing that several Cabinet ministers were in her next batch of guests, he delayed his departure to meet with them.[8]

To all, Lyons counselled non-intervention. He stayed away from the Commons on 18 July when William Lindsay called for "serious and immediate attention" to Anglo-French mediation. That would be both premature and unwise, Lyons privately warned, for not enough was known of the extent of the new military defeat the Union had suffered. There was, in fact, precious little likelihood of an immediate reversal of non-intervention. Neither Palmerston nor the Tory leadership favoured a change of course. Lord Stanley, Derby's son and heir, considered mediation useless and premature. "If we want to protract the war – to stimulate the combatants to the utmost, let us talk of interfering to stop it," he remarked to Benjamin Disraeli, the party's spokesman in the Commons. Derby showed no signs of wavering in his general support of the government's decision to recognize Confederate belligerency and withhold full diplomatic recognition of the South. Nothing would be achieved without active interference in the conflict the leader of the opposition contended, and mediation was, as his son argued, utterly pointless because its rejection by the Union was certain.[9]

How could Britain act as a mediator and escape the acute moral embarrassment of aiding the establishment of a slave republic? Charles Sumner pointedly asked British friends. Where would they divide the Union? Would the slave republic include all the slave states or only the cotton states, or the cotton states and others? What would be the condition of slavery and would the free states be obligated to return fugitive slaves? The moral dilemma was exploited by Lyons, who insisted that only a request for mediation from both belligerents would warrant action. To act as Stoeckl had proposed and back an offer of mediation with a threat to recognize the Confederacy if it was refused would in the eyes of Northerners make mediation the equivalent of recognition. At the very least the Union would break off diplomatic relations, and worse might follow. The moment Britain was distracted by European problems, he had warned the ministers he met at Lady Marian's, the Union would "go against her." Indeed, diplomatic recognition would be a mere *brutum fulmen* unless it was so perfectly timed that it brought the war to an end. If the conflict continued, the North would discover that it had done them little harm, the South that it had done them little good, and the European states that it had cost them prestige and had earned them the hatred of the Union. The Civil War should be decided by the belligerents, and if it ended in disunion the North must not be allowed to claim that foreign nations were responsible. Knowing Mercier as well as he did, Lyons expected him to be in full cry for mediation and so urged Stuart not to give him any encouragement. If the Frenchman had a point it was that it would be useless to recognize the Confederacy except at a moment when that decision would end the conflict. Where he and Mercier were at odds was over the moment. He doubted it would ever come.[10]

Lyons had left Lady Marian Alford's home reassured that the Cabinet was not champing at the bit of intervention, but opinion was more fluid than he realized. The influential Clarendon, who had waited three years for Russell to fall flat on his face as foreign secretary, and would have been dismayed had he known he was to wait another three before regaining possession of the Foreign Office, admitted to Edmund Hammond that he hated Confederates almost as much as he did Federals. He hoped for a continuation of the war until complete exhaustion prevented the Americans from uniting against Britain. Then, when Russell submitted to Cabinet the draft of his reply to James Murray Mason's request in July for recognition of Confederate independence, several ministers led by Gladstone objected to it. The foreign secretary and Lyons had met for another weekend-long discussion, and the draft appeared to require Union recognition of the Confederacy before any action by

foreign powers. Although reflective of Lyons's opinion, the Cabinet critics considered it too restrictive and Mason was informed that Britain
would continue to wait but not indefinitely.[11]

William Gladstone, who liked to think of himself as a moral voice
in politics, deemed the conflict "foolish and wicked." Convinced by the
first Battle of Bull Run that the South could not be forcibly dragged back
into the Union, and contemptuous of Salmon Chase's management of
Union finances, he understood that the situation in the textile districts
was becoming "explosive." There had been unrest and protest by unemployed operatives, and Walter Bagehot of *The Economist* was urging hm
to speak out. A conversation with Henry Hotze had made an impression
on him, the Confederate propagandist justifying "the Confederate effort
at nation-building" by placing it "in the framework of nineteenth-cen-
tury revolution." Gladstone was attracted by the idea of joint mediation
with France and Russia, and was confident he had brought Palmerston
to his view. Certainly, on 8 August, Russell indicated to Stuart the government's willingness to take a look in October at the "disposition" of
the North. However, he admitted that if the Unionists were then determined to fight on it would be pointless to propose that they stop. Nevertheless, a majority of Cabinet ministers appeared to have concluded that
the Union was fast wearying of the war.[12]

Then came the reports of further Union military reverses culminating
in a second morale-shattering defeat at Bull Run. "Even you will I think
now agree," Stuart wrote somewhat presumptiously to Lyons, "that the
South has earned its recognition nobly." He enclosed a copy of his private
dispatch of the same date to Russell in which he reported that Mercier had
advised the French government that the time for mediation was fast approaching but had not quite arrived. What the French minister proposed
was that Thouvenel and Russell come to an understanding on a joint
course of action and quickly dispatch Lyons back to Washington with the
instructions. His unexpectedly early return, Mercier and Stuart agreed,
would prepare the American people for mediation. The chances of its acceptance would undoubtedly be improved by Russian involvement, but
Stuart thought they would be good if made at a favourable moment by
Britain and France alone. A crisis was fast approaching and a risk would
have to be incurred sooner or later, he added. Sooner suddenly appeared

to be the preference of Tories. On 5 August, in the final hours of the parliamentary session, Malmesbury raised the possibility of recognition or mediation in association with France and perhaps other powers. Russell responded that he desired the involvement of all the Great Powers in any representations and had faith in the "perfect discretion" of Lyons, who would be returning to Washington in early October.[13]

Towards the end of August Lyons retreated to Arundel for rest and relaxation in the company of Minna and her children. There was little danger of his being bothered, for the castle was rarely open to visitors. This the Austrian ambassador and one of the imperial archdukes discovered when they arrived unannounced and were turned away at the door. After a month Lyons did hear from Russell, who hinted at a possible change of policy. Mercier was again looking for an opportunity to offer mediation, the foreign secretary revealed, adding that "this time he is not so much out in his reckoning." Russell may have been influenced by a group of financiers, among them the Rothschilds. They deplored the bloodshed and the disruption of the Atlantic trade, and given the absence of a Union commitment to rid the nation of slavery they joined the ranks of those who questioned whether the conflict was a moral one. Russell was turning over in his mind the possibility of mediation leading to recognition of Confederate independence or of an armistice without mediation. Lyons went up to London on 1 October to meet with him, and they agreed he should delay his departure for the United States and spend the weekend of 18–19 October at Woburn Abbey. There they could talk matters over at some length shortly before what might prove a crucial Cabinet meeting.[14]

Much had happened since Lyons left the Republic. Robert E. Lee had led a Confederate army across the Potomac into Maryland, an invasion seen by Stuart as a decisive moment in the war. Were the Union to suffer yet another defeat it would surely be more receptive to a diplomatic proposal that promised to end the fighting. Stuart suggested that Lyons return to Washington with the discretionary authority, in concert with Mercier, to offer mediation. The choice of the right moment would be a heavy responsibility, but Stuart was confident that Lyons's "good judgment" would carry him through. The news that Lee had been repulsed did not cause him to rethink this recommendation. The Confederates had re-crossed the Potomac in good order with all their artillery and baggage trains, had captured Harper's Ferry, and had taken a number of prisoners and guns. This he reported on 19 September, and three days later Lincoln issued a preliminary Proclamation of Emancipation.[15]

When on 17 July Lincoln signed the Second Confiscation Act concerning rebel-owned slaves who escaped to Union lines or lived in Confederate territory that the Union recovered, he already had in hand a proclamation freeing all the slaves of the rebel South. It had been delayed, as Stuart was aware, by Seward, who had warned that after repeated Union military defeats it would be seen not as a great act of humanity but as the Union's "last *shriek,* on the retreat." With Lee's retreat from Maryland, Lincoln as commander-in-chief gave notice on 22 September of his intention as a military measure to declare free all slaves held in rebel states on New Year's Day, 1863. He realized that it might encourage not prevent foreign intervention to end the war, for any such measure had long been condemned in Britain, and by some Northerners, as an incitement to servile rebellion which would disrupt cotton production. Again on Seward's recommendation, Lincoln had added to the document a clause urging slaves to abstain from violence except in self-defence. The proclamation was also vulnerable to the criticism that it emancipated slaves where the Union could not free them and left them in bondage where they might have been liberated. Indeed, the administration found itself under attack by enemies on several fronts. Lincoln issued a second proclamation suspending the writ of habeas corpus "for anyone arrested or imprisoned by any military authority." This measure, conservative Democrats charged, provided for the incarceration of the "free white people of the North" who opposed the Emancipation Proclamation.[16]

The Confederates' retreat from Maryland dampened British hopes that the Union would soon recognize the war's futility while the Emancipation Proclamation delivered a heavy blow to Britons hostile to the North. Union nationalism had finally embraced the cause of freedom. Moreover, many Britons understood that Lincoln had been obliged to approach emancipation cautiously given popular opinion, the racial prejudice of his troops, and his own constitutional scruples. The fear remained that racial "calamities" would mark and mar this social revolution. *The Times* accused the Lincoln administration of organizing a series of Cawnpores, a reference to the massacre of British women and children during the Indian mutiny. There was much wild talk of "Santo Domingo massacres," and *Punch* depicted Lincoln playing his final card the Ace of Spades. Ironically, to one supporter, the president had described the Emancipation Proclamation as his last trump card.[17]

This was the background to the Cabinet ministers' debate on American policy. Should they adopt mediation and recognition of the South's independence as Mercier and Stuart had proposed? There was little likelihood of a consensus, for sitting at the table were Union sympathizers, advocates of diplomatic action to stem the bloodletting and ease the employment crisis in Lancashire, and a group whose attitude was best expressed in the adage "They who in quarrels interpose are sure to get a bloody nose." Thanks in large part to Lyons, ministers were aware of the danger of a conflict with the Union. The North would retaliate for intervention. Britain's embarrassments in Europe and the vulnerability of British North America would be exploited, Britain would lose its "most important trading partner" and probably much of its merchant marine. Bearing all of this in mind, Russell declared himself happy to wait and allow Lincoln to spend his recently raised 600,000 men before asking him to listen to reason. When the time came to act they should reaffirm Britain's neutrality and ensure that its troops in Canada were concentrated at defensible points. News of a second Bull Run had prompted a brief Palmerston flirtation with mediation but only on the condition that the Confederates pushed on to capture Washington and Baltimore. Lee's failed invasion of the North convinced him that it would be better to remain "lookers on." Russell did dally with the idea of proposing an armistice backed by an implied readiness to recognize the Confederacy if it was refused by the North, but he also had conditions in mind. He would act only if Russia, Austria, Italy, and France joined with Britain, and this was never a likely combination. Nor was there an enthusiastic public response to a speech by the chancellor of the exchequer, the most dogged ministerial interventionist.[18]

Gladstone set out for Tyneside on 4 October, having promised Palmerston to be discreet in his public comments. The prime minister had reason to be apprehensive. The chancellor was deeply affected by the suffering in the textile industries. He was providing employment for a number of men on his own estate, Hawarden, on the border of North Wales, and had arranged for women operatives to be trained for domestic service. Speaking at Newcastle on 7 October, he decided to open the public's eyes to the "facts." The Confederate leaders had made an army, were making a navy, and what was even more significant they had made a nation. Thus the separation of the Southern states from the Union was as certain as any future event could be. The press dismissed his assertions, the prime minister angrily complained that he had behaved as if he were the authorized "organ" of the government," and his public contradiction by a highly respected colleague exposed the Cabinet's divisions.[19]

Speaking in Hereford, Sir George Cornewall Lewis, the secretary of state for war, neatly reduced the government's options to the Lyons alternatives. They were strict neutrality or recognition of the Confederacy and war with the Union. Meanwhile, Russell was circulating among Cabinet ministers a lengthy memorandum and documents which revived the armistice proposal. On his way to Woburn Abbey for a final consultation with the foreign secretary before returning to Washington, Lyons called at Clumber, where he seems to have influenced the colonial secretary, whose dukedom bore the name of the town where Gladstone had delivered his unfortunate speech. Much to Russell's surprise, Newcastle did not support the armistice proposal. Premature action, he warned, echoing his recent house guest, would merely strengthen the North's resolve to fight on. By the time Lyons reached the Bedfords' mansion it is likely that Lewis's detailed response to the memorandum had arrived there. The Lincoln administration was so committed to reunion that it would never take a step towards Confederate independence, Lewis contended, and its rejection of an armistice would probably result at best in a severance of diplomatic relations. This would compel Britain to dispatch at great expense additional troops to Canada. Palmerston, an armistice skeptic, had been reminded by Derby of the Tories' opposition to a more interventionist policy. Even Russell had not changed his mind that the proposal's success would depend on the always-improbable collective support of France, Russia, Prussia, and Austria. Lyons had never made any secret of his grave doubts that the Russians would co-operate, and little assistance could be expected at this particular moment from Paris, where Thouvenel had been shuffled out of the foreign ministry and replaced by Edouard Drouyn de Lhuys. A former diplomat, a former foreign minister, a former ambassador to the court of St James's, he endorsed the cautious American policy of his predecessor. France had problems enough not only in Mexico but also in Italy, where the emperor could ill afford to take "French leave" of the pontiff, whose person and authority it was protecting.[20]

The well-advertised Cabinet differences over American policy, the absence of a solid partnership with France for which the deep and enduring suspicion of Napoleon provided one explanation, the unlikelihood of Russian association with any approach to the belligerents, and Stuart's most recent recommendation of no action until the results of the upcoming Congressional elections were known, persuaded Palmerston to cancel the special Cabinet meeting he had summoned to consider the American question. Lyons was relieved to be returning to Washington without instructions on armistice, mediation, or recognition. "I am quite satisfied with the course the government means to take with regard to American politics, which diminishes the annoyance of going back," he informed Minna, who did not mask her anguish at his departure. He assured her that he would seek to end his transatlantic mission just as soon as he could do so with credit and propriety.[21]

Before leaving the American capital for home, Lyons had invited his young staff to send him, during his absence, "personals," private letters on legation and social life. Ernest Clay, the son of the member of Parliament for the fishing town of Hull, wrote frequently, and his letters suggested the mission's genuine family atmosphere. He and Stuart were established very comfortably in Lyons's house, reading their chief's back numbers of the *Revue des Deux-Mondes*. Another bonus was the vacationing Mercier's generosity in loaning them his French cook, who each evening prepared appetizing "delicacies." Unfortunately, the depreciation of the paper currency fuelled inflation and the rate at which pounds were converted rarely kept pace. Prices were adjusted accordingly by tradesmen and even by the company that insured the house and its contents. Temperature inflation undoubtedly played a part in emptying the capital of its few remaining "ladies" – Clay made no reference to the legions of streetwalkers – which contributed to its "general air of dejectedness." The requisition of public buildings, including the Capitol, to house the wounded was a constant reminder of the demoralizing second defeat at Bull Run. Thankfully, the closing of barrooms and retail liquor stores by the local Federal commander prevented the able-bodied troops from drowning in drunken despair. Public works were continuing. An aqueduct was constructed to bring fresher water to the capital, additions were being made to the Treasury, War and Navy Departments, and the completion of the Capitol was again under way. What most impressed Clay was the opening of the street railway that ran down the middle of Pennsylvania Avenue from the Capitol to the State Department. By mid-August the streetcars were in full operation, ruining the hacks whose prices had always been "iniquitous" and throwing "a few more idle black men on the town." His chief's delight in these "Household Words" brought Clay a reward. Lyons selected him as the temporary manager of his household when Monson, who had sailed home with him months earlier, remained in Britain to sit his civil service examinations. His return was then delayed by the collapse of his health following a succession of family crises and deaths, though he put some of his time to good use hunting up excellent wine bargains. He forwarded *"Liebefraumilch"* [sic] at fifty shillings a case, confident Lyons would like it and that it would be popular in Washington, and arranged for claret to be shipped in bulk directly from Bordeaux. Finally, in Paris, he engaged a French cook for the legation.[22]

Lyons did have a young companion on his return voyage. He was Edward Malet, twenty-five, who over the next decade was to play a large role in the older man's life. Malet had, like Lyons himself, gained a foothold in the service as an unpaid attaché to his own father, Sir Alexander Malet, the British minister to the German Confederation. Transferred to Brussels in 1858, Malet had on passing the civil service examination two years later been raised to the ranks of the paid attachés. Sent first to the Argentine Confederation, he had quickly moved on to the Empire of Brazil and the court at Petropolis, where he amused himself and others by organizing amateur theatricals. The imminent return from extended leave of the British minister, whose reputation was that of a "beast" in his treatment of juniors, spurred the ambitious Malet to seek greener pastures. He accepted the proposal of the disgraced Brodie, who was still formally attached to the Washington legation, that they exchange posts. The dispatch of his soldier brother to Canada during the *Trent* crisis had increased greatly his interest in North America, and Washington was not only a far more interesting posting, but as the "most important mission next to the embassies" it would benefit his career.[23]

Similarities in their family and professional backgrounds, and of their personalities, saw Lyons and Malet develop the close and affectionate relationship of mentor and pupil. The older man undoubtedly saw something of himself in this young, quiet, self-contained gentleman. He appeared on introduction "to be 'rather stiff in manner' and something of 'a stickler for etiquette'" but possessed charm, was somewhat unconventional, a little over-imaginative, and had an "artistic temperament." He proved to be a diverting companion for a chief who expected his juniors to entertain and amuse him. Malet's enthusiasm for amateur theatricals ensured his ready acceptance by his new colleagues, and he possessed those basic attributes for which Lyons looked in young diplomats. He had a good hand for copying, was industrious, and his private life was "well-conducted."[24]

Lyons and Malet sailed for New York aboard the *Scotia* on 25 October. "We have no doubt," the press commented, that "the ability and discretion" of Lyons "will continue to stand the country in good stead, and that our intercourse with the President's government will remain as peaceful and uninterrupted as the best friends of England and America could wish." Very rough seas made the passage another vision of hell for Lyons. Even when they came in sight of New York they had to stand off for thirty-six hours because of a snowstorm. Finally able to disembark on 8 November, they found Clay waiting for them and remained in the city for three days perhaps to allow Lyons to recover his land legs and settle his stomach. He and his young companions reached Washington on the evening of 12 November. Malet was pleasantly surprised by the Americans he encountered. "The Yankees are exceedingly civil to us and treat us with the greatest kindness personally," he wrote home. "One has been told so often that they hate England that I suppose one should believe it but it makes their civility to individuals speak all the better for their manners." He found chancery life hectic and the workload heavy, for in the first two months he and his colleagues copied almost eighty dispatches. Yet such was the affection with which the staff regarded their chief, and the loyalty he inspired, that few complained. Clay later wrote to him: "There is little merit in doing the best one can for you, and that from the first to the last of the men I have served with under you, I do not think there has been one who would not do more work, and do it more cheerfully, for you than for any other Chief that can be found." Lyons continued to make legation life as pleasant as possible. Malet and his colleagues were invited to dine with him three or four times a week, and chief and juniors celebrated Christmas together in fine style, though Malet regretted that, Lyons being a bachelor, ladies did not call upon him. He did host large dinners to which "plenty of ladies" were invited.[25]

Charles Sumner welcomed Lyons back to his "great duty" of maintaining peace between the two nations. Another heartfelt greeting came from Governor General Monck, who shared Lyons's relief that no change of British policy was presently contemplated. This was proof, he observed, that the course pursued so far had been right and politic. As it happened, Lyons had been closely followed to Washington by a private letter from Russell. In it the foreign secretary described a French proposal received at the Foreign Office shortly after the *Scotia* sailed. Napoleon had outlined it to his old friend Malmesbury while they were both guests of the interior minister, Persigny, at his seventeenth-century chateau near Paris. The emperor, who once described the Comte de Persigny as the only genuine Bonapartist and thus insane, had been reminded by him of the deepening depression and swelling unemployment in the textile and export industries. These difficulties, well reported by the Paris press, represented an obvious threat to a regime that was a plebiscitary dictatorship. What Napoleon envisaged, having admitted his "very strong" Southern sympathies to Malmesbury, was a joint approach by France, Britain, and Russia to the American belligerents, urging an armistice of six months during which the blockade of the Confederacy would be lifted. Once the fighting ceased, Napoleon argued, it would be difficult if not impossible for either belligerent to resume it. But Malmesbury thought there was little chance of the Union accepting a suspension of hostilities so advantageous to the South.[26]

Russell's initial response to the emperor's proposal was one of skepticism, his Cabinet colleagues having so recently shown no interest in pressing for an armistice. Nor had he detected any evidence to support the emperor's optimism that both belligerents would accept it. On the contrary, preaching peace to them would be like "speaking to mad dogs." Nevertheless, when the Cabinet met on 11 November to consider the French proposal, Russell backed it. Stuart had suggested that a moderately and courteously worded Anglo-French proposal would, "after a certain amount of threats and howlings by the violent portion of the press, be favourably received by a majority of the Public." Perhaps even more influential was Mercier's information that Stoeckl was seeking "to bring about a French-Russian mediation with an aim to separate France from England." This reading of Russian intentions was one to which Lord Napier, now ambassador to Russia, gave some credibility. But Russell's inclination to work with France was a response also to the Democrats' successes in the Congressional elections, which had raised in Stuart's mind the possibility of a "relaxation in the conduct of the war." The foreign secretary had not forgotten Seward's casually brutal remark to Stuart that he expected a war of mutual extermination from which the Union would emerge victorious because of its vastly greater population. This "is the most horrible thing I ever heard," an appalled Russell commented. But on 11 November, despite half-hearted backing by Palmerston, and the full-hearted support of Gladstone and Lord Chancellor Westbury, he could not persuade the Cabinet to act. The government's diplomatic inaction, Malmesbury predicted, would "act unfavourably on the subscriptions for the distressed manufacturers." That the subscriptions were needed Cobden did not doubt. He estimated at £10 million the losses in wages of cotton operatives alone and calculated the employers' losses at much the same figure. He feared the distress would soon spread to other industries. You "cannot remove a great plank from the bottom of a vessel, without impeding the sailing powers of the whole ship," he remarked. If the war continued another year he feared the effects would be felt in every English household, and he remained convinced that the North's attempt to subjugate so vast a region as the slave South was "the most chimerical project that ever entered the mind of man."[27]

Russell, in his reply to the French foreign minister, did not exclude the possibility of some form of intervention at some future date, and this diplomatic gesture was appreciated in Paris. But his decision not to close the door on diplomatic action had been taken with an eye to the situation in Lancashire and Cheshire. When Seward protested the Europeans' discussion of American affairs without consulting the Federal government, Russell retorted that the distress in the two counties gave him reason enough to discuss them in Europe. Furthermore, Lincoln's preliminary proclamation might cause massive disruption of cotton production. Privately, Russell was keen to learn what the Democrats, who had done well in the Congressional elections, would do to promote the gradual and peaceful emancipation of the slaves. Their answer to this question might very well revive the idea of mediation, he believed. Lyons quickly scotched it.[28]

During his three days of recuperation in New York, Lyons had taken political soundings. They were based, he cautioned the foreign secretary, on discussions with several leading Democrats who were anticipating the return of constitutional government at least in New York. They could not believe that Federal authorities would now dare ignore or resist writs of habeas corpus. However, their confidence that Lincoln would seek to catch the breeze of electoral change by strengthening the moderate and conservative elements in the Cabinet was severely dented by his removal of the conservative McClellan not only from command of the army but also from military service. Another moderate and conservative figure who had lost influence was the secretary of state. Here was a "new difficulty to contend with in managing matters," Lyons grumbled. The source of his information was the welcoming Sumner, whose detestation of the secretary of state had been increased by Thurlow Weed's ill-advised advice to the people of Massachusetts not to return the "impracticable" Sumner to the Senate. But senatorial hostility to Seward was broadly based. The publication of his dispatches for the past year confirmed Radical Republicans in their belief that he had never recognized or welcomed the war's abolitionist character. The final straw for them was the humiliating and bloody repulse of yet another Union advance towards the Confederate capital. The defeat at Fredericksburg on 13 December was likened by Sumner to the British Crimean War catastrophe of the Charge of the Light Brigade but "on a much larger scale." There was a "terrible depression" across the North, and for this someone had to pay. With the covert assistance of secretary of the treasury Chase, the Republicans in the Senate sought to oust Seward and force Lincoln to reconstruct the Cabinet. Were Seward to be driven from office Lyons believed it would signal the triumph of Radical Republicans, who were willing to risk a foreign war in order to cling to power. They were deftly outmanoeuvred by the president, who in retaining both the loyal Seward and the disloyal Chase demonstrated anew his dexterity in the management of men. Seward's survival was an immense relief to Lyons. Their relations were "friendly and cordial," whereas any new secretary would almost certainly be less disposed to peace. "I should hardly have said this two years ago," he wryly admitted.[29]

Lyons did not think that an offer of "simple mediation" would cause serious diplomatic inconvenience, yet by the same token he could not see that it would do any good. If nothing followed a Union rejection they would have played a good card without making a trick. Indeed, he dealt Russell a full hand of objections to immediate action. Little was to be expected of the Democrats, for no matter their increased strength in Congress, the executive remained in Lincoln's hands at least until March 1865. The party's leaders opposed a "premature proposal of foreign intervention" out of fear that it would give the "Radical Party" the means of "reviving the violent war spirit." Timid on the subject of peace, they cried for war even more loudly than Republicans. They privately intimated that European recognition of Confederate independence, following a Union rejection of mediation, would be "disastrous to their moderate plan." It would undoubtedly be followed by a quarrel with the Union, Lyons continued to warn, yet it would be of no benefit to the South unless it was followed by "strong measures with regard to the blockade." In short, intervention "short of the use of force" would make matters worse. Britain had the security of Canada to consider, and the president's call in his message to Congress for the great canals of New York and Illinois to be enlarged carried in this context a warning. Armed vessels would be able to use the canals, thereby circumventing the Anglo-American agreement to restrict the naval forces on the Great Lakes.

Lyons held fast to his belief that the war's outcome should be decided by the belligerents themselves. Even those Democrats who acquiesced in European diplomatic intervention did so conditionally, he noted. His understanding of their position, as it had been explained to him in New York, was that they might look favourably on mediation "if it appeared to be the only means of putting a stop to the hostilities," and if Britain were not prominently involved. "The bitter portion of the draft would be the English portion, and the more it is diluted by a mixture of foreign elements the better," Lyons advised Russell. He would rather France mediated alone than France and Britain go ahead without Russia. The impressionable Stuart, whom he dispatched to New York to assess the political situation, reported violent abuse of president and Cabinet and a level of public despondency that battlefield victories alone could reverse. Yet the Democrats were still unwilling to take the lead in admitting the necessity of peace, and they continued to cling to the illusion that their return to power would bring the South voluntarily back into the Union. All of the while, Stuart claimed, the Proclamation of Emancipation was having so divisive an effect on popular opinion that come spring Lincoln would in all likelihood be compelled to grant an armistice. Here was another way in which the belligerents themselves might settle the Civil War.[30]

The Democrats would have difficulty taking a position on gradual and peaceable emancipation, Lyons explained to Russell, because "they repudiate the notion of the Federal Government having any right to deal with the question at all, and because they desire above all things to conciliate the South, which shrinks from all mention of interference" with slavery. This attitude he contrasted with that of the president, who in his message to Congress had proposed a compensated, gradual emancipation scheme. In the states that returned to the Union and agreed to liberate slaves by the beginning of the twentieth century owners would be compensated. Slaves freed by the chances of war would remain free. The Democrats' praise of this plan was in the opinion of Lyons merely a political tactic to allow them to charge Lincoln with inconsistency or to oblige him to withdraw what they termed the "Servile War Proclamation." However, if issued as promised at the beginning of the new year the proclamation would in his opinion prove to be a "very unsuccessful move for its authors." He expected it to unite the South and further divide the North. Where it did appear to be having a beneficial effect was overseas. Seward, who privately considered both proclamations – emancipation and the general suspension of habeas corpus – unfortunate, defended them publicly as proof that a Union triumph would end slavery. There was "no prospect of foreign intervention now," he confidently assured one senator on 22 January 1863. France and Britain were so jealous of each other that neither had any intention of interfering in the conflict. Even Stuart admitted that the definitive Proclamation of Emancipation, dated 1 January 1863, might bolster the ranks of Union sympathizers in Britain. More certain was the acute discomfort any British government would now experience if it aided Confederate independence. "If an attempt were made by the government in any way to commit us to the South," Cobden assured Sumner in mid-February, "a spirit would be instantly aroused which would drive our government from power." Recognition of the slave South as a nation was impossible unless the Union had done so first. This had long been the position of Lyons, who required that both sides request foreign mediation, and Russell now agreed with it. "I should like any thing better than being obliged to take the part of the Confederates," he admitted. This thought was undoubtedly in the back of his mind when he dismissed the Democrats as no better than the Republicans and on slavery much worse. He suspected that when Congress met they would make some move in favour of slavery, and dismissed as ridiculous their talk of restoring the Union. The war "must run its bloody course unchecked for some time to come," he wrote to Lyons on 24 January. Until both parties were "entirely tired and sick of the business," he could see "no use of talking of good offices." Should Mercier be keen to act, he accepted Lyons's advice to allow him to "have all the honour and glory of being the first."[31]

His residence in Georgetown having been destroyed by fire months earlier, Mercier had during Lyons's leave moved into an elegant house on H Street only a short distance from the British legation. But physical proximity brought no unity of minds on mediation. Lyons did not share the Frenchman's confidence that Northern public opinion could be rallied behind it. He did agree that an element of intimidation, "felt, if not seen," in the form of a threat to recognize the South would be needed to ensure the administration's acceptance but drew from this an entirely different conclusion. For Mercier it was a reason to act immediately whereas for Lyons it was the clinching argument for standing still unless there was a will "to make the consequences serious if it be rejected." This he knew his government did not have. The American public's antipathy towards Britain despite its refusal to support the French initiatives on an armistice and a temporary lifting of the blockade was acknowledged by Mercier. Stoeckl, who had received discretionary authority to back a renewal of the French proposal, agreed with Lyons that the present was "particularly unfavourable to an offer of mediation." What the Russian had in mind, whenever a more promising moment arrived, was nothing more than an offer to put the belligerents "into communication with each other." This Lyons dismissed as a waste of time. A successful mediation depended "upon military events" and the bringing of the conflict to an end "without the intervention of England." No settlement was possible that would not be galling to Northern pride, he constantly reminded the foreign secretary, and the "wounded self love" of exasperated Americans would see them round on Britain. Consequently, "the less conspicuous the part" Britain played the more quickly would irritation subside.[32]

Lyons watched calmly as Mercier, encouraged by the influential editor of the *New York Tribune*, Horace Greeley, approached Seward on 3 February 1863 with the futile proposal that, without an armistice, the Union "enter immediately into direct negotiation with the Confederate Government." Lyons viewed it as an exercise in French domestic politics, an effort by Napoleon as distress deepened in France's textile industries to show his people that he was "doing his best for them." Nevertheless, Lyons recognized the diplomatic benefit it might have for his own country. First, it promised to breed Union uneasiness about the intentions of the Europeans and make the administration more cautious about antagonizing foreign powers. Second, it would heighten American distrust of France. Union ire had already been aroused by the republication in Northern newspapers of the dispatches found in the French "Yellow Book," and the public's temper had not been improved by the reports of French troops on the march in Mexico. A government and people angry with France might find less fault with Britain.[33]

Spring brought three anniversaries, not one of which Lyons was inclined to celebrate. April marked his fourth year in the United States, the end of the second year of civil war, and his forty-sixth birthday. Middle age was leaving its characteristic mark upon him. The expansion of his girth was all the more evident because of his small stature. A photograph, taken by Matthew Brady, suggests a sober, stolid, and serious man, though eyes and mouth hint at a capacity for humour. Yet the face also hints at the toll, physical and psychological, that the stress of keeping relations with the Union on an even keel was taking. Lyons found some comfort in the evidence that Britain was a "shade less unpopular" largely because of the growing ill will towards France. There was little doubt at whom Sumner was principally taking aim with the resolutions he introduced in the Senate on the last day of February. They declared foreign interference in the war to suppress the rebellion an "unfriendly act," regretted the failure of foreign powers to inform the leaders of the rebellion that they were engaged in "hateful" work, and affirmed that the war would continue until the rebellion was suppressed. Lyons hoped that by the summer the fighting would languish if it did not end, convinced as he was that the mass of the people of the North were weary of war but were as yet unwilling to accept a peace which required acquiescence in Confederate independence. Given the popular mood, however, he doubted the Union's ability to replenish its military ranks by volunteers or even by conscription unless it began to enjoy success in the crucial eastern theatre of military operations.[34]

CHAPTER NINE

Marking Time

Lyons was increasingly afflicted by severe headaches caused by the nerve-wracking tension. It was clear by the spring of 1863, however, that European intervention to halt the Civil War was highly unlikely, and for this an embittered South held Britain responsible. The London Emancipation Society and its provincial affiliates were staging impressive meetings of support for the Union as freedom's standard bearer. This campaign seemed certain to have a political effect as did the redefinition of Confederate nationalism to embrace slavery as a basis of social stability and a source of "peculiar strength." The Union, Russell stated in Parliament on 23 March 1863, would regard British recognition of the Confederacy as an unfriendly act. The belligerents, he added, paraphrasing Lyons, should be left to settle the conflict themselves. Neither the ongoing distress nor occasional disturbances in the textile towns excited serious talk of intervention as the means of obtaining cotton.[1]

Europe's political turmoil was briefly a greater concern than the American war. The Russians had responded brutally to the revolt by the Poles, and the problem was "burning," Russell wrote to Lyons on 7 March. He had quickly voiced moral support for the insurgents, and Palmerston, having doffed his hat to Czar Alexander II as the emancipator of Russia's serfs and a ruler keen to improve the condition of his Polish subjects, damned the "*barbarous*" conduct of the Russian authorities and censured the Prussians for their willingness to co-operate with them. One listener thought the speech "must raise the House of Commons in the estimation of the world," but, as *The Times* reminded its readers, words were not action and amounted to little more than a "well meant but fruitless protest." Nobody in Britain believed the Poles capable of self-government, Cobden assured Sumner, but their insurrection was diplomatically helpful to the Union. So also was the sudden flaring into flame of the dispute which had been smouldering for some time between Denmark and Prussia over the duchies of Schleswig and Holstein. Austria, as a German power, joined Prussia in remonstrating against the Danes' decision to integrate Schleswig into the state. As tension mounted the question asked was which side Britain would support. The Prince of Wales married Princess Alexandra of Denmark on 10 March, and Britain soon placed her younger brother on the vacant Greek throne. Queen Victoria, on the other hand, was stoutly pro-German. She was the widow of a German prince and their eldest daughter had married the crown prince of Prussia. While the government's position was far from clear, the Conservative opposition demanded that Denmark be protected from Prussian aggression.[2]

The knowledge that Britain was unlikely to meddle in the American conflict was likely to make Seward more difficult to deal with, Lyons fancied. What made this possibility so unwelcome was the lengthening list of problems which might entangle the two nations in confrontations. The escape of the Confederate commerce raider *Alabama* from Liverpool, and its roaming the seas armed with British guns and crewed by British seamen, to burn, sink, and destroy the vessels of a friendly nation, were a "scandal & a reproach," sufficient "to *rile* a more temperate nation," Russell privately admitted. Lyons repeatedly reported the growing "exasperation against England on account of the proceedings of the 'Alabama' and still more on account of the fleet of new vessels for the Confederates." Seward sent his friend William Evarts, "a lawyer of great eminence," to London to assist the American legation in its efforts to persuade the British to seize suspect vessels. The danger was of an angry Union overreaching in its response by reviving legislation to authorize letters of marque. When Lincoln signed such a law early in March, Seward informed Lyons and Charles Francis Adams assured Russell that

Union privateers would only hunt Confederate commerce raiders. But would their captains resist the temptation to target blockade runners? They would be easy pickings and rich prizes.[3]

Unionists bitterly resented British blockade running and had little difficulty convincing themselves that it enabled the Confederacy to arm, clothe, and feed its troops. The Union navy had tripled in size by the fall of 1862 with one-third of its 266 ships assigned to blockade duty. One measure of their success, and of the volume of trade, was the 141 blockade runners sold at auction in New York during the first two years of war. Lincoln's irascible secretary of the navy, Gideon Welles, a forbidding figure, noted in April that 200 vessels were sitting off the mouth of the Rio Grande whereas before the war it had been rare for half a dozen to be there at any one time. Their papers invariably named the neutral Mexican port of Matamoros as their destination, but just across the river stood the Confederate town of Brownsville. Another booming entrepôt of trade was the British colony of the Bahamas, whose colonial government was accused by the "highly excitable" American consul of stretching the letter of neutrality to the very limits in favour of the South. The governor, whose support of the first Palmerston government as a journalist for *The Times* had seen him rewarded first with a consulship in Mauritius and later with the governorship, dismissed his critic as a "drunken maniac" and a "nervous dyspeptic." He called for him to be replaced by a "man of experience, tact, good temper, good breeding, shrewdness and sagacity." These were not the attributes associated with the commander of the American naval squadron. Charles Wilkes intimidated traders by hovering outside the port of Nassau, which had become a focal point of the blockade runners because of its relative proximity to the coast of the South. He and his officers next turned their attention to St Thomas, in the Virgin Islands, where again by "means both fair and foul" they disrupted the thriving trade with Matamoros. The interception and seizure of the *Peterhoff*, a British vessel ostensibly travelling between these two neutral ports, sparked a highly charged parliamentary debate in Britain. Newspapers raised the spectre of war, stocks slumped, and maritime insurance rates rose dramatically.[4]

To calm the "insane fury" on the American side of the Atlantic, Lyons stressed the need for action to halt the construction of Confederate vessels in British yards and to prevent the escape of any ready to sail. On 4 April the foreign secretary ordered the detention of the *Alexandra*. Although a bizarre interpretation of the Foreign Enlistment Act by the presiding judge when the case went to trial saw him issue an order for the vessel's release, a bill of exceptions ensured its continued detention. This decision convinced Evarts of Britain's good faith, and Cobden drove home the point in his correspondence with Sumner. Britain had been "the only obstacle to what would have been almost a European recognition of the South," he wrote, for had it agreed to joint action with France they would have been followed by much of the Continent. On the issue driving many Britons to "insane fury," the licensing of privateers, Russell looked to Lyons and his "great influence with Seward" to prevent a crisis from developing. Gideon Welles, scornful of the secretary of state's "constant trepidation" of trouble with Britain, respected the "cool and sagacious" British minister, who appeared able to induce Seward to yield "almost everything." Hence Lyons's dismay when he suddenly found himself in danger of losing the personal goodwill he had worked so hard to earn. Russell had approved the publication in the Blue Book of dispatches in which Lyons had failed to express "blind confidence" in the complete restoration of the Union. Equally unfortunate was the disclosure of his conversations with New York Democrats, for they were men whose loyalty many Republicans questioned. His vexation was shared by the Queen, who pointedly asked why dispatches were published that were certain to have a prejudicial effect on a minister's position. Russell's reply was the familiar and feeble one that the Foreign Office had an obligation to keep members of Parliament fully informed of the conduct of the government and its diplomatic agents. The news that Palmerston had appointed the Marquis of Hartington, heir to the Devonshire dukedom and the member for one of the family's parliamentary seats, to a junior office only added to Lyons's troubles. Hartington, during a recent visit to the United States, had infuriated Unionists by attending a New York ball with a "secesh badge in his button-hole."[5]

While holding fast to the belief "that the best safeguard against an attack from the Americans is firmness at resisting them at the outset," Lyons deplored unnecessary irritation of their "ever-sensitive vanity." Determined to prevent "disagreeable questions" from developing into serious disputes, he returned in his private correspondence with Russell to the subject of the construction and fitting out in British shipyards of vessels for the Confederacy. If there was to be an American quarrel, he observed with some asperity, the Foreign Office would do well to find some "better ground" on which to make a stand than the government's inability or failure to enforce the Foreign Enlistment Act. The American threat to retaliate by licensing privateers, the prospect of being presented with bills for the damage done to the American merchant marine by British-built commerce raiders, and the realization that inaction would establish a dangerous precedent for Britain as a naval power, concentrated minds in London. The detention of the *Alexandra* and the assumption that the pair of powerful ironclad rams being built at Birkenhead would not be permitted to sail if evidence were found that they were intended for Confederate service promised to rescue Britain, at least temporarily, from that embarrassment. This encouraging news, along with the calm and insistent warnings issued by Lyons of the danger of a collision should "lawless adventurers intent only on plunder" interfere with legitimate British commerce, led to the decision not to issue letters of marque. Both president and secretary of state desired "to keep on terms of peace with England," while Welles and Sumner were opposed to a resort to privateering. Lyons, learning of the decision on the eve of his forty-sixth birthday, welcomed the present.[6]

Having quickly regained Seward's good opinion, Lyons lost no time raising another highly sensitive issue, the manner in which the blockade was being enforced. He told the secretary of state that a few more *Peterhoffs* might rouse among his fellow countrymen feelings more dangerous to peace than the "ebullitions of anger here which rise and fall with equal speed." He took care to ensure that British naval commanders were ordered to deal calmly and carefully with their American counterparts. "They are rather prone to be suspicious of us these days, and therefore unusual circumspection is necessary," he wrote to one captain, but "they are almost always courteous if properly approached." The conciliatory Milne understood the annoyance of Welles when he read reports of British steamers loaded with contraband sitting in neutral ports waiting for a favourable opportunity to run the blockade. The admiral instructed his officers "to abstain from any act likely to involve England in hostilities" and was quick to reprimand any who commented on the right of blockade or criticized its effectiveness. His patience was sorely tried, however, by aggressive American captains who detained British steamers without reference to their cargoes or ports of destination, fired into British merchantmen, and even on occasion put a shot across the bows of British men-of-war. This "exceedingly outrageous" conduct, he warned, was an affront to the world's mightiest naval power and might provoke the unwanted confrontation.[7]

Intent on keeping open to the very last minute a door to "spontaneous" American action to lessen the irritation of the blockade, Lyons made no demands and refrained from "embarrassing observations." He was constructing a "golden bridge" across which the Americans might retreat from their "national vanity" with composure and without loss of dignity. He pointed out to Seward the diplomatic benefit of taking corrective steps before strong foreign remonstrances were made and persuaded him to return unopened the mail bag found aboard the *Peterhoff*. Welles secretly admired this success, though it also infuriated him. The bag might have revealed evidence of the detained vessel's illegal activities. Ironically, the Palmerston government had belatedly concluded that Britain's future interests as a maritime belligerent would be better served if the right to open seized mail bags was established. Another American concession to Britain was the removal of Wilkes from the West Indies. Welles in this instance was only too happy to oblige her, having wearied of this egotistical, "eccentric, impulsive, opinionated, somewhat arbitrary" officer who was "disinclined to obey orders" and had failed in his primary mission, which was to capture the *Alabama*.[8]

A further British gain was the reaffirmation, which Lyons extracted from the secretary of state, of what had long been the American rule that the goods of neutrals not contraband of war were exempt from confiscation whether carried by "a neutral or disloyal vessel." Seward's assurances would have been more reassuring had the instructions on how to enforce the blockade not been "set at naught" by many of the recipients. At the urging of Lyons, and the direction of the president, "additional instructions and of a more explicit character" were issued. The language, Welles angrily observed, was almost identical to that used by Lyons, who was shaping blockade policy to a "mortifying extent."

Too much was being conceded to the British minister, he groused. He learned that the president wished to bolster the Palmerston ministry, which had recently beaten back another ill-conceived parliamentary charge towards recognition of the Confederacy. It had been led by an eccentric Radical, John Roebuck, a vituperative critic of the "insolent and overbearing" conduct of the Union on the high seas.[9]

Even though the storms over commerce raiders, privateers, and the rules of blockade showed signs of abating, Lyons was unable to relax. Everybody who got into trouble, he moaned, suddenly discovered he or she was a British subject and wrote to him as if he were "the United States Government, or at any rate had at hand the means of engaging immediately in war against the United States with superior forces" and obtaining a settlement of all their demands. Extraordinary measures, especially the suspension of habeas corpus, were in his opinion bringing about a "total change of the system of government." Appalled by the evidence that the common law principle of an accused's innocence until proven guilty had in cases of military arrests been stood on its head, Lyons created a procedure for handling the appeals of British subjects who claimed to have been coerced into military service or imprisoned for refusing to enlist. The aggrieved were to apply for assistance to the closest British consul, and if he was unable to obtain a satisfactory result the case was to be referred to Lyons, who would take it up with the Federal government and if necessary pass it on to the Foreign Office. In the Confederacy, where anti-British sentiment was more intense and the treatment of British subjects often extremely unpleasant, consuls were far fewer in number and Lyons was virtually powerless. Communication by him with the Southern consuls excited suspicion in the North and was denounced in the South as offensive. He had lost the valued if unofficial services of Robert Bunch in February, when he and his family had been carried to safety by a British warship on the eve of an expected Federal attack on Charleston. When Lyons summarily dismissed the consul at Mobile for allowing shipment on a British man-of-war of Confederate specie believed to be the payment for British munitions, the Confederate secretary of state retaliated by revoking the exequatur of consul Moore in Richmond. Then, learning of the failure of the Roebuck motion, he dismissed the remaining British consuls and formally withdrew James Murray Mason as Confederate commissioner in Britain.[10]

Conscription, which had become law on 1 March 1863, caused Lyons to be "beset with terrified British subjects" and he admitted that those of them who had declared an intention to become naturalized, or had voted in an election, had reason to be afraid. For those who had made a declaration but not completed the formalities of naturalization, he obtained a temporary period of grace during which they were permitted to return home. This concession persuaded Lyons of the Federal government's desire to behave "fairly towards aliens in the Draft," a judgment which much to his irritation many a British subject assailed. "I have given myself a world of trouble to make the burthen of proving their exemption as light as possible," he protested, and his resentment of their "ingratitude" found release in the blunt notice he gave those who had freely enlisted that by doing so they had forfeited his protection.[11]

Claims for exemption from conscription promised to increase exponentially in late June, when Robert E. Lee again led his troops into the North, perhaps in hopes that a victory would spur foreign recognition of the Confederacy. Lyons considered the advance into Pennsylvania a "perilous move," and he was proven correct when it came to a bloody halt at Gettysburg on 3 July. Additional good Union news came from the west, where victories at Vicksburg and Port Hudson had given the Federals complete control of the vital Mississippi. But Lincoln's decision now to commence the military draft sparked four days of savage and destructive rioting in New York City. The violence was strongly coloured with racism. Lincoln's recent commitment to organize black regiments had been welcomed in many parts of the North but had brought threats of retaliation from the South. White officers who commanded these regiments were threatened with execution on capture and the rank and file with enslavement. The Union countered with a threat to execute Confederate prisoners of war in retaliation. These were fresh examples, a grim Lyons observed, of the conflict's descent into a ferocity that did not respect "the usages of civilized warfare." Fugitive slaves who escaped to freedom behind Union lines would, he believed, be sacrificed without scruple if the belligerents came to an understanding. So he made plans to get as many of them as possible to safety in Britain's nearby territories only for this good intention to be checked by the concern that it would lead to trouble with the Americans. But his fear for their safety was not illusory, as New York's murderous rioters proved. Although blacks were a minuscule proportion of the city's population, racial enmity had been inflamed during the summer by the use of black men to replace striking Irish dockers and by rumours of whites being discharged from the Brooklyn Navy Yard to permit the employment of freed blacks. Even black British seamen were not safe on board their ships, and until the arrival of the British man-of-war ordered there by Lyons they were obliged to seek refuge on a French warship.[12]

Lyons had not wished to return to Washington at the end of his leave, but fear of jeopardizing career and pension had deterred him from revealing this. A succession of colds and "atrocious" January weather had discouraged him from venturing out for exercise and fresh air, and with the arrival of spring, heat and dust became the deterrents. Increasingly, he was compelled to undertake humdrum legation work. The head of chancery, Percy Anderson, was suffering from an inflammation of the eyes, which for more than three months prevented him from either reading or writing. Three of the legation's staff were in England preparing for their civil service examinations, and without at least two replacements he would "break down," he informed the Foreign Office. The arrival of a pair in April raised his hopes of getting through the summer, and with the expected return of Monson and Frederick Warre the total would be raised to ten. But neither of the pair planned to return to the "inferno on earth." They had been yearning for a war with the United States, Warre only half-jokingly wrote, for they shuddered at the prospect of another tour of duty in the American capital. Monson decided to enter political life by standing for Parliament in the next general election, scheduled for 1865, and so secured a more convenient posting in Germany. In a touching parting, he wrote to Lyons: "No one can ever feel more devotion for you, nor greater desire to please you, than I have always felt. From the first you have treated me with confidence and consideration which won all my regard, as much as did the spectacle of all your ability my respect and admiration. I have learned to look upon you as a true friend." This heartfelt tribute was further proof of Lyons's ability to win the affection and loyalty of his young charges.[13]

The heat and humidity of the "inferno" kept Lyons from sleeping well, depleting his energy and stamina. Russell recommended a voyage to Halifax to consult Milne followed by a visit to Canada or an American watering place. But Lyons felt he could not leave Washington until Stuart came back from a shooting expedition to the west, where he had to be satisfied with wild turkeys instead of the buffalo he had hoped to slaughter. Even when the refreshed and reinvigorated Stuart returned, Lyons did not immediately slip away. He considered himself duty bound to await the outcome of Lee's invasion of Pennsylvania and was reluctant to leave the capital without Russell's authorization to travel north on "public service." The thought of any of his time in the United States failing to count towards his pension was intolerable.[14]

He planned for his absence from the capital to coincide with Seward's summer vacation, only to be surprised when the secretary of state insisted "pertinaciously" on taking him and a group of fellow diplomats on a scenic tour of his home state. Seward's purpose was to impress them with the resilience and strength of the North, and Lyons agreed to join an expedition he expected to be more fatiguing than pleasurable because the host deserved his consideration. He doubted Britain would have managed to keep the peace without Seward and arranged to remain in touch with Stuart, whom he ordered to consult him on all important matters. Lyons was accompanied by the recovered Anderson, a pair of young attachés, one of them George Sheffield, and two servants. In New York, he and his small party joined their guide and the other diplomats, and Lyons quickly realized that this would be an enjoyable experience. They advanced via the historic spa village of Sharon Springs, where Thurlow Weed had a summer retreat, to Cooperstown, the home of James Fenimore Cooper, then to Trenton Falls, which Lyons described as the "most picturesque" in the country, and from there to Seward's hometown of Auburn. Its two institutions of greatest interest were the theological seminary and the prison, the latter's inventive staff having recently improvised a "water cure" to discipline unruly prisoners. The final stop was Niagara Falls, where three years earlier Lyons had watched "The Great Blondin" cross the rapids on a tightrope 1,100 feet long and 160 feet above the water. Seward and his guests spent the weekend of 22 and 23 August at the Cataract House Hotel on the American side of the Falls, whose thunderous roar was no lullaby. There, Lyons parted from them. The journey had increased his liking of Seward and it had agreed with him physically. He was feeling well, had enjoyed the countryside, and welcomed the return to British territory. "The curiosity of the Americans is a little fatiguing," he allowed, "but they are essentially so kind and hospitable that one cannot complain."[15]

Happy "to be with his own people" again, Lyons and his companions spent two nights at the port city of Hamilton at the western end of Lake Ontario and were provided with a special rail carriage for the onward journey of no great distance to Toronto. After a night at the Queen's Hotel, Lyons and the attachés, minus Anderson, who had returned to Washington, continued by train to Kingston, which the presence of the Orange Order had prevented him from visiting in 1861. At Montreal they passed a relaxed weekend in the company of several of the Guards officers who from time to time had visited Washington and on 31 August boarded the morning train for Quebec City. After a brief visit with the Moncks, they sailed on the comfortable steamer which the governor general had placed at their disposal for a trip downriver to the Saguenay, "the only place of consequence in Canada" that Lyons had not seen on his previous visit. Unfortunately the St Lawrence was so rough on the first day that almost everyone was sick, another instance of misery loving company. The two following days were far more enjoyable, yet Lyons, perhaps because he was still suffering the after-effects of the previous day's torment, was no more than modestly impressed with the natural beauty. The scenery was very fine, he granted, but not so fine or "peculiar" to justify a long journey merely to see it. But the trip to Canada had been useful in that he and Monck had laid the foundations of an excellent relationship. On a special train provided by the Grand Trunk Railway, he set off for Rivière-du-Loup, from where he travelled by coach in four easy stages to the capital of New Brunswick. The roads were tolerable, the inns by no means uncomfortable, and the scenery "sufficiently pretty and characteristic to make the journey pleasant." The lieutenant-governor, Arthur Gordon, who came to meet him, was a nephew of his one-time mentor the late Sir Robert.[16]

During his brief stay in Fredericton Lyons declined invitations to dinners at which speeches might be given, for in a region of British North

America where Confederate sympathizers were believed to be numerous he had reason to be apprehensive of remarks that would cause him embarrassment in Washington. On 22 September he travelled down to the colony's major port of St John to await the warship that Milne had assigned to ferry him to Portland, Maine. He sailed three days later on HMS *Medea*, another appropriately named transport for a man who had begun his career in Greece, and happily the passage across the Bay of Fundy was "tolerably smooth." He took the train to Boston, where he stopped only briefly. In New York City he dined with the Archibald family and then with the shipping magnate Sir Samuel Cunard. Quickly tiring of hotel living, even though he was staying at Brevoort House with its very modern conveniences, and finding little diversion in the theatre or pleasure in the local sights, he left on 8 October for Philadelphia, where he was joined by Sir Alexander Milne and a pair of his staff officers. Lyons ordered legation staff by telegraph to prepare "first rate dinner for twelve" for the following evening, a "great dinner" on Saturday evening, and a third meal for as many as fourteen on Sunday. At his dinners, Lyons boasted, "the eating and drinking parts are excellent" for his French cook was the best if not "the only good cook in America."[17]

With Seward as an escort, Lyons and Milne visited the Navy Department on Saturday to introduce the admiral to the secretary. At the great dinner that evening, attended by Seward, Attorney General Bates, and a clutch of foreign diplomats, Lyons thoughtfully sat Milne beside Welles. "The whole was well-timed and judiciously got up for the occasion, and with a purpose," the American admiringly noted. He was impressed with Milne's physical presence, for he was "tall – six feet two – strongly built, not fleshly yet not spare, – a good physique in every respect," and proved a captivating conversationalist. By way of an appetizer, Milne briefly commented on his own efforts "to preserve harmony and good feeling, and [to] prevent, as far as possible, irritation and vexatious questions between us," and then heaped dollops of praise on Welles's plate for the secretary's management of the blockade and administration of naval affairs. They were swiftly consumed. Then, on Monday evening, Lyons, Milne, and Welles were guests at Seward's home. He introduced to them his house guest the actress Charlotte Cushman, with whom Lyons had become acquainted at Rome. She and the Seward family were invited to dine at the legation a week later, and Lyons had a "delightful time" reminiscing with her about Rome. No doubt he attended her benefit performance as Lady Macbeth at Grover's Theatre, as did the Lincolns and the Sewards. Her same-sex amatory relationships outraged Stuart, who privately grumbled that he and Lyons had acted as good Samaritans to a woman who provided another reason to rejoin the "Misogymist [sic] Society." Amid this diverting company Lyons admitted to feeling very well. His "holiday" had been restful and recuperative, his "personal acquaintance" of Monck and Gordon was sure to prove "advantageous and satisfactory with regard to the public service," while Milne's visit to Washington had been an unqualified success. Even the weather co-operated, but Lyons's optimism about the state of his health quickly faded.[18]

His spirits drooped with the departure of several of the men with whom he had lived and worked closely. William Stuart left for home in late October with every intention of never returning. Percy Anderson soon followed, much to his chief's regret, having been "very much more than merely an efficient head of chancery." A grateful Anderson declared that he never expected again to be a member of such a "happy, jovial, family party." Another loss was Ernest Clay, who in Monson's absence had been acting as Lyons's private secretary, and Lyons missed him greatly and not least for his society. When Clay wrote early in the new year to inform Lyons of his impending marriage, he apologized for "falling away so from the traditions of the legation," aware as he was of Lyons's belief that a woman would be a "firebrand" in the happy male family. To his immense relief he received a handsome wedding gift. Lyons was soon to learn, however, that Stuart, who had secured the post of secretary of embassy at Constantinople, was to be replaced by a nephew of the legendary Scottish maverick Radical Joseph Hume. This family connection, Earl Russell assumed, would make J. Hume Burnley particularly acceptable to Americans. But Burnley had a wife, "which is a horrible thing to me," Lyons moaned. His hope that she would be good enough to remain at home was quickly dashed, leaving him with the even fainter hope that she would avoid involving the legation staff in "incessant quarrels." While plainly no misogynist, Lyons was not entirely free of the taint.[19]

He cobbled together a functioning legation from what remained of his staff. He named Edward Malet, who had "plenty of ability" if little experience in the management of business, as a temporary head of the chancery. The Foreign Office "must" therefore be patient, he told Edmund Hammond, "if *things* don't go on correctly at first." He installed George Sheffield, a younger son of the recently deceased Sir Robert Sheffield, as his private secretary. The family had ducal connections, and thus Sheffield had the social attributes required for membership in the profession. Handsome and boyish, he looked a full decade younger than his twenty-seven years. Another misogynist, he welcomed Lyons's desire for an exclusively male establishment and had proven during the recent tour to be "remarkably pleasant and attentive & very companionable." He was a gifted anecdotist and an unparalleled teller of "delightful stories." Lyons pronounced him a "very good private secretary."[20]

A loss for whom there was no immediate and reassuring replacement was Henri Mercier, who announced he would sail for home at the end of the year. He was "very agreeable and has been a very good Colleague to me," Lyons acknowledged. "He won't come back if he can possibly help it." Mercier's departure, following so hard on the heels of that of the members of the legation staff with whom he had been most comfortable, made Lyons "more than ever weary" of his "exile to this place." The Frenchman had been essential to the "strict concert" which had, Lyons still believed, deterred the Americans from carrying their anger at Britain to extremes. Would it survive his departure? This was a serious even vital question with the development of problems that were more exclusively Anglo-American.[21]

Charles Sumner had, to the dismay of British friends, delivered a blistering attack on British policy at New York's Cooper Institute on 10 September while Lyons was in British North America. Was it politic, Cobden asked the American, "to array us in hostile attitudes just at the moment when the hopes of the South were mainly founded on the prospect of a rupture between yourselves and Europe"? Lyons was so "disappointed and disgusted" by the remarks that his relationship with the chairman of the Foreign Relations Committee was damaged beyond full repair. An angry Russell responded to the senator's "vile" misrepresentation of his conduct before a hastily assembled and no doubt mystified audience of Highland crofters. He defended British neutrality, his recent detention of the powerful ironclad rams nearing completion across the Mersey from Liverpool, and announced that the Foreign Enlistment Act would, if necessary, be amended. Stuart had informed the State Department more than a week earlier of the decision to prevent the departure of the rams but he had cautioned that there might be difficulty obtaining the legal proof of their Confederate ownership. Liverpool was a port "specially addicted to Southern proclivities, foreign slave trade & domestic bribery," so it was late October before the rams were formally detained. Even then, lingering legal doubts of the validity of the decision saw them purchased by the government for the Royal Navy.[22]

Lyons found himself facing a full meal of problems at a time when he had lost his appetite. The correspondence for a single year filled sixty large folio volumes."The work here is more wearisome than ever," he wrote to Odo Russell in Rome, "and as time goes on the sharp edge of one's interest in things wears off." To Odo's uncle at the Foreign Office he declared that he had as much diplomatic business as he could manage. "The correspondence with Mr. Seward, which requires minute care in many cases, grows more and more burdensome," he explained. There were the multiplying appeals from British subjects for his protection, among them the crews of seized blockade runners, and disturbing reports of Confederate agents using Canada as a base from which to launch attacks on the Union. Their clear intent was to embroil the province with the Union, but on this topic Lyons was somewhat hamstrung in his dealings with Seward. He was expected to protect the identity of informants and respect Monck's aversion to creating the impression that he enjoyed an "extraordinary intimacy with Washington." That would rile the many Canadians who sympathized already with the South, the governor general warned, and perhaps goad them into co-operating with the Confederacy's agents. His quiet ordering of Canadian confidential agents to investigate Confederate activity, his dispatch of troops to the border town where the Southerners were most heavily gathered, and a personal visit to Buffalo by the province's premier to discuss the problem with the local American authorities dampened these embers.[23]

Another fire quickly flared up with the arrest in November of the American consul general, Joshua Giddings. He had made himself deeply unpopular by his abrasive manner and suspected involvement in the recruitment of Canadians to serve in the Union armies. Charged with complicity in the kidnapping and false arrest of a British subject, he was saved from extended detention by a pair of Canadian friends who put up his bail and by a medical diagnosis of a serious heart condition. Knowing Giddings to be an influential Republican, Lyons asked Monck to intervene. The case was dropped. Already another serious incident had taken place. Southern passengers aboard a Union coastal steamer, the *Chesapeake*, had seized control of the vessel and sailed it into British waters. A Union warship had then entered those waters, retaken the *Chesapeake*, and put into Halifax where the locals made plain their Southern sympathies. Lyons painstakingly explained to the colonial authorities the importance of behaving as good neighbours of the Union. The Reciprocity Treaty would be up for renewal before long, he reminded them.[24]

The rash of incidents did focus hostile American attention on the treaty. Early in the new year, Senator Justin Morrill, who had given his name to the protective tariff of 1861, introduced a resolution that looked to give Britain notice of the treaty's termination. Lyons followed Seward's advice on how to respond. He recommended silence to the Canadians and advised them to send someone to Washington to lobby the Cabinet and Congress. At the same time, he was insistent that the Canadian who came did not presume to advise him. That would amount to precedent-setting colonial diplomacy, he told Monck, for which there would be time when Canadian ministers provided themselves with an army and a navy. He did work closely and effectively, however, with the able Canadian agent John Young, who played his part "very judiciously" by urging the Canadian government to establish an Anglo-American commission to investigate possible changes to the treaty.[25]

Looking further into the future, Lyons was uneasy over the rapid growth in the military and naval strength of the United States. It would be worthwhile, he advised the foreign secretary, to keep a close eye on what was happening. The Union might not be preparing for an early quarrel with Britain but the better prepared Britain was for the possibility the safer it would be. Russell arranged for the dispatch of military and naval investigators to the North, and they confirmed Lyons's impression that the Americans were "seriously preparing for a foreign war" and that Britain would be the target of choice if it could be waged "with tolerable safety." The Americans, Lyons warned, believed they could throw overwhelming force into Canada, attack Bermuda and the Bahamas, and inflict enormous injury to British commerce. Their animosity towards Britain was in his opinion "utterly unreasonable and utterly regardless of facts or arguments," but it could not be ignored, and he withdrew his earlier objection to the appointment of naval and military attachés. They were to keep London so well "informed of the state of preparation, and of the position of the Naval and Military Forces of the United States, that if war were to break out at a moment's notice, our Admiralty and War Office would know exactly what to do." Ironically, Russell was at this very moment foreshadowing what came to be called the "special relationship." He recommended that Lyons go on "quietly" with Seward, for "violent demonstrations of friendship" might turn sour if there was a thunderstorm. "But I am more and more persuaded," he confessed, "that amongst the Powers with whose Ministers I pass my time there is none with whom our relations ought to be so frank and cordial as the United States."[26]

Russell could not believe that the Union would cavalierly add to its massive debt by quarrelling with Britain. That did not preclude "a great deal of buncombe" during the presidential and Congressional elections to take place in 1864, but he anticipated no greater abuse than usual of Britain. Moreover, Britain had grievances of its own: the imprisonment of the crews of blockade runners, which was contrary to the Law of Nations; the enticing of British subjects into the Union armies with whisky; and violations of the treaty obligations governing trade between Nassau and New York. Of course, none of the grievances were to be pressed to the point of a quarrel. Russell was too preoccupied with the crisis over Schleswig-Holstein to write often to Lyons, although he appeared confident in February 1864 that the dispute would be resolved peacefully with some loss of Danish territory. The peace of Europe was the "preeminent consideration," but Britain was becoming ridiculous, Richard Cobden argued, "by *talking* so loudly while never meaning to *do* anything." British diplomatists were striving to preserve a status quo for which Britain would not fight. "So we shall more and more stand aside," he predicted, "and leave Continental affairs to those who are interested in them." The policy of all future British governments, he cheerfully concluded, would be one of non-intervention.[27]

Lyons continued to be fully occupied with routine diplomatic business because of the legation's chronic understaffing. A replacement who arrived in January had to be sent home after four months for reasons of health; a second attaché quickly followed him because of a family death; and Lyons vetoed a third possible addition to his staff because of his Confederate connections. His only useful employment, he sarcastically commented, would have been as the courier to carry dispatches home. Increasingly, he felt unable to come to the rescue of his overworked juniors. He was already working daily to the point of exhaustion and finding the work "troublesome, wearing, [and] uninteresting" and rejected Hammond's proposal that young attachés be instructed not to seek leave whenever the pressure of business was intense. That would be tantamount to a ban on leave, he pointed out. Appointment to Washington would become, he quipped without genuine humour, the diplomatic equivalent of the favourite sentence of American courts martial – "Confinement at hard labour during the war." Russell interpreted Lyons's complaints of overwork, physical exhaustion, and ill health as pleas for home leave. They were, in reality, excuses for his "total cessation of political and military despatches." Lyons had no intention of going home before August, which would mark five years' residence at a first-class mission and thus ensure a higher pension in the event of retirement.[28]

Disappointment that the rumours of his being moved to Constantinople with the rank of ambassador had come to nothing may explain his sour mood at the opening of the social season with the New Year's Day reception at the White House. He, like the other guests, was kept waiting an hour before Mrs Lincoln put in an appearance. He persevered with his "great dinner parties" though he no longer enjoyed them. Those he attended he dismissed as far worse, being "interminable in length, execrable in quality, and rarely amusing by way of society." He was irritated by Sheffield's decision to attend a ball at the headquarters of the Army of the Potomac, moaning to Minna that he was "quite dull without him." He found himself under pressure over the "Black House." His landlord, Hamilton Fish, reported that he had been offered $35,000 for it by a New York congressman but gave Lyons first refusal since he had paid out of his own pocket for several costly improvements to the residence. Unable to bear the thought of moving, yet anxious to escape the United States, Lyons declined to purchase but negotiated an increase in the rent.[29]

Lyons had always been money conscious. At his final meeting with Russell at Woburn Abbey before returning to the United States in 1862 he had mentioned the insufficiency of his salary. Like Napier before him, he was given permission to draw annually from the secret service fund on the understanding that some more permanent arrangement would eventually be made. "This contingency has now arrived," he informed Russell in May 1864. "The expense of living in Washington is beyond all comparison greater than it was in 1862, and the incidental expenses occasioned by the War, and the enormous increase of the business of the legation, get larger and larger. The rise of prices in this place is out of all proportion to the depreciation of the currency." This appeal served as the introduction to another brief essay on his physical and mental exhaustion after five years of service in the American capital. He declared himself uncertain of his ability to get through another summer "without breaking down in health and without getting into any very serious scrapes." Declaring the profession too important and too interesting to him to be abandoned, he asked to be considered "for an equal or superior position in Europe." Hence the boost to his spirits with the arrival of Russell's assurance that he would take the first opportunity to transfer him to a better and more comfortable post. In the meantime, he recommended another jaunt to Canada on the "public service," sending Burnley out immediately to take charge of the legation. In Canada, Lyons might discuss the Reciprocity Treaty and the defence of the province in the event of a Union invasion, and determine what the Canadians would be willing to do for themselves. "The defence of Quebec both by land & sea is one of the most important points for the consideration of the Cabinet," Russell revealed. Lyons would have an opportunity to become acquainted with Milne's successor, Sir James Hope, and with him and Monck he might go on an extended tour of the St Lawrence and the lakes to assess Canada's interior lines of communication and defence. He might also form an opinion on the viability of a British

North American Confederation. If the French Canadians were secure in the enjoyment of their laws and usages a general parliament for all the provinces would, Russell wrote, have more national spirit than the separate parliaments. United, they would be better prepared to help defend themselves.[30]

Once a torrent, the flow of Lyons's dispatches and private letters had become a trickle and the contents more perfunctory. Russell's promise to be on the lookout for a more suitable post did briefly reinvigorate him. He sent to the Foreign Office thoughtful analyses of military and political developments. General Grant's campaign to take Richmond was costing so many lives and making so little progress that it was infusing the "Peace Party" with strength and boldness. It sought peace "*with the Union*" intact, he emphasized, and thus held little promise of bringing the conflict to a swift end. In July, he assessed Lincoln's prospects of re-election as poor but was scornful of the Democrats, who lacked "principles" and sought a candidate whose sole object was to turn out the Republicans. George B. McClellan was the party's most likely presidential nominee but he was no favourite of the thoroughgoing peace Democrats, who threatened secession if he secured the nomination. Lyons drew Russell's attention to the Democrats' geographical division. Those in the western and border states were "really anxious for peace at any price," while those in the east were "still nearly unanimous in preferring war to separation for the South." He read correctly the reaction of the people of the Northern states to the news in September that General Sherman had taken Atlanta, thereby exposing the Confederacy's soft underbelly. "The vast majority of them ardently desire to reconquer the lost territories," he recognized. "It is only at moments of despair of doing this, that they listen to plans for recovering the territory by negotiations." With the capture of Atlanta, it was widely assumed that Lincoln would be re-elected and the war continue.[31]

Lyons was relieved to see Burnley arrive with only another attaché in tow, for he had thoughtfully deposited his wife and children at a seaside resort for the summer. Lyons welcomed escape from a Washington as hot at midnight as it was at midday. So hard was he working that instead of dining at noon as he preferred he ate in the evening. All the men were ailing, and as he was either the least unwell or the most patient he had been "fixed" in the legation. But "tired of this, indeed worn to death," fearful of Washington's notorious fevers which had taken one of the president's sons and more recently had been the death of the former Norfolk House servant brought over from England, Lyons gratefully delivered the legation, if a little nervously, into the hands of Burnley. Accompanied by Sheffield and Malet, he set off on 25 August for Canada.[32]

"I find myself wonderfully revived already by rest and fresh air," Lyons assured Russell from New York just five days after leaving Washington. "I intend to stay here a few days, in order to pick up a little political intelligence." As he had the previous year, he stayed at the Brevoort House, where there was always a possibility of encountering a visiting European aristocrat. "We are very jolly living on the fat of the land – going to the Theatre and dining out every night – and making the most of the change of air," a happy Malet informed his mother. They made an excursion to New London to visit Madame de Stoeckl, but the journey gave Lyons a severe headache. The train's shaking was the cause, he believed, though it surprised him since it had been his experience that American trains ran too slowly to shake a great deal. The trio advanced on Quebec in easy stages, stopping at Albany, Trenton Falls, and Saratoga, before spending a few days with Fenwick Williams in Montreal. They reached Quebec on 20 September, two days later than they had planned. The reason was that 18 September was a Sunday, and on the Sabbath neither steamers nor trains operated. Lyons found Spencer Wood, the Moncks' residence, something of a menagerie reminiscent of the Dresden legation.[33]

Stricken with another severe headache the day after his arrival, Lyons nevertheless proved his value as a member of the small touring party organized by the Moncks. There were picnics at beauty spots seen in all the glorious colours of the Canadian autumn, and at one of them, the Shawinigan Falls, Lyons exhibited an unexpected informality by removing boots and socks to scramble across the rocks that extended into the water. He dined with several prominent provincial politicians, among them George-Étienne Cartier and John A. Macdonald, who were preparing for the conference scheduled to open in the city on 10 October to discuss a federal union of the colonies. Lyons undoubtedly endorsed the project but was coming to the conclusion that Britain did not have the means of defending British North America against the

United States – indeed, that without "very strong provocation" it did not have the spirit to try.

Lyons was a social success. The other members of the party found him "most delightfully agreeable" with his fund of anecdotes told with a straight face and in a "gravely accented tone" of voice which made the commonest remarks sound amusing. He participated in the after-dinner sing songs, played "old maid" with the ladies rather than whist with the gentlemen, recited poetry, and talked a great deal about books. He declared a fondness for children's books and revealed that he and Malet always travelled with a copy of Elizabeth Gaskell's *Cranford*. He was relaxed, was free of headaches, and again showed himself, despite his prejudices, at ease in female company. On two occasions the closeness of his relationship with Sheffield was apparent – his describing him as his baby, and the private secretary taking the largest cabin on a steamer on which they were to travel, consigning Lyons to "a little inferior" one. Perhaps to ease the embarrassment of his companions, Lyons made a joke of being "*neglected* and offended." The party made for Ottawa via Montreal, finding the future capital rather squalid looking, the hotel clean but third rate, and the food "uncivilized." The unfinished Parliament buildings promised to be magnificent when completed, the setting sun turning the greystone pink. Then it was a train to Prescott to board another appropriately named steamer, the *Grecian*, for passage to Toronto. However, Lyons opted for terra firma at Kingston. The last stop was Niagara, where it was agreed the party would stay at the Cataract House on the American side of the Falls, having discovered that Confederates were staying at the Clifton House on the Canadian side. Lyons had no wish to be seen in their company. On 12 October, he and his two companions bid goodbye to the others and began their long return trek to the American capital.[34]

Lyons had repeatedly assured his sister of his resolve "to leave America for good and all." The task was to "get out of the whole thing" without endangering his career prospects. By the time he reached New York on 15 October he was again suffering from severe headaches and moaning of his imminent loneliness in Washington. Most of the men with whom he had been comfortable were either soon going home (Malet) or planning to do so (Sheffield). He could not bring himself to ask them to remain in "so intolerable a place" if they had a chance of getting away. So he parted with attachés, or secretaries as they were now more correctly known, one after another always to their joy but never to his. There would be no one to act as his private secretary, he groused to his ever-sympathetic sister, and he could not go on without one. He resolved to join the exodus so long as by doing so he did not jeopardize his standing in the profession.[35]

In New York, on 19 October, Lyons dined with General John Adams Dix, who as a youth had fought the British in the War of 1812, had quit the military to follow the well-trodden path from law to politics, had been a senator from New York and very briefly a secretary of the Treasury before returning to the army with the outbreak of the Civil War. He commanded the Department of the East. Their meal was interrupted by an aide who delivered a telegram reporting the raid on St Albans, Vermont, by Confederates based in Canada. The raiders had crossed the border, robbed banks, and attempted to set fire to the town before fleeing back to the province. Dix ordered their hot pursuit despite a warning by Lyons that this would play into the hands of the raiders, who he guessed were hoping to provoke an international crisis. It would be far better, he counselled the general, if Canada arrested the raiders, treated them as criminals, and handed them over to the United States under the terms of the Extradition Treaty. He telegraphed Burnley to urge Seward to guard against violations of British territory, only to learn that the secretary of state was in no haste to countermand Dix's order. No doubt Seward saw this episode as an opportunity to revive his campaign to persuade Britain to withdraw its recognition of Confederate belligerency, but, in what proved to be his last full commentary on American developments, Lyons informed Russell on 1 November of the bloody repulse of Grant's latest advance on the Confederate capital. He found a "gleam of consolation" for the carnage in the doom of slavery. A desperate South appeared willing to free large numbers of slaves and grant them land if they would serve in the Confederate army. This would surely be followed by the emancipation of them all, Lyons reasoned. Of the slave states that had remained loyal, Maryland on this very same day abolished the institution. Lyons ought to have drawn Russell's attention also to the proposed 13th amendment to the Constitution abolishing slavery everywhere. This was one of the planks of the platform on which Abraham Lincoln was on the verge of re-election.[36]

That first day of November saw Lyons also send Russell word of his inability to continue as British minister. His health had not recovered and he could no longer perform his duties. He reminded the foreign secretary of his assurance that another mission worthy of his talents would be found for him. Less than three weeks later Russell regretfully agreed to Lyons's return home. "You will come away at once," he wrote on 19 November. What ailed Lyons? He was certainly desperate to leave the United States after three years of intense pressure, severe strain, and hard work. He saw the prevention of a breach in his nation's relations with the United States as his primary duty and was thus always aware of the heavy burden of responsibility he bore. Charles Sumner wrote of him that he was "just & loved peace" but had "no facility in business or intercourse – so that his heavy work told upon him." Tell on him the work did, in the form of painful and debilitating headaches, but Sumner's criticism of Lyons's handling of business may have been influenced by the chasm that had opened between them following the Cooper Institute speech. It would have been difficult to get through the work, Burnley acknowledged, having compared it to that of a galley slave, but for the admirable way in which papers were classified and the efficiency with which the chancery functioned. This was a tribute to Lyons's handling of business. Being a bachelor, he had given up the entire bedroom floor of the house to the chancery and had employed at extra personal expense domestic servants to wait upon the overworked attachés. Were the post to be filled by a married man with a family, Lyons noted, he would need an allowance for chancery servants and messengers and would encounter difficulty finding a house in which to keep the chancery on its present scale. His successor proved to be another bachelor.[37]

Equally suspect was Sumner's claim that the Foreign Office was Lyons's "absolute guide," for Sumner was in no position to appreciate the extent to which he interpreted his instructions. Nor was he aware of the degree to which the minister's private correspondence and dispatches had shaped British policy throughout the war. Lyons had assumed Britain would remain a neutral long before it was officially declared. He had adopted a strict concert with France, had urged demonstrations of

Britain's resolve to defend her national interests, had handled the *Trent* crisis and negotiated the Anti-Slave Trade Treaty with great skill, had established a productive relationship with Seward, and had argued that the conflict should be settled by the belligerents. His recommendation of non-intervention had been forcefully backed by the warning that meddling would lead to war with the Union. If he had misjudged Lyons's influence, Sumner respected him, as did Seward, as a "sincere, truthful person." These had long been the watchwords of his diplomatic conduct. At least one American newspaper agreed, distinguishing him from a long line of predecessors. He was not haughty like Richard Pakenham, it commented, not an idler like Henry-Stephen Fox, not a crafty casuist like Henry Bulwer, not a bon vivant like John Crampton, not a ladies' man like Lord Napier, but an honest sympathizer with anti-slavery, "a sturdy representative of the lords and gentlemen of England," and a diplomat who shunned covert activities. Deception was not in his character, and there is no reason to believe that he feigned illness in order to escape the United States. His headaches had become so bad, he wrote to Minna on 6 November, that he had been obliged to turn over all business to Burnley. Sheffield was so alarmed by his condition that he considered sending to New York for the best available American physician. In Washington, gossips spoke of typhoid and of a caged Lyons confined to his room and unable to see visitors. His doctor diagnosed neuralgia and dyspepsia, although the patient was convinced the headaches were bilious in origin. Biliousness was all too common in the marshy, unhealthy American capital. One concerned and sympathetic correspondent offered him a cure for neuralgia in the form of a strict regimen: abstinence from high living and from the injurious use of wine and spirits; open air, especially on horseback; a daily wine glass of tonic perhaps in the form of port before each meal, to which he might add small doses of quinine and laudanum which could then be increased according to his ability to endure them. Lyons credited a strict diet and the abandonment of work with the improvement in his digestion, but the severe headaches persisted if somewhat more intermittently. He did not remain in bed longer than usual because lying down made the pain worse, and on fine days took short walks, whereas carriage rides were ruled out because he could not stand the jolting on the abominable roads.[38]

Painful as he found it even to write, Lyons wrote personally to Seward on 3 December to announce his imminent departure and to make arrangements to call at the State Department to "shake him by the hand" and then to pay his respects to the president. Seward agreed that it was best that he go home for a rest but hoped it would not be for long. His own difficulties would be increased, he fancied, by Lyons's absence. On 5 December he escorted the Englishman to the White House to bid farewell to Lincoln, who received him with "sincere kindness and sympathy." Four months later, on learning that Lyons would not be returning to the United States, Seward expressed his "sincere sorrow" at the news. Years later he was to write that he had become "warmly attached" to Lyons "by reason of his honourable and upright conduct as Minister of Great Britain to the United States in the early years of our civil war." Seward, influenced by Lyons's conduct, advanced his own concept of a "special relationship." The Union's interests were common to all branches of the British family, he declared, so he did not doubt that when the Civil War ended the United States and the United Kingdom would be reconciled and become better friends than ever. Lyons was in Seward's considered opinion entitled to a full share of the credit for this because he had played so great a role in controlling the international strains of the domestic conflict. Lyons also advised Governor General Monck, the lieutenant-governors of Nova Scotia and New Brunswick, and the British naval and military commanders of his imminent return home. He left domestic matters to Sheffield, through whom a more flexible rental agreement for the house was negotiated. Lyons was to pay $250 a month on the understanding that the agreement could be terminated with a month's notice. On 14 December 1864 Lyons and Sheffield boarded the *China* in New York for the voyage home. The sale by auction a few days earlier of his horses, carriages, wines, and brandies was proof he was leaving for good.[39]

Lyons was carrying from the United States a well-tested set of personal rules of diplomatic conduct. A legation should be an expression of British wealth and power, it should be administered much like a family to inspire loyalty to its head, and women should be excluded. Straightforwardness and honesty should be the basis of dealings with the host nation. There should be no involvement in "underhand activities." There should be no interference in matters over which the British government could not exercise effective control, and there should be no meddling in the internal affairs of the country to which he was accredited. This had won for him from the *New York Tribune*, no voice of anglophilia, the accolade of the "Model" minister. By minute attention to detail he prevented causes of difference growing up, and when disagreeable questions had arisen the same response had prevented them from developing into serious disputes. Confrontation should be avoided whenever possible, as should unnecessary irritation of national vanity, and the other nation should be offered a dignified and even graceful means of retreat from disputes. Hence his stress on providing it with the time and space to make a "spontaneous" decision and his construction of a "golden bridge." He disdained, as in the case of the Anti-Slave Trade Treaty, confidential semi-official conversations on the grounds that they usually ended badly by getting one into trouble and complicating the problem. He pushed for a treaty whose provisions could not be easily repudiated. Similarly, he considered it wise to look for a diplomatic partner when seeking to restrain a host nation from behaviour that might end in a collision. Lyons had selected the French representative as his ally, and it was a national preference to which he was to remain true. Finally, in certain critical circumstances, he accepted that Britain needed to show that it had both the will and the means to protect by force its national interests.[40]

CHAPTER TEN

Ambassador to
the Sublime Porte

The *China* arrived off Ireland on Christmas Day, but few of its passengers were in a festive mood after eleven storm-tossed days. The rough passage had taken its predictable toll on Lyons, though his headaches were less painful, surprisingly, despite the vessel's pitching and rolling. He and Sheffield docked at Liverpool on Boxing Day, from where they sped directly to the capital and Norfolk House. On 27 December 1864 Lyons went out to Richmond Park to confer with Russell and on his return consulted Dr Ferguson, whom Minna had recommended. He then retreated to Arundel, where he was guaranteed the quiet prescribed by the American doctor whom he had consulted in New York City. Following a more thorough examination in January, Ferguson concluded that the patient had expended too much nervous energy over the past several years. This was the cause of his severe headaches, and the prescription of no more than a physic reassured Minna that her brother's general health was sound.[1]

During the first long weekend in February, which he spent at Pembroke Lodge, Lyons learned of the Cabinet's impatience to have full representation in Washington. The Civil War was plainly drawing to a close and its end might release pent-up Union irritation with Britain. The decision of a Canadian magistrate to release the St Albans raiders "on the absurd pretext that it was necessary for the governor general to have issued a warrant for their arrest" had provoked another eruption of American bellicosity. With the Reciprocity Treaty almost certain to be terminated by the Americans at the earliest opportunity, Lord Derby was among the British politicians who saw in the Confederation of the North American territories a more formidable barrier to their annexation by the United States. Lyons realized that there was in Britain far greater interest in American affairs than in 1862 when he had last been home. He submitted his formal resignation in late February, news the press regretted. Britain had lost the services of the man who had "smoothed the roughness and adjusted the difficulties which arose" with the United States, it lamented. Lyons, Russell added, had discharged "the most difficult duties with which any Diplomatic agent can be entrusted."[2]

The ever-ambitious Lyons made plain his lack of interest in the Lisbon mission when it was raised as a possible posting. Portugal would be a significant step down from the United States. To ensure that he was not overlooked by the Foreign Office, he remained in the capital. He went out to Windsor Castle to be sworn into the Privy Council, attended the first levee of the season, and dined with the Prince of Wales, the Duke of Cambridge, Granville, and Palmerston. He went up to Oxford to add another ironic punctuation mark to his dismal university undergraduate career, an honorary DCL. He helped to secure a Companionship of the Order of the Bath for Edward Archibald and wound up his personal affairs in the United States by selling unwanted furniture and household effects to his successor as minister the amiable and affable Sir Frederick Bruce. The tragic news from Washington of President Lincoln's assassination, which was reported in Britain on Lyons's forty-eighth birthday, and Bruce's private account of its consequences, which included mass arrests, confirmed for Lyons his decision to resign the post. Still plagued by severe headaches, he consulted the "chemical doctor" Henry Bence Jones, who had built a large and profitable society practice with the aid of his marriage to the daughter of an earl. Jones agreed with the earlier diagnosis, prescribed a pill of his own manufacture to be taken with a tonic, and strenuously opposed the visit Lyons had been planning to make to his elder sister in Germany. The weather would be too hot and the waters of no benefit, the good doctor explained.[3]

At loose ends, Lyons went back up to Oxford in June to spend a few days first with Richard Michell, his old tutor, and then with Edmund Monson at All Souls. Back in the capital he made contact with Malet, who was on a temporary assignment at the Foreign Office, and they exchanged dinners. Malet hosted his at the new Clubhouse of the Garrick Club, the appropriate haunt of an amateur thespian. But this interlude of relaxation came to an end soon afterwards. On 22 July Lyons learned he was to succeed Sir Henry Bulwer as ambassador to the Sublime Ottoman Porte. Promotion to ambassadorial rank at the relatively young age of forty-eight brought him within touching distance of the diplomatic ladder's top rung, Paris. He requested the addition of Malet and Sheffield to his staff as insurance that he would not again find himself engaged in chancery labour and semi-official business. Advised that the Constantinople embassy was already grotesquely overstaffed, Lyons neatly solved this problem by proposing, naturally in the interest of the public service, a thorough cleansing of this "Augean stable" and the introduction of new stock. He summoned William Stuart from Scotland, where he was enjoying leave, to discuss the embassy's "efficiency, respectability and pleasantness."[4]

The Lyons appointment was for his friends a moment to savour, he being in their opinion the perfect choice. His "solid and direct character, and resolute perseverance in that straight and manly line of conduct" which he had made his own, and his "quiet abrogation of self interest" had earned him the "high and responsible situation as director and controller of the Turks." He would be returning, after thirty-five years, to a region which threw "far into the shade the more homely spectacles, and more familiar events of the western world." Even the climate was more to his taste, the heat of summer tempered at Therapia by cooling breezes which blew down the Bosporus from the Black Sea. There were, of course, the problems associated with living in an "uncivilized" country, but he would be surrounded by men whom he trusted.[5]

The plan was to leave for Turkey in mid-September, and in preparation for departure he called on Stratford Canning at Hemel Hempstead. Now Viscount Stratford de Redcliffe, he had played a large part in the removal of Edmund Lyons as chief of mission in Athens but was too valuable a source to be overlooked. He had during his time at

Constantinople become its most influential foreign diplomat and in retirement still commanded great respect for his knowledge of Turkish affairs. From him, Lyons sought information on personalities and problems and the names of locals on whom he might rely. The task of identifying "intriguers" the former ambassador left to Lyons himself.[6]

Edmund Hammond was confident that Lyons would keep the embassy's clique of intriguers and hangers-on in their place and would do everything "for the benefit of Turkey and for the honour and interest of England." This was an allusion to Bulwer's failure to behave honourably and practise economy. His bitter dispute with his initial secretary of embassy had obliged the Foreign Office to intervene with a circular establishing a more formal relationship between ambassador and diplomatic staff. This effectively terminated the tradition of the so-called "Family Embassy" in which the head of mission and the secretary were the only two members of the diplomatic profession. Another of Bulwer's sins was his financial extravagance. He had raised Foreign Office hackles by charging to it the entire expense of a "very large" dinner in honour of the Queen's birthday. His justification had been the exceptional role of the ambassador as chief of a very large staff and head of a colony of expatriates. Britons were members of thriving merchant houses, had their own chamber of commerce, their own post office; they staffed local banks, the Supreme Consular Court, the British Seamen's Hospital, the Ottoman Mint, and the British High School for Girls founded by Lady Stratford. They constituted a diverse society whose members were "all more or less in equal position," and as a result it was almost impossible, "without giving offence," to draw a line between fifty and one hundred and fifty people.

The size of Bulwer's "Extraordinaries" was far from being the most serious Foreign Office criticism of his conduct. He was accused of not dealing openly with Lord Cowley in Paris by counselling the Turks sent on missions there to keep their distance from the British embassy. He was charged with failing to stiffen the Sultan's resistance to land grabs by the French along the banks of the Suez Canal being constructed by a company headed by Ferdinand de Lesseps. Bulwer was believed to have been party to a loan scheme which would have converted domestic Turkish debt into foreign debt, thereby propping open a little wider the door to foreign intervention in the empire, and to have participated in a shady real estate speculation. He had purchased an island in the Sea of Marmara ostensibly to transform this barren rock into a profitable farm "to show the Turks what could be done where there was a will," but had sold it to the Egyptian viceroy. He should never have acquired the island, Russell complained, and in selling it had mixed private with public interests in a way that appeared to place him in the Khedive's debt. His extended visit to Egypt, allegedly for health reasons, deepened this suspicion. His reputation as an unscrupulous schemer and trickster gained him few friends in the British community. The ambassador, an American missionary remarked, was "a brilliant but unprincipled man, who was ready to sacrifice anything to his own personal interest." Among Lyons's tasks was the restoration of the faith of the British community in their ambassador and to inspire the embassy staff with loyalty and affection. He brought to this challenge his reputation for running missions as a different kind of family affair.[7]

Lyons was going to Constantinople at a time when British foreign policy had been a less than spectacular success. The Palmerston government's passive response to the Polish rebellion had done further damage to the uneasy Anglo-French alignment. The Schleswig-Holstein crisis had ended in humiliation. Cabinet divisions fomented by the Queen, and the absence of popular support for physical involvement, had allowed Bismarck to call Palmerston's bluff on intervention. Denmark, swiftly crushed, had ceded the duchies jointly to Austria and Prussia on 1 August 1864 only for them quickly to become a source of tension between the two powers. Lord Stanley put something of a gloss on Britain's conduct with his declaration in Parliament that neutrality and non-intervention were the elements of a safe, respectable, and honourable foreign policy. Ironically, just as European troubles had constrained Britain's response to the American Civil War, so the uneasy Anglo-American relationship at its end strengthened the aversion to involvement in European squabbles.[8]

What did non-intervention mean for Britain's traditional policy of protecting the integrity of the Ottoman Empire? It was said that Lord Chatham, a heroic statesmen of the previous century, had declined to discuss the East with anyone who failed to accept that the empire's independence was a "question of life and death to Great Britain." Could Britain now stand aside and watch the once mighty "Mohammedan colossus" disintegrate and new states rise on its ruins? Britain, Austria, and France had "jointly and severally" guaranteed the empire's independence and integrity only nine years earlier while all the powers attending the Congress of Paris had given a solemn assurance of non-interference in its internal administration. When the unreliable French emperor showed signs of ignoring his own commitment, Foreign Secretary Malmesbury had cautioned him that Britain's "determination to maintain Turkey against all comers" was unshakable. His Liberal successor at the Foreign Office avowed a preference for the Turks over their restless subject nationalities because "they have more notions of good faith, of truth, of friendship, and of the great art of government than any of the other races." Britain would stand by the commitments it had given in 1856 so long as the Sultan honoured his promises of imperial reform, Russell added, for it could not "guarantee the Sultan against his own disenchanted subjects." Yet he despaired of the Porte's adoption of the needed reforms and was mindful of the declining parliamentary and public sympathy for the Turks. Britain would wage no more wars in defence of the Turks, Richard Cobden confidently asserted. A "Slavonic Garibaldi" seeking to throw off Ottoman oppression would have the support of the British public and the Foreign Office would bow to popular opinion.[9]

Russell drew up an agenda for the Sultan. He was to live within his means, do justice to his subjects, behave much like an English gentleman who succeeds to an indebted estate, and name to office men of unquestioned integrity and honesty. A soundly based regular system of finance and a well-organized, well-officered, and well-disciplined army would enable Turkey to remain a power. This push for administrative reform was driven in part by economic interest. Turkey was an important market for British goods and a promising source of raw materials. The empire consisted of countries whose resources Britain wished to develop, Bulwer had admitted, and to that end it sought order and justice. A universal code of law was one essential, as were severe restrictions on the ability of foreigners to claim the protection of the laws of their respective countries. These "capitulations" had resulted in a legal hodge-podge, with different consuls administering different laws, following different procedures, and imposing different sentences for similar if not identical offences.[10]

The dominant British strategic concern was the Suez Canal. Robert Stephenson, the nation's leading civil engineer, had knowledge of Egypt, and his profitable involvement in railway construction there may have influenced his judgment that construction of a canal was impossible. Indeed, he had declared a willingness to stake "his reputation and whole fortune upon that opinion." He did not live long enough to realize how costly a wager this would have been. Russell and Palmerston were also skeptics, though this did not prevent them from striving to ensure that the French company engaged in the enterprise did not deliver Egypt into Napoleon's hands. Ferdinand de Lesseps, at the company's head, was a cousin of Empress Eugénie. The army of French directors, engineers, workmen, and soldiers who descended on the viceroyalty were believed to be seeking land grants, which if secured would leave the Sultan, already no more than the nominal suzerain, with little sovereignty and Britain with little prospect of securing unrestricted free passage through the canal. The Turks made no objection to the project, perhaps influenced by Lesseps's artful argument that the canal would preserve the empire by compelling the Great Powers to sustain Turkey as the guarantor of its neutrality. Palmerston was not persuaded, least of all by the French government's assurances that it had no connection with the project. Why then, he asked himself, was Napoleon seeking to dole out Egyptian land to his countrymen despite being a guarantor of the Ottoman Empire's territorial integrity? If they permitted "so arrogant an instance of injustice to be consummated," and the French to gain the idea that Britain was indifferent to the fate of Egypt, the British Empire in the East would be lost, Bulwer had warned. Hence his resentment of the criticism that he had been lethargic in his response to the canal question.[11]

When Lyons met with Palmerston on 16 August 1865 the canal was a prime topic of conversation. The prime minister continued to believe that the project was political not commercial and Lesseps merely a "blind" for the French government. If the French secured territorial control of both ends of a canal they would in a conflict with Britain command the Indian Seas. The task the prime minister handed to Lyons was to convince the weak and apathetic Turkish government not to alienate any territory. The same topic loomed large in Russell's instructions. He and Palmerston agreed that the emperor was hoping to make Egypt a French dependency, and the foreign secretary suspected the Porte of quietly cultivating the goodwill of France by acquiescing in Napoleon's disposal of Egyptian land. Hence Russell's resolve to prevent any canal fortifications being occupied by the French company, for that would in his opinion amount to their control by the French government. Lyons was to watch the project's progress "narrowly" to ensure that neither Turkey's apathy nor Egypt's ambition to be independent compromised the promised freedom of passage for all nations. Although Napoleon III's current prudent posture suggested that he was unlikely to sanction "any glaring violation of international equity," he was too opportunistic and too responsive to popular opinion to be trusted.[12]

In dispatches that Lyons consulted in the Foreign Office's archives, Bulwer claimed a large share of the credit for the new Anglo-Turkish Commercial Treaty and for the Sultan's decision to permit European advisers to overhaul his empire's finances. The tasks of reducing the imperial debt and of increasing revenues was in Bulwer's judgment a "simple question of knowledge and will." Abuses and poor administration had to be identified and the will found to root them out. The Sultan's denial of personal extravagance could be taken with a pinch of salt given the size of the harem and the costs of its protection, and his expenditures on palaces. Abdul Aziz was credited by Bulwer with good sense, honesty of purpose, vanity, fickleness, and a "burning desire to restore the glory of his empire." Although he was physically imposing, his chronic ill health was attributed to his residence in the newest of his palaces, which was so damp that water trickled down the walls; to his excess in the matter of food, for he consumed vast quantities of cherries; and to his resort to a female "quack" for medical attention because she was less involved than recognized physicians in palace intrigues. The cares of empire weighed heavily on his mind, and the stress was turning his hair prematurely grey. His educational deficiencies obliged him to depend on ministers whom he never truly trusted nor effectively controlled. Lyons would be operating in a complex and conspiratorial political society if not quite a nest of vipers.[13]

Russell was counting on Lyons's good sense and temper, "his patience and discretion in which subjects he had graduated with honours from the 'University of Washington,'" to protect and advance British interests. Although he disclaimed knowledge of Eastern questions, Lyons was better informed than he admitted. John Green, whose Athens consulate had been his refuge from the tensions of the Wyse mission, was now in Bucharest, where his consulate was effectively a diplomatic mission. He had been providing Lyons with regular updates on the chronic problem of the Danubian Principalities of Moldavia and Wallachia. Commanding the great river, they were thus strategically important. Their citizens disliked Turkish suzerainty and were Russian in their religious affiliation and political sympathies. They desired union and the creation of a Romanian state and could count on the support of both France and Russia. Britain, on the other hand, opposed further dismantling of the Ottoman Empire. A step towards union had been taken in 1859 when both principalities elected the same man, Alexander Couza, as *hospodar* or governor, and two years later the United Principalities of Romania had been formed with France acting as its patron. But the disturbances that broke out in the summer of 1865 hardened Green's opinion that they would remain a perpetual nuisance. However, so long as the present government of "Moldo-Wallachia" was agreeable to its inhabitants and accepted the Sultan's suzerainty the Foreign Office opposed intervention.[14]

Lyons, Sheffield, and Malet took a late-afternoon train to Dover on 18 September. Malet entertained his companions with an account of the large dinner party he had attended which a member of the Cabinet, the Duke of Somerset, had hosted. Malet had an eye for the kind of detail that would amuse his chief, describing the duchess unflatteringly and ungallantly as "a large woman with a black wig – a garden of geraniums round such an expanse of bosom as you see only in England." He supposed his invitation was to enable the Turkish ambassador to get a close look at him but his table companion had been the "amusing and queer" Charles "calculator" Babbage, the designer of the first automatic calculating engine. Following a calm crossing of the Channel and a night in Calais, they arrived in Paris in the early evening. On 21 September Cowley presented Lyons to the French foreign minister. In his second term as the Second Empire's tenant of the Quai d'Orsay, Drouyn de Lhuys

knew what the Briton wished to hear. Their two nations should work
together to sustain the Ottoman Empire, he declared, assuring Lyons
that the Suez Canal was an entirely commercial endeavour in which the
emperor had no political interest, that it would never be under exclusive
French control, and Britain's full and equal use of it was guaranteed. He
then professed a desire to prevent the Danubian Principalities from becoming an "inconvenient discussion" among the Great Powers, arguing
that it would be better to improve the present deplorable regime than
to replace it. The French position, Cowley explained to Lyons, was the
result of Napoleon's promise to protect Couza. His domestic prestige
damaged by the imminent collapse of the foreign adventure in Mexico,
the emperor could not afford in the ambassador's opinion to abandon
Couza. Lyons emerged from the interview resolved to keep a very close
eye on his French counterpart in Constantinople.[15]

Along with his two companions, Lyons left Paris on 22 September for
Strasbourg, where they were joined by his old friend Gozze, who was
to accompany them as far as Trieste. At the port they embarked on the
small but very comfortable HMS *Caradoc*. Foul weather caused its captain to put in at the Austrian port of Pola, much to the relief of the violently ill Lyons. An arsenal open only to foreign vessels in such emergen-
cies, it had been one of the "petty extravagances" of the former governor
general of Lombardy-Venetia, Archduke Maximilian, who was soon to
meet his end before a Mexican firing squad. It boasted a third-century
amphitheatre whose exterior walls were remarkably perfect, prompting
the three British visitors to agree that it was an "immense place and
worth coming to see from a long distance." Soon on its way again, the
Caradoc coaled at Corfu before cruising the Greek coastline and finally
docking at Constantinople on 12 October. "I have dwelt much on what it
must have been to see it again," Minna wrote. "That time at Constantinople I have often thought was for us and for you especially a beginning
of a different life and how much came to an end for us there or in connection with it." She was alluding to Moubray's death, and the day after
his arrival Lyons made the short journey up the Bosporus to Therapia to
view his brother's grave, which happily he found well tended.[16]

The embassy staff had come aboard the *Caradoc* to greet their new
chief and escort him safely ashore in an extraordinarily decorated boat.

On landing he found colourfully dressed embassy guards waiting to accompany him to the embassy. There, to his private dismay, Lyons found
Bulwer still in residence. He had requested a few extra days to put his
affairs in order, their settlement having been delayed by an outbreak of
cholera. They knew each other well from Italy, Bulwer was on his very
best behaviour, and Lyons's anodyne personality ensured there would be
no unpleasantness. Bulwer advised him that he had arranged for them
to present his letters of recall and Lyons's credentials to the Sultan on
18 October. Abdul Aziz sent six carriages to transport the party to his
palace, and Lyons surely thought back more than thirty years to the day
he had acted as a page of another British ambassador. They travelled at
a snail's pace, for to have gone faster would have jolted them "to bits" on
the "villainous" pavement. Deposited at the palace gates, they walked
through two courtyards to enter a building and a world reminiscent of
the *Arabian Nights*. The Sultan's room proved to be surprisingly simple,
and was likened by Lyons to a sparsely furnished French drawing room.
Abdul Aziz was plainly dressed but wearing on his head a "fez of significantly ugly shape" like a "saucepan without the tail." After their brief
speeches Lyons and Bulwer withdrew to the drawing room overlooking
the Bosporus where Bulwer mournfully remarked that he might now
consider himself a man in his coffin. A lugubrious Lyons responded: "in
sure and certain hope of the Resurrection." Coincidentally, Palmerston
died that same day.[17]

Bulwer finally sailed on 23 October. While his views on Turkish politics had been helpful, his constant postponing of his departure had irritated Lyons, who politely but firmly discouraged the idea of his returning in the spring as a private citizen. The state of the embassy was
an immediate concern to a man who believed that the houses of British
chiefs of mission should express the power and wealth of the nation,
and in Constantinople he was taking possession of the "very first gov-
ernment-owned and built embassy house." Although immense in size,
it was likened by Malet to a "plain Club house in Pall Mall" and with an
absurd interior. The rooms had high and ugly ceilings, the walls were
covered with "hideous" papers much like the "worst designs of German
Hotel rooms," the furniture was dilapidated if not unserviceable, and the
elaborate heating system did not function. Lyons immediately dismissed

the architect employed to keep the house in good order with the aid of a generous annual grant from the Treasury and briefly supervised expenditures himself. He was relieved, however, when an English officer of engineers, Colonel E. Gordon, arrived from Britain to take care of the building. Lyons made some minor improvements out of his own pocket, but its size made the embassy expensive to inhabit and he was unable to find "any compact corner" in which to live "moderately and comfortably." He quickly discovered that the state of the villa at Therapia was even worse. A structure built of wood that was plainly rotting, the building was held together by paint alone. In this "tottering condition," every high wind from the Black Sea threatened to blow it down.[18]

The day-to-day management of the embassy was in the hands of a steward who was no "cheap treasure." Lyons, a man who thought quiet a thing for which one had to pay, as with any luxury, preferred paying the steward to the alternative of incurring "the annoyance of constant changes in the household and contentions about the way to manage it." The suggestion by Malet's mother that this male household hire a "lady housekeeper" was never considered, for Lyons still refused to have women around him, and a married applicant for a diplomatic position was bluntly told that there was no place for him. This resistance to women was encouraged by Sheffield, who "is also a woman hater," Malet grumbled. Thus Lady Bulwer, left behind by her husband at his house in Scutari, threatened to become a headache. A daughter of Lord Cowley, with whom Lyons had immediately established a private correspondence, thereby correcting another of Bulwer's mistakes, and who was expected soon to retire from the service's most prestigious post, she could not be ignored and evoked sympathy as a "lone woman in the middle of the Turks." Happily, she proved to be wonderfully cheerful and independent and asked only for the loan of novels.[19]

Lyons welcomed the return of William Stuart on 22 November. As secretary of embassy, he dealt directly with the handful of consuls-general and scores of consuls and vice-consuls scattered throughout the empire. Unfortunately, the Oriental secretary immediately beneath Stuart in the staff hierarchy imposed on Bulwer by the Foreign Office was "an impulsive fretful creature always anxious to be doing something and never doing it." Another of the secretaries created tensions because of his undisguised resentment of the British aristocracy from whose ranks so many of his colleagues came. The head of the chancery, Count Pisani, who ranked fourth, impressed as a "good little man, a gentleman, a man of one idea – the one idea being how to keep his Chancery in good order." His misfortune was his relationship, brother, to the chief dragoman, translator Etienne Pisani, who while "certainly very sharp" and the "best witted" of the staff was also "very corrupt." There were three other dragomen, one of whom was a chronic invalid and another a "fawning Greek." Only the youngest of them had a "good deal of good in him." Palmerston had introduced a scheme more than twenty years earlier to send out young Englishmen nominated by the vice-chancellors of Oxford and Cambridge to serve as translators and thus make the embassy independent, in sensitive political discussions, of foreign dragomen. The arrangement had failed because of Stratford de Redcliffe's distrust of them as interpreters. Russell, as an alternative, had urged Lyons to deal directly with the Sublime Porte, which took its name from the decorated gate of the building which housed the offices of the grand vizier, the ministers of foreign affairs and of the interior, and those of the Supreme Council of Judicial Ordinances or Grand Council of Justice. Since both the grand vizier and the minister of foreign affairs had a command of French, Lyons hoped that by his direct dealing with them he would eventually lead the entire diplomatic corps in the abandonment of the dragoman system.[20]

Grand Vizier Fuad and Foreign Minister Aali were the odd couple of the Sublime Porte. Fuad was "tall and handsome," Aali "small and frail." Fuad was "expansive," "loquacious," "enterprising," and "decisive" but inattentive to detail; Aali was "self-contained," "silent," "circumspect," "hesitant," "meticulous," and conservative. Both were devoted to the "service and preservation of the state," both manoeuvred to avoid European intervention, both struggled to preserve the integrity of the empire, and to these ends both advocated a measure of administrative reform. Aali welcomed the appointment of Lyons, a family name well known to Turks from the Crimean War, and applauded his resolve to dispense with the services of dragomen. Lyons found the pair "agreeable and satisfactory" but quickly despaired of ever fully understanding "the complicated system of managing things." He was, he suspected, a fish out of water in this sea of diplomatic intrigue. "I am too stupid even to comprehend the multifarious intrigues in which everybody says everybody else is engaged," he admitted with more than a hint of false modesty. He had quickly realized that the Turks deliberately fomented discord within the diplomatic corps, telling him evil things about its other members which led him to assume that they were saying the same about him to them. His French counterpart was reputedly the most notorious intriguer. Bulwer had assessed Léonel, the 5th Marquis de Moustier, as "cleverish and voluble" but a casuist "who can never look at any matter in a plain straightforward way and constantly undertakes to show you that a horse chestnut and a chestnut horse are one and the same thing." Nor did the Frenchman cut a noble figure. Malet ridiculed him as "a coarse looking Frenchman of the hairdresser type or rather like a French circus clown." Apart from their unimpressive physical appearances – for Lyons was short, rotund with a faintly hangdog face – he and Moustier appeared to have little in common. Lyons's reputation was that of a laconic, "plain straightforward" person.[21]

Several members of the diplomatic community, notably the Russian minister, did not hide their dislike of the "swaggering" French ambassador. Nikolai Ignatiev warned Lyons that Moustier was a colleague with whom it was impossible to do business. He was "insupportably arrogant in conferences," the Russian complained, and needed to be resolutely resisted. Lyons chose not to enlist in the resistance, for Moustier had given him no cause to complain of either his manner or conduct, and it would not help him to resist successfully the French ambassador on matters of real importance, such as the Suez Canal, if out of pique he alienated him unnecessarily. He decided to follow the line of conduct that had proven so successful with Mercier in Washington. He would do his very best to get on well with this Frenchman and act in concert with him as much as possible. It was a tribute to his diplomatic skill and distaste of personal flamboyance that he and Moustier quickly became "very good colleagues." He was helped by his understanding that the French could achieve little alone, and thus Moustier had limited options. He could either co-operate with him to prop up the empire, or with Russia to hasten its collapse. The latter option was the less attractive of the two because Russia would be its principal beneficiary.[22]

Lyons welcomed the choice of foreign secretary when the government at home was restructured following Palmerston's death. Russell became prime minister and Clarendon finally regained possession of the Foreign Office. "We certainly have never had to protect the Turks from the consequences of firm resistance, for they knock under the moment that France speaks," Clarendon griped. That Moustier appeared to make greater headway in his dealings with the Porte than he did himself with his calm but persistent representations did not concern Lyons unduly. From the outset, he had decided to do business in a different manner by forgoing "the use of many of the old methods of acquiring information and exercising influence." As he later admitted to Edmund Hammond, "I have perhaps gone a little far in this direction, but thought it necessary at first in keeping to the direct path." He was also faced with the fact that the Turks considered France an enemy and Britain at best a "lukewarm and weak friend." "They think we are too friendly for them to have anything from us, and not friendly enough, or resolute enough," to protect them from France or Russia. Britain was paying a high diplomatic price, he recognized, for its ineffectual response to the Schleswig-Holstein crisis. The perception that Britain's bark was "more to be dreaded than her bite" meant that there was a great deal to do "to recover reputation lost in the Danish business."[23]

Lyons had no need to worry about his personal reputation. "I hear," Clarendon wrote, that "your Colleagues all write in high praise of your judgment and fairness and your determination to oppose intrigues of all kinds, rather a novelty at the British Embassy." Lyons doubted that the representatives of other nations would follow his example. He made sure he was well informed of what was happening throughout the empire by utilizing the same source of legitimate intelligence that had proven so useful in the United States. Although Stratford had undoubtedly advised him during their meeting that if Turkey was the sick man of Europe the British consuls, numbering close to fifty, were equally sick, Lyons invited those in sensitive locations, such as restless Crete, to correspond privately with him. As John Green approvingly wrote, this confidential relationship sharply distinguished him from Bulwer, who had been "universally detested" for his conspicuous lack of interest in the consuls' activities and opinions. Lyons, on the other hand, was quickly held in "general estimation" because of the flattering regularity with which he attended to their problems and replied to their letters. Lyons did emulate Bulwer in coming to an understanding with the editor of the *Levant Herald and Eastern Express*, who claimed that his newspaper was the only one in English in the empire and had the second-largest circulation in its capital. With deniability in mind, Lyons used Sheffield as the conduit for tidbits of social information and the occasional "guiding hint" on British policy. Slowly but surely Lyons was mastering both his work and his strange surroundings. "Seriously I am well pleased with this place and the whole thing," he admitted early in the new year.[24]

One delicate and difficult challenge was that of restoring and enhancing British influence without exciting French jealousy. Or as Lady Stratford had expressed it in a none-too-subtle allusion to her husband's career, he should revive the "right principles and honest upright practices" that would regain for Britain its rank as the leading power at Constantinople. With this ambitious objective in mind, Lyons needed to finesse French obstructionism and resist Russian subversion. Edward Erskine, the British minister in Athens, forwarded credible information that Russian emissaries were busily promoting panslavism in Thrace, exciting Bulgarian hatred of Turkish rule, and encouraging the Serbian peasantry to rise in revolt, free themselves, and "unite with their Servian brethren." Only Lyons, Erskine's informant asserted, could counter these subversive activities. Nor should he overlook the French, Erskine advised, for the French minister in Athens was encouraging the Greeks to expand territorially at the empire's expense. How was the influence of the French at Constantinople to be explained, Erskine asked, given their encouragement of Greek aggression especially in Crete? Lyons replied that the Turks, having studied the fate of Denmark, unfortunately placed little trust in Britain's friendship and protection.[25]

After decades of administrative, legal, commercial, and religious reforms that were intended to modernize the state and better equip it to resist both domestic dissidents and external enemies, the heterogeneous empire remained a ramshackle, vulnerable structure. The substantial measure of autonomy enjoyed by areas within it, and the rise of ethnic nationalism among its 6 million Slavs, 4 million Moldo-Wallachians or Romanians, and 2 million Greeks, amounted to an Achilles heel. But it was the empire's misfortune that it had a pair of heels, the result of the reformers' failure to create an efficient, centralized financial system. With British and French support an Imperial Ottoman Bank had been established and its founders had negotiated a foreign loan in 1862. A permanent financial council, on which a Briton, a Frenchman, and an Austrian sat as representatives of the guaranteeing powers of 1856, had drawn up a first budget, but the continued deterioration of the empire's financial position during a period of increasing trade, relative tranquility, and guaranteed territorial integrity was attributed to "ministerial ignorance, inveterate habits of abuse, too much facility of borrowing, and too little prudence at the Porte."[26]

Lyons quickly raised the issue with Fuad. Failure to keep faith with creditors would do untold damage to Turkey's credit and to its reputation with the British public, he repeatedly warned. The grand vizier appointed Mustapha Fazil, brother of the Khedive of Egypt but long a resident of Constantinople, as chair of a Council of Treasury. It was tasked to examine fiscal policy. Fuad spoke of secularizing religious endowments, though Lyons assumed that in that event the bulk of the property would be diverted by corrupt agents into their own pockets. "Honesty and Economy" were necessities, and herein lay a problem for Lyons. Abdul Aziz had developed a passion for ironclad frigates which the British had encouraged because he placed the orders with British shipyards. To remonstrate against this immense expense would be undesirable, Lyons admitted, but they could expect to hear much of the ironclads in any European discussion of Turkish finances.[27]

The Sublime Porte, "absolutely without money" and ever ready to resort to temporary expedients, opened negotiations for another foreign loan. But Fuad recognized that the solution to the recurring problem of an empty treasury was a combination of extraordinary retrenchments and richer revenues. Lyons recommended, as a first step, the preparation of a real as opposed to a fictional financial statement. Its likelihood, never great, effectively disappeared with Mustapha's dismissal for revealing to the Sultan the full extent of corruption. Fuad's promise that certain branches of the revenue would be paid into the Ottoman Bank to cover the interest on foreign loans failed to reassure Lyons. The deposits, he calculated, would never amount to more than an insignificant portion of what was needed, and there was every likelihood of their diversion to other government projects. The news that Ismail Pacha, the Khedive, was seeking exemption from the Ottoman Law of Succession so that his son rather than his brother Mustapha would inherit the viceroyalty raised the possibility that in exchange he would increase substantially the annual tribute to the Sultan. He agreed to increase it from £363,000 to £681,000, but this offered only brief respite and the situation was further complicated by the sudden and unexpected dismissal of Fuad. The grand vizier paid the price for having vetoed Abdul Aziz's marriage to a daughter of the Khedive, which he had done out of fear it would give Ismail too much influence at the palace. The new grand vizier was the unimpressive Mehemid Ruchdi, who was "slow, obstinate, abundantly self-confident" and advocated the printing of money as a solution to financial shortfalls. The collapse of the loan negotiations effectively obliged the Porte to declare bankruptcy. The Foreign Office and Lyons had known at the time of his appointment that his prospects of convincing the Turks to implement fiscal discipline were not good, so his reputation survived this setback. The Turks, he concluded, required pressure as well as encouragement to behave sensibly.[28]

The two less intractable problems with which he had to deal almost from the day of his arrival in the Turkish capital were the Suez Canal and the Danubian Principalities. At his meeting with Aali on 18 October, he had argued that his nation as the empire's friend and benefactor had a right to expect that the Sultan would thwart French plans with respect to the canal that were "evidently designed in hostility to British interests." Moustier's professed lack of interest in the canal was, Lyons believed, merely a screen behind which the French were probably seeking to steal a march on Britain. The news that Ismail Pacha, having prohibited France from employing its troops as labourers on the canal, had agreed to contribute "negroes" to the French forces operating in Mexico alarmed Lyons. Would the Khedive now permit the French to secure lands along the banks of the waterway? Under strong pressure from Lyons, Aali instructed the Porte's canal commissioner to limit severely the land ceded, ordered the Turkish ambassador in Paris to request that the French government put a stop to the efforts of the Canal Company to occupy and dispose of land, and promised to press the Khedive to keep a close eye on its "insidious proceedings." These interventions resulted in a "tolerably satisfactory" settlement and thus a modest success for Lyons, who saw in the French concessions evidence that Lesseps and his associates were in need of cash. When the Khedive arrived in Constantinople to purchase the *firman* altering the line of succession in Egypt, Lyons impressed upon him the protection Egypt enjoyed as part of the Ottoman Empire, the need for constant vigilance in his dealings with the French, and his opportunity to exploit the French company's financial troubles to buy back concessions granted earlier. Not for a moment, however, did Lyons think that the canal problem was solved. He did not trust "these Orientals to look out for themselves" and remained "constantly on the watch."[29]

Watchfulness was also Lyons's response to the chronic problem of the Danubian Principalities. Their restlessness was an obvious and serious threat to the integrity of an empire administered by men whom he judged "supine and careless." Ignatiev had approached him with a proposal for the separation of Wallachia and Moldavia, the removal of Couza, and the election by each territory of its own prince. Moustier had countered with the suggestion that Britain, France, and the Porte combine to frustrate this Russian design. It would be far better, the Frenchman argued, adhering to the line taken by Drouyn de Lhuys in Paris, to maintain the union of the Principalities and retain Couza as the ruler rather than search for a replacement which might revive Great Power jealousies. Aali also raised the Principalities with Lyons, declaring tranquility the Porte's objective. Hence it wished to "correct" Couza not oust him. From Couza's agent in the capital Lyons received a copy of a letter detailing the "insidious character" of Russia's conduct. Sensibly, he declined to commit himself to any course of action before gaining a clearer picture of the situation. He sent for John Green.[30]

Green was a severe critic of the Couza regime. The corruption and poor administration were in his experience unprecedented. In a land where people had once slept behind unlocked doors, and had travelled everywhere unarmed and in safety, brigandage was rampant thanks to the protection it received from the "highest quarters." The prefect of police dismissed by the minister of the interior for harbouring brigands had been reinstated by Couza, a prince living in a "fool's paradise." Discontent

was so general and disorganization so great, Green reported, that catastrophe was inevitable and intervention that did not cut to the root of the
evil would be mischievous. He had not welcomed the instructions from
the Foreign Office to act in close partnership with the French consul
general, Tillos, because of the "malign influence" of Colonel Librecht, "a
Belgium ex-waiter and billiard maker" who had been appointed director
general of posts and telegraphs. He was the "vile and disgusting" agent
of Couza's enjoyment of the favours of Madame Tillos, who had been the
Frenchman's mistress before becoming his wife, and Green believed that
she and Librecht were the means by which Couza had full knowledge of
every single word of his French counterpart's instructions.[31]

Green reached Constantinople on 25 November, and Lyons arranged
for him to meet with Aali, Fuad, Moustier, and Ignatiev. The consul
warned them that revolution was imminent. Couza would be deposed,
he predicted, and power taken by a provisional government dominated
by the "Red Republican Party." He doubted that there was a native of
the Principalities who could govern more ably than Couza, and since
Britain, France, and the Porte had no successor in mind Lyons endorsed
Green's advice that it would be wiser to wait and watch, leaving "things
to accident." Then, on 24 February 1866, word reached Constantinople
that Couza had been compelled to abdicate and a provisional government formed, but it was not the "Red Republican" regime Green had
foretold. The inhabitants of the Principalities were virtually unanimous,
however, in their desire for union and rule by a foreign prince. The del-
egation they dispatched to Constantinople declared such a prince essential for peace and stability, and exhibiting good diplomatic sense the delegates avowed that their surest protection against powerful neighbours
was the continued connection of the United Principalities to the empire.
These assurances of fealty and homage won them an audience with the
Sultan but failed to remove the Porte's opposition to a foreign prince.[32]

Clarendon in London and Lyons in Constantinople discouraged the
Turks from intervening militarily in the Principalities. The foreign secretary proposed, instead, the summoning of a conference to be held in
Paris. The French capital was a convenient location, the meeting there
would be a courtesy to Napoleon III, and Clarendon believed that this
concession would improve Britain's prospects of restraining the French.

The removal of Couza had caused the French to lend their support to the selection of a foreign prince as his successor, but the Turks feared that this would be seen as a national humiliation and would excite demands for greater independence by other remote provinces. The Russians were reported to be sending arms into Serbia and Montenegro, and not to be outbid in the struggle for local influence the Austrians were matching them. Meanwhile, the French were ominously elevating their support for the selection of a foreign prince to a "culte nationale." Cowley suspected that they doubted finding anyone acceptable and were keeping the problem simmering until they thought the time right for the Principalities to throw off their allegiance to the Sultan. For his part, Lyons allowed that a prince of ability, industry, honesty, prudence, and vigour would be a treasure but considered even more important the establishment of constitutional government. No head of government was the worse for being under some control, he believed. A prince of Romania should govern as well as reign, otherwise the Greek mistake would be repeated.

His efforts to calm and comfort the Turks without saying anything that could be interpreted as a personal or British pledge of support saw them accuse Britain of caring more for its relationship with France than for the integrity of the empire. They bitterly resented British accusations of weakness for failing to stand up to French bullying when Britain was plainly unwilling to protect them physically from the consequences of firm resistance. Thinking themselves powerless, the Turks, Lyons informed Clarendon, were rumoured to be contemplating the sale of the Principalities to Russia in the hope that this would satisfy the czar's craving for territory. The Turks were certainly indignant when they heard on 22 May that Prince Charles of Hohenzollern-Sigmaringen had arrived in Bucharest. He was the foreign prince favoured by the Principalities' liberals and by the French, and had passed through Austria disguised as a travelling salesman. The angry and dismayed Turks threatened to resort to force, for they were already under pressure to evacuate the fortresses they held in Serbia, which, while of little military value, they clung to as symbols of suzerainty. Lyons and Moustier were both instructed to counsel the Turks to weigh carefully their options. Would it not be better and less dangerous to acquiesce in the selection of Prince

Charles, rather than trust to the mercy of the Russians, so long as he did homage in the traditional manner, promised to be loyal, and agreed to observe the treaties made between the Porte and other powers? "Unless the Porte soon makes up its mind to recognize Prince Charles at once," Clarendon telegraphed on 21 June, "it must be prepared for his recognition by Russia without reference to the Porte." But by this date the Eastern question had been overshadowed by the events in Central Europe.[33]

Austria and Prussia were at war, though Edmund Hammond had difficulty determining the conflict's rights and wrongs because of the "maze of lies, duplicity and equivocation on all sides." He considered Bismarck the most dangerous figure, for the king of Prussia appeared to be infatuated with him. But the permanent undersecretary's inherent distrust of the French led him to suspect that they would seek to exploit the situation in either the Rhineland or Italy. As for the Russians, their desire to secure compensation for their "discomfiture in the East" in the Crimean War settlement promised to be checked by the shock of the attempted assassination of the czar on 4 April by a fellow Russian. Britain could watch the turmoil on the Continent "with a certain degree of unconcern" so long as Napoleon III made no attempt during the upheaval to annex Belgium, an overconfident Hammond argued. Indeed, he was convinced of the merit and value of Britain's policy of non-intervention. British trade might experience some disruption during the war but if they kept clear of it all the other nations would have to come to Britain for "the supply of their ordinary wants," and eventually it would be the great gainer "from the ruin of manufacturing abroad." Of course, what no one anticipated was a swift Prussian victory. Equally false were Hammond's domestic assumptions. The Russell government would carry second reading of its controversial Reform Bill, he confidently predicted, because the Conservative opposition would not dare fight an election on the issue. Instead, a group of conservative Liberals, whom John Bright scornfully dismissed as troglodytes dwelling in a Cave of Adullam, voted with the opposition, and after some confusion and indecision Russell resigned. Clarendon regretted leaving office with the "vile" problem of the Principalities still unresolved but he advised his Tory successor that the more he left Eastern affairs in the capable hands of Lyons "the better it would be for them and for himself."[34]

CHAPTER ELEVEN

To the Diplomatic Summit

Lyons found his headaches returning within three months of his arrival at Constantinople, and they concerned his closest staff. "I trust we shall have no troubles here to make the work harder than it is," Edward Malet wrote to his mother, "for our chiefs [*sic*] head is not as much cured of headaches as to prevent one from feeling alarm at the idea of strain upon it." Her suggestion that a clairvoyant be consulted he sensibly did not pass on. The visit in April by Lyons's young nephews, Henry, Duke of Norfolk, and Louis Wurtzburg – the former "a good little fellow," the latter a "nuisance" – provided a welcome distraction from his political headaches. The youths attended the celebration of the Queen's birthday on 24 May, and Lyons did not repeat his predecessor's mistake. He invited only forty Britons to dinner. Following another dinner, this one for the visiting Khedive, Ismail Pacha, "a round podgy little man rather lively and very animal looking," Lyons, his nephews, and staff steamed up the Bosporus in June to the ambassador's villa at Therapia. Called a palace, it remained despite recent repairs a "tumbledown house." The flimsy structure meant that any noise was heard everywhere. The windows forming three sides of the drawing room rattled loudly in the wind and were a sore trial for a man who prized quiet and was cursed with headaches. Bugs, beetles, ants, moths, and slugs were additional annoyances, and Lyons made plain his distaste by likening the experience to shipboard life. However, he and his party soon boarded the *Caradoc* for the short voyage across the Sea of Marmara to the port of Mondanieh (Mudanya). He had decided to lead an expedition to the local Mount Olympus, which rose more than 8,000 feet above the city of Broussa (Bursa) in the ancient province of Bithynia. The party rode on horseback from the port to the inland city, where they visited mosques and toured the famed silk "manufactories." Rested, they began the ascent and after hours of hard hiking reached a plateau where tents had been erected on the orders of the local governor to provide them with shelter overnight. An extremely cold night and a heavy fall of snow caused Lyons to abandon the expedition, and two days later the entire group was again happily basking in the warmth of Therapia.[1]

Thanks to the London-Constantinople telegraph line Lyons soon learned of the change of government at home, where the Tories had again taken office under Lord Derby. His choice of his son Lord Stanley as foreign secretary raised eyebrows. The appointment was welcomed by Clarendon, to whom the Conservative leader had first offered the Foreign Office. In refusing, the Whig had worried that Disraeli might be his replacement. His selection would give offence to every foreign power, Clarendon privately sneered, for while previous holders of the seals had varied in fitness and intellect, all had at least been gentlemen. No doubt it was knowledge of Disraeli's strenuous opposition to Malmesbury's return to the Foreign Office that had alarmed Clarendon, but as it happened the Tories' Commons' spokesman strongly supported the choice of Stanley. He argued that the foreign secretary should be in the Commons since the prime minister was in the upper house. Derby had already decided not to send his middle-aged son back to the India Office he had occupied in his previous administration because it took the minister "more or less out of the general course of European politics." Nor was Stanley especially ill-equipped for his new responsibilities. He had travelled extensively, had served as Malmesbury's parliamentary undersecretary in the first Derby government, was "clever, industrious and just," and even looked the part, being a "tall, pale, Saxon-looking man." The lingering doubts of his fitness had more to do with his ideological non-interventionism and chronic indecisiveness. Not that foreign affairs were the first concern of the new government. Until the unresolved domestic issue of parliamentary reform was settled, it was assumed that international affairs would be a secondary concern.[2]

One problem that did arise almost immediately was the selection of an ambassador to the Second Empire, Cowley having announced his intention to resign. It presented "a great difficulty," Derby admitted, for the Paris embassy was one that might be given "in or out of the regular service." An appointee from outside the profession would need to be a figure of recognized political importance. Malmesbury met that requirement but was excluded from serious consideration because of his old friendship with Louis Napoleon, which stoked fears that he would be putty in the hands of the crafty emperor. Of the senior and experienced diplomatists who came to mind Sir John Crampton was considered "worn out," Henry Bulwer was tarnished by scandal, and Lord Kimberely, who had been an undersecretary for foreign affairs, a diplomat, and a successful Lord Lieutenant of Ireland, was politically unacceptable. "I am not myself a votary of the ultra-professional spirit in diplomatic appointments," Disraeli later remarked, conveniently overlooking Kimberley's service as envoy extraordinary to Russia after the Crimean War, "but the system certainly ought not to be broken into in favour of a violent partisan on the wrong side, and who, according to my personal judgment of him, is vain, shallow and incapable." The talk of transferring Lord Bloomfield from Vienna to Paris was again silenced by Disraeli and with a characteristic jibe. In "both handwriting and matter," he wrote of Bloomfield's dispatches, they "are those of a greengrocer."[3]

The shortlist of acceptable candidates had only two names. Lord Strathnairn, the former Sir Hugh Rose, had combined soldiering and diplomacy, winning high marks as a liaison officer with the French during the Crimean War. His military reputation had been made during the Indian mutiny, and he had become the Tories' favourite soldier despite staging a macabre mass execution of 140 sepoys. Arrogant, vain, and selfish, he was unloved by subordinates and made few friends. His attraction, Disraeli believed, was his military reputation, which would be his greatest asset in France, where a general enjoyed greater respect than any other figure. Nevertheless, his appointment would be a risk. His hospitality was often a source of embarrassment because of his tendency to forget such important details as the date of the meal and the number of guests. "This caused the poor cook much tribulation as sometimes an enormous feast was prepared and hardly anyone turned up, whilst at other times people flocked in when there was nothing to eat." This would not be a welcome British eccentricity in Paris. Another liability was his suspect "*temper*," and it was Derby's opinion that an ambassador to France required "a considerable stock" of good humour and self-control. Moreover, there was doubt whether he could be safely spared from his current military command in Ireland, where an insurgency appeared imminent.

Lyons was the other candidate. There would be little trouble replacing him in Constantinople, and his temperament was not suspect. He was capable, cautious, tactful, prudent, and reserved. The doubts were of his ability to do "the social part well," or gain a great deal of information. He shunned ungentlemanly intelligence activities, despising such "dirty matters" whose importance he disputed. As for his want of a "sufficient social position," which Disraeli fastened on, Stanley considered the criticism more than a little rich given the source. Nevertheless, the lack of a wife was a "more real drawback." Clarendon, when consulted, spoke of Lyons's "extreme shyness, want of initiative, [and] fear of responsibility," but this was more a mistaken identification of his reserve. He had not shirked responsibility in Rome, Washington, or Constantinople. Significantly, Clarendon still recommended him highly, and Derby agreed that Lyons was the best man for the post. He had played a vital role in securing a solution to the problem of the Danubian Principalities and had regained for the embassy much of the respect it had lost under his predecessor. The prime minister admired the skill, shrewdness, and subtlety with which Lyons had established a good working relationship with a French ambassador in Constantinople who was heartily disliked by every other member of the diplomatic corps, and it had made possible his modest successes. That same Frenchman was now Napoleon III's foreign minister.[4]

No sooner had Derby and Stanley decided to send Lyons to Paris than Cowley expressed a wish to remain there for at least another year. He professed to be acting in response to a request from the Queen that he be on hand to manage the visits of the Prince of Wales and the Duke of Edinburgh to the Paris Exhibition of 1867. The heir to the throne was leading an "utterly foolish frivolous life," displaying a fondness for "actresses" and an aversion to sober advice. Cowley's presence was to prove no deterrent to fresh indiscretions, the Prince becoming one of the many intimates of the current sensation of the Paris stage, Hortense Schneider. As the ambassador admitted, "it would not do to enquire too closely" into the behaviour of the Prince and his brother the Duke when they were not in society. Stanley, convinced that Cowley had manoeuvred the Queen into seeking an extension of his tenure in the hope that the delay would benefit Bloomfield's candidacy, stuck to his choice of Lyons. He knew from his discussion with Clarendon that were the Liberals quickly to regain office they would appoint Lyons to the Paris embassy. Although he received no formal notification, Lyons was soon aware that the most prestigious post in the profession was soon to be his. Stanley had mentioned his intention to the Turkish ambassador in London and he forwarded the news to Aali, who congratulated Lyons. In the meantime, the foreign secretary was pleased that Lyons would be remaining in Constantinople during a "critical" period. Equally pleased was Minna, who thought a short extension of her brother's residence in the Ottoman capital would strengthen his health and thus better prepare him for the challenge of Paris.[5]

Meanwhile, Edmund Hammond's "pleasurable excitement" at the prospect of a German war was short-lived. He had expected Britain to profit from the conflict between Austria and Prussia, one in which he assumed the Austrians would do well. Instead, they suffered a swift and crushing defeat. Stanley's immediate concern was France. Bismarck had persuaded Napoleon III to remain on the sidelines with the hint that he would not stand in the way of French annexation of Belgium and Luxembourg, only for the unforseen speed and totality of Prussia's victory to greatly alter the situation. A preliminary peace was signed on 26 July 1866, and the awesome demonstration of Prussian military might, and the shock it delivered to the French public, alarmed Napoleon. France was submitting to the new European power structure with "great reluctance and disgust," Cowley admitted, but he was confident peace would endure at least until the closing of the Paris Exhibition of 1867. Yet it was plain that a Franco-Prussian war would be a means of completing the work of German unity only partially accomplished with the signing of the final terms of Prusso-Austrian peace at Prague on 23 August. It established Prussian hegemony in a Germany from which Austria was excluded. The old German Confederation was abolished and a North German Confederation led by Prussia created. Two months later Austria surrendered Venetia to the French emperor, who then handed it on to Prussia's ally, Italy. The Risorgimento was nearing fulfilment, and only the presence of French troops in and around Rome prevented it from becoming the capital of the Kingdom of Italy. Would the French seek to annex Belgium and/or Luxembourg? "We live in dangerous times for small States," Stanley observed, but the news that Napoleon was recovering only slowly from a mysterious illness made imminent French action unlikely.[6]

What of the Eastern question? In Crete the rebels were receiving aid from Greece, a kingdom with which they sought union. Stanley considered the "Eastern Christians" fanatical and intolerant, thus little different from the Turks and at no higher "point of civilisation." His father, being of the same opinion, did not think the condition of the Cretan Christians would be improved through union with the "wretched little Kingdom of Greece, whose utter incapacity of government at home [was] only equalled by its activity for mischief abroad." He suspected the Cretans of being mere pawns of Russians committed to the subversion of Ottoman sovereignty. But armed intervention would be "exceedingly impolitic" in the present state of affairs. The Ottoman Empire, although "worn out and unable to maintain itself," had no natural heir. Were Greece a well-governed and civilized country, like Piedmont and Prussia, the solution would be obvious and simple. Instead, it was "bankrupt, anarchical, without an honest politician or class which can be trusted with power." Therefore, sooner rather than later, they would be faced yet again with the Eastern question, and Stanley had no desire for Britain always to be on the losing side. "I don't mean that we should take part against the Turks," he assured his father, "but only that we should avoid doing anything that looks like giving them direct assistance. Remember that nothing can be done to remedy such a state of feeling as exists throughout Greece, short of an occupation by an armed force." With Europe rapidly returning to peace, all attention would soon be fixed on the East as "the only disturbed question," Stanley told Lyons, before assuring him that he remained committed to a policy of non-intervention.[7]

The struggle to rescue the finances of the Ottoman Empire had effectively been lost, so the Turks remained a "dangerous element." The personally honest grand vizier lacked the ability to improve the administration of the empire's finances and thus the means to pay the dividends
on the foreign loans. Another problem was the Principalities, which
threatened to emerge as "source of future confusion in Europe." Much
of the credit for the fact that they did not belonged to Lyons. He alone of
the members of the diplomatic corps had maintained "very cordial and
confidential relations" with the volatile and difficult Moustier and had
drawn him into a co-operative arrangement reminiscent of the one he
had pursued with Henri Mercier in Washington. He had found it easier
and more agreeable to work with the French "than with most other foreigners," and saw in his co-operation with Moustier the best means of
keeping the Ottoman Empire quiet. Collaboration with the Frenchman
ensured that both the Romanian prince and the Turks attended to his
advice that a stable and honest government in the Principalities – "with
just so much connection to Turkey to maintain the principle of the integrity of the Empire" – was the best solution for all parties. It would
deny the Russians a pretext for intervention, and containment of their
influence in the Balkans was a prime objective of British policy. Lyons
and Moustier sent "identic" telegrams to Bucharest announcing the refusal of both their nations to countenance either independence or repudiation of Turkish suzerainty. They pressured the government of the
Principalities to agree to Charles's investiture on "the reasonable and
moderate terms" offered by the Porte, and dissuaded him from seeking
to exercise the powers tantamount to political independence conferred
on him by the new Romanian Constitution, a document which Green
considered a "bombastic act of aggression against the Porte" drafted by
"silly and incapable" men. And to ensure unified representation in Bucharest, Lyons instructed Green to announce that he and the French
consul general were acting in concert. Fortunately, co-operation had
been made easier by the recall of Tillos. His clever replacement, Baron
d'Avril, a former *rédacteur* in the French Foreign Office and a scribe for
the *Revue des Deux Mondes*, exhibited "none of the presumption which
frequently renders Frenchmen unpleasant colleagues."[8]

The settlement of the squabble over the investiture of Charles as
prince was effected by Lyons, and following Moustier's departure home

he was careful to associate the French chargé d'affaires with every move he made. He informed Charles that in writing to the Sultan he needed to acknowledge that the Principalities were an integral part of the Ottoman Empire and to omit any demand that he be received "unconditionally" in Constantinople. The Turks would interpret this proviso as a lack of interest in a compromise solution, he warned. Compromise being a two-way street, Lyons convinced the Porte to withdraw its demands that the Romanians acknowledge its "right" both to maintain an agent in Bucharest and to veto any substantial increase in the size of the Romanian army. Charles then came to Constantinople, where his reception was cordial and hospitable. He met on 24 October with the Sultan, from whom he received the carefully negotiated *firman* of investiture, and called on Lyons the following afternoon to thank him for his assistance. Naturally, Lyons was irritated by Moustier's boast in Paris that he alone was responsible for the Turks' recognition of Charles as prince. However, the foreign secretary recognized his larger contribution. These things "are French nature, and the French are only surprised that we don't do the same," Stanley wryly observed. He knew the truth and congratulated Lyons handsomely on his excellent management of the question and the "judicious manner" with which he had smoothed over the difficulties. His diplomatic discretion and the "straightforwardness" of his dealings were sources of his burgeoning influence with the Porte, evident in Aali's habit of talking with him confidentially and fully. Nor was Lyons a man to forget a loyal ally. He called to Stanley's attention John Green's complaint that he cut a shabby figure in Bucharest because his salary did not approach those of the French and Russian consuls. Green was awarded an additional £300 a year.[9]

There are "no questions of much interest or importance in the office," Stanley wrote Lyons in mid-October. He calculated that six hours a day would be more than enough time to get through what he needed to do were it not for the "curiously unbusiness like habits of diplomatists." They never went straight to the point but insisted first on talking of "indifferent things." Their calls on him were driven, he supposed, by a desire to find out what was "passing and get materials for a despatch." This did not deter him from keeping Lyons, as the prospective ambassador to France, abreast of what was happening in Western Europe. Fully one-half of the alarming accounts of the state of the French emperor's health were spread for "stock-jobbing purposes," Stanley suggested. He expressed bemusement at the French belief that at its current strength of 600,000 men their army was incapable of defending the nation. French troops had been demoralized by the massive casualties suffered by the Austrians in the recent war, victims of the Prussians' breech-loading weaponry, he had been told, yet the French infantry was being re-equipped with a superior rifle named for its inventor Antoine Chassepot. Troop strength was on the rise. Unfortunately, the plan announced in December, which called for a regular army of 800,000 men and a reserve militia of 300,000, risked the alienation of the peasantry, who were the popular backbone of the Napoleonic regime. Plainly, a "plebiscitary dictator" in uncertain health, aware of an erosion of his popular support, and given to foreign adventures, was not a reassuring actor on the international stage. Long used to being surrounded by weak states, the French regarded a Prussian neighbour of equal strength a threat. Deepening the foreign secretary's unease as year's end approached were the stories of the collapse of Bismarck's mental health and the dire predictions that without his master hand to settle its affairs Germany would descend into anarchy. Then there was the decision of the Prince of Wales to travel to St Petersburg to attend a royal wedding where he was likely to be indiscreet in expressing his anti-Turkish sentiments. Stanley discreetly advised the Russians that Edward's opinion was "not necessarily that of the Cabinet."

The Eastern question continued to simmer. John Green had warned that in Serbia and Bulgaria, where Russian influence was most apparent, the populations were ripe for rebellion. The Russians were also at work in Romania, he reported, stirring up sedition in the belief that confusion there would open wider the door to their intervention elsewhere. Paris, meanwhile, was rife with rumours of a Franco-Russian understanding on the fate of the Ottoman Empire. When questioned by Cowley, Napoleon responded that in working with a Russia humiliated and isolated as a result of the Crimean War he was endeavouring to restrain that nation. His contention that Russia had no present intent to dismember the Ottoman Empire was immediately contradicted by its proposal for Greek annexation of Crete. As the island suddenly emerged as "the European question of the moment," Lyons found himself at its heart.[10]

Fearful that bloodshed and atrocities would excite disturbances elsewhere among the Sultan's heterogeneous subjects, which might result
in the destruction of the Ottoman Empire in Europe (for the plight
of Christian victims was certain to excite European sympathy), Lyons
sought as ever to calm the situation. On the one hand he disabused the
Greeks of the idea that Britain would rush to the aid of the Cretans, and
on the other he stressed the need for the Turks to redress grievances,
adopt salutary measures of reform, and prevent confrontations between
Muslim troops and the Christian populace. Unless the problems in Crete
were addressed, he warned Aali, the disorder would spread to other
provinces leading to "the 'destruction of Ottoman Rule in Europe.'" The
Porte promptly announced the dispatch of a special commissioner to
the island. Although he suspected that the widely distributed reports
of Muslim atrocities had been exaggerated, Lyons worried that violence
"incompatible with the usages of civilized warfare" might become inevitable. He counselled Aali to announce an investigation of alleged atrocities and dissuaded him from withdrawing the Ottoman minister and
consuls from Greece on the news that Turks residing there were being
roughly treated. The severing of diplomatic relations would simply convince the Greeks of Ottoman weakness, he cautioned, and thus cause
additional trouble among the empire's Hellenic minority, who were already exhibiting rebel sympathies.[11]

A storm was brewing in the East, Lyons advised Stanley, and Russia
was at its centre. It was seeking to reassert its self-proclaimed role as special protector of the Sultan's Christian subjects. Hence it welcomed the
disruptive conduct of the Greeks, knowing that a forcible response by
the Turks might spark European intervention. Lyons's nagging fear was
that serious disturbances by ethnic Greeks would spell the empire's end
at a time when it was by no means clear what would replace it. What was
certain was a European crisis because the Turks would put up a fight,
during which "carnage, devastation and every kind of horror" would
ensue. The way to avoid these calamities was to prop up the Turks and
oblige them "go on tolerably well for some years longer." Lyons denied
being one of those who thought that the empire should be sustained at
all costs. Rather, he wished to let it down "gently." If this subtle policy
was to succeed, the Turks "must be prudent and behave well towards

all their subjects." Hence his pressing the Porte to go to considerable
lengths to avoid conflict with Greece over the support being given the
Cretan rebels, and his strong recommendation that it appease Serbia by
evacuating the fortress in Belgrade.[12]

Stanley's commitment to non-intervention dictated Britain's response
to the problems of the Ottoman Empire. After considerable hesitation,
the foreign secretary joined the French in proposing local autonomy for
Crete. He refused even to hint at coercion, however, in order "that the
very offer of friendly advice [might] be made the occasion for laying
down the doctrine of non-interference." His intention, he admitted to
Lyons, was to be "as little mixed up in the quarrel as we can." But the
question became "more perplexing" when Moustier unexpectedly endorsed the Russian call for Greek annexation of the island. The foreign
minister appeared to be reacting to rumours of a Russo-Prussian agreement directed against his nation. Moustier was seeking to use Crete as
an element in a "masterly policy" designed to transfer Russian sympathies from Prussia to France, the Foreign Office suspected. "It is incon-
ceivable how these people are playing the Russian game *with their eyes
open*," a scornful Cowley commented. Britain's clear duty was to "stand
aloof" from the intrigues. "We have no personal ends to serve, and all
the world knows it," Stanley wrote to Lyons on 7 March. "We have the
strongest reason to suppose that every other power has some such ends:
and the experience of the Mexican expedition, into which England was
drawn simply by a wish to get her just claims settled, while France aimed
at founding a new empire, is a warning for the future." Britain's object
should be the avoidance of entanglements. But Lyons was not a fully
committed non-interventionist. The advantages of not interfering in the
politics of the Continent came at a price, he observed, and it was the loss
of influence with the European states. Benjamin Disraeli was another
questioner of non-intervention in Europe, observing: "I doubt whether
this country would see any further glaring case of public violence and
treachery with composure. Reaction is the law of human affairs and
the reaction from non-intervention must sooner or later set in. I would
rather however try to prevent mischief."[13]

Stanley's decision to follow the French lead on Crete threatened to
cause him acute political embarrassment when Moustier suddenly

endorsed annexation, but from this he was rescued by other dramatic developments which caused the island to "drop out off men's minds." At home, the government found itself in "a bit of a mess" over the Reform Bill, for the measure Disraeli was piloting skilfully through the Commons was more liberal than that which had brought down the Liberals. Abroad, a crisis seemed imminent over France's desire to acquire the Grand Duchy of Luxembourg. That it coincided with Cowley's resignation as ambassador meant that Lyons would be arriving in Paris at a time when, in Stanley's words, "the eastern question seems likely to be suspended by even more serious difficulties at home." On a visit to France, Clarendon detected and reported grave public anxiety, a deepening distrust of the emperor's wisdom, an uneasiness at the loss of international prestige, a jealousy of Prussia, and even a vague fear of revolution. There were rumours of an arrangement between the French and the Prussians which would see France annex Belgium in exchange for not opposing Prussian absorption of southern Germany. Stanley could not believe that Bismarck would make so direct a proposal, though he thought it the kind of wild idea that would appeal to the emperor, whom he likened to the gambler who having lost half his fortune sought to recover it with a single coup that was more likely to prove fatal. In this instance the coup was not Belgium but Luxembourg. Napoleon planned to purchase it from an impecunious Dutch monarch who was its grand duke, only for Bismarck to block the sale. The Grand Duchy had been a member of the recently dissolved German Confederation and its massive fortress was still occupied by Prussian troops, so the Dutch monarch did not dare complete the transaction without Prussian consent. Stanley thought it rich of the Prussians to cavil over so modest an increase of French territory when they had so recently swallowed up half a dozen German states. Stymied, Napoleon sought to save face by demanding the withdrawal of the Prussian troops from the fortress. The "irritation against Prussia is so strong," Cowley advised Lyons, "that I can hardly see how war is eventually to be avoided."

The nervous Belgian king suspected that in the event of war France would seize his nation and allow the Prussians to occupy Holland. The time had come for a little "reaction," Disraeli suggested, and for Britain "to dictate a little to Europe." The foreign secretary was willing to support Belgium diplomatically but would not pledge to fight in defence of that nation's independence. The Grand Duchy's neutralization was "the indispensable condition of peace," he believed, and if established, and the Prussian troops withdrawn, the terms of a settlement would be in place. Both he and the Queen appealed to the Prussians to make the "slight" concession required of them, and the several governments responded favourably to a Russian call for an international conference to meet in London. There, on 11 May 1867, a treaty was signed. The fortress was to be demolished, the Prussian troops withdrawn, the Duchy's neutrality reaffirmed, but it was to be included in the German Customs Union, which Prussia dominated, and it was to remain a personal possession of the Dutch monarch.

This peaceful resolution of the crisis won Stanley "golden opinions" for his management of foreign affairs, though skeptics warned that a Franco-Prussian war had merely been postponed. The mutual irritation and distrust of the two nations had not lessened and neither of them exhibited any inclination to reduce their massive military establishments. But in this instance Stanley placed his faith in time as an instrument of peace. It would allow "irritation to subside," new questions to come to the fore which would divert attention from the problem, and would provide an opportunity for the expression of public opinion, which he unwisely assumed would always be pacific. Furthermore, the success of the London Conference appeared to contradict those critics of non-intervention who claimed that Stanley's policies led to everything being arranged or disarranged without Britain. Instead, Hammond boasted, other nations "begin to find they cannot do without us, and the less forward we are the more anxiety do they show to secure our goodwill and cooperation." This was a dangerously optimistic conclusion. Edward Erskine, writing to Lyons from Athens, urged the abandonment of Britain's attitude as a mere spectator of the Crete rebellion. Convinced that the Foreign Office would turn a deaf ear to the croaking of so obscure an agent as himself, he urged Lyons to make the case to Stanley for a more active policy.[14]

Lyons had remained at Therapia throughout the summer and autumn of 1866 impatiently awaiting the repair and redecoration of the embassy in Pera. The "palace" on the Bosporus was more habitable yet still in "very bad repair," and he described residence there as a form of bivouacking. He welcomed the cool temperatures and the companionship of Malet and Sheffield, which ensured his life went on "quietly and contentedly." They made a flying visit to Constantinople, where on 12 September Lyons hosted a "farewell family dinner" for Moustier, his wife, their three children, and four French embassy secretaries. The meal, prepared by Lyons's cordon bleu cook, presumably pleased French palates. Lyons found Therapia cold and uncomfortable on his return there and complained of his enforced residence in a "miserable house" in this "bleak place," but it was early November before the embassy was fit for occupation. He found that the troubles of the Ottoman Empire were multiplying. Instead of offering amnesty to Greeks taken prisoner in Crete, as he had advised, the Porte continued to imprison them. From Belgrade there were reports of warlike preparations financed by the Russians. More surprising and disturbing was the evidence of Muslim disaffection. Troops and bureaucrats had not been paid and there was popular resentment of both increased taxation and the Principalities' settlement, which many Turks considered an Ottoman humiliation.[15]

The new year saw Malet go on leave and Sheffield complain incessantly of poor health. Even though he had concluded that Sheffield was a hypochondriac, Lyons granted him a month's vacation in Egypt. This left him with the comfort only of his dog "Toby" and brought the return of his "bad headaches." He encountered few English people with whom he wished to spend much time, too many of them being insignificant merchants "with few ideas beyond the place." He was growing disheartened over the empire's chronic malaise and was reduced to hoping that another crisis might be avoided until matters were ripe for either the patient's recovery or his "dying gently." The formation of a new government in February 1867 was welcome but did little to raise his spirits. Aali became grand vizier, and the energetic and enterprising Fuad returned to office as foreign minister but had become in the opinion of Lyons a "humbug" far more interested in appearances than in progress. Lyons joined the new and young French ambassador in pressing the Porte to introduce internal reforms in the belief that if things were made at least more tolerable for the empire's subjects its collapse would be slower and more gradual, thereby lessening the consequent "shock and the damage."[16]

The problem of Crete dragged on. Stanley, who thought the Porte had little chance of long retaining the island, did not consider it the business of Britain "to help in the work of separation." What he recommended was the adoption of an administrative system similar to that of Lebanon, where a Christian governor with executive powers was assisted by a council on which Muslims and Christians had an equal say. The Turks rejected this possible solution. The French proposal that Crete be handed to Greece and that nation expand to its "natural frontiers" of Thessaly and Epirus would in the judgment of Lyons bring the empire nearer than ever to ruin without satisfying the Russians. They, he argued, were determined to prevent a reconciliation of the Porte and the Sultan's Christian subjects in the hope thereby of draining its finances preparatory to a seizure of territory. A second British proposal was for the Porte "spontaneously" to grant Crete real autonomy and confer on the Christian population a positive share in the government. This the Porte rejected as imperial suicide. Aali did, as Lyons advised, send a relief commissioner to the island bearing gifts of clothes, tents, provisions, and medical stores, but Lyons, frustrated by the lack of progress towards a lasting solution of the problem, and by his inability to persuade the Porte to introduce reforms to slow the empire's disintegration, welcomed his escape to France. On 7 May 1867, he formally accepted the Paris embassy. "I cannot but rejoice at our being free from the tangled meshes of recent French and Russian policy here," he wrote Stanley. "I have taken no step and offered no advice which in the least degree pledges Great Britain either to the Porte or to the Powers. When the time comes, if come it does for our acting, we shall be entirely free to act for the good of all parties." Here was another hint of his less-than-full commitment to non-intervention.[17]

Lyons had been cheered by the return of Malet and Sheffield in March, the latter not looking especially well but at least in better spirits. They in turn had found him "pretty near well," and thanks to fewer headaches "very lively." He hosted a large dinner in April for the visiting Prince of Serbia, "a very presentable savage, tall, smart figure and good manners." Following the annual dinner in celebration of the Queen's birthday, he retreated to a more habitable Therapia. The balconies had been repaired and the dining room improved, so it was a little less uncomfortable. There he read the many letters of congratulation on his new appointment. Cowley flattered him that he had never known of one so young reaching the summit of the service. Lyons had celebrated his fiftieth birthday a month earlier. Minna could scarcely contain her joy that he was at last to be within easy reach, but her boast that he had reached the pinnacle of his profession entirely on his own merits glossed over the "influence" that had from time to time been exerted on his behalf. Undoubtedly, his performances in Rome and Washington had paved the path to this goal, and he had done as well in Constantinople as could reasonably be expected. One piece of well-intentioned advice that he ignored was offered by Monson, who suggested that he take Cowley's second daughter, Lady Feodorowna, "a discreet maiden of some 30 summers," to Paris as Lady Lyons. Her residence there during the fifteen years of her father's tenure guaranteed that she would make a "commendable ambassadress." She was to return there in that role in 1905. Lyons preferred the company of Malet and Sheffield. "I shall be very uncomfortable and be very much at a loss even in business matters," he warned Hammond, "if I do not have them with me." Sheffield was immediately appointed, but only with time and persistence were Malet's services secured. Eventually, he was named a supernumerary second secretary.[18]

Having gratefully accepted the Paris embassy, Lyons immediately and characteristically began to fret over the expense. He was only just beginning to recover from the cost of setting up in Constantinople, and while the salary in Paris was £2,000 higher, he worried he would not be able to afford to have things done well there. "I want to do Paris well," he assured Hammond, "but it will be a great strain upon my means at first and you must manage to let me have as much pay as the regulations will admit of. My experience here and at Washington has convinced me that a very great deal depends upon keeping a good house and establishment – a notion which I used to contest in theory, but which I have acted upon in practice since I have had the means of doing so." He was disappointed to learn that he was to receive only a very modest outfit allowance of £2,000, news that Hammond endeavoured to put into perspective. Horses and carriages would be cheaper to purchase in London in the early autumn than at any other season, and since Lyons was a

bachelor he would avoid "a very expensive item, namely lady's dress."
Hammond wrote with the authority of a father of three daughters. "It is
bad enough in London," he moaned, "but ruinous in Paris." For the first
time in his career someone had found an advantage, if only monetary,
in the refusal of Lyons to take a wife. As for the knotty question of the
date on which his larger salary would commence, Lyons was assured
that he would be dealt with as liberally as possible. He promptly claimed
the leave for which he was eligible after twenty uninterrupted months
in Constantinople.[19]

The Sultan had accepted an invitation to visit the Paris Exhibition,
and his wish to then visit Britain added a sensitive item to the Lyons
agenda. The Foreign Office was anxious to know whether his suite
would be modest in number and as little representative as possible of
the "peculiarities of Oriental life." Would Abdul Aziz, the first Sultan to
pay a friendly visit to Western Europe, be accompanied by concubines
and slaves? Lyons answered that he would not. However, his reception
in England should match that given him in France. Much the same rule,
Lyons added, should govern the reception of the Khedive of Egypt, who,
inconveniently, would be visiting at much the same time and whose territories were of such strategic importance to Britain. Hence *The Times*
questioned the decision to put the Viceroy up at an "inn," Claridge's,
which sat in the "midst of a crowded and noisy thoroughfare consisting
of a few second-rate Brook-street houses" and was surrounded by buildings where there was no pretence of a garden "so constant an accompa-
niment of an Oriental residence." In the event, his reception was perhaps a little too royal. Ismail Pacha dined and slept at Windsor Castle,
whereas the Sultan, who was provided with apartments at Buckingham
Palace, was invited for lunch only.[20]

Aware that not a single member of the Sultan's party had a command
of English, Lyons added to it a young member of his staff who spoke
Turkish and mixed well with the Turks. Every effort should be made,
Lyons advised the Foreign Office, to impress Abdul Aziz with Britain's
wealth and naval might. The Turk's passion for ironclads suggested that
the sight of a fleet of battleships might have even greater influence than
the glitter and magnificence of the City of Light. He was escorted across
the Channel by some of the Royal Navy's finest ships, and on arrival

in London found several state carriages with their "gorgeously-arrayed attendants" and an escort of household cavalry ready to transport him in royal style along the Guardsman-lined route to Buckingham Palace. Unfortunately, not all of the functions went off smoothly. The reception organized by the Turkish ambassador, Constantine Musurus, lacked its host because Madame Musurus had dropped dead at a ball held a few days earlier. The foolish Lord Cardigan then created a scene when, peeved that he had not been identified as he considered he ought to have been when introduced to the Sultan, yelled that he had led the charge at Balaclava. This notorious Crimean War disaster was not one for which most men would have wished to claim the credit. As Lyons recommended, a massive naval review which included fifteen ironclads was staged at Spithead, and the Queen was prevailed upon to invite both the Sultan and the Khedive to view it from her yacht. Unfortunately, pelting rain so reduced visibility that the guests saw little. Lyons had also emphasized the desirability of demonstrating to the Sultan the joys of constitutional monarchy by showing him that it increased popular loyalty to and reverence of the sovereign. This objective led to cancellation of the planned military review in Hyde Park. The scandalous gossip concerning the nature of the Queen's relationship with her Scottish gillie, John Brown, and the knowledge that the London mob was beginning "to speak very disrespectfully of her," caused the Cabinet to ban Brown from the spectacle. Ministers feared his presence would produce "hoots" from the crowd. Victoria then refused to attend without him, using as her excuse the news of Emperor Maximilian's execution in Mexico. Instead, the Prince of Wales and the Sultan reviewed a brigade of the household cavalry, four battalions of foot guards, and a mass of volunteers on Wimbledon Common only for another rainstorm to terminate the ceremony abruptly.[21]

Lyons was not in Britain during the Sultan's visit. He remained at Therapia, where he was able to economize in preparation for Paris and avoid the farewells organized by Constantinople's appreciative British community. Some 146 members of it signed a farewell address in which they declared that "the better moral atmosphere" of his embassy had instilled in them a "universal feeling of attachment and respect." The Cricket Club thanked him for the handsome donation which ensured the success of the coming season. The Protestant community thanked him for his "cordial sympathy," which had secured for them the privileges and rights bestowed on his subjects by the Sultan. The American missionaries seeking to establish a Christian college in the capital thanked him for his vigorous backing of their project. In the same vein was the order issued by Aali at Lyons's prompting admitting Protestants to the *medjlisses* that had been created to limit the power of provincial pachas. But the continued domination of these conciliar bodies by local notables prevented them from becoming, which was the intent, organs of administrative reform. Similarly, the negotiation of another foreign loan shortly before Lyons's departure was a reminder that the old unsatisfactory system of state finances continued. The money covered the interest on the old debts by adding to them.[22]

Lyons and Sheffield sailed from Therapia aboard the *Caradoc* on 25 July. They made for Varna, the former British and French headquarters and naval base during the Crimean War, and were thankful for a calm Black Sea. From there they took the train to Rustchuk (Ruse) on the right bank of the Danube. Then it was up the river to Pesth, which they reached on the last day of July. The arrival that very evening of the Sultan on his way back to his capital allowed Lyons to take formal leave of him. This he did on 2 August before setting off for the resort spa of Bad Kissingen, where he and Sheffield met up with Annie. From there their route took them via Mayenne, Cologne, Brussels, and Calais to London, which they reached in mid-August. They were in good time for Lyons to brief his successor at Constantinople, who was waiting for the cooler autumn temperatures before setting off. Lyons then went down to Arundel to spend time with Minna and her family. The quiet and undisturbed atmosphere of castle life provided him with a very welcome, restful environment. On his return there in mid-September he brought a supply of reading material. He had purchased the recently published *Early Years of His Royal Highness the Prince Consort*, written by Victoria's private secretary, General Charles Grey, and the far lighter read, if not in hand, Trollope's *Last Chronicle of Barset*.[23]

On his first arrival in the capital, Lyons may have encountered the Clevelands, whose townhouse in St James's Square was only a few yards from Norfolk House. Friends and family were urging Lyons to marry, perhaps aware of Clarendon's remark that in Paris the lack of a wife would be a serious diplomatic disadvantage. They recommended Cleveland's "very clever and ladylike" step-daughter. Malet, who privately admitted that a marriage would be "rather disastrous" for his own future prospects as his chief's companion, nevertheless approved. He and Sheffield could not be with Lyons forever, and the time would certainly come when he would "feel the want of a wife to take care of him." Cleveland was allegedly willing to settle £100,000 on the young lady, and in the event of a quick change of government, and thus perhaps Lyons's loss of the Paris embassy, "it would be a great thing for him to have her as company and her money to ensure his comfort." The visit Lyons paid at the end of September to Cleveland's County Durham seat, Raby Castle – "a noble pile of stately towers, retaining all the appearance of ambiguity and giving the most perfect idea of a great baron's palace in feudal ages" – was interpreted by Malet as evidence that the union was about to be finalized. But the absence of any mention of marriage in Lyons's letter to him of 5 October led him to surmise that it would "all end in smoke." From the outset, he had doubted that Lyons would "make up his mind to bring himself to the scratch." The confirmed bachelor had long contended that no man should marry after the age of thirty-five. He was now fifty, a quarter of a century older than Cleveland's step-daughter. Furthermore, he was neither very wealthy nor physically very attractive. One acquaintance described him unkindly as a little fat figure "like a pumpkin with an apple on the top." Moreover, he remained faithful to his preference for male company. In all likelihood the young lady was less than enthusiastic about a match, while the duke may not have had the large rumoured financial settlement in mind. He was, after all, abstemious, very careful about his finances, and was saving hard to buy out the reversionary claims of the two wastrels who would otherwise inherit his more than 100,000 acres. The failure of Lyons to wed this young lady did not immediately ease the matrimonial pressure. Minna and their aunt Caroline Pearson attacked him on the subject. They nominated Clarendon's daughter, Lady Emily, as a possible spouse. Lyons objected to her on the grounds that she had no money and insisted with the authority of a man who had just spent several days in her company at the former foreign secretary's Watford home that she had no desire to marry a man who was more than double her age. He was, in short, "inexorable" in his opposition to wedlock. Lady Emily did wed the following year, accepting Odo Russell, who had been another of the house guests. Handsome and gifted, he was considerably younger than Lyons.[24]

Lyons went up to Scotland to spend a few days at Balmoral with the Queen, then called at Knowsley outside Liverpool for discussions with the prime minister and his son the foreign secretary, and continued his country house tour with visits to the Salisburys at Hatfield and the Carnarvons at their modern castle, Highclere, near Newbury. But his first call, on 2 September, had been on Cowley at his recently inherited country seat of Draycot House, Chippenham. There he received a briefing on French affairs from a man who had been dealing with Louis Napoleon for a decade and a half. Although the French had in Cowley's opinion a "latent antipathy" to the British, and the emperor was a ruler who did not consider any promise however firmly made binding under changed circumstances, the former ambassador was another of those who considered Napoleon III the friendliest ruler of France that Britain was likely to encounter. On the other hand, the emperor recognized "what little assistance England with her present policy would be to him." If his confidence in the country had weakened, he still desired to "keep well" with Britain even though he could no longer feel sure of its sympathy and support. But Cowley was apprehensive. German press insinuations that France would eventually be obliged to relinquish Alsace and Lorraine to Germany – they had been taken by France more than two centuries earlier and Prussia had failed to recover them for "Germany" at the Congress of Vienna in 1815 – was contributing, Cowley warned, to the deepening popular discontent with imperial rule. The regime appeared less stable and less secure. An electoral system of "directed" manhood suffrage was no longer comfortably controlled by an army of prefects, mayors, and gendarmes. The premature death at the age of fifty-three, two years earlier, of the emperor's illegitimate half-brother, the Duc de Morny, had dealt the regime a serious blow. The cause of death was listed as pneumonia but was probably arsenic poisoning, for in an effort to improve his complexion or his sexual stamina, or to treat syphilis, de Morny had taken arsenic pills prescribed by Sir James

Olliffe, the physician to the British embassy. The Duc for all of his many faults had at critical moments been an adviser of "great calmness and firmness." Following his death, Napoleon increasingly solicited the support of disaffected liberals. The debate on the annual speech from the throne was liberalized "by the right of *interpellation*" and by the requirement that ministers participate. Would such modest reforms reverse the decline in Napoleon's popularity? His unpopular Spanish-born empress, Eugénie, was evidently skeptical, according to gossip.[25]

Lyons had in his discussions with Cowley evinced great interest in embassy detail, which was not surprising given his lack of a wife, his belief in social diplomacy, and his monetary concerns. Cowley estimated that he had never spent less than £13,000 a year in Paris, but this sum included the expense of supporting his family and maintaining a summer retreat at Chantilly. Lyons hoped to do as much with his salary of £10,000 and the allowance of £1,000 for lighting and heating. Hence he was quick to order five dozen bottles of Maraschino at a knock-down price, for if it proved to be a good liqueur it might be offered as an everyday *petit verre* with cognac instead of the far more expensive Curacao. Initially, he planned to have frequent evening receptions and host large dinners only occasionally. Aware of his predecessor's unfortunate reputation as the host of "the worst served dinners" in Paris, Lyons paid minute attention to the adequacy of the silver plate and even to the size of the entree dishes. The current cook, Fort, came highly recommended by both the Cowleys and the Clarendons as the best in Paris except in point of economy. He demanded exclusive control of his accounts and all other matters connected to the kitchen. Fear of lavish expenditures prompted Lyons to instruct Sheffield to seek other opinions of Fort's current performance "as people are not always the best judges of their own dinners."[26]

Assured by Cowley that the "entire house" was in good order, Lyons nevertheless asked Sheffield and Malet to make an inspection for him. It being the second state-owned embassy, an official of the Board of Works arrived from London to report on the furniture and fittings, and Lyons assigned to Sheffield the task of meeting with the proper department of the board to discuss the repairs "indispensably necessary for the embassy to be made fit for occupation." The news that the smell of paint would not have left the building before the middle of October convinced Lyons to remain in England at least until then. He also sought information on what items for his personal use he might bring into France free of duty, since they included carriages, horses, harnesses, saddles, glass, and china. In some countries ambassadors were permitted to import a large quantity of such items on first entry but only a limited quantity afterwards. The pantechnicon carrying his household effects was not expected in Paris until 24 October, and it would take several days to unload. The date of his arrival was also influenced by his desire to be formally installed before the closing ceremonies of the Paris Exhibition in mid-November. Revealingly, he obtained from the Foreign Office the precise number of days he would need to reside in the French capital in order to qualify for an ambassador's pension. He was probably reacting to the expectation of the return of a far less conservative Parliament in the first general election fought under the provisions of the Tories' Reform Bill. William Gladstone, who would in all probability head a Liberal government, was rumoured to have earmarked the Paris embassy for Earl Granville. However, when he met with Stanley on 19 October, Lyons was instructed to leave almost immediately for France. Since the Board of Works had pulled the embassy kitchen to pieces and it would be unusable for another fortnight at least, Lyons resigned himself to breakfasting and dining temporarily in French cafés.[27]

He would not arrive as the agent of a more interventionist British foreign policy. As a senior Liberal privately grumbled, it "is difficult to say which has made the greatest diplomatic blunders during the last 3 years, England or France or which has lost weight and reputation the most. The influence of both is incalculably lessened." Britain was handicapped by its unresolved difficulties with the United States and by the "standing danger of Ireland." It had little choice but to remain "not only inactive but almost silent upon the affairs of Europe." Were it to become involved in a Continental crisis, Irish American nationalists would surely seek to provoke an Anglo-American conflict. This might not be difficult because the manner in which American politicians pandered to anti-British sentiment was in Derby's opinion "hardly within the limits even of international courtesy." "In foreign affairs, nothing gives me real uneasiness except the negociations [sic] with America," his son admitted;

"it is impossible to say what may happen in that country, where the Irish vote is powerful and parties are utterly reckless of consequences, if they can secure a momentary advantage." A Franco-Prussian conflict on the other hand, while "disagreeable," would not in his opinion be dangerous for Britain. He ignored the Queen's wish for the appointment of Robert Morier as British ambassador in Berlin. He was the favourite of her daughter, the Crown Princess of Prussia, who heartily disliked Bismarck and saw Morier as the man to undermine his influence. "I can conceive nothing more inconvenient as regards the British Embassy," Stanley informed his father. "We have nothing whatever to do with the internal politics of German States. By meddling in these, we only destroy our proper and legitimate [influence] in matters affecting Europe." In making diplomatic appointments, he attached "considerable importance to the selection of such individuals as would thoroughly understand and act upon this principle."[28]

Stanley realized that the French were nervous. Napoleon's "growing indolence and irresolution" had been documented by Cowley, while the French ambassador in London hinted that he seldom received instructions. "I do not know that we have cause to regret that state of things," the foreign secretary commented, but by October there were disturbing signs. Across the Channel a crisis loomed, both commercial and political. The Crédit Mobilier, which had played a significant role in the financing of French industrial growth, was failing, and its collapse threatened to excite a general panic. Protectionists were targeting the liberal trade treaty with Britain, while criticism of Napoleon's foreign policy was striking a responsive public chord among Frenchmen who were disgusted with the failure of the Mexican adventure and alarmed by Prussian hegemony in Germany. "The public vacillates and the Emperor dare not take the initiative," Stanley jotted in his diary on 9 October. Would Napoleon embark on a "middle course" of greater political freedom at home and peace abroad? Would Britain find in French antagonism to German unification greater "security and repose"? The French would eventually come to terms with the idea of a German empire, the foreign secretary comforted himself. "They won't like it, any more than we like the growing power of the United States: but they will accept the inevitable, as we all do, if they have leisure to get used to it." The visit of the Prussian king and Bismarck to Paris during the Exhibition had been a success, but there was no sign of an improvement in the attitude of the French public towards Prussia, and Stanley could only hope that Lyons would become initiated in the requirements and duties of his post "before any fresh complications turn up." One that immediately resurfaced was Rome. Garibaldi had announced at the Geneva Peace Congress of European democrats and revolutionaries in early September, of which he was elected honorary president, his intention to launch an invasion of the Papal States. Napoleon's response was to threaten to return to Rome the French troops he had only recently withdrawn, and it prompted the Italian prime minister, Urbano Rattazzi, to detain Garibaldi. However, he was immediately compelled by an outraged public to release him. On 23 October, Garibaldi led 8,000 Red Shirts on a march towards Rome, inflicting a defeat on the papal forces at Monterotondo. The news did not concern Stanley unduly, as he had long believed that the Roman question "has only sentimental interest for Englishmen." He was content to instruct Julian Fane, the chargé d'affaires in Paris, to advise Napoleon that Britain would frown on the return of French troops to Rome for that might lead to trouble with Italy. At the same time he counselled the Italians not to be drawn into hostilities with France, for the contest would be an unequal one in which they would have little foreign help. Certainly, Britain had no intention of becoming involved.[29]

CHAPTER TWELVE

Ambassador to a Liberalizing Empire

Lyons arrived in the French capital early in the evening of 25 October. Built in 1722, the embassy had an impressive pedigree and shared with the neighbouring Hôtel d'Évreux (Élysée Palace) the distinction of being the only substantially unaltered mansion of that era on the fashionable Faubourg Saint-Honoré. It was sold in 1803 by the widowed Duchesse de Charost to the widowed Pauline Leclerc, the first Napoleon's favourite sister, who sold it in 1814 to her brother's military nemesis, the Duke of Wellington, now the British ambassador to France. Much of the furniture dated from her ownership, which may explain why Lyons considered it "shabby." His almost obsessive concern with the embassy's appearance was yet again a matter of national pride, but the miserly Treasury advanced a mere £1,245 for its redecoration and the purchase of new furniture. The clerk of works was another problem, making in Sheffield's words "a dreadful hash of things from employing his own creatures who are described as drunkards, incompetents, and rogues." He had to be removed. As work progressed Lyons was only tolerably satisfied because not a single room was completely redecorated and the new furniture accentuated the shabbiness of the old.[1]

Lyons reserved the afternoons for making calls and gathering material for his dispatches, which he drafted in the two hours before dinner at 7 p.m. He also wrote privately and at length to the foreign secretary and more occasionally to Bloomfield in Vienna, Paget in Florence, Odo Russell in Rome, Crampton in Madrid, Elliot in Constantinople, and Erskine in Athens. Surprisingly absent from the list of regular correspondents was Lord Augustus Loftus in Berlin, perhaps because he was "pompous, conceited, indiscreet," "perfectly ridiculous," and "personally disagreeable." But disagreeableness invaded the embassy. Malet grew irritated with Sheffield's low tolerance of pain whenever his gout flared up, and he began to liken Lyons's demands upon his time to a form of servitude. After a day's labour in the chancery, he was expected to accompany Lyons on afternoon drives, dine with him and Sheffield most evenings, sit with him until he retired, or accompany him to one of the *café chantants* on the Champs Élysées, where the singing and dancing by the "outrageously overdressed" performers were often "of a coarse nature," and the refreshment "usually of an inferior quality."[2]

During his first fortnight in Paris, Lyons paid three visits to the Great Exhibition, becoming one of its more than 13 million visitors. The venue was a huge iron-framed oval structure designed by Jean-Baptiste-Sébastien Kranz, assisted by a younger engineer, Gustave Eiffel, who was later to utilize the metal to greater dramatic and enduring effect. Of the 50,000 exhibits, one-third were French artifacts illustrative of the nation's industrial progress and culture. Among the eye-catching inventions on display, appropriately on the Champs de Mars, was the breech-loading chassepot rifle and the breech-loading rifled steel artillery which the Prussians had used to such devastating effect during the recent Austrian war. Yet what most impressed Lyons was the statue depicting the first Napoleon during his last days on St Helena. He had his own prized bust of the former emperor which he put on prominent display at the British embassy.[3]

Lyons found the French capital transformed thanks to Georges-Eugène Haussmann, prefect of the Seine, who had made the capital a healthier, more beautiful, and more modern city with more "air, light, space and mobility." Among his accomplishments were: ensuring a supply of clean water; expanding public parks; planting chestnut trees on the Champs-Élysées for their early foliage and spring blossoms; replacing narrow streets with broad boulevards lined with impressive apartment buildings; linking the new thoroughfares to give easier access to railway termini and make it possible "to move through the city from monument to monument"; doubling of the streets radiating out from the Arc de Triomphe, which made it "the most dramatic and monumental place in Paris"; and purchasing the Hôtel Carnavalet to convert it into a museum of the city's history, On the other hand, Paris had become more a centre of luxury and curiosity than a place of true usefulness, and the social costs and financial expense of these improvements excited popular unrest and scorching criticism.[4]

The rapid growth of the city's population as hundreds of thousands poured in from depressed rural areas in search of work ought to have made their plight a prime Haussmann concern. Instead, the working classes became his victims. Low-cost housing did not feature in his plan for the city centre, so the workers employed there lived either in ghastly shantytowns or made a long daily trek in from the periphery. The result was increasing "spatial segregation" of labourers and middle classes, the wealthier bourgeois occupying the new distinctive apartment buildings. Since one-fifth of the workforce was engaged in construction, whenever public works slowed as they were to do after 1868, insecurity of employment bred worker radicalization. Coinciding as the unrest did with a liberal relaxation of the law on public meetings, there was greater opportunity for mass expressions of worker discontent. Moreover, in his haste to deindustrialize the centre of Paris, Haussmann added industrialists to an ever-lengthening list of enemies. A journalist, Jules Ferry, emerged as a trenchant critic. His *Les Comptes fantastiques d'Haussmann* documented the staggering size of the city's debt, and Napoleon's association with the hugely expensive projects swelled the ranks of the regime's critics also.[5]

On a foggy, damp early November afternoon, Lyons travelled the short distance from the embassy to the Tuileries Palace to present his letters of credence. Napoleon, as described by Mark Twain, was a "long-bodied, short-legged man, fiercely mustached, old wrinkled, with eyes half closed, and *such* a deep, crafty, scheming expression about them." Following his audience, Lyons made the customary calls in his heavy ambassadorial uniform to the other members of the corps diplomatique. On 15 November he made the longer journey to the emperor's suburban retreat of St Cloud, which was redolent of the First Empire, and before long he and Napoleon were on "intimate terms." The following afternoon he hosted a full-dress reception for his fellow diplomats, French ministers, and court functionaries. Then, accompanied by Sheffield and Malet, he spent a weekend with Baron James de Rothschild at the banker's large, luxurious residence some fifteen miles east of the city. Completed in 1859, and designed by the British architect Sir Joseph Paxton, who had designed the Crystal Palace, the exterior of the Château de Ferrières was mock Italian Renaissance but the interior was a trove of genuine treasures. "Everything that can be imagined in the way of splendid furniture and stuffs and decorations reigns within," one awed guest recalled. "The great hall is a fine room, but overcrowded with magnificence; the salons are superb, and even the bedrooms are full of paintings and treasures." Not that Malet considered the artwork "very remarkable" or the members of the family very impressive, although he did exempt their host from censure. The meal, despite the Rothschilds' reputation for staging "sumptuous feasts," he dismissed as disappointingly "bourgeois." He was similarly critical of the dinner Moustier hosted for Lyons at the richly decorated Quai d'Orsay. The food, he remarked, was "by no means first rate."[6]

There was talk of a plot hatched by elements of the English and Continental press to attack Lyons for his alleged neglect of society, and women were believed its inspiration. "They complain that, socially speaking, the Cowleys did more for them than the current regime does," Edmund Monson advised Malet. Lyons had certainly decided against staging balls, having calculated their cost at £1,000 an evening. He abandoned evening receptions on learning that they were considered "intolerably dull" and decided to remain true instead to the often ridiculed maxim that good dinners defined a diplomatist. He began in a small way while the kitchen was still a construction site. Among his first guests were Lord Normanby and the French admirals and generals who had served alongside his father in the Crimean War. They were able to admire the portrait of the first Lord Lyons which had been shipped over from Arundel. His first large dinner was for senior members of the French government and visiting British lords. Two other guests were Thomas Gibson, a Radical member of Parliament and former Cabinet minister, and his wife. After the meal Malet, the enthusiastic amateur thespian, performed scenes from *The Rivals* with the assistance of Mrs Milner Gibson, who proved to be an "exquisite" Mrs Malaprop. Lyons, far from being a social misfit in the French capital, was, as Stanley soon discovered, universally and deservedly popular. "He entertains as if he had all of Lord Cowley's arrears to make up," the admiring foreign secretary remarked. Particularly surprising was his popularity among the British residents, who numbered some 9,000, many of them belonging to the monied classes, and "who always used to be in antagonism with the Embassy and had nothing but abuse of it." How, Stanley wondered, had Lyons worked this magic? It was not a mystery. Sensibly, he did not ignore the "small English," those without great names or great influence. They were invited to dine in groups of perhaps forty, an experience that one guest likened to a "dream of fairyland."[7]

There was more talking and much going from place to place but less reading and writing in Paris than there had been in Washington, Lyons assured his anxious sister, so there was less strain on his health. At his initial meeting with Moustier on 28 October, Rome was the first item on the agenda. The latest French expedition to defend and protect the pontiff had sailed just as Lyons reached the French capital, and he was struck by the unanimous applause given the emperor's reference to it in his speech opening the new legislative session on 18 November. Napoleon had as president of the Second Republic and then as emperor of the Second Empire cultivated the support of France's ultramontane clergy, who had such influence in the countryside, and he had every intention of holding onto it as liberals became more vocal in their criticism of his autocratic rule. Unfortunately, the Roman Church's identification with illiberalism, which Pius IX had promoted with his *Syllabus of Errors*, nourished in France an anti-clerical republicanism which did not bode well for the emperor. The troops sent back to Rome would prevent revolution and disorder and would be withdrawn just as soon as order was firmly established, Moustier assured Lyons. The problem, as Stanley saw it, was that in avoiding "momentary embarrassment" by rushing to the pope's aid Napoleon had stored up "heavy trouble for the future." For Britain, the "practical question" was how to use its diplomatic influence to best effect to prevent a Franco-Italian conflict.[8]

Lyons contacted Augustus Paget in Florence to ensure that the Italian government was impressed with the need to avoid a collision. Next, he allowed Moustier to believe that Britain would give serious consideration to participation in an international conference on the Roman question although he knew that Stanley would have little interest in the proposal. Outright rejection of the idea, however, might further erode Napoleon's diminished domestic prestige and damage Anglo-French relations. Lyons identified foreign setbacks and domestic "inconstancy" as the twin sources of the regime's current vulnerability. After more than fifteen years of imperial rule the French public desired "novelty," he believed. Stanley followed Lyons's lead on Rome. He agreed that when in difficulty a conference was the first idea that crossed Napoleon's mind. Yet such gatherings were in his opinion utterly useless unless those planning to attend knew beforehand what was to be proposed and the likelihood of an agreement. Britain's presence at a conference on the pope's temporal powers was particularly essential, a devoutly Catholic Empress Eugénie repeatedly emphasized during a meeting with Lyons on 11 November. Four days later the emperor raised the possibility of a collective decision to preserve the pope's temporal power at least in the city of Rome while permitting the annexation of the other papal territories by the Kingdom of Italy. When Lyons politely asked what means were available to induce Pius IX to accept such a settlement, Napoleon replied "moral influence." Lyons doubted that this would suffice. His own experience in Rome had taught him that the papal court would never agree to a conference unless it was understood that the pontiff was to retain his temporal domains.[9]

In declining the French invitation to a conference, Stanley followed Lyons's advice to sweeten the pill by ostensibly leaving ajar the door to further discussions. They were agreed that the emperor had no plan and was "following his usual hand-to-mouth policy of staving off present at the cost of future embarrassments." Lyons was not persuaded by the report that Napoleon intended to defend the temporal power of the pope, trifurcate the peninsula, and install the pontiff as sovereign of one of the divisions. He realized, however, that the Italians might not share his skepticism and warned them through Paget not to act rashly. There existed in France a large party which was hostile to Italians and Italy, he emphasized, but there was nothing to fear "at present" if the Italian government kept "decent order at home" and was "conciliatory towards French public opinion." The French war materiel en route to Rome was entirely precautionary, he wrote, and was to provide for the defence of the city and the port of Civitavecchia in the event of a Franco-Prussian conflict and the creation by the Italians of a diversion in favour of the Prussians. There was no guarantee, of course, that French behaviour, increasingly characterized by improvisation and opportunism, would not suddenly change direction.[10]

During the winter Lyons found himself drawn against his will into covert activities. On 13 December 1867, a Friday, Irish revolutionary nationalists, known as Fenians, attempted to bomb one of their leaders out of London's Clerkenwell Prison. The casualties among the unfortunate residents of houses close to the prison wall led Stanley to observe cynically that the incident "has had, and still more will have, a very good effect on English opinion." However, the knowledge that Paris was a hive of Fenian conspirators, and a belief that they were allying with the local Red Republicans, brought the head of a Home Office special anti-Fenian unit, Colonel Percy Feilding, to the French capital. He met with Lyons and set up a surveillance operation supervised by an agent working out of a local hotel. The information gathered was telegraphed in the embassy's cipher to London. With a plea of incompetence in such matters, and an admission of his profound dislike of dealing "with the sort of people who give secret intelligence," Lyons scrupulously kept his distance from the operation. He did authorize payments from the Secret Service fund to informers but delegated to Sheffield the task of maintaining contact with the agent in charge of surveillance. What made this near association with an intelligence operation acceptable in this instance to Lyons was the co-operation of the French authorities. French secret police reports on the Fenians' contacts with "Reds" and "foreign anarchist societies" were passed to him, this being one way for Napoleon to place the British in his debt at a time when he had cause to be anxious about both his personal safety and the survival of his dynasty. Reportedly, the French section of the (First) International, or the International Workingmen's Association, which had been organized in London in 1864 with the objective of uniting left-wing groups, was plotting his assassination.[11]

Stanley's confidence that the Fenian panic in England had by the end of January completely passed away was matched by his roseate view of foreign affairs. "I never knew this office quieter, which is fortunate since our parliamentary troubles are about to begin," he informed Lyons. The task of handling those troubles fell to a new prime minster. Derby's resignation due to ill health saw Disraeli succeed him with the assistance of a "benign conspiracy" of Queen and departing first minister. If in London the transition was smooth and the ministerial changes few, in Paris the political situation was less tranquil. Distrust of Prussia explained the emperor's anxiety to withdraw his troops from Rome, and Bismarck's objection to a conference that might allow him to do so without further loss of prestige was inevitably regarded as malign as well as strategic. A France in "hot water" with Italy would be less inclined to resist the unification of Germany. In the opinion of the emperor's cousin, Prince Napoleon, who impressed Lyons as intelligent and liberal, war with Prussia would be dangerous if not disastrous for the regime. This explained the contradictory conduct of its political opponents, who while professing a commitment to international peace inflamed public opinion with the charge that France was being humiliated by Bismarck. Adolphe Thiers quickly came to mind. A bellicose minister during the reign of Louis Philippe, and the man who in 1848 had dismissed Louis Napoleon as a cretin who would be easily managed as president of the Second Republic, he and other critics were plainly seeking to topple the Bonaparte dynasty. On the subject of war, Clarendon offered some reassurance. Passing through Paris in mid-March, he dined with the emperor and informed Lyons and Stanley that Napoleon had decided that France's best chance of curtailing Prussia was patiently to permit a festering of the reported discontent in the provinces it had annexed in 1866. A war on the other hand would assuredly unite Germans. Meanwhile, Stanley was convincing himself that Bismarck had no wish to break with France. The Prussian, he advised Lyons, insists that his policy is "wholly pacific" because its object was "to secure the leisure necessary for arranging the internal affairs of Germany."[12]

The arrival of spring in 1868 had no dove as its messenger. The meeting of the Zollverein (Customs Union) Parliament fuelled French concerns of a Prussian move to annex South Germany. When Moustier suggested that Britain caution Bismarck against provoking France, Lyons counselled Stanley against any step that might effectively pledge Britain to take the French side in a conflict. He was preaching to the converted. Stanley, the ideologue of non-intervention, had no intention of offering advice "which would certainly be uncalled-for, probably useless, and perhaps altogether out of place." Moreover, Lyons was of the opinion that Napoleon's multiplying domestic troubles were the greater danger to European peace. His plebiscitary autocracy was threatened by economic stagnation as capitalists withheld investment in response to the talk of war with Prussia by the bellicose minister of war, Marshal Adolphe Neil. The deepening distress among the working classes brought from them ever louder rumblings of discontent. The peasantry resented military conscription. Liberals deplored the emperor's identification with the "Clerical Party," which was demanding the dismissal of the minister of public instruction for the "venial sin" of supporting the attendance of unmarried females at lectures on chemistry and other natural sciences. There was evidence of disaffection among the the emperor's traditional supporters. Hide-bound conservatives were angered by the relaxation of press censorship, which they viewed as evidence that Napoleon had become weak and vacillating. Ironically, he inadvertently fed their palpable unease with his release of an "injudicious" pamphlet on his dynasty. The other worrying developments identified by Lyons were: the establishment of two additional camps of military instruction, which promised to see two additional army corps ready to take to the field at short notice; reports that the War Department was frantically preparing maps of the Rhenish Provinces; and the news that a large store of salt meat had been laid in, perhaps to feed campaigning troops. Napoleon's hasty explanation, that it was required to test an American invention for its preparation, was far from persuasive. Although Lyons credited the emperor with a desire for peace, he feared becoming "overborne by the war party in the army and navy," whose confidence in the superiority of French troops and weaponry apparently knew no bounds. They saw in war the means to burnish the tarnished imperial prestige, but Lyons suspected it would bring instead either a return to "personal government," a euphemism for autocracy, or destroy the dynasty. He found neither alternative attractive, convinced as he was "that Europe, and England in particular, are more interested in maintaining the emperor than in almost anything else."[13]

A furious attack in the Corps législatif on the Commercial Treaty of 1860 was another disquieting development. The talk of war, Lyons believed, had by damaging trade and industry sparked the attacks on free trade, though behind them he saw something other than simple protectionism. Once persuaded that their suffering was a direct result of the emperor's commercial policy, working people could be expected to rally to opponents of his regime. The debate in the legislature ended well enough under the circumstances. Nevertheless, the government's spokesman, Eugène Rouher, with a reputation for "parliamentary compromise and suppleness rather than intellectual penetration or political adroitness," and who excelled in the art of "damage control," had been obliged to give a "sort of pledge" that future tariff changes would be effected by legislation not imperial decree. Lyons advised the Foreign Office not to initiate a discussion of the treaty, fearful it would imperil Napoleon's evolving liberalism. The press had been freed from direct executive government control. Certain public meetings were now permitted. Ministers were required to defend in person government legislation and take part in debate. And greater influence on policy had been granted to both chambers of the legislature. Would these concessions strengthen the regime? Would greater freedom of discussion be compatible with a form of government in which the emperor had all the responsibility? These were the serious questions awaiting answers, Lyons informed the foreign secretary.[14]

The reception given the emperor on 14 August when he reviewed the troops in the parade staged annually to commemorate the birth of the first Napoleon was expected to reveal whether his popularity was on the wane. Lyons was astonished at the great importance attached by the regime's friends and its enemies to the review, apparently unaware that it had been the hostility of the National Guards during a military parade on 24 February 1848 that had caused Louis Philippe to ride directly into exile. He noted the generally good-natured attitude of the civilian spectators, and while loud cries of "Vive l'empereur" from the ranks of the National Guardsmen "elated" Napoleon, they did not impress Lyons. They had clearly been encouraged by ambitious officers seeking to catch the emperor's eye and came from detachments formed of citizens wealthy enough to provide their own equipment. In short, unrepresentative of the working classes, they were not evidence of a broad satisfaction with the regime. On the other hand, Lyons did not doubt that Napoleon continued to command the support of rural France.[15]

In a sudden period of "diplomatic calm" which not even the assassination of Prince Michael of Serbia disturbed, a relaxed Lyons prepared for a royal visitor. The Queen planned to rest for twelve hours at the embassy before continuing her journey to a vacation in Switzerland. To his relief, the Scrooge-like Treasury now released the funds needed to decorate the embassy's bedrooms. Having requested from the emperor a special rail carriage in which the Queen might travel, Lyons received instead an entire train. Although her arrival was to be "in so very strict an incognito" that only Lyons in plain clothes was to greet her at the rail terminus, an entourage of two princesses, a prince, five attendants, and fifteen servants ensured it would not go unnoticed. Paris being a haven for Fenian conspirators, Lyons employed extra guards to protect the royal person. Unfortunately, her brief stay in the capital gave him a diplomatic headache. She had agreed to receive the empress at the embassy in the mid-afternoon of 7 August but with a plea of ill health failed to return the call. Since Eugénie was barely a stone's throw away at the Élysée Palace, this apparent snub was gleefully seized upon by the dynasty's enemies. They "maliciously" cited it as proof that the imperial couple were no longer treated with consideration by Europe's ancient royal houses and then rubbed salt into the wound by implying a British partiality for the Orléans family. "Our Embassy are disgusted, and the French Court sore," Stanley, who was in attendance on the monarch, reported to Disraeli. "Lyons did what he could but without a chance of success." The Queen did write a personal letter to Eugénie from Lucerne, a copy of which she showed to Lyons when she passed back through Paris on her way home in September. On this occasion she gave physical exhaustion as her excuse for not travelling out to Fontainebleau to call on the empress, who was yet again "a little put out." In the words of the visiting Malmesbury: "With the French Court anything like a want of respect of it, reacts upon their people, and the emperor at this moment is far from popular in consequence of his mismanagement of foreign affairs. He is therefore doubly jealous of our public appreciation of his dignity and importance."[16]

If by her ungracious conduct Victoria caused problems for Lyons, she was "particularly gracious and agreeable" in all her dealings with his staff and servants. Before departing in August she had the diplomatic personnel presented to her, speaking a word or two to several of them and asking Malet about his parents. Most of the young men were intrigued by the Queen's accompanying gillie, about whom there had been such salacious gossip. He made a favourable impression on Malet, who described John Brown as "a well grown very respectable looking man, rather a red face and grizzly grey hair," plain spoken and sensible, and thus a "comfortable man to have about one." On her return in September, despite her pleas of exhaustion, Victoria proved to be "more animated and cheerful than before." She gave £200 for distribution among the embassy's domestic staff and presented a set of studs and "wrist buttons with diamonds in them" to its head steward. Understandably, the servants were thoroughly pleased with the visit.[17]

Stanley lingered in Paris after the Queen's departure. He met with Moustier and judged him "a shrewd pleasant man of the world, who talked much and well" without ever saying anything new. He and Lyons went out to Fontainebleau to dine, finding the emperor "in good spirits, but rather nervous and uneasy about the future," especially "as to the result of universal [male] suffrage." Napoleon was confident he retained the support of the country districts but admitted that all the towns were against him. Hence the sensation when in an August by-election in the agricultural district of Jura an opponent of the empire won a landslide victory. He was Jules Grévy, a prominent lawyer who had achieved political prominence during the Second Republic and had been arrested during the coup d'état of 1851. What did this result mean for the empire's hitherto successful manipulation of the electoral system? What impact would it have on the regime's future direction? Would the timid prevail with their argument that absolute power was the only security against anarchy? Or would bolder spirits carry the day with their contention that the dynasty's permanence and stability were to be found in a "prudent but continued advance towards liberal government"? Napoleon would make the decision, but he had angrily remarked to Stanley and Lyons that the freer press dealt only in scandal. Another factor was his poor health. "He may live for years," Stanley observed, "but will never be a healthy man again." Convinced of the emperor's physical inability to govern as he once had, and sharing with Stanley the opinion that Britain "can never expect to have a warmer friend or more faithful [French] ally," Lyons hoped the bolder spirits would prevail. Under parliamentary government, the opposition might take office and power without a revolution.[18]

Napoleon's unpredictability, his reputation for "sudden and surprising acts," was for Lyons a further cause of concern. Did the emperor lack the steady application necessary for the gradual introduction of liberal measures? Disraeli had heard from a friend, probably a Rothschild, that the French were planning to pick a quarrel with Prussia. "Lyons believes in peace," Stanley informed his father, the former prime minister, after the success of the "official" candidate in a Var by-election revived confidence in Napoleon's rural popularity. Unfortunately, a speech by the Prussian king, and the bellicose reaction of that element of the French press most closely identified with the government, sparked turmoil on the Paris Bourse and a corresponding increase in international tension. Moustier immediately sought to lower the temperature. "The two governments should be as civil as possible, but should abstain from discussions in the present state of public feeling," he declared, and "should take off their hats to each other with marked civility, but should not enter into conversation." However, revolution in Spain saw a matronly Isabella II driven from her throne, creating a succession problem that was not to lend itself to hat doffing and civility.[19]

"Pleasant work for diplomacy in 1869," an ironic Stanley predicted to Lyons. He was relieved to be leaving office following the Liberals' widely anticipated victory in the general election held under the terms of the Tories' Reform Bill. The decrepit state of the Ottoman Empire remained a simmering problem. The revolution in Crete was staggering on, and its leaders in Greece were believed to be willing to go to any lengths to effect their object. Edward Erskine in Athens reduced the options of Britain and France to the stark choice of either occupying and governing Greece for an extended period or standing to one side while the Turks taught the Greeks and their "wretched government" to respect the law of nations. More trouble was brewing in Romania, from where John Green wrote that Prince Charles was "little better than an idiot," having been convinced that he had been sent by Providence to create the greater Romanian nation. He was accumulating an arsenal and, as a

Hohenzollern, was seeking to replace French with Prussian military instructors. Moustier, who had long suspected Bismarck of having a finger in that pie, began talking to Lyons more about Romania than any other problem. A Romanian declaration of independence, Lyons predicted, would cause the Turks to cross the Pruth, leaving Britain in a predicament uncomfortably similar to that on the eve of the Crimean War. Would Britain's new Liberal foreign secretary adopt "a decided course of action"? He would have to bear in mind the meaning for foreign policy of the passage of parliamentary reform. The newly enfranchised middle classes, it was assumed, desired "economy at home and abstention abroad."[20]

The tense Franco-Prussian relationship showed no sign of improvement. Clarendon had informed Lyons that during his private visit to Berlin both the king and the chief of the Prussian General Staff, General Helmuth von Moltke, had spoken of peace and had vowed that if war broke out they would make it clear to the world that France was the "unprovoked aggressor." However, it may not have been politic of the then-former foreign secretary in speaking with the pair, and thus indirectly to Bismarck, to stress the extreme danger of provoking France. Napoleon, he had warned them, would be unable to resist anything like a challenge from Prussia because of the feeling in the French army and among the French public. This was almost two years before the Ems telegram. "When the newspapers speak with bitterness and suspicion of Prussia they do no more than give expression to the feelings prevalent among Frenchmen," Lyons later agreed. But during dinner at St Cloud on 19 October Napoleon had given Clarendon the germ of an idea for reducing tension. "Subject both nations to international pressure to slow their military preparations," he suggested.[21]

Meanwhile, in Madrid, the French minister, Henri Mercier, had assured his British counterpart that Napoleon had no wish to intervene in Spain. In Paris, Moustier affected total indifference to the succession question there, but Lyons was not deceived. Two possible solutions to the Spanish conundrum were as he knew entirely unacceptable to France: the establishment of a republic and the placing of the Duc de Montpensier on the vacant throne. The youngest son of Louis Philippe, the Duc was married to Isabella's younger sister. The close family connection had not prevented him from supporting the insurgency led by Francisco Serrano and Juan Prim that drove his sister-in-law into exile. Both generals declared their support for a constitutional monarchy and both were thought to favour the Frenchman, but Napoleon hated the Orléans family. Britain's attitude was less personal and more material. The Tories had seen no reason to delay recognition of the de facto government established by the generals so long as it was willing to improve the commercial relationship. In leaving office, Stanley declared it almost imperative that his Liberal successor "commit the country as little as possible to any line of action not already laid down." After all, he was aware that the convention he had recently negotiated to settle the Civil War claims of the United States was unravelling, and that Ireland remained a problem.[22]

Stanley and Lyons parted on the very best of terms, the former thanking the latter for "the constant supply of information – always interesting and accurate – which you have never failed to furnish." Gladstone named Clarendon to the Foreign Office. He was the Liberal party's acknowledged expert on international affairs, and having once been a senior diplomat himself he understood diplomatic procedure. He envied Stanley's good fortune to be "taking the boat as the tide was turning." The new government, he moaned, would be meeting Parliament "with a parcel of difficulties for not one of which we are responsible." His choice did not please a Queen angered by his "great love of scandal and gossip, not without malice." He had, one colleague observed, "the spice of the 'devil' in him without which no one can attain the high position he held." There was something almost feline about him, and in this instance he had sunk his claws into Victoria's relationship with John Brown. She recommended the discreet and reserved Lyons as a more acceptable foreign secretary, but Gladstone declined to humour her. Lyons remained in Paris, Clarendon took possession of the Foreign Office, and the pair enjoyed an excellent relationship. Clarendon had recommended him to Stanley as Cowley's successor in Paris and while out of office had been a frequent guest at the embassy. Lyons, wary of repeating his Washington experience, immediately asked Clarendon to promote Malet to secretary of legation so that he could head the chancery. He was a "hard working man" who would keep routine business "straight," and by his attention to the "small affairs of British subjects" keep the embassy in "good odour" with this clientele. But Clarendon declined to promote a junior over the heads of several more senior men. Concern that this would damage service morale may have played its part in his decision but so did the availability of Henry Wodehouse, the younger brother of his Cabinet colleague Kimberley. Lyons delegated to the ever-present Sheffield the "important departments of the kitchen," the stables, and relations with the press. Not that he himself ignored public relations. He liked and met often with the "dispassionate, friendly and agreeable" Felix Whitehurst, the Paris correspondent of Britain's most popular newspaper. His clever letters in the *Daily Telegraph* had made him a favourite at the Tuileries. Another influential representative of the fourth estate whom Lyons helped was Henry Reeve, the editor of the *Edinburgh Review*. He returned home "charmed" with the British ambassador. "The Editors and Correspondents are most hospitably treated by the ambassador," Malet later observed, "and on the whole I think that no hospitality pays better – they are grateful and friendly."[23]

Meanwhile, the "endless rumours and surmises" of French ministerial changes suddenly acquired substance. The talk was of Charles Félix, Marquis de La Valette, replacing Moustier at the Quai d'Orsay. A rather prim looking man with a sharp nose and pursed lips, he had considerable diplomatic experience, and his had been a voice of caution and restraint when the swift Prussian victory over Austria in 1866 led Drouyn de Lhuys to advocate French intervention in the conflict. France was not yet militarily strong enough to confront Prussia, he had argued persuasively. Following Drouyn's departure, La Valette had acted as caretaker of the Foreign Office while Moustier was summoned home from Constantinople. Scandal was the explanation given for Moustier's dismissal after he had dutifully followed to the letter the emperor's instructions. He stood accused of making "violent" efforts to secure for a lady with whom he was reportedly "very intimate" a very large share of the profits of the Turkish tobacco monopoly. He was replaced by La Valette in December 1867, but Lyons was confident there would be no change in French policy. After spending a week at Compiègne with Napoleon, he assured the foreign secretary of the emperor's improved health, good spirits, and desire to maintain the "cordial understanding" with Britain.

Clarendon made clear, in turn, the Liberal government's intention to persist with the foreign policy pursued by the Tories. What else could Britain do? Its military was minuscule compared to the huge armies of the major Continental powers; its Navy could make little impression on events in Central Europe; it had an empire to protect, and barely a decade had passed since the Indian mutiny; Ireland's problems remained unsolved if not insoluble; and the Americans were still angry. Indeed, the Gladstone Cabinet was very gloomy about the state of Anglo-American relations. Another settlement of the Civil War claims had been rejected by the Americans, and the uncertain situation in North America helped to convince ministers of the wisdom and necessity of the non-interventionism that the Tories had so "strictly observed" to "general approval." It received a Gladstonian gloss with the promise that Britain would support the "principles of political morality" and international law.[24]

Shortly after Napoleon mentioned to Lyons that he harboured a measure of sympathy with Greek nationalism, La Valette proposed a six-power conference on the Greco-Turkish problem. The rebellion in Crete was again threatening to develop into a European crisis. A Turkish ultimatum had been rejected by Greece; diplomatic relations between the two nations had been severed; the Turks had adopted a number of anti-Greek measures; and the Greeks were reported to be seeking war materiel from friendly nations such as Russia. The czar's niece had recently wed the Greek king. The idea of a conference may have originated in Berlin, where Bismarck saw in a possible conflict between Russia and Austria over the "Slavonic question" a serious impediment to German unity. For Napoleon, the attraction of an international conference in Paris was the helpful impression it would foster among the French that their nation was still the arbiter of Europe and their emperor the Continent's dominant figure. The Gladstone government, preoccupied with Ireland, preferred a simple understanding between Britain, France, and Russia as the protecting powers of Greece, but Lyons argued that it would be wise for Britain to encourage the professed desire of Prussia and Russia to avert a "disturbance of European tranquillity" by agreeing to attend a conference.[25]

As Britain's delegate, Lyons had a delicate role to play. He needed to come to an understanding on the agenda with La Valette, who was to be in the chair. The Russians must not be permitted to introduce those articles of the 1856 treaty ending the Crimean War which they wished annulled. Their denials of any intention of doing so were not believed by Clarendon. "This is likely as not to be a lie for the object of covering a contrary intention," he wrote to Lyons. Another of Lyons's tasks was to ensure that the Greeks were not rewarded for their humiliation of the Turks and for the trouble they had given the international community. They had in his personal opinion produced an "absolutely intolerable" state of things. But he had been dealt a weak negotiating hand. His instructions required him to announce the refusal of "moral" Britain to undertake "ignoble" police work. A resort to force, the Gladstone Cabinet feared, would provide the Russians with too many opportunities to meddle in the affairs of the Ottoman Empire. Finally, Lyons had to keep in mind the use to which the Americans might put his language. Thus in his criticism of Greece for sending men and arms to Crete aboard the symbolically named *Enosis* he must not strengthen the Americans' contention that Britain was entirely responsible for the damage inflicted on Union commerce by the *Alabama*.[26]

The conference formally opened in the late afternoon of Saturday, 9 January, and was immediately thrown into confusion by the Greeks, who announced that they would participate only on terms of equality with the Ottoman Empire. They had been granted, with the approval of Lyons, a "consultative" not a "deliberative" voice. Lyons offered a diplomatic solution by promising to support La Valette if he proposed a "deliberative voice" for Greece, since there was not to be any voting in the conference. It would be ludicrous to allow the conference to "break down on the imperceptible difference between consultative seat and voting seat," Gladstone agreed. He was also aware that on this point British public opinion might side with Greece. In Paris, where the conference was going ahead without the sulking Greeks, Lyons recommended that they be given every opportunity to comment on the deliberations and insisted that there be no Turkish signature on any finding condemnatory of Greece. Its presence would allow the Greeks to bring a charge of unfairness which might influence British opinion since the Turks would have served as both judge and jury.[27]

Crete and its Christian majority were granted a measure of autonomy within the Turkish Empire, and Greece was rebuked for its support of the rebellion. The Turks, who had only attended the conference with the "utmost distrust," were delighted to find themselves judged in the right. "The sick man has behaved very well & ought to have credit given to him," Clarendon agreed. But in the back of Lyons's mind had been his nation's unsettled relations with the United States. Condemnation of the recruitment of armed bands to disturb another nation's territories would be useful, he believed, in the light of the invasion of Canada by American Fenians in the summer of 1866. However, the British law officers insisted on the amendment of the draft text. They objected to wording implying a duty on the part of the Greek government "absolutely to ensure" that no vessel hostile to Turkey sailed from its ports. "Such a construction might to a certain extent be inconvenient to us with reference to the Alabama claims," the foreign secretary reminded Lyons. Nevertheless, he warmly praised Lyons's general performance. The Greeks had not been rewarded, the Russians had not managed to reopen the terms of the 1856 settlement, and Lyons had gained the trust of La Valette, who had entered office by no means well disposed towards him. It was an achievement made possible by his straightforward and frank dealings with the Frenchman. They had, by the conference's end, "established relations between themselves more intimate and real than has been the case for a long time past." If "the complete understanding" of the two nations had been made manifest to the world, it was immediately under pressure. Yet another crisis was simmering, this one over Belgian railways.[28]

Early in 1868, the French Compagnie de l'Est had acquired the right to run a rail line into Belgium. It then set its sights on the Grand Luxembourg and the Ligeois-Limburgeois companies and before year's end had negotiated the purchase of the former. Ever mindful of ulterior French designs on their country, the Belgians appealed for British protection. Their nation's independence and neutrality had been guaranteed in the Treaty of London signed by the Great Powers thirty years earlier, but Stanley had opposed any de facto British protectorate of Belgium. Why throw away the military benefits of Britain's insular position and create a second Hanover whose personal union with the British Crown had only dissolved with a woman's accession, Victoria's, to the throne in 1837? Yet Lyons had noted and reported a disturbingly prevalent opinion in the French capital that as Prussia had grown, and Hanover had been one of the annexations in 1866, so must France. Belgium might be annexed without danger, a number of influential Frenchmen argued, because Prussia would not care to intervene and Britain could not. Indeed, when France had sought "compensations" for maintaining its neutrality during the Austro-Prussian war, Bismarck had appeared to promise not to stand in the way of French annexation of Luxembourg and Belgium. This unratified arrangement, so secret that Vincent Benedetti, the French ambassador in Berlin, had written it up in his own hand, became a diplomatic time bomb. One of the two copies was entrusted for safekeeping to the French minister of state, the other was in Bismarck's pocket. He was holding it for a more opportune disclosure of its terms.[29]

In mid-January 1869, at the urging of her cousin Leopold II, the Belgian monarch, Victoria expressed to the new Liberal government her belief that France had designs on Belgium. Clarendon, as yet not entirely convinced of this, instructed Lyons to drop the occasional hint in La Valette's ear that the small country was under Britain's special protection. But the febrile French response to the Belgian government's introduction of legislation to veto the French rail company's acquisitions precipitated a crisis. The French press, led by the *Peuple*, a regime organ, assailed the Belgian government "with extraordinary violence and bitterness" and accused it of acting at the instigation of Prussia. This accusation, which in private both Napoleon and La Valette repeatedly made, was disputed by the British ambassador in Berlin. Then again, Napoleon's insistence that the railway contract be ratified, thereby humiliating Belgium, deepened the Gladstone government's resentment of his "impolitic" conduct. At the very moment when the danger of a Greco-Turkish conflict had been swept under an international rug, Napoleon was bringing "another to the carpet and thus deny[ing] mankind time to enjoy peace." His foolishly provocative appointment of a former journalist as the French minister in Brussels increased British anger, for Lyons learned that he was a handsomely paid agent of the opponents of a peaceful settlement. It was the Mexico story all over again, Clarendon fumed. Napoleon was allowing himself "to be dragged through the mud & to imperil the most manifest interests of France," and it was happening at a time when the British public were growing restless over their government's unassertive international conduct. Clarendon persuaded the editors of *The Times* and the *Daily Telegraph* not to dwell upon the Belgian crisis. *The Times* "pooh poohs (very judiciously) the alarmists" and encourages the belief that "the quarrel is a mere dispute about railway tariffs" not a French attempt "to obtain an exclusive political influence over Belgium," an appreciative Cabinet colleague noted. Unfortunately, the relief was only temporary. Before long, John Delane at *The Times* and other "good judges of public opinion" were warning of a "tremendous explosion" should France attempt to crush or annex Belgium.[30]

The Cabinet gave to Lyons the task of dissuading Napoleon from advancing so far down the road to annexation that he would find it impossible to retreat with dignity. It was time for him to build another of his "golden bridges." Clarendon provided him with several helpful arguments – the emperor would alienate British opinion, would cause an estrangement between the two nations, would destroy the confidence the British felt in him, and would play into the hands of Prussia. "I believe nothing would be more agreeable to Prussia," the foreign secretary observed, "than that the intimacy between [Britain and France] … should be disturbed by a territorial encroachment that would run on all fours into Prussian aggrandizement." From Berlin, Loftus forwarded unverifiable information of an understanding between Napoleon and Bismarck which would see France annex Belgium and Prussia absorb South Germany. French purchase of the Belgian railways was to be the first step. This suspect intelligence, which may have been an initial test by Bismarck of the diplomatic usefulness of the terms of the secret draft treaty, appears to have removed any lingering doubts in the minds of Gladstone and his colleagues that the French had "ulterior" designs on Belgium. Bismarck's "ways are inscrutable & he is never to be relied upon but he has had a union with us against France in his head ever since the Belgian business began," the foreign secretary wrote. Although he and Gladstone considered Prussian talk of joint action with Britain in defence of Belgium neutrality a ruse to separate it from France, Clarendon admitted that "it may come to this after all."[31]

Lyons approached the Belgian question in an "amicable spirit," determined to keep "Lavalette and his Master out of an 'inchoate scrape.'"

Convinced of the foreign minister's ardent desire to preserve peace, he took every opportunity to remind him of Britain's profound interest in the integrity and independence of Belgium and to stress the "improbability of the charge that the Belgians had acted at the instigation of Prussia." He persuaded La Valette to tone down a dispatch in which he accused the Belgians of "bad dealing," a small but not insignificant diplomatic gain. He preached caution to the Belgian minister in Paris, who called frequently at the embassy to discuss his government's evidence of the French government's deep involvement in the "whole transaction" between the railway companies. Privately, he deplored Napoleon's "dangerous, and foolish, if not incomprehensible" insistence that ratification of the railway contract was for him "a personal question." By risking his own prestige the emperor was according the dispute "a gravity out of all proportion to its intrinsic importance." Moreover, the longer a settlement was delayed the greater the danger of the British press repeating the mistake of the Schleswig-Holstein affair. Then it had misled the Danes into believing that Britain would do wonders for them; hence their subsequent sense of betrayal, not to mention the blow to Britain's international prestige, when Bismarck called its bluff. So, working through the Belgian minister in Paris, and through Clarendon in London, Lyons pressed the Belgian government to go as far as possible to "satisfy the supposed susceptibility of the Emperor." The Belgians offered tariff concessions beneficial to France, only to receive the ominous reply that this was no longer a question of material interests but of "national dignity." The French proposed a joint examination of the contract instead of its immediate ratification, but this the Belgians refused. All the while Lyons was impressing on La Valette his government's "great anxiety" to see the affair settled, but he did so with subtlety rather than menace. "The fear of being ill with us acts as a restraint the more from being left a little vague," he explained to an increasingly impatient Clarendon. "If we pull the string tight it will snap." Although the rumoured pact between France and Prussia to sacrifice Belgium would in his opinion be an "iniquity equal to the partitions of Poland," he insisted that Britain's "present cordial and intimate terms" with France were the best means of protecting Belgium because British cordiality was "highly valued" by the French and there was a "great desire to preserve it."[32]

An explosive note from Clarendon, implying a willingness to abandon non-intervention, was pocketed by Lyons. The Cabinet having granted him great discretion saw no reason to withdraw it. "I entirely concur in your views & advice, they are words of wisdom that I shall endeavour to instill into the Belgian Government," Clarendon later confessed. Lyons had received from Felix Whitehurst an account of his interview with the emperor on 19 March, during which Napoleon had declared a settlement of the affair imminent. A mixed commission was to examine it. The prudent and ever-cautious Lyons intended to watch with "zealous attention" both the composition and proceedings of this body. To stymie any arrangement that would leave Belgium a dependent of France he took the opportunity of his audience with the imperial couple on 3 April to remind them tactfully but firmly of the importance Britain attached to that nation's independence and neutrality. Clarendon applauded his remarks. Napoleon now understood the situation, he wrote. He might be sore at being found out in his annexationist ambition "but our displeasure is the parent of his discretion."[33]

When the Belgian premier and finance minister, Hubert Frere-Orban, arrived in Paris to negotiate the terms of reference of the mixed commission, Lyons briefed him on Napoleon's "peculiarities" and the best means of dealing with them. Known at home as the "Iron Bar," the Belgian proved as inflexible on certain crucial points as this nickname implied. He ruled out any discussion of his government's right to invalidate contracts or veto the cession of railways and made sure that the mixed commission was denied "any political or diplomatic character." He did promise his full co-operation in securing for France commercial and traffic advantages equivalent to those lost with the vetoing of the contract. The imminence of a French general election played its part in Napoleon's acceptance of this face-saving preliminary settlement. There were hiccups before a final agreement was announced in July, by which time the French government was keen to extract itself from the mini-crisis with an arrangement that could be credibly represented as neither "nugatory nor ridiculous." This caused Lyons a moment of apprehension for he believed it "quite consonant with the French Character to endeavour to drown ridicule by turning an unimportant affair into a serious one." Hence his relief on learning of Napoleon's willingness to accept anything, such as the promise of tariff concessions, that the French public might consider satisfactory. However, the insertion in the final *procès verbal* of a phrase designed to limit any damage to the emperor's personal prestige risked producing "a discussion in the press desirable to be avoided."[34]

As ever, success had many parents. Clarendon boasted that his frank remarks to the French ambassador in London had convinced the emperor to accept a reasonable settlement. In distant Vienna, Count Friedrich von Beust, now the minister-president of the Austro-Hungarian Empire, claimed that it was his support of France that had convinced Belgium to yield. But the lion's share of the credit belonged to Lyons. He had defused the crisis by patiently exploiting the French obsession with Prussia and by capitalizing on Napoleon's obsessive preoccupation with the survival of his dynasty. The nervous emperor, as Lyons had grasped from the outset, could ill-afford to antagonize or alienate Britain. It "never can be sound policy in the Emperor," Clarendon also recognized, "to keep so many interests in a state of continuous anxiety & force them to regard him as a common enemy." By moving "in a most decided and decisive fashion to influence events," Lyons had played a crucial role in the maintenance of peace. He had worked effectively with La Valette, deepening the Frenchman's trust in the process, had discouraged Napoleon from recklessness or blatant bullying of Belgium, and had discreetly exerted pressure on the Belgians to offer the French economic gains that masked the political reverse suffered by the prestige-preoccupied emperor.[35]

A diplomatic success which attracted so little public attention at home afforded Lyons no protection from British critics of the diplomatic service. During a debate on the diplomatic estimates, MPs deplored the cost of the Paris embassy and held Lyons personally responsible for expenditures they decried as excessive. Although he was defended on both sides of the Commons, a difficult night ended with the deletion of the £300 assigned to the Paris embassy's chaplaincy. This did not dismay Lyons, besieged as he was by applicants for the vacant post. But parliamentary pressure drove the Foreign Office to practise "all sorts of small economies." It scrutinized the budget for newspaper subscriptions and wished them to be restricted to the press of the nation to which an ambassador or minister was accredited. It demanded a reduction in the cost of postage, which prompted Malet to warn his mother that she might have to prepay her letters to him. "The reason, is that they pay double on delivery if not prepaid," he explained. His chief adamantly refused, however, to give ground on the cost of mailing certain dispatches. His own were carried by the regular messenger, Lyons pointed out, while those coming to the embassy from other missions, and then forwarded to London, were only sent by post if their contents were either too interesting or too important to be delayed until the next regular messenger set off for the Foreign Office. Were the long-standing arrangement changed whereby such dispatches came first to Paris, enabling him to peruse them, then he would be deprived of "a great deal of useful information." Less easily dismissed was the innuendo, implicit in the allusions of the freshly freed Paris press, concerning his relationship with Malet and Sheffield. They were dubbed "Le Petit Brun" and "Le Petit Blond," but these suggestive descriptions hinting at the "English disease" were quickly forgotten as France entered an extended period of momentous political change.[36]

Shortly before the French general election Lyons became aware of deepening uneasiness in the business community. The monied and commercial men were beginning to fear for the survival of peace with Prussia once the ballots had been counted. Panics, he reported, "appear to increase in frequency and intensity," and he listed the factors contributing to them: the military preparations of the previous year that seemed to have put France in a position to go on a war footing "at a very short notice"; the adamant opposition of the French government to any reduction in armaments; the "extraordinary irritability of the French with regard to Prussia," which convinced the regime that it would be politically unsafe to tolerate any Prussian action which displeased the French public; and the emperor's volatile character. Lyons asked his military and naval attachés to investigate the rumoured French preparations for immediate hostilities, and while they found none they reported a constant state of military and naval readiness. "Mischief is brewing," Lyons and his military attaché Colonel Claremont agreed, despite their inability to discover any "tangible foundation" for this belief. Lyons did observe that the language reportedly used in Berlin was a mirror image of that heard in Paris. France was saying that there would be no war so long as Prussia did not do anything it disliked. Prussia was effectively saying that there would be peace so long as France allowed the fatherland to do as it pleased. Both nations insisted that peace depended on an announcement by Britain of its willingness to come to the aid of the victim of aggression, statements that served to reinforce Lyons's commitment to a rigorous neutrality. Were Britain to declare its support for either France or Prussia, he argued, that nation would immediately pursue its objectives and draw it into war with the other.[37]

The immense public interest in the coming French election was for Lyons "remarkable evidence of a revival of political life," and all but the Republicans seemed content with the dynasty and the progress towards parliamentary government. A government majority was expected to be returned to the Corps législatif, but one considerably more independent in spirit and tone than its predecessor. Equally, it was assumed that Napoleon would select and dismiss ministers with an eye to their influence in the lower chamber and that he would take greater care to support only those measures certain of passage. Although "the very peculiar system of government" made the forming of a "trustworthy opinion" difficult, and each party massaged figures to prove "that universal suffrage [had] pronounced in its favour," Lyons provided Clarendon with a thorough account of the election and an astute analysis of its meaning. Approximately two-thirds of the new chamber, or 216 of the 292 members so far returned, were supporters of the government, but only 118 of them were "official" candidates. Of the remaining third, half were moderate opponents of the government and the rest were Ultra Republicans "pledged to irreconcilable hostility to the Dynasty." Since the system of personal government and official candidates guaranteed that the Constitution and the dynasty were "virtually brought into question at every election," the results on this occasion were "far from entirely satisfactory to the Imperialists." The opposition was now approaching the government in popular ballots. Admittedly supporters of a Bourbon restoration, whether Orléanists or Legitimists, had been defeated as had many moderate Republicans, but the success of Red Republicans and Socialists in the capital and other great cities and towns was a stark reminder of the failure of the regime's "painful endeavours" to bind the working classes to the dynasty. Riots and strikes in Paris, St Étienne, Bordeaux,

Marseilles, and Nantes, and the evidence that they were on a larger scale than those that had taken place before the proclamation of the Second Empire with its commitment to order, were additional "uncomfortable symptoms" of a regime whose grip on the nation was weakening. Even the success of the official candidates could not be taken at face value. There had been "unscrupulous and unsparing government influence on their behalf." Furthermore, to secure election, many had felt it necessary to avow a desire for the country to have a greater share in the management of affairs, more effective control of extravagant expenditures, and for there to be less unpredictability in government policy.[38]

What conclusions did Lyons draw? First, that Napoleon remained personally popular with the bulk of the population but his reputation for "sagacity, energy and good fortune" had diminished. Second, that neither of the fallen dynasties had popular appeal and if there was a dynastic attachment it was to the Bonapartes. Third, that there was an almost universal belief that the system of personal government should be "abated." Fourth, that most of the supporters of parliamentary government on the British model hoped to obtain it from the emperor, or were willing to try to do so. Fifth, that the Red Republicans who sought "violent revolution and a total subversion of society" were uncomfortably large in number but the bulk of the French nation wanted reform not revolution. Nevertheless, Lyons feared that the government had committed a "serious mistake" by discreetly helping Reds in order to crush Orléanists.[39]

How would Napoleon respond to the election results? Would he launch a coup d'état at home or abroad in an effort to recover popularity? Clarendon thought that the French "Caesar" obsessed with his dynasty's survival saw responsible government a greater threat than war. "It is not surprising," he wrote to Lyons, "that the French people would be exasperated at always living on a Volcano & never knowing when it may burst out & what mischief it may do them." Lyons had reported the talk that war was the surest means of restoring the emperor's personal prestige. Other Bonapartists were recommending that Napoleon posture as the saviour of society and resort to another bout of "Caesarism." A more careful analysis of the returns from provinces where official candidates had done poorly convinced Lyons that there had been no popular endorsement of "personal government." It was less a case of the French preferring "English parliamentary government," he concluded, and more one of them tiring of the uncertainty and disquiet which resulted from everything being dependent on the "inscrutable will of one man" whom they no longer considered "infallible." The dynasty's best hope in his judgment was liberal government. Consequently, he welcomed the news that the emperor was moving in that direction. Prince Napoleon, a liberal, had reportedly been offered the presidency of the Council of Ministers but had demanded as his price of acceptance the dismissal of La Valette. This his cousin had declined to pay. Similarly, Émile Ollivier, a respected moderate Republican, had been offered the post of minister of public instruction but had declined to serve with Eugène Rouher, popularly dubbed the vice-emperor. Liberal pressure on the emperor continued to mount, however. Forty-two deputies, among them "officials," signed a manifesto calling for the more effective association of the country with public affairs, a peaceful foreign policy, the abrogation of the general security law, and electoral reform. Several days later they added to the manifesto a requirement that ministers be politically responsible to the Corps législatif and that it be granted the right to elect its own officers. Then on 6 July the 42 signers of the manifesto swelled to 116, and the signatures of a pair of courtiers were interpreted as a signal that the emperor was not opposed to the reforms. Two days later he decided to sacrifice Rouher, and on 12 July, in his speech opening an extraordinary session of the Corps législatif, Napoleon announced the resignation of the entire ministry and his endorsement of the manifesto. Lyons was astonished at this rapid collapse of both the personal power and reputation of the "Oracle of St Cloud."[40]

The Chamber's privileges were to be greatly extended. It was to make its own standing orders, elect its own presiding officers, enjoy greater latitude in the amendment of bills, and exercise comparatively unfettered power to question the government; all Ministers were to attend its sessions. This would establish their "virtual responsibility" to the legislature. The changes would remove almost all the restrictions which had made the Corps législatif less important than the popular legislatures in constitutional governments, and they suggested to Lyons that Napoleon had listened to the voice of a country which opposed personal government and war. Consequently, a war to maintain personal government "would have been a desperate expedient indeed." Napoleon evidently intended to respect the will of the nation. This "constitutional coup d'état" caused something of a sensation in Britain and produced a "striking unanimity of good feeling" for the emperor. But as Lyons cautioned and reminded the Foreign Office, it "remains for reasonable and patriotic Frenchmen to give him the support for averting revolution, and to show that liberty in France is not incompatible with peace abroad and order at home."[41]

CHAPTER THIRTEEN

The Fall of
the Second Empire

The disestablishment of the Church of Ireland (Anglican) was a central plank of Gladstone's platform as he strove to conciliate Ireland's Catholic majority. Passage through the Commons sent the bill to the Lords, where the Cabinet feared "suicidal" hereditary peers would reject it, precipitating a constitutional conflict with the elected lower chamber. This prospect sent Earl Granville, the government's leader in the upper chamber, trawling for votes, or "contents," on the bill's decisive second reading. Clarendon approached Lyons in early June to ask if he would return to London to vote for the measure. The question revived the sensitive issue of the relationship between professional diplomats and partisan politics. Malet counselled abstention as the safest course, whereas Sheffield recommended support. He pointed out that even some Tories of "stature" were planning to do so in order to avoid a constitutional crisis. When Lyons resisted the summons, citing his career-long non-involvement in politics, and his belief that a "regular diplomatist could only impair his efficiency by entanglement in home politics," Clarendon was queried by his Cabinet colleagues on the ambassador's political sympathies. Although Lyons had appeared on the Whip's list as either a Whig or a Liberal, perhaps because of his family's earlier associations, Clarendon disclaimed any sure knowledge of his political sentiments but guessed that they were Conservative. "I think it of advantage to the diplomatic service and profession," he added as a former member of it himself, "that men in important places should not be political and therefore change with the Government. I am sure that this is the case as regards Paris."[1]

Granville and Gladstone did not agree. "I do not think it would be right to ask a man to vote against his political opinions," the former responded, "but I am sure it is a very dangerous doctrine for the House of Lords that peers should abstain from taking one line or another in politics on account of personal convenience." Had not earlier ambassadors to France always been in the "political confidence of the Home Government"? he asked rhetorically. Certainly his own father had. Gladstone, he informed Clarendon, was "if anything more strongly of this opinion." So, writing from the Cabinet room, and by the "unanimous desire" of those present, the foreign secretary effectively summoned Lyons home to vote for the bill. Aware that this would not be another instance of absence making the heart grow fonder, and not wishing to imperil his future in Paris, Lyons returned to London, and in the early hours of Saturday morning, 19 June 1869, the bill was read a second time. A year later, when he was again summoned to vote on legislation, Lyons successfully avoided doing so.[2]

In July, Napoleon announced a new French government. He did not select its members as parliamentary custom dictated from the 116 signatories of the manifesto. Instead, he appointed an interim team of "technicians." Lyons regretted the loss of La Valette, with whom he had established an excellent relationship and was appalled by the thought that Drouyn de Lhuys would be his successor. Instead, La Valette exchanged posts with the French ambassador in London, Prince la Tour d'Auvergne. The Prince brought to the Quai d'Orsay a "mild and conciliatory character," "very attractive manners," and a reputation for straightforward and honourable conduct. But did this transitional ministry truly indicate the emperor's acceptance of liberal government? Would his acceptance solidify popular support for his dynasty? Might conservatives, who comprised "all the timid of the nation," desert the regime if they concluded that the emperor had neither the strength nor the will to protect them from disorder and socialism? Some generals, uncertain of Napoleon's resolve to resist the demands of the Left for a reduction in the size and cost of the army, were reportedly wavering in their support.

The Paris National Guard was becoming troublesome, clamouring for the election of its officers, and when their commander resigned Napoleon had difficulty finding a successor. Not even the lavish celebrations of the centenary of the birth of the founder of the dynasty moved Parisians en masse to a show of enthusiasm.[3]

The ministry's transitional character, the announcement of an amnesty for all those convicted of political and press offences, and the arrival of the traditional holiday month, August, brought a welcome "languor" to public affairs. This persuaded some Frenchmen that liberal change was possible without revolution, but France remained in "a very critical situation." Napoleon had now been emperor for some eighteen years, and the nation's recent history suggested that this was a regime's normal lifespan. The restored Bourbons had lasted for sixteen years, and the Orléanist branch for another eighteen. Perhaps classical scholarship had taught Lyons that there was a natural life cycle to French regimes as there was to some states. What concerned him was the emergence of an impatient younger generation without personal experience of the bloodshed and misery of the Revolution of 1848 and thus eager for change and excitement. Indeed, Liberal accusations that Napoleon had sponsored reform only with great reluctance were feeding the very well-grounded fear among some of his friends that the lurch to liberalism would end in the overthrow of the dynasty and the establishment of a Republic. What they saw, Lyons told Clarendon, was an emperor being led from concession to concession until he had "no power left to keep the Republicans in check." Others feared that, "finding it impossible to reconcile himself in practice to his altered position," he would have "recourse to some violent expedient such as war or a coup d'etat to extricate himself from it." Adding to the uncertainty and uneasiness was Napoleon's chronic poor health.[4]

Rheumatism, gout, and hemorrhoids were the common enough complaints from which the emperor was suffering, and the third of them provided a convenient explanation of his absence from Paris. A bumpy coach ride, or a horse ride, from St Cloud would cause him considerable discomfort. In addition to these painful conditions, Napoleon, unknown to the public, had a very large stone in his bladder. The team of physicians who attended him had planned to use the procedure developed earlier in the century, lithotipsy, only to get cold feet when Marshal Niel died under the treatment. His death called a halt to his military reforms, and this was soon to have disastrous consequences. Unaware of the true nature of Napoleon's suffering, Lyons was inclined to be unsympathetic. "He bears up so little against pain and is so apt to get into bed at all hours," he observed, "that there is no counting on seeing him even when he has made an appointment." However critical of the emperor's pain threshold, Lyons did not doubt that he had been tormented politically by recent foreign reverses. Hence his anxiety for the Gladstone ministry to bolster the emperor's reputation for "sagacity and influence" by responding to problems in a way that might help him. For example, the British Cabinet, aware that Napoleon's decidedly liberal commercial policy was in difficulty in the Corps législatif, ought to react with extreme caution to the proposed changes to the French tariff.[5]

Clarendon forwarded to Lyons an article from the *Economist* which detailed the striking and mutually beneficial growth of trade produced by the Commercial Treaty. The export of French wines had increased exponentially and there had been a boom in the French silk industry and, more surprisingly, a substantial rise in the shipment overseas of French textiles. Of course, there had been losers: since the weakest branches of manufacturing were the most vulnerable during any depression the arrival of hard times had put a number of them to a "rude test." Unfortunately, hard-pressed Frenchmen did not subscribe to the notion that the experience now gained would, when the economy rebounded, enable them to profit more handsomely "by the greater general prosperity incidental to freedom of trade." Protectionists were "very active and very hopeful," but at an audience on 24 November the emperor assured Lyons that his personal zeal for freer trade was not weakening. Nevertheless, his government did not intend to obstruct a parliamentary inquiry into the consequences of the Cobden Treaty. Why sacrifice the material interests that had grown up, and the "friendly and cordial feeling" they had promoted, "to the short sighted and selfish clamours" of certain French manufacturers? Lyons asked. Napoleon replied that he would outflank protectionism by reducing the burdens on industries and by launching public works to facilitate the rapid and cheaper shipment of goods.[6]

A debate which stretched over eleven consecutive days ended with a decisive vote in the Corps législatif against denunciation of the treaty. There was, however, unanimous agreement on the need for an investigation. Sentiment, Lyons realized, was moving ominously in the direction of protective duties to aid a number of suffering domestic industries. His consolation was that no one had spoken "disparagingly of England, or [had] undervalued the importance of a cordial union between the two countries." Furthermore, he believed the introduction of the parliamentary system had "much diminished the hostility" towards free trade. Again, his own contribution had been significant. By his calm and patient conduct, and his quiet and persuasive argument that to be "fair and complete" the inquiry needed to gather evidence from every quarter, he had ensured a hearing for British witnesses. Less promising was the choice of an enemy of the Cobden Treaty to chair the inquiry.[7]

The future of the Commercial Treaty was but one of the handful of items on Lyons's agenda. Tunis was threatening to become a problem, the Bey's indebtedness to the French nourishing the suspicion that as in Mexico this would be used as the excuse for an extension of French influence. Lyons considered a crude grab of Tunisian territory unlikely, but he impressed upon the French the "very great and very just offence" any action of this kind would give to the other powers concerned. A squabble at the heart of the Ottoman Empire was another threat to "cordial" relations with France. There had long been a danger that the Khedive of Egypt would take advantage of the Porte's *laisser-aller* policy to move towards full independence, and Ismail Pacha's semi-royal reception and independent actions during his second tour of Europe raised Turkish hackles. He had discussed with his hosts the neutralization of the Suez Canal, had issued the formal invitations to its ceremonial opening, and had entered into negotiations for a foreign loan. All of this had been done without the Porte's prior permission. On his return home he had ignored telegrams sent to him in the Sultan's name, had commissioned provocatively a statue to commemorate an Ottoman defeat, and had selected as his representative in Constantinople a person who had been convicted of corrupting high Turkish officials and was believed to be subsidizing a party of Turkish reformists dubbed "Young Turkey." What was more, the Khedive had imported modern munitions, including rifles and multi-barrelled rapid-fire weapons, with which to re-equip his army. Was he planning to declare independence? The Porte would resist, Ambassador Elliot advised Lyons, for it continued to consider Egypt an integral part of the empire and knew that with its loss the Sultan would lose control of the Holy Places of Islam. Surrounded by persons notoriously hostile to the Khedive, Elliot added, Abdul Aziz might draw Britain into all the disagreements and dangers of an Eastern question.[8]

Lyons appeared to signal an approaching sea change in British policy. He and Clarendon had in their separate meetings with Ismail Pacha warned him not to seek independence. Why exchange lax Turkish suzerainty for the control of a powerful nation such as France? they asked. Lyons, who considered the Khedive a silly, vain, "contumacious vassal," was confident the Egyptian would instinctively shy away from the risks inherent in the pursuit of independence. Clarendon was no more admiring of the Sultan, who in his opinion differed "little from an Oriental savage" and thus had to be "kept under control." Abdul Aziz needed to understand that completion of the Suez Canal, which Empress Eugénie was to open formally on 17 November 1869, had created great interests in Egypt which the Great Powers would not neglect simply because the Khedive had failed to respect the Sultan's dignity. Nor would Britain back any foolish Turkish attempt to exercise more effective control over Egypt. Consequently, it was in Britain's interest to convince both rulers to maintain the status quo. This was another Lyons recommendation accepted by Clarendon.[9]

When it came to convincing the Sultan and the Khedive to behave as Britain wished, Lyons decided to adhere to the course he had followed so successfully in Washington and Constantinople. He realized that a French government, whose first concern was its tense relationship with Prussia, had no interest at this moment in stirring the Eastern pot, and he assumed that Sultan and Khedive would do as they were told if Britain and France were "firm, united and earnest." Lyons still considered the French easier to work with than any other nationality, and although Clarendon urged him always to keep in mind the possibility that they would play him false, he was soon claiming that the Egyptian business had cemented the Anglo-French entente. He expected difficulty on the issue of the canal's neutralization, but the inability of the Gladstone Cabinet to agree on the best means of ensuring free passage for all ships of all nations at all times prevented the development of a clear British policy. But the problem of the waterway's usage was set aside with the plunge of Franco-Prussian relations into a crisis.[10]

"I am afraid we shall never again either in political or commercial affairs have as good times as we had under the pouvoir personnel of the Emperor," a wistful Lyons wrote to the foreign secretary on 3 December 1869. The transitional French ministry sought to resign, being aware that only a "Parliamentary Ministry" would convince liberals of the emperor's genuine commitment to constitutional government. Napoleon's delay in appointing one simply fostered the perception that his "energy and decision" were not what they had once been. Finally, on 2 January 1870, Émile Ollivier took office as the head of a new government. He held the justice portfolio not the presidency of the Council of Ministers, and was one of several members who entered office with "curious antecedents." A Republican *préfect* of Marseilles following the fall of the Orléanist monarchy, he had withdrawn from politics with the failure of the Revolution of 1848 and the imprisonment and deportation of his father by President Louis Napoleon. Ollivier, who then made a career at the bar, became convinced of the merits of constitutional monarchy and of the compatibility of the empire and political liberty – "Liberty without anarchy, order without despotism" was his motto. He had also served as a confidential liberal adviser of the emperor. His choice to lead the new government, whose members were drawn from the Centre Left and Centre Right, was therefore no bolt from the blue. Another curiosity was Count Daru, the new tenant of the Quai d'Orsay. Son of one of the most respected figures of the First Empire, indeed a godson of the first emperor, and now an Orléanist of the Centre Left, he had once presided over a public meeting which had called for the impeachment of Napoleon III. Daru is a "very disagreeable cross grained fellow," Lyons informed Clarendon, yet he accepted his appointment as proof of the emperor's resolve to play the part of a constitutional sovereign.[11]

The ministry had little by way of a political honeymoon. The "horrid affair of Prince Pierre Bonaparte" caused it immediate trouble. Dubbed the "wild boar of Corsica," he was an unsavoury character with a taste for violence. He forsook Republicanism once Napoleon named him a prince and awarded him an annual pension of 100,000 francs. His exchange of insults with organs of the newly liberated "satirical and scurrilous" left-wing press controlled by Paschal Grossuet and Henri de Rochefort, the latter the "son of a Legitimist marquis," brought a pair of "seconds," Victor Noir and Ulrich de Fonvielle, to Bonaparte's door with a demand for satisfaction. The Prince, who invariably carried a revolver and practised with it regularly in his garden, shot Noir fatally during a scuffle in which Fonvielle drew a weapon. The Radical Republicans of the capital staged a massive funeral demonstration for the "martyr" and vehemently protested the refusal to permit his interment in the Père-Lachaise cemetery. The demonstrators "looked murderous" and sported sprigs of *immortelle* as they passed the Tuileries Palace loudly singing the "Marseillaise." The troops Ollivier had ordered onto the streets ensured they did not become too unruly. In the Chamber, he calmly answered the questions of the "extreme left" and announced the arrest of Bonaparte and an Imperial decree ordering his trial. As befitted his rank, the Prince was to be tried in the High Court and the jury was to be composed of thirty-six councillors. Also, Ollivier secured the withdrawal of Rochefort's parliamentary immunity from prosecution. His subsequent arrest did briefly produce disturbances, with the throwing up of barricades and the invasion of armouries, but Lyons could detect no sign of a widespread readiness to revolt. "There is some uneasiness," he admitted, "and the change of system is too recent to enable one to judge how it will work in the end." Indeed, he understood that the empress believed that the affair would have been far more disastrous under the old system of government.[12]

The French were not well fitted for the representative system of government, at least in all its liberties, and probably never would be, a pessimistic Clarendon observed. They "may train themselves up to fitness, if they do not abuse the new power given to the Corps Legislatif" but were "too impatient to give themselves a chance of obtaining the liberty they pretend to desire & that they are unfit for." He was similarly skeptical of Ollivier's leadership abilities, dismissing him as deficient in judgment, tact, experience, firmness, and knowledge of men. The talent he did possess, he acidly remarked, was that of "indisposing people to him."

But following the Noir episode, he was persuaded by Lyons that Ollivier had created a general belief in his capacity to deliver, legally and quickly, all the freedom Frenchmen could desire. The "Parliamentary ministry," Lyons reported reassuringly, was winning by its resolute and energetic conduct the support of all who desired liberty and abhorred violence and revolution.[13]

Ollivier acted swiftly to enhance his liberal credibility. He promised the decentralization of administration, electoral and municipal reform, jury trials for newspapermen accused of political offences, greater liberty of education, and the abandonment by the present ministers of the despised system of naming "official" candidates at elections. The proposed changes to the Constitution announced a month later signalled a constitutional imperial monarchy but with a number of "peculiarities" which Lyons duly noted. The emperor was responsible to the people and retained the right always to appeal to them; ministers were appointed by him and he would continue to preside in the Council of Ministers; and the principle of ministerial responsibility was asserted, if curtly and vaguely, with the phrase "*Ils sont responsables*." But having lost the support of the Right with these liberal measures, Ollivier forfeited that of the Left by failing to invest the power to amend the Constitution exclusively in the legislature and by granting the emperor the right to appeal over its head to the people via plebiscites. The moderate Republican Jules Favre, who had distinguished himself as the defence attorney for Felice Orsini, the attempted assassin of the emperor in 1858, was one of many deputies who saw in this provision the means by which Napoleon might return to the system of personal government. When the deputies of the Centre Left made the deletion of this provision the price of their support of the Constitution, and it was not paid, they inadvertently ensured that the approval or rejection of the Constitution would, as Napoleon wished, be decided through the very instrument they deplored and feared.[14]

The public was briefly distracted by the trial of Pierre Bonaparte. Acquitted of murder, he was required to pay compensation to the parents of the deceased, their court costs, and the costs of the trial. There would have been greater satisfaction, Lyons remarked, had the Prince been convicted of murder under severe provocation. Nevertheless, the charge levelled by Radical Republicans that he had escaped conviction as a result of imperial pressure failed to resonate. It was common in France for juries to acquit an accused who had killed the assailant immediately after being struck, as Bonaparte had been in the incident. Even the efforts of the Republican press to arouse passions by concentrating on the fact that Bonaparte had walked away free while Noir's companion, Fonvielle, had been sentenced to ten days' imprisonment for contempt of court, met with little success following the revelation that Noir was less a journalist than a thug who had been employed by Rochefort and other left-wing journalists as a bodyguard and to bully those they disliked.[15]

"To pass in so short a time from a virtually absolute monarchy to a practically free government without producing a great amount of agitation among so excitable a people as the French is of course impossible," Lyons wrote in a dispatch clearly intended for publication in the Blue Book. He was seeking to generate British public support for the new, more liberal, imperial regime. "It is the good faith of the Emperor, and the honesty and ability of the Ministry," he declared, "that have hitherto enabled France to pass through this revolution without violence and without bloodshed." But the resort to the "sense or nonsense of universal suffrage" on questions drafted by the emperor was widely regarded in Britain as the means of setting aside the legislature. The plebiscite, Clarendon growled, ought to have been one of the ships Napoleon burned when he embarked on liberalism, while Gladstone considered it an "absolute mockery" of constitutional government[16]

The question framed for the electorate was naturally a leading one: The people approve the liberal reforms carried out in the Constitution by the emperor with the assistance of senior institutions of the state. Thus to vote in the affirmative was to vote for the dynasty. To ensure he received the 6 million votes that had been "fixed upon as the figure of a decided success," Napoleon resorted to a range of manipulative measures. He circulated 10 million copies of his proclamation; men of property and bankers were induced to contribute money to the cause or to exert themselves in support of a "decided majority"; strikes and occasional eruptions of social disorder were well publicized to bring the timid to the polls; and the dread of disorder and revolution was cynically exploited with the altogether too opportune discovery of another alleged plot to assassinate the emperor. Even an aspect of foreign policy was a fraction in the political equation. The French government had long been agitated over the proceedings of the Ecumenical Council convened by Pius IX, whom the French foreign minister ridiculed as "lost in mysticism and not amenable to practical reasoning." Several of the decrees, and primarily that of papal infallibility, were in Daru's words "hostile to the laws and feelings prevalent among civilized nations and subversive of the rights and authority of the Civil Power." Moreover, in many quarters, France was held in large part responsible for the "measures" since its troops, by their presence, had made the Council possible. Instead of pressuring the pontiff by threatening to leave him to the "tender mercies" of the Italians, or by summoning home the French bishops, it chose to do neither because of the looming plebiscite on the Constitution. The ultramontane French inferior clergy, which continued to exercise great influence over rural voters, would resent any coercion of the pope. France had better not bark at the pope while it could not bite him, Lyons and Odo Russell agreed.[17]

At first glance, the ends had justified the means. In excess of 7 million affirmative votes had been cast on 8 May 1870, while a further 3 million were divided almost equally between noes and abstentions. This was an "undoubted triumph for the Emperor and his Ministers," Lyons concluded, but Clarendon fastened on the rejection of the Constitution by the electors of Paris and other large urban centres. Moreover, 50,000 army votes had been against the emperor, although this was attributable, in part, to the cunning strategy of Republicans. They supplied soldiers with free passes to brothels only for them to be angered at being confined to barracks in the expectation of being needed to suppress disturbances. An empire "based on soldiers and peasants is not a solid foundation," Clarendon observed, and "no effort should be spared to enlarge the basis." Sensibly, given British criticism of the regime's exploitation and manipulation of universal manhood suffrage, Lyons dismissed as "preposterous" the proposal that the diplomatic corps collectively congratulate the emperor on the result. This would amount to an unacceptable interference in the internal affairs of France, he informed his fellow diplomats. But convinced as he still was that Napoleon was the best security for free trade and cordial relations, Lyons trod the delicate line between overt, enthusiastic support of the outcome and implied disapproval of the dubious means by which it had been secured. He was present in the diplomatic gallery when the result was formally announced in the Corps législatif and made a little speech to Napoleon at a ball on 23 May that "hit the Emperor's taste." At the same time, he was providing the skeptical Clarendon with a thoughtful analysis of the Second Empire's lingering problems. The Ollivier ministry had little press support and was weak in both chambers, while among senior army officers there was a dangerous mood which equated war with promotion and glory. Nor, with Daru's departure when the Centre Left defected, was Lyons cheered by the appointment of Antoine Agenor Duc de Gramont as foreign minister even though he called at the embassy to express profusely his fondness for Britain. In Rome, where they had first become acquainted, Gramont's profound religious faith had seen him take a "supremely ludicrous view" of the papal regime. His subsequent transfer to Vienna had led to his infection with Prussophobia and he had declared a Franco-Prussian war unavoidable. He saw himself as the man of action providentially destined to "arrest the decline into which French prestige had fallen." Gramont was proof of the extent to which "the French mind" had become "less than ever cool and unprejudiced about Prussia," Lyons fretted, while Clarendon derided the new foreign minister as "an empty headed unreliable coxcomb quite unfit for the post." This was the man who now faced a long, simmering crisis which showed signs of rapidly coming to the boil: the Spanish succession.[18]

Sir John Crampton had retired as British minister to Spain in the autumn of 1869. After forty years in the diplomatic service he was weary, tired especially of the incessant "intriguing and lies" in the Spanish capital, and of the possible daily embarrassment of encountering his former wife. The post was offered to Austen Henry Layard, first commissioner of works in the Liberal government. But Layard had become a political liability. Unpopular in the Commons, far from trusted by a number of his ministerial colleagues, he was later dubbed "Liehard" by the Queen, whose abuse of him prompted a listening Disraeli to describe her language as "Billingsgate" (the fish market in London's east end that had long been notorious for the foul language of its traders). The office he held was wanted for another. The Madrid mission would provide a convenient, face-saving means of being rid of him. Despite his considerable knowledge and experience of foreign affairs gained as parliamentary undersecretary to Russell and Clarendon, his selection was "questionable" in the opinion of Stanley, who considered him so "wholly wanting in discretion and tact" that diplomacy was the last profession for which he was suited.[19]

The Layards called on Lyons on their way to the Spanish capital, and from him the new minister gained an insight into the situation in Spain. The willingness of the Great Powers of Europe to look on as the crown of a great country went begging was astonishing, Lyons thought. On reaching Madrid, Layard was flabbergasted when he found that the population was seemingly indifferent to the identity of their future monarch. "Altogether we are in a mess and no one seems to see the way out of it," he informed Lyons. Alfonso, the Prince of Asturias, the young son of the deposed queen, was reputed to be Napoleon III's choice as monarch. Isabella had established a court in exile in Paris, where the emperor assumed the boy would be exposed to French influence that would continue during a regency. A second candidate was Montpensier, who had seemingly found an influential backer in General Prim. A Frenchman, he was not a popular figure among the Spanish people, nor was he acceptable to the French emperor, and he exhibited little good sense. He fought a duel as a result of which his adversary, Don Enrique de Bourbon, who was certainly devoid of commonsense if not mentally ill, suffered a fatal wound to the head. "There appears to have been a kind of pretence of a judicial enquiry," Edith Layard noted, which concluded that "Don Enrique died from his pistol going off in his hand & hitting him in the head." The duel effectively killed Montpensier's chance of securing the throne, something guaranteed by the passage through the Cortes of a resolution to exclude anyone of Bourbon descent. This applied to Alfonso as well. On 11 June, Prim mentioned in the Cortes another, as yet unidentified, candidate. This was the first public allusion to the Hohenzollern prince with whom negotiations had been conducted for several months. He was unacceptable to Napoleon.[20]

Clarendon, ably assisted as ever by Lyons, had striven for months to lessen the tension between France and Prussia. During a visit to the British embassy on 30 January, Ollivier discussed his wish to do something for the nation's agricultural population on which his government depended for support as it battled urban socialism. A saving on the military budget by reducing the annual intake of recruits by 20 per cent would make possible a lowering of taxation while easing the burden of conscription. Unfortunately, the emperor and his generals countered that it would be dangerous to reduce the strength of the army while that of Prussia remained at current levels. The obvious solution was a mutual reduction of the men annually conscripted. Having twice proposed this, and having twice been rebuffed, France could not in dignity renew the proposal, Ollivier told Lyons. On the other hand, Britain might take the lead and use its good offices as a friendly power in the cause of disarmament. Lyons was amenable, recognizing as he did the danger inherent in the two nations being ever ready for war.[21]

Clarendon could have been in no doubt that this proposal originated with the emperor, for Napoleon had discussed such an initiative with him privately while the Tories were still in office. Massive standing armies were a threat to peace, were at odds with the "civilization of the modern age," and the heavy taxes levied to provide for their maintenance were a source of popular discontent, the foreign secretary readily agreed. However, he was sure that a private and confidential approach to Prussia was the only one likely to be treated seriously, so the French insistence that it be made in a regular and publishable dispatch fed his and Lyons's suspicions that their objective was less disarmament than the embarrassment of Bismarck by saddling him with the responsibility for the continuing arms race. In short, to follow the course demanded by the French would precipitate the very crisis they were seeking to avoid. If the negotiations became public, Bismarck would rally German nationalism with the cry of foreign intervention, and France would declare that it had been rebuffed yet again. Such an announcement, Ollivier admitted, would excite such shrill French cries of anger that a government accountable to a popularly elected legislature would have grave difficulty resisting them. Lyons shared Clarendon's pessimism that anything truly useful could be achieved since a disarmament proposal would not complicate Bismarck's task of inducing Germans to remain heavily armed. Another problem, which he identified, was the semantic one of what constituted conquest and what aggression. The Prussians, Lyons pointed out, denied that their annexation of South German states would be either, whereas the French insisted it would be both. Plainly, Prussia would never give a commitment to refrain from the completion of German unity and France would never promise peacefully to accept it. If mutual declarations of non-interference were made the condition of disarmament, it would never be brokered. Clarendon agreed with this analysis yet did not believe that German political unity would alter significantly the strategic relationship between the two nations. The South German states were already military allies of Prussia, and any attempt by France to prevent them from uniting with the North would simply weld Germany more closely together.[22]

Initially, Bismarck used King William as his excuse for maintaining a massive army. The monarch, who from the age of six had been dressed in a military uniform, would never agree to a reduction in the number of his troops, he insisted. Next, Bismarck cited his country's peculiar vulnerability to attack. There were three empires on its three borders – French, Austrian, and Russian – all infected with anti-Prussian sentiment, all parading remodelled armies, and the most dangerous of them, France, having an army much larger than that of Prussia. When Lyons raised Bismarck's "concerns" with the then foreign minister, Daru, he dismissed them as "simply ridiculous." Clarendon agreed. He considered the Prussian's fears "weak and absurd." The Russians, he argued, posed no threat to Germany because they were seeking to extend their influence and commerce eastwards into Asia not westwards into Central Europe. The Austrian threat was another fiction because the alarmingly disorganized dual monarchy of Austria-Hungary, created in 1867, could in an emergency put no more than 250,000 men into the field, and its finances were in a sorry state. As for France, only by including the French troops dispersed in North Africa, in Rome guarding the Pope, and in the nation's large urban areas to maintain order could Bismarck claim that the army facing Prussia was the larger of the two. Also, the chancellor had failed to take into account the new liberal government of the Second Empire. As the people of France and elsewhere gain more influence over the administration of their affairs "the chances of causeless wars will diminish," the foreign secretary airily predicted, for they understood the horrors of war and knew that they not their rulers would be its victims. Bismarck countered that Clarendon miscounted the number of French troops in Algeria and failed to recognize the uncertain future of liberal government in France. War cries could be raised there at the drop of a hat, he complained, and for proof of this cited the Prussophobia of the provincial press. He had not forgotten Napoleon's ominous comment to him during the Paris Exhibition, that to ensure his regime's survival he could either allow more domestic liberty or fight a war and if necessary would resort to both. To Clarendon and Lyons it was clear by early April that there was no immediate prospect of disarmament as a means of lessening tension.[23]

Two months later Clarendon was dead. He had been in poor health for some time and had along with his wife visited Wiesbaden in 1869 to take the waters. During their stay at the Paris embassy, he and his wife had been given Lyons's room on the first floor because they were too "Rhumatic" to climb stairs. Clarendon also suffered from gout and by the spring was in such pain in both knees that he kept briefly to his Watford home. By June he was suffering from a chronic bowel disorder and collapsed soon after returning home from the House of Lords on 26 June. He died the following morning. Gladstone described him as "an incomparable colleague, a statesman of many gifts, a most lovable and genial man." He made a less sensitive remark to the chronically unwell John Bright: "He is gone where we shall soon follow him." Lyons was quite overwhelmed by the news and felt the loss profoundly.[24]

Only Granville of the members of the Cabinet knew anything of foreign affairs, and Gladstone "really believed in Cobden's theory that men were growing too civilised for war," Disraeli remarked with characteristic mocking asperity. In fact, Kimberley, the colonial secretary, had served in the Foreign Office, been minister plenipotentiary to St Petersburg in the difficult immediate aftermath of the Crimean War, and, had he acquired a fondness for irony, might have cited his viceroyalty of Ireland as both a diplomatic and foreign posting. Gladstone gave the office, however, to his friend and confidant Granville, declaring that he possessed not only the deep calm of an Aberdeen but also "a strong sense of justice, much foreign knowledge, and singular tact." In arguably the most significant particular, he was embellishing Granville's qualifications. He had been briefly a parliamentary undersecretary thirty years earlier, and even more briefly foreign secretary when Russell had named him, to considerable surprise, as Palmerston's replacement in 1851. Granville was a "very able man in many ways, and shrewd & ready when he fairly gives his mind to the business before him," the overlooked Kimberley later acknowledged, before criticizing him as "a hand to mouth man who trusts to the chapter of accidents, and never reasons out any matter completely or goes into it enough to master its details." The new foreign secretary, whose cherubic countenance was consistent with his small stature, though the downturn to his mouth and prominent nose created an impression of looking down it, affected a suitable modesty. "Remember what a novice I am, and give me any advice that strikes you," he wrote to Lyons. Indeed, he professed embarrassment at issuing instructions to such an experienced and successful diplomat and promised to be "a better boy for the future."[25]

His development of an effective foreign policy was hampered by the poisonous atmosphere within the Foreign Office. Contributing to this mood were the hearings of the parliamentary select committee that was looking to improve the office's organization and consolidate the professional character of the diplomatic and consular services via a "formal clarification of ranks and salaries." The undersecretaries were at daggers drawn, Lyons learned from his former head of chancery in Washington, Percy Anderson, who was later to be knighted and to head the Africa Department. Arthur Otway, an old Lyons friend, and the parliamentary undersecretary, was so "idle, careless, and utterly incapable of work and so jealous of Hammond that his guiding principle [appeared] to be to counter order any suggestion" of his permanent counterpart. He made matters worse by appearing before the parliamentary committee to extol John Bidwell, the ineffectual head of the German department, thereby ensuring that he kept the position. Anderson likened the pair to the chemist's assistant in the *Pickwick Papers* who had the fixed idea that Epsom salts meant prussic acid. Neither man would permit any challenge of his convictions. Anderson was similarly unimpressed with Granville, whose reputation for indolence compromised him as an authority figure. His illegible handwriting obliged him to employ an amanuensis, while his literary ability was equally suspect. The syntax and grammar of his draft of one dispatch to the British ambassador in Berlin had been corrected so heavily by Gladstone that, according to Anderson, it was as if he were "cutting up a schoolboy exercise." Robert Lowe, a former leader writer for *The Times*, and now chancellor of the exchequer, had been so "peppery" in his criticism of a dispatch to Layard that the Cabinet required the submission of all instructions before they were sent. Of course, Anderson's criticisms may have been sharpened by resentment. The foreign secretary shared the making of policy with Gladstone not the Office, whereas Clarendon had not only acted to improve the position and prospects of his staff but had thanked them for providing him with "such valuable memoranda." However, neither prime minister, foreign secretary, nor their Cabinet colleagues were likely to stray from the non-interventionist path trodden earlier by Stanley and Clarendon. The government's preoccupation with domestic reform, especially in troubled Ireland, was again limiting discussion of foreign policy issues by a Cabinet which met only weekly.[26]

It was not until the day of Clarendon's funeral, 2 July, that Gladstone informed the ministers of Granville's appointment, and it was another four days before he received the seals of office. Already a crisis was brewing. Isabella's melodramatic abdication in May while standing on the balcony of her Paris residence had failed to advance her son's claim to the throne. Prim now announced in Madrid that the Cortes would assemble on 20 July to elect Leopold of Hohenzollern-Sigmaringen king. A Catholic, married to a Portuguese infanta, ironically a nearer relation of Napoleon III than of King William of Prussia, and a brother of Prince Charles, whom the French had helped to place on the Romanian throne, he seemed destined to be little more than a figurehead. According to reports, his letter accepting the nomination was accompanied by one from Bismarck, whom Clarendon had long suspected of having "an eye on Spain as an auxiliary," which indicated Prussia's support of his decision. The overwhelming majority given to the Bonaparte dynasty in the French plebiscite may be the explanation of this provocative intervention. Before the plebiscite Bismarck had probably counted on the Ollivier ministry to acquiesce, if reluctantly, in both the peaceful unification of Germany and the placing of a Hohenzollern on the Spanish throne. Had not Napoleon and Ollivier both earlier admitted that the moment had "irreparably passed" for calling a halt to the growth of Prussia? Following the plebiscite, however, Bismarck could expect a greatly strengthened and more confident emperor to be far less accommodating, and this was seemingly confirmed by his appointment of the Prussophobic Duc de Gramont as foreign minister.[27]

Napoleon informed his ministers on 6 July that unless the Hohenzollern candidature was withdrawn it would mean war, and Gramont advised the Corps législatif later that same day of the government's absolute refusal to accept a Hohenzollern on the throne of Spain. Lyons telegraphed the news to London and in a remarkable tour de force quoted Gramont's statement almost word for word from memory. "I doubt any one else having been able to do such a thing," an admiring Malet commented. Granville and Gladstone were startled by the vehemence of the French reaction, although Hammond understood the anger in Paris and the readiness to make this a *casus belli*. At the same time he feared the peremptory language of the French government would leave Prussia with no means of escaping its support of Leopold's candidature save at the expense of national honour. Ambassador La Valette, during a hastily arranged interview, urged the foreign secretary to use all of Britain's influence to stop the nomination going ahead, and Granville immediately telegraphed Layard: "Use every pressure which will not offend the Spanish Government but which in your opinion will promote the abandonment of the Hohenzollern project." Representations were also made in Berlin and pressure exerted on Prince Leopold's father to withdraw his son's candidacy, but it was in Paris where war or peace was most likely to be decided.[28]

Lyons listed the factors that were deepening the crisis: French chauvinism; their exaggeration of the injury to their interests; the talk of national honour; the anxiety of liberal ministers to exhibit "spirit" and to demonstrate that a parliamentary government would hold high the nation's flag; their belief that they had an advantage in the "forwardness of their preparations" for war; and their conviction that a confrontation with Prussia was inevitable and that this was a favourable moment to have it. Gramont's contention that France's "energetic language" and military preparations would make possible the success in Berlin of British counsels of peace was rejected by Lyons. Instead, he thought that French belligerence was more likely to thwart peace efforts. But as the excitement in Paris continued to mount he began, presciently, to fear that even a renunciation of the Hohenzollern candidacy would not suffice, that the French would then pick a quarrel over the form of the renunciation, and that the French and the Prussians would end up hating each other more than ever. "Nothing can be better than your work in Paris," Granville wrote encouragingly. However, Gladstone wanted him to use even stronger language to Gramont since "no nation is powerful enough in these times to stand up against the [peaceful] public opinion of Europe."[29]

The announcement on 12 July of the withdrawal of the Hohenzollern candidacy saw Lyons's worst fear realized. During a lengthy conference with Eugénie and Gramont at St Cloud, Napoleon agreed to demand a Prussian guarantee of Leopold's renunciation of the Spanish throne. Ambassador Benedetti was to present it to King William at Ems, where he was taking the cure. On learning from Lyons of this latest development, a sardonic Edmund Hammond noted the difficulty experienced by the French in fixing a quarrel on Prussia. "If there is nothing which has not been made public of a more damning character against Prussia," he observed, "it will be a most reckless proceeding on the part of France to force on a war." On the other hand, he considered Bismarck's conduct "somewhat suspicious" and the Prussian's "evil genius" potentially "destructive of peace." He was reported to have left his estate in East Prussia for Berlin not for Ems to confer with the King.[30]

Lyons spent a hectic day running Gramont to earth. He urged him, without success, to accept the family's renunciation of the candidacy as an end to the crisis. He then attended the discussion in the Corps législatif. As a result, he had not had time to consider carefully whether Prussia could or should meet the French demand. Nevertheless, he freely admitted in private that in the cause of European peace and of good Anglo-French relations he would be happy for the Gladstone government to support the French "request" and endeavour to secure Prussian compliance with it. The French "are always horribly suspicious that we have a leaning to Prussia," he advised Granville. The foreign secretary, on the other hand, stressed the "immense responsibility" of France should it decline to accept unconditionally Leopold's withdrawal. He did not see how he and his colleagues could bring more pressure to bear on Prussia, especially after King William politely declined to provide the guarantee demanded by France. The monarch telegraphed his reply to Bismarck, who was conveniently dining with the chief of the Prussian army, Helmuth von Moltke, and the minister of war, Albrecht Graf von Roon. Assured by them that the Prussian army was ready for war, Bismarck engaged in the kind of provocation against which Clarendon had warned the Prussians only two years earlier. He edited the king's refusal to make it appear brusque and disrespectful of the French ambassador, and its immediate publication in a special edition of Bismarck's most faithful organ was proof that he knew exactly what he was doing. Republished in Paris on the evening of 14 July, it carried the headline "Public Insult to Our Ambassador," and the streets were filled with Parisians shouting "On to Berlin." This episode convinced Lyons that the Prussians were bent on conflict. French mobilization quickly followed, and two days later, with only ten dissenting votes, the Chamber of Deputies voted funds for war. All his diplomatic skill would now be required, he predicted, to prevent a rapid deterioration in relations with France.[31]

In a last-gasp effort to preserve peace, Lyons recommended that London invoke Protocol 23 of the Crimean War settlement. It provided for the referral of serious disputes by the parties concerned to the good offices of a third party "before having recourse to arms." Always a forlorn hope, given the wars of 1864 and 1866 and the depth of Franco-Prussian animosity, Lyons was authorized to make the effort, but by then the French had for all intents and purposes declared war. Gladstone and Granville sent a telegram to Berlin proposing mediation, which allowed them to claim that they had left no stone unturned in the quest for peace. Edmund Hammond had already advised them that there was no prospect of the mediation of a friendly power being accepted. Bismarck rejected the proposal and deliberately discouraged future British efforts by inspiring press attacks on Britain for selling war materiel to France and by circulating the preposterous claim that Britain might have forbidden France to declare war. Lyons, his notes on the Protocol unanswered, and as the representative of a nation occupying "the hardly tolerable position of a country neutral and impartial," recalled his "painful experience of this sort of thing in Washington." The French were already "sore" over Britain's failure to go "wholly with them," he admitted on 16 July, and so it would be a miracle if after six months of "this wretched war" friendly Anglo-French relations survived. Tact and prudence, assets he possessed in abundance, and sensitive "consideration of French susceptibilities," would be required to prevent their severe deterioration. To this end, he effectively demanded a decisive say on the diplomatic correspondence published in the Blue Books and indicated his intention to consult Gramont on the contents. In the same spirit, he was uncooperative when newspaper correspondents and "amateur travellers" who wished to accompany the French armies applied to him for passes. He feared Britain would be held responsible for any damaging indiscretions they committed. With an eye to generating favourable French opinion, he suggested that the British embassy in Berlin volunteer to take charge of the interests of French subjects trapped by the war in Prussia.[32]

Public opinion was a potentially mighty force in international relations, Granville believed; hence his intimacy with the editor of *The Times*. The "feeling" in the lobby of the House of Commons, he informed Lyons, was very strong against French "precipitation." The French public had gone mad about Spain and Prussia, Earl Russell wrote to his daughter-in-law, and Napoleon had favoured the popular madness "for the sake of his diadem, & his dynasty." "He knows as his uncle did," the former prime minister and foreign secretary added, "that what the French like is not liberty but military glory." In an effort to improve their public image in Britain, and damage that of Prussia, the French leaked to the press on 17 July details of Clarendon's proposals for mutual Franco-Prussian disarmament. Bismarck swiftly retaliated. On 19 July, the day the French formally declared war, the German ambassador to Britain, Count Bernstorff, revealed to Gladstone the provisions of the secret draft treaty with France on Belgium and Luxembourg. He evidently expected the prime minister to mount his moral high horse, deplore so immoral an agreement, and reveal it to the world. Instead, seeing it as another Prussian snare, Gladstone initially shared the information only with Granville. A frustrated Bernstorff then leaked it to *The Times* on 25 July, causing the security of Belgium to become an immediate British concern. Accusations by the French press that the king of the Belgians had connived at the Hohenzollern candidacy had already revived British suspicions that France had designs on its northern neighbour. Lyons, faithful to his policy of avoiding wherever possible issues with France, had recommended that Belgium be vigilant, on guard, and quiet, but that was a line now more difficult for Britain to adhere to. "The French have behaved abominably," an angry Earl Russell spluttered, and "our Govt are too civil and mealy mouthed about them."[33]

Gladstone and his colleagues were driven by political and public opinion to seek from both belligerents a commitment to respect Belgian neutrality. The publication of the draft treaty convinced Lyons that both had been parties to a "scandalous iniquity" worse even than the earlier partitions of Poland. At least in that case the country had been turbulent, ill-governed, populated by serfs, and an inconvenient neighbour, whereas Belgium and Holland were free, extremely well governed, and perfectly inoffensive neighbours. In pursuit of a binding agreement, Lyons counselled against any clear British commitment to dispatch troops to Belgium should its neutrality be violated. A force less than 100,000 would in his opinion be "laughed at" in this age of massive armies, and where was Britain to find even that number of men? Consequently, its best course was to create a "vague apprehension" that the Royal Navy would act against any nation that offended Britain in this matter. Gramont's sudden production of a draft Anglo-French Treaty for the defence of Belgium he dismissed as a ploy to embroil Britain in the war, and he ensured that negotiations with France and Prussia on Belgium took place in London. Protocols guaranteeing the belligerents' respect of Belgium's neutrality and independence were signed on 9 and 11 August, and both bound themselves to co-operate with Britain against any violator of the agreement.[34]

While dutifully respecting the Gladstone government's resolve to avoid involvement in the European conflict at almost any price, distracted as it still was by troubles in Ireland and difficulties with the United States, Lyons was more sympathetic to the French cause than were his masters in London. He did not dispute that the French had "enormously exaggerated" the injury of the Hohenzollern candidacy to their national interests, that their press had been violent in its rhetoric, and that war had been forced on the emperor by his own party in the Chamber and by ministers who would otherwise have found themselves in a minority and obliged to resign. He deplored, however, the stridently anti-French attitude of *The Times*, which he considered a "wilful

perversion" of the facts and dangerous because the French understood
it to be very much under Granville's influence. He rejected the newspaper's claim, undoubtedly Prussian inspired, that France had sought,
after the opening of the crisis, to revive the project of dividing the Low
Countries with Prussia, and described as a "pathetic trick" Bernstorff's
attempt to make Granville vouch for the authenticity of the "business."
Edward Malet accurately reflected his chief's view when he observed
that everybody knew that a banked-up fire was there and that on the
poke of a stick it would burst into flame. Thus responsibility for the war
rested with the power that poked it, and this was Prussia and Leopold
its stick. All that had been required following his renunciation of the
throne was a "civil word from the King of Prussia." All that Gramont had
actually said on 12 July, Lyons reminded Granville, was that if Leopold
should "on the advice of the King" withdraw his name the affair would
be over. Instead, Bismarck had ensured that the French ambassador was
publicly humiliated and had slammed the door on mediation by convincing the French, via the article in the *North German Gazette*, that he
was intent on war. Revealingly, although he did not consider it proper
for a neutral to take part in the rejoicing of expected French victories,
the francophile Lyons secured permission to illuminate the embassy if
he judged that necessary to avoid its damage by celebrating Parisians.[35]

This was a decision, it was soon painfully clear, he would not have to
make. The news filtering back to Paris from the front made a darkened
embassy the more appropriate response. "*Nous marchons à un désastre*," a
prescient Marshal Bazaine had commented as he boarded a train to take
command of one French army. A week later, on 28 July, Napoleon left St
Cloud to assume supreme command. He was in no physical condition to
do so. His "face was ashen, his eyelids puffy, his eyes dead, his legs wavering, his shoulders bowed." His kidney stone and piles made riding an
agony, and it was not long before he had to stuff his trousers with towels
to mask his incontinence. His spirits were not improved by the realization that his forces were under strength and unready for battle. Prussia
had mobilized more than double the poorly organized, poorly supplied,
poorly officered, and poorly led French troops. Napoleon himself was
likened by one critic to a circus ringmaster discharged for drunkenness.
By 7 August the French had suffered a string of defeats, though as yet

these were not decisive, and the Prussians and their German allies had suffered heavy casualties. So "tardy, scanty and uninteresting" was the military news coming back to the capital that Lyons and much of the populace looked for the evening edition of British newspapers for the latest intelligence. Writing to Granville on 8 August, Lyons observed: "If the panic in the army is as great as that in the capital all is over with France. One would think the Prussians were already on Montmartre." The Chambers were convoked, the Department of the Seine was declared in a state of siege, Ollivier's residence in the Place Vendôme required the protection of the National Guard, and the Empress, regent in Napoleon's absence, hurriedly arrived from St Cloud. She, at least, was behaving with spirit but not wisdom.[36]

Lyons reported the empress-regent's forlorn efforts to save the rapidly disintegrating regime, for without a quick and significant military victory it seemed to him, and to many others, that the fall of the dynasty and the establishment of a third republic was "inevitable." The Corps législatif had a stormy opening on 9 August, the emperor being harshly criticized while not a voice was raised in his defence. Jules Favre called for all power to be taken into the hands of the legislature, and his motion recommending the arming of the population passed without a division. The military disasters, Thiers declared a couple of days later, were products of "insufficiency of preparations and absolute incapacity of direction." Eugénie issued a "spirited Proclamation" and in response to the reports that the Prussians were advancing on the capital in overwhelming numbers steps were taken to bolster the ranks of the National Guard, cannon were mounted on the city's fortifications, trees were toppled to clear the line of fire for the fortifications in the Bois de Boulogne, railway tunnels were blocked, bridges across the river were dismantled, thousands of sheep and cattle were brought in to graze in the Bois and the Luxembourg Gardens, art treasures were evacuated, and arrangements made for the installation of a provisional government in Tours should Paris fall. This was the work of a new administration. Ollivier and his colleagues had been replaced by a ministry led by the Comte de Palikao, a veteran of Algeria, the Crimea, and the Second Opium War against China – hence his title taken from the Beijing suburb where he had won his most significant victory. The general's colleagues were drawn from the ranks of the veterans of the emperor's years of personal government and from the Chamber's "extreme Right." Only military victories would allow the new government to survive, Lyons realized. Instead, the situation continued to deteriorate, and on 12 August he advised the Foreign Office that, no matter what happened on the field of battle, the dynasty was doomed.[37]

That same day Napoleon transferred supreme command to François Achille Bazaine, a soldier's soldier. He had indeed carried a marshal's baton in his knapsack, having risen through every rank to the very highest. He had reached that pinnacle in Mexico, where he had distinguished himself and organized a well-conducted withdrawal of his troops from the foolhardy imperial adventure. But when he predicted disaster as he left Paris for the front almost a month earlier, Bazaine may not have foreseen the personal ignominy that was to be his own fate. "Everybody appears to be looking for the authoritative mediation of the great powers," Lyons had noted a few days before the change in overall command, and in the event that the French made a successful stand before Paris he would have liked Britain, Russia, Austria, and Italy collectively to insist on a moderate peace. The settlement he envisaged would include the independence of the small non-German nations of Belgium, Holland, and Denmark, would exclude territorial sacrifices by a defeated France, and would oblige France to pay a substantial war indemnity and accept a Germany constituted as Prussia and its allies wished. Peace on this basis might well have prevented the bitter and enduring postwar tension between vanquished and victors. However, as Lyons recognized, his nation and the other powers lacked both the will and the might to impose these terms. Furthermore, on his arrival from Vienna to replace Gramont as foreign minister, the Prince de la Tour d'Auvergne belligerently rejected mediation before the Prussians had been driven from the soil of France.[38]

By the middle of the month the situation at the front and in the rear had gone from bad to worse. A French military retreat to Chalons caused confusion and chaos in the capital. The empress sent her nieces abroad for safety and called the Bonaparte clan to the Tuileries and advised them to look out for themselves. The Corps législatif dithered over whether to suspend sittings in order to give ministers more time to attend to their administrative duties and to prepare the capital for a possible Prussian siege, while no group was willing bravely to step forward and accept responsibility for negotiating a peace that admitted defeat. Count Constantino Nigra, the Italian ambassador, and Prince Richard Metternich, his Austrian counterpart, approached Lyons with a warning that "France and indeed all Europe would be at the feet of the Prussians, if the Neutral Powers did not intervene in time." Although he could see no sign of either belligerent welcoming an offer of mediation, Lyons agreed to approach La Tour. The foreign minister responded that neutrals might press "prudent and moderate" advice on the Prussians and "exert themselves to preserve the balance of power in Europe." In short, the French would not object to the other powers bringing pressure to bear on the Prussians so long as France was neither committed nor consulted. In the diplomatic equivalent of carrying coals to Newcastle, Lyons advised the Gladstone government not to act. Popular animosity towards Britain and the British had become very "disagreeable," he reported, thanks to the unsympathetic articles in *The Times*. There were no terms of peace that they could offer which would be acceptable to the French and no likelihood of the Prussians offering "very moderate terms" which the French might be pressured into accepting. "As for putting pressure on Prussia," he was "unwilling to discuss even theoretically a proposal so likely to draw all Europe into the war."[39]

With his personal influence and the future of Anglo-French relations in mind, Lyons had no wish to be the channel through which Prussian complaints of alleged French firings on field hospitals and violations of flags of truce were presented to the Quai d'Orsay. The American minister was in charge of Prussian interests, he reminded Granville. Why should he undertake the unpleasant work of messenger, which might damage his position and prejudice his ability to effect much in the event of an emergency? The foreign secretary refused to let him off the hook, however. He was unwilling to leave the Prussians with the idea that the American was their only friend. Lyons approached La Tour with his customary sensitivity, serving the dish "with a palatable sauce," and his reward was an understanding that he would not give offence by communicating the Prussians' charges so long as there was no hint that either he or his government endorsed them. Relieved, Lyons undertook the task.

Granville wholeheartedly approved not only of this arrangement but also of the advice Lyons gave his former Roman physician, who arrived in Paris as a special agent of the Italian government. Dr Pantaleone, a man of letters and science and a skilled politician, was seeking information on how the Italian cabinet might acquire the Papal States and even Rome either during the war or in the peace settlement. Lyons discouraged any thought of Italian military assistance to France and counselled continued neutrality, but he understood from Pantaleone that in the event of the Bonaparte dynasty's collapse Italian troops would seize Rome.[40]

Only three days later, following the surrender of Napoleon and an entire army at Sedan, the emperor was declared deposed, a Republic proclaimed, and a provisional government of National Defence formed. Reporting the Italians' occupation of papal territories, their annexation of the Eternal City, and their naming it the capital of the Kingdom of Italy, Sir Augustus Paget doubted that there had ever been in the history of the world so "sudden and woeful" a collapse as that of the French. In the opinion of the pro-German and sententious British monarch, France's defeat was a "judgment from heaven" and a "*just* retribution on a very guilty government and a very frivolous vain-glorious people." During the last hours of the Second Empire his staff marvelled at Lyons's sang-froid. He was quite in his element, an admiring head of chancery wrote to a friend, making no change to his daily routine. He drove through the streets of the capital in an open carriage with stepping horses as usual, and returned to the embassy in the midst of all the frantic excitement to draft a dispatch on Tunisian finances. To Granville, in a letter on 7 September, Lyons wrote: "This Revolution has been accomplished without bloodshed, and so far as I know without even a political arrest, and up to this time order has not been disturbed in Paris." Jubilant Parisians were "smiling and calling each other citoyen and shouting Vive la Republique," while soldiers were marching "with flowers in their muskets." Nevertheless, every one who could not speak French was likely to be treated as a Prussian spy, while respectable bourgeois worried that if they manned the ramparts against the advancing Prussians the "Reds" would in their absence pillage the city. When the siege began there would be no change at the embassy, Lyons informed his staff, except that the staff serving dinner would be allowed to wear trousers instead of formal dress. More importantly, on the basis of an understanding reached by the other representatives of major powers, he intended to remain in Paris so long as the French government did so. When it departed he would follow, and the care of besieged Britons would become the responsibility of the consular service.[41]

CHAPTER FOURTEEN

Monarchy or Republic?

As the Prussians approached Paris, "dangerous characters" and "useless mouths" were expelled by the city's authorities and panicked Britons besieged the embassy in search of advice and assistance. What would become of them and their property when the Prussians arrived? They were already encountering hostility on the streets because of the pleasure some British newspapers appeared to find in the misfortunes of France. Lyons recommended they leave, especially the women and children, but he did not publish a general notice to this effect for fear of antagonizing a government which was plainly uninterested in issuing a timely depart notice to "inoffensive subjects of Neutral Powers." Were foreign subjects seen as pawns in the approaching crisis? Assistance for Britons too poor to pay their own way home, and relief for those who for whatever reason remained, was left largely to the British Charitable Fund. One of its principals was Dr Alan Herbert, a personal friend of Lyons as was his brother and Tory politician the Earl of Carnarvon. The charity's cash reserves were modestly padded by funds forwarded on Granville's instructions by the Foreign Office and by a very modest personal donation by Lyons, who was authorized to advance upwards of another £1,000 from the Secret Service Fund.[1]

    "What stupendous events, and what a moment of anxiety for you," Granville wrote, but he offered Lyons little guidance. He did instruct him not to follow the empress out of the city in the event that she endeavoured to maintain a shadow government, but she had already flown via the back door of the Louvre. The symbolism of this undignified exit could not have escaped her. Lyons had asked Malet to be ready at a moment's notice to escort her to safety in Britain, but her escape there had been organized and effected with all the panache of Baroness Orzcy's fictional hero of the great French Revolution. The Pimpernel in this instance was Dr Thomas Evans, an American who had been the imperial dentist. Lyons remained in the capital dealing discreetly and informally with a new de facto Republican government led by General Jules Trochu, a distinguished soldier who had declined a field command but had accepted the governorship of Paris. Jules Favre was his deputy and acting minister of foreign affairs, while Adolphe Thiers was another prominent figure whose presence was an assurance that this was no radical revolutionary regime. The minister of the interior, Léon Gambetta, was admittedly something of a firebrand, but Favre assured foreign nations that this Republic would not be a missionary of revolution.[2]

Favre and Thiers each called at the embassy seeking to stir Britain into diplomatic action. They announced their nation's readiness to pay a large war indemnity and accept foreign mediation, but not to surrender a foot of territory. If British inaction led to humiliating German terms of peace, Thiers warned, the result would be Prussian domination of Europe and conceivably a seizure of power by Radicals in France. Britain would then find itself confronted by a "violent Red Republic, with Revolutionary propaganda, and principles subversive of [all] society." A moderate peace settlement, on the other hand, would preserve France from anarchy and protect the rest of Europe from the contagion of "subversive principles." Neither argument moved the Gladstone Cabinet, several of whose members considered German supremacy "less dangerous to Europe than that of France," and few of them favoured aiding France with a demand for mediation. Odo Russell, who had accepted a transfer from Rome to the Foreign Office, had passed on to them the information that Prussia would reject it. The source was Harry, Count von Arnim, Odo's former Prussian colleague in Rome and a former school friend of Bismarck. His government, Arnim revealed, was determined to "recover" Alsace and Lorraine. Britain, if it wished to be useful, should ensure that France understood this. Lyons thought "that the loss of territory and the humiliation of France and the great diminution of her power and influence would be great evils and great sources of danger," but if Britain had not the means to prevent them it would be folly to aggravate them by encouraging in the French hope that through mediation it could lessen them.[3]

Granville recognized the absence of a basis on which peace might be negotiated. French insistence on the inviolability of territory was in Gladstone's opinion "out of all proportion to the present distribution of good and ill fortune in military matters." Yet as a political moralist he soon deplored the "annexation of Alsace & Lorraine contrary to the wishes of the inhabitants." The European norm, he insisted, citing the plebiscites held in the former Papal States before their annexation by Italy, was consultation of the people concerned. His timid colleagues, however, would do no more than approve Britain's delivery to the Prussians of French peace proposals that had a "certain elasticity." Unfortunately, elasticity was still too great a stretch as Favre proved with a vainglorious circular declaring that France would never yield either an inch of territory or a single stone of a fortress. Malet and Sheffield, intimates of Lyons, were both contemptuous of their government's "supine" policy. "I must say I hardly think there is a tree high enough to hang Lord Granville on," the former commented, while Sheffield groaned that "England has now sunk into the humiliating position of German defending and newspaper writers and Stockjobbers seem to have reached the zenith of their aspirations." These comments may reflect the private sentiments of their chief, but his duty was to implement government policy, and the adamant refusal of the French to listen to reason on the loss of territory convinced him that Britain should continue to steer clear of the "mess." Nevertheless, he declined an invitation from the diplomatic corps to lead its members to provincial Tours, where several departments of government were already up and running. He was clinging to the hope that the French would soon cease evading their plight, and in that event he might be of greater use in the capital.[4]

Lyons agreed to inform the Prussians of the French government's desire for an end to the war and he selected Malet as the messenger. Malet's father and Bismarck had served as representatives to the old

German Confederation in Frankfurt, where they became friends, and the son was well known to the Prussian and spoke German. Bismarck spoke excellent English. Crossing into Prussian-occupied France under the cover of a "white handkerchief," Malet caught up with the Prussian at Meaux. They dined, smoked cigars, and "liquored up," but Bismarck made crystal clear his rejection of an armistice which as he pointed out would benefit the French alone. Nor, he emphasized, would neutrals be permitted to rescue the French in the guise of mediators. The French had attacked Germany twenty-seven times in scarcely two centuries, he informed the young Englishman, so any peace that left their territory intact would be a mere armistice, which they would terminate just as soon as they were able to strike back. Alsace and Lorraine were going to be taken from them, and if they failed to seek terms Paris would be shelled into submission or destroyed. Furthermore, continued obduracy might cause him to settle with his prize prisoner, Napoleon, and restore him to his throne. A third option was the restoration of the Legitimist monarchy in the person of the Comte de Chambord. He had approached the Prussian monarch, but to seat him on the throne would involve generous territorial terms of peace and Bismarck had no intention of surrendering the prize of Alsace. When Malet returned with his grim news, Lyons gave Favre a heavily edited version of Bismarck's comments for fear the full account would discourage the Frenchman from sitting down with the Prussian. But Lyons was certain the victors would eventually have reason to rue ruthless terms of peace.[5]

In Paris, which the Prussians progressively encircled, radical elements elected a city council or Commune, which prompted Lyons to instruct his staff not to accept for safekeeping the valuables of expatriate Britons. Reports that the embassy was being used as a safe deposit might make it the target of pillagers in the event that the city descended into lawlessness. All of the while he was continuing quietly to counsel Britons to leave the capital. Those who remained were told that they did so at their own risk, but he did not leave himself when the Austrian, Russian, Italian, and Ottoman ambassadors hurried off to Tours. Only when Favre personally urged him to follow the others did he board a train on 17 September, and it was as well that he did for two days later the Prussians cut the capital's last rail and telegraph links to the outside world. Lyons turned over the embassy to Henry Wodehouse, who, when he ventured out onto the streets, was careful never to speak to anyone, never to stand still, never to stare about him, and always to carry identifying documents. Irregulars and "marauders" were stopping and illtreating everyone whom they suspected of being German spies. Nor did he see any point in writing dispatches, for they had to be left unsealed in order to pass through Prussian lines. Soon, thanks to the progress of photographic miniaturization, the pigeon post was his principal means of communication with the world beyond the capital.[6]

In Tours, its numerous convents and seminaries serving as reminders of the city's long religious associations, Lyons had difficulty finding suitable accommodation even at the extortionate rents being demanded. He took the Château de Rigny with some reluctance because it was several miles from the city. A modern house, built only four years earlier for the widow of a wealthy lawyer, its lack of carpets and reliance on open fires for heating made it "uncommonly cold." Life was also dull, for the inconvenient distance from Tours discouraged evening receptions and visits. Lyons and his staff whiled away most evenings playing whist and then retiring early. The absence of diplomatic activity was in the opinion of the provisional government's delegate for foreign affairs, Jean-Baptiste, Comte de Chaudordy, the result of the "overly comfortable" lives of the diplomatic corps. Lyons did have time on his hands. Since the Queen's messengers now spent so long on the road, he abandoned the writing of daily dispatches. Meanwhile, the "clever and agreeable" Thiers, behaving "almost as a mendicant seeking support for his country," set off on a tour of European capitals beginning in London, where he requested Britain's moral influence in support of the French quest for an "honourable" peace. If Britain took the lead by announcing formal recognition of the provisional government other nations would follow, he argued but to little effect. The Gladstone Cabinet still had no intention of providing "active" diplomatic assistance. Several ministers had yet to forgive France for precipitating the war and were keenly aware of the "present position of the belligerents."[7]

When Lyons also turned a deaf ear to their pleas for action, the angry French accused him and his government of "coldness and unkindness." Britain was jeopardizing the future relations of the two nations, Favre warned. Word of Léon Gambetta's dramatic flight from Paris in a balloon, identified as he was with war to the bitter end, caused Lyons to half-regret that the basket had not capsized. As minister of the interior, Gambetta postponed indefinitely the election of a Constituent Assembly and began to form an Army of the Loire out of the troops scattered across the countryside. The intention was to use them to help lift the siege of Paris, but this was a pipe dream, Lyons learned from General Denis Bourbaki. The Prussians had permitted this Crimean War hero to escape encircled Metz in the expectation that he would support the formation of a compliant French regime with whom they could negotiate on their terms. His sister was Eugénie's prime lady-in-waiting, and he travelled to England seeking the exiled empress's signature on a treaty of peace. She refused. Nevertheless, Bourbaki wished to see the war brought to an end while Metz and Paris were still in French hands.[8]

The difficulty was the obduracy of the French on the subject of "territorial sacrifices." General Philip Sheridan, whose dubious distinction it had been to help transform the American Civil War into a total war in which civilians were deliberately targeted, was at the Prussians' headquarters advocating the bombardment of the capital as a means of destroying the morale of French civilians. Horrified by the thought of indiscriminate shelling of the city, Lyons suggested to Granville on 17 October that the time had finally arrived for neutrals to make their voices heard. He was, he admitted, too anxious for peace and too disturbed about Paris "to criticise any mode of halting hostilities." He favoured an armistice during which a Constituent Assembly could be elected, believing that the certainty it would favour peace would make it acceptable to the Prussians. Moreover, once the fighting stopped he was confident it would be extremely difficult to resume hostilities.[9]

Granville authorized Lyons to inform Chaudordy of Britain's desire for an armistice, which would save the inhabitants of Paris from possible disaster and permit elections to be held. Reports that the morale of the homesick, hungry, and cold German troops was faltering gave hope that the Prussian high command, which was also having difficulties with Bismarck, might be amenable to a suspension of hostilities. Thiers volunteered to enter Paris to obtain the approval of that branch of the bifurcated French government. He was in Lyons's judgment the man to open the eyes of the ministers there to the hopelessness of the military situation. Bazaine's surrender of Metz and his entire command made the point even more emphatically. Since Alsace and Lorraine would be the sticking point of any peace, Lyons urged Thiers to skate around that delicate topic in the negotiations.[10]

Bismarck, counting on the news from Metz to make the French more pliable, briefly withheld the safe conduct Thiers required for his mission into Paris. The Prussians' pressure point was the capital, and anticipating its bombardment Lyons instructed Wodehouse via a "pigeon-gram" to leave before shelling began and to take with him as many Britons as possible. Their escape was obstructed first by the French and then by the Prussians, the former perhaps seeing the civilians as "human shields" while the latter may have calculated that the British would lean harder on the French to capitulate if their subjects remained trapped in the beleaguered capital. However, on 8 November, Wodehouse finally escorted 120 Britons to safety. The armistice negotiations which had eventually opened at Versailles were then broken off by the Prussians when they learned of the radical turn of events in the city they were besieging. The confusion there allowed Bismarck to question the legitimacy of the provisional government and to stiffen his terms. For his part Lyons had been angered by wild French talk of a "war to the knife." The likes of Gambetta were to his mind refusing to give negotiation a fair trial.[11]

When Bismarck suddenly offered to resume the discussions for an armistice and even to facilitate the holding of elections for a National Assembly, Lyons was witness to an unseemly argument. Thiers, a new Republican, sarcastically remarked during a heated exchange with Chaudordy that voting would be freer under the occupiers than under the prefects appointed by Gambetta. The primitive system of communication between Paris and Tours added to the confusion. As Lyons observed, a government "strange in its origins" was even "stranger in its duality." The unreliability of wind-driven hot-air balloons contributed to the failure of the uncoordinated French attempt to break out of Paris while the Army of the Loire occupied the Prussians in and around Orléans. The triumphant Prussians were now advancing on Tours, where officials and diplomats were hastily packed aboard a special train on 9 December which took them to Bordeaux. Lyons found rooms at what, under the circumstances, he must have considered the ironically named Hôtel de la Paix. These "migrations" were both inconvenient and expensive, and the Foreign Office offered him an allowance for "entertaining" his staff. This he indignantly rejected as repugnant to his principles and destructive of discipline. He was not a "hotel keeper for subordinates," he haughtily responded. Instead, he obtained for them a per diem allowance of thirty shillings for the time they were obliged to spend away from Paris. For himself, he accepted payment of his travel and lodging expenses. The move to Bordeaux did not restore rapid communication with the Foreign Office. "A pretty fix we are in without a direct telegraph to you," Hammond remarked, for the only open lines were from Lisbon or via an American telegraph in Brest. Nor was the messenger service to be depended upon. The longer road journeys, and the danger of messengers being mistaken by French irregulars for German spies, led to its suspension.[12]

The refusal of the French to admit defeat did stir in Lyons admiration of their wonderful elasticity of character. The "terrible question," however, was whether it was "leading them to weal or woe." He thought he detected "a vague feeling that any international complication in Europe might be of advantage in the present circumstances of France," and fortuitously it emerged with Russia's demand for an end to the neutralization and demilitarization of the Black Sea. The Foreign Office had dispatched Odo Russell to Versailles to discover whether Prussia and Russia had reached an understanding. "He is very Bismarckian in his sentiments as far as he is able to express them," being unable to write or spell English, an envious Malet wrote of this Russell, whose "one great talent," in his opinion, was the ability "to impress paltry outsiders such as newspaper correspondents." Once he arrived at the Prussian headquarters Odo quickly fell under Bismarck's spell, but his extended presence in Versailles deepened French suspicions of Britain. Was it planning to acquiesce in the German annexation of Alsace and Lorraine? Hence the British concern that the French remain ignorant of the fact that it was at Bismarck's instigation that they were seeking French consent to a Black Sea conference. The conference had to be seen as a British initiative and should be convened in London, Lyons stressed.[13]

As it happened, Bismarck lost interest in a French presence at the conference once they made plain their intent to press for the addition of the conflict to the agenda. He ensured that difficulties over a safe conduct prevented Favre from attending. Not that the absence of the French foreign minister displeased Granville, who thought he would have made tiresomely long speeches and would have fraternized with British republicans. At the Congress, Russia regained the right to maintain a fleet on the Black Sea, Turkey was restored to its sovereign rights there, and the French Republic "was admitted to the council of the Great Powers." Yet, or so he informed Lyons, the foreign secretary lay in bed at night with "his heart bleeding" for the misery of France and especially for the plight of Paris. Lyons believed the residents of the capital would be able to hold out until mid-January on a basic diet of bread and wine, but he foresaw considerable suffering and a jump in infant mortality. In fact, the general death rate rose sharply as food rations were cut, domestic animals and vermin became sources of meat, and intestinal diseases consequently flourished. The undernourished population then suffered an arctic winter. The situation left Lyons defensive over the plight of trapped Britons. Not that they had been abandoned. Edward Blount, a banker, who was serving as the acting consul, had cash with which he financed relief.[14]

Lyons evaluated for Granville the principal players in the final act of the French tragedy. Bismarck, ruthless and brutal, was fomenting the "desperate hatred and zeal" of the French and thus assisting the "violent party" led by Léon Gambetta. The French radical, in turn, was either a "great man or merely an energetic demagogue," but as yet it was not clear which. Jules Favre was more of a known quantity. A true patriot who was willing to sacrifice his personal interest for what he understood to be the good of the nation, mild and agreeable in private but fierce and truculent in debate, always liable to put his foot in his mouth, he had not exhibited skill as a negotiator. Adolphe Thiers was pressing for a National Assembly and the founding of a moderate, conservative Republic. This he expected to succeed the provisional regime once the capital, which the Prussians commenced shelling indiscriminately on 5 January 1871, surrendered. Negotiations for an armistice to permit the election of a National Assembly to ratify a Prussian-imposed peace resumed at Versailles three weeks after the opening of the bombardment. At long last, Lyons sighed, some Frenchmen were willing to "face the daylight" and admit the futility of fighting on. His hope that the terms would not be "intolerably humiliating" was immediately dashed. The Germans had already delivered a "crushing insult" to France by staging in the Hall of Mirrors of the Palace of Versailles the coronation of the Prussian king as emperor of the second German Reich.[15]

With the signing of an armistice agreement by Bismarck and Favre on 28 January, the British acted to "relieve the wants of Paris." Lyons was credited with being among the first to procure provisions for the capital's famished residents. The more affluent British survivors ordered food hampers from fashionable Fortnum and Mason's in Piccadilly, while London's Lord Mayor collected provisions for the less fortunate which the Royal Navy shipped to France. The acts of generosity smoothed the rougher edges of French anglophobia, but popular hatred of Germany was visceral and intense following the publication of a "blundering telegram" which implied that Favre, to secure the armistice, had agreed to disastrous provisional terms of peace. Gambetta issued a "violent and warlike" proclamation urging their rejection, but Lyons regarded as illusory the Radical's hope of winning a Republican and a rejectionist majority in the elections on 8 February for an Assembly. Only the residents of the very largest urban areas were Republicans and Socialists, Lyons assured London. Indeed, less than one-quarter of the deputies returned proved to be genuine Republicans. The great majority were Monarchists, but they owed their election more to the peasantry's craving for peace than to its enthusiasm for a restoration of the Bourbons, either in the person of Henri de Chambord or the Orléanist branch headed by the Comte de Paris. Clearly, the Assembly would have difficulty settling swiftly and definitively the political identity of the postwar French state. All of the Monarchists regarded the Republic as provisional and merely neutral ground on which, temporarily, they could safely meet. Recognizing this, Lyons was consoled by the thought that, at least for the time being, the moderate Republic envisaged by Thiers was the regime most likely to hold the nation together and accept with gritted teeth the Prussians' terms.[16]

The conviction that France was aching for revenge was the justification trundled out by Bismarck for the annexation of Alsace and much of Lorraine. Those provinces, he declared, would make the Reich secure. The irony, which did not escape Lyons, was that their acquisition nourished the enmity against which they were the supposed protection. Pondering the likelihood of an extended period of European instability, and anxious to revive the "old cordial state" of Anglo-French relations, he suggested Britain give the French a little "help," or a "little *patent* sympathy in their misfortunes." What he had in mind was some overt effort, however fruitless, to moderate the terms of peace, and swift recognition of the government established by the Assembly. Advised by Odo Russell that any British criticism would simply harden German resolve, the Cabinet rejected Gladstone's proposal that they protest the cession of Alsace and Lorraine against the will of the provinces' peoples. In Bordeaux, protected from local rejectionists by a heavy military guard, Thiers organized the Assembly, formed a government broadly representative of its three largest factions, and secured for himself the clumsily named post of chief of the executive authority of the French Republic. That evening, 17 February 1871, Lyons was the first foreign representative to call on Thiers and "open official relations" with him.[17]

The German terms were harsh. Alsace with the exception of Belfort was to be ceded, as was much of Lorraine including Metz, an indemnity of 5 billion francs was to be paid within three years, France was to pay the costs of the large German occupation force until the indemnity was discharged, and above the Loire it was to maintain only a small military force. The Assembly had no option, Lyons recognized, but to ratify the settlement, which he considered "monstrous." He admired the skill with which Thiers managed the legislature and secured its massive endorsement of the peace preliminaries, but when as chief executive he proposed that the government return to the nation's capital he encountered stiff resistance. Conservative Deputies of all shades had no intention of entering a city they considered a hotbed of Red Republicanism and where the "mob" had set up a new local government, the Commune. They preferred Versailles, now vacated by the Germans. But several of Lyons's staff, led by Wodehouse, had returned to the embassy. The building was "rather uncomfortable, lacking both fuel and gas, while the provisions forwarded by the Lord Mayor's Relief Fund for needy Britons, and stored in the embassy's kitchen, were being devoured by the regiment of rats using the building as a billet. The city was "miserable and dismal," its residents "supremely wretched," especially during the victory parade staged by the Germans, to which cafés and wine shops made a silent protest by remaining shuttered. As a result, Paris briefly became the City of Darkness in which there was a palpable sense of menace. The working people of Belleville and Montmartre were known to be armed, and in the judgment of Lionel Sackville-West, who had recently joined the mission as secretary of embassy, were a threat to social order and needed to be swiftly suppressed. Unfortunately, in the absence of Lyons, he was another who had difficulty with Granville's private instructions, which were "remarkable only from the impossibility of understanding them." Sackville-West was soon relieved of that responsibility. He received leave to be with his ailing common-law spouse and mother of his several children. A former Spanish dancer known as "Pepita," but calling herself La Comtesse de Sackville-West, she had been living for some time in a coastal resort south of Bordeaux, and there she died on 10 March. Four days later Lyons returned to Paris and, it being the Ides of March, found himself threatened with verbal assassination in Parliament.[18]

Sir Robert Peel, bearer of an illustrious name, and a critic of the first Lord Lyons during the Crimean War, accused Lyons of "unmanly" behaviour, of abandoning thousands of British subjects when he left Paris the previous September. Eighteen other diplomats had remained within the besieged city, Peel told the House of Commons. Both Gladstone and Granville mounted effective defences of Lyons in their respective chambers, a task eased by Peel's reputation for insolence and vulgarity and by his record of stupidity and incompetence while serving a decade earlier as Ireland's chief secretary. The Foreign Office then quickly published the correspondence explaining Lyons's conduct. However, Peel's wounding criticism was not without effect. Lyons had been hoping that a heavy fall of snow would "cool the ardour of the Belleville patriots," whom Thiers dismissed as the "vile multitude." Their hatred of him dated from his brutal suppression as an Orléanist minister of a workers' rising in 1834, but it had recently been reinvigorated by the Germans' victory parade and the passage through the Assembly of a string of measures which greatly worsened the plight of the capital's poor. The moratoria on the suspension of payments due on promissory notes and house rent was terminated, bringing fresh hardship to heavily indebted shopkeepers as well as artisans. Consequently, Lyons considered "discreditable" the failure of the Thiers government to assert its authority by disarming the Paris Radicals. Troops were sent to haul away the cannons commanding the capital from the heights of Montmartre, and to detain Radicals, but the operation was bungled and two senior officers were executed in the streets by Republican National Guards. With Radical Republicans effectively in control of Paris, government ministers who had gone there, among them Thiers, fled to Versailles. He asked the diplomatic corps to follow but Lyons delayed, fearful that his sudden departure would excite a fresh outcry at home. When he was ordered to leave, he vowed to return as frequently as possible so as to be near British subjects. It was a promise made easier by dislike of Versailles, where he counted himself fortunate to find a "poky lodging au troisième" for himself, Sheffield, and Wodehouse.[19]

Malet, aided by three even younger men, had been left in charge of the embassy. Lyons appointed him *chargé des archives*, not chargé d'affaires, because there could be no official communication with the Commune. Malet was granted the run of the building on the understanding that he did not dip into the wine cellar's small stock of "irreplaceable" '48 and '54 clarets. No restriction was placed on his consumption of the "Lafitte of 64." In permitting Malet to entertain anyone he wished, and by encouraging him to suppress any scruples over dealing discreetly with the Commune, Lyons hoped to obtain intelligence. Malet, who had some understanding of the French working classes, having earlier written a report on them, believed that the Reds' control of the city might endure because the men at the Hôtel de Ville were maintaining order. The bourgeoisie, on the other hand, who composed the party of order, were proving arrant cowards. When he called on the Commune's delegate for external affairs, who was none other than Paschal Grousset, he encountered a perfectly obliging "good looking young man" who willingly issued the pass that enabled Lyons to enter and leave the city almost at will even though it had been closed by the Commune as the government's forces began to encircle and squeeze it. During his visits Lyons learned that the Commune had granted rent cancellations and remissions, made generous lease concessions to lodgers, extended by three years the grace period on overdue bills, suppressed the organs of the "party of order," detained a number of prominent individuals, among them the arch-bishop of Paris, "debaptized" much of the city's largest hospital, Hôtel-Dieu, ordered the removal from public view of "liturgical objects and religious images," and had converted a number of churches into "po-litical clubhouses, arsenals, or military posts." Were the Communards a later version of the Jacobins? Several of their measures were in Malet's opinion "reckless" and all breathed "defiance to the Government instead of extending the hand of reconciliation." When Thiers suggested that the British volunteer their services as mediators, Lyons sensibly left the decision to Granville because by intervening Britain might find itself responsible for the fate of the "Communists." "Instruct Malet if applied to act cautiously according to Thiers wishes," the foreign secretary tel-egraphed, only for the decision to appall and horrify the Queen, for whom, as for respectable British society, the Communards epitomized evil.[20]

When he slipped into Paris on 14 April for a personal reconnaissance, Lyons detected neither divisions within the Commune nor the loss of popular support on which Thiers was counting heavily. One week later, however, he noted deserted streets, shuttered shops, a steep rise in the price of provisions, and the heavy firing of cannon and musketry throughout the night. The relief supplies sent over from Britain had been seized by the Commune, Malet reported, and were to be issued as rations to the "insurgent National Guards." Furthermore, it was not long before he discerned dissension within the leadership of the Com-mune and a sharp slump in popular morale. This news made Lyons im-patient for a more determined military effort by the forces of the French government, which would, irony of ironies, oblige them to storm the formidable defences whose construction Thiers had supervised as a minister of Louis Philippe. Another impatient observer was Bismarck. He may have suspected that the large French force which with German consent the government had concentrated around Paris would become a weapon in a French diplomatic struggle to secure some softening of the terms of peace to which the unfortunate Favre would be putting his name at Frankfurt. Hence Bismarck's warning: act swiftly or German troops would storm the capital and suppress the Commune. Almost im-mediately, Thiers ordered the shelling of Paris.[21]

Lyons was actively engaged in the effort to save the life of Georges Darboy, the archbishop of Paris. The Commune had offered to exchange him for Auguste Blanqui, a prisoner of the government. The archbishop supported the exchange, arguing that no principle would be compromised, but Thiers and his ministers vetoed it. They feared that Blanqui was the one Republican Socialist who might reinvigorate the Commune. Another factor was Darboy's reputation as "a Gallican anti-infallibilist," which did not endear him to the Assembly's Monarchist right wing. The conservative Le Figaro, showing its ultramontane colours, had declared it no coincidence that the first military defeats in the Prussian War had occurred at the very moment the withdrawal of the French troops from Rome had left the pope defenceless. When government troops finally began pouring into Paris, and they were followed by Lyons on 24 May, the city presented a "heartbreaking sight." He heard constant firing in the evil-smelling, smoke-filled streets, and saw fires everywhere. Was this a vision of hell? he asked himself. The Tuileries Palace was among the ruined buildings, while St Cloud had been destroyed by fire the previous October during the Prussian siege. The Rue de Rivoli was aflame, as was the Ministry of Finance, the Palais de Justice, the Prefecture of Police, and the Hôtel de Ville. Happily the art collections of the Louvre had escaped destruction as had the Imperial National Library in its new buildings on the Rue Richelieu, where it would soon revert to its former name of Bibliothèque nationale. Lyons urged the Papal Nuncio to beg the Germans to intercede on behalf of the archbishop, thinking they were more likely to intimidate the insurgents. But the ferocity of the government's troops, their mass slaughter of persons merely suspected of being radicals, speeded the Commune's retaliatory executions and the archbishop was one of the victims. Between 21 and 29 May the Commune put fifty-six hostages to death, but the killings – and those by the government tended to be utterly indiscriminate – eventually exceeded 20,000. Only with greatest difficulty was Lyons able to prevent the execution of a score of Britons who had, usually without good cause, been detained as Communards. The "Versailles party," one member of Gladstone's Cabinet noted, had been guilty of "unheard of wickedness & cruelty." Hell, Lyons agreed, seemed "to have broken loose in that accursed city."[22]

Although the government was again in control of Paris, Versailles remained the seat of government and Lyons soon grew heartily sick of commuting between them. Toothache further frayed his temper. However, in an age when brass bands were employed by some dentists to mask from potential clients the torment of their patients, Lyons was able to consult Thomas Evans. The American had returned to Paris having in his homeland become experienced in the use of nitrous oxide, popularly known as "laughing gas" because of its euphoric properties. Evans was credited by appreciative patients, like Lyons, with a "miraculous ability" to ease suffering. The more comfortable Lyons concentrated on a few domestic problems such as the restocking of his impressive wine cellar. He bought a dozen bottles of the finest cognac, fifty bottles of Chateau Lafitte '58, fifty bottles of Chateau Margaux '58, and another fifty of the '69, while his wine merchant reserved an additional 275 bottles for him. When a bibulous "Willy" Russell and two friends came to dinner, for Lyons was still courting influential newspapermen, they enjoyed his fine wines. The journalists were soon followed by hordes of British visitors keen to view the city's "heart rending spectacle" of destruction. The embassy had suffered minimal damage, although Parliament voted £1,600 for repairs, but a sensitive Edith Layard found the condition of far humbler dwellings more affecting. "In some places where the destruction was not so complete," she noted, "it was curious to see an open cupboard with its plates and cups – or a kitchen stove with saucepan & pots as if the inhabitants had been surprised while preparing their food & these things remained perched up in the air just clinging to one wall."[23]

Were the Communards who managed to escape the horror of the government's brutal campaign of suppression seeking refuge in Britain? It was a notion Thiers and his colleagues fostered. To "palliate their own errors," Lyons privately fumed, French ministers were laying the horrors committed by the Commune at the door of the International Workingmen's Association headquartered in London. The French press had seized upon the speeches of Britons sympathetic to the refugees and had publicized a ridiculous claim, traced to Bismarck, that 8,000 British subjects had been active in the Paris insurgency. The International, Thiers and Favre insisted, was committed to a war against society and thus membership of it should be made a criminal offence. Patiently,

Lyons responded that in Britain the "whole system was opposed to the exercise by the Government of any arbitrary or inquisitorial powers in such matters." However, the French remained in a "dangerous state of mind." There was, Lyons groaned, "nothing too preposterous" for them to believe "with a regard to the hostility or contemptuous feeling of foreign nations" in general, and of Britain in particular. Hence, the necessity for extreme care. Thiers would avoid "idle displays of irritation" and would restrain subordinates from "foolish acts," Lyons was confident, because his overriding concern was to pay off as speedily as possible the massive war indemnity in order to free France of German occupation. How was he to raise the five billions? A large loan was negotiated, but, disliking the income tax as a source of additional revenues, Thiers sought levies on tobacco, alcohol, coffee, and sugar, and changes to the tariff still controlled by the Treaty of 1860. His assurances to Lyons that the customs duties would be for revenue only were not believed, given his earlier declaration: "We are protectionists by conviction, we ought to be so by duty." Equally suspect was the minister of finance, Thomas-Augustin Pouyer-Quertier, who like many another textile manufacturer assailed the Commercial Treaty as the principal source of his own business troubles. He cited as proof the five-fold increase in the import of British cloths. Aware that free traders were too few in number to prevent passage of a protectionist tariff, Lyons concluded that his country's best option was to retreat from its current position of holding on to the treaty from year to year effectively at the pleasure of the French. They should, instead, seek a most-favoured-nation agreement similar to that inserted by Bismarck into the Treaty of Frankfurt ending the war. British manufacturers and merchants would thereby be protected from the danger of being left out in the cold in the event of a French denunciation of the Commercial Treaty. Absent clear instructions from Granville, who laconically conceded that his comments were "meagre and superfluous," Lyons recommended avoidance of a commercial dispute. If it developed, he was sure the French would blame it on the "unaccommodating spirit of the English."[24]

What was to be the future organization of the French state? Having lived in the United States during the Civil War, Lyons questioned the ability of a Republic to provide its citizens with stable and liberal government. But Thiers appeared far more interested in securing for himself the title of President. An amused Lyons considered "astonishing" the speed with which this former Orléanist had fallen in love with republicanism. His presidential ambition was boosted by a Republican landslide in the elections held in July to fill the 120 vacant Assembly seats. Bourbon, Orléanist, and Imperialist divisions militated against the success of Monarchism. Legitimism of the Bourbon variety had a broad social base of support because of the belief that a restoration would stabilize politics and society, yet within its ranks there was an ideological gulf between moderates and extremists which the Comte de Chambord deepened. Just as Pius IX had opened his reign with the promise of liberal reform which he failed to honour so Chambord had repeatedly pledged his allegiance to liberal freedoms. He did this to counter Republican propagandists who depicted Monarchists as reactionaries and charged that torture chambers were being prepared under Notre-Dame to be used on Republicans following a restoration. Then, during a brief visit to his Loire Valley château in July 1871, Chambord signed a manifesto which he gave to the Royalist press in Paris. He announced that he would never abandon the white flag of Henry IV. That ancestor had uttered one of the most famous pragmatic sentences in French history when, raised a Protestant, he had remarked that Paris was worth a Mass. The white flag had floated over his cradle and it would be draped over his tomb, the foolish Chambord declared. For him, it was the proof that the Assembly and the nation had accepted his authority and convictions. Instead, it became the tomb of his hopes. In twenty-four hours, a distraught Royalist editor remarked, the pretender had frittered away twenty years of prudence. With his declaration he had blocked fusion with the Orléanists, who had long accepted the tricolour, one of them observing that Chambord had taken the position of Henry IV before the Mass. Pius IX remarked that the tricolour had restored him to Rome following the 1848 Revolution, and then allegedly went on to ask who had ever heard of a man giving up a throne for a napkin? A gleeful Thiers commented that he was accused of seeking to establish a Republic but Chambord had done it for him.[25]

Chambord had upset the Monarchist coach, a rueful Lyons admitted. Many Orléanists accepted a moderate Republic for the time being, and worked with the Centre Left headed by Thiers in the Assembly. He was, after all, committed to repairing the damage done by the war, to paying off the indemnity, to reinvigorating the economy, and to rebuilding the army. In late June a motion was introduced to name him president of the Republic, but when it finally passed two months later he was also president of the Council of Ministers and a member of the Assembly. This arrangement did not convince Lyons that irreversible progress had been made towards the "definite establishment of a Republic." Too much authority had been concentrated in the president's hands, he feared. By denying ministers responsibility for the details of ordinary legislative measures, and by remaining a member of the Assembly, Thiers might be driven from office merely by an adverse vote on some incidental question.[26]

Lyons welcomed Favre's removal as foreign minister. Not only had he become deeply unpopular as the unfortunate signatory of the Treaty of Frankfurt, but he also had a poor understanding of the commercial problems that increasingly dominated relations with Britain. In his dealings with Lyons he had been irritatingly muddled, whereas his replacement was far more businesslike. Charles de Rémusat, lawyer, journalist, historian, and author, had made no secret of his wish to see his country adopt an English system of government. He quickly developed an "excellent rapport" with Lyons yet failed to establish truly cordial relations with Britain. The reasons, he concluded, were the British weakness for the Second Empire, the economic prejudices of Thiers, and the undiplomatic behaviour of the French ambassador in London, Albert, Duc de Broglie. Although adept at dry, ironic banter which ought to have appealed to the British, Broglie committed the cardinal crime of making no secret of his dislike of his hosts. He believed that British "ill-will" in 1870 had been almost as fatal to France as Russian neutrality, and tactlessly remonstrated against the presence of Napoleon and Eugénie at a Buckingham Palace reception to celebrate the recovery of the Prince of Wales from a near fatal illness.[27]

Learning that as soon as the Assembly adjourned Thiers would go off to the country, Lyons took some leave of his own. He had been at his post for twenty-two months, was worn out, and feared a recurrence of his "sick headaches." Following a family holiday with Minna and several of her children in Switzerland during the second half of September, he made his way to London. He met at the Foreign Office on 7 October with Hammond, Edmund Monson, and Percy Anderson. He learned that Malet's reward for his sterling conduct in Paris was a posting to the farthest reaches of civilization, if not beyond, Peking. It did not pay, Anderson bitterly complained, to rise above mediocrity, having himself been shunted aside "to provide for a pauper peerage" in the person of Lord Tenterden. Granville was abandoning seniority in favour of "selection" in matters of promotion, Anderson moaned, pointing to the advance of Tenterden and the appointment of Odo Russell as ambassador to Berlin. Lyons, who met with the foreign secretary nine days later, was even more anxious to confer with Gladstone. For a variety of reasons they were not able to get together until 8 November, when he gave the prime minister a sombre assessment of the political situation in France. The French "have no reverence for any institutions or any dynasty," he regretted, "and therefore nothing to distinguish opposition from revolution." In short, constitutional opposition was not a concept they understood. He warned that the "inevitable failure" of customs duties to produce the revenues that Thiers anticipated might cause the government's collapse. However, were Thiers and his colleagues to be driven from office they would be able in his opinion to claim a number of worthwhile achievements. They had maintained order, had disarmed the "mobs" who as National Guards had terrified towns, had pursued a prudent foreign policy, and had advanced the day when France would be free of German troops. Thus Britain would be wise to anticipate the re-emergence of France as a formidable military power.[28]

Lyons had an audience with the Queen at Windsor on 5 December 1871, and that same evening dined with Malet and Sheffield at the Traveller's Club. About to depart for China, and having been awarded, thanks largely to Lyons, a Companionship of the Order of the Bath, Malet added his own to the tributes his former chief had received from former members of his diplomatic family. "If I ever get further in the service than I am now," he declared, "it will be owing to the training I have had under you so that I am not only indebted to you for past happiness but for any future success I may achieve." The next morning, accompanied as ever by Sheffield, Lyons returned to Paris in order to be present when Thiers addressed the Assembly on 7 December. The president spoke to a chamber in which the monarchist majority was steadily shrinking. Radical Republicans were still making significant electoral gains, and there was evidence of a Bonapartist revival which Lyons attributed to shopkeepers' fond memories of brisk trade, the workers' memories of employment on huge public works, and the peasantry's recollections of domestic peace and tranquility. All of which brought him to a number of conclusions as 1871 drew to a close. The Thiers government was "supported heartily by none, but accepted by all" as a temporary expedient; the Commercial Treaty would in all likelihood soon be denounced, which as matters stood would leave Germany enjoying a far more favourable trading relationship with France than either Britain or Belgium; and recent heavy military expenditures were giving rise in Berlin to menacing talk of having it out with France before it again became strong. From Whitehurst, Lyons learned that in a recent interview a belligerent Bismarck had threatened to attack France if the French continued to talk "nonsense."[29]

The French Army Bill, which made military service obligatory, included loopholes through which many might pass. "Family breadwinners, elder sons of widows, brothers of serving soldiers, educational administrators, and priests" were all exempt. Colonel Conolly, the embassy's new military attaché, who at the request of Lyons had made a countrywide tour to assess the nation's military progress, advised him that Thiers had made a mistake in going for numbers with the draft without ensuring these men would be properly equipped. Until great improvements were made, Conolly concluded, a French war of revenge would be folly. Nevertheless, Lyons welcomed the strengthening of France, which promised eventually to correct the imbalance of power in Europe. For that reason the bill angered the Germans. The sooner the indemnity was paid and the German troops left France the better, Lyons observed. "Europe might then settle down."[30]

Britain's direct dealings with the Thiers government focused on the Commercial Treaty, although the Gladstone Cabinet was divided on its value. Under pressure from Lyons, who was striving to encourage French supporters of freer trade, Granville agreed to exhibit an interest in negotiations. At the same time, Lyons was impressing on Thiers and

Rémusat the wisdom of avoiding "vexations" on the subject. But Rémusat declined, understandably, to contradict the Protectionist who stood at the head of the government. This, together with the refusal of the French to examine the trade figures for the past decade or so, lending support as they did to the argument for freer trade, left Lyons regretting Britain's inability to threaten retaliation. "Our free trade principles being sincerely held and acted upon make us defenceless," he groaned. What he could do he did, which was to warn the French of the danger they would run of exciting francophobia if they treated Britain as the "*least favoured nation.*" Surely it deserved to be no worse off commercially than the Germans, and by the time he set off home on leave in August 1872, trade negotiations were "fairly underway." [31]

The principal objectives of French foreign policy were clear. They sought to restore their nation to its old position of international influence, to recover the lost territories, and to be revenged on Germany. They were hoping, Lyons suspected, for a Russo-German confrontation in the East, and thus would seek to divert or incapacitate any power inclined to back Germany in resisting Russian ambitions in that region. That support would lessen the likelihood of a collision. Hence his call for a close eye to be kept on the French legation in Washington, lest it be tempted to paralyze Britain by encouraging American designs on Canada. Anglo-American ill feeling had resurfaced with the Union's submission of a massive bill to the Geneva arbitration of its Civil War claims. That bill was rooted in the notion that Britain had by its conduct significantly extended the conflict. There were dark mutterings in Britain of American bribery of the arbitrators, while Cabinet divisions on how to respond to the "monstrous" claims briefly threatened the government's survival. Lyons, who naturally had a keen interest in the settlement, responded swiftly to American propaganda in support of these "indirect claims." The material they were circulating, he discovered, was being printed in the French National Printing Office. His counter efforts helped to convince everyone, or so he flattered himself, that the claims were "simply preposterous in themselves." He certainly went out of his way to make a friend of one of the arbitrators rumoured to be sympathetic to the American position, Baron d'Itajuba, the Brazilian minister to France. Before long he had persuaded him of the strength of the British counter

case, and Gladstone and Granville were able to announce in Parliament
the withdrawal of the "indirect claims." However, the settlement was still
so costly – $15.5 million – that one outraged British commentator asked
if they had fallen prey to the strange mania of eating dirt.[32]

On the first full day of his leave Lyons lunched at his new Club, the
Athenaeum, although the meal was so mediocre that he did not become
a habitué. He met with Gladstone and Granville and repeated his earlier
warnings of chronic French political instability if Thiers failed to establish a more permanent form of government. On the negotiations for an
extension of the Commercial Treaty, he labelled "very objectionable" the
French proposal that the two countries come to a tacit agreement. Britain needed a regular convention, signed by plenipotentiaries, and ratified by the French National Assembly, he insisted. When the articles of
a proposed draft treaty were subsequently forwarded to him he secured
more binding language with respect to the most-favoured-nation clause
and added wording which "clearly and unambiguously" provided for the
renunciation of specific provisions without terminating the treaty. His
amendments were adopted with flattering ease and a draft treaty was
signed on 5 November. The Tariff of 1860 was to continue, under certain
specified conditions, until 1 January 1877, and alterations to it could only
be made after "twelve months notice and of continuing thereafter most
favoured nation treatment." The agreement had been made possible by
Thiers, who had instructed the French negotiators to make the concessions the British considered necessary. The treaty was not as protectionist as he would have wished, the president admitted, but it would have to
do for the time being. Lyons had ensured that his country was protected
from commercial discrimination.[33]

He returned to Paris on 7 November 1872, having spent the previous
evening with Granville at Walmer Castle. A week later Charles Kennedy,
the head of the Commercial Department in the Foreign Office, arrived
to complete the negotiation of the Commercial Treaty. Although signed
more than a week earlier, it was not sealed for several months. The delay was due in part to the labours of the commission sitting in Paris to
settle details, and to the anger of the National Assembly's Protectionists, who charged Thiers with surrendering too much. "In order not
to furnish arguments to the opponents of the Treaty in the National

Assembly it would be as well," Kennedy cautioned his Foreign Office colleagues, "not to insist more than strictly necessary on the advantages obtained in negotiation in the Commission, or on the points hereafter to be discussed."[34]

While commissioners haggled and deputies balked, Lyons fell ill. When his decision to drink only plain water with his meals failed to effect an improvement he summoned Sir John Cormack. Author of several texts, a free lecturer at the oldest of the capital's hospitals, Hôtel-Dieu, he had arrived in Paris in 1869 to fill the vacancy in British medical ranks created by the death of Sir James Oliffe. For his heroics during the siege and the Commune, Cormack had the previous year been named a Chevalier de la légion d'honneur, and had more recently been knighted by the Queen. Although he was admired as a "careful clinical observer," it is not clear what he determined Lyons's ailment to be. Whatever it was, Cormack called every other day for a fortnight and restricted the patient to the embassy. It was the eve of Christmas before Lyons resumed walking for exercise. The news barely two weeks later of the death of Napoleon at the hands of British surgeons created a new political dynamic in France. Thiers was no longer needed by monarchists as their protector against the return of the former emperor and they began to talk excitedly of "fusion" and of a government administered by Marshal Mac-Mahon during the restoration of the monarchy. The problem was still Chambord, who as Lyons reported was continuing to work with "perfect success to make himself and fusion impossible." Would the Legitimists, when they finally admitted this, rally to the cause of empire as a bulwark against Red Republicanism and "anarchy"? Bonapartism quickly found an attractive figure in the youthful Prince Imperial, and Lyons saw two great political parties now taking shape. One was formed of "Red Republicans and Socialists"; the other, committed to strong and resolute government, would look to the young prince as its natural leader. Both parties could only have welcomed the remarks of the German ambassador, Count von Arnim, that Thiers had lost favour in Berlin. A source of the president's domestic strength had been the perception that he was the French leader most acceptable to Bismarck and thus the best man to secure the complete removal from France of German troops. Now that assumption had been called into question. Thiers had also become alarmed at the possibility of German meddling in Spain where Amadeo, who had mounted the Spanish throne on the very day that Metz surrendered, now abdicated under a threat of assassination. When the alarmed Thiers suggested that Britain, France, and Russia come to some understanding on Spain, Lyons cautioned him against seeking an international understanding apparently hostile to Germany. The "smallest result" of such an agreement, he predicted, would be a delay in the withdrawal of German troops.[35]

The "one object of Diplomacy," Lyons and Odo Russell agreed, "was to re-establish the balance of power in Europe on a peace footing." One difficulty was German ambition. By neutralizing the power and influence of the Latin race in France and elsewhere, Odo acknowledged, the Germans were seeking to establish their political supremacy in Europe and that of their race globally. A second problem was their "invincible" military position. "Germany is in reality a great camp ready to break up for war at a week's notice with a million men," Russell warned. Furthermore, Bismarck had during a meeting in Berlin negotiated an offensive-defensive alliance between the three European emperors which "completed Britain's international isolation." Then there was the Germans' unshakable belief that the French were preparing for a war of revenge. This explained, to Russell's satisfaction, Germany's massive military spending. It was, he opined, "merely the result of prudence and foresight, the wisdom of nations." Without denying French hunger for revenge, Lyons accused the Germans of exaggerating it, and he argued that by so doing they drove the French to match them in a dangerous arms race. As a result, both nations were "alike unreasonable." He had not altered his opinion of Bismarck, whom he considered unscrupulous. He did greet the Franco-German agreement on the final payment of the war indemnity and consequent German troop withdrawal as real progress towards a "normal state of affairs," but noted its failure to strengthen the position of the weakened Thiers. Following a debate on a report of the Committee on Constitutional Affairs, known as the committee of thirty, the deputies refused to declare the Republic permanent and rejected a proposed extension of the president's powers.[36]

With the approach of the Assembly's Easter recess, Lyons again took a brief holiday in Britain. He left the embassy in the hands of his new first secretary, Robert Bulwer-Lytton. A nephew of Sir Edward Bulwer, under whom he had begun his diplomatic career at the age of eighteen in Washington, the son of the novelist Edward Bulwer-Lytton, he was very like his father, being handsome and "very dreamy in manner" as befitted an aspiring poet. Privately, he had been critical of Lyons during the Franco-Prussian War, accusing him unfairly of recommending "an excessively prudent policy for fear of losing his reputation as a safe man." Despite this, they got along well enough. Having presented him to Thiers, and having instructed him to keep an especially close eye on Bismarck, Lyons set off at the end of the second week of April for Walmer Castle, where in a few hours he brought the foreign secretary up to date on the unstable political situation in France and the thrust of its foreign policy. Thiers had disclaimed any idea of entering into a special alliance with any foreign power, or even of giving any appearance of intimacy with any one nation, yet was engaged in a "little outward" coquetting with Russia. From Deal, Lyons travelled cross country to Arundel, where every day he walked the short distance uphill to the Roman Catholic cathedral, now nearing completion, which his nephew had commissioned in the French Gothic style. Perhaps he was already thinking of a conversion to Catholicism. On 26 April, 1873, his fifty-sixth birthday, he went up to Norfolk House and with one of his nieces toured some of the capital's sights. They visited the Botanical Gardens in Regent's Park, the Kensington Museum, and the Sir Richard Wallace Art Collection which was on temporary display at Bethnal Green Museum.[37]

On his return to Paris in mid-May 1873, Lyons found Thiers fatally weakened. The agreement which had set in motion the departure of the remaining German troops, for the final payment of the indemnity was to be made in September, reminded many deputies that he was no longer needed. They restricted his opportunities to address the Assembly and on those occasions when he was permitted to speak required him to leave the chamber before any debate ensued. Then with Rémusat's defeat by a Radical Republican in a Paris by-election, and the return of eleven additional Republicans elsewhere, Thiers was charged with "impotence" in the face of radicalism. "Society is dying of universal suffrage," the novelist Edmond de Goncourt wrote in his journal. "Everyone admits that it is the fatal instrument of society's imminent ruin."

Pouyer Quertier rallied the Protectionists against Thiers, while Albert de Broglie, who had resigned his ambassadorship the previous year, led the attack on the government for its failure to be more resolutely conservative. The passage of Broglie's non-confidence motion, thanks to a brief cynical alliance of Bonapartists and Monarchists, left Thiers little choice but to resign. Lyons paid the "old man" a generous tribute, admitting that he could reflect on his record with pride. He had made peace with Germany, had reversed the drift to communism, had restored and maintained public order, had reorganized all branches of the public administration, had raised an army formidable at least in size, had quickly paid down the indemnity, and had secured the imminent withdrawal of the German troops. The "whole credit of the liberation of the country must still be given to him," Lyons maintained.[38]

Monarchists and Bonapartists immediately voted MacMahon into the presidency, each believing him to be one of their own. He was, one senior Foreign Office official commented, the kind of man the French required, "an officer and a gentleman and a good policeman." He promised "moral order." Lyons was more caustic. The French, he growled, preferred a man on horseback to one who mounted the Tribune. Yet if MacMahon was to preside over the restoration of the monarchy, which of the three pretenders did he favour? He was believed to favour Chambord, but Broglie, whom he appointed vice-president of the Council of Ministers and foreign minister, was an Orléanist, while three Bonapartists held Cabinet posts, one of them the experienced and eloquent Pierre Magne. As finance minister, his history suggested he would support ratification of the most-favoured-nation provision which would protect British trade with France until 1877. Lyons spent three hot and uncomfortable days in "poky lodgings" in Versailles in late July finalizing the commercial agreement. Ever the anodyne diplomat, he recommended an acknowledgment of the conduct of the French. They had merely treated Britain with common justice, he conceded, but had done so "with considerable sacrifice of their [Protectionist] prejudices." With Kennedy's aid, he had ensured that Britain would not be at their mercy for another four years. "We are much indebted to you for it," Granville wrote, and authorized him to flatter Broglie, who "likes a little butter, although he is not extravagant in its use."[39]

Broglie conducted business in a straightforward and decided manner, exercised greater discipline over his subordinates, and made himself agreeable to the diplomatic corps in general and to Lyons in particular. Welcome as this was, so was his assurance that there would be no change in foreign policy. But Broglie's response to what he perceived to be a Radical Republican threat did not bode well for a harmonious relationship between the conservative government and an increasingly Republican Assembly. Twenty Republican prefects were replaced; Republican newspapers were kept under close surveillance and their public sale restricted; civil burials were hampered in favour of religious; busts of the Republic, of Marianne, which during the Thiers years had been placed in many city halls, were removed; Republican municipal councils were suspended; avowed enemies of the Republic were appointed to the bureaucracy; and persons suspected of involvement in any way with the Commune were detained.[40]

The Monarchists, it seemed, were preparing the ground for decisive action when the deputies returned in November. So Lyons expected them to negotiate the oft-discussed "fusion" during the summer recess. However, the obstacles to a restoration of the monarchy were in his opinion more formidable than ever. Chambord's "fanaticism" had still not been tempered "by any eager desire to take so uneasy a seat as the French throne." Moreover, neither Legitimists nor Orléanists understood or respected "the feelings ingrained in the majority of Frenchmen on the subjects of religion and social equality." Recent by-elections suggested a popular sentiment favourable to a hereditary monarchy, but the French press was exhibiting less enthusiasm for "fusion" given the inability of its supporters to bring Chambord "up to scratch." As obdurate as ever, he still refused to pledge himself, if king, to wise and liberal government.[41]

Lyons had taken advantage of the recess to return home for another holiday, at the end of which he held hurried discussions with Granville and the French ambassador, the Duc Decazes. And when he met with Broglie on 25 October he undoubtedly learned of the Orléanist pretender's decision to recognize Chambord as the "representative of the monarchical principle." Since Chambord was childless and likely to remain so, the Comte de Paris became his heir, but the arrangement prevented him from challenging for the throne without Chambord first abdicating his claim. This was no more likely than Chambord's acceptance of terms that might make his accession "humanly possible." Consequently, the eroding Monarchist majority in the Assembly decided that an extension of MacMahon's presidency was their only option at least for the time being. Unknown to them Chambord had arrived secretly in Versailles and had sent for MacMahon. Although the marshal declared himself a Legitimist in his soul, he listened to his wife and refused to wait upon the pretender. The Monarchists received unexpected help from Thiers and elements of the Centre Left, he calculating that the marshal could not long survive in office and that he would then be begged to return to the vacant presidency. Even more bizarre was the talk of making the MacMahon regime "provisionally definitive," while a strange alliance of Radicals and Bonapartists demanded popular endorsement of the extension via a plebiscite. But the evident increase in Republicanism in response to Chambord's foolish manifestos, and disquieting evidence of an alliance of "Reds" and moderate Republicans, drove conservatives of all shades to extend for seven years MacMahon's presidency. On hearing this, Chambord left France never to return. The Orléanists "have sacrificed their separate position as a political party (the only French representatives of constitutional monarchy), for the sake of a fusion which has come to nothing," the 15th Earl of Derby, a former and a future Tory foreign secretary commented.[42]

Lyons adhered to the principle "that it is better [for diplomats] to avoid as far as possible manifesting an opinion, to a foreign government, on political matters which give rise to great difference of feeling in the country in which they occur." Hence his relief when his government did not instruct him, as some of his colleagues in the diplomatic corps had been by theirs, to congratulate MacMahon on the extension of his term. He did welcome the appointment of Louis duc Decazes as foreign minister, Broglie having decided to take the Interior portfolio instead. The new man, who dismissed MacMahon as a *crétin*, was an experienced diplomat, an Orléanist, and was admired by Broglie for his "great pliancy of mind, his charm and grace of manner, his skill in managing men." Decazes had served the Second Empire and as a representative of the Gironde was something of a free trader. Protectionists were far from being his only critics. He was accused of being "unrestrained in conversation," too good-natured and obliging, of lacking industriousness, and of speculating on the Bourse. If the suspicion that he was frequently short of money led to questions about his fiscal trustworthiness, he and his wife were a lively and agreeable couple with whom Lyons swiftly became friends. And during this ministerial transition, the Derbys arrived in Paris for a brief visit only to delay their departure to attend the court martial of Marshal Bazaine. He was on trial for the surrender years earlier of Metz and an entire army. After he had been convicted and sentenced to death and degradation, his life was spared by MacMahon, who reduced the sentence to imprisonment for twenty years. The disgraced general's wife then swiftly organized his escape. Her personal participation gave the incident a romantic touch. In the words of one mordant observer, French patriots were relieved to learn that a single man had been responsible for the military humiliation suffered at the hands of the Germans. The scapegoating of Bazaine, and the transformation of the army from the symbol of crushing defeat to an instrument of social order with its suppression of the Commune, now placed it "at the heart of the national revival."[43]

Granville advised Lyons on 23 January 1874 of an imminent general election in which the Liberal government faced defeat. For some time Lyons had been seeking to focus the foreign secretary on Franco-German relations. The Germans were complaining of the hostile tone of the French press and Ambassador Arnim had warned that a Legitimist restoration would be considered an unfriendly act. Although Bismarck, seeing him as a rival, was scheming to drive Arnim from the diplomatic service in disgrace, having placed a spy in his embassy, and this Lyons knew thanks to Odo Russell, there were other signs of a German willingness to quarrel with France. Bismarck disliked France's "too rapid convalescence" from the war and was continuing to work for its diplomatic isolation. Another source of tension was the cultural struggle, *kulturkampf*, he had launched in 1871 on the grounds that "ultramontanism vitiated the power of Prussia and retarded the growth of the German nation." However, the harsh anti-Catholic legislation sowed sectarian and cultural divisions instead of fostering national unity. "Thinking himself more infallible than the Pope," Odo Russell dryly remarked, Bismarck "cannot tolerate two infallibles in Europe." When French bishops criticized the repressive measures they ran the danger of providing the chancellor with a pretext for an attack on France. Since all the women and half the men of France were Roman Catholics, a French government could not follow "a strong anti-Catholic line." To head off danger, Decazes made a statement in the Assembly clearly designed to appease the Germans, and a French newspaper that had printed the episcopal criticism was briefly suspended from publication. Lyons trusted that Bismarck's francophobia would subside when he secured passage of his latest army bill, for a sudden economic depression was causing problems in a Reich where virtually the entire budget was spent on the military. A German wolf was confronting a French lamb, Lyons observed, and he hoped the latter would not be "skittish." One possible way to buy off Bismarck was "obedience to his requests with respect to the ultramontane question," but the chances of doing so would be greatly enhanced if it was the work of a secure and stable French government. Unfortunately, the Assembly's Committee on Constitutional Laws was making little progress in that direction. How was it possible to preserve universal suffrage and obtain a conservative legislature in a nation where the lowest class was "Socialist"? Lyons asked himself. Was it possible to create an influential upper chamber in a nation where no one would admit the superiority of anyone else? In short, was parliamentary government even possible in a nation where political stability was in exact proportion to the prevalence of the belief that its chief executive possessed not only the means but also the will to support himself by force against all comers?[44]

CHAPTER FIFTEEN

The Third Republic

Lyons drove out to Versailles on New Year's Day, 1874, to attend the president's reception, and two weeks later MacMahon, Broglie, and Decazes were guests at his first large dinner of the new season. Spring was celebrated appropriately with an embassy wedding, the union on 15 April of Lord Randolph Churchill, third son of the Duke of Marlborough, and Miss Jennie Jerome, the second daughter of an American financier. The premature birth only seven months later of their son Winston may have been the result of their determination to overcome, come what may, parental reservations. The Granvilles were next to arrive followed in quick order by Anthony Trollope, with whom Lyons had become acquainted in Washington, Sir John Michel, who had taken command of the British troops in Canada shortly after he quit the American capital, and his old adversary William Henry Seward. Entertaining visitors was a source of pleasure, and a duty at which he excelled, but Lyons wasted valuable hours responding to the silly requests of British friends to find them French cooks. A time-consuming, irritating, and unwelcome assignment was his membership of the Anglo-French commission examining the possibility of a Channel tunnel. Toothache, a recurrence of eye trouble, happily no more than "pink eye," and Sheffield's "Mental 'idiosyncrasy'" and "hypochondriasis" did not improve his temper, but there was one compensating diplomatic achievement. He and Charles Kennedy signed a supplementary agreement to the Commercial Convention on 24 January 1874. "The Treaty is quite finished," a relieved Lyons sighed.[1]

His principal diplomatic worry was the tense Franco-German relationship which he considered the "one great cause of peril to Europe." Odo Russell wrote that nothing would save France if Bismarck decided on war, for the kaiser was little more than the chancellor's "signature machine." But he was confident that Bismarck had Austria's German provinces in his sights and that his talk of a hostile France was designed merely to arouse and sustain German war spirit. This analysis ignored the extent to which Austro-German friendship was being converted by the chancellor "into a formal alliance." Furthermore, Bismarck's "anti-ultramontane mania" was as Russell admitted another means whereby at a convenient moment he might pick a quarrel with any Catholic power. To be sure of peace France needed to gag its press, imprison its bishops, quarrel with Rome, cease organizing a massive army, and shun foreign alliances. As for Protestant Britain, what influence could it exert? Military action was out of the question. The British Army had slipped far behind the German in quality and organization, commanded as it still was by a royal duke who lacked the resolve required to correct obvious deficiencies. Although the purchase of commissions had ceased, the military was riddled with administrative problems. The senior officials of the War Office were in a "dilapidated condition." They were either chronically ill, hobbled by gout, afflicted with cancer, cursed with a weak heart, or sojourning on the Riviera. Was Odo Russell correct, therefore, when he suggested that the only safe policy for Britain was to let Bismarck do as he pleased and submit to the consequences until he died?[2]

The British Conservatives who took office in February 1874 were led by a man who sensed "that political capital could be made out of a programme of imperial pride and diplomatic boldness." Disraeli was determined to "reassert Britain's power in Europe," yet in returning Derby to the Foreign Office he was entrusting policy to a devout non-interventionist who appeared infuriatingly oblivious to popular restlessness over Britain's diminished international influence. Lyons's dispatches on Franco-German relations did convince Derby that there was a "good deal of loose powder about" and Britain's "diplomatic wet blankets" might not be "sufficient to prevent an explosion," but he opposed involvement in matters of no immediate concern to Britain. At most, he envisaged a tinkering with non-interventionism. They could work for peace, he wrote to Lyons, by using their role as "impartial lookers-on to check misunderstandings, and represent the feelings of each country towards the other in as favourable a light" as truth allowed.[3]

Britain had in France an ally in the cause of peace, Lyons assured the foreign secretary. Decazes accepted with greater equanimity and temper than did the vast majority of his countrymen the humiliating relationship with Germany. Devoid of "stiffness," as Lyons put it, he was able to "bend in the German storms [that] might wreck the ship." Any government for which he spoke would be prudent. Lyons made his own contribution to the easing of tension by reminding French politicians that with the final departure of the German troops there was no longer an excuse for "manifestations of impotent resentment as undignified as impolitic." However, any hint of a foreign alliance would play into the hands of those Germans keen to finish off France as a major power once and for all.[4]

Lyons welcomed the "happy lull in foreign politics" on hearing that Bismarck was restricted to his bed and unable to attend to business. Unfortunately, the political situation in France remained volatile. The current government lacked that appearance of permanence which he considered essential if it was to win and retain popular support. In the Assembly, it was dependent on a Monarchist majority continually shrivelling as by-elections were held to fill vacant seats. The elections on the first day of March 1874 added to the uncertainty. The newly appointed conservative prefects and mayors failed to halt either a drift to the Left or, conversely, "the progress of Imperialist ideas." The resurgence of Bonapartism as the Prince Imperial came of age led the Centre Left to pull in its horns on constitutional change for fear it would be the beneficiary. From all of this Lyons drew four conclusions. First, that there was an aversion to the white flag of the Bourbons and the aristocratic and clerical influences of which it was the emblem. Second, that the great majority of Frenchmen were currently Republican in sentiment. Third, that Imperialists were the most numerous party after the Republicans. Fourth, that the MacMahon *septennat* was merely acquiesced in. As for a "definitive" French system of government, Lyons doubted that "moderation and good sense" would carry the day. "Despotism and Communism" remained, he thought, alternatives.[5]

Derby accepted "entirely" Lyons's analysis of French political instability and took to heart his assessment that the French ascribed to Bismarck "whatever goes wrong in the world." Consequently, he could not have been surprised when the long-simmering ministerial crisis finally boiled over on 16 May 1874. Monarchist deputies, detecting a decline in Legitimism, no decrease in Republicanism, and an increase in Imperialism, vented their fury on Broglie and his "snubbing ways." They brought down the government and replaced it with one that was identical except for the absence of the unpopular Broglie. These Monarchists were driven by "transcendental motives, too far above all considerations of ordinary human policy and good sense, to be comprehended by me," a frustrated Lyons commented. The chronic problem was the presence in the Assembly of six political factions not one of which commanded a majority and no two of which could even agree to co-operate for any length of time. MacMahon named a fellow soldier, General Ernest Courtot de Cissey, to head the new government, but his public "taciturnity" and personal indolence did not inspire confidence in his longevity as premier. But the retention of Decazes as foreign minister gave Lyons some hope that a ministry otherwise "so colourless as not to offend the weakest eyes and allow the Assembly to do what it chooses about constitutional laws and all political questions" might survive a little longer than most observers anticipated.[6]

The government's "very military air," with a marshal as president, a general as premier, and a second general as minister of the interior, conjured up for Lyons the unwelcome image of a military solution of the French problem. Was MacMahon thinking of staging a coup, or would he applaud a pronunciamento by senior army officers convinced that it was the only viable alternative to Radical Republican government? It would be an evil day for France if troops intervened in this manner, Lyons observed, believing as he still did that it would eventually re-emerge as a great nation and that Britain should behave accordingly. He welcomed the news that the Assembly was going to prorogue and had decided to put off until its next session the introduction of constitutional laws. This promised at least a lull in the squabbling. A by-election in Calvados in which a Bonapartist triumphed was equally welcome. It eased Conservative concerns of an inexorable Radical Republican march to power. Indeed, the unlikelihood of anything of importance occurring during the recess saw Lyons take another leave.[7]

In London, which he and Sheffield reached on the evening of 9 September, he met with Odo Russell "to exchange ideas on the situation that cannot be written down." They agreed that the only safe French policy was to continue to avoid giving Bismarck a pretext for a quarrel. He took a ride on the capital's underground railway, the first line of which had opened eleven years earlier, before embarking on a country house tour with the usual stops. At Raby Castle, he and the other guests had an evening of whist followed by an evening of charades. At Knowsley, he and Derby discussed the danger of Bonapartism, associating it as they did with military aggression, and the attractions of a Conservative French Republic. If it evolved as a constitutional presidency it would not be too far removed from constitutional monarchy. Joined by Sheffield, he set off for Highclere Castle, the home of the Carnarvons. Sheffield had already met with the colonial secretary, from whom he gathered that Disraeli's health was shattered. He was suffering from bronchitis, asthma, gout, and a kidney problem which did not benefit from the glasses of port he took on the advice of the Queen's personal physician. If Disraeli resigned, Carnarvon expected Derby to become prime minister and hoped to secure the Foreign Office himself. Instead, Disraeli soldiered on. Lyons called at the Foreign Office to assess its management, which both Carnarvon and Percy Anderson had described as lamentable. There was a need for a thorough reorganization from top to bottom, they argued, for Tenterden, who on Hammond's retirement the previous year had been promoted to permanent undersecretary, lacked the necessary knowledge of society and of the world. He was industrious but overrated and lacked his predecessor's "lofty dictation." Contempt of the permanent undersecretary, disloyalty to the secretary of state, the promotion of a "small clique of privileged pets," and staff antagonism were becoming persistent and damaging problems.[8]

On the first day of December Lyons and Sheffield returned to Paris, where Lyons immediately fell ill with a severe bilious attack. It kept him close to the embassy for several uncomfortable days. Dr Cormack's prescription of a footbath appeared somewhat eccentric, although it did prepare him for the resumption of walking as a form of exercise. He accompanied the visiting Granvilles to the Comédie-Française; he attended the president's New Year's Day reception and the opening of the Charles Garnier–designed opera house with its 1,600 seats. But French politics remained a "mess." Imperialists, Legitimists, Orléanists, and Moderate Monarchists were still unable to unite or make common cause, while the varieties of Republicans – Conservatives, Moderates, and Radicals – gave every appearance of being "very nearly as widely separated from each other as ever." Even more disheartening was the related irresponsibility of the Assembly, which skirted "burning topics" and ousted ministers without giving the slightest thought to their replacements. To govern on "parliamentary theory" with such a body was simply impossible, Lyons concluded, and he began to fret that a new Assembly "would be, immediately or soon, socialist." He had detected a revived restlessness among senior military figures and their increasing interest in Bonapartism. This was not welcome news. How could a successor to Napoleon III forget Sedan? Derby asked. How could he be content with the reduced territory of defeated France? What would he represent other than the traditions of a military dynasty, with a defeat to avenge and an army to restore to its once glorious reputation? France needed a government which did not talk of one day marching into Berlin. This awareness did not herald a change of British policy. They could do no more than "look on," Derby continued to insist, and, by maintaining between the French and the Germans "a position sufficiently neutral," perhaps gain the trust of both. For all of Disraeli's talk of a more active and assertive foreign policy, nonintervention remained the foreign secretary's mantra.[9]

Fear of Bonapartism did finally induce the Assembly to organize "something like a definitive republic." By the slimmest possible majority it provided on 30 January 1875 for the election of the President of the Republic by an absolute majority of a Senate and a Chamber of Deputies sitting together as a National Assembly. France was at last "officially republican in name," and its legislature was to be bicameral. The 300 members of the Senate were to be at least forty years of age, and seventy-five of them were to be elected for life by the Assembly. The form of election of the remainder, and the distribution of seats, "perpetuated the dominant influence of rural France." The upper house in combination with a president armed with the powers of a constitutional monarch, and who was not accountable to either house, could be expected to check the potential political radicalism of the more than 600 deputies returned to the Chamber by "direct universal suffrage." Having watched this constitution made in just three afternoons, Lyons remained unconvinced that the Conservative Republic envisaged by Thiers had at last been created. Instead, what had transpired was merely "an experiment in Republican institutions," and the constitutional laws were "more a guide to procedure than a proper constitution." MacMahon did surprise him by showing an unexpected grasp of political tactics. He named Louis Buffet to head the new ministry. He had a liberal reputation, having served in Ollivier's government before the war, and his recent presidency of the Assembly explained his broad acceptability. Decazes continued as foreign minister, much to Lyons's delight, but there was little joy for the political Left since Buffet failed either to persecute Bonapartists or restock the public service with Republicans. The French would have done better to go on for the time being as they were, Lyons believed, while the 15th Earl of Derby questioned the purpose of a Senate. There was nothing to represent in France except the people, he remarked with aristocratic hauteur, and they were to be fully represented in the Chamber of Deputies.[10]

The spring of 1875 brought in addition to "a sort of constitution" a sort of war crisis. The Germans revealed to the French government the threatening language they had used when protesting to the Belgian government the conduct of Belgian ultramontanes. In Paris, the disclosure was interpreted as an implied threat. This, Decazes told Lyons on 11 March, together with the Germans' prohibition of the export of horses so vital to battlefield operations ought to concern all governments committed to the preservation of international peace. But the reorganization and enlargement of the French army, its strength growing by an estimated 144,000 men, a massive printing of currency which might serve as a war chest, and the importation by France of thousands of horses from eastern Europe, undoubtedly spurred Bismarck's effort to unnerve the French. He was determined "to reduce France to a second-class status." His resentment of their plans "to reassert their claims to a place among the Great Powers" was plain enough, but what Derby saw also was an effort to sow disunity among European states. Knowing that the German Empire was far stronger than any other individual power, the German chancellor was intent on preventing a "combination" as his League of Three Emperors demonstrated. Yet Lyons could not suppress the suspicion that the "inscrutable" Bismarck might seek to finish with the French before tackling another victim.[11]

When the French Assembly adjourned for almost two months on 21 March, Lyons persuaded himself that a conflict was not imminent and with Derby's consent travelled to London to enjoy the season. At his meeting with the foreign secretary on 9 April he added little to what he had already written about French war fears. Eight days later he dined with Disraeli and found him reassuringly well briefed especially on the danger if France aroused the "jealousy of Bismarck" by seeking an understanding with Britain. By early May the "war in sight crisis" appeared to be deepening. An ominous article in the Berlin Post, which was believed to be government inspired, Moltke's talk of a preventive war, which he leaked to the press, a report that Bismarck had spoken to the Austrian ambassador of taking the initiative against France, and his belief, according to the German ambassador to France, that the French were preparing to make war on Germany, heightened the tension. Astutely, Decazes provided the Paris correspondent of The Times with the documents for a withering exposure of Bismarck's conduct, and pointed out to the German ambassador how difficult it was for any rational person to believe that the French "could be so mad as to think of another war." France certainly desired to recover Alsace and Lorraine, Decazes admitted, but it was committed to a diplomatic pursuit of that objective. Then, to calm the ragged nerves of his fellow countrymen, he ostentatiously attended the horse races.[12]

Lyons called at the Foreign Office on 8 May to ask if he should return early to Paris and was undoubtedly surprised when Derby said there was "nothing urgent." The Russian ambassador, Shouvaloff, had informed him of the czar's intention to travel to Berlin "to insist on peace being maintained." This demand by one of the Three Emperors, the Austrian being the third, was a heavy blow to Bismarck as the League's founder. It was "the first serious reverse he had suffered." By 11 May the crisis had passed and Disraeli was quick to claim for Britain a share of the credit, as Derby had in a widely circulated dispatch instructed Russell by telegraph to support the czar's intervention. It had, Odo reported, taken Bismarck by surprise. Before long the chancellor was claiming that the crisis had been manufactured both by Decazes, for stockjobbing purposes, and by the ultramontane press. The profuse French expressions of gratitude for saving "them from attack" were interpreted by Lyons as an attempt to imply that the British had become "partisans of theirs instead of good but impartial friends." As one such friend, Lyons impressed upon Decazes the danger of dedicating ever larger budgetary appropriations to the military. Why strengthen German suspicions that the French were planning an early war of revenge? he asked. The foreign minister ensured that military appropriations in the current budget did not exceed those of the previous year. This was, as Lyons knew, a piece of legerdemain. The deleted items would be restored later in a supplementary bill.[13]

Now at the summit of his profession, which he had scaled from its base, ambition was no longer Lyons's driving force. His interest in his duties was beginning to flag, for Berlin had become Europe's most important capital. Furthermore, the certainty that France would not for some time re-emerge as a great power was insurance that it would not push disputes to extremes. The French had no wish to quarrel with Britain, "for to do so would be almost a fatal blow to their foreign policy since the Prussian War." News of fresh trouble in the Ottoman Empire did arouse Lyons's interest, familiar as he was with its problems and with the long-standing French involvement in the region. From small beginnings in Herzegovina, a revolt by Christians spread across the Balkans. Personally, Lyons hoped the risings would end or be suppressed before the European powers decided to intervene because a lasting solution required measures that would hasten the empire's collapse. It was simply impossible, he believed, "to reconcile the Christian population to the Turkish yoke." But the instability, if it resulted in Russian control of Constantinople, would open the door to Russian domination also of the eastern Mediterranean and thus control of the approaches to the Suez Canal. Neither Disraeli nor Derby were among the select group of British politicians who believed that if liberated the Balkan Christians would prove a "more effective bulwark" than the Turks against Russian expansion. Yet Derby did not re-evaluate the policy of non-intervention, for it enjoyed considerable public support, and like many of his country-men he had no wish to fight another war in defence of the integrity of the Ottoman Empire.[14]

In developing diplomatic strategy, Derby did not count on help from France. He knew from Lyons that Decazes was obsessed with the no-tion that the turmoil in the Balkans would so preoccupy both Russia and Austria that Bismarck would have a free hand to deal as he wished with France. This was a "respectable" cause of apprehension, Derby conceded, but it was rooted in the Frenchman's "absurd" notion that the Prussian was a being of "superhuman power and superhuman ma-lignity." In fact, the Frenchman's judgment was in this instance sounder than that of the foreign secretary. Derby was equally dismissive of the Queen's concern that Britain would find itself "isolated." The Cretan re-bellion was his proof that Britain had "generally been most successful" when it had been isolated. So in this instance it should promote fair play and discourage foreign interference. That would not be easy given the "apathy and helpless laziness" of the Turks. They might have crushed the rebellion with minimal losses had they only acted quickly, he moaned. Now its suppression would be expensive in lives. "So much for the hu-manity of delay in such cases," the foreign secretary commented with unintentional irony, being so resolute a procrastinator himself. He also did not waste much sympathy on bondholders, who began to agitate for intervention as soon as it became clear a default was imminent on the payment of the interest on the Turkish debt. They knew the risk when they loaned money at a high rate of interest, he observed, and would still have a "fair return" on the reduced rate the Turks could af-ford to pay. But it would be hard to hold fast to non-intervention when the French bondholders set up a clamour for action, Lyons fretted, for their weak government was likely to be more responsive. Nor would it be wise to count on the czar standing aside, since by doing so he would open himself to the emotive charge that he was neglecting the welfare of his fellow Slavs. Equally, would the Austro-Hungarians remain pas-sive when Slavs made trouble on their frontier? If the summoning of an international conference was the obvious response, Lyons did not envy its British representative. Germany and France would each bid for Russian favour, Austria-Hungary would be too afraid to make a stand, so the Briton would be consistently outvoted. Yet the British representative, according to Sheffield who wrote from England, would be under intense public pressure to achieve "two definite objects." The first was to ensure that no great power, and Russia in particular, gained control of Constantinople. The second was to establish British control of the Suez Canal.[15]

Disraeli, soon after his return to Downing Street, had offered to purchase the shares of Ferdinand de Lesseps, and while the Frenchman had declined to sell he needed cash for additional works. An increase in tolls was the simplest means of raising it, but the Khedive blocked him. Britain being the waterway's heaviest user, Lesseps approached Lyons in May 1875 in search of an understanding. Lyons said little and "opposed a friendly imperturbability" to the Frenchman's "agitation." Five months later Disraeli and Derby became disturbed on hearing that the impecunious Khedive, Ismail Pacha, was negotiating the sale of his massive block of shares to a French group. An unacceptable exclusive French interest in the waterway was raising its ugly head again. The consul general was instructed to protest any such sale and intimate Britain's willingness to be the purchaser if acceptable terms could be arranged. Derby still hoped to avoid "the purchase expedient." He doubted the financial value of so large an investment and feared Britain's acquisition of the shares would lead to unpleasantness with France and the Porte. But, as he emphasized to Lyons, the Khedive's shares "must not be allowed to get into French hands." Lyons played his part. He maintained a studied indifference to the Khedive's plight lest curiosity arouse French nationalism and spur French action. On 23 November he warned London by telegraph that Ismail Pacha was still seeking to raise money in Paris on the shares. The very next day the government learned from Cairo that Lesseps had offered £4 million for them. Disraeli's Cabinet immediately matched the offer, the money loaned by Lionel de Rothschild, and on 25 November 1875 the contract of sale was signed. Ironically, the "complete political success" of the purchase caused Derby considerable uneasiness over future policy. It shows, he noted apprehensively, "the intense desire for action abroad that pervades the public mind, the impatience created by long diplomatic inactivity, and the strength of feeling which might under certain circumstances take the form of a cry for war."[16]

Decazes complained bitterly to Lyons that he and the French government had been deeply embarrassed by the British diplomatic coup, cultivating as it did in the mind of the French public the belief that Egypt would soon be in Britain's hands. Not that this protest alarmed Lyons, who recognized that the French could ill afford to behave provocatively following Bismarck's support of the British action. Furthermore, they were able to console themselves financially. There was a sharp rise in the value of the shares they controlled and also of the Egyptian securities in which they had invested. To ease their impotent resentment, however, he ensured that Britons took no part in the general meetings of the Canal Company in Paris. Here was a discreet assurance that Britain was not seeking a controlling influence over the canal now that it owned almost half the shares.[17]

That the French did not make more of an "ugly face" over the shares had much to do with their domestic preoccupations, which included the organization of the Republic's legislature. Writing on 7 December 1875, Lyons described France as "perfectly tranquil." The Assembly had voted a "very Conservative Electoral Law," which provided for the return of deputies from single-member districts where local and government influence, a Lyons euphemism for prefects and mayors, might be exerted to produce a desired result. He hoped, therefore, that the new Chamber would be sufficiently conservative to work with MacMahon only to watch in disbelief as the Right behaved "stupidly" during the election by the Assembly of seventy-five life senators. The several factions by their mutual skullduggery during the voting allowed the more united Left to win an unexpectedly high proportion of the seats. Lyons could only shake his head in disbelief, reporting that by their divisions "they have made monarchical government in any form impossible at the moment, and yet they will not acquiesce even temporarily in the mild monarchical kind of Republic which has been established." Worse still, they had opened the door to a Red Republic.[18]

The French elections early in 1876 "brought a state of political chaos." Republicans, many of them "ultra Radicals," appeared to be well placed to control the Chamber. Panicked by the thought that they planned to free the imprisoned Communards and allow those who had been exiled to return, that they would re-establish the National Guard and introduce a progressive income tax, rich Parisians began to send their money abroad. If more confident of "tolerable tranquillity," at least until the expiry of the presidential *septennat* in 1880, Lyons was startled by the failure of Louis Buffet, the government leader and minister of the interior, to be returned. No previous holder of that portfolio had suffered that indignity. Jules Dufaure, at seventy-eight a true veteran in every sense, succeeded him as head of the government, a post he had held twice before. His choice suggested that MacMahon was selecting a ministry representative of the more moderate members of the Chamber, and Dufaure's title of President of the Council announced the president's exclusion from the Cabinet and thus another step towards a constitutional presidency. However, both Left and Right damned Dufaure.[19]

Lyons considered Léon Gambetta the most "important personage," commanding as he ostensibly did the allegiance of almost two-thirds of the Republican deputies. But the Left was as schismatic as the Right. A good number of Republicans were plainly determined to remain at arm's length from Gambetta's Union Républicaine. Jules Ferry, a "bourgeois, son of a bourgeois, brought up correctly in the bourgeois manner," lacked Gambetta's enthusiasm for social mobility and was dismissive of his notion that the peasantry could be inculcated with Republican values. In an effort to gain a better understanding of the Radical Republican, Lyons sent Sheffield to dine with him. His private secretary was a popular figure despite his "atrocious" French accent, and his close relationship with Lyons was widely known. Sheffield duly noted Gambetta's statements: that the premiership was rightly his, for he had been the organizer of the Republicans' electoral triumph; that Bonapartism would expire as soon as a moderate Republic was truly established; that no true Republic could have been established under Thiers; that he could keep the extreme Radicals in order; that he had no intention of issuing a general amnesty to Communards; and that he did not intend to re-establish the National Guard. Finally, he declared that it was his ambition to serve as premier under MacMahon. Republics, like misery, "may prompt a man to have strange bedfellows," Lyons allowed, but it was unimaginable that the very conservative MacMahon would accept this firebrand as his first counsellor. Understanding this, Gambetta began to moderate his rhetoric. His expression of support for the Commercial Treaty with Britain persuaded Lyons that a Cabinet headed by him would not do anything "dreadful." Reasonable and moderate government was still possible in France, he assured Derby, who replied that matters there "were in a fair way to settle down." "I have never understood," he admitted, "why a republic should be difficult to establish in a country where social equality is pushed very far, and where dynasties have lost their influence: nor why it should not be conservative, when the general feeling of the nation so evidently is so." The problem, Lyons patiently explained, was the willingness of French Conservatives to risk violent social revolution rather than allow the current system to work well.[20]

An unresolved international problem was the Balkans' rebellion. Shortly before Christmas, the Porte published the reforms it had promised as a response to the widespread unrest. Then, shortly before the New Year, the so-called Andrássy Note, named for the Austrian foreign minister, was circulated. Vienna, St Petersburg, and Berlin, the capitals of the Three Emperors, agreed that pressure should be exerted on the Porte to implement reforms that addressed the rebels' grievances. To ensure implementation, the Note called for the creation of a supervisory mixed commission of Muslims and Christians. Derby was willing for Britain to adhere, if not too closely, to a movement which France and Italy were soon expected to join. They might, otherwise, find themselves "isolated in Europe," he advised Disraeli again without a hint of irony. From Berlin, Russell wrote in favour of Britain doing so, but the prime minister was initially resistant. Britain should lead not follow, he growled. The measures of pacification were almost certain to fail, and in that event Britain might be drawn into "ulterior measures as a remedy to the failure." He preferred the summoning of another congress.[21]

When asked by Derby for his opinion the ever-cautious Lyons stressed that it was formed in ignorance of "two important elements": knowledge of British public opinion and of the real feelings of the three emperors. Decazes had been alarmed, he knew, by reports that Derby had cooled towards the Andrássy Note, that the British public was hostile to involvement, and that the Tory Cabinet was sharply divided. Britain's non-involvement, the French foreign minister warned, would feed the czar's suspicion, and he hinted his own, that the Porte had agreed to abandon Egypt to Britain in return for its support in resisting foreign interference in the empire's internal affairs. Although he dismissed as absurd the talk of "sinister" British designs, it helped to convince Lyons that his nation had little option but to endorse the Note. Here was a way to leave the other powers with less of an excuse to attack Turkey. This argument was certain to resonate with Disraeli, who feared a Russian march into Constantinople. There were grave objections to every course, Derby characteristically observed, having thanked Lyons for his "valuable letter," but on this occasion "still graver ones against doing nothing." Three days later the Cabinet agreed "to give [only] a general support to the note." Britain had not been its author, had not been consulted over its wording, and the reforms it specified differed little from those the Porte had promised. Turkey accepted the Note on 15 February.[22]

Having contributed to the government's decision to endorse the Andrássy Note at least half-heartedly, Lyons also contributed to the rejection of Bismarck's proposal of close Anglo-German co-operation on the Eastern question. Odo Russell recommended acceptance, observing that an "ambitious, irresponsible, unaccountable genius with a million soldiers at his back" was a desirable friend. On receiving a copy of Russell's dispatch, Lyons urged caution on a foreign secretary who shared his doubts of the German's sincerity and suspected he had "other plans in contemplation." Lyons was willing to believe that Britain's co-operation with Russia in the "war in sight" crisis, and its acquisition of the Suez Canal shares, had demonstrated that it still had the will and the means to play a "foremost part in European politics." However, he reminded Derby of the chancellor's efforts since 1870 to divide Britain and France. Then there was the possibility of Germany quarrelling with Russia, and of the French siding with the czar. In that event, Bismarck would wish to have the British Navy on his side to prevent his enemies "being all powerful at sea." Furthermore, support of Britain on the Eastern question was his best hope of embroiling Britain with Russia. So, the Queen's enthusiasm for an Anglo-German understanding notwithstanding, which did not increase its allure for Derby, and despite Disraeli's musings that it might be a good idea, the foreign secretary declined to give Bismarck "anything more than fair words." Britain desired no exclusive alliances,

Russell was instructed to inform the chancellor, and the principles of British policy did not admit of any being entered into.[23]

By the spring, the ill health that had plagued Lyons intermittently throughout his adult life was chronic. Bad colds developed into persistent coughs, and Dr Cormack was a regular caller at the embassy. When the Derbys arrived in early April for a short visit they found their host suffering from influenza and bronchitis, and three days after they departed he followed them to England. He rested at Norfolk House, called on Disraeli and several friends, went to Westminster Abbey on Easter Sunday to hear Dean Stanley preach, but quickly realized that foggy London was no place for him despite his use of the bronchial steam kettle to improve the atmosphere in a room. Following a flying visit to Paris in mid-April to greet the Queen on her arrival there, he consulted her physician, Sir William Jenner, on his return to London. Jenner recommended a trip to the seaside, and accompanied by two of his nieces Lyons took rooms on 22 May at the new Highcliffe Mansions Hotel in Bournemouth. Equipped with all the "novelties and conveniences" required by first-class patrons and commanding magnificent views, it was a magnet for ailing aristocrats. Daily walks in the bracing sea air worked their therapeutic magic, and by month's end Lyons appeared to be in somewhat ruder health and fit enough to return to duty.[24]

When he called at the Foreign Office on 1 June he learned of the latest developments in the East. The Cabinet agreed that same day to congratulate the new Sultan, Murad V, a nephew of the deposed and soon to be murdered Abdul Aziz. Only a fortnight earlier it had rejected the Berlin Memorandum, which revised the Andrássy Note by calling for a brief armistice during which the Turks were to negotiate with the insurgents, whose ranks had swollen with the enrolment of the Bulgars. The Memorandum was effectively an ultimatum, for its demands were backed by a threat of great power coercion. It was also unfair in the sense that the signatory powers were promising the rebels better terms if they rejected those offered by the Porte. Britain's rebuff of the document was followed by a modest naval demonstration, a squadron entering Besika Bay at the southern end of the Dardanelles. The problem for Derby as a non-interventionist was the extent to which the fate of the Ottoman Empire involved vital communications with India and even the "balance of power in Europe." He identified three options. The Turks might agree to the demands of the insurgents, which would mean autonomy if not independence for Bosnia and Herzegovina; an international conference might be summoned but its success would depend on a prior understanding among the powers, and there was little likelihood of it being reached; or the Sultan might be granted additional time to reach reasonable terms with his rebellious subjects. This option was unlikely to involve Britain in a dispute with the other interested nations and it would leave the door ajar to mediation; hence it was Derby's preferred choice. It was also Disraeli's, initially. Another palace revolution which deposed Murad V had put his brother Abdul Hamid II on the throne, and it was the prime minister's understanding that he would place himself entirely in Britain's hands. What was more, Disraeli had heard that he had abandoned the "old Seraglio life" for monogamy, having married a "very pretty" Belgian "modiste" whom he had encountered in Pera. Suspect as this romantic tale was, the stories of Turkish atrocities were all too credible.[25]

Shortly after Lyons returned to Paris the press reported the slaughter of Bulgaria's Christian peasants by Turkish irregulars. There were horrifying accounts of dogs feeding on the remains of humans, of headless skeletons, and of women wailing for their dead. As an appalled British public agitated for a reversal of policy, Disraeli unwisely strove to fend it off by minimizing the scale of the horrors. The result was acute embarrassment when Gladstone published a passionate indictment of the Turks. His *Bulgarian Horrors and the Question of the East* sold in excess of 200,000 copies in a mere three weeks. "I have never seen a more sudden or vehement outbreak of feeling than that which is making itself heard against the Porte just now," an uncomfortable Derby admitted to Lyons. "It will blow over like all other popular gusts, but meanwhile it strengthens Russia and weakens us abroad." Lyons was reduced to hoping that the "unfairness and extravagance" of the "Atrocitarian" protests would cause the public agitation to lose steam. "Diplomatists need thick skins if they are to work themselves to death in the public service and then meet with this sort of return," he grumbled. Opposition politicians, anti-Turks, women, and clergy, whom he identified as the protestors, had in his opinion no understanding of foreign politics. They failed to appreciate how difficult the Turks were to deal with, it being impossible to tell them to their faces that they were "a set of savages, who must not expect to be treated as if they were really members of the civilized community of European nations."[26]

Lyons was heartened by the evidence that the French were at last recovering from the extended postwar depression, with its wild, unreasoning cry for revenge on Prussia. Hope and confidence were steadily returning. The nation's finances were prosperous, commerce was thriving, the army was experiencing an astonishing "resurrection," and the high levels of taxation required to implement near-universal military service were being cheerfully borne. This revival of French military strength was a welcome development, Lyons again stressed, seeing it as he still did as one means of correcting the imbalance of power in Europe. France would, of course, continue to avoid a premature quarrel with Germany. It would also continue to maintain friendly relations with Britain if only to ensure the British did not fall into a German embrace. Less welcome was France's cautious wooing of Russia as a possible ally, for that objective might induce France, in the current Eastern crisis, to make "great sacrifices of western interests in the Levant."[27]

The six powers that had been signatories of the Treaty of Paris in 1856 agreed each to send two representatives to Constantinople to seek a settlement. Thought was given in London to naming Lyons as the lead British delegate, but continuing political turmoil in Paris, and the probability that the new government led by Jules Simon would be short-lived, kept him where he was. Instead, Lord Salisbury was named. Salisbury being secretary of state for India, the discussions would involve his area of responsibility, he would as a member of the government speak with greater authority than a diplomat, he would be able to defend any settlement in Parliament, and he was unlikely to be "easily talked over." He stopped in Paris on his way to the East to confer with Lyons, who introduced him to Decazes and persuaded him to add Rome to his travel itinerary. The reform proposals on which Salisbury and the other delegates subsequently agreed were quickly rejected by the Porte despite the certainty that the decision would be followed by war with Russia.[28]

With the outbreak of fighting in April, Lyons was surprised by the more assertive French policy on Egypt. The German ambassador in

London had earlier encouraged Britain to take advantage of the Eastern crisis to occupy a country attached so tenuously to the Ottoman Empire. Derby assumed, reasonably enough, that Bismarck was seeking to divide Britain from France and draw it "into a close alliance with Germany." Lyons had suggested that pride would cause the French to hide from the world their mortification at being ousted from Egypt, but with the Turks hard pressed by the Russians he discovered they were quietly discouraging the Khedive from assisting the Sultan even with money. This not only ensured that he retained the funds to pay French bondholders, but it also promised to please the Russians and frustrate British efforts to aid the Porte. If as a result they gained Russia as an ally, Lyons expected the French to strive to recover their influence in Egypt. To guard against this possibility, he recommended the maintenance of British naval superiority in the Mediterranean.[29]

Decazes, in leaning towards Russia, was in Lyons's opinion playing a "dangerous game." Germans keen to attack France before it became more powerful would welcome this fresh supply of ammunition. But the hope that fear of Germany would induce the French to be more anxious to appease Britain in matters of trade was quickly snuffed out by yet another ministerial crisis. MacMahon dismissed Simon – as Lyons admitted he had been a comprehensive failure as premier – the president giving as his reason Simon's concessions to the Left, which included the failure to close newspapers that attacked Germany. The new premier was Broglie. MacMahon had turned out a ministry which commanded a majority in the recently elected Chamber of Deputies, an incredulous Lyons remarked, and had replaced it with one composed of men personally and politically obnoxious to that majority. Broglie later defended the decision as the inevitable consequence of a presidency that was both elective and irresponsible. Elected by conservative Monarchists, the marshal had suddenly found himself "debarred from serving that cause, nay, ordered as it were, to desert and betray that cause." However, MacMahon's provocative conduct, and his securing Senate consent for a dissolution, united the normally fractious 363 Republican deputies. They issued a manifesto denouncing the president's actions, and Lyons again shook his head in disbelief when the Right depicted the confrontation as one between the *canaille* and the aristocracy. Conservatives were "thereby wounding the sentiment of equality which is the strongest political and social sentiment in France," he observed, and the crisis "is increasingly regarded as the last struggle of the old society against the new."[30]

On the day the potentially far-reaching political crisis erupted in Paris, 16 May 1877, the British Cabinet was preoccupied with the danger of a Russian advance into Constantinople. On learning what was happening in the French capital, Derby must have complimented himself on declining to send Lyons, as Disraeli proposed, on a mission to Vienna. "In the critical state of the world," the foreign secretary considered this fresh complication a misfortune. The news that Decazes had again survived as foreign minister did offer hope of continuity in French policy, but Lyons was becoming suspicious of the ever-friendly Frenchman. He had used his influence to secure a loan for Russia in Paris, and this prodded Bismarck, keen to maintain Russian friendship, to further the czar's policy in the East. Lyons suspected the Frenchman of seeking to involve Britain in a quarrel with Germany and of manoeuvring to prevent any increase of British naval power in the Mediterranean. Do not make an agreement with Decazes on the Suez Canal, Lyons cautioned the foreign secretary, listing the "numerous objections" to the foreign minister's proposal of an Anglo-French protectorate of Egypt and Syria: it was designed to prevent Britain acting alone in its own interests; France would prove an untrustworthy partner should Russia, against whom they would be acting, offer it hope of help to recover Alsace and Lorraine; the two nations would almost certainly fall to quarrelling over a protectorate; and Britain would still lack absolutely secure swift communication with India.[31]

With the French government committed to spending three months preparing for the elections, and having remained at his post for fourteen months, Lyons summoned to Paris the new secretary of embassy, Francis Adams, to act in his absence. Adams was currently at a Swiss spa recovering from bouts of heavy drinking. Lyons, suffering still with a painful infected throat, declined to expose himself to the risk of typhoid, which he believed the repair of the embassy's drains would present. At his meetings with Disraeli and Derby in early August he argued for greater British intervention in the Eastern crisis. Russia should understand that Britain would act if certain limits were "overpassed."

Personally, he favoured the creation of a rapid reaction force of 60,000 men but doubted it would be funded by Parliament. "When the danger is actually at the door, there may be unanimity in England," he admitted, "but then it may be too late." At least the Mediterranean fleet was strengthened as he had recommended. France, he recognized, wished to extricate Russia from the war with Turkey without any loss of its usefulness as a potential ally against Germany. However, the French approach to a settlement of the conflict promised to be shaped also by a resolve to halt the growth of British influence in Egypt. Hence this might be the moment for Britain to acquire that country. Not surprisingly, the non-interventionist Derby "opened on him at once as to Egypt" when they met on 6 August. Lyons, the foreign secretary complained, had "half-persuaded" Sir Stafford Northcote, the chancellor of the exchequer, when they had met in Paris earlier in the year, that Britain should take the country. Derby disdained this "very diplomatic view" of property acquisition by questionable means in order not to be thought outwitted. Lyons replied: "This is the point of view from which we learn to look at things."[32]

On leaving the Foreign Office Lyons went directly to the consulting rooms of Sir William Jenner, who referred him to Dr Hermann Weber, a German authority on "consumption" with a practice in London. The referral suggests a suspicion that this was a possible root cause of Lyons's persistent coughing and shortness of breath. After a round of official and social calls, he set out on Weber's advice for Bad Ems. He was accompanied, as ever, by Sheffield, Giuseppe, the faithful manservant, and Toby the dog. Lyons was so attached to the animal that whenever there was a spare chair at the embassy dining table, and no guests, Toby was seated. Prostration was the initial and usual effect of his daily consumption of several glasses of the water, and inhalations were subsequently added to the regimen. He had companionship even after Sheffield fled to England complaining that the town's atmosphere was so "close" that he felt like "a plum pudding in a bag." Lyons's elder sister Annie and her husband joined him until Sheffield returned in mid-September to escort him back to England. He arrived there "sound of limb but still not of wind" yet still undertook his annual country house trek. His night at Hughenden Manor proved to be less comfortable than he had anticipated.

"We have not a servant in the house," his host, the prime minister, wrote to a female friend, "all being engaged in a grand cricket match in the park with a neighbouring parish. It is impossible to disturb them. We are at our wit's end." At Woburn Abbey, where Disraeli and Odo Russell were fellow guests, there was an opportunity to discuss French and German affairs. France was "where what may happen God, or rather Satan, only knows," Disraeli remarked, whereas Bismarck "might figure, indeed, as Satan himself." The prime minister probably told them of the chancellor's astonishingly frank statement of his objectives on the eve of becoming minister-president of Prussia in 1862. He planned, he told Disraeli, to reorganize the army, seize the first pretext for declaring war on Austria, dissolve the German Diet, and give national unity to Germany under Prussian leadership. The fulfilment of the last resolve had required the removal of the French obstacle. Disraeli's confidence in the current instance that "determined language" would deter a Russian occupation of Constantinople was in the opinion of Lyons misplaced. It meant war if it failed to have the desired effect, he remarked to a receptive foreign secretary, because "a mere game of brag never succeeds." Furthermore, Disraeli grossly overestimated Britain's military capability when he spoke of dispatching "100,000 men to the east."[33]

Lyons returned to Paris on 20 October 1877 and he found it still mired in a political crisis. The unpopular government, in a desperate search for a majority, had revived the manipulative electoral practices and devices of the Second Empire. In response, the Chamber's elected Republican majority invalidated seventy returns on the grounds of administrative and electoral intervention. The ensuing by-elections inflated their number to almost 400, leaving Bonapartists the largest segment of the Conservative minority. That the crisis dragged on for two months was the result of MacMahon's stubborn refusal to name a government acceptable to the Republicans. Then, in early December, the former marshal made an "ignominious surrender." He affirmed loyalty to parliamentary rules, acknowledged that dissolution was not acceptable as a method of government, and named Jules Dufaure to form a Centre Left ministry. Explaining his political capitulation to Lyons, MacMahon claimed he had been driven to it by a German threat to take action if he retired or set up an ultramontane administration. None of this reassured

Lyons that France had finally achieved political stability because no single party commanded a majority in a Chamber where factions united to pull down but not to prop up. This, he sadly admitted, was the "ordinary course of French politics." He fully expected the political extremes, the "Reds" and the Bonapartists, to ally to topple the Dufaure government. The "motives of the Legitimists and their Roy" remained, he mocked, "too transcendental for any ordinary calculations."[34]

There was no government for him to deal with, he complained. Decazes, on his return from his remote Gironde constituency, had the haunted look of a condemned man and went quickly to the political gallows. His successor, the Marquis de Banneville, another former diplomat, was a political nonentity with whom Lyons considered it pointless to engage. He concentrated instead on sprucing up the embassy before the opening of the Paris Exhibition in May, took more exercise by walking to the Arc de Triomphe and back, no great distance, and the length of the Champs Élysées, and consulted Dr Noël Guéneau de Mussy, a specialist in diaphragmatic pleurisy, the symptoms of which were all too familiar: chest pain, cough, and shortness of breath. After thirteen consultations, Mussy halted the arsenic pills which were supposed to aid hill walkers and mountain climbers and instructed Lyons to return to inhalations. Meanwhile, the arrival of William Henry Waddington at the Quai d'Orsay had revived Lyons's interest in diplomacy. Son of a wealthy British textile manufacturer who had chosen to become a French subject and had married a French woman, the young Waddington had been sent to England for the education of a gentleman. Public school, in his case Rugby, where he had been a friend of Francis Adams, had been followed by Cambridge University, where he had excelled athletically as well as academically. He had been a member of the crew which won the boat race against Oxford, an event which was being transformed into an annual event. In 1876 his election to the Senate saw him begin a political career in middle age, and his reputation was that of "an able & moderate man, with great self confidence, quite ignorant of Foreign Affairs, and likely to take unexpected steps." Of course, his English background, his friendship with Lyons, whom his American wife condescendingly described as a "big simple schoolboy," aroused the suspicions of members of his own party and of the officials of his ministry. He would, Lyons realized, have to demonstrate that he was truly French.[35]

Waddington would be less Russian than Decazes, would avoid quarrelling with Germany, and would give as little offence as possible to any other power, Lyons predicted. As no doubt he expected, the foreign minister was especially assertive on Egypt, where the Khedive was "getting matters into a terrible mess possibly in hopes of escaping his promises and engagements by means of a financial catastrophe." British occupation of Egypt would create bitter feeling in France, Waddington warned, but Lyons remained confident that the French, still "paralysed" by fear of Germany, would not risk conflict to prevent it. Should Britain decide to confront Russian aggression in the East, however, there was a possibility that the popular craving in France for territorial expansion, which in Europe was blocked by Germany, might focus on Egypt. But the talk in London's diplomatic community of Britain drifting towards war with Russia served to reawaken in the minds of French ministers the unpleasant possibility of suddenly finding themselves facing Germany alone. Derby's determination to avoid war at almost any price had seen him fall out of royal favour and at loggerheads with Disraeli, and the strain of resisting actions that might heighten the danger of a conflict was taking its toll on him. There were rumours of heavy drinking, although Lady Derby, whose personal conduct was a source of much society gossip, assured Lyons that the problem was a severe intestinal attack. Derby and Carnarvon then resigned from the Cabinet in protest to the measures it adopted but returned when they were rescinded. This decision was made easier by the armistice negotiated by the Turks and the Russians and the signing of "ambiguous and elastic" provisional terms of peace which opened the door to a congress on the Eastern question.[36]

Derby declined to represent Britain. He had yet to recover fully from his illness and with his recent Cabinet difficulties clearly in mind had no wish to find himself implementing at the end of a telegraph line policies which he might not have influenced. Lyons was the "fittest person," he insisted. He did his best to reassure Lyons, who had earlier expressed sympathy for the plight of a Briton at a Congress where the French and the Germans would be competing for the good opinion of the Russians. He would not be alone, Derby wrote, for the Austrians and the Italians would in this instance be allies and the French benevolent neutrals. Even if the Russians entered Constantinople this would not be made a *casus belli*, and the presence of the fleets of neutrals would ensure the maintenance of order. Barely a week later, and ignoring the fears of a terrified Sultan that the appearance of a British squadron would goad the Russians into seizing his capital, six Royal Navy ironclads anchored near the city. Their arrival was an immense relief to Austen Henry Layard, who although a Liberal had been transferred from Madrid to Constantinople by Disraeli. The Russians, he reported, had by tricks and manoeuvres of "the most utter barbarians" made themselves masters of the Ottoman capital. Would they be prevented from occupying it? Lyons, as he told the pacifist Derby, was "far from thinking peace at any price compatible with the interest or even the safety of England." Russia needed to be left in no doubt that other powers were "in a position to interfere with her arrangements by material force." Unless Austria was "ready for war and determined to use force if necessary, and Britain equally determined and ready," and unless the Russians were convinced of this, he doubted they would make concessions. In short, he was now aligned more closely with Disraeli than with Derby.[37]

The news that Lyons was to be Britain's lead representative at the Congress to be held in Berlin saw his fitness questioned in the Commons by the obnoxious Sir Robert Peel, who accused him of being willing to accept the dissolution of the Ottoman Empire. The attack fizzled, and Lyons was soon inundated with requests from persons of influence keen to join his staff. These he tactfully declined. Determined to be as well prepared as possible, he submitted to the Foreign Office requests for a mass of documents – protocols, treaties, parliamentary papers, population returns showing different nationalities, ethnographical maps, and travel books. Since all telegrams sent via Paris to the Foreign Office were copied and studied by France's *cabinet noir*, and supposing that other countries behaved in the same way, he stressed the necessity of a secure cipher. He drafted a long memorandum on the issues which so impressed Derby that he had it printed and circulated to his Cabinet colleagues. Meeting with the ministers on 7 March Lyons explained to them that "France wants quiet, no conference or no active part in it. Wishes to act with us as to Egypt or to prevent our acting alone." He joined the small Cabinet committee struck to draft his instructions, and when he and John Bright were fellow dinner guests of the banker Frederick Hankey he impressed the old Radical as a "sensible man, calm of temper and serious." Had Lyons been at Constantinople, Bright jotted in his diary, "affairs might have been different." However, when the Russians refused to allow the terms of peace they had imposed on the Turks to be added to the Congress's agenda, the Cabinet on 27 March decided to take "further drastic measures." Derby resigned.[38]

Both the Queen and Stafford Northcote suggested Lyons as Derby's replacement, but Salisbury was Disraeli's choice. He had emerged as the most eager supporter in Cabinet of the prime minister's proposals for action and exhibited a degree of cynicism, realism, and ruthlessness that appealed to him. "Diplomacy which does not rest on force is the most feeble and futile of weapons," Salisbury had responded to one critic of the government's foreign policy, "and except for bare self-defence we have not the force." In Cabinet, he had been contemptuous of the moral scruples voiced by some of his colleagues, remarking that had their ancestors cared for the rights of other people "the British empire would not have been made." Decisive and practical, he accepted the halt in the preparations for the Congress while additional naval and military pressure was applied to Russia. By early June the path to the German capital had been cleared with the negotiation of three secret treaties. An Anglo-Turkish Convention provided for Britain's occupation of Cyprus and a defensive alliance; Austria-Hungary was assured of Britain's support for its annexation of Bosnia-Herzegovina and the creation of a smaller Bulgaria; while Russia secured Bessarabia and a number of minor gains in Asia. But there were strong doubts that the Balkans would long remain calm, for the survival of the Ottoman Empire appeared even more problematic. Lyons now learned that Disraeli and Salisbury were going to Berlin to complete the settlement, for the "threads" of the recent negotiations had been in their hands, news he greeted with a sigh of relief. But to ease any discomfort he might experience, he was assured that he was needed in Paris, where dangerous questions were again looming.[39]

Britain's acquisition of Cyprus was causing great irritation in France "from high society down to strong Republicans." Layard's letters from Constantinople were full of the "extreme susceptibility and the jealous suspicion of England" exhibited by a devious French ambassador and his staff. Lyons speculated that French agents would soon be scheming to trip his country up in Egypt. Do not drive France into a Russian embrace "by rejecting or even receiving with coldness" any friendly overtures from Paris, he advised Salisbury. If Britain ensured that French holders of Turkish and Egyptian bonds profited it might reconcile the French to both its occupation of Cyprus and its defensive "protectorate" of Ottoman Asia Minor. In Egypt, where the French motto was "share and share alike," it was important not to behave as if Britain controlled the administration. Lyons's objective was to protect Waddington, whom he feared might be made the scapegoat for the perceived reverses suffered by France in Berlin. The foreign minister's loss of office would be a personal and political blow. "English blood and English education mean he is more straightforward than most Frenchmen, that he understands and shares many English feelings, and sees the force of arguments advanced in an English way," Lyons impressed on Salisbury. If forced out of office it would be because he was regarded as insufficiently tough in his dealings with Britain, and his successor would behave accordingly.[40]

Lyons did his own part by making good use of the £2,000 he received from the Treasury to cover "partially" the costs of entertaining during the Paris Exposition. He had an enthusiastic partner in the Prince of Wales, who invited the Ultra Republican Gambetta to breakfast, during which he declared himself an enthusiast of a Franco-British alliance. Lyons had Waddington to lunch with the Prince, though the latter was politely reminded by Salisbury that he had trespassed upon Cabinet business when at a public dinner he declared an entente cordiale essential to the peace of Europe. But frantic fence mending taxed Lyons's depleted physical resources. So when Waddington, like so many of his fellow countrymen, went on vacation in August, the French chambers recessed, and Parliament was up at home, Lyons followed his doctor's orders to take his ease. He decided to sample the waters of Wootten Hall, Henly In Arden. Wootten Warwen was a classic English village five miles north of Stratford upon Avon, its main street an attractive collection of fifteenth- and sixteenth-century buildings. After three weeks of his retreat, a rested Lyons returned to London, where he met briefly with Salisbury before embarking again on the country house circuit. But reports that the Egyptian question was becoming troublesome in Paris led him to make a hurried return there at the end of September. At his meeting with Waddington, the Frenchman asked for concessions that would allow him to claim that France had not lost ground in Egypt. That he sought French control of the port of Alexandria and of Egyptian railways as the British sacrifices to his nation's vanity was peculiarly unfortunate because, as Lyons pointed out to Salisbury, France would then be in a position to threaten important British interests. Half of Egypt's imports came from Britain and four-fifths of its exports went there. He did not forget that the purchase of the Canal shares notwithstanding, the waterway remained in French hands. He resolved, therefore, to avoid discussion of Egypt and was able to utilize as an excuse the persistent ministerial instability. The Centre Left government was hoping that the Senate elections in January would free it of Gambetta's "oppressive protection." Then, on the eve of those elections, the government gave the required notice of the termination on 1 January 1880 of the Commercial Treaty with Britain. The minister of commerce was more than half a protectionist and Waddington less than half a free trader, Lyons moaned.[41]

In the general election, Republicans won 66 of the 82 Senate seats being contested. Then on 28 January 1879 Lyons learned from a "good source," probably Waddington, that MacMahon, rather than sign the decrees submitted by Dufaure which removed "old comrades" from their military commands, was resigning the presidency. With impressive speed, Jules Grévy, "a drab, cautious, tightfisted lawyer" with "impeccable republican credentials," and currently president of the Chamber of Deputies, became "the first president of the Third Republic to be elected according to the forms defined by the laws of 1875." On the political spectrum, Lyons placed him somewhere between Gambetta's Union Républicaine and the Centre Left. Clearly the Republicans were at long last "masters of the government." Gambetta took the presidency of the Chamber that Grévy had vacated, which elevated him out of the "Bohemian ruck" and was considered a stepping stone to higher office. Waddington added the presidency of the Council of Ministers to the Foreign Ministry only for his relations with Gambetta to be complicated by Bismarck's expression of esteem for the new premier. The German's mischievous intervention added to Lyons's skepticism about the government's chances of survival. Waddington's limitations as a speaker, his slight English accent, and his English education prevented him from having "exactly French modes of thought and French ways," which meant that he was "never completely in tune with the feelings of his listeners." The insults and intimidation to which he and his ministers were subjected in the legislature by Bonapartist bullies underscored their inability to dominate it. In the country at large, the ministers were dismissed as mere "warming pans" for Gambetta. Not surprisingly, Lyons found it difficult to conduct much business with a foreign minister who was also the leader of a government chronically in crisis.[42]

There was no shortage of issues, however. The denunciation of the Commercial Treaty could not be allowed to pass without a British protest. French anger over the conduct of the British consul general in Tunis eventually required the deletion of the post from the service to get rid of the objectionable individual. Waddington's suggested nominee as ambassador to the Court of St James's, Emmanuel-Henry, Marquis de Noailles, was objected to vehemently by the Queen. His wife, a Pole, had notoriously been his mistress while married to an elderly gentleman. Neither the pair's prompt union on her being widowed, nor her acceptance by French society, made them acceptable to Victoria. The French were further aggrieved at the news that the Prince Imperial was accompanying a British force sent to South Africa to suppress the Zulus. His death during the campaign, which aided the Republicans by dismaying Bonapartists, created another storm in a teacup when several members of the British royal family attended his funeral. Their presence did not give the obsequies an official character, Salisbury patiently explained. "In a purely constitutional country it is the action of the government not that of the Royal Family which gives an official character to any proceeding." But the most persistent Anglo-French problem was the "blessed Egyptian question" on which Lyons complained he was beset with "telegrams, interviews and whatnot."[43]

Egypt would never prosper so long as one-quarter of its revenues were earmarked to pay the interest on the debt, Salisbury realized. Two European controllers had been appointed in 1876 to supervise income and expenditures, and two years later a Briton and a Frenchman took the key financial positions in the Khedive's Cabinet. European influence should be confined to positions of criticism and control, Salisbury believed, and he rejected, as the French seemingly did not, going into partnership with unhappy bondholders. To serve as their "sheriff's officer" would be a new and embarrassing sensation for Britons, he disdainfully remarked. Similarly, he was determined to prevent the French from gaining a special ascendancy in Egypt. His objective was a firm British hold on the Egyptian government but without the assumption of "any overt responsibility." They needed to exchange the nominal authority of ministers for "real inspectorship," and, having taken to heart a Lyons warning, he informed the new commissioner of the Egyptian debt, Evelyn Baring, that the country would be run under Anglo-French dual authority.[44]

Unfortunately, articles in the British press nourished French suspicions that Britain was planning to throw them over in Egypt. "How often do newspapers thwart the efforts of government and their agents to promote good will among nations," a weary Lyons remarked. Even articles intended to be conciliatory rubbed the French the wrong way, while editorials often had an annoyingly patronizing and pedagogical tone. They should, he advised, "humour French diplomats abroad, and the French public at home, who are beginning to think France has become too strong to play a secondary part any longer." But the French must not be allowed to gain control of Egypt's finances, nor be permitted to introduce their language and system of accounting, for they might prove more dangerous and lasting.[45]

It had been another hectic year for Lyons. The Prince of Wales had made yet another of his private visits only to scorn the new president on hearing that he had married his cook. Lyons was more appreciative of Madame Grévy, who on one occasion loaned to him the presidential box at the Opera. The Queen's decision to stay at the embassy while travelling to and from the Italian Piedmont resort of Baveno obliged him to arrange for additional police protection, concerned as he remained for her safety in a city where Irish revolutionary nationalists were known to be present. By this time the monarch had been assigned a metropolitan police detective inspector for her European vacations. He was George Greenham, who spoke several European languages and whose mother had been an intimate friend of the Queen of Naples, which made him socially as well as linguistically acceptable. Victoria rewarded Lyons for his attention to her safety and comfort with a pair of prints of herself and Princess Beatrice, which she suggested he hang in one of his rooms. The government, as a mark of its appreciation of his public services, awarded him the Grand Cross of St Michael and St George.[46]

CHAPTER SIXTEEN

Endings

Lyons detected an almost universal feeling of unease in Paris on his return there from leave in November 1879. Were the "Ultra Reds" gaining power? Waddington was driven from office on 28 December and replaced by Charles de Freycinet. The former minister of public works, he had served under Gambetta in the Provisional government of 1870–1. Lyons dubbed his Council of Ministers the "Gambetta Cabinet." Yet he hoped for a period of relative calm, assuming that nothing "great" would be attempted until Gambetta took the premiership himself. However, the policy that had been identified closely with the late Thiers – that of preserving as far as was possible with an elective presidency the traditional institutions, laws, and administrative system of France – seemed dead and buried. The Conservative Republic envisaged by Thiers had required for its successful establishment an able and energetic president, which it had failed to find. As a result, Lyons was anticipating a French experiment, one he considered dangerous, with "real democratic and republican government."

The weather in Paris throughout the winter had been "unendurable," and he had again been laid up with influenza. Increasingly, his chronic poor health saw him take leave every July or early August and return around the middle of October. Gladstone, who "had fallen into a vicious habit of regarding diplomatic health as varying conveniently with the seasons and always hitting the proper holiday," noted during a stay at the embassy with his wife that their host was not "in strong health." Occasionally, Lyons visited Germany for the *Kur*, or sought rest in Switzerland, but more often than not he went home. The country air, he believed, reinvigorated him, relieved his bronchitis, and was therapy for his "violent and painful cough." With large-scale reconstruction under way at Arundel Castle, Minna had leased Heron's Ghyll, a large house if not a mansion near Uckfield in East Sussex. It now became her brother's country retreat. The owner's second wife, a woman of nun-like devotions and habits, had required his conversion to Catholicism as the price of her consent to marry him, and this association suited the dowager duchess. But Lyons's family connection briefly threatened to be embarrassing when his young nephew, the duke, met the Comte de Chambord, and this led to talk of Britain's ambassador to France being a Legitimist sympathizer. Such gossip threatened to harm his relations with elements of the Liberal party, which returned to office shortly before his sixty-third birthday in 1880.[1]

Troubles in South Africa and the murder in Kabul of the British minister and his staff by mutinous Afghan soldiers had taken much of the shine off the Tories' imperial policies. An increase in the income tax did not cover the increased expenditures, and the resultant budget deficit unfortunately equalled the surplus inherited from the Liberals six years earlier. During the election campaign, the Marquis of Hartington, the nominal Liberal leader, promised a foreign policy of non-intervention. He declared that Britain would preserve peace by remaining free of alliances with foreign powers. Little wonder Derby soon joined the Liberal caucus. All of the while Gladstone was not behaving like a retired former leader. He announced six "right principles of foreign policy" without making "absolute commitments" to them and without disavowing the agreements entered into by the Tories. The equal rights of all nations, good government at home, the preservation of peace abroad, the maintenance of the Concert of Europe, the avoidance of needless entanglements, and an undertaking to be guided by the love of freedom made up his package. As for the long-simmering problem of Egypt, he was on record as having rejected the inevitability of Britain's occupation of that country. Once the election results were in, the Queen invited

Hartington to form a government. This decision was motivated by her
intense personal dislike of Gladstone and in response to the advice of
Disraeli. She discovered to her chagrin that the party was determined
to have Gladstone at the head of the government and he accepted her
commission on 23 April.[2]

For the office of foreign secretary, three names were on most lips:
Hartington, Kimberley, and Granville. The Marquis was generally considered unqualified, for he reportedly knew little of foreign affairs,
spoke poor French, and was "insufficiently married." This was a delicate allusion to the Duchess of Manchester, his paramour of many years.
They were eventually to wed in 1892, following the death of her husband and Hartington's succession as Duke of Devonshire. Kimberley
was dismissed as a "chattering idiot," leaving Granville, who had held
the porfolio in the previous Gladstone administration. Although still
regarded as somewhat indolent, a reputation first acquired years earlier as undersecretary, he had a close relationship with Gladstone and
was identified with "moderation." This promised to be of value in the
current state of foreign relations. Convinced that the Ottoman Empire
would soon fall to pieces, he was anxious to know from Lyons whether
the French had any decided views on what should then be done. Was
Freycinet dependent upon or independent of Gambetta? he asked, and
what was known of the latter's views? Was the current French ambassador in London, Léon Say, trustworthy? What were his views on foreign
problems, and would he truly represent Freycinet? Rather than commit
himself on paper, Lyons returned home on 4 May and discussed these
matters personally with Granville. Then, having paid his respects to the
Queen, and having met with Hartington, Kimberley, and Gladstone, he
returned to Paris.[3]

Léon Say's decision to accept the presidency of the French Senate
obliged the French to name a successor as ambassador. They first revived the Noailles candidacy only to discover that Victoria's objection
to him had been strengthened by the stories that he had been only one
of his wife's four lovers before their marriage, "one for each season of
the year." The marquise was "dull, large and very pious looking, the
most respectable of women, as she had been since her marriage," Say
assured the British. Although Granville denied any personal hostility

to "Magdalenes," he was sure the Queen was right to keep diplomatic standards high. Objections might have been made also to Paul-Armand Challemel-Lacour, an intimate of Gambetta indeed the former editor of his newspaper, *République Française*, who had been serving as ambassador to Switzerland. He inspired dread in the members of the French embassy in London, perhaps because of his associations with the Extreme Left in French politics. Nervous juniors may have spread the stories that he was living with a washerwoman who posed as his grandmother, and that while prefect of the Rhône in 1870 he had executed a number of monks. Nevertheless, Lyons intervened forcibly to ensure he was accepted. He had been named by the French "with their eyes open," he impressed upon the Foreign Office. Challemel-Lacour's greatest fault, the Prince of Wales learned, perhaps making inquiries on his mother's behalf, was a violent temper.[4]

France had embarked, with Bismarck's blessing, on a "spirited colonial policy." The German chancellor, Lyons suspected, was seeking to confirm the Reich's supremacy in Europe by shuffling Austria into the Levant, Russia into Asia, France into Africa and the Mediterranean, and confining Britain to its islands. Odo Russell considered the policy defensive. By diverting the French from Alsace and Lorraine, he explained, Bismarck was gratifying their vanity at little cost to Germany and dispersing overseas their ever more formidable army. Furthermore, French imperial adventures promised to create irritants in their relationship with Britain. The likelihood of this did not escape Lyons. Scattered around the globe were islands and territories whose annexation by France might be prejudicial to British interests, and places where an extension of French influence might prove dangerous to Britain or where high-handed French conduct might lead to quarrels. Thus in Somalia and Burma the French consuls were proving the "worst of bedfellows." The French protectorate of Tunis, to which they believed Salisbury and Disraeli had agreed at Berlin, was creating problems for the new Liberal government because of the suspicions of the British press that the French would seek to curtail British trade there. Jealousy of France was excited not by its possession of "barbarous districts," Granville agreed, but by its establishment of differential privileges to the benefit of its own subjects. Beyond commercial concerns lay the strategic threat of French imperialism. Colonel Brackenbury, a former military attaché in Paris, now a member of the War Office staff, slipped a secret memorandum to his former chief. The French, it warned, were putting themselves in a position to threaten Sierra Leone, which in the event of war would be an important coaling station between Gibraltar and the Cape. On the other side of Africa, their control of Madagascar and the Mozambique Channel would allow them to threaten the route from the Cape to India. Similarly, they were well positioned in the Gulf of Aden to threaten communications with India via the Suez Canal and the Red Sea.[5]

Lyons was convinced that in French imperialism there was a "vast amount of dirty pecuniary stockjobbing interests at the bottom, which have been the real motive power." Tunis he considered a "very bad augury" in that it might encourage the French to engage in other overbearing proceedings whenever the risk appeared to be slight. Borrowing imagery from Gambetta, he described Tunis as a glass of wine for a convalescent France whose taste might tempt it to try stronger stimulants. However, so long as French chauvinism was not nourished by British condemnation of the "spirited Colonial policy," it might eventually fall into "great discredit." Lyons sought to apply this policy to the "hideous traffick" of the controversial "Coolie trade" between India and the French sugar island of Réunion. *The Times* stoked the fire of British indignation with its exposure of the appalling French treatment of the Indian labourers. Yet Lyons supported France's request for the removal of the British consul on the island, arguing that he was ill-suited to the delicate nature of the position and endangered amicable relations. When the Indian government still halted the shipment of coolies, demanding that the French adopt the safeguards required of British colonies, Lyons successfully recommended that the French be assured the trade would resume just as soon as they agreed to the conditions of the Indian government. Otherwise, he warned, there was a possibility that they would revive, if on a small scale, the "Negro Slave Trade" with Portuguese Africa. Of course, Britain did not have the same responsibility for "Portuguese negroes" as it did for "our own Indian fellow-subjects."[6]

If French colonial policy raised "ticklish" problems, the Commercial Treaty and Egypt remained the dominant issues in the relationship. Holding both Treasury portfolios, Gladstone rejected as chancellor of the exchequer a "supplicating attitude" on trade. The Treasury would have the last word on revenues. Bearing in mind the deficit inherited from the Tories, there would be no immediate reduction of the current duty on French wines. Indeed, his interest in negotiations weakened as the French "spirit of Protection" deepened with the worsening of their economic recession. Léon Say, while still ambassador, had evidently been "instructed to dance on the edge of a razor, which for a person of his ample proportions is difficult." But Lyons cautioned against allowing the French to blame British "diplomatic dilatoriness" for any suspension of negotiations. The instability of French ministries meant that a change of government was always possible, and if a new government found the treaty under discussion it might agree to acceptable terms. Consequently, negotiations should be pursued "as seriously and as steadily as is compatible with not committing ourselves to any decidedly objectionable duties so definitively as to be hampered in subsequent negotiations if we find the new Government fairly disposed towards us." This sound diplomatic advice was spurred by the desire to maintain good relations and the hope that Gambetta would soon take office. What Lyons envisaged was a "simple most favoured nation Treaty," leaving it to nations unencumbered with a commitment to free trade to extract with threats of retaliation better terms from France. Britain would then benefit from these.[7]

The bargain being contemplated by the Gladstone Cabinet was a reduction of wine duties at some future date in exchange for a more liberal French treatment of British textiles. The phylloxera ravaging the vineyards made such an exchange impossible because France became an importer of wines. And even when Gambetta briefly took office he was only willing to offer, given the protectionism rampant in the Chamber, a modest adjustment of the general tariff. This fell well short of British requirements. What remained was the Lyons option, only for the French to demand a major concession in exchange. They insisted that Britain freeze its tariff, causing Lyons to bemoan his involvement in such a tiresome and labourious business. When the British balked, the French neatly secured their objective by extending most-favoured-nation treatment via legislation not a treaty. Lyons spotted the catch. "If the legislation is special to England," he explained, "the object of it will probably be to subject us to the severest possible penalties if we were to touch our own Tariff." In short, Britain remained at the mercy of the French. It had not been granted most-favoured-nation standing for a definite period, and were Britain to do anything to which the French took exception the Protectionists would demand the repeal of the law of 27 February 1882. This should be kept in mind, he advised the Foreign Office, even as it congratulated him on achieving "as great a success as was possible under the circumstances."[8]

Egypt was the other major issue. Writing to Granville shortly after a nationalist military revolt led by a Colonel Arabi deprived the Khedive of effective power and called into question the survival of the Anglo-French Dual Control, Gladstone summarized his response. Britain was "to act in concord with France, to aim at a *minimum* of interference, and to work for the good of Egypt itself." Edward Malet, now British consul general in Egypt, assured his former chief a few weeks later that things were "going smoothly at present." He did admit to being worried by talk of an Anglo-French invasion, for the lapse in time between the organization of an expeditionary force and its landing in Egypt would be "sufficient for fanaticism to deal a great mischief to a defenceless Christian population." The risk of "lighting up" Muslim extremism would be far less, he wrote, if under British supervision the Sultan intervened as suzerain. Granville agreed, as he made clear in his response to the French proposal of joint intervention. Action by Britain alone was certain to be opposed by the Egyptians, antagonize the French and the Turks, and perhaps excite European jealousy.[9]

Lyons had expected Egypt to be "the most perplexing question." The French, he believed, were anticipating Tewfik's ouster by Arabi as Khedive and his replacement by Halim Pacha, a grandson of Mehemet Ali. To prevent this he proposed an Anglo-French joint statement making plain their refusal to tolerate either Tewfik's removal or the dismantling of the current system of government. If the two nations were in a position to resort to force, Lyons was confident the situation might be rescued. Gladstone's plan for a Concert of Europe he effectively quashed in a "very able letter." He warned that it would amount to the abandonment of the exceptional position the two nations enjoyed and would have a "very bad" effect on relations with France. The French would suspect that Britain intended to use the other powers to help it push France out of Egypt. Their union in that country, he reminded the Cabinet, was the principal symbol of their good understanding, and for this reason alone the French attached great significance to it. Anyway, he would far prefer to deal with France than with a group of other powers. As for the idea of employing Turkish troops in the belief that they would not excite Muslim fanaticism, a new French prime minister, Charles de Freycinet, was insistent that any Turkish intervention not be by force of arms. Once there, he argued, they would prolong their presence in order to get their hands on the Treasury and interfere with the administration. This possibility had no appeal for Lyons or for French bondholders. Equally unattractive to him was the "strictly confidential, personal, private and academic" manner in which the French accepted limited, non-violent Turkish intervention. These "between ourselves" talks invariably "cause mischief," he warned Granville.[10]

The killing of several Europeans by nationalists in the port city of Alexandria, and rumours that "the Military Egyptian party or roving bands of Bedouins" were threatening an attack on the canal, provided activists in the Gladstone Cabinet with the excuse for "decisive measures." Auckland Colvin, the British chancellor of Egyptian finance and acting consul general in the absence of Malet, who was in Venice recuperating after a fever, added to the pressure for action. Things were as bad as they could be, administratively, financially, and commercially, he telegraphed Lyons on 26 June, and unless prompt measures were taken to restore order and confidence the ruin would be intensified. The Gladstone government demanded the execution of the nationalists who had killed the Europeans and compensation for the injured, for the families of the dead, and for the owners of destroyed property. In addition, the Egyptians were to stage ceremonial salutes of the British flag in Cairo and Alexandria. When, instead, the nationalists fortified Alexandria and the Royal Navy bombarded the port city, there were fresh riots. In response, the Gladstone Cabinet ordered the assembly of an expeditionary force of 15,000 men. The French were invited to participate and thought was given to inviting the Italians also, but Lyons argued successfully that the Cabinet should wait for the French response before extending other invitations. Freycinet's organ, La France,

had announced that he would act with the British only so long as they
acted in accordance with the decisions of the conference of ambassadors currently meeting in Constantinople. This the French defined as
intervention latérale. When the conference declined to sanction British
military action, Freycinet found himself twisting in the wind, and he resigned when the Chamber denied him the funds to assist in the protection of the Canal. Granville welcomed the news, having tagged him an
"Anglophobist" who was "intriguing with Arabi Bey." This was an idea
Lyons had unfortunately planted in his mind. Where did all of this leave
the relationship with France? Lyons listed three requirements for "good"
relations: Britain's prompt action and success in Egypt; the avoidance of
Turkish intervention; and the dissolution of the ambassadors' conference in Constantinople. By the middle of September 1882, Britain was
the "*de facto* ruler of Egypt."[11]

The Anglo-French rapprochement that Lyons had worked so hard to
achieve was in jeopardy. In a midnight telegram to Granville on 6 November 1882, he expressed alarm at the thought of the Gladstone government, without prior consultation with the French, responding to the
Khedive's request for abolition of Dual Control. "If we leave them bitterly discontented with arrangements in Egypt," he telegraphed, "I hardly
see when we shall be able to withdraw our troops and still maintain the
influence which is a necessity to us." Although the Liberal government
issued a circular to other powers on 3 January 1883, announcing Britain's
resolve to withdraw from Egypt "as soon as the country was settled," the
French government was not appeased. It would now "work against English influence in Egypt by every means in its power," Lyons predicted.
Britain's more influential role on the canal's directorate, and the assertive language of the British press, merely made matters worse. The canal,
Lyons emphasized, was the "really hazardous point in relations" because
it united French "pecuniary and sentimental interests." Hence his relief
when over dinner Gladstone gave an assurance that in his dealings with
Lesseps he would not take unfair or ungenerous advantage of Britain's
commanding influence in Egypt. Unfortunately, the parlous state of that
country's finances further endangered the understanding with France.
Britain, unwilling to assume greater responsibility for Egyptian debt, proposed a reduction of the interest being paid on Egyptian bonds. France

refused. As a result, the conference of interested powers that gathered in London in June 1884 in order to resolve the issue was dismissed by Liberal activists as a "fiasco." Britain's problem was how to keep France out of Egypt without formally annexing that country itself.[12]

The problem of Egypt's finances was clearly having a "disastrous effect" on Anglo-French relations. Lyons welcomed as a "great blessing," therefore, the Cabinet's acceptance of a French proposal – but only after a fierce debate which almost led to its disintegration – for the canal's neutralization and for an Egyptian loan guaranteed by all the powers. This gave those powers "complete control of Egyptian finances and made any further attempt at Egyptian reform dependent on European cooperation." Signed in March 1885, the agreement granted Egypt a "two-year breathing space" during which to put its finances in order by establishing levels of taxation adequate to make the reduced payments bondholders were now required to accept. That the entente cordiale with France had not yet been restored was apparent two years later when Lord Salisbury, prime minister and foreign secretary, complained that he could not see how Britain could devise terms on Egypt that would be acceptable to the troublesome French. They were seeking to terminate the arrangement on the Somali coast, were continuing to occupy New Hebrides, were destroying British fishing tackle off of Newfoundland's French shore, and were endeavouring to elbow Britain out of places on the West coast of Africa. "Can you wonder," he asked Lyons, as another Franco-German crisis loomed, "that there is, to my eyes, a silver lining to the great black cloud of a Franco-Prussian War"?[13]

Despite the prominence he had given foreign relations during the general election of 1880, Gladstone had hoped on assuming office to concentrate again on the Irish problem. The creation of the Irish Land League, committed to the abolition of "landlordism," and its melding with the radical element of the Home Rule movement led by the young Protestant gentleman Charles Stewart Parnell, had created a new sense of urgency. Parnell was thought to be involved with the American remnants of Fenianism, and in November 1880 a French newspaper, the *Gaulois*, reported that he was about to confer with the Fenians in Paris. Lyons was asked to discover all he could about Parnell's visit, but his intense dislike of covert activities had not diminished. He recommended the dispatch to Paris of British agents familiar with the Irish nationalists, that they be instructed to communicate with the embassy only in cases of absolute necessity, and that they be cautioned against approaches to the French authorities. Were they to do so, he informed the Foreign Office, Britain could expect a reciprocal request with respect to French political refugees living in London. So when Parnell complained in the Commons that he had been followed in Paris by a pair of detectives who reported to the embassy, Lyons immediately telegraphed an emphatic denial. Armed with this, Granville, Gladstone, and William Forster, Ireland's chief secretary, agreed to contradict Parnell only to be dissuaded from doing so by Sir William Harcourt, the home secretary. He had employed the detectives and preferred to allow the issue quietly to fade away. The surveillance of the Irish leader did uncover his liaison with Katharine O'Shea, the wife of a member of his own party in the Commons.[14]

Gladstone's hope of pacifying Ireland was quickly dashed by murder. He had agreed to the detention of Parnell on a charge of inciting violence, but by the following spring, that of 1882, he reached an understanding with the home ruler. Parnell, who wished to be out of prison in time to be in attendance when Mrs O'Shea gave birth to their first child, agreed to a suspension of agitation in Ireland in return for an assurance that something would be done to help tenants who faced ejection for arrears of rent. Gladstone took this opportunity to reorganize the Irish administration, appointing Earl Spencer as lord lieutenant and replacing Forster as chief secretary. This latter change was simplified by Forster's resignation in protest to the arrangement with Parnell, which he considered tantamount to the appeasement of terrorism. Gladstone named one of his own relations, and a younger brother of Hartington, to the office. On the day of his arrival in Dublin, Lord Frederick Cavendish went walking in Phoenix Park with his undersecretary, Thomas Burke, where both were literally butchered to death by a group of Irish nationalists in the Fenian tradition. Lyons's former military attaché, Brackenbury, informed him of the wild rumours of ministerial resignations, of officials refusing to venture onto the streets without armed escorts, and of a new chief secretary so afraid for his personal safety in London as well as in Dublin that he went to the dinner table armed. The Liberal government responded to the Phoenix Park horror with coercion.[15]

The presence of Fenians and other violence-prone political radicals in Paris, the passage of a bill excluding from France princes of old reigning families, the bitterness of "ultra parties" against "constituted dignities," French anger at Britain, and the surge in anglophobia as a result of the dispute over Egypt caused Lyons to fear for the safety of British royal visitors to France. Over the next few years the Prince of Wales scurried through Paris whenever suspicious characters were spotted in the neighbourhood of his hotel. Precautionary measures were adopted at Royat in the Auvergne when he tested the thermal springs, and he was dissuaded in 1885 from attending the Nice Carnival where all the sybarites were to be masked. The following year it was the widely rumoured purpose of the Prince's frequent visits to France that attracted unwelcome public attention. In Paris and Nice a large number of "scandalous" placards were posted advertising a pamphlet entitled "Les amours du Prince de Galles." Much to Lyons's disgust, the recent liberalization of the press laws had left the government little power over such scurrilous publications, while an action for libel could only be launched at the request of the government of the foreign sovereign. In fact the Prince's mother was another victim of scandal sheets. Lyons had suffered a miserable Christmas in 1883 because of the "foul slanders" about the Queen's private life. They first appeared in *La République démocratique et sociale*, but worse followed when Henri de Rochefort returned to France following the Communard amnesty. He edited *L'intransigeant*, which published all the salacious gossip about Victoria and her son and heir. The newspaper claimed that the Queen had taken one of her domestics, John Brown, as her lover while the Prince had built a château with special padded rooms in which to rape small girls as young as eight years. The object of libellers, Lyons stressed, was notoriety and the profit made from the great sale of "calumnies." Hauled before the courts, the authors of the libels would make every possible scurrilous assertion and through the cross-examination of witnesses create even greater scandal and annoyance. The best policy was to ignore them. Granville and Gladstone accepted his advice. A public trial in France might see the monarch's "personal morals" discussed before all Europe, while Gladstone, who understood that one "Libel on the Queen" had "recommended assassination" by "lighting a train," feared that a trial "might again set-a-going the impulses of some feeble and morbid mind & thus cause real danger."[16]

In 1885, at Victoria's request, Lyons attended the state funeral of Victor Hugo, whom, in the opinion of the French press, he had insulted the previous year by addressing the literary giant merely as "Senator." The criticism may have influenced his opinion that there had been nothing "splendid or appropriate in the monstrous catafalque erected beneath the Arc de Triomphe," though he was obliged to admit that the crowds had been impressive in number and the procession through the capital's finest thoroughfares had taken five hours to complete. But he claimed to have detected a general weariness and unconcern, a "chilling" absence of strong feelings, and a lack of solemnity. This last he attributed to the studied absence of any recognition of religion. Again at the Queen's personal urging, Lyons wasted time investigating her information that the brains of the last Stuart king, James II, deposed in the "Glorious Revolution" of 1688, were being held in a leaden box in the Scottish College of Paris. She wanted them returned to Britain. Lyons informed her, perhaps with unintentional irony, that there was no "external evidence" of the box's contents, and that the college's administrator seriously doubted that if it held brains they were those of James II.[17]

Lyons encountered two other problems largely beyond his control. They were the state of French public opinion and the instability of French governments. He was, he believed, a witness to a society in transition. American agricultural competition was producing a curious change in the rural population of France. He understood that peasants were no longer clinging to small plots of land but were selling them off and investing the money in speculations as they sought a more pleasant and comfortable existence than that of slaving morning to night for a bare existence. What he failed to note was the capitalist development of large farms and the crisis in the wine industry as phylloxera ravaged the vines. He did record the erosion of the "ultra-conservative labouring class" and the filling of towns "with idle and frequently disappointed and discontented speculators." France, in the words of a historian, was entering "one of the most serious depressions that have ever marked the history of an industrialized nation," and its severity did not escape Lyons. The collapse of the Union Générale in February

1882, having been founded seven years earlier as an investment fund to consolidate "the financial strength of Catholics," had been the signal. People in Paris were very gloomy, Lyons reported towards the end of the following year. Building and manufacturing were apparently "in a bad way," while the poor harvest would inevitably bring the sharp rise in the price of bread, which was always a dangerous situation in France. Public works and railroads, begun with little system since their purpose was to please deputies and their constituents, were ruining French finances, yet they could not be halted for fear of disturbances by labourers thrown out of work. The discontented and distressed work-men of Paris, such as the capital's furniture makers, were being taught that it was the duty of the government to relieve them through such improvisations as the re-equipment of public offices. Lyons suspected that these expedients would ensure that the crash, when it came, was serious and irremediable and would arm political demagogues with heavier weapons.[18]

Paris was alive with fear that quiet and orderly government was un-der threat, and Lyons provided the Foreign Office with a thorough anal-ysis of the situation. Two deaths had proven particularly unfortunate, he wrote. That of Léon Gambetta at the young age of forty-four on the last day of 1882 had removed the one man of marked ability in the Republi-can Party. His popularity might have seen the public acquiesce in his ex-ercise of the central power that Lyons considered essential for political stability. The reins of authority had become so loose, he observed, that their "sudden pick up" by a strong hand was necessary if anarchy was to be avoided. The other misfortune was the passing a few days afterwards of General Chanzy. He had been the one military figure who, having emerged from the Franco-Prussian War with his reputation intact, had possessed the authority and influence to keep the army united and to have employed it effectively in the event of a grave domestic political crisis. Monarchists and other Conservatives had seen in him the man to stop "the too rapid progress of the Republican car." Lyons expected little of the president, Jules Grévy, who lacked energy, appeared to be in poor health, and was a political nonentity. The Chamber of Depu-ties, the "preponderant power in the state," had been discredited by a sharp increase in violence and the emergence of "professedly anarchical parties." The lower orders cared nothing for a Republic that had failed to realize "their dreams of absolute equality with, or rather predominance over, the rich and the educated," Lyons had concluded. Discontent, he warned, was seeping through the ranks of the upper classes. They were convinced that material prosperity was a delusion, were fearful for the security of their property, and were contemptuous of a regime run by a ceaseless succession of ministers. Added to this were the daily shocks experienced by those "committed to religion." The Jesuits had again been expelled, all teaching orders were required to apply for legal residence, the law forbidding Sunday work had been annulled, and no longer were cemeteries to be denominational. Much of this had been the work of Jules Ferry, who as minister of education was committed to the secularization of the Republic.[19]

Political instability fostered public anxiety and was a diplomatic curse. Although there was a measure of hidden stability in that the politicians who headed governments were relatively small in number, and ministerial successions were rarely followed by radical changes of policy, it was well nigh impossible to settle urgent and "great affairs" with ministers whose grip on power was always tenuous. In a mere seven years Lyons had dealt with nine separate premiers and twelve governments. Francis Adams saw France heading in the direction of that "rough democracy" the United States, in which politicians worked the government while taste and manners faded away. The tenure of office by the influential, able, and intensely ambitious Léon Gambetta, of whom Lyons remarked it was "better to do business with God than with the angels," had been brief because important figures such as Freycinet and Léon Say had refused to serve under him. His proposal to revise the constitution and institute the *scrutin de liste* instead of what were in effect single-member constituencies was the issue on which he fell after less than seventy days in office. Things were "in a terrible mess," a gloomy Lyons acknowledged. Freycinet succeeded Gambetta as premier only for the reins to be snatched from his hands barely six months later for his doing too much or too little. The new Cabinet was led by a minor figure, Charles Duclerc, whom Lyons liked personally but whose tenure was so uncertain that he did not consider it worth his while to establish a close diplomatic relationship with him. Armand Fallières, who had been serving as minister of the interior, then cobbled together a ministry in which he held four portfolios, one of them foreign affairs. For almost a month there was no one with whom Lyons could deal because Fallières, having fallen ill in the middle of his speech to the Chamber, became a virtual political recluse. With everything at sixes and sevens, his government collapsed after a few weeks.

The return of Jules Ferry to the premiership in February 1883 did produce a measure of stability. He held office for almost twenty-six months, yet he never commanded a dependable majority in the Chamber, and thus his hold on power was never firm. The Ultra Left, with Georges Clemenceau in the vanguard, was violently hostile to him personally, and the Ultra Right was ever ready for mischief. It sought to discredit Republicanism by making government virtually impossible and came to hate Ferry for his suppression of religious communities. His additional misfortune was the disloyalty of the members of his own party. In London, his fall went unlamented. "He arrived at the Quai d'Orsay, quite ignorant of Foreign Affairs," Granville remarked, and "the more he learnt of them, the more subservient he became to Bismarck, and the more tricky to us." Freycinet, whom Lyons had come to consider a particularly good personal friend, returned again as chief minister, but his majority was always suspect and the government did not see out the year. Two other men, René Goblet and Maurice Rouvier, held the premiership during 1887. Toting up the presidents of the Council with whom he had dealt in less than two decades, Lyons discovered they numbered an astonishing twenty-two.[20]

As he strove to improve Anglo-French relations under these trying circumstances, Lyons was aware of another problem. Three of the four tenants of the Foreign Office during his final years in Paris subscribed to the traditional, profound Foreign Office distrust of the French. The permanent undersecretary, Tenterden, angrily disparaged them as uninformed and was confident that one day they would pay for their "ignorance and selfishness." The Liberal foreign secretary, all of whose dispatches Tenterden allegedly drafted, which explained Granville's difficulty in defending them in Cabinet, wrote of the French that from time to time no concession would satisfy them. "The difficulty of keeping on friendly terms with France is not to be underrated," he admitted, which increased his admiration of Lyons. Archibald Primrose, the fifth Earl of Rosebery, who suddenly emerged as a senior Liberal with Gladstone's formation of another government in 1886, and during its brief life held the Foreign Office, was another cynic about the French. He had taken the Office, he avowed, with a sincere wish to be friendly with France and so considered it a great pity that "our cordiality should be poisoned at source." Nor was the animus confined to the Foreign Office. James Bryce, Regius Professor of civil law at Oxford, Liberal member of Parliament, and Rosebery's parliamentary undersecretary, had been struck, he informed Lyons, by a silently growing public distrust and dislike of France. He traced it to unjustified French hostility and jealousy of Britain. Should the French again find themselves in a critical situation they would enjoy less active British friendship, Bryce predicted, than they had received in the Franco-Prussian War. Salisbury, the Tory foreign secretary, described by Granville as strong and very clever but far from prudent, was blunt: "The French are inexplicable," an "incessant vexation," he fumed, and they did not need to manufacture enemies, having been well provided with them by nature. They seemed bent on aggravating every patient heart in Britain by every insult and inventiveness their ingenuity could devise. Across the Channel, there was a corresponding "special bitterness towards Britain."[21]

Chronic ministerial instability convinced many observers that the Third Republic was doomed. It had survived for sixteen years, and that, according to Lyons, was approximately the length of time it usually took the French to tire of a form of government. The Republic could not boast that it had put the nation's finances on a secure foundation, or that agriculture was thriving, or that trade flourishing, or that it had won a reputation for efficiency and purity. "So there is plenty to croak about for those who are inclined to croak," Lyons admitted in the summer of 1886. Increasingly, his attention was drawn to the popular General Georges Boulanger. His connections were Anglo-Welsh on his mother's side and he spoke perfect English. A graduate of the Saint-Cyr military academy, he had seen service in French colonial conflicts, in the Mexican disaster, the Austrian War, and the Prussian disaster. He had led one of the columns that entered Paris to suppress the Commune and had an eye for the main chance. When looking to the Right for advancement he had been an ardent clerical and a questioner of the parliamentary system and the Republican constitution. When turning to the Republicans and Gambetta he had become a fervent anti-clerical Republican. Appointed inspector of infantry in 1882, thanks to Gambetta's influence, he had four years later found a second sponsor in Georges Clemenceau, who secured for him the Ministry of War in the Freycinet administration As minister, he tightened the system of compulsory national military service, insisting that the nation's 55,000 priests bear arms, and politicized the army by removing from important commands officers identified with the Right and replacing them with his own men. He curried favour with the rank and file by making the life of ordinary soldiers easier, replacing straw pallets with mattresses and making uniforms more comfortable and the food far more edible. He courted a more general popularity by travelling the country making speeches, by permitting troops to fraternize with striking miners, by having sentry boxes painted in the national colours, and by staging a magnificent military review on 14 July. Republicans had designated the day of the storming of the Bastille in 1789 a national holiday. In addition, they had adopted the "Marseillaise" as a national anthem, renamed streets, and engaged in "statuemania." Across the capital, granite likenesses of Republican heroes had been erected. At the 1886 military review the cries of *"Vive Boulanger"* were far louder than those of *"Vive la République,"* prompting Lyons to ask himself whether Boulanger intended to be a French Cromwell or a French Monck. Did he intend to become something of a dictator, or did he plan to restore the monarchy, and if so which dynasty?[22]

Boulanger's alliance of the rank and file and the mob in support of his authoritarianism, militarism, and *revanchisme* made him a domestic and international danger. Was he planning to march higher politically by "violent revolutionary means," or would he welcome war as a path to a military dictatorship? He certainly excited fears that he was imperilling peace with Germany, having been dubbed "General Revenge." He demanded a large increase in the military budget, which in February 1887 the Chamber augmented by 86 million francs for additional "war expenses." He increased the size of the army and re-equipped the troops with more sophisticated weaponry. He stockpiled the new high explosive, melinite, and established stores at strategic locations. He made an arrangement with railways to ensure the rapid movement of troops. He strengthened border fortifications and banned the export of horses to Germany. All of these measures, together with his movement of troops and artillery around Paris seemingly en route to the German frontier, were red rags to the German bull. Reminding the Reichstag that Napoleon III had embarked on war in 1870 largely in the belief that it would strengthen his hold on France, Bismarck suggested that Boulanger, if he came to power, would behave in exactly the same way. Seventy thousand German reservists were moved to the frontier, the number of men under arms was increased, and a defensive alliance was signed with Italy. The seizure by German police of a French customs official heightened tension, and the public gave Boulanger the credit for securing the officer's release. But there was panic on the Bourse and an alarming run on savings banks. A frightened Alphonse de Rothschild came to Lyons with a letter from someone, perhaps Bismarck's son Herbert with whom Rothschild had become friendly, in which the chancellor was reported to be committed to resort to force if the French continued their warlike preparations.

Conflict was inevitable, the Germanophile Rothschild argued, if Boulanger remained in office. Frightened politicians, their anxiety heightened by a signal from London that in the event of war and a temporary German violation of Belgium neutrality Britain would not intervene, formed a government from which Boulanger was excluded. The ministry which took office in May 1887 had no policy of its own, Lyons reported dismissively, and showed no evidence of vigour or clear intelligence on relations with foreign powers because its raison d'être was to reassure Germany by removing Boulanger from the War Ministry. Even so, fearful of unpopularity, Prime Minister Rouvier declared that his minister of war would equal the departed Boulanger in energy. And the evidence of the general's popularity was on display at the Gare de Lyon, from where he left to assume a provincial military command. People threw themselves on the tracks to prevent the train from leaving and pasted posters on the carriages emblazoned with the promise "He will return." At the Bastille Day military review there were again loud cries of "*Vive Boulanger*" and "down with Grévy," the president, but Lyons welcomed the fact that they had not come from the troops. Boulangerism was the new French word for jingoism, and it was spreading, he noted, not only among reckless radicals who were enemies of the Rouvier government, such as Henri Rochefort, but also among the better classes. A dangerous belligerence was developing in a generation of Frenchmen without experience or practical knowledge of war. Revenge had been rejected in favour of colonialism, but to many Frenchmen this seemed evidence of their nation's weakness in the face of the German enemy, and Boulanger had capitalized on this sentiment.[23]

Long a francophile, Lyons had become disenchanted with French politics and even with the people of France, who were evidently dissatisfied with their moderate Republic. He was reduced to hoping that at some point there would be a change for the better. The senatorial elections of 1885 had resulted in the defeat of both monarchist parties, and he feared that "Extreme Radicals" with the aid of "Extreme Monarchists" intended to make stable government utterly impossible. He was irritated not only by the difficulty of dealing with governments that were playing a form of musical chairs but also by their habit of referring international problems to Berlin for Bismarck's approval before acting. He resented the resurgent anglophobia that was sparked by the differences over Egypt. When Rochefort in his newspaper urged the taking of vengeance on Lyons personally, who happily was at home on leave at the time, the embassy was given a police guard. In the country at large he saw an erosion of authority, a decrease in respect for law, and moral decay. "One of the causes and one of the effects, for things turn in a vicious circle," he brooded, "is the practice of juries to acquit criminals in absolute defiance of evidence and law in response to the attitude of a low class of newspapers and even the public in court." Another was President Grévy's commutation of the sentences of atrocious criminals. Then scandal enveloped the presidency. Daniel Wilson, Grévy's son-in-law, was accused of selling honours, including membership of the Legion of Honour, to wealthy bourgeois. He conducted the business from the Élysée Palace on presidential stationery, which reminded Lyons of the abuses and corruption of the Second Empire. The scandals at the heart of the government fed the popular pessimism.[24]

In recognition of his "singular fairness, his great perspicacity, and the perfect balance of his mind," the Liberals awarded Lyons a viscountcy and exempted him, as they did Odo Russell, now Baron Ampthill, from their decision to apply a five-year rule to ambassadors. These honours did not make Lyons any more responsive to the Liberals' request that he come home to vote on a franchise bill which would add 2 million voters to the rolls. His resistance fed their suspicion that he was at heart a Conservative. Salisbury as the Tory leader was demanding a redistribution of seats as the price of Conservative acquiescence in the legislation. In this crisis, Lyons was not swayed by Gladstone's familiar argument that since some Tory peers were going to vote for the bill there was no reason why ambassadors of "no party" should not do the same. He was similarly unmoved by the talk of a constitutional crisis if, in the event of the bill being defeated in the Lords, the Liberals in the Commons made hostility to the hereditary house a leading issue at the next general election. Nor was he unduly alarmed by the dark warnings that Britain would experience political instability similar to that in France. Salisbury might turn out the government with the help of the Irish home rulers, Granville suggested, only to be ousted himself six months later by the Liberals and the Irish. Something like this did indeed briefly happen only for Gladstone to divide his own party by adopting the cause of home rule. This allowed the Tories to return to power for a full Parliament. Lyons first evaded returning to London to vote on the bill with the explanation that he had yet formally to take his seat as a viscount, and then with the plea that he was suffering from a painful condition of the throat. A compromise between the Liberals and the Tories finally removed the pressure on him to attend.[25]

When forming his second and stable government in July 1886, Salisbury decided not to repeat the brief experiment of the previous year when he had been both prime minister and foreign secretary. He invited Lyons to become foreign secretary, no doubt aware that both the Queen and Northcote had proposed him as a replacement for Derby in the Disraeli government. His knowledge and experience of foreign affairs were unequalled, Salisbury flattered Lyons, and no Tory could claim a "tithe of his fitness." His appointment would exercise a great "moral authority" in Europe. On learning of the offer, friends rushed to counsel him to think twice before declining it. He was still "in full vigour" and was no older than Palmerston had been when he became prime minister, one reminded him. Of course, he was not in full vigour. He continued to suffer from bronchitis and a "violent and painful cough." He had no interest in public speaking, which would be painful, and certainly had no desire to be on his feet in the House of Lords explaining and justifying foreign policy. He valued quiet. And he did not have a wife to preside at Foreign Office entertainments.[26]

Lyons immediately telegraphed Salisbury from Paris 27 July 1886 citing his age and health as his reasons for declining the high office. He needed rest, he wrote. He could not begin a new life of hard work and could not undertake new and laborious duties with any confidence of being able to discharge them efficiently. Rosebery understood his decision, describing the Foreign Office as a "weary post." Lyons may have been influenced also by a greater awareness of mortality. The death of his uncle William in 1881 could not have been a surprise, since he was a very old man, but the sudden death of Odo Russell in August 1884 had been a shock for he was twelve years younger than Lyons. Then in the late summer of 1885 his "faithful old servant," Giuseppe, had suffered a stroke while they were at Blenheim on the annual country house tour. Lyons arranged for him to have the best available medical attention, first in Woodstock, then in London, and finally in Paris. Once it was clear that Giuseppe would be unable to continue in his service, Lyons checked with his solicitor to ensure that he had made generous provision for him in his will and forwarded a modest sum to him when he returned home to Rome. His other constant companion, who "lived entirely" with him, George Sheffield, underwent a "beastly operation" for a urinary problem in the spring of 1886. Far more unsettling had been the state of Minna's health. Soon after he returned to Paris in October 1885 she informed him that she had been diagnosed with a "contraction of the liver" and a tendency to dropsy. In all probability she was suffering from congestive heart failure, as had their mother, and very quickly fell into "invalid ways." The news in December that she was seriously ill brought Lyons swiftly to London to be with her at Norfolk House, but when she survived "a critical day" early in January, and although he privately admitted that "the decline continues," he appears to have been unable to bear the stress of being on a death watch and in mid-January returned to Paris. There he learned of her passing in March. Her last letter to him, written in pencil and in painfully large characters, informed him of her inability to read beyond a few pages but that every word of his letters were read to her. "I am in great affliction and I may want very much to come to England in a day or two," Lyons wrote to the foreign secretary on 23 March. He left Paris six days later. On arrival he stopped only the night in London before going down to Heron's Ghyll, and returned to France the following week. A cousin, in one of the many consoling letters, declared that her heart turned for him in his loneliness and the "terrible blank" in his future. Five months later he heard of the death in Clermont-Ferrand of his old friend Mercier.[27]

Shortly after Minna's death an old friend wrote: "I wish I could convince you that marriage is the right thing for you, now that your position is more isolated than it was by your having lost your English home, and is likely ere long to be a more private one than it has for some many years been." "You are still young for your age and many women would be glad to have you." Late marriage was not only better for a man, it was his duty. A "good help-mate" was an "inestimable blessing" for one of advanced years whose relations had "died off." "Disparity of 20 or 30 years is nothing at our time of life," the friend concluded. Lyons had no intention, nor had he ever had, of marrying. He did with Sheffield's assistance search for a London home. He thought seriously of a house in Berkeley Square but rejected it because of shabby furniture and the sorry condition of the drains. Another, in South Audley Street, owned by Lord Cardogan, was priced too high, as was a third in fashionable Park Lane. The "pretty house" of Sir William Gregory, the former governor of Ceylon and a man who had in his advanced years married a much younger woman, was available for rent in St George's Place, Hyde Park Corner, and there was an excellent club, the Wellington, only one hundred yards away. It appeared ideal, being comfortable and small, but Lyons failed to take it, perhaps because he had been persuaded by Salisbury to delay his resignation until the end of 1887 and had assumed the remainder of his dead sister's lease on Heron's Ghyll.[28]

His seventieth birthday barely a month away, Lyons advised Salisbury on 22 March 1887 that the time of his superannuation could not come soon enough. Ill with chronic bronchitis, he announced that the labour and responsibility of the ambassadorship were too much for him. The prime minister persuaded him to remain in place at least until year's end. "The loss which the Diplomatic Service will suffer by your retirement will be profound and for the time hardly possible to repair," he hurriedly wrote. His presence in Paris, Salisbury continued, had given the public mind a sense of security. There is a European crisis, he reminded Lyons, alluding to the threatening German response to Boulanger, and if a fateful decision was going to be taken it would be within the next three or four months. Public anxiety would only increase if the reins in Paris were then in the hands of an inexperienced diplomatic coachman. Lyons remained, but unwillingly, and the crisis eased following Boulanger's departure from the War Ministry. Lyons received the customary retirement reward of an earldom and on 1 November formally tendered his resignation and requested the usual retiring pension. His last act of "fidgettiness" was to make sure that the insurance on the embassy, which came due in November, had been paid. His last letter, dated 20 November, was a note of thanks to the Chamber of Commerce for its "gratifying communication" on his retirement.[29]

How did contemporaries mark the resignation of a diplomat who considered quiet a luxury for which one should be willing to pay and had long deliberately avoided popular attention? The Northern Whig lauded him as a "prince of diplomatists," while the Liberal Daily News feared the nation would look in vain among the emerging generation of diplomats for his equal in tact and experience. He had been a "representative not only of England but of Englishmen." Above board and fair in all his dealings, he had quietly pocketed instructions which in his judgment it would be injudicious to execute. Charles Dilke, once a rising political star until brought to earth by a sex scandal, had as a parliamentary undersecretary in the Foreign Office worked closely with Lyons. He praised his patience, his splendid hospitality, and the high quality of his dispatches. They had matched in number those of all the nation's other ambassadors and ministers combined. Lyons had plainly fulfilled his primary diplomatic duty, which was to keep the Foreign Office fully informed of what was happening in the nations to which he was posted. This was the information that shaped policy.

The London Standard claimed that it was his self-effacing successes that explained why Lyons had been so little heard of by the British

people. He had served the country so ably in France, a nation of frequently changing regimes and ministries, that he had remained there
for twenty years and had managed to maintain cordial relations despite
a very difficult political environment. The Paris correspondent of *The
Times* offered a more nuanced appraisal. He acknowledged Lyons's immense capacity for work, his industry, his discretion, his affability, his
correctness and precision, and his lack of ostentation, and attributed his
failure to become a public figure to a lack of ambition to be popular. But
Lyons had in his opinion also lacked flair and imagination. He charged
him with being too dispassionate, of watching with indifference the excitement around him, of failing to take into account human stupidity,
and of an incapability of going beyond the intentions of the government he was currently serving. This was a criticism echoed privately by
his less successful former colleague A.H. Layard. Lyons, he wrote to a
friend, was an example of the modern diplomat who sat at the end of the
telegraph line and followed his instructions to the letter. This charge has
found its way into modern histories of the British diplomatic service,
causing one historian to offer a curiously conflicted assessment of Lyons. He labels him a bureaucrat, "self-effacing, subordinate, and anonymous," a fit person "to execute the policy of the foreign secretary at the
behest of the electric telegraph," only later to admit his brilliance as a
mediator and his "well-deserved reputation as Britain's greatest mid-
century ambassador."[30]

Lyons overcame emotional and psychological problems that could be
traced to his upbringing and might have blighted his career. The intensity of his relationship with his mother went far to explain his refusal to
marry, which threatened to impede his professional advancement. The
strength of his aversion to wedlock was such that it even overwhelmed
the fear of failure and the craving for promotion that long bordered on
the obsessive. That he did succeed was attributable, at least in part, to
the set of rules of diplomatic conduct that he wrote for himself, progressively updated, and to which he doggedly adhered. He emerged from
Greece with a handful of lessons learned during his unhappy experience
under Thomas Wyse. He believed that the residence of a British minister should as a matter of national pride always symbolize the wealth

and power of Britain and that it was important that a diplomat be liked by the fellow members of the diplomatic corps. In addition to personal affability, he needed to win their good opinion by giving excellent dinners. Within a legation, only a foolish junior was disagreeable to his chief even when the fault was all on the latter's side. Equally, a wise chief contrived to win the loyalty and affection of his staff. Finally, his tense relations with the Wyse women, the minister's sister-in-law and niece, confirmed Lyons in his resolve to exclude women from any mission of which he was chief. A Lyons mission was a family of sorts, if more like a boys' school in which he was headmaster. The social chasm that divided foreign secretary and perhaps his political or parliamentary undersecretary from the permanent staff of the Foreign Office – which the latter, considering themselves gentlemen, resented, leading to disharmony – was mirrored in some foreign missions such as Constantinople under Bulwer. It was not found in a Lyons house. When running a peripatetic embassy during the Franco-Prussian War he did bridle at what he interpreted as a Foreign Office suggestion that he act as a "hotel keeper for subordinates," but with the exception of a few worthless juniors he manifested a genuine interest in the well-being and careers of his staff. While away in England in 1862, he encouraged them to send him "personals." They responded with affection and loyalty. He it was who recommended Malet as the successor to Odo Russell in Berlin. Malet, like Odo, helped himself in a way Lyons never had. He proposed to a young lady of high society. Odo had married a daughter of the Earl of Clarendon and Malet was to wed a daughter of the Duke of Bedford.

As Britain's unofficial representative in Rome, an anomalous position but one of greater importance than superficially it appeared to be, Lyons added to his diplomatic handbook. He intended always to be straightforward and honest in all his diplomatic dealings and shunned "underhand activities," or ruse, having concluded that all was give and take in diplomacy. Information or intelligence should be gained by mutual exchanges with colleagues not by covert means. And while it has recently been asserted that nothing was so abhorrent to successive generations of British diplomatists as the penchant for underhanded methods, though foreign secretaries were frequently less scrupulous, as their secret service accounts indicated, Lyons was in the vanguard of those adhering to this version of the "Foreign Office mind." Other Rome dictums were: non-interference was crucial in matters over which the British government could not exercise effective control; prudence was more indispensable than zeal in minor disputes, which suggested a familiarity with the remarks of the notorious French cynic Talleyrand; and tact and temper were vital to the settling of trifling disputes which had the potential to develop into serious quarrels.[31]

The curriculum of what came to be called the "Lyons school" was further augmented in the United States, where at last he was chief of an important mission and where he did his most important and effective diplomatic work. He named as his primary responsibility the seemingly simple task of providing his superiors in London with ample material from which to develop policies. His duty was to implement that policy without reference to his personal opinion. Here was the origin of the claim by contemporaries and historians that the Foreign Office was his "absolute guide," and in support of it he has been described as "painfully shy." Lyons had conquered his youthful shyness thanks to his obligatory participation in the amateur theatricals at the Bedfords' stately home of Woburn Abbey. He did not enjoy nor did he excel in the art of public speaking, often suffering as he did from throat infections and pulmonary problems, but he followed the advice of Francis Bacon, who had stressed the importance of the art of listening. Moreover, if the quality of his dispatches from Rome had made his reputation at the Foreign Office, he had exercised a certain interpretive latitude with respect to his instructions. His conduct was no different in Washington and was in this sense anticipatory of diplomats who were at the end of a telegraph line or equipped with far more rapid means of communication. He weighed how receptive the Union government was likely to be against what he had been instructed to say and considered the local developments that made the latest dispatch less relevant. He selected language with care and watered down, and on occasion did not deliver, his instructions. "This interpretive function of the diplomatist is of real importance," a twentieth-century Foreign Office insider wrote, because "seemingly small differences of procedure and phraseology are apt to have large results" in international relations.[32]

Learning from the mistakes of his immediate predecessor in Washington, Lyons declined to engage in confidential, quasi-official conversations with American officials. Nine times out of ten, he remarked, they complicated matters, and one of those involved usually found himself in a "scrape." He avoided as far as possible in his dealings with a host government any expression of his personal opinion on its controversial political problems. Committed to easing tensions and avoiding whenever possible confrontations and collisions, he was on occasion willing to sidestep questions of principle and stoutly resisted the temptation to write spirited notes that if published in the Blue Book would have earned popular applause at home. He was certain that nothing had so bad an effect on relations as the delivering of remonstrances which were not enforced. When demands were made he sought to provide the host government with an opportunity to depict any concession as a spontaneous action on its part, and constructed a "golden bridge" across which it might withdraw with a measure of dignity and certainly without unnecessary humiliation. In a crisis he was determined to preserve an unruffled calm yet advocated military demonstrations of Britain's will and power to defend its national interests.

Like those politicians at home who were identified with certain newspapers – Palmerston with the *Morning Post* and Granville with *The Times* – Lyons saw in the press an adjunct of diplomacy. In Washington, Constantinople, and Paris, he used journalists to advance policy but invariably did so with great discretion. Usually, he remained one step removed from direct contact, utilizing his private secretary and dogsbody, Sheffield, as the conduit. An exception to this rule was Felix Whitehurst, the Paris correspondent of the *Daily Telegraph*. He had influence at the Tuileries Palace and was willing to report fully and in person on interviews conducted with European giants such as Bismarck. Of course, the press could be a two-edged sword. It often complicated Lyons's diplomatic life with articles and leaders that were deeply resented in the nation to which he was accredited. William Russell, whom he had been using in an effort to restrain policies of the Lincoln administration harmful to British commercial interests, was eventually driven from the Union by the hostility of Americans infuriated by his reports. In France, the unsympathetic comments of British newspapers, and especially *The*

Times, during the Prussian War reinvigorated the traditional anglophobia at a time when Lyons was struggling to prevent a deterioration in Anglo-French relations.

Lyons had been described by the *New York Tribune* as the model ambassador. If this tribute was one measure of the success of his approach to diplomacy, he continued to tinker with his rule book on reaching the service's highest rank. An ambassador should be acquainted with diplomatic business and transact it accurately and diligently. In short, it was a profession thus unsuitable for amateurs. This lesson he had first been taught in Athens and Naples. An ambassador should desire to remain long at his post, should be able to take part in society, and should form friendships with the statesmen of the nation to which he was accredited. Lyons certainly practised what he preached. He endeavoured to improve relations and smooth difficulties by personal influence. This, in the opinion of the American secretary of the navy, he had done all too well in Washington. He should not be an aspiring politician and thus forever thinking of his image at home. He should ensure that he understood completely the wishes and views of the government he served that were unlikely to be expressed fully and frankly in dispatches. Consequently, he should engage in an extensive confidential correspondence with the foreign secretary. He should possess the confidence of the government and share its sentiments but not be a political partisan.

Lyons would have been proud of posterity's judgment that he was "the first major diplomat who owed his appointment to the highest post in diplomacy," the Paris embassy, "to professional rather than political considerations." Arguably, that distinction might have been backdated to his appointment to the United States, a major post by 1859. In Paris, on several occasions, he faced the sensitive issue of the relationship between his profession and partisan politics. He resisted the pressure exerted by two Liberal governments to return to London to vote in the House of Lords for controversial legislation. Clarendon as a former diplomat recognized the benefit to the service if men in important posts were not political. Gladstone and Granville admitted that it was not right to ask a man to vote against his political opinions, but the prime minister denied Lyons the right to refuse to take a political position on the grounds of personal convenience. Gladstone assumed that Lyons was disinclined to make the inconvenient and uncomfortable journey from Paris to London simply to vote. He failed to recognize that Lyons was intensely proud of his reputation as a diplomat of "no party," and that his resistance was principled and pragmatic. He had seen Normanby unceremoniously pushed out of Florence because of his political colouring and may have heard of Malmesbury's boast that he had appointed men of the right political affiliation. Both Whigs and Tories had traditionally selected men from their own ranks to represent the nation abroad, but this road led to a dead end: the disruption of the service with every change of government. So Lyons was again a vanguard figure. The modern diplomat must be careful to avoid "showing his personal bias and predilections in regard to the party politics in his own country."[33]

What were the achievements that brought Lyons recognition as perhaps "the most famous diplomat of the middle years of the nineteenth century"? One of the most enduring, for it long survived his death, was the "Lyons school." A great many young men served under him in Washington, Constantinople, and Paris, and he became their role model. Their dubbing him "Fetish" was undoubtedly a magical rather than a sexual allusion. They learned from him how to behave diplomatically and how to conduct diplomacy. Many went on to senior positions, and a handful rose to the very top of the profession. Laurels were won, he had shown, by a "combination of industry with quiet zeal and unerring tact." The *London Standard* commented at the time that he was "one of those men – happily the race is not extinct – who acquire the confidence of their superiors and the respect of their countrymen by solid rather than shining qualities." Where Lyons had excelled was "not in the brilliancy of a phrase or novelty of conception, but in sound and quick judgment."[34]

In Athens, Lyons had played an important role in the resolution of the Don Pacifico affair but it was unknown outside the Foreign Office and went unrecognized within. Rather than seek popular attention, as others might have done, he continued to work within the system using his extended family's political connections in his drive for recognition and promotion. They helped him secure the post that set his career on its rapid rise. As Britain's unofficial representative in Rome, Lyons lacked the standing to negotiate formal agreements. He did complete a commercial arrangement, secured the release of provocative Protestant evangelicals, and dissuaded the papacy from moving on the creation of a Scottish hierarchy. This, he warned, would reignite the anti-Catholicism touched off only a handful of years earlier by the re-establishment of the Catholic hierarchy in England and Wales. By his personal conduct, his tact and good sense, Lyons won unexpected personal influence. His meetings with the pope were always friendly and his working relationship with Cardinal Antonelli, the secretary of state, was excellent. He was unable to persuade the Vatican to open official relations with Britain, or to reform the papal government, but through observation and association he gained a depth of knowledge of the Papal States and of Italy that greatly impressed both an architect of the Risorgimento, Count Cavour, and his masters in London. The clarity and intelligence of his analyses of the problems and policies of the papacy won him admirers in the Foreign Office, as did the skill with which he settled the *Cagliari* affair. So impressed was Lord John Russell by his performance in Rome, having named him to the post, that he charged his nephew Odo, who now held it, to emulate Lyons. But after twelve years he had yet to match his predecessor's performance and took a position in the Foreign Office.

"Seldom has there been a more important post at a more critical time," the press later remarked of Lyons's tour of duty in Washington during the Civil War. These years marked the peak of his diplomatic effectiveness. The "main object" of all he did, he avowed, was to avert conflict between his nation and the Union, and his peaceful settlement of the Mason and Slidell affair was widely regarded as a great achievement. It established his "well-deserved reputation as Britain's greatest mid-century ambassador." But long before this crisis Lyons had acted to deter the Americans from behaviour that might, if only through miscalculation, lead to a confrontation. He assumed his nation's neutrality before it was proclaimed. He entered into a "strict concert" with his French counterpart and friend Henri Mercier, knowing that the Americans would think twice before provoking both powers. He urged military demonstrations in the form of a strengthened North American naval squadron and the dispatch of troop reinforcements to Canada to impress upon the Americans his nation's will and power to defend its interests. He established with the American secretary of state, as he had done with the Papal, an excellent working relationship which made his persuasiveness all the more effective. He consistently counselled his own government to allow the belligerents to decide the war's outcome themselves, believing that the Union would ultimately triumph. He preached non-intervention and personally carried the message home to Britain in the decisive year of 1862. The cost of meddling, he warned Cabinet ministers, was likely to be war with the Union. His recommendations and measures shaped the policy of the Palmerston government, and this significant achievement won him the respect and admiration of Secretary of State Seward and perhaps inspired his talk of a special Anglo-American friendship. Another achievement was the negotiation of the Anti-Slave Trade Treaty that carried both their names.[35]

The proven ability to deal with difficult diplomatic problems took Lyons to Constantinople as ambassador. He arrived fully aware of the damage done to his nation's prestige and influence by its humiliation at the hands of Bismarck in the Danish crisis of 1864. At the British embassy he inherited a dysfunctional family that the large expatriate community did not hold in high regard. Nevertheless, during his comparatively short tenure he restored order within the embassy and regained the lost respect of his fellow countrymen. Also, by dealing directly with the grand vizier and the foreign minister, instead of relying on a dragoman, he set in motion the recovery of British influence with the Sublime Porte. The defence of the integrity of the Ottoman Empire was the traditional British policy but there was little enthusiasm in Britain for another Crimean War. Lyons modified the policy. He settled for propping up the empire so that it could go on "tolerably" for a number of years and decline "gently." To implement this subtle strategy he made another concert with the French. He worked with a French ambassador that few members of the diplomatic community could abide and with his assistance resolved the problem of the Danubian Principalities. At the same time he quietly utilized his improved relations with the Porte to persuade it to oppose additional concessions to the French building the Suez Canal. He helped to ensure that they did not secure absolute control of what was certain to be a vital line of communication to India and beyond. What Lyons could not do was persuade the Turks to implement desperately needed reforms or make limited concessions to the rebellious Cretans. Unless checked the turmoil would spread, he feared, to the empire's other Christian provinces.[36]

An even temper, great patience, "detachment, coolness, and foresight" were some of the qualities that brought Lyons to the pinnacle of his profession. His two decades in Paris, however, saw a decline of his influence on policy-making as Berlin emerged as the focal point of European power politics. France's defeat in the Prussian War and consequent loss of international standing were accompanied by domestic confusion. The country experienced regime change as Republic replaced Empire and then prolonged uncertainty as the possibility of a monarchical restoration remained a political factor. The Republic was also cursed with chronic ministerial instability that compromised and complicated diplomatic activity. His energy sapped by persistent ill health, satiated ambition, and weakening francophilia in the face of rising anglophobia, Lyons succumbed to fatigue. Yet he continued almost to the end to forward to the Foreign Office admirably clear and astute analyses of the problems of France, and these recommended him to the Queen as a fit candidate for the office of foreign secretary. The portfolio was offered to him shortly before he retired from the foreign service. By following his rule book, he left with a solid record of achievement. He established excellent personal relations with the great majority of foreign ministers with whom he dealt. He played a constructive role in the temporary settlement of Turko-Greek relations and a vital one in the resolution of the crisis over French purchase of Belgian railways.[37]

As the commercial relationship with France emerged as the major issue, Lyons advocated a most-favoured-nation agreement to protect British trade from economic discrimination, and this became the solution. His most significant achievement, however, was his success in preventing a dangerous deterioration in relations during one of the most tumultuous periods in the modern history of France. On the eve of the Franco-Prussian War he had glumly suggested that it would be a miracle if in its aftermath the two nations remained good friends. Tact, prudence, and consideration for French susceptibilities would be required to prevent the improved feeling of the past two decades from being destroyed, he predicted. He may not have been greatly loved by French Republicans, one of Britain's popular newspapers acknowledged, but he was "universally esteemed." Radical Republicans did seek to deliver a stiletto thrust with their claim that Lyons might have tutored the Count of Monte Cristo in magnificent living. They alleged that he had spent £45,000 a year, kept 34 footmen and stabled 25 horses, and squandered 2,000 guineas on the banquet to celebrate Queen Victoria's Jubilee. These were, of course, "fantastic calculations" for Lyons had never been given to lavish expenditures.[38]

After a lifetime of fretting about his pension, Lyons did not live to enjoy it. Edmund Hammond had written to him on 11 November to thank him for his numerous acts of kindness and consideration over the many years of their association, and to express his hope that he would enjoy health and happiness for many years to come. He did not. Lyons suffered a seizure, probably a stroke, at Norfolk House following breakfast on Monday 28 November. Sir William Jenner was one of the three physicians immediately summoned, but after lingering in a paralytic state for a week he died at 8 a.m. on Monday 5 December. At the end George Sheffield was at his bedside, along with three of Lyons's nieces. One of them was a Carmelite nun and a second was a sister of charity. He had for some time expressed a desire to enter the Roman Catholic Church, and the previous year following the death of Minna had, with Salisbury's permission, embarked on a study of Catholicism. On occasion, he had attended Mass and according to the *Weekly Register* "had placed himself under instruction, and had begun to regularly attend Roman Catholic services several weeks prior to his paralytic seizure." Indeed, it claimed that he had been received into the Roman Catholic Church by the Right Rev. Dr Butt, Bishop of Southwark. Whether or not he had completed the conversion, the bishop did administer to him extreme unction. This quickly stirred the sectarian pot. The Rev. T. Howard Gill, the incumbent at the English Church in the rue d'Aguesseau, denied that as a regular congregant Lyons had ever been in secret sympathy with the Roman Catholic faith. Lyons had resisted the efforts of the person closest to him, Minna, to convert, Gill assured his congregation. But with his powers failing, and living alone among his Roman Catholic relatives, without a wife or son or daughter to confirm him in his allegiance to the Church of England, he had been persuaded by those learned in polemics to discuss conversion with priests. The worry this caused had perhaps hastened

his end, Gill implied. Then advantage had been taken of his condition
to proselytize him. Speechless and inarticulate on his deathbed, he had
only been able to nod his head in consent, in a moment of lucidity, to a
conditional baptism. "And, however confidently that Church may claim
him as her own," Gill thundered, "we say that he never gave his adhe-
sion to her Communion" and had never really abjured his Church. The
publication of the sermon in the English-language *Galignani's Messenger* ensured that it was recopied in the British press.[39]

Lyons was not leaving life as quietly as he had lived it. His body in a
coffin of polished oak with brass handles was taken in a hearse drawn
by four horses from St James's Square to Victoria Station. The hearse was
followed by Lyons's brougham carrying two of his nephews, the Duke
of Norfolk and Father von Wurtzburg. By train the body was carried
to Arundel and then in another hearse up the hill to the small Fitzalan
Chapel. At the weekend, a special train left Victoria at 9:30 a.m. carrying the distinguished mourners. Among them were representatives
of the Queen and the Prince of Wales, of the diplomatic corps, of the
government, of the Foreign Office and of the Paris embassy. The friends
included Malet and Monson and Sheffield. Dr Butt celebrated the Req-
uiem Mass, assisted by several clergy, and then those present gathered
around the bier for the burial service. The coffin was covered in a black
velvet pall, a gold cross traversing it, and on it was a viscount's coronet,
the patent of creation of an earldom not having arrived by the time of
Lyons's death. The body was then interred in the Howard family vault.
On the same day a service was held at Brompton Oratory "for the repose
of the soul of the deceased." *The Times* obituary ran to two columns,
and the passing of Lyons was widely commented upon in the provincial press. In Paris, *Le Temps* and *La Nation* joined other newspapers
in regretting his death and extolled his "high qualities and conciliatory
spirit," his winning as few other Englishman had "the sympathy of all
those in social and diplomatic relations with him," and his success in so
getting into the ways of Paris that he became almost a Parisian. When
Parliament opened in February Granville paid a brief tribute. "A great
diplomatist has died, of the highest public and private reputation," he
declared, "a man of consummate prudence and judgment. He must have
made mistakes, but I know of none during his long career. An excellent

adviser, and, from the confidence which he inspired both in his own Government, whatever Party was in power, and in that of the country to which he was accredited, Lord Lyons was able to render great services to both nations."[40]

After a lifetime of worry about means, Lyons left a personal estate valued at £114,000.

Notes

INTRODUCTION

1   Raymond A. Jones, *The British Diplomatic Service, 1815–1914* (Waterloo, ON, 1983), 117; Beckles Willson, *Friendly Relations: A Narrative of Britain's Ministers and Ambassadors to America (1791–1930)* (New York, 1934), 202.
2   Lord Strang, *The Foreign Office* (London, 1955), 91.
3   T.G. Otte, *The Foreign Office Mind: The Making of British Foreign Policy, 1865–1914* (Cambridge, 2011), 123.

CHAPTER ONE

1   Jane Austen, *Persuasion* (Scarborough, ON, 1964), 24; Vere Langford Oliver, *The History of the Island of Antigua*, 3 vols (London, 1894), 2:211–17; Richard B. Sheridan, *Sugar and Slavery: An Economic History of the West Indies, 1623–1775* (Barbados, 1994), 188; Sidney W. Mintz, *Sweetness and Power: The Place of Sugar in Modern History* (New York, 1985), 39, 49, 67, 73, 106, 118; Elizabeth Abbott, *Sugar: A Bittersweet History* (Toronto, 2008), 69–71; S. Eardley-Wilmot, *Life of Vice-Admiral Edmund, Lord Lyons* (London, 1898), 2–4.
2   Lease of St Austens, L337, Lyons Papers, WSRO; Will of John Lyons, 5 October 1804, L340; Richards to E. Lyons, 13 December 1827, B61/1; Eardley-Wilmot, *Lyons*, 4–6, 13; William R. O'Byrne, *A Naval Biographical Dictionary*, 2 vols, 3rd ed. (Polstead, 1990), 1:687–8; H.C.G. Matthew and Brian Harrison, eds, *Oxford Dictionary of National Biography*, 60 vols (Oxford, 2004), 5:654–5; Bickerton to E. Lyons, 21 March [1812], B60/1.
3   Anne Lyons to E. Lyons, 14 April, 22 May 1813, B60/1; Marriage Settlement, 16 July 1814, L301; *Salisbury and Winchester Journal*, 3 April 1815; Cole to E. Lyons, 9 June 1819, 18 January 1820, 11 June 1821, B59/1; G. Lyons to E. Lyons, 9 January 1817, 19 April 1821, L309; H. Lyons to E. Lyons, 15, 23 May 1818, L307, 24 September 1823, B61/1, 27 November 1824, L308.

4   E. Lyons, pocket books, 1816, 1819, 1820, box 220; Jonathan Duncan, *The History of Guernsey: With Occasional Notices of Jersey, Alderney and Sark and Biographical Sketches* (London, 1841), 190–2; John Jacob, *Annals of Some of the British Norman Isles Constituting the Bailiwick of Guernsey, Part 1* (Paris, 1830), 347, 350, 355–7, 363, 368–9, 398; Bickerton Lyons, student journals, 1827, 1828, box 221; R.B. Lyons to E. Lyons, 23, 24 April, 2 May 1827, box 281; Jacob, *Annals*, 400–1; Kidd to E. Lyons, n.d. [June 1828], B599/2.

5   Clarence to E. Lyons, 14 January 1828; Cockburn to E. Lyons, 15 January 1828, B76/2; Lyons Log Books, box 35; Saumarez to E. Lyons, 24 April 1828; Lady Bickerton to E. Lyons, 17 June 1828, B76/2; E. Lyons to A. Lyons, 2 July 1829, B77/1; Michael Mitchie, *An Enlightenment Tory in Victorian Scotland: The Career of Sir Archibald Alison* (Montreal and Kingston, 1997), 25; Bickerton Lyons, student journal, 25 August 1828, box 221.

6   A. Lyons to E. Lyons, 24 October 1828, 18 August 1832, box 280; A. Lyons to R.B. Lyons, 4, 21 July 1830, box 217.

7   Asli Cirakman, *From the "Terror of the World" to the Sick Man of Europe": European Images of Ottoman Empire and Society from the Sixteenth Century to the Nineteenth* (New York, 2002), 22, 105, 109, 157–8, 164, 167, 198, 207; Martin Sicker, *The Islamic World in Decline: From the Treaty of Karlowitz to the Disintegration of the Ottoman Empire* (Westport, 2001), 90, 93, 100–2, 105, 107–8, 113; *Blackwood's Magazine*, 16 (1824), 444, 450; 23 (1828), 26, 29–32.

8   Eardley-Wilmot, *Lyons*, 44; E. Lyons to A. Lyons, 16 October, 13 November 1828, B76/1; R.B. Lyons to A. Lyons, 1,2, 9, 10 February, 12, 13, 25, 30 March, 2 April, 22 May 1829, box 215; A. Lyons to R.B. Lyons, 22 March, 26 April, 21 June, 25 July, 4 September, 1829, 9 December 1830, box 217; R.B. Lyons to A. Lyons, n.d. [July 1830], box 215.

9   Muriel E. Chamberlain, *Lord Aberdeen: A Political Biography* (New York, 1983), 213, 206, 214, 216, 57–8, 80, 113, 173; Eardley-Wilmot, *Lyons*, 45; R.B. Lyons to A. Lyons, 10, 15, [20] June 1829, box 215; Gordon to Aberdeen, 8 August 1829, BL Add. Ms. 43210; Bernard Lewis, *The Emergence of Modern Turkey* (London, 1965), 92, 101, 27, 13–14, 31, 54–61, 70; Carter V. Findlay, *Bureaucratic Reform in the Ottoman Empire: The Sublime Porte, 1789–1922* (Princeton, 1980), 134–5, 141; J.M. Hussey, ed., *The Journals and Letters of George Finlay*, vol. 1: *The Journals* (Athens, 1995): 21, 12–13; R.B. Lyons to A. Lyons, 6 October 1830, box 215.

10 R.B. Lyons to A. Lyons, [20], 21, 26 June 1829, box 215; Miss [Julia] Pardoe, *The City of the Sultan and Domestic Manners of the Turks in 1836*, 2 vols

(London, 1837), 1:278–9 405–21; E. Lyons to A. Lyons, 30 June, 21 July, 2 August, 18 September, 15 October, 15 December 1929, B77/1; R.B. Lyons to A. Lyons, 21, 23 June, 19 July, 1 October 1829, box 215.

11 E. Lyons to A. Lyons, 20 August, 16 September 1829, B77/1; Gordon to Aberdeen, 20 August, 2 September 1829, BL Add Ms. 43210; Chamberlain, *Aberdeen*, 219; R.B. Lyons to A. Lyons, 23 June, 1 July 1829, box 215; Pardoe, *City of the Sultan*, 1:56, 58, 64, 23; E. Lyons to A. Lyons, 24 October, 20 November 1829, B77/1; R.B. Lyons to A. Lyons, 1 July, 4 August, 10 December 1829, 7 June 1830, box 215; 24 August 1830, box 281.

12 E. Lyons to A. Lyons, 10 June 1829, B77/1; R.B. Lyons to A. Lyons, 7 June 1830, box 215; R.B. Lyons to E. Lyons, 24 August 1830, B75/2; Gordon to E. Lyons, 26 September 1830, B59/2; Warren to E. Lyons, 9 August 1830, B75/2; Villiers to E. Lyons, 26 November, 27 December; Gordon to E. Lyons, 27 November 1830, B75/2; Villiers to E. Lyons, 29 January; Gordon to E. Lyons, 9 February, 25 March 1831, L116.

13 E. Lyons to A. Lyons, 22 December 1830, B75/1; 26 November, 2, 6 December 1831, B84/1; C. Grey to E. Lyons, 19 November [1831], 3 July 1832, B120/3; E. Lyons to A. Lyons, 2 December 1831; Wheatly to E. Lyons, 6 December 1831, B84/1; James Chambers, *Palmerston: The People's Darling* (London, 2004), 158; Dawkins to E. Lyons, 29 May 1832, B120/3.

14 E. Lyons to A. Lyons, n.d. [December], 27 November, 22 December 1831, B84/1; Augusta Lyons, pocket book, 31 January 1832, B131; R.B. Lyons to A. Lyons, [1], 5 February, 3 March, 26 April, 3 June 1832, box 215; R.B. Lyons to E. Lyons, 4 March 1832, box 217; Lord Newton, *Lord Lyons: A Record of British Diplomacy*, 2 vols (London, 1913), 2:213.

15 R.B. Lyons to A. Lyons, 5 February, 29 April, 3 June 1832, box 215; R.B. Lyons to E. Lyons, 30 April, 4 June 1832, box 213; Bayly to E. Lyons, 5 March 1832, box 215.

16 R.B. Lyons to A. Lyons, 5 February, 3 March, 1, 2, 21, 30 July, 4, 24 August 1832, box 215; Villiers to R.B. Lyons, 29 May, 1832, box 117.

17 G.W. Clarke, ed., *Rediscovering Hellenism: The Hellenic Inheritance and the English Imagination* (Cambridge, 1989), 163; *Quarterly Review* 52 (1834): 128, 35, 174; Elizabeth Gaskell, *North and South* (Oxford, 1982), 113; David Newsome, *The Victorian World Picture: Perceptions and Introspections in an Age of Change* (New Brunswick, NJ, 1997), 1, 3, 67; John Chandos, *Boys Together: English Public Schools 1800–1864* (New Haven, 1984), 133, 37, 42; A. Lyons to E. Lyons, 25 August 1832, box 280; E. Lyons to R.B. Lyons, 24 April 1834, box 95; R.B. Lyons to E. Lyons, 17 May 1834, box 213; R.B. Lyons to A. Lyons, 25 February, 30 March 1833, box 215.

18 Roundell Palmer, *Memorials: Part 1 – Family and Personal 1766–1865*, 2 vols (London, 1896), 1:86, 90; Williams to E. Lyons, n.d. [December 1833], box 215; Gordon to E. Lyons, 1 April, 3 July 1833, B119/3; A. Lyons to R.B. Lyons, 22 November 1834, box 213.

19 R.B. Lyons to A. Lyons, 25, 28 February, 3, 30 March, 5 May, 28 October 1833, 26 April 1834, box 215; for a brief discussion of the "mother complex" and its consequences see Daryl Stamp, *Jung Lexicon: A Primer of Terms and Concepts*, website of the New York Association of Analytical Psychology (nyaap.org); E. Lyons to A. Lyons, 8 January, 1 May 1835, B78/1.

20 E. Lyons to A. Lyons, 8, 31 January 1835, B78/1; Clarke to E. Lyons, 29 January 1835; Lady Bickerton to E. Lyons, 1, 6 February 1835, B78/3; Williams to E. Lyons, 28 February 1835, B78/1.

21 A. Lyons to R.B. Lyons, 22 October [1835], box 217; R.B. Lyons to A. Lyons, 31 May 1834, 31 March, 5 May 12, 25, 27 October, 30 November, 30 December 1835, 30 January, 29 February, 31 March, 26 April 1836, box 215; Villiers to R.B. Lyons, 1 November, 29 September 1836, box 215; 30 April, 1 June, 1 July 1837, box 225; 7 June 1837, box 117; Bickerton Lyons, pocket books, 1837, box 220; R.B. Lyons to A. Lyons, 26 April 1837, box 215.

22 R.B. Lyons to E. Lyons, 3 May 1837, box 213; Bickerton Lyons, pocket books, 1837, box 220; R.B. Lyons to A. Lyons, 23 June, 2, 30 July, 1 August, 28 September 1837, box 215; A. Lyons to R.B. Lyons, 26 April 1838, box 217; R.B. Lyons to A. Lyons, 31 August 1838, box 215; Michell to R.B. Lyons, 10 October 1838, box 117.

23 R.B. Lyons to A. Lyons, 12 October 1838, box 215; E. Lyons to R.B. Lyons, 10 October [1838], box 95; R.B. Lyons to A. Lyons, 26 October, 9, 22 November 1838, box 215.

24 Lynn E. Williams, "The Career of Sir Edward Malet, British Diplomat, 1837–1908" (PhD thesis, University of Wales, 1982), 1; T.G. Otte, *The Foreign Office Mind: The Making of British Foreign Policy 1865–1914* (Cambridge, 2011), 10–13.

25 E. Lyons to Lady Bickerton, 28 February 1839, B116/2; Raymond A. Jones, *The British Diplomatic Service, 1815–1914* (Waterloo, ON, 1983), 14, 16; A. Lyons to R.B. Lyons, 25 March, 23 May 1837, 26 April, 31 August 1838, box 217; Lord Strang, *The Foreign Office* (London, 1955), 34; Roger Bullen, ed., *The Foreign Office, 1782–1982* (Frederick, 1984), 46, 19–38; Staveley to E. Lyons, 1 September 1815, box 51; F.T.A. Ashton-Gwatkin, *The British Foreign Service* (Ann Arbor, MI, 1967), 13-14.

26 Edward Hertslet, *Recollections of the Old Foreign Office* (London, 1901), 90; Kenneth Bourne, *Palmerston: The Early Years, 1784–1841* (New York,

1982), 332, 335; Robert Gildea, *Barricades and Borders: Europe, 1800–1914* (Oxford, 2003), 57–60, 69; Kenneth Bourne, *Foreign Policy of Victorian England, 1830–1902* (Oxford, 1970), 8, 11, 20, 28–9, 34–9; John Clarke, *British Diplomacy and Foreign Policy, 1782–1923* (London, 1972), 41; Douglas Dakin, *The Unification of Greece, 1770–1923* (London, 1972), 25, 52–3, 58, 62; David Brown, *Palmerston: A Biography* (New Haven, CT, 2010), 214.

27 Palmerston to E. Lyons, 3 July, 1 August, 21 September, 3, 23 October, 2 November, 1 December 1835, box 51; E. Lyons to Palmerston, 2, 29 June 1835, B78/2; for the three medical opinions see L408; Bourne, *Palmerston*, 556; Dakin, *Unification of Greece*, 71; Hussey, *Journals and Letters of Finlay*, 1:174; Jasper Ridley, *Lord Palmerston* (London, 1970), 369.

28 Minna Lyons, pocket diary, 1838, box 223; E. Lyons to Lady Bickerton, 3 January 1839, B116/2; Fitzalan to E. Lyons, 16 January, 22 February 1839, box 96; Surrey to E. Lyons, 23 February 1839, B116/2; Villiers to E. Lyons, 13 April 1839, box 225; A. Lyons to E. Lyons, 30 June, 24 August 1839, box 280; J. Lyons to E. Lyons, 26 March 1839, L307; R.B. Lyons to Minna, 19 August 1839, box 298.

29 Hertslet, *Recollections*, 51, 77, 80; A. Lyons to Minna, 9 June 1840, 31 March, 31 December 1841, 28 September 1842, 29 June 1843, box 290; Hertslet, *Recollections*, 77; R.B. Lyons to A. Lyons, 20, 27, 30 June, 4, 10 August, 21 July 1841, 8 July 1842, 20, 31 August, 6 September 1843, box 216.

30 Dakin, *Unification of Greece*, 75–80; Eardley-Wilmot, *Lyons*, 96–9; Chamberlain, *Aberdeen*, 358–9; Hussey, *Letters and Journals of Finlay*, 1:95, 117–18; A. Lyons to Minna, 31 January, 20 April, 9 May, 20 June 1844, 19 March 1845, 10, 20 June, 20 July, 19 September 1847, box 290.

31 Hussey, *Letters and Journals of Finlay*, 1:65, 88; Donald Sassoon, *The Culture of the Europeans: From 1800 to the Present* (London, 2006), 30; A. Lyons to Minna, 30 January, 12, 26 March, 10, 23, April, 21, May 1840, 20 January, 30 April 1841, box 290; Griffith to Minna, 27 March, 21 May, 27 October 1841, 30 September 1842, box 302; R.B. Lyons to A. Lyons, 24, 27 June 1841, box 216; A. Lyons to Minna, 19 February 1842, box 290.

32 Graham Robb, *Strangers: Homosexual Love in the Nineteenth Century* (New York, 2005), 12, 52, 70, 80, 91–3, 200; Peter N. Nardi, *Men's Friendships* (London, 1992), 42–5; Mark C. Carnes and Clyde Griffin, eds, *Meanings of Manhood; Constructions of Manhood in Victorian America* (Chicago, 1990), 185–6; Reay Tannahill, *Sex in History* (New York, 1982), 378–81.

33 R.B. Lyons to A. Lyons, 9 October 1843, box 216; A. Lyons to Minna, 20, 31 January, 8 March, 20 April 1844, box 290; R.B. Lyons to A. Lyons, 25, 31 May, n.d.[June], 1 August, 22 October 1844, box 216; Bickerton Lyons, pocket book, 1844, box 220.

34   R.B. Lyons to E. Lyons, 1 August 1844, box 216; E. Lyons to Aberdeen, 27 August 1844, box 284; Lady Bickerton to E. Lyons, 19 August 1844, L390; A. Lyons to R.B. Lyons, 19 August 1844, box 217; R.B. Lyons to Minna, n.d.[October 1844], box 298.

CHAPTER TWO

1   R.B. Lyons to A. Lyons, 7, 15 February 1845, box 216; *The Times*, 11 June 1845; R.B. Lyons to A. Lyons, 7, 15, 23 April 1845, box 216; R.B. Lyons to Minna, 1 June 1846, box 298.

2   R.B. Lyons to A. Lyons, 15, 23 November, 2, 12, 25 December 1844, 6, 25 January, 7 February 1845, box 216; R.B. Lyons to E. Lyons, 8 July 1846, box 213; R.B. Lyons to Minna, 9 September 1846, box 303; R.B. Lyons to A. Lyons, 21 October 1846, box 216; Jonathan Steinberg, *Bismarck: A Life* (Oxford, 2011), 47; R.B. Lyons to Minna, 25 June, 5, 24 July, 5 August 1847, box 298; R.B. Lyons to A. Lyons, 7 April, 16, 26 August, 24 December 1847, 8 May 1848, box 216.

3   R.B. Lyons to E. Lyons, 23 December 1846, box 213; Karina Urbach, *Bismarck's Favourite Englishman: Lord Odo Russell's Mission to Berlin* (London, 2001), 14; R.B. Lyons to E. Lyons, 15 December 1846, box 213; R.B. Lyons to A. Lyons, 24 December 1847, box 216.

4   R.B. Lyons to A. Lyons, 3 February 1848, box 298; M. Lyons to E. Lyons, 18 January, 8 February 1848, box 282; M. Lyons to A. Lyons, 18 April 1848, box 283; R.B. Lyons to A. Lyons, 8 May 1848, box 216; A. Lyons to Minna, 13, 21, 29 March, 8, 9, 29 April, 8, 18 May 1848; box 217; Canning to E. Lyons, 12 June 1848; E. Lyons to Palmerston, 12 June 1848, L121; Palmerston to E. Lyons, 31 January 1849, B132/1; R.B. Lyons to Minna, 21 February 1849, box 298.

5   E. Lyons memorandum, n.d. [1849], B58/3; E. Lyons to R.B. Lyons, 17 July 1849; Arundel and Surrey (Fitzalan) to Grey, 19 June 1849; Russell to Arundel and Surrey, 9 July 1849; Palmerston to E. Lyons, 28 July 1849, LE122; R.B. Lyons to E. Lyons, 3, 7, 8 June 1849, B132/3.

6   R.B. Lyons to A. Lyons, 8, 24 June, 8 July, 18 August, 30 October, 7 December 1849, 7 August, 7 October, 18, 29 July 1851, box 216; R.B. Lyons to E. Lyons, 6 April 1852, box 214; R.B. Lyons to Minna, 18 July, 18 August, 27 November, 7 December 1851, box 298; Bruce Knox, "British Policy and the Ionian Islands, 1847–1864: Nationalism and Imperial Administration, *English Historical Review* 99 (1984): 506–9; David Hannell, "A Case of Bad Publicity: Britain and the Ionian Islands, 1848–51," *European History*

Quarterly 17 (1987): 131–43; David Hannell, "Lord Palmerston and the 'Don Pacifico Affair' of 1850: The Ionian Connection," *European History Quarterly* 19 (1989): 495–7; R.B. Lyons to E. Lyons, 13, 18 January 1850, box 214.

7   R.B. Lyons to E. Lyons, 22, 29 January 1850, box 214; Bickerton Lyons, pocket book, 1850, box 221; Ridley, *Palmerston*, 379, 381; Hannell, "Lord Palmerston and the 'Don Pacifico Affair,'" 495; A. Lyons to M. Lyons, 13 February 1850, box 282; R.B. Lyons to E. Lyons, 30 January, 8, 18, 19, 28 March, 27 April 1850, box 214; R.B. Lyons to A. Lyons, 18 June 1851, box 216.

8   R.B. Lyons to E. Lyons, 8 March, 27 April, 28 May; Palmerston to Wyse, 7 May 1850; R.B. Lyons to E. Lyons, 18 May, 18, 19 March 1850, box 214; R.B. Lyons to Minna, 18 February 1850, box 298.

9   A. Lyons to Minna, 14 February 1850, box 290; A. Lyons to E. Lyons, 9 April 1850, box 280; Lady Bickerton's will, L299; A. Lyons to R.B. Lyons, 14 February 1850, box 217; A. Lyons to E. Lyons, 21 March, 20 May 1850, box 280; E. Lyons to A. Lyons, 27 March, 21, 23 April 1850, box 280.

10   Bickerton Lyons, pocket book, 1850, box 221; Minna to A. Lyons, 13 June 1850, box 289; Hertslet, *Recollections*, 72–3, 29; Ridley, *Palmerston*, 383–5; R.B. Lyons to A. Lyons, 25, 29 June 1850, box 216.

11   R.B. Lyons to A. Lyons, 31 August, 9, 10, 12, 19, 22, 25 September, 29 December 1850; Bickerton Lyons, pocket books, 1851, 1852, box 221; R.B. Lyons to Wyse, 11 December 1851, box 118; R.B. Lyons to A. Lyons, 19, 20, 22, 23, 27, 30 January 1852, box 214.

12   R.B. Lyons to Minna, 20 April 1851, 9 March 1852, box 298; A. Lyons to R.B. Lyons, 24 February 1852, box 217; R.B. Lyons to E. Lyons, 30 March 1852, box 214.

13   Addington to R.B. Lyons, 10, 13 April 1852, box 174; R.B. Lyons to E. Lyons, 12, 15 March, 6, 9 April 1852, box 214; Hertslet, *Recollections*, 99; Geoffrey Hicks, "An Overlooked *Entente*: Lord Malmesbury, Anglo-French Relations and the Conservatives' Recognition of the Second Empire, 1852," *History* 92 (2007): 191–2, 194, 198; Angus Hawkins, *The Forgotten Prime Minister The 14th Earl of Derby*, vol. 2: *Achievement 1851–1869* (Oxford, 2008), 8–9, 18, 32, 45, 42; *Oxford Dictionary of National Biography*, 25: 435, 439.

14   R.B. Lyons to Malmesbury, n.d. [April 1852], box 192; R.B. Lyons to E. Lyons, 9, 13, 23, 26, 30 April, 1, 21 May 1852; 8 January 1850, 25 November 1849, 9 September, 7 October, 4, 18 November 1851, box 214; Hertslet, *Recollections*, 205–6; Ashton-Gwatkin, *British Foreign Service*, 6.

15   Jones, *British Diplomatic Service*, 39; R.B. Lyons to Forbes, 22, 24 April 1852, box 118; R.B. Lyons to E. Lyons, 18 May, 7, 28 August, 9 September, 12

October, 6 November 1852, box 214; Bickerton Lyons, pocket book, 1852, box 221; Richard Mullen and James Munson, *The Smell of the Continent: The British Discover Europe 1814–1914* (London, 2009), 74–5 142; Sassoon, *Culture of Europeans*, 262–3.

16 John Prest, *Lord John Russell* (London, 1972), 353–8; Chamberlain, *Aberdeen*, 442–9; Malmesbury to Bulwer, 15 August 1852, BUL 1/103/17, Bulwer Papers, NRO; James P. Flint, *Great Britain and the Holy See: The Diplomatic Relations Question 1846–1852* (Washington, DC, 2003), 13, 35, 83, 98, 159-61; R.B. Lyons to E. Lyons, 18 March, 16 May 1853, box 214; Addington to R.B. Lyons, 9 February 1853, box 174.

17 John Pemble, *The Mediterranean Passion: Victorians and Edwardians in the South* (Oxford, 1987), 2, 1, 8: Maura O'Connor, *The Romance of Italy and the English Political Imagination* (New York, 1998), 13–14, 18, 38–9; R.B. Lyons to E. Lyons, 13 February, 3, 18 March 1853, box 214; Addington to E. Lyons, 18 March 1853, box 174; R.B. Lyons to Minna, 12, 13, 19, 25 February, 3, 4, 8 March 1853, box 298; R.B. Lyons to E. Lyons, 18, 19, 21, 25 March 1853, box 214.

18 Bulwer to Derby, 8 June 1852, BUL 1/100/12; Bulwer to Malmesbury, 23, 31 October, 6 November 1852 FO 79/160; Bulwer to Russell, 18 January 1853, FO 79/165; *The Times*, 24 June 1857; Ivan Scott, *The Roman Church and the Powers 1848–1865* (The Hague, 1969), 53; Frederick Brown, *For the Soul of France: Culture Wars in the Age of Drefus* (New York, 2010), 10, 13; C.T. McIntire, *England against the Papacy 1858–1861: Tories, Liberals and the Overthrow of Papal Temporal Power during the Risorgimento* (Cambridge, 1983), 18–21; Pierre Milza, *Napoléon III* (Paris, 2004), 237–8; Scarlett to Granville, 4, 19 February 1852, FO 79/157; *News of the World*, 22 March 1857.

19 Bickerton Lyons, pocket book, 1853, box 220; R.B. Lyons to E. Lyons, 6 April 1853, box 214; Flint, *Britain and the Holy See*, 123-4, 88; R.B. Lyons to Minna, 19 February, 18 April 1853, box 298; Matthias Bruschkuhl, *Great Britain and the Holy See, 1746–1870* (Blackrock, 1982), 84–5; R.B. Lyons to E. Lyons, 18, 19 March 1853, box 214.

20 R.B. Lyons to Addington, 20 June 1853, box 174; Mullen and Munson, *Smell of the Continent*, 158, 171, 186–7, 194; R.B. Lyons to E. Lyons, 14 April 1853, box 214; R.B. Lyons to Minna, 14 April 1853, box 298.

21 Bickerton Lyons, pocket book, 1853, box 220; R.B. Lyons to E. Lyons, 18 April, 31 May 1853, box 214; R.B. Lyons to Minna, 18, 20 April, 4 May 1853, box 298; *The Times*, 24 June 1857; Scarlett to R.B. Lyons, 1 June, 2 May 1853, box 118; R.B. Lyons to Scarlett, 23 April 1853, FO 79/166; for Antonelli see Frank J. Coppa, *Cardinal Giocomo Antonelli and Papal Politics in European Affairs* (Albany, 1990).

22 R.B. Lyons to Minna, 11 May 1853, box 298; R.B. Lyons to Addington, 28 April 1853, box 174; R.B. Lyons to E. Lyons, 31 May, 30 June, 19 July, 26 October, 11, 16 November, 1853, box 214; R.B. Lyons to Minna, 13 July 1853, box 298.

23 R.B. Lyons to Scarlett, 3, 7 June, 28 July 1853, FO 79/167; 23 September 1853, FO 79/168; 29 October, 5 November, FO 79/169; 26 November 1853, FO 79/170; E.E.Y. Hales, *Pio Nono: A Study of European Politics and Religion in the Nineteenth Century* (New York, 1954), 142; Jonathan Steinberg, *Bismarck: A Life* (Oxford, 2011), 129.

24 R.B. Lyons to Scarlett, 27 May 1853, FO 79/166.

25 R.B. Lyons to Minna, 13 July 1853, box 298; R.B. Lyons to E. Lyons, 19 July 1853, box 214; Addington to R.B. Lyons, 18 October, 15 November 1853, box 174; Charles Beatty, *Ferdinand de Lesseps, a Biographical Study* (London, 1956), 28–9.

26 R.B. Lyons to Addington, 4 November 1853, box 174; O'Connor, *Romance of Italy*, 20 51, 54; McIntire, *England against the Papacy*, 40; Pemble, *Mediterranean Passion*, 18, 43, 81; Mullen and Munson, *Smell of the Continent*, 89–91; R.B. Lyons to Addington, 28 April 1853, box 174; R.B. Lyons to Minna, 28 April, 11, 18 May, 24 September 1853, box 298; R.B. Lyons to E. Lyons, 16 May, 14 June 1853, box 214.

27 R.B. Lyons to Addington, 4 November 1853, box 174; Bickerton Lyons, pocket book, 1853, box 220; R.B. Lyons to Minna, 4, 18 May 1853, box 298; R.B. Lyons to E. Lyons, 14 June, 14 July, 10 August 1853, box 214; R.B. Lyons to Addington, 24 February 1854, box 106; R.B. Lyons to Minna, 4, 20 November, 14 December 1853; 10, 20 January, 10 February 1854, box 298.

28 Scarlett to Clarendon, 31 January 1854, FO 79/176; R.B. Lyons to Scarlett, 13 December 1853; Scarlett to Clarendon, 16 December 1853, FO 79/170; R.B. Lyons to Scarlett, 23 January, 9 February, 2 May 1854, FO 43/58; R.B. Lyons to Bulwer, 15 August 1854, BUL 1/101/20; 13 November 1854, BUL 1/101/22; George Leveson Gower, *Mixed Grill* (London, 1947), 170; R.B. Lyons to Addington, 4 November 1853, box 174.

29 Clarendon to R.B. Lyons, 24 February 1854, FO 43/59; R.B. Lyons to E. Lyons, 31 May 1858, box 214; R.B. Lyons to Addington, 14 March 1854, box 106.

30 R.B. Lyons to Addington, 18 April 1854, box 106; Addington to R.B. Lyons, 2 May 1854, box 174; R.B. Lyons to E. Lyons, 21 June 1854, box 214; Bulwer to R.B. Lyons, 17 April, 30 July, 17 November 1854, box 118; R.B. Lyons to Bulwer, 27 July, 2 August 1854, box 106.

31 Constance Wright, *Fanny Kemble and the Lovely Land* (New York, 1972), 1–3, 10, 25, 42, 126, 136–7, 144–5; Bickerton Lyons, pocket book, 1854, box

220; Frances Anne Kemble, *Further Records, 1848–1883: A Series of Letters,* 2 vols (London, 1890), 2: 180–5, 1: 262.

32 Bickerton Lyons, pocket books, 1854, 1855, box 220; R.B. Lyons to Bulwer, 27 July 1854, BUL 1/101/18a; R.B. Lyons to Minna, 5 December 1854, box 298; 30 November 1857, box 299; R.B. Lyons to Moubray, 3 January 1855, box 284; R.B. Lyons to E. Lyons, 14 March 1855, box 214.

33 Bickerton Lyons, pocket book, 1854, box 220; R.B. Lyons to Bulwer, 11 December, 5 November 1854, FO 43/58; private note, 26 November [1854], box 106; Clarendon to Bulwer, 3 January 1855, FO 79/179.

34 Clarendon to Bulwer, 23 November 1854, FO 79/175; Bulwer to Clarendon, 6 November 1854, FO 79/179; R.B. Lyons to Bulwer, 10 November, 2 December 1854, FO 43/58; 11 January 1855, FO 43/60; R.B. Lyons to Normanby, 16 June 1855, FO 43/60; Bulwer to Clarendon, 6 November 1854, FO 79/179.

35 Bulwer to Clarendon, 4 January 1855, FO 79/183; Bulwer to Lyons, 3 [February] 1856, BUL 1/140/38; 3, 15, 21 January 1855, box 118; R.B. Lyons to Minna, 7, 29 March 1855, box 298; Bickerton Lyons, pocket book, 1854, box 220; Clarendon to R.B. Lyons (telegram), 27 June 1855, FO 43/61.

36 E. Lyons to Corbett, 20 August 1855; E. Lyons to Clarendon, 17 November 1855, box 294; Frederick Grey to [E. Lyons], 24 June 1855, L297; R.B. Lyons to E. Lyons, 14 July 1855, box 214.

37 Minna to E. Lyons, 26 October 1855, box 96; Bickerton Lyons, pocket books, 1854, 1855, box 220; J.B. Conacher, *Britain and the Crimea: Problems of War and Peace* (New York, 1987), 110, 138; Andrew D. Lambert, *The Crimean War: British Grand Strategy, 1853–1856* (Manchester, 1990), 312–13; E. Lyons to Clarendon, 17 November 1855, box 294.

38 E. Lyons to Clarendon, 17 November 1855, box 294; R.B. Lyons to E. Lyons, 7 October, 25 November 1855, 19 March 1856, box 214; R.B. Lyons to Hammond, 22 February 1856, box 118.

39 Brown, *Palmerston*, 394; Bickerton Lyons, pocket book, 1856, box 220; R.B. Lyons to Normanby, 4 February 1856, box 106; R.B. Lyons to E. Lyons, 4 April 1856, box 214.

40 Lister to R.B. Lyons, 31 March 1856, box 118; Bourne, *Foreign Policy of Victorian England*, 79–80; William E. Echard, *Napoleon III and the Concert of Europe* (Baton Rouge, LA, 1983), 58, 62–3; Winfried Baumgant, *The Peace of Paris 1856: Studies in War, Diplomacy and Peacemaking* (Oxford, 1981), 147, 149, 144, 139, 150–1; *Illustrated London News*, 17 May 1856; Paul W. Schroeder, *Austria, Great Britain and the Crimean War: The Destruction of the European Concert* (Ithaca, NY, 1972), 374–5, 377; R.B. Lyons memorandum, 16 April 1856; Clarendon to R.B. Lyons, 16 April 1856, box 106; R.B.

Lyons to Normanby, 29 May 1856, FO 43/63; Clarendon to Normanby, 20 May 1856, box 195.

41 Bickerton Lyons, pocket book, 1856, box 220; R.B. Lyons to Minna, 20 May, 2, 26 June 1856, box 298; Norfolk to E. Lyons, 30 November 1855, L298.

42 Bickerton Lyons, pocket book, 1856, box 220; R.B. Lyons to Minna, 20 May 1856, box 298; R.B. Lyons to E. Lyons, 28 April 1856, box 214; R.B. Lyons memorandum, 14 May 1856, box 106; Dennis Mack Smith, *Mazzini* (New Haven, CT, 1994), 116; R.B. Lyons to Normanby, 21, 28 June 1856, box 106; Hudson to R.B. Lyons, 6 June 1856, box 118; R.B. Lyons to E. Lyons, 9, 16 July, 17 September, 15 October 1856, box 214; Normanby to R.B. Lyons, 25 June 1856, box 195.

43 *News of the World*, 27 March 1857; Moore to R.B. Lyons, 2, 7, 18, 22 September 1856, 24, 28 November, 16, 25 December 1857, box 195.

44 R.B. Lyons to Minna, 10, 14 January 1857, box 299; Normanby to R.B. Lyons, 26 February 1857, box 195; Bickerton Lyons, pocket book, 1857, box 220; R.B. Lyons to Minna, 28 May, 18, 27, 29 June, 6 July 1857, box 299; Normanby to Clarendon, 6 July 1857, FO 79/193; R.B. Lyons to Minna, 22 August, 6 September, 30 November 1857, box 299; R.B. Lyons to E. Lyons, 23 October 1857, box 214;

45 R.B. Lyons to Clarendon, 30 August 1857, FO 79/194; R.B. Lyons to Normanby, 11 October 1857; R.B. Lyons to Hudson, 11 October 1857, box 106; R.B. Lyons to Clarendon, 25 August, 9 October 1857, FO 79/194.

46 R.B. Lyons to Conyngham, 5 December 1857, FO 43/66; E. Lyons to Minna, 1 July 1856, box 96; R.B. Lyons to Minna, 4 December 1856, box 298; Scott Thomas Cairns, "Lord Lyons and Anglo-American Diplomacy during the American Civil War, 1859–1865" (PhD thesis, London School of Economics, 2004), 34, 40; R.B. Lyons to Minna, 24 January 1857, box 299; R.B. Lyons to E. Lyons, 28 January, 4, 11 March 1857, box 214; E. Lyons to Minna, 6 April 1858, box 96.

CHAPTER THREE

1 R.B. Lyons to Minna, 30 November 1857, box 299; Bickerton Lyons, pocket book, 1857, box 220; Hudson to R.B. Lyons, 29 August 1857, box 118; Lyons to Normanby, 6 January 1858, box 106.

2 Lyons to Normanby, 6 January, 6 March 1858, box 106; Frank J. Coppa, *Cardinal Giacomo Antonelli and Papal Politics in European Affairs* (Albany, 1990), 97; Henry Reeve, ed., *The Greville Memoirs*, 3 vols (London, 1874), 1:356, 334, 338; *The Times*, 21 August 1857.

3 Malmesbury to R.B. Lyons, 3 March 1858, box 192; *Daily Telegraph*, 18 March 1857; *Reynolds's Newspaper*, 29 March 1857; *Glasgow Examiner*, 11 April 1857; *The Times*, 29 August 1857; Malmesbury to R.B. Lyons, 11 March 1858, 9M73/54, Malmesbury Papers, Hampsire Record Office (HRO).

4 Derby to Malmesbury, 14 April 1858, 920 DER (14) 184/1, Derby Papers, Liverpool Public Library (LPL); Malmesbury to Cowley, 14 March 1858, 9M73/54; Gavin B. Henderson, "Palmerston and the Secret Service Fund," *English Historical Review* 53 (1938): 485–7; Henry E. Carlisle, ed., *A Selection from the Correspondence of Abraham Hayward, Q.C.: From 1834–1884*, 2 vols (London, 1886), 1:294–5, 305; Harold Acton, *The Last Bourbons of Naples (1825–1861)* (London, 1961), 328–9, 334.

5 Hudson to Clarendon, 10 July 1857, FO 70/293; *Illustrated London News*, 18 July 1857; Barbar to Clarendon, 30 June 1857, FO 70/293; Hudson to Clarendon, 17 January 1858, FO 70/295.

6 William Watt to Clarendon, 21 July, 1 September 1857; see also Charles Park to Clarendon; Barbar to Clarendon, 11 August, 8 October 1857; see Palmerston Memoranda, 27 October 1857, FO 70/293.

7 *Reynolds's Newspaper*, 9 January 1858; *Leeds Mercury*, 16 April 1858; Hammond to Barbar, 8 October 1857; George Ridley, M.P. to Clarendon, 12 November 1857; Clarendon to Carafa, 14 November 1857; Barbar to Clarendon, 17, 23 November 1857, FO 70/293; Diarmaid MacCulloch, "Evil Just Is," *London Review of Books* 33 (2010): 24; Barbar to Clarendon, 28 November 1857, FO 70/294; *The Times*, 23 January 1858.

8 Barbar to Clarendon, 19 December 1857, 12, 27 January 1858, FO 70/294; Malmesbury to Cowley, 10 April 1858, 9M73/54, Malmesbury Papers.

9 Hawkins, *Forgotten Prime Minister*, 2:166–8, 197; *The Times*, 13 March 1858; Malmesbury to Cowley, 1 March, 30 October 1858, FO 519/196, Cowley Papers, NA; Derby to Cowley, 21 August 1858, 920 DER (14) 184/1, Derby Papers.

10 R.B. Lyons to Malmesbury, 12 March 1858, box 106; Bickerton Lyons, pocket book, 1858, box 220; Barbar to Clarendon, 2, 15 February 1858, FO 70/295; T.A. Jenkins, ed., *The Parliamentary Diaries of Sir John Trelawny, 1858–1865*, Camden 4th series, vol. 40 (London, 1990): 28–9; Earl of Malmesbury, *Memoirs of an Ex-Minister: An Autobiography*, 2 vols (London, 1884), 2:107; R.B. Lyons to Malmesbury, 21 March 1858, FO 70/297.

11 *Dundee Courier*, 24 March 1858; *The Times*, 13 March 1858; Malmesbury to Hudson, 15 March 1858, 9M73/54, Malmesbury Papers; Malmesbury to R.B. Lyons, 18 March 1858, box 192; Bickerton Lyons, pocket book, 1858, box 220; R.B. Lyons to Malmesbury, 27 March 1858, box 106; R.B. Lyons

to Minna, 30 March, 10 April 1858, box 299; R.B. Lyons to Malmesbury, 27 March 1858, FO 70/297; Park to R.B. Lyons, 17 October 1879, box 151.

12 Carafa to Malmesbury, 27 March 1858, FO 70/297; Malmesbury to R.B. Lyons, 1 April 1858, box 192; R.B. Lyons to Minna, 30 March 1858, box 299; R.B. Lyons to Malmesbury, 17 April 1858, FO 70/297; *The Times*, 19 March 1858; *Stirling Observer*, 31 March 1858; Bidwell to R.B. Lyons, 25 March 1858, box 119; R.B. Lyons to Bidwell, 3 April 1858, box 106.

13 R.B. Lyons to Malmesbury, 25 March 1858; *The Times*, 11 March 1858; Malmesbury to R.B. Lyons, 15 April 1858, box 192; Malmesbury to Cowley, 16 April 1858, 9M73/54, Malmesbury Papers.

14 Derby to Malmesbury, 12 April 1858, 920 DER (14) 184/1, Derby Papers; Malmesbury to Cowley, 13 April 1858, FO 519/196, Cowley Papers.

15 Malmesbury to Cowley, 13, 15, 16, 17, 29 April, 1 May 1858, FO 519/196; Cowley to Malmesbury, 18 April, 1858, FO 70/297; Malmesbury to R.B. Lyons, 21, 30 April 1858; Malmesbury to Hudson, 24 April, 6 May 1858, 9M73/54, Malmesbury Papers.

16 *The Times*, 13 March 1858; Malmesbury to R.B. Lyons, 30 April 1858, box 192; R.B. Lyons to Minna, 11 May, 1 June 1858, box 299; *Morning Post*, 26 May 1858; *The Times*, 12 June 1858; Malmesbury to Normanby, 17 May 1858, 9M73/54, Malmesbury Papers; Malmesbury to R.B. Lyons, 31 May, 3 June 1858, box 192.

17 R.B. Lyons to Malmesbury, 12 June 1858, box 106; Malmesbury to R.B. Lyons, "private and confidential," 8, also 3 June 1858; Malmesbury to Azeglio, 11 June 1858, 9M73/54, Malmesbury Papers; Malmesbury to Carafa, 25 May 1858, FO 70/295; FO to Treasury, 22 July 1858, FO 70/299; R.B. Lyons to Minna, 19 June 1858, box 299; *Lancaster Gazette*, 19 June 1858; *The Times*, 12 June 1858.

18 Derby to Pakington, 2 May 1858; Derby to Cowley, 13 August 1858, 920 DER (14) 184/1, Derby Papers; Cowley to Derby, 20, 27 August 1858; Derby to Malmesbury, n.d., 2 September 1858, 920 DER (14) 144/2; Disraeli to Derby, 3 October 1858, 920 DER (14), 145/5; Malmesbury to Derby, 27 October [1858], 920 (14), 144/2; Hawkins, *Forgotten Prime Minister*, 2:198.

19 Malmesbury to Derby, 17 December 1858, 920 DER (14) 144/2, Derby Papers; R.B. Lyons to Minna, 10 April 1858, box 299; *The Times*, 20 March 1858; R.B. Lyons to Minna, 25 May 1858, box 299.

20 R.B. Lyons to Minna, 25 May, 1 June 1858, box 299; Normanby to R.B. Lyons, 16 April 1858, box 195; R.B. Lyons to E. Lyons, 31 May 1858, box 214; Fenton to R.B. Lyons, 25 May 1858, box 178; Malmesbury to Cowley, 1 June 1858, FO 519/196.

21 R.B. Lyons to E. Lyons, 31 May 1858, box 214; Malmesbury to Derby, 4 April 1858, DER (14) 144/2, Derby Papers; Raymond A. Jones, *The British Diplomatic Service, 1815–1914* (Waterloo, 1983), 99–100, 24; R.B. Lyons to Minna, 2 September 1860, box 299; Odo Russell to R.B. Lyons, 2 January 1859, box 197; Lord Strang, *The Diplomatic Career* (London, 1962), 17, 19; Russell to Odo Russell, 30 November 1858, FO 918/7, Odo Russell Papers.

22 Malmesbury to R.B. Lyons, 8 June 1858, box 192; Jenkins, *Parliamentary Diaries of Trelawny*, 36–7; Bickerton Lyons, pocket book, 1858, box 220; Strang, *Diplomatic Career*, 33; R.B. Lyons to Malmesbury, 13 July 1858, box 106.

23 R.B. Lyons to Lady Normanby, 29 June 1858, box 192; Bickerton Lyons, pocket book, 1858, box 220; Normany to Malmesbury, 12 July 1858, FO 79/199; R.B. Lyons to Minna, 25 July 1858, box 299; L540, box 272; Addington to R.B. Lyons, 26 July 1858, box 174.

24 Corbett to Malmesbury, 6 October 1858, FO 79/199; Hudson to R.B. Lyons, 29 June 1858, box 119; R.B. Lyons to Hudson, 13 July 1858, box 106; R.B. Lyons to Minna, 26 June, 25, 31 July, 30 September 1858, box 299; Malmesbury to R.B. Lyons, 5 October 1858, box 106.

25 Minna to R.B. Lyons, 16, 23 July, 29 September, 2, 4, 7, 8 October 1858, box 293; R.B. Lyons to Minna, 25, 31 July, 28 August 1858, box 299; Bickerton Lyons, pocket book, 1858, box 220; Malmesbury to Derby, 22, 28 December 1858, 920 DER (14) 144/2, Derby Papers; S. M. Eardley-Wilmot, *Life of Vice-Admiral Edmund, Lord Lyons with an Account of Naval Operations in the Black Sea and Sea of Azov 1854–56*, replica edition (London, 2005), 411–15; Hertslet, *Recollections*, 14–15.

26 Eardley-Wilmot, *Lyons*, 411–15; *Wells Journal*, 26 November 1858; R.B. Lyons to Cleeve, 9 March 1875, box 141; Jones, *The British Diplomatic Service*, 127–8.

27 *Oxford Dictionary of National Biography*, 40:165; Napier to Malmesbury, 26 October 1858, 9M73/18, Malmesbury Papers; James J. Barnes and Patience P. Barnes, *Private and Confidential: Letters from British Ministers in Washington to the Foreign Secretaries in London, 1844–67* (London, 1993), 179.

28 Napier to Malmesbury, 26 October 1858, 9M73/18, 15 February 1859, 9M73/19, Malmesbury Papers; Allan Nevins, *The Emergence of Lincoln: Douglas, Buchanan and Party Chaos 1857–1859*, 2 vols (New York, 1950), 1:126–7; Beverly Wilson Palmer, ed., *Selected Letters of Charles Sumner*, vol. 1 (Boston, 1990): 486, 490; *Glasgow Examiner*, 16 May 1857; *Illustrated London News*, 16 May 1857; *Daily Telegraph*, 12 February 1857; Glyndon Van Deusen, *William Henry Seward* (New York, 1967), 257; Malmesbury to Napier, 30 April 1858, 9M73/54.

29 Malmesbury to Derby, 26 April [1858], 920 DER (14) 144/2, Derby Papers; Barnes and Barnes, *Private and Confidential*, 174–5; Malmesbury to Cowley, 20 November 1858, FO 519/196.

30 Barnes and Barnes, *Private and Confidential*, 182–3, 202; Wilbur Devereux Jones, *The American Problem in British Diplomacy, 1841–1861* (Athens, GA, 1974), 100, 166, 169, 115; Derby to Malmesbury, 20 August, 11 October 1858, 9M73/20, Malmesbury Papers.

31 See Phillip E. Myers, *Caution and Cooperation: The American Civil War in British-American Relations* (Kent, OH, 2008); Derby to Malmesbury, 15 September, 11 October 1858, 9M73/20, Malmesbury Papers; Malmesbury to Derby, 18 September 1858, 920 DER (14), 144/2, Derby Papers; *Oxford Dictionary of National Biography*, 8:462; Malmesbury to Buchanan, 18 November 1858; Malmesbury to R.B. Lyons, 20 November 1858, 9M73/54; Jones, *British Diplomatic Service*, 127; M.S. Anderson, *The Rise of Modern Diplomacy, 1450–1919* (New York, 1993), 199.

32 Malmesbury to R.B. Lyons, 8, 14, 21 November 1858; R.B. Lyons to Malmesbury, 9, 15 November, 1858, box 192; Lynn William, "The Career of Sir Edward Malet, British Diplomat, 1837–1908" (PhD thesis, University of Wales, 1982), 20; Griffith to R.B. Lyons, 12 July, 21 August, 24 October 1852, box 185.

33 Malmesbury to Napier, 26 November 1858, 21 January 1859, 9M73/54, Malmesbury Papers; George Mifflin Dallas, *A Series of Letters Written from London*, ed. Julia Dallas, 2 vols (Philadelphia, 1869), 1:131, 138; John Bassett Moore, ed., *The Works of James Buchanan*, reprint ed., 12 vols (New York, 1960), 10:317; Napier to Malmesbury, 15, 21 February 1858, 9M73/19; Nevins, *Emergence of Lincoln*, 1:431–2.

34 Moore, *Works of Buchanan*, 10:317; Dallas, *Series of Letters Written from London*, 2:87–8; Sarah Agnes Wallace and Frances Elma Gillespie, eds, *Journal of Benjamin Moran*, 2 vols (Chicago, 1948), 1:505; *Illustrated London News*, 4 December 1858; Minna to R.B. Lyons, 29 March 1859, box 293; Malmesbury to Napier, 26 November 1858, 9M73/54, Malmesbury Papers.

35 For the will of the first Lord Lyons see box 119, and L395; Cleeve to R.B. Lyons, 5, 8 December 1858; 15 January, 1, 2, 8, 15 February 1859, box 175.

36 R.B. Lyons to Minna, 1, 26 March, 11 April 1859, box 299.

37 *Morning Chronicle*, 25 April 1859; R.B. Lyons to Minna, 11 April 1859, box 299; Derby to Malmesbury, 20 August 1858, 9M73/20, Malmesbury Papers; Malmesbury to Derby, 17 December 1858, 920 DER (14), 144/2, Derby Papers; Malmesbury to Napier, 30 April, 26 November 1858, 9M73/54; Barnes and Barnes, *Private and Confidential*, 174, 198; Napier to Malmesbury, 15 February 1859, 9M73/19.

38 Napier to R.B. Lyons, 27 May 1859, box 119; R.B. Lyons to Bayley, 20 July 1859, box 106; Griffith to Lyons, 16 January 1859, box 185.

39 R.B. Lyons to Malmesbury, 30 May 1859, box 106; Brian Jenkins, *Britain and the War for the Union*, 2 vols (Montreal and London, 1974, 1980), 1:83; *Daily Telegraph*, 24 February 1857; Barnes and Barnes, *Private and Confidential*, 113.

40 R.B. Lyons to Malmesbury, 30 May 1859, box 106; Jones, *American Problem in British Diplomacy*, 172.

CHAPTER FOUR

1 Hawkins, *Forgotten Prime Minister*, 2:217; John Prest, *Lord John Russell* (Columbia, SC, 1972), 385–6; Brian Jenkins, *Britain and the War for the Union*, 2 vols (Montreal and London, 1974, 1980), 1:82, 85; Jenkins, *Parliamentary Diaries of Trelawny, 1858–1865*, Camden 4th ser., 40 (London, 1990): 221; Algernon Cecil, *Queen Victoria and Her Prime Ministers* (London, 1953), 124; David F. Krein, *The Last Palmerston Government: Foreign Policy, Domestic Politics, and the Genesis of "Splendid Isolation"* (Ames, IA, 1978), 14–16; Paul H. Scherer, "Partner or Puppet? Lord John Russell at the Foreign Office, 1859–1862," *Albion* 19 (1987): 348–9, 352; Cobden to Chevalier, 5 March 1864, Cobden 47, Cobden Papers, WSRO; Jenkins, *Parliamentary Diaries of Trelawny*, 158; Brown, *Palmerston*, 439, 434.

2 Scherer, "Partner or Puppet?" 348; John Clarke, *British Diplomacy and Foreign Policy 1782–1865* (London, 1989), 261–4; Jenkins, *Parliamentary Diaries of Sir John Trelawny*, 106, 141; Prest, *Lord John Russell*, 386–8.

3 Lord Redesdale, *Memories*, 2 vols (London, 1915), 1:109; Wilbur Devereux Jones, *The American Problem in British Diplomacy, 1841–1861* (Athens, GA, 1974), 164; Hammond memorandum "at the close of Lord Derby's Administration," 9M73/75, Malmesbury Papers; Hammond memorandum "at the close of the Year 1858," 1 January 1859, 920 DER (14) 144/2, Derby Papers.

4 Robert E. May, *Manifest Destiny's Underworld: Filibustering in Antebellum America* (Chapel Hill, NC, 2002), 218–19, 221, 230–1, 244–5, xii; Gordon T. Stewart, *The American Response to Canada Since 1776* (East Lansing, 1992), 62–71; Reginald C. Stuart, *United States Expansionism and British North America* (Chapel Hill, NC, 1988), 194–5, 203, 206–9.

5 Crampton to Bulwer, 20 March 1858, BUL 1/100/8, Bulwer Papers.

6 *The Times*, 11 May 1857; Jones, *American Problem in British Diplomacy*, 2, 160; Jasper Ridley, *Lord Palmerston* (London, 1970), 548, 457; C.P. Villiers

to Bright, 25 January 1862, BL Add. Ms. 43386, Bright Papers; *The Times*, 24 March, 11 May 1857; Brown, *Palmerston*, 450–1; Robert Kagan, *Dangerous Nation* (New York, 2006), 213; Jay Sexton, *Debtor Diplomacy: Finance and American Foreign Relations in the Civil War Era, 1837–1873* (Oxford, 2005), 40; Jenkins, *Britain and the War for the Union*, 1:83–4; Phillip E. Myers, *Caution and Cooperation: The American Civil War in British American Relations* (Kent, OH, 2008), 8–28; *Illustrated London News*, 13 November 1858; *The Times*, 24 February 1857; David Brown, *Palmerston and the Politics of Foreign Policy* (Manchester, 2002), 27, 41; George Mifflin Dallas, *A Series of Letters Written from London*, ed. Julia Dallas, 2 vols (Philadelphia, 1869), 1:31, 39; Palmerston to Hammond, 4 October 1859, 4 April 1861, FO 391/7, Hammond Papers; May, *Manifest Destiny's Underworld*, 246; S.M. Ellis, ed., *A Mid-Victorian Pepys: The Letters and Memoirs of Sir William Hardman* (London, 1923), 8.

7   Stanley to Derby, 9 September 1866, 920 DER (15) 12/3/7, Derby Papers; Stanley Diary, 31 December 1867, 920 DER (15); Sexton, *Debtor Diplomacy*, 73; Moore, ed., *Works of Buchanan*, 10:102; Willard Karl Clunder, "Lewis Cass and Slavery Expansion: 'The Father of Popular Sovereignty' and Ideological Infanticide," *Civil War History* 33 (1986): 293–317; *New York Daily Times*, 25 February 1857; *The Times*, 20 December 1858.

8   *The Times*, 20, 22 December 1858; *Illustrated London News*, 25 September, 13 November 1858, 8 January 1859; Martin Crawford, *The Anglo-American Crisis in the Mid-Nineteenth Century: The Times and America, 1850–1862* (Athens, GA, 1987), 23, 17, 18, 26, 28, 48, 50; *The Times*, 20 November, 1858, 24 February, 11 May 1857, 18, 20, 22, 23 December 1858.

9   Charles Adams, *Slavery, Secession and Civil War: Views from the UK and Europe, 1856–1865* (Lanham, MD, 2005), 28, 33,14, 27, 29, 2; Crawford, *Anglo-American Crisis*, 63; Beverly Wilson Palmer, ed., *Selected Letters of Charles Sumner*, 2 vols (Boston, 1990), 1:492, 498, 502–3, 506; see Richard Huzzey, "The Moral Geography of British Anti-Slavery Responsibilities," *Transactions of the Royal Historical Society* 22 (2012): 111–39.

10 *The Times*, 22 June 1857; James J. Barnes and Patience P. Barnes, eds, *Private and Confidential: Letters from British Ministers in Washington to the Foreign Secretaries in London, 1844–67* (Toronto, 1993), 174; R.B. Lyons to Minna, 11, 17, 24 April; 2 May; 25 July 1859, box 299; R.B. Lyons to Barbar, 25 April 1859, box 106.

11 Sexton, *Debtor Diplomacy*, 76; Jenkins, *Britain and the War for the Union*, 1:44; R.B. Lyons to Minna, 24 April, 2, 10, 16, 24 May, 13, 21, 27 June, 22, 30 August, 27 September, 17 October, 26 December 1859, box 299; Cobden to

Kate Cobden, 20 March, 30 April 1859, Cobden Papers 81; 30 June 1859, Cobden Papers 82, WSRO; Conyngham to R.B. Lyons, 19 August 1859, box 175; Barnes and Barnes, *Private and Confidential*, 172.

12 George Augustus Sala, *My Diary in America in the Midst of War*, 2 vols (London, 1865), 2:68–70, 77; *The Times*, 17 March 1857; Dallas, *A Series of Letters*, 1:197, 2:30–3; *Illustrated London News*, 24 July 1859; R.B. Lyons to Minna, 25 July; 2, 10, 16, 24 May 1859, box 299.

13 R.B. Lyons to Minna, 27 June; 2 August 1859, box 299; *Weekly Arizonian*, 14 July 1859; R.B. Lyons to Malmesbury 11 July 1859, box 106; Russell to Lyons, 29 June; 28 July; 30 August; 25 November 1859, box 196; R.B. Lyons to Minna, 2 August 1859, box 299; Malmesbury to R.B. Lyons, 6 May, 25 March, 29 April 1859, box 192; R.B. Lyons to Russell, 16, 22, 30 August, 5 September 1859; R.B. Lyons to Wyke, 1 September 1859, box 106; Wyke to R.B. Lyons, 15 September 1859, box 119; Dallas, *A Series of Letters*, 1:93.

14 R.B. Lyons to Bunch, 13 October, 15 November 1859, 2 June 1860, box 106; Eugene H. Berwanger, *The British Foreign Service and the American Civil War* (Lexington, KY, 1994), 4–6; D.C.M. Platt, *The Cinderella Service: British Consuls since 1825* (London, 1971), 19, 62.

15 Berwanger, *British Foreign Service*, 8–9; Edith J. Archibald, *Life and Letters of Sir Edward Mortimer Archibald: A Memoir of Fifty Years of Service* (Toronto, 1924), 100, 91; R.B. Lyons to Archibald, 8, 16, 24 June 1859, box 106; Platt, *Cinderella Service*, 36.

16 R.B. Lyons to Minna, 8 November 1859, box 299; R.B. Lyons to Hammond, 23, 28, 30 November 1859, box 106; Berwanger, *British Foreign Service*, 8–9.

17 R.B. Lyons to Hammond, 30 August 1859, box 106; R.B. Lyons to Minna, 17 April 1859, box 299; R.B. Lyons to Hammond, 30 August 1859, box 106; Edward Malet to mother, 2 December 1862, Malet Papers, Duke University; R.B. Lyons to Minna, 20 December 1859, 5 March 1860, box 299.

18 Jones, *British Diplomatic Service*, 161; R.B. Lyons to Hammond, 15 December 1858, FO 79/200; Conyngham to R.B. Lyons, 11 December 1858, box 175; R.B. Lyons to Napier, 21 June; R.B. Lyons to Warre, 1 July 1859, box 106; R.B. Lyons to Minna, 30 August, 11, 31 October, 28 November 1859, box 299; R.B. Lyons to Monson, n.d. [December 1859], box 106; Monson to R.B. Lyons, 22 December 1859, 19 January, 26 April, 10 May 1860, box 193; R.B. Lyons to Minna, 9, 22 January, 14 May 1860, box 299; R.B. Lyons to Monson, 17 July 1860, box 106; R.B. Lyons to Odo Russell, 5 March 1860, FO 918/52, Odo Russell Papers.

19 Virginia Clay-Copton, *A Belle of the Fifties: Memoirs of Mrs. Clay of Alabama*, new edition, ed. Ada Sterling (Tuscaloosa, AL, 1999), 139, 115; R.B. Lyons to Minna, 14 February 1860, box 299; Gozze to R.B. Lyons, 26 March 1860, box 181; R.B. Lyons to T. H. Farrer, 18 February 1860, box 106; Philip Shriver Klein, *President Buchanan: A Biography* (University Park, PA, 1962), 246; Cobden to Bright, 29 April 1859, Cobden 45, Cobden Papers; R.B. Lyons to Minna, 8 May 1860, 4 June 1861, 17 April, 20 December 1859, 28 February 1860, box 299.

20 Sterling, *Belle of the Fifties*, 141; Amanda Foreman, *A World on Fire: An Epic History of Two Nations Divided* (London, 2010), 12; R.B. Lyons to Minna, 30 April 1860, box 299; R.B. Lyons to Bunch, 3 May 1860; R.B. Lyons to T. H. Farrer, 18 February 1860, box 106.

21 R.B. Lyons to Minna, 9, 17, 22 January, 19 March, 10 April 1860, box 299; Palmer, *Selected Letters of Sumner*, 2:17, 19; R.B. Lyons to Odo Russell, 5 March 1860, FO 918/52, Odo Russell Papers.

22 R.B. Lyons to Mure, 1 February; R.B. Lyons to T. H. Farrer, 18 February 1860, box 106; F.T.A. Ashton-Gwatkin, *The British Foreign Service* (Ann Arbor, MI, 1967), 4; Barnes and Barnes, *Private and Confidential*, 219, 218; Alston to R.B. Lyons, 12 May 1860, box 195.

23 Russell to R.B. Lyons, 24 June 1859, box 196; Scherer, "Partner or Puppet?" 370–1; Malmesbury to Derby, 13 January 1860, 920 DER (14) 144/2a, Derby Papers.

24 Russell to R.B. Lyons, 24 June, 28 July, 5 August, 21, 30 September, 11 November, 23 December 1859, box 196.

25 Russell to R.B. Lyons, 23 December 1859, box 196; R.B. Lyons to Mure, 1 February 1860, box 106; Barnes and Barnes, *Private and Confidential*, 221–2; Philip M. Hamer, "British Consuls and the Negro Seamen Acts 1850–1860," *Journal of Southern History* 1 (1935): 166–7.

26 For a succinct account of "the pig war," see the internet site of the San Juan National Historical Park; E.C. Coleman, *The Pig War: The Most Perfect War in History* (Stroud, UK, 2009), 63–4, 88, 77.

27 Russell to R.B. Lyons, 21 September 1859, box 196; Myers, *Caution and Cooperation*, 30.

28 Coleman, *The Pig War*, 97, 130; R.B. Lyons to Baynes, 16 September 1859; R.B. Lyons to Russell, 13, 19 September, 17 October, 8 November 1859, box 106; Barnes and Barnes, *Private and Confidential*, 219.

29 Baynes to R.B. Lyons, 28 January, 10 February, 25 March 1860, box 120; R.B. Lyons to Baynes, 2, 30 May, 12 June, 24 October, n.d. [9 November] 1860,

box 106; Russell to R.B. Lyons, 30 September, 28 October 1859; 25 February 1860, box 196; Barnes and Barnes, *Private and Confidential*, 230, 237, 241.

30 Michael C. Meyer and William H. Beezley, *The Oxford History of Mexico* (Oxford, 2000), 371–3; Russell to R.B. Lyons, 28 October 1859, box 196; Klein, *Buchanan*, 321–3.

31 Aldham to R.B. Lyons, 6 May 1859, 2 February 1860, box 106; Barnes and Barnes, *Private and Confidential*, 220, 223, 226, 228; R.B. Lyons to Archibald, 21 May 1859; R.B. Lyons to Russell, 5 September 1859; Mathews to R.B. Lyons, 19 December 1859, box 119; Meyer and Beezley, *Oxford History of Mexico*, 379.

32 Aldham to R.B. Lyons, 3 March 1860, box 120; Barnes and Barnes, *Private and Confidential*, 233; Aldham to R.B. Lyons, 1 January 1860; Wyke to R.B. Lyons, 23 June 1861, box 121; Meyer and Beezley, *Oxford History of Mexico*, 376–7.

CHAPTER FIVE

1 Moore to R.B. Lyons, 1 December 1859, box 194; Laura A. White, "The South in the 1850's as Seen by British Consuls," *Journal of Southern History* 1 (1933): 30, 37–40, 44–5.

2 R.B. Lyons to Moore, 16 December 1859; R.B. Lyons to Tulin, 21 December 1859; R.B. Lyons to Bunch, 7 December 1859, 14 January 1860, box 106; Moore to R.B. Lyons, 19 December 1859, box 194.

3 R.B. Lyons to Mure, 1 February 1860, box 106; Irvine to R.B. Lyons, 31 January 1860, box 120; Edward K. Spann, *Gotham at War: New York City, 1860–1865* (Wilmington, DE, 2002), 125; Barnes and Barnes, *Private and Confidential*, 218, 220–2; R.B. Lyons to Moore, 23 October 1859; R.B. Lyons to T.H. Farrer, 18 February 1860; R.B. Lyons to Bunch, 3 May 1860, box 106; R.B. Lyons to Minna, 26 April 1859, box 298.

4 Barnes and Barnes, *Private and Confidential*, 222; R.B. Lyons to Kortwright, 4 January 1860, box 106.

5 R.B. Lyons to Minna, 5 March, 16 April 1860, box 299; Archibald Alison, *Some Account of My Life and Writings: An Autobiography*, 2 vols (Edinburgh, 1883), 2:488–9; Jenkins, *Britain and the War for the Union*, 1:192; J.M. Mason to R.B. Lyons, 17 March 1860, box 120; R.B. Lyons to Wigfall, 11 April 1860; R.B. Lyons to Bunch, n.d. [12 April 1860], box 106; *Holmes County Republican*, 19 April 1860.

6 Minna to R.B. Lyons, 23 August 1859, and her correspondence for early 1860, box 299; Minna to R.B. Lyons, 9 May 1860, box 293; R.B. Lyons to

Wilkins (consul at Chicago), 28 April; R.B. Lyons to Edmund Head, 28 April, 22 June 1860, box 106; Barnes and Barnes, *Private and Confidential*, 227, 229.

7   Barnes and Barnes, *Private and Confidential*, 227–34.

8   R.B. Lyons to Minna, 3, 9, 17, 31 July 1860, box 299; Barnes and Barnes, *Private and Confidential*, 234–6; R.B. Lyons to Hammond, 5 June; R.B. Lyons to Archibald, 29, 30 May, 8, 19 June 1860, box 106; R.B. Lyons to Newcastle, 14 May 1860; Newcastle to R.B. Lyons, 11 July 1860, box 211; Harold Holzer, *Lincoln President-Elect: Abraham Lincoln and the Great Secession Winter, 1860–1861* (New York, 2008), 278.

9   R.B. Lyons to Minna, 31 July, 7, 10, 17, 19 August, 2 September 1860, box 299; Matthew Hale Smith, *Sunshine and Shadow in New York* (Hartford, 1869), 43; Benjamin Feldman, *Butchery on Bond Street* (New York, 2007), 64, 66; Allan Nevins, ed., *Diary of the Civil War: George Templeton Strong* (New York, 1962), 49.

10 R.B. Lyons to Wilkins, 1 September 1860; Hilliard to R.B. Lyons, 28 August 1860; Irvine to R.B. Lyons, 5 September 1860; R.B. Lyons to Irvine, 9 September 1860, box 211; R.B. Lyons to Minna, 19, 23 August, 11, 17 September 1860, box 299.

11 Stanley Weintraub, *Edward the Caresser: The Playboy Prince Who Became Edward VII* (New York, 2001), 49–59; R.B. Lyons to Minna, 19, 23 September 1860, box 299; Cairns, "Lord Lyons and Anglo-American Diplomacy," 126.

12 Weintraub, *Edward the Caresser*, 62–79; *Nashville Union and American*, 9 October 1860; Lloyd Morris, *Incredible New York: High Life and Low Life of the Last Hundred Years* (New York, 1951), 24; Archibald, *Life and Letters of Sir Edward Archibald*, 112; Monson to R.B. Lyons, 27 December 1860, 18 January 1861, box 193; R.B. Lyons to Minna, 23, 30 September, 8, 14, 23 October 1860, box 299.

13 R.B. Lyons to Griffith, 10 November 1860, box 106; R.B. Lyons to Minna, 23 October 1860, box 299; R.B. Lyons to Newcastle, 29 October 1860, box 106; Nevins, *Diary of the Civil War*, 51, 45, 52; Scott to R.B. Lyons, 18 October 1860, box 211; Palmer, *Selected Letters of Sumner*, 2:36; R.B. Lyons to Russell, 7 October 1860, box 211; Barnes and Barnes, *Private and Confidential*, 236–7; Nelson D. Lankford, *Cry Havoc: The Crooked Road to Civil War, 1861* (New York, 2007), 16.

14 Russell to R.B. Lyons, 20 November 1860, box 160; Minna to R.B. Lyons, 22, 29 November, 17 December 1860, box 293; R.B. Lyons to Minna, 6, 25 November 1860, 1, 7, 15 January 1861, box 299.

15 William J. Cooper, *We Have the War upon Us: The Onset of the Civil War* (New York, 2012), 20; James J. Barnes and Patience P. Barnes, *The American Civil War through British Eyes: Dispatches from British Diplomats*, vol. 1: *November 1860–April 1862* (Kent, OH, 2005), 2–3; R.B. Lyons to Newcastle, 10 December 1860, box 106; Barnes and Barnes, *Private and Confidential*, 236–7; Walter Stahr, *Seward: Lincoln's Indispensable Man* (New York, 2012), 272; Moore to R.B. Lyons, 7 December 1860, box 194.

16 R.B. Lyons to Bunch, 14, 28 November, 7 December 1860, box 106; Bunch to R.B. Lyons, November 1860; 21 March 1861, box 208; Barnes and Barnes, *American Civil War through British Eyes*, 1:40; R.B. Lyons to Mure, 8 December 1860, box 106.

17 *The Times*, 12 October 1857; David G. Surdam, *Northern Naval Superiority and the Economics of the American Civil War* (Columbia, SC, 2001), 198; R.B. Lyons to Bunch, 12 December 1860, box 106.

18 Barnes and Barnes, *American Civil War through British Eyes*, 1:8–11, 13–14; William Lee Miller, *President Lincoln: The Duty of a Statesman* (New York, 2008), 11–12; Cooper, *We Have the War upon Us*, 38–9; Bunch to R.B. Lyons, 20 December 1860, box 208.

19 William H. Freeling and Craig M. Simpson, eds, *Secession Debated: Georgia's Showdown in 1860* (New York, 1992), xix, xxi; White, "The South in the 1850's as Seen by British Consuls," 46; Moore to R.B. Lyons, 28 December 1860, box 194; Lankford, *Cry Havoc*, 12; Barnes and Barnes, *American Civil War through British Eyes*, 1:19; Bunch to R.B. Lyons, 22 May 1861, box 208; Archibald to R.B. Lyons, 2 January 1861, box 205; Holzer, *Lincoln President-Elect*, 57.

20 Holzer, *Lincoln President-Elect*, 25, 41–2, 131, 73; Russell McClintock, *Lincoln and the Decision for War: The Northern Response to Secession* (Chapel Hill, NC, 2008), 10, 19, 39–40, 121; Cooper, *We Have the War upon Us*, 73–4, 78–9; Maury Klein, *Days of Defiance: Sumter, Secession, and the Coming of the Civil War* (New York, 1997), 238; Barnes and Barnes, *Private and Confidential*, 239; Palmer, *Selected Letters of Charles Sumner*, 1:40–1.

21 Cooper, *We Have the War upon Us*, 130; Barnes and Barnes, *American Civil War through British Eyes*, 1:20–3, 25, 27–8; Barnes and Barnes, *Private and Confidential*, 241; Holzer, *Lincoln President-Elect*, 158, 342; Michael Burlingame, *Lincoln: A Life*, 2 vols (Baltimore, 2008), 2:1, 5, 14, 16, 35. McClintock, *Lincoln and the Decision for War*, 182.

22 Orville Vernon Burton, *The Age of Lincoln* (New York, 2007), 122; Cooper, *We Have the War upon Us*, 190; Surdam, *Northern Naval Superiority*, 119; R.B. Lyons to Bunch, 27 January 1861, box 106; Monson to R.B. Lyons, 18

January 1861, box 293; Barnes and Barnes, *American Civil War through British Eyes*, 1:31–2, 34.

23 Napier to R.B. Lyons, 27 May 1859, box 119; Barnes and Barnes, *Private and Confidential*, 240–1.

24 Russell memorandum, 19 December [1860], FO 319/7, Hammond Papers; Andre M. Fleche, *The Revolution of 1861: The American Civil War in the Age of Nationalist Conflict* (Chapel Hill, NC, 2012), 82; Sexton, *Debtor Diplomacy*, 80, 4; Charles M. Hubbard, *The Burden of Confederate Diplomacy* (Knoxville, TN, 1998), xv; Russell to R.B. Lyons, 29 December 1860, 16 February 1861, PRO 30/22/96, Russell Papers; Russell to R.B. Lyons, 10, 22 January 1861, box 196; Crawford, *Anglo-American Crisis*, 88.

25 Cobden to Bright, 25 March 1861, Cobden 45, WSRO; Ronald C. White, *A. Lincoln: A Biography* (New York, 2009), 299; R.B. Lyons to Minna, 4, 12 March 1861, box 299; Sala, *My Diary in America*, 2:147–8.

26 *New York Daily Tribune*, 5 March 1861; R.B. Lyons to Minna, 4, 12 March 1861, box 299; Holzer, *Lincoln President-Elect*, 455–7, 460; Roy P. Basler, ed., *Collected Works of Abraham Lincoln*, 8 vols (New Brunswick, NJ, 1953): 4:271.

27 Archibald to R.B. Lyons, 11 March 1861, box 205; Nevins, *Diary of the Civil War*, 106; Moore to R.B. Lyons, 9, 28 March 1861, box 194.

28 Kenneth M. Stampp, *America in 1857: A Nation on the Brink* (New York, 1990), 232; R.B. Lyons to Griffith, 6 April 1861; R.B. Lyons to Head, 7, 10 March 1861, box 106; Head to R.B. Lyons, 3 April 1861, box 181; Basler, *Collected Works of Lincoln*, 4:266; Russell to R.B. Lyons, 9 March 1861, box 196; Alfred Grant, *The American Civil War and the British Press* (Jefferson, NC, 2000), 98; Barnes and Barnes, *American Civil War through British Eyes*, 1:40; Bunch to R.B. Lyons, 21 March 1861, box 208; Hubbard, *Burden of Confederate Diplomacy*, 31.

29 Monson to R.B. Lyons, 10, 19 April 1861, box 193.

30 Glyndon Van Deusen's *William Henry Seward* (New York, 1967) remains the best of the modern biographies, but John M. Taylor's *William Henry Seward: Lincoln's Right Hand* (New York, 1991) is useful as is Walter Stahr's *Seward: Lincoln's Indispensable Man*; there is also a lively discussion of him in Doris Kearns Goodwin's *Team of Rivals: The Political Genius of Abraham Lincoln* (New York, 2005); Martin Crawford, ed., *William Howard Russell's Civil War: Private Diary and Letters, 1861–1862* (Athens, GA, 1992), 22; Ilana D. Miller, *Reports from America: William Howard Russell and the American Civil War* (Stroud, UK, 2001), 57; Cobden to Bright, 6 November 1861, Cobden 45; Napier to R.B. Lyons, 27 May 1859, box 119; R.B. Lyons to Seward,

20 June 1860, W.H. Seward Papers, Rush Rees Library, University of Rochester; R.B. Lyons to Stanley, 19 February 1868, box 108

31   Dean B. Mahin, *One War at a Time: The International Dimensions of the American Civil War* (Washington, DC, 1999), 2, 4, 12.

32   Taylor, *Lincoln's Right Hand*, 113, 31, 89; Frederic Bancroft, *The Life of William H. Seward*, 2 vols (New York, 1900), 2:151; Van Deusen, *William Seward*, 105, 148, 166–7, 183, 208–9.

33   Cooper, *We Have the War upon Us*, 220–1; Barnes and Barnes, *American Civil War through British Eyes*, 1:37–41; R.B. Lyons to Bunch, 19 March 1861, box 106.

34   Barnes and Barnes, *Private and Confidential*, 1:242–4; Stahr, *Seward*, 263–4.

35   Barnes and Barnes, *Private and Confidential*, 242–4; Barnes and Barnes, *American Civil War through British Eyes*, 1: 42–4.

36   Russell to R.B. Lyons, 6, 20 April 1861, box 196; Basler, *Collected Works of Lincoln*, 4:317–18; Palmer, *Selected Letters of Sumner*, 2:64.

37   Patrick Sowle, "A Reappraisal of Seward's Memorandum of April 1, 1861, to Lincoln," *Journal of Southern History* 33 (1967): 234–9; Stahr, *Seward*, 272; Basler, *Collected Works of Lincoln*, 4:316–18.

38   Barnes and Barnes, *American Civil War through British Eyes*, 1:45–6; Barnes and Barnes, *Private and Confidential*, 245; Archibald to Lyons, 9 April 1861, box 205; Basler, *Collected Works of Lincoln*, 4:323–4; Klein, *Days of Defiance*, 391, 411.

39   Basler, *Collected Works of Lincoln*, 4:331–2; Archibald to R.B. Lyons, 15 April 1861, box 205; Archibald, *Life and Letters of Sir Edward Mortimer Archibald*, 120–1; Palmer, *Selected Letters of Sumner*, 2:65; Moore to R.B. Lyons, 18, 25 April 1861, box 194.

40   Barnes and Barnes, *American Civil War through British Eyes*, 1:49; R.B. Lyons to Minna, 27 April 1861, box 299; R.B. Lyons to Bunch, 17 April 1861, box 106; Barnes and Barnes, *Private and Confidential*, 245–7.

41   Crawford, *Russell's Civil War*, 198; R.B. Lyons to Head, 15, 18 April 1861, box 106; Head to R.B. Lyons, 11 May 1861, box 181; Archibald to R.B. Lyons, 23 April 1861, box 205; R.B. Lyons to Archibald, 27 April 1861; R.B. Lyons to Mulgrave, 27 April 1861, box 106.

CHAPTER SIX

1   Granville to R.B. Lyons, 20 February 1861, box 182; R.B. Lyons to Bunch, 12 April 1861, box 106; Miller, *Reports from America*, 38; Crawford, *Russell's Civil War*, 23–4, 26–33.

2 Miller, *Reports from America*, 13, 35; R.B. Lyons to Bunch, 12 April 1861, box 106.

3 Bunch to R.B. Lyons, 16, 19, 29 April, 30 June 1861, box 208; Crawford, *Russell's Civil War*, 42–3, 45, 46, 49, 75–6, 56–8.

4 R.B. Lyons to Head, 4 May; R.B. Lyons to Bunch, 1 May 1861, box 106; Barnes and Barnes, *American through British Eyes*, 1:64, 77–80, 83; Barnes and Barnes, *Private and Confidential*, 247; Crawford, *Anglo-American Crisis*, 117; R.B. Lyons to Russell, 6 May 1861, PRO 30/22/35; R.B. Lyons to Milne, 12, 17 May 1861, box 106.

5 Cobden to Bright, 19 May 1861, Cobden 45; Bright to Cobden, 29 July, 24 October 1861, Cobden 20, WSRO.

6 Kevin J. Logan, "The *Bee-Hive* Newspaper and British Working Class Attitudes towards the American Civil War," *Civil War History* 22 (1976): 337–41; Hubbard, *Burden of Confederate Diplomacy*, 21; Charles Adams, ed., *Slavery, Secession and Civil War* (Toronto, 2007), 100, 102–3, 112–14, 422–4, 122–3; Fleche, *Revolution of 1861*, 73; Grant, *American Civil War and the British Press*, 157, 156, 38–9, 28; Donald Bellows, "A Study of British Conservative Reaction to the American Civil War," *Journal of Southern History* 51 (1985): 505–26; R.J.M. Blackett, *Divided Hearts: Britain and the American Civil War* (Baton Rouge, LA, 2001), 7, 9, 13.

7 Russell to R.B. Lyons, 20 April 1861, box 160; Fleche, *Revolution of 1861*, 60, 76, 84; Sexton, *Debtor Diplomacy*, 79, 88–90.

8 Russell to R.B. Lyons, 4 May 1861, box 160; Jenkins, *Britain and the War for the Union*, 1:92–4; Grant, *American Civil War and the British Press*, 77–80.

9 Jenkins, *Britain and the War for the Union*, 1:99; Russell to R.B. Lyons, 18 May 1861, box 160.

10 Russell to R.B. Lyons, 21, 25 May, 3 June 1861, box 160; Lord Newton, *Lord Lyons: A Record of British Diplomacy*, 2 vols (London, 1913), 1:323.

11 Archibald, *Life and Letters of Archibald*, 125–6; Archibald to R.B. Lyons, 21, 23 May 1861, box 205; Stephen C. Neff, *Justice in Blue and Gray: A Legal History of the Civil War* (Cambridge, MA, 2010), 19, 21, 168; Palmer, *Selected Letters of Sumner*, 2: 69; Stahr, *Seward*, 293.

12 R.B. Lyons to Granville, 19 September 1870, box 109; Barnes and Barnes, *American Civil War through British Eyes*, 1:84–5; Barnes and Barnes, *Private and Confidential*, 251–2; *Illustrated London News*, 12 September 1857; Van Deusen, *Seward*, 301; Goodwin, *Team of Rivals*, 363.

13 R.B. Lyons to Archibald, 25 May 1861, box 106; Moore to R.B. Lyons, 31 August 1861, box 194; Crawford, *Anglo-American Crisis*, 106–8, 116–17; Duncan Andrew Campbell, *English Public Opinion and the American Civil War*

(Rochester, NY, 2003), 17–18, 30–3; Adams, *Slavery, Secession and Civil War*, 56–7, 139; Archibald to R.B. Lyons, 28 May 1861, box 205.

14   R.B. Lyons to Wodehouse, 16 July 1861, box 106; Berwanger, *British Foreign Service*, 35; R.B. Lyons to Head, 22 May, 4 June 1861, box 106; Barnes and Barnes, *America through British Eyes*, 87–8, 86.

15   R.B. Lyons to Head, 22 May 1861, box 106; Head to R.B. Lyons, 26 May 1861, box 181; Jenkins, *Britain and the War for the Union*, 1:98–9.

16   Barnes and Barnes, *American Civil War through British Eyes*, 1:87, 104, 109; R.B. Lyons to Minna, 10 June 1861, box 299; Lynn M. Case and Warren F. Spencer, *The United States and France: Civil War Diplomacy* (Philadelphia, 1970), 127, 50–1, 67; Berwanger, *British Foreign Service*, 29; George M. Blackburn, *French Newspaper Opinion on the American Civil War* (Westport, CT, 1997), 6.

17   Barnes and Barnes, *American Civil War through British Eyes*, 1:106–7, 115–18; Case and Spencer, *United States and France*, 79.

18   Barnes and Barnes, *American Civil War through British Eyes*, 1:92, 94–5, 99, 121–3; Barnes and Barnes, *Private and Confidential*, 248–50.

19   Barnes and Barnes, *American Civil War through British Eyes*, 123–4, 126–7, 196–7; Jenkins, *Britain and the War for the Union*, 1:138–9, 136–7; Taylor, *Seward*, 164; Lyons to Russell, 2 September 1861, FO 5/770; Archibald to R.B. Lyons, 29 August 1861, box 205; Berwanger, *British Foreign Service*, 37–47; Crawford, *Russell's Civil War*, 151–2; Hammond to R.B. Lyons, 24 October 1861, box 187; Milne to R.B. Lyons, 14 October 1861; R.B. Lyons to Milne, 24 November 1861, box 106.

20   R.B. Lyons to Minna, 4 June, 13 May, 18 October, 5 November 1861, box 299; Sala, *My Diary in America*, 2:142–3; Jenkins, *Britain and the War for the Union*, 1:105–6; Berwanger, *British Foreign Service*, 24–5.

21   R.B. Lyons to Alston, 21 June; R.B. Lyons to Wodehouse, 16 July 1861, box 106; R.B. Lyons to Stuart, 5, 12 July 1862, box 107: R.B. Lyons to Hammond, 8 July, 8, 18 October 1861, box 106; Hammond to R.B. Lyons, 24 October 1861, box 187.

22   Barnes and Barnes, *American Civil War through British Eyes*, 1:120, 123, 113, 107, 87; Jenkins, *Britain and the War for the Union* 1:110; Crawford, *Russell's Civil War*, 80; R.B. Lyons to Minna, 22, 26, 30 July 1861, box 299; Bunch to R.B. Lyons, 30 September 1861, box 208; R.B. Lyons to Crawford, 12 September 1861, box 106.

23   R.B. Lyons to Kortright, 23 July 1861, box 106; Bunch to R.B. Lyons, 30 September 1861, box 208; R.B. Lyons to Minna, 26 July 1861, box 299; Crawford, *Russell's Civil War*, 94; Barnes and Barnes, *American Civil War*

through British Eyes, 1:147–52; Barnes and Barnes, *Private and Confidential*, 256; R.B. Lyons to Head, 7 October 1861, box 106; Head to R.B. Lyons, 11 October 1861, box 181.

24 R.B. Lyons to Minna, 23, 2, 12 August 1861, box 299; Jenkins, *Britain and the War for the Union*, 1:113; Cowley to Russell, 2 July 1861, PRO 30/22/57; Hammond to R.B. Lyons, 21 September 1861, box 187; R.B. Lyons to Russell, 8 October 1861, box 106.

25 James F. Simon, *Lincoln and Chief Justice Taney: Slavery, Secession and the President's War Powers* (New York, 2006), 207; Barnes and Barnes, *American Civil War through British Eyes*, 1:142; Palmerston memorandum, 9 July 1861; Russell memorandum, 30 July 1861, PRO 30/22/27, Russell Papers; Russell to R.B. Lyons, 24 July 1861, box 106; Case and Spencer, *United States and France: Civil War Diplomacy*, 157; Theodore Calvin Pease and James G. Randall, *Diary of Orville Hickman Browning*, 2 vols (Springfield, IL, 1925), 1:489; R.B. Lyons to Russell, 2 September 1861, box 106.

26 Berwanger, *British Foreign Service*, 53–4; R.B. Lyons to Head, 7 October, 12 September; R.B. Lyons to Mulgrave, 29 September 1861, box 106; Barnes and Barnes, *American Civil War through British Eyes*, 1:166; Barnes and Barnes, *Private and Confidential*, 262; Simon, *Lincoln and Chief Justice Taney*, 192–7; Stahr, *Seward*, 305; Crawford, *Russell's Civil War*, 158.

27 Barnes and Barnes, *Private and Confidential*, 264; Crawford, *Russell's Civil War*, 173; R.B. Lyons to Head, 7 October 1861; R.B. Lyons to Russell, 22 October 1861, box 106; R.B. Lyons to Seward, 15 October 1861, Seward Papers; Michael F. Hughes, "'The Personal Observations of a Man of Intelligence': Sir James Ferguson's Visit to North America, 1861," *Civil War History*, 45 (1999): 245.

28 Daniel B. Carroll, *Henri Mercier and the American Civil War* (Princeton, 1971), 126; Barnes and Barnes, *American Civil War through British Eyes*, 183–7; Barnes and Barnes, *Private and Confidential*, 263, 265; R.B. Lyons to Russell, 22 October 1861, box 106.

29 Palmerston to Milner Gibson, 7 July 1861, BL Add. Ms 48582, Palmerston private letterbooks; Jenkins, *Britain and the War for the Union*, 1:148–50; Roundell Palmer, *Memorials: Part 1 – Family and Personal 1766–1865* (London, 1896), 377; Hammond to Lyons, 5 October 1861, box 187; Cobden to Lindsay, 22 October 1861, Cobden 123, WSRO.

30 Jenkins, *Britain and the War for the Union*, 1:171–4; Russell to R.B. Lyons, 26 October, 2 November 1861, box 196.

31 Russell to R.B. Lyons, 26 October 1861, box 196; Wyke to R.B. Lyons, 29 September 1861, box 121; Jones, *Blue and Gray Diplomacy*, 76; Hammond

to R.B. Lyons, 5 October 1861, box 187; Jenkins, *Britain and the War for the Union*,1:175–6.

32 Jenkins, *Britain and the War for the Union*, 1:176–7; Palmerston memorandum, 20 October 1861, FO 391/7, Hammond Papers; Wyke to R.B. Lyons, 27 October, 28 November 1861, box 121; Russell to R.B. Lyons, 2 November 1861, box 196.

33 Palmerston to Russell, 9 September 1861, PRO 30/22/21, Russell Papers; G.F. Lewis, ed., *Letters of Sir George Cornewall Lewis* (London, 1870), 401; Monck to R.B. Lyons, 25 October 1861, box 192; Head to R.B. Lyons, 6 August 1861, box 181; Mulgrave to R.B. Lyons, 4 October 1861, box 195; Stahr, *Seward*, 306; Crawford, *Russell's Civil War*, 154–5, 159; Archibald to R.B. Lyons, 13 November 1861, box 205; R.B. Lyons to Russell, 8 November 1861, box 106.

34 Barnes and Barnes, *Private and Confidential*, 266–7; Russell to R.B. Lyons, 16 November 1861, box 196.

CHAPTER SEVEN

1 Crawford, *Russell's Civil War*, 163, 175; Case and Spencer, *United States and France: Civil War Diplomacy*, 177–9; Barnes and Barnes, *American Civil War through British Eyes*, 1:206–7; John Fisher and Antony Best, eds, *On the Fringes of Diplomacy: Influences on British Foreign Policy, 1800–1945* (Farnham, UK, 2011), 127–54; Barnet Schecter, *The Devil's Own Work: The Civil War Draft Riots and the Fight to Reconstruct America* (New York, 2005), 78.

2 Barnes and Barnes, *American Civil War through British Eyes*, 1:206; Crawford, *Russell's Civil War*, 61; William Howard Russell, *My Diary North and South* (New York, 1863), 237; Hubbard, *Burden of Confederate Diplomacy*, 56; Mahin, *One War at a Time*, 25.

3 Hubbard, *Burden of Confederate Diplomacy*, 58; Jenkins, *Britain and the War for the Union*, 1:189, 193–4; Anne Sarah Rubin, *A Shattered Nation: The Rise and Fall of the Confederacy, 1861–1868* (Chapel Hill, NC, 2005), 44; Howard Jones, *Abraham Lincoln and a New Birth of Freedom: The Union and Slavery in the Diplomacy of the Civil War* (Lincoln, NE, 1999), 8; Grant, *American Civil War and the British Press*, 104–5.

4 Jenkins, *Britain and the War for the Union*, 1:195–7; Coleman, *The Pig War*, 31; for Shufeldt's involvement see F.C. Drake, "The Cuban Background of the *Trent* Affair," *Civil War History* 19 (1973): 29–49; Philip E. Myers, *Caution and Cooperation: The American Civil War in British-American Relations* (Kent, OH, 2008), 71.

5   Anthony Trollope, *North America*, reprint edition (London, 1968), 1:294, 2:36; Palmer, *Selected Letters of Sumner*, 2:81–4; Victor H. Cohen, "Charles Sumner and the *Trent* Affair," *Journal of Southern History* 22 (1956): 206–8; Margaret Leech, *Reveille in Washington, 1861–1866* (New York, 1941), 122; Trollope, *North America*, 2:37.

6   Crawford, *Russell's Civil War*, 180, 183, 177, 179, 207–8, 203–4; Stahr, *Seward*, 308.

7   Crawford, *Russell's Civil War*, 187, 190; Arthur Irwin Dasent, *John Thadeus Delane, Editor of "The Times": His Life and Correspondence*, 2 vols (New York, 1908), 2:36–7; Jenkins, *Britain and the War for the Union*, 1:209; Hammond to R.B. Lyons, 16 November 1861, box 187; Pease and Randall, *Diary of Browning*, 1:513–14; Stahr, *Seward*, 312.

8   R.B. Lyons to Milne, 25 November; R.B. Lyons to Hammond, 2 December 1861, box 107; Crawford, *Russell's Civil War*, 197; R.B. Lyons to Russell, 3 December 1861, box 107; Monck to R.B. Lyons, 25 October, 5 December 1861, box 192.

9   R.B. Lyons to Monck, 9 December 1861, box 107; Barnes and Barnes, *American Civil War through British Eyes*, 1:225–8; Barnes and Barnes, *Private and Confidential*, 267–8; Jenkins, *Britain and the War for the Union*, 1:200–2.

10 Jenkins, *Britain and the War for the Union*, 1:211–12; Taylor, *Seward*, 182.

11 Hammond to R.B. Lyons, 1 December 1861, box 187; Hawkins, *Forgotten Prime Minister*, 2:263–4; Malmesbury to Derby, 3 December 1861, 920 DER (14), 144/2a, Derby Papers; Jenkins, *Britain and the War for the Union*, 1:214–16; Hammond to R.B. Lyons, 14 December 1861, box 187; George M. Blackburn, *French Newspaper Opinion on the American Civil War* (Westport, CT, 1997), 47–51; Case and Spencer, *United States and France: Civil War Diplomacy*, 195–207; Henry Adams, *The Education of Henry Adams*, reprint edition (Boston, 1960), 119.

12 Seward to Adams, 27 November 1861, NA/M77/77; *New York Times*, 30 November, 3 December 1861; Barnes and Barnes, *Private and Confidential*, 270–1; Pease and Randall, *Diary of Browning*, 1:515; Case and Spencer, *United States and France: Civil War Diplomacy*, 215; Goodwin, *Team of Rivals*, 398; Jenkins, *Britain and the War for the Union*, 1:222; Stahr, *Seward*, 316; Crawford, *Russell's Civil War*, 206; Cohen, "Charles Sumner and the *Trent* Affair," 209–10; Palmer, *Selected Letters of Sumner*, 2:88–9.

13 Case and Spencer, *United States and France: Civil War Diplomacy*, 216; R.B. Lyons to Russell, 27 December 1861, box 107; Russell to R.B. Lyons, 7 December 1861, box 196; Barnes and Barnes, *Private and Confidential*, 271–2;

Barnes and Barnes, *American Civil War through British Eyes*, 1:250; Carroll, *Mercier and the Civil War*, 109–110.

14   Barnes and Barnes, *American Civil War through British Eyes*, 1:250, 254–6; Barnes and Barnes, *Private and Confidential*, 271–3.

15   Crawford, *Russell's Civil War*, 213; Pease and Randall, *Diary of Browning*, 1:516–19; Sumner to Cobden, 31 December 1861, Cobden 106, WSRO; Case and Spencer, *United States and France: Civil War Diplomacy*, 221–2; Stahr, *Seward*, 318; Jenkins, *Britain and the War for the Union*, 1:227–8; R.B. Lyons to Russell, 27 December 1861, FO 5/777.

16   Jenkins, *Britain and the War for the Union*, 1:228; Moore, *Works of Buchanan*, 11:244–5; Cohen, "Charles Sumner and the *Trent* Affair," 214; R.B. Lyons to Russell, 27 December 1861, box 107; R.B. Lyons to Hewitt, 29 December, 1861, box 107; R.B. Lyons to Seward, 30 December 1861, Seward Papers; Barnes and Barnes, *American Civil War through British Eyes*, 1:257.

17   Sumner to R.B. Lyons, 1 February 1862, box 122; R.B. Lyons to Minna, 3 February 1862, box 299; Russell to R.B. Lyons, 28 December 1861, 11, 14 January 1862, box 196; Hammond to R.B. Lyons, 11 January 1862, box 187; G.C. Lewis to Russell, 14 January 1862, PRO 30/22/25; Minna to R.B. Lyons, 16, 30 January, 6 February 1862, box 294; R.B. Lyons to Minna, 31 December 1861, box 299; Kenneth Bourne, *Britain and the Balance of Power in North America, 1815–1908* (London, 1967), 246.

18   R.B. Lyons to Minna, 31 December 1861, 31 January, 3, 7 February 1862, box 299.

19   Barnes and Barnes, *Private and Confidential*, 274, 278; Monck to R.B. Lyons, 13, 22 January 1862, box 192; R.B. Lyons to Monck, 17 January, 1 February 1862, box 107.

20   Normanby to R.B. Lyons, 15 November 1861, box 195; R.B. Lyons to Normanby, 10 January 1862, box 107; Pease and Randall, *Diary of Browning*, 1:527–9; R.B. Lyons to Minna, 11, 21 February, 31 March, 22 April, 6 May 1862, box 299; Minna to R.B. Lyons, 8 May 1862, box 294.

21   Barnes and Barnes, *American Civil War through British Eyes*, 1:277, 274–5, 285–6; *New York Tribune*, 4 April 1862; Bunch to R.B. Lyons, 5 April 1862, box 208

22   Barnes and Barnes, *American Civil War through British Eyes*, 1:288–9, 276, 301–2, 293; Crawford, *Russell's Civil War*, 237.

23   Barnes and Barnes, *Private and Confidential*, 276–7, 279–81; Palmer, *Selected Letters of Sumner*, 2:93; Van Deusen, *Seward*, 330.

24   Barnes and Barnes, *Private and Confidential*, 276–7, 279; R.B. Lyons to Hammond, 7 February 1862, box 107; Barnes and Barnes, *American Civil*

War through British Eyes, 1:291–2; R.B. Lyons to Milne, 27 February 1862, box 107.

25 Barnes and Barnes, *American Civil War through British Eyes*, 1:303–5; Barnes and Barnes, *Private and Confidential*, 280–1; R.B. Lyons to Monck, 1 February; R.B. Lyons to Normanby, 17 March 1862, box 107; Jenkins, *Britain and the War for the Union*, 1:258.

26 Jasper Ridley, *Lord Palmerston* (London, 1970), 555; Russell to R.B. Lyons, 15 February 1862, box 196; Jenkins, *Britain and the War for the Union*, 1:239–41.

27 Jenkins, *Britain and the War for the Union*, 1:242–3, 255–8; R.B. Lyons to Crawford, 23 May 1862, box 107; Hammond to R.B. Lyons, 11 January 1862, box 187; Russell to R.B. Lyons, 8, 15, 22 February 1862, box 196; Hubbard, *Burden of Confederate Diplomacy*, 76; see also Brian Jenkins, "William Gregory, Champion of the Confederacy," *History Today* 28 (1978): 322–30.

28 Russell to R.B. Lyons, 1 March 1862, box 196; Sexton, *Debtor Diplomacy*, 100–3; R.B. Lyons to Archibald, 11 June 1859, box 106; see Harold E. Landry, "Slavery and the Slave Trade in Atlantic Diplomacy, 1850–1861, *Journal of Southern History* 27 (1961): 184–207.

29 Jenkins, *Britain and the War for the Union*, 1:249–50; Taylor, *Seward*, 215; Jones, *Blue and Gray Diplomacy*, 122; Palmer, *Selected Letters of Sumner*, 2:93, 100–1; Pease and Randall, *Diary of Browning*, 1:530–1.

30 Barnes and Barnes, *Private and Confidential*, 280; A Taylor Milne, ed., "The Lyons-Seward Treaty of 1862," *American Historical Review* 38 (1932–3): 516–19; Archibald, *Sir Edward Mortimer Archibald*, 138; Conway W. Henderson, "The Anglo-American Treaty of 1862 in Civil War Diplomacy," *Civil War History* 15 (1969): 311; Barnes and Barnes, *American Civil War through British Eyes*, 1:310–11; Louis P. Masur, *Lincoln's Hundred Days: The Emancipation Proclamation and the War for the Union* (Cambridge, MA, 2012), 46; Eric Foner, *The Fiery Trial: Abraham Lincoln and American Slavery* (New York, 2010), 196.

31 Milne, "The Lyons-Seward Treaty of 1862," 519–22, 524–5; Barnes and Barnes, *Private and Confidential*, 281–2.

32 Masur, *Lincoln's Hundred Days*, 47; Henderson, "The Anglo-American Treaty of 1862 in Civil War Diplomacy," 313–15; Barnes and Barnes, *Private and Confidential*, 282; Richard Carwardine, *Lincoln: Life of Purpose and Power* (New York, 2007), 201–3; Palmer, *Selected Letters of Sumner*, 2:111; Jenkins, *Britain and the War for the Union*, 1:256–7; Case and Spencer, *United States and France: Civil War Diplomacy*, 251, 269–74; Russell to R.B.

Lyons, 15, 22 March, 26 April, 14, 17 May 1862, box 196; Jones, *Blue and Gray Diplomacy*, 132; Hubbard, *Burden of Confederate Diplomacy*, 81.

33 Carroll, *Henri Mercier*, 148–54; Case and Spencer, *United States and France: Civil War Diplomacy*, 277–9; Barnes and Barnes, *American Civil War through British Eyes*, 2:14–18; Malmesbury to Derby, 11 May 1862, 920 DER (14), 144/2b, Derby Papers; R.B. Lyons to Milne, 24 April 1862, box 107.

34 Barnes and Barnes, *American Civil War through British Eyes*, 1:320, 299; Wyke to R.B. Lyons, 3 March, 4 May 1862; Bigelow to Seward, 28 April 1862, box 122; Russell to R.B. Lyons, 17 May 1862, box 196; Jones, *Blue and Gray Diplomacy*, 128.

35 R.B. Lyons to Milne, 24 April 1862, box 107; Barnes and Barnes, *American Civil War through British Eyes*, 2:27–31, 58; Carroll, *Henri Mercier*, 175, 181, 195; *London Standard*, 6 May 1862; *Belfast News-Letter*, 8 May 1862; *Morning Post*, 9 May 1862; *Sheffield Independent*, 9 May 1862; Palmer, *Selected Letters of Sumner*, 2:120.

36 Barnes and Barnes, *Private and Confidential*, 286–8.

37 Minna to R.B. Lyons, 16 January, 19 May 1862, box 294; R.B. Lyons to Minna, 16 May 1862, box 299; Barnes and Barnes, *Private and Confidential*, 285–6; R.B. Lyons to Milne, 8, 15 June 1862, box 107; Barnes and Barnes, *American Civil War through British Eyes*, 2:76–80.

38 Russell to R.B. Lyons, 22 March 1862, PRO 30/22/96; R.B. Lyons to Milne, 15 June 1862, box 107; Barnes and Barnes, *American Civil War through British Eyes*, 2:7–9, 11, 53–4; Frank J. Merli, *"The Alabama," British Neutrality and the American Civil War*, ed. David M. Fahey (Bloomington, IN, 2004), 17; *New York Tribune*, 20, 22 May 1862; Jones, *Abraham Lincoln and a New Birth of Freedom*, 57; R.B. Lyons to Head, 22 May 1861, box 106.

39 Barnes and Barnes, *Private and Confidential*, 288–9; R.B. Lyons to Stuart, 5 July 1862, box 107; Jenkins, *Britain and the War for the Union*, 2:29.

CHAPTER EIGHT

1 Russell to R.B. Lyons, 27 June 1862, box 96; R.B. Lyons to Stuart, 5 July 1862, box 107; Edward L. Pierce, ed., "Letters of Richard Cobden to Charles Sumner, 1862–1865," *American Historical Review* 2 (1897): 306; see R.J.M. Blackett, *Divided Hearts: Britain and the American Civil War* (Baton Rouge, LA, 2001); Sheldon Vanauken, *Glittering Illusion: English Sympathy for the Confederacy* (Worthing, 1988), 2; Jenkins, *Britain and the War for the Union*, 2:33, 46–9; Duncan Andrew Campbell, *English Public Opinion and the American Civil War* (Toronto, 2003), 104–5; Adams, *Slavery, Secession and*

Civil War, 347–9, 355, 359; Jenkins, *Parliamentary Diaries of Trelawny*, 195, 219.

2 Surdam, *Northern Naval Superiority*, 187–8, 148; Grant, *American Civil War and the British Press*, 59–63; Jenkins, *Britain and the War for the Union*, 2:52–3, 56–7; Sexton, *Debtor Diplomacy*, 151; Jenkins, *Parliamentary Diaries of Trelawny*, 212; Pierce, "Letters of Richard Cobden to Charles Sumner," 306–7.

3 Pierce, "Letters of Richard Cobden to Charles. Sumner," 307; Russell to R.B. Lyons 31 May 1862, box 196; Barnes and Barnes, *American Civil War through British Eyes*, 2:142; Merli, *"Alabama," British Neutrality*, 17; R.B. Lyons to Granville, 16 July 1870, box 109; Cobden to Chevalier, 7 August 1862, Cobden 46, WSRO; Jenkins, *Britain and the War for the Union*, 2:35; Campbell, *English Public Opinion*, 148.

4 Jenkins, *Britain and the War for the Union*, 2:62, 103–6; Jenkins, *Parliamentary Diaries of Trelawny*, 219, 216–17; Hawkins, *Forgotten Prime Minister*, 2:277–80.

5 R.B. Lyons to Stuart, 5, 12, 19 July 1862, box 107; Stuart to R.B. Lyons, 30 June 1862, box 201; Barnes and Barnes, *Private and Confidential*, 290–2.

6 Barnes and Barnes, *American Civil War through British Eyes*, 2:131, 133–6, 140, 148, 152–5; Pease and Randall, *Diary of Browning*, 1:555; Barnes and Barnes, *Private and Confidential*, 293.

7 Stuart to R.B. Lyons, 15, 21, 29, 31 July, 8 August 1862, box 201; Barnes and Barnes, *Private and Confidential*, 293–4.

8 Archibald to R.B. Lyons, 30 July 1862, box 205; R.B. Lyons to Minna, 12, 19 21, 22 July, 8 August 1862, box 299; R.B. Lyons to Stuart, 19 July 1862, box 107.

9 Jenkins, "William Gregory, Champion of the Confederacy," 328; R.B. Lyons to Stuart, 19 July 1862, box 107; Case and Spencer, *United States and France: Civil War Diplomacy*, 306–7; Jenkins, *Britain and the War for the Union*, 2:82, 99; Vanauken, *Glittering Illusion*, 131; Hawkins, *Forgotten Prime Minister*, 2:279.

10 R.B. Lyons to Stuart, 5, 12, 19, 25, 29 July, 8, 15, 22 August 1862, box 107; Palmer, *Selected Letters of Sumner*, 2:119.

11 R.B. Lyons to Stuart, 8, 15 August 1862, box 107; Jenkins, *Britain and the War for the Union*, 2:63, 110–11.

12 Richard Shannon, *Gladstone: God and Politics* (London, 2007), 143–4; Sexton, *Debtor Diplomacy*, 155; Fleche, *Revolution of 1861*, 85–6; Russell to Stuart, 8 August 1862, PRO 30/22/96; Malmesbury to Derby, 19, 31 August 1862, DER (14), 144/2a, Derby Papers.

13 Stuart to R.B. Lyons, 10, 20 August, 5, 9 September 1862, box 201; Barnes and Barnes, *Private and Confidential*, 297; *Memphis Daily Appeal*, 29 August 1862.

14 Edward Malet to Lady Malet, 25 October 1867, Malet Papers, Duke University; Russell to R.B. Lyons, 24 September, 4 October 1862, box 196; Sexton, *Debtor Diplomacy*, 151–4; Hubbard, *Burden of Confederate Diplomacy*, 115; Lyons to Stuart, 3, 10 October 1862, box 107.

15 Bunch to Stuart, 20 August 1862; Stuart to R.B. Lyons, 19 September 1862, box 201; Barnes and Barnes, *American Civil War through British Eyes*, 2:186–8.

16 Foner, *Fiery Trial*, 215–9; Barnes and Barnes, *Private and Confidential*, 296; Basler, *Collected Works of Lincoln*, 5:433–7; Carwardine, *Life of Purpose and Power*, 207, 211–13; Robert May, ed., *The Union, the Confederacy and the Atlantic Rim* (West Lafayette, IN, 1995), 33; Van Deusen, *Seward*, 333; Stahr, *Seward*, 338; Alan C. Guelco, *Lincoln's Emancipation Proclamation: The End of Slavery in America* (New York, 2004), 225; Masur, *Lincoln's Hundred Days*, 5, 114, 117–8; Schecter, *Devil's Own Work*, 90.

17 Jenkins, *Britain and the War for the Union*, 2:152–8; Adams, *Slavery, Secession and Civil War*, 429, 214–15; Cobden to Chevalier, 2 December 1862, Cobden 46, WSRO; Grant, *American Civil War and the British Press*, 21, 28–9.

18 Case and Spencer, *United States and France: Civil War Diplomacy*, 308, 335; Jenkins, *Britain and the War for the Union*, 2:166–71; Sexton, *Debtor Diplomacy*, 156; Kinley J. Brauer, "British Mediation and the American Civil War: A Reconsideration," *Journal of Southern History* 38 (1972): 51, 54–5.

19 Jenkins, *Britain and the War for the Union*, 2:171–3; Shannon, *Gladstone: God and Politics*, 150; Robert L. Reid, ed., "William Gladstone's 'Insincere Neutrality' during the Civil War," *Civil War History* 15 (1969): 293–307; Bright to Cobden, 8 October 1862, Cobden 20, WSRO; Campbell, *English Public Opinion and the American Civil War*, 177–8; Jones, *Blue and Gray Diplomacy*, 238.

20 Jenkins, *Britain and the War for the Union*, 2:173–6; R.B. Lyons to Malet, 28 September, 15 October 1862, Malet Papers; Brauer, "British Mediation and the American Civil War," 58–60; Hubbard, *Burden of Confederate Diplomacy*, 122; Case and Spencer, *United States and France: Civil War Diplomacy*, 347–51.

21 R.B. Lyons to Milne, 11 November 1862, box 107; Minna to R.B. Lyons, 23 October 1862, box 294; R.B. Lyons to Minna, 24 October 1862, box 299.

22 Clay-Seymer to R.B. Lyons, 11 July, 4, 18 August, 11 September, 5 November

1862, box 197; for reinsurance of the legation see box 123; Leach, *Reveille in Washington*, 182–3, 206, 261; Monson to R.B. Lyons, 9, 16, 31 October, 7, 20 November, 20 December 1862, 23 January, 7 February 1863, box 193; Monson to Minna, 23 January 1863, box 294.

23   R.B. Lyons to Stuart, 12 July 1862, box 107; Calvin D. Davis, "A British Diplomat and the American Civil War: Edward Malet in the United States," *South Atlantic Quarterly* 77 (1978): 160–3; Malet to his parents, 6 July, 2 August, 8, 22 December 1861, 24 January, 6 February, 2 March 1862, Malet Papers.

24   Lynn E. Williams, "The Career of Sir Edward Malet, British Diplomat, 1837–1908" (PhD thesis, University of Wales, 1982), 6, 22–3.

25   *London Daily News*, 26 October 1862; *Kentish Chronicle*, 31 October 1862; Minna to R.B. Lyons, 21 November 1862, box 294; Davis, "A British Diplomat and the American Civil War," 159, 164–5; *Athens Post*, 7 November 1862; Malet to father, 20 November 1862, Malet Papers; Clay-Seymer to Lyons, 1 February 1869, box 197; Malet to mother, 2 December 1862, 26 January 1863, Malet Papers.

26   Sumner to R.B. Lyons, 12 November 1862, box 122; Monck to R.B. Lyons, 18 November 1862, box 192; Malmesbury to Derby, 1 November 1862, 920 DER (14) 144/2b, Derby Papers; Case and Spencer, *United States and France: Civil War Diplomacy*, 376–7.

27   Russell to R.B. Lyons, 1 November 1862, PRO 30/22/96, see also 1, 8 November 1862, box 196; Barnes and Barnes, *Private and Confidential*, 303–4; Hammond to R.B. Lyons, 15 November 1862, box 187; Jenkins, *Britain and the War for the Union*, 2:180–1; Malmesbury to Derby, 17 November 1862, 920 DER (14) 144/2b, Derby Papers; Cobden to Chevalier, 2 December 1862, Cobden 46, WSRO.

28   Jones, *Blue and Gray Diplomacy*, 272; Case and Spencer, *United States and France: Civil War Diplomacy*, 386; Barnes and Barnes, *American Civil War through British Eyes*, 2:290; Russell to R.B. Lyons, 15 November 1862, box 196.

29   Barnes and Barnes, *Private and Confidential*, 306–7, 309, 312; Palmer, *Selected Letters of Sumner*, 2:120–1, 127–9, 131–3; Van Deusen, *Seward*, 343–4; Pease and Randall, *Diary of Browning*, 1:597–603; Russell to R.B. Lyons, 3 January 1863, box 196; R.B. Lyons to Russell, 19 December 1862; R.B. Lyons to Milne, 22 December 1862, box 107.

30   R.B. Lyons to Russell, 18 November 1862, box 107; Barnes and Barnes, *Private and Confidential*, 307–8, 314, 317; Barnes and Barnes, *American Civil War through British Eyes*, 2:236–8, 240, 255; Malmesbury to Derby, 1

November 1862, 920 DER (14) 144/2b, Derby Papers; Stuart to R.B. Lyons, 29 January 1863, box 201.

31 Barnes and Barnes, *Private and Confidential*, 310–11, 313; Pease and Randall, *Diary of Browning*, 1:618–19; Stuart to R.B. Lyons, 29 January 1863, box 201; Russell to R.B. Lyons, 13 December 1862, 24 January, 7 February, 28 March 1863, box 196; Pierce, "Letters of Richard Cobden to Charles Sumner," 308–9; Russell to R.B. Lyons, 14 February, 7 March 1863, box 196.

32 Carroll, *Henri Mercier*, 304–5; Barnes and Barnes, *Private and Confidential*, 310; Barnes and Barnes, *American Civil War through British Eyes*, 2:248, 253–5, 311.

33 Barnes and Barnes, *American Civil War through British Eyes*, 2:325; Barnes and Barnes, *Private and Confidential*, 317; Carroll, *Henri Mercier*, 269–72.

34 Palmer, *Selected Letters of Sumner*, 2:144–5; Carroll, *Henri Mercier*, 266; Barnes and Barnes, *Private and Confidential*, 319; R.B. Lyons to Russell, 6 February 1863; R.B. Lyons to Milne, 14 February 1863, box 107.

CHAPTER NINE

1 Jenkins, *Britain and the War for the Union*, 2:203–4, 215, 221, 229; Fleche, *Revolution of 1861*, 133–5.

2 Russell to R.B. Lyons, 7 March 1863, box 196; Jenkins, *Trelawny Diaries*, 226–7; Laurence J. Orzell, "A 'Favorable Interval': The Polish Insurrection in Civil War Diplomacy, 1863," *Civil War History* 24 (1978): 332–8; Pierce, "Letters of Richard Cobden to Charles Sumner, 1862–1865," 313; Jenkins, *Britain and the War for the Union*, 2:239–40, 263, 282; *The Times*, 2 March 1863; Russell to R.B. Lyons, 16 April 1863, box 196; Hawkins, *Forgotten Prime Minister*, 2:281–2.

3 Orzell, "A 'Favorable Interval,'" 344; Russell to R.B. Lyons, 20 December 1862, 28 March 1863, box 196; Barnes and Barnes, *Private and Confidential*, 319–21; Barnes and Barnes, *American Civil War through British Eyes*, 3:10, 25–6, 34–7; Stahr, *Seward*, 372.

4 Stephen R. Wise, *Lifeline of the Confederacy: Blockade Running during the Civil War* (Columbia, SC, 1988), 3, 112, 63–4; Howard K. Beale, ed., *Diary of Gideon Welles*, 3 vols (New York, 1960), 1:283; Kenneth J. Blume, "Coal and Diplomacy in the British Caribbean during the Civil War," *Civil War History* 41 (1995): 140; Fisher and Best, *On the Fringes of Diplomacy*, 42; Bailey to R.B. Lyons, 20 December 1862, 5 July 1863, box 122; Kenneth J. Blume, "The Flight from the Flag: The American Government, the British Caribbean, and the American Merchant Marine, 1861–1865," *Civil War History*

32 (1986): 55; R.B. Lyons to Milne, 11 May 1863, box 107; Jenkins, *Trelawny Diaries*, 242–3; Stuart L. Bernath, "Squall across the Atlantic: The *Peterhoff* Episode," *Journal of Southern History* 34 (1968): 386.

5 Russell to R.B. Lyons, 14, 21 March, 11, 25 April 1863, box 196; Jenkins, *Britain and the War for the Union*, 2:254–5, 274–5; Pierce, "Letters of Richard Cobden to Charles Sumner, 1862–1865," 309–12, 313; Russell to R.B. Lyons, 7 March, 11, 25 April 1863, box 196; Beale, *Diary of Welles*, 1:398–9; R.B. Lyons to Russell, 13 April 1863, box 107; *National Republican*, 4 April 1863; Argyll to Russell, 22 May 1863, PRO 30/22/26; *National Republican*, 7 April 1863.

6 Barnes and Barnes, *American Civil War through British Eyes*, 3:37; R.B. Lyons to Russell, 13 April 1863, box 107; Stahr, *Seward*, 374; Palmer, *Selected Letters of Sumner*, 1:146–52; Beale, *Diary of Welles*, 1:275, 287; R.B. Lyons to Russell, 17, 24 April; R.B. Lyons to Milne, 27 April 1863, box 107; Barnes and Barnes, *American Civil War through British Eyes*, 3:44.

7 R.B. Lyons to Russell, 24 April; R.B. Lyons to Monck, 25 April; R.B. Lyons to Milne, 27 April; R.B. Lyons to Thrupp, 19 April 1863, box 107; Stuart L. Bernath, "British Neutrality and Civil War Prize Cases," *Civil War History* 15 (1969): 330; Bernath, "Squall across the Atlantic: The *Peterhoff* Episode," 388; Milne to Lyons, 1 January, 20 March, 5, 25 April, 11 May, 20 July 1863, box 192.

8 Barnes and Barnes, *Private and Confidential*, 322–3; R.B. Lyons to Milne, 11 May 1863, box 107; Jenkins, *Britain and the War for the Union*, 2:272–3; Beale, *Diary of Welles*, 1:270, 298–9, 304.

9 Seward to R.B. Lyons, 13 August 1863, Seward Papers; Blume, "The Flight from the Flag," 55; R.B. Lyons to Milne, 11 May 1863, box 107; Beale, *Diary of Welles*, 1:398, 409; Case and Spencer, *United States and France: Civil War Diplomacy*, 408–19; Jenkins, *Britain and the War for the Union*, 2:160–1, 310–12; Russell to Lyons, 30 May 1863, PRO 30/22/96; Mark E. Neely, Jr, "The Perils of Blockade Running: The Influence of International Law in an Era of Total War," *Civil War History* 32 (1986): 117; R.B. Lyons to Milne, 8 June 1863, box 107.

10 R.B. Lyons to Archibald, 11 June 1863; R.B. Lyons to Milne, 5 March 1863; R.B. Lyons to Hammond, 29 March 1863; R.B. Lyons to Archibald, 2 April 1863, box 107; Berwanger, *British Foreign Service*, 90–1, 108; Moore to R.B. Lyons, 16 January, 17 February, 6 June 1863, box 194; Barnes and Barnes, *American Civil War through British Eyes*, 3:23, 21, 68, 65.

11 Berwanger, *British Foreign Service*, 60; Barnes and Barnes, *Private and Confidential*, 320; Barnes and Barnes, *American Civil War through British*

Eyes, 3:9–10, 16, 48–51, 60–1, 122; R.B. Lyons to Milne, 11 May 1863; R.B. Lyons to Kortwright, 13 August 1863, box 107; Barnes and Barnes, *Private and Confidential*, 331.

12	Barnes and Barnes, *Private and Confidential*, 328; R.B. Lyons to Russell, 17 July 1863, box 107; Spann, *Gotham at War*, 96, 126; James M. McPherson, *Drawn with the Sword: Reflections on the American Civil War* (New York, 1996), 78–9, 91, 94; Barnes and Barnes, *Private and Confidential*, 324–6; Barnes and Barnes, *American Civil War through British Eyes*, 3:65, 70, 82–3; for a recent account of the Draft Riots see Barnet Schecter, *The Devil's Own Work: The Civil War Draft Riots and the Fight to Reconstruct America* (New York, 2005).

13	R.B. Lyons to Minna, 9, 13, 19, 25, 27 January, 2, 6, 24 February, 5, 15 May, 26 June 1863, box 300; R.B. Lyons to Hammond, 23 February, 21 April 1863, box 107; Warre to R.B. Lyons, 10 May 1863, box 203; Monson to R.B. Lyons, 1 March, 10, 18 July, 14 August 1863, box 193.

14	Goodwin, *Team of Rivals*, 540; R.B. Lyons to Milne, 20 July 1863, box 107; Russell to R.B. Lyons, 30 May, 13 June 1863, box 196; R.B. Lyons to Russell, 12, 30 June, 4 July 1863, box 107; Davis, "A British Diplomat and the American Civil War: Edward Malet in the United States," 173.

15	Barnes and Barnes, *Private and Confidential*, 332–3; Stahr, *Seward*, 379; R.B. Lyons to Stuart, 16 August 1863, box 107; R.B. Lyons to Minna, 15, 16, 24 August 1863, box 300; R.B. Lyons to Monck, 24 August 1863, box 107.

16	R.B. Lyons to Monck, 24 August 1863, box 107; R.B. Lyons to Minna, 25, 30 August, 2, 7, 11, 19 September 1863, box 300; R.B. Lyons to Stuart, 3 September 1863, box 107; Monck to R.B. Lyons, 12 September 1863, box 192; Sheffield to Brydges, 19 September 1863, box 107.

17	R.B. Lyons to Russell, 29 September 1863, box 107; R.B. Lyons to Minna, 29 September, 3 October 1863, box 300; R.B. Lyons to Gordon, 4 October; R.B. Lyons to Stuart, 3 October; R.B. Lyons to Stanfield, 4, 5 October; R.B. Lyons to Kortwright, 5 October 1863, box 107; Charles Lockwood, *Manhattan Moves Uptown: An Illustrated History* (Boston, 1976), 173; R.B. Lyons to Minna, 22 January, 23 February 1863, box 300.

18	Beale, *Diary of Welles*, 1:467–9; Barnes and Barnes, *Private and Confidential*, 335; R.B. Lyons to Minna, 20 October, 17, 27 November, 7 December 1863, box 300; Stahr, *Seward*, 382; Stuart to R.B. Lyons, 7 January 1863[4], box 201; R.B. Lyons to Odo Russell, 6 November 1863, FO 918/52, Odo Russell Papers.

19	Barnes and Barnes, *American Civil War through British Eyes*, 3:104; R.B. Lyons to Anderson, 4 October 1863, box 107; Anderson to R.B. Lyons, 6

October 1863, box 123; R.B. Lyons to Clay, 16 August 1863, box 107; Clay to R.B. Lyons, 12 February, 12 May 1863, box 197; Warre to R.B. Lyons, 23 April 1864, box 203; Stuart to R.B. Lyons, 27 May 1863, box 201; Russell to R.B. Lyons, 18 June, 16 July 1863, box 196; R.B. Lyons to Minna, 4 July 1863, box 300.

20 R.B. Lyons to Anderson, 4 October; R.B. Lyons to Hammond, 7 October 1863, box 107; W. L. Morton, ed., *Monck Letters and Journals 1863–1868: Canada from Government House at Confederation* (Toronto, 1970), 125; Hare to Sheffield, 30, 11 June 1863, box 200; R.B. Lyons to Minna, 16, 20 October 1863, box 300.

21 Barnes and Barnes, *Private and Confidential*, 338; R.B. Lyons to Minna, 26 December 1863, box 300; Minna to R.B. Lyons, 15 January 1864, box 294; Barnes and Barnes, *American Civil War through British Eyes*, 3:127, 94.

22 Palmer, *Selected Letters of Sumner*, 2:203–4, 210–11, 277; Pierce, "Letters of Richard Cobden to Charles Sumner, 1862–1865," 313–14; Jenkins, *Britain and the War for the Union*, 2:299–300, 304–5; Barnes and Barnes, *Private and Confidential*, 337; Russell to R.B. Lyons, 2, 24, 31 October 1863, box 196; Barnes and Barnes, *American Civil War through British Eyes*, 3:101–2; David F. Krein, "Russell's Decision to Detain the Laird Rams," *Civil War History* 22 (1976): 158–63.

23 *Leeds Mercury*, 1 March 1865; R.B. Lyons to Odo Russell, 6 November 1863, FO 918/52; Barnes and Barnes, *American Civil War through British Eyes*, 3:107; R.B. Lyons to Seward, 4 January 1864, Seward Papers; Bernal to Stuart, 14 September 1863; Monck to R.B. Lyons, 22 October, 12, 18 November 1863, 14, 25, 26 January 1864, box 192.

24 Jenkins, *Britain and the War for the Union*, 2:346; R.B. Lyons to Monck, 11 February 1864; R.B. Lyons to Gordon, 17 December 1863; R.B. Lyons to Milne, 10 January 1864, box 107; Barnes and Barnes, *Private and Confidential*, 338–9.

25 Barnes and Barnes, *American Civil War through British Eyes*, 3:140; Barnes and Barnes, *Private and Confidential*, 340; R.B. Lyons to Monck, 1 March 1864, box 107; Jenkins, *Britain and the War for the Union*, 2:348–9.

26 R.B. Lyons to Russell, 3 November, 7 December 1863, box 107; Barnes and Barnes, *Private and Confidential*, 342; Barnes and Barnes, *American Civil War through British Eyes*, 3:157–8; Russell to R.B. Lyons, 21 November 1863, box 196.

27 Russell to R.B. Lyons, 16 January, 6 February, 23 April, 21, 14 May, 30 January 1864, box 196; Cobden to Chevalier, 4 January, 26 February, 5 March, 5 November 1864, Cobden 47, WSRO.

28 R.B. Lyons to Anderson, 4 October 1863; R.B. Lyons to Hammond, 17 May, 14 June 1864; R.B. Lyons to Elliot, 5 April 1864; R.B. Lyons to Gordon, 13 April 1864; R.B. Lyons to Hammond, 5 April 1864; R.B. Lyons to Stuart, 28 March 1864, box 107.

29 R.B. Lyons to Minna, 21, 31 December 1863, 12, 22 January, 23 February 1864, box 300; Malet to mother, 4 January 1864, Malet Papers; R.B. Lyons to Stuart, 29 September 1863; R.B. Lyons to Stanfield, 29 September, 2 October 1863, box 107; Fish to R.B. Lyons, 31 December 1863, box 123; R.B. Lyons to Fish, 6 January 1864, box 107; Burnley to R.B. Lyons, 6 February 1865, box 124.

30 Barnes and Barnes, *Private and Confidential*, 343–4; Russell to R.B. Lyons, 4, 18 June, 16, 23 July, 20 October 1864, box 196; Bourne, *Britain and the Balance of Power in North America*, 278.

31 Barnes and Barnes, *Private and Confidential*, 345–9.

32 R.B. Lyons to Minna, 4, 8, 12, 29 July, 1, 19, 23, 30 August 1864, box 300; Barnes and Barnes, *Private and Confidential*, 346.

33 Barnes and Barnes, *Private and Confidential*, 348; Malet to mother, 30 August 1864, Malet Papers; R.B. Lyons to Minna, 30 August, 6 September, 9 October 1864, box 300; R.B. Lyons to Monck, 31 August 1864, box 107; F.E.O. Monck, *My Canadian Leaves* (Dorchester, 1873), 15.

34 For Lyons's visit to Canada see F.E.O. Monck's *My Canadian Leaves* and her journals published as part of *Monck Letters and Journals*, edited by W.L. Morton (Toronto, 1971); Newton, *Lyons*, 1:291.

35 R.B. Lyons to Minna, 18, 21, 24 October 1864, box 300; R.B. Lyons to St Germans, 23 September 1864, box 107.

36 R.B. Lyons to Burnley, 19 October 1864, box 123; Jenkins, *Britain and the War for the Union*, 2:359–60; Stahr, *Seward*, 411, 414; R.B. Lyons to Russell, 1 November 1864, box 107.

37 Barnes and Barnes, *Private and Confidential*, 350; Russell to R.B. Lyons, 19 November 1864, PRO 30/22/97; Palmer, *Selected Letters of Sumner*, 2:277; Burnley to R.B. Lyons, 26 July, 7, 24 September 1864, box 123; R.B. Lyons to Hammond, 3 January 1865, box 107.

38 Palmer, *Selected Letters of Sumner*, 2:277; Adland to R.B. Lyons, 14 January 1865, box 124; R.B. Lyons to Minna, 6, 15 November, 5 December 1864, box 300; B. Ogle Taylor to R.B. Lyons, 5 December 1864, box 123; Davis, "A British Diplomat and the American Civil War: Edward Malet in the United States," 177.

39 R.B. Lyons to Seward, 3 December 1864, box 107; Seward to R.B. Lyons, 4 December 1864, box 123; Seward to R.B. Lyons, 20 March 1865, box 124;

Wickham Hoffman to R.B. Lyons, 17 April 1874, box 139; R.B. Lyons to Alexander Malet, 3 December; Sheffield to Kennedy, 12 December; Sheffield to Burnley, 12 December 1864, box 107; *National Republican*, 10 December 1864.

40 Beckles Willson, *Friendly Relations: A Narrative of Britain's Ministers and Ambassadors to America (1791–1930)* (New York, 1934), 205.

CHAPTER TEN

1 R.B. Lyons to Minna, 25, 26 December 1864, box 300; Russell to R.B. Lyons, 27 December 1864, box 196; Minna to R.B. Lyons, 26 December 1864, 31 January 1865, box 294.

2 R.B. Lyons to Minna, 3 February 1865, box 300; Burnley to R.B. Lyons, 15 December; Seymour to R.B. Lyons, 16 December 1864, box 123; Hawkins, *Forgotten Prime Minister*, 2:291–2; R.B. Lyons to Burnley, 24 February 1865, box 107; *Leeds Mercury*, 1 March 1865; *Liverpool Mercury*, 1 March 1865; Russell to R.B. Lyons, 25 March 1865, box 196; R.B. Lyons to Stuart, 6 March 1865, box 107.

3 Malet to mother, 24 May 1865, Malet Papers; Bruce to R.B. Lyons, 1 March 1865, box 123; R.B. Lyons to Minna, 19, 21 February, 5 June, 1, 11 July 1865, box 300; Bruce to R.B. Lyons, 4 May, 4 June 1865, box 123; R.B. Lyons to Michel, 29 May 1865, box 107.

4 R.B. Lyons to Minna, 5 June 1865, box 300; R.B. Lyons to Malet, 21 June; Malet to mother, 22 June; R.B. Lyons to Malet, 14 July 1865, Malet Papers; Russell to R.B. Lyons, 22, 28 July 1865, box 196; Stuart to R.B. Lyons, 2 September 1864; 8 February 1865, box 201; R.B. Lyons to Russell, 24 July 1865; R.B. Lyons to Stuart, 14, 17 August 1865, box 107.

5 Russell to R.B. Lyons, 10 August 1865, box 196; Malet to mother, 10 November 1865, Malet Papers; Farrar to R.B. Lyons, 14 August 1865, box 123; Addington to R.B. Lyons, 16 September 1865, box 174; *Blackwood's Magazine* 46 (1839): 100; Stuart to R.B. Lyons, 4 August 1865, box 201.

6 R.B. Lyons to Minna, 16, 31 August, 4, 7 September 1865, box 300; Lady Stratford to R.B. Lyons, 2 September; Stratford to R.B. Lyons, 17 September 1865, box 123.

7 Jones, *British Diplomatic Service*, 83–96, 51; Hammond to R.B. Lyons, 15, 18 August 1865, box 187; Bulwer to Russell, 23 May 1865, BUL 1/166/1a, Bulwer Papers, NRO; Bulwer to Russell, 24 May 1865, BUL 1/166/2a; Bulwer to Layard, 15 August; Russell to Layard, 11 September 1865, BL 39116, Layard Papers; Philip Mansel, *Constantinople: City of the World's Desire, 1453–1924*,

pb ed. (London, 1997), 285; Malet to father, 24 October; Malet to mother, 3 November 1865, Malet Papers; Angus Hawkins and John Powell, eds, *The Journal of John Wodehouse, First Earl of Kimberley for 1862–1902*, Camden 5th series, vol. 9 (London, 1997), 240; George Washburn, *Fifty Years in Constantinople and Recollections of Robert College* (Boston, 1911), 1, 11; Jones, *British Diplomatic Service*, 89–96; Stuart to R.B. Lyons, 2 September 1864; Russell to Stuart, 6 April 1865; Stuart to R.B. Lyons, 8 February 1865, box 201.

8 For the late foreign policy setbacks of the Palmerston ministry see David F. Klein, *The Last Palmerston Government: Foreign Policy, Domestic Politics, and the Genesis of "Splendid Isolation"* (Ames, IA, 1978); Russell to R.B. Lyons, 6 August 1865, box 196.

9 *Blackwood's Magazine* (46): 102, 115; Christopher Howard, *Britain and the Casus Belli, 1822–1902* (London, 1974), 25; Alan Palmer, *The Decline and Fall of the Ottoman Empire*, reprint ed. (New York, 1994), 135; Malmesbury to Cowley, 16 December 1858, FO 519/196, Cowley Papers; Russell to Bulwer, 4 September 1859, 22 November 1860, 25 April 1861, PRO 30/22/116, Russell Papers; Cobden to Chevalier, 2 June 1863, Cobden 47, WSRO.

10 Russell to Bulwer, 5 November 1861, 4 January 1862, 4 September, 16 July 1859, PRO 30/22/116, Russell Papers; Ann Pottinger Saab, *Reluctant Icon: Gladstone, Bulgaria and the Working Classes, 1856–1878* (Cambridge, MA, 1991), 18–19; L.S. Stavrianos, *Balkan Federation: A History of the Movement towards Balkan Unity in Modern Times* (Hamden, 1964), 15; Bulwer to Clarendon, 5 March 1869, BUL 1/368/9.

11 Charles Beatty, *Ferdinand de Lesseps: A Biographical Study* (London, 1956), 84, 122–3; Malmesbury to Derby, 15 November 1859, 920 DER (14) 144/2a, Derby Papers; Bulwer to Bulwer Lytton, 15 January 1860, BUL 1/25518, Bulwer Papers; undated memorandum to Bulwer Lytton, BUL 1/255/19a; Bulwer to Russell, 20 June 1865, BUL 1/167/16a; Russell to Bulwer, 17 November, 15 December 1859, PRO 30/22/116, Russell Papers; Bulwer ro Russell, 7 September 1865, BUL 1/167/9.

12 Palmerston to Hammond, 4, 20 September 1864, FO 391/7, Hammond Papers; Russell to Bulwer, 10, 28 September 1864, PRO 30/22/116, Russell Papers; Russell memorandum, 24 November 1864, FO 519/7; Russell to R.B. Lyons, 18 September 1865, FO 78/1854.

13 Bulwer to Russell, 15 June, 16 August 1865, PRO 30/22/93, Russell Papers; n.d. [1865], BUL 1/347/20b; Bulwer memorandum, [1865], BUL 1/352/8, Bulwer Papers; Washburn, *Fifty Years in Constantinople*, xviii; Palmer, *Decline and Fall of Ottoman Empire*, 130–1, 135; Bulwer to Russell, 16 March 1864, PRO 30/22/93; 1 July 1865, BUL 1/166/12a.

14　Barbara Jelavich, *A Century of Russian Foreign Policy, 1814–1914* (New York, 1964), 137–9; Pottinger, *Reluctant Icon*, 18; Bulwer to Russell, 16 March 1864, PRO 30/22/93; Green to R.B. Lyons, 3 May 1861, box 184; *Illustrated London News*, 15 August 1857; *The Times*, 24, 26 August 1865; Russell to R.B. Lyons, 18 September 1865, FO 78/1854.

15　Minna to R.B. Lyons, 18 September 1865, box 294; Malet to mother, 15 September 1865, Malet Papers; R.B. Lyons to Minna, 19 September 1865, box 300; R.B. Lyons to Russell, 21 September 1865; Russell to R.B. Lyons, 5 October 1865, box 196.

16　R.B. Lyons to Minna, 21, 26, 30 September, 5, 8, 13 October 1865, box 300; Malet to mother, 5 October 1865, Malet Papers; Minna to R.B. Lyons, 4, 25 October 1865, box 294.

17　Malet to father, 13 October 1865, Malet Papers; Bulwer to R.B. Lyons, 16 August 1865, BUL 1/255/11, Bulwer Papers; September n.d., box 124; R.B. Lyons to Minna, 6 December 1865, box 300; Malet to father, 24 October; Malet to mother, 18 October 1865, Malet Papers.

18　Jones, *British Diplomatic Service*, 83; Malet to father, 24 October 1865, 26 January 1866, Malet Papers; R.B. Lyons to Minna, 8 November 1865, box 300; Malet to mother, 29 October, 3 November 1865, 5, 11 January 1866, Malet Papers; Lady Layard's Journal, 20 April 1877, Armstrong Browning Library of Baylor University, http://fleetwood.baylor.edu/layard/calendar/1861calendar.php; R.B. Lyons to Hammond, 24 October 1865; R.B. Lyons to Lady Cowley, 27 October 1865; R.B. Lyons to Clarendon, 22 November 1865, box 107.

19　Malet to father, 24 October 1865; Malet to mother, 3 November, 15 December 1865, 5 January, 6 April, 18 June 1866, Malet Papers.

20　Malet to mother, 23, 10 November 1865, 2 May 1867, Malet Papers; Michael Diamond, *Victorian Sensation*, pb ed. (London, 2004), 191–3; Jones, *British Diplomatic Service*, 84, 87, 92–3, 96; Roderic H. Davison, *Reform in the Ottoman Empire, 1856–1876*, 2nd ed. (New York, 1973), 35–8; Platt, *Cinderella Service*, 164; R.B. Lyons to Hammond, 24 October 1865, box 107; Clarendon to Lyons, 29 January 1866, FO 78/1903.

21　Hammond to R.B. Lyons, 5 October 1865, box 187; R.B. Lyons to Clarendon, 22 November 1865; R.B. Lyons to Hammond, 24 October 1865, box 107; R.B. Lyons to Cowley, 25 October 1865, FO 519/201, Cowley Papers; R.B. Lyons to Salisbury, 2 January 1880, box 111; Bulwer to Russell, 16 March 1864, PRO 30/22/93, Russell Papers; Malet to mother, 10 November 1865, Malet Papers; Davison, *Reform in the Ottoman Empire*, 83–90.

22　R.B. Lyons to Russell, 8 November 1865, box 107; Malet to mother, 3

November 1865, Malet Papers; R.B. Lyons to Minna, 5 September 1866, box 300; Otte, *Foreign Office Mind*, 34.

23 Clarendon to R.B. Lyons, 5 April 1866, box 176; R.B. Lyons to Hammond, 14 May 1867, FO 391/13, Hammond Papers; R.B. Lyons to Clarendon, 22 November 1865; Erskine to R.B. Lyons, 7 February 1866, box 178; R.B. Lyons to Erskine, 4 July 1866, box 107.

24 Clarendon to R.B. Lyons, 1 March 1866, box 176; R.B. Lyons to Erskine, 22 November 1865, box 107; Sheffield to R.B. Lyons, 20 February 1867, box 199; Platt, *Cinderella Service*, 154–5; McCowan to Sheffield, 13 November 1865, 8 May, 1 October 1866, box 200; R.B. Lyons to Odo Russell, 16 January 1866, FO 918/52, Odo Russell Papers.

25 Seward to R.B. Lyons, 24 September 1865; Lady Stratford to R.B. Lyons, 8 February 1866, box 124; Erskine to R.B. Lyons, 4, 20 June 1866, box 178.

26 Davison, *Reform in the Ottoman Empire*, 61, 112; see also, Niyazi Berkes, *The Development of Secularism in Turkey* (Montreal, 1964), and Bernard Lewis, *The Emergence of Modern Turkey* (London, 1965); Halil Inalcik and Donald Quataert, *An Economic and Social History of the Ottoman Empire, 1300–1914* (Cambridge, 1994), 826; Stratford de Redcliffe to R.B. Lyons, 13 December 1865, box 124.

27 R.B. Lyons to Russell, 25 October, 8 November 1865, box 107; Serif Mardin, *The Genesis of Young Ottoman Thought: A Study in the Modernization of Turkish Political Ideas* (Princeton, NJ, 1962), 28–31; R.B. Lyons to Clarendon 14 February 1866, box 107.

28 R.B. Lyons to Clarendon 6 December 1865, box 107; Clarendon to R.B. Lyons, 16 December 1865, FO 78/1854; R.B. Lyons to Clarendon, 3, 17 January, 14 March, 6 June 1866, box 107; Davison, *Reform in the Ottoman Empire*, 91; R.B. Lyons to Clarendon, 18 July 1866, box 100; see also private letter of same date, box 107; R.B. Lyons to Russell, 25 October 1865, box 100.

29 R.B. Lyons to Russell, 25 October 1865, box 100; R.B. Lyons to Granville, 21 November 1870, box 109; Bulwer to Russell, 27 September 1865, BUL 1/166/24, Bulwer Papers; R.B. Lyons to Clarendon, 19 (confidential), 26 December 1865, 22 May, 6 June 1866, box 100; R.B. Lyons to Russell, 8 November, 1865; R.B. Lyons to Cowley, 14 February; R.B. Lyons to Clarendon, 28 February; R.B. Lyons to Stanton, 8 March 1866, box 107.

30 R.B. Lyons to Cowley, 14 February 1866, box 107; R.B. Lyons to Russell, 7 November (confidential); R.B. Lyons to Clarendon, 22 November (confidential) 1865, box 100; see also private letter of same date, box 107; Green to R.B. Lyons, 7 October 1865, box 184.

31 Green to R.B. Lyons, 7, 10, 13, 17 October 1865, 2, 9, 16 January 1866, box 184.

32 R.B. Lyons to Clarendon, 25 November (confidential) 1865, box 100; R.B. Lyons to Clarendon, 6 December 1865, box 107; R.B. Lyons to Clarendon, 28 February 1866, box 100; see private letter of same date, box 107; R.B. Lyons to Clarendon, 28 March 1865, box 100.

33 Clarendon to R.B. Lyons, 25 February 1866, FO 78/1903; Foreign Office circular, 25 February 1866, FO 78/1903; Cowley to R.B. Lyons 6 April 1866, box 178; R.B. Lyons to Clarendon, 28 February, 14 March, 23 May 1866, box 107; R.B. Lyons to Clarendon, 28 March, 11 April, 22 (confidential), 30 May, 17 June (confidential) 1866, box 100; Clarendon to R.B. Lyons, 21, 22 June 1866, box 107; R.B. Lyons to Clarence Paget, 20 June 1866, box 107; Cowley to R.B. Lyons. 29 June 1866, box 178.

34 Hammond to R.B. Lyons, 22 March 1866, box 187; Clarendon to R.B. Lyons, 21, 22 June 1866, box 170.

CHAPTER ELEVEN

1 Malet to mother, 19 January, 9 March, 28 May, 4 June 1866, Malet Papers; Frederick St John, *Reminiscences of a Retired Diplomat* (London, 1905), 106–8.

2 *The Times*, 24 March 1857; Clarendon to R.B. Lyons, 28 June 1866, box 176; Derby to Stanley, 24 April 1866, 920 DER (15), 12/3/7, Derby Papers; Sarah Agnes Wallace and Frances Elma Gillespie, *The Journal of Benjamin Moran,, 1857–1865*, 2 vols (Chicago, 1948), 1:290; Kenneth Bourne, "Great Britain and the Cretan Revolt, 1866–1869," *Slavonic and East European Review* 35 (1956): 75; Otte, *Foreign Office Mind*, 30–1.

3 Malet to mother, 27 June 1866, Malet Papers; Derby to Stanley, 23 September 1866, 920 DER (15) 12/3/7; Stanley to Derby, 8 August, 19 September 1866, 920 DER (15) 12/3/7, Derby Papers; Disraeli to Stanley, 14 October 1867, 12/3/7; 17 August 1866, 12/3/8.

4 Brian Jenkins, *The Fenian Problem: Insurgency and Terrorism in a Liberal State 1858–1874* (Liverpool, 2008), 50–1; Stanley to Derby, 8 August, 19, 26 September 1866, 920 DER (15) 13/2/3, Derby Papers; Otte, *Foreign Office Mind*, 26; George Leveson Gower, *Mixed Grill* (London, 1947), 127; R.B. Lyons to Erskine, 12 September 1866; R.B. Lyons to Cowley, 7 November 1866, box 107; Stanley to Disraeli, 22 August 1866, 920 DER (15) 13/2/4; Derby to Stanley, 23 September 1866, 13/3/7; Stanley to Malmesbury, 5 September 1866, 13/2/1; Hon F.A. Wellesley, ed., *The Paris Embassy during the Second Empire* (London, 1928), 315, 321.

5 Stanley to Cowley, 28 September 1866, FO 519/182, Cowley Papers; Derby to Stanley, 5, 6 October 1866, 920 DER (15) 12/3/7, Derby Papers; Angus

Hawkins and John Powell, eds, *The Journal of John Wodehouse First Earl of Kimblerley for 1862–1902*, Camden 5th ser., vol. 9 (London, 1997), 196; Weintraub, *Edward the Caresser*, 145; Wellesley, *Paris Embassy during the Second Empire*, 322; Desmond Seward, *Eugenie: The Empress and Her Empire*, pb ed., (Stroud, 2005), 169; Hammond to Stanley, 16 August 1866, 12/3/9; Stanley to Derby, 5, 6 October 1866, 13/2/3; Minna to R.B. Lyons, 24 October 1866, box 294.

6 Hammond to R.B. Lyons, 22 March 1866, box 187; Malet to mother, 27 June 1866, Malet Papers; Cowley to R.B. Lyons, 13 July 1866, box 178; Diary of 15th Earl of Derby, 30 July 1866, 920 DER (15), Derby Papers; Stanley to Malmesbury, 15 August, 13 September 1866, 920 DER (15) 13/2/1; Stanley to Cowley, 30 August 1866, FO 519/182, Cowley Papers.

7 Maureen M. Robson, "Lord Clarendon and the Cretan Question, 1868–9, *Historical Journal* 3 (1960): 40; Derby to Stanley, 23 September, 12 October, 21 December 1866, 920 DER (15) 12/3/7, Derby Papers; Stanley to Derby, 22 December 1866, 13/2/3; Stanley to Cowley, 15 September 1866, FO 519/182; Stanley to R.B. Lyons, 6 September 1866, box 179.

8 R.B. Lyons to Stanley, 20 September, 31 July, 5 September 1866, box 100; R.B. Lyons to Stanley, 12 September 1866, box 107; Otte, *Foreign Office Mind*, 46, 51; R.B. Lyons to Reade, 12 October 1866, box 107; Green to R.B. Lyons, 12 August 1866, box 184; R.B. Lyons to Green, 10 October 1866, box 107; Green to R.B. Lyons, 17 October 1866, box 184.

9 R.B. Lyons to Stanley, 26 September, 1, 25 October 1866, box 100; R.B. Lyons to Stanley, 7 November 1866; R.B. Lyons to Cowley, 7 November 1866, box 107; Stanley to R.B. Lyons, 25 October 1866, FO 78/1904; Stanley to R.B. Lyons, 1, n.d., November 1866, box 179; R.B. Lyons to Stanley, 19 March 1868, box 108; Green to R.B. Lyons, 15 January, 19 February, 6 October 1867, box 184.

10 Green to R.B. Lyons, 22 January, 5 February 1867, 11 December 1866, box 184; Diary of 15th Earl of Derby, 26 January 1867, 920 DER (15), Derby Papers; Cowley to Stanley, 29 April 1867, box 178; Stanley to Cowley, 25 September 1866, FO 519/182.

11 Otte, *Foreign Office Mind*, 34; R.B. Lyons to Erskine, 22 August 1866; R.B. Lyons to Stanley 29 August 1866, box 107; Otte, *Foreign Office Mind*, 43; R.B. Lyons to Stanley, 31 July, 23 August, 3, 9 October, 7, 28 November, 5 December 1866, box 100.

12 R.B. Lyons to Stanley, 11 September 1866, box 100; R.B. Lyons to Stanley, 5, 19 December 1866, box 107.

13 Stanley to R.B. Lyons, 9, 17, 23, 31 January, 7 March 1867, box 179; Fane to R.B. Lyons, 8 February 1867, box 178; Cowley to Stanley, 30 June 1867, FO 519/234, Cowley Papers; R.B. Lyons to Stanley, 12 September 1866, box 100; Malet to mother, 28 January 1867, Malet Papers; Disraeli to Stanley, 30 December 1866, 920 DER (15) 12/3/8, Derby Papers.

14 Hammond to R.B. Lyons, 7 March, 2 May 1867, box 187; Cowley to R.B. Lyons, 5 April 1867, box 178; Stanley to R.B. Lyons, 21 March, 4, 24 April, 16 May 1867, box 179; Diary of 15th Earl of Derby, 24, 25 January 1867, 920 DER (15), Derby Papers; Disraeli to Stanley, 30 December 1866, 3, 22 April 1867, 12/3/8; Stanley to Disraeli, 31 December 1866, 23 April 1867, 13/2/4; Diary 15th Earl of Derby, 17 May 1867; Stanley to Malmesbury 23 April 1867, 13/2/1; Malet to mother, 27 March 1867, Malet Papers; Otte, *Foreign Office Mind*, 53; Hammond to R.B. Lyons, 30 May 1867, box 187; Erskine to R.B. Lyons, 15 May 1867, box 178.

15 R.B. Lyons to Paget, 6 August 1866; R.B. Lyons to Monson, 8 August 1866, box 107; Malet to mother, 11 September 1866, Malet Papers; Longworth to R.B. Lyons, 12 November 1866; Pisani to R.B. Lyons, 1 November 1866, box 125; R.B. Lyons to Stanley, 29 August 1866; R.B. Lyons to Cowley, 14 October 1866; R.B. Lyons to Blake, 24 October 1866, box 107.

16 R.B. Lyons to Minna, 2 January, 5, 13, 27 February 1867, box 301; R.B. Lyons to Malet, 30 November 1866, Malet Papers; R.B. Lyons to Lady Russell, 23 February 1867, box 107; Diary of 15th Earl of Derby, 26 January, 22 February 1867, 920 DER (15), Derby Papers; R.B. Lyons to Hammond, 1 January 1867, FO 391/13; R.B. Lyons to Stanley, 13, 27 February 1867, 920 DER (15) 12/1/21; Bourne, "Great Britain and the Cretan Revolt, 1866–1869," 83.

17 Stanley to Cowley, 28 June 1867, FO 519/182; Stanley to R.B. Lyons, 17 January 1867, FO 76/1954; Stanley to R.B. Lyons, 3, 12, 21 June 1867, FO 76/1955; R.B. Lyons to Hammond, 23 July 1867, FO 391/13, Hammond Papers; R.B. Lyons to Stanley, 29 January, 6 February 1867, box 100; R.B. Lyons to Stanley, 13 March 1867, box 107; Diary of 15th Earl of Derby, 17 May 1867, 920 DER (15), Derby Papers; R.B. Lyons to Cowley, 8 May 1867, box 107; R.B. Lyons to Stanley, 8 May 1867, 920 DER (15) 12/1/21.

18 R.B. Lyons to Minna, 7, 30 May, 18 June 1867, box 301; Malet to mother, 27 March, 10, 11 April 1867, Malet Papers; R.B. Lyons to Sanderson, 24 October 1876, box 110; Cowley to R.B. Lyons, 17 May 1867, box 178; Clarendon to R.B. Lyons, 30 May 1867, box 176; Minna to R.B. Lyons, 22 May 1867, box 294; R.B. Lyons to Hammond, 14 May 1867, box 107; Monson to R.B. Lyons, 12 August 1867, box 193; R.B. Lyons to Hammond, 14, 25 June 1867,

FO 391/13, Hammond Papers; Malet to mother, 12 July 1867, Malet Papers.

19 Minna to R.B. Lyons, 7 March 1867, box 294; R.B. Lyons to Minna, 7 May 1867, box 301; Hammond to R.B. Lyons, 18 June, 4 July 1867, box 187; R.B. Lyons to Hammond, 16, 25 June 1867, FO 391/13, Hammond Papers.

20 Malet to mother, 22 May 1867, Malet Papers; R.B. Lyons to Stanley, 18 May, 3 June 1867, box 100; Stanley to R.B. Lyons, 30 May 1867, box 179; R.B. Lyons to Stanley, 10 June 1867, box 107; *The Times*, 3 July 1867; Hammond to R.B. Lyons, 4 July 1867, box 187.

21 R.B. Lyons to Stanley, 10 June; R.B. Lyons to Hammond, 10 June 1867, box 107; *The Times*, 13 July 1867; Hawkins and Powell, *Journal of John Wodehouse, First Earl of Kimberley*, 205, 207; Hawkins, *Forgotten Prime Minister*, 2: 349–50; Hammond to R.B. Lyons, 11 July 1867, box 187; Michael Diamond, *Victorian Sensation*, pb ed. (London, 2004), 29.

22 E. Gordon to Sheffield, 11 July 1867, box 200; Gilbertson to R.B. Lyons, n.d. [July 1867], box 107; George Washburn, *Fifty Years in Constantinople and Recollections of Robert College* (Boston, 1911), 11; R.B. Lyons to Stanley, 8 October 1866, box 100.

23 R.B. Lyons to Stanley, 25 June 1867, box 100; Cowley to R.B. Lyons, 28 June 1867, box 178; R.B. Lyons to Minna, 19, 27 July, 2, 10 August 1867, box 301; R.B. Lyons to Hammond, 23 July 1867, box 107; Hammond to R.B. Lyons, 11 July 1867, box 187; R.B. Lyons to Minna, 3 September 1867, box 301.

24 Malet to mother, 27 September, 2, 5, 15 October 1867, Malet Papers; *Northern Echo*, 22 August 1892; John Vincent, ed., *A Selection from the Diaries of Edward Henry Stanley, 15th Earl of Derby (1826–1893) between September 1869 and March 1878*, Camden 5th series, vol. 4 (London, 1994), 113; Karina Urbach, *Bismarck's Favorite Englishman: Lord Odo Russell's Mission to Berlin* (New York, 2001), 12–13.

25 Wellesley, *The Paris Embassy*, 165, 281, 314–15, 318–19; Hon. F.A. Wellesley, *Secrets of the Second Empire: Private Letters from the Paris Embassy* (London, 1929), 313, 317, 319, 324; Otte, *Foreign Office Mind*, 34; Ross King, *The Judgment of Paris: The Revolutionary Decade That Gave the World Impressionism* (New York, 2006), 146; Roger Price, *The French Second Empire: An Anatomy of Political Power* (Cambridge, 2001), 50.

26 Clay Ker-Seymer to R.B. Lyons, 28 December 1865, 5 September 1867, box 197; R.B. Lyons to Sheffield, 3 September, 8, 15, 16 October 1867, box 199; R.B. Lyons to Alston, 11 October 1867, box 107.

27 R.B. Lyons to Sheffield, 3 September 1867, box 199; R.B. Lyons to Malet 15 September 1867, Malet Papers; Lord John Manners to R.B. Lyons, 1, n.d. [23] October 1867; R.B. Lyons to Fane, 14, 29 September, 7 October 1867;

R.B. Lyons to Staveley, 20 October 1867, box 107; Sheffield to R.B. Lyons, 29 September, 17 October 1867, box 199; R.B. Lyons to Malet, 19 October 1867, Malet Papers; R.B. Lyons to Minna, 24 October 1867, box 301.

28 Hawkins and Powell, *Journal of John Wodehouse*, 201; Derby to Stanley, 9 September 1866, 920 DER (15) 12/3/7, Derby Papers; Derby Diary, 31 December 1867, 920 DER (15); Wellesley, *Paris Embassy*, 315; Stanley to Derby, 3 October 1867, 920 DER (14) 105/8.

29 Stanley to Derby, 4 January 1867, 920 DER (14) 105/8; Derby Diary, 9 October 1867, 920 DER (15), Derby Papers; Stanley to Cowley, 12 December 1866, 28, 29 June, 28 May 1867, 27 November 1866, FO 519/182, Cowley Papers; Cowley to Stanley, 16 June 1867, FO 519/234; Milza, *Napoléon III* (Paris, 2004), 512; Stanley to Fane, 22 October 1867, FO 27/1655.

CHAPTER TWELVE

1 R.B. Lyons to Minna, 26 October 1867, box 301; R.B. Lyons to Cowley, 28 October, 30 November 1867, box 107; Alston to R.B. Lyons, 3 February 1870, box 195; Stanley to R.B. Lyons, 10 January 1868, FO 27/1696; Sheffield to R.B. Lyons, 18 October 1869, box 199; Malet to mother, 27 November 1867, Malet Papers; R.B. Lyons to Minna, 18 January, 22 February 1868, box 301.

2 R.B. Lyons to Minna, 9, 15 November 1867, 5, 6 January, 6, 22 June 1868, box 301; Hannah Pakula, *An Uncommon Woman: The Empress Frederick* (London, 1996), 141; Rupert Christiansen, *Paris Babylon: Grandeur, Decadence and Revolution 1869–1875*, pb ed. (London, 2003), 9; Vincent, *Diaries of 15th Earl of Derby*, 42; Lytton to Sheffield, 16 April 1869, box 200; Sheffield to R.B. Lyons, 11 November 1871, box 199; Malet to mother, n.d [1867], 18, 22 June 1868, Malet Papers.

3 R.B. Lyons to Minna, 9 November 1867, box 301; Robert Gildea, *Children of the Revolution: The French, 1799–1914* (London, 2008), 195; King, *The Judgment of Paris*, 185, 193–4, 206.

4 David P. Jordan, *Transforming Paris: The Life and Labors of Baron Haussmann* (New York, 1995), 175, 203; Christiansen, *Paris Babylon*, 101, 106.

5 David Harvey, *Paris, Capital of Modernity*, pb ed. (London, 2006), 180, 135–6, 139, 144–5, 150–1, 165–6, 178–80, 187, 198, 296; Jordan, *Transforming Paris*, 305, 238, 298; Christiansen, *Paris Babylon*, 99.

6 R.B. Lyons to Minna, 9, 15 November 1867, box 301; Newton, *Lyons*, 1:188; S.C. Burchell, *Imperial Masquerade: The Paris of Napoleon III* (New York, 1971), 131; Sheffield to R.B. Lyons, 17 October 1867, box 199; Lord Randolph Sutherland Gower, *Records and Reminiscences: Selected from "My*

Reminiscences" and "Old Diaries" (London, 1903), 341; Malet to mother, 16, 19, 27 November 1867, Malet Papers.

7 Monson to Malet, 7 May 1868, Malet Papers; M.S. Anderson, *The Rise of Modern Diplomacy 1450–1919* (New York, 1993), 126; R.B. Lyons to Minna, 6, 27 February 1869, 1 December 1867, 20 April, 6 June 1868, box 301; Malet to mother, 19 April, 8 August 1868, Malet Papers; Odo Russell to R.B. Lyons, 11 December 1869, box 197.

8 R.B. Lyons to Minna, 6 February 1869, box 301; Dacros to R.B. Lyons, 27 October 1867, box 126; R.B. Lyons to Stanley, 28 October 1867, box 107; Malet to mother, 19 November 1867, Malet Papers; Michael Burleigh, *Earthly Powers: The Clash of Religion and Politics in Europe from the French Revolution to the Great War* (New York, 2005), 208–11; R.B. Lyons to Stanley, 28 October 1867, box 100; Stanley to R.B. Lyons, 29 October 1867, box 179.

9 R.B. Lyons to Paget, 30 October 1867; R.B. Lyons to Stanley, 1, 11 November 1867, box 107; Stanley to R.B. Lyons, 2, 6 November 1867, box 179; R.B. Lyons to Stanley, 8, 11, 14 16 November 1867, box 107.

10 R.B. Lyons to Stanley, 14 November 1867, box 107; Stanley to R.B. Lyons, 14, 16 November 1867, box 179; R.B. Lyons to Odo Russell, 19 November 1867, box 107; Stanley to R.B. Lyons, FO 27/1655; R.B. Lyons to Stanley, 28 November, 6 December 1867; R.B. Lyons to Paget, 10 December 1867; R.B. Lyons to Stanley, 17 December 1867, box 107; R.B. Lyons to Paget, 7, 21 January 1868, BL Add. Ms. 51231, Paget Papers; R.B. Lyons to Stanley, 11 February 1868, box 100.

11 Stanley to R.B. Lyons, 16, 18 December 1868, 4, 6, 25 January 1868, box 179; Feilding to Sheffield, 5 January 1868; Trelawney to Sheffield, 6 January 1868, box 127; R.B. Lyons to Hammond, 22 December 1867; R.B. Lyons to Pietri (emperor's private secretary), 5 January 1868, box 108; Brian Jenkins, *The Fenian Problem: Insurgency and Terrorism in a Liberal State 1858–1874* (Liverpool, 2009), 170–1.

12 Stanley to R.B. Lyons, 24 February, 4 March 1868, box 179; Fane to R.B. Lyons, 12 February 1867, box 178; Jenkins, *Fenian Problem*, 210; R.B. Lyons to Stanley, 26 November 1867, box 107; Stanley to R.B. Lyons, 6 January 1868, box 179; R.B. Lyons to Stanley, 2 January 1868, box 100; R.B. Lyons to Stanley, 24 December 1867, 19 March 1868, box 108; Gildea, *Children of the Revolution*, 58; Derby Diary, 22 March 1868, 920 DER (15); Stanley to R.B. Lyons, 4 February 1868, box 179; Stanley to R.B. Lyons, 25 March 1868, FO 27/1696.

13 Stanley to R.B. Lyons, 14 April 1868, FO 27/1697; Bourne, "Great Britain and the Cretan Revolt," 75; R.B. Lyons to Stanley, 17 April, 16 January, 4, 21

February, 3, 19, 20 March, 2, 21 April, 5 May 1868, box 108; Stanley to R.B. Lyons, 21 March, 7, 14, 24 April 1868, box 100.

14   R.B. Lyons to Stanley, 27 March, 2 April, 2, 13, 14, 22 May, 12 June 1868, box 108; Jordan, *Transforming Paris*, 306; R.B. Lyons to Stanley, 18 August 1868, box 100.

15   R.B. Lyons to Stanley, 18 August 1868, box 100; Stanley to Disraeli, 20 August 1868, 920 DER (15) 13/2/4.

16   R.B. Lyons to Bloomfield, 17 June 1868; R.B. Lyons to Stanley, 23 June 1868, box 108; Stanley to R.B. Lyons, 14 July 1868; Biddulph to R.B. Lyons, 4 June 1868, box 127; R.B. Lyons to Lord John Manners, 13 July 1868; R.B. Lyons to Hammond, 1 October 1868, box 108; Manners to R.B. Lyons, 14 July 1868, box 127; R.B. Lyons to Biddulph, 23 July 1868, box 108; Biddulph to R.B. Lyons, 1, 2 August 1868, box 127; Stanley to Disraeli, 8 August 1868, 920 DER (15) 13/2/4; R.B. Lyons to Stanley, 27 August, 8, 11 September 1868, box 108; Malmesbury to Derby, 16 September 1868, 920 DER (14) 144/4.

17   R.B. Lyons to Stanley, 11 August 1868, box 108; Malet to mother, 8 August, 12 September 1868, Malet Papers; R.B. Lyons to Minna, 8 September 1868, box 301.

18   R.B. Lyons to Minna, 11 August 1868, box 301; Malet to mother, 8 August 1868, Malet Papers; Stanley to Disraeli, 8, 20 August 1868, 920 DER (15) 13/2/4; Vincent, *Derby Diaries*, 37; R.B. Lyons to Stanley, 11 August 1868, box 108; R.B. Lyons to Stanley, 21 August 1868, box 100.

19   R.B. Lyons to Stanley, 13 August 1868, box 108; Stanley to Disraeli, 12 September 1868, 920 DER (15) 13/2/4, Derby Papers; R.B. Lyons to Stanley, 6 September, 8 October 1868, box 100.

20   Jenkins, *Fenian Problem*, 240; Stanley to Derby, 28 November 1868, 920 DER (14) 105/9, Derby Papers; Stanley to R.B. Lyons, 25 November 1868, box 179; Erskine to R.B. Lyons, 7 January 1869, box 178; Stanley to Derby, 30 November 1868, 920 DER (14)105/9; Green to R.B. Lyons, 21 September 1868, 29 January 1869, box 184; R.B. Lyons to Stanley, 6, 25 November 1868, box 108; R.B. Lyons to Stanley 28 November 1867, box 100; Stanley to R.B. Lyons, 11 December 1868, box 179; Otte, *Foreign Office Mind*, 31.

21   R.B. Lyons to Stanley, 13, 18, 20 October 1868, box 108; Stanley to R.B. Lyons, 11 December 1868, box 179; R.B. Lyons to Clarendon, 2 February 1869, box 100.

22   R.B. Lyons to Stanley, 5, 6, 7, 13, 18 October, 5 November 1868, box 108; Stanley to Hardy, 1 October 1868, 920 DER (15) 13/2/2, Derby Papers; Stanley to Derby, 30 November 1868, 920 DER (14) 105/9.

23   Vincent, *Derby Diaries*, 66; Derby Diary, 6, 11 December 1868, 920 DER (15), Derby Papers; Clarendon to Odo Russell, 11 January 1869, FO 918/1, Odo

Russell Papers; Hawkins and Powell, *Journal of Wodehouse*, 251; Bernard Gerard Sasso, "The Embassy of Lord Lyons in Paris, 1867–1887" (D.Phil. thesis, University of Wales, 1991), 1; Maureen M. Robson, "Lord Clarendon and the Cretan Question, 1868–9," *Historical Journal* 3 (1960): 55; R.B. Lyons to Clarendon, 15 December 1868, box 108; Clarendon to R.B. Lyons, 15 April 1869, box 176; Alston to R.B. Lyons, 3 February 1870, box 174; Malet to mother, 12 February 1870, Malet Papers.

24 R.B. Lyons to Clarendon, 17, 24, 18, 19 December 1868, box 108; Clarendon to R.B. Lyons, 28 December 1868, 2 January 1869, box 176; Paul Kennedy, *The Realities behind Diplomacy: Background Influences on British External Policy, 1865–1980* (London, 1981), 75–6; Hawkins and Powell, *Journal of Wodehouse*, 234.

25 R.B. Lyons to Clarendon, 15, 20 December 1868, box 108; Loftus to Otway, 23 January 1869, box 129; Clarendon to R.B. Lyons, 19 December 1868, box 176; R.B. Lyons to Clarendon, 20, 21 December 1868, box 101; Bourne, "Great Britain and the Cretan Revolt, 1866–1869," 90.

26 R.B. Lyons to Clarendon, 2 January 1869, box 108; Newton, *Lyons*, 1:206; Lord Augustus Loftus, *Diplomatic Reminiscences, 1862–1879*, 2nd ed. (London, 1894), 2:209; R.B. Lyons to Clarendon, 24, 26, 29, 30 December 1868, box 108; Clarendon to R.B. Lyons, secret and confidential, 5 January 1869, FO 27/1739.

27 R.B. Lyons to Clarendon, 10 January 1869, box 101 Clarendon to R.B. Lyons, 12, 14, 15, 16, 19, 23 January 1869, box 176.

28 For detailed discussions of the Cretan rebellion and Paris Conference see Robson, "Lord Clarendon and the Cretan Question," 38–55, and Bourne, "Great Britain and the Cretan Revolt, 1866–1869," 74–94; Elliot to R.B. Lyons, 26 January 1869, box 129; Clarendon to R.B. Lyons, 20 January 1869, box 176; 5 February 1869, FO 27/1739; 23 January 1869, box 176; R.B. Lyons to Clarendon, 7 January 1869, box 108; Clarendon to R.B. Lyons, 15 January 1869, FO 27/1739; R.B. Lyons to Hammond, 29 January, 2, 25, 28 February 1868, box 108; Clarendon to R.B. Lyons, 19 April 1869, box 176.

29 R.B. Lyons to Bloomfield, 28 April 1869, box 108; Stanley to Disraeli, 1 October 1868, 920 DER (15) 13/2/4, Derby Papers; R.B. Lyons to Clarendon, 26 January 1869, box 108.

30 Clarendon to R.B. Lyons, 15 January 1869, box 176; R.B. Lyons to Clarendon, 16 February 1869, box 100; Clarendon to R.B. Lyons, 21 February, 2 March, 17 May, 10, 13, 20 March, 19 April, 18 February 1869, box 176; Hawkins and Powell, *Journal of John Wodehouse*, 233.

31 Clarendon to R.B. Lyons, 18 March, 17 February 1869, box 176; Loftus to Clarendon, 27 February 1869, box 130; Clarendon to R.B. Lyons, 9 March, 20, 19, 29 April 1869, box 176.

32 R.B. Lyons to Clarendon, 17 February 1869, box 108; R.B. Lyons to Clarendon, 23 February 1869, box 101; R.B. Lyons to Clarendon, 16 February, 2, 5, 4, 8, 18 March 1869, box 108.

33 Sasso, "Embassy of Lord Lyons," 65; Clarendon to R.B. Lyons, 6,10 March 1869, box 176; 19 May 1869, box 177; Whitehurst to R.B. Lyons, 20 March 1869, box 130; R.B. Lyons to Clarendon, 23 March, 6 April 1869, box 101; Clarendon to R.B. Lyons, 10 April 1869, box 176.

34 R.B. Lyons to Clarendon, 19 March 1869, box 108; Daniel Thomas, "English Investors and the Franco-Belgium Railway Crisis of 1869," *Historian* 26 (1964): 234; R.B. Lyons to Bloomfield, 28 April 1869, box 108; R.B. Lyons to Clarendon, 27, 30 April, 25, 29 June 1869, box 101; Clarendon to R.B. Lyons, 9 July 1869, FO 27/1741.

35 Clarendon to R.B. Lyons, 27, 1 April 1869, box 176; Bloomfield to R.B. Lyons, 6 July 1869, box 174; Clarendon to R.B. Lyons, 3 May 1869, box 177; Sasso, "Embassy of Lord Lyons," 64.

36 Otway to R.B. Lyons, 30 July 1869, box 130; Sasso, "Embassy of Lord Lyons," 10; Malet to mother, 7 September 1869, Malet Papers; R.B. Lyons to Clarendon, 13 September 1869, box 101.

37 R.B. Lyons to Clarendon, 2, 11 March, 6 April 1869, box 101; 30 April 1869, box 108.

38 R.B. Lyons to Clarendon, 20 April, 11, 25 May, 3, 8 June 1869, box 108; 14 June 1869, box 101; Milza, *Napoléon III*, 557; Gildea, *Children of the Revolution*, 100–1; King, *Judgment of Paris*, 255.

39 R.B. Lyons to Clarendon, 14 June 1869, box 101; Clarendon to R.B. Lyons, 26 May 1869, box 177.

40 Clarendon to R.B. Lyons, 9 June 1869, box 177; R.B. Lyons to Clarendon, 27 May, 3, 8, 20 June, 7, 9 July 1869, box 108; Milza, *Napoléon III*, 557, 560.

41 R.B. Lyons to Clarendon, 13 July 1869, box 108; 14 July 1869, box 101; Clarendon to R.B. Lyons, 13 July 1869, box 177.

CHAPTER THIRTEEN

1 Clarendon to R.B. Lyons, 5 June 1869, box 177; Newton, *Lyons*, 2:10–11; Clarendon to Granville, 11 June 1869, PRO 30/29/55, Granville Papers.

2 Granville to Clarendon, 11 June 1869, PRO 30/29/55, Granville Papers;

Clarendon to R.B. Lyons, 12 June 1869, box 177; Hawkins and Powell, *Journal of John Wodehouse*, 236.

3   Milza, *Napoléon III*, 561–2; Newton, *Lyons*, 1:241; R.B. Lyons to Clarendon, 13, 20, 21, 23, 27, 30 July, 4 August 1869, box 104.

4   Peter H. Wilson, *Europe's Tragedy: A History of the Thirty Years War* (London, 2009), 123; R.B. Lyons to Clarendon, 27 August 1869, box 101.

5   Malet to mother, 7 September 1869, Malet Papers; King, *Judgment of Paris*, 273; R.B. Lyons to Clarendon, 31 August 1869, box 108; R.B. Lyons to Clarendon, 27 August 1869, box 101.

6   Lister to R.B. Lyons, 22 February 1869, box 129; R.B. Lyons to Clarendon, 23, 26 November 1869, 2 January 1870, box 101.

7   R.B. Lyons to Clarendon, 6, 11, 25, 30 January, 23 April 1870, box 102; Chevalier to R.B. Lyons, 16 February 1870, box 131.

8   R.B. Lyons to Clarendon, 9 January, 8 April 1869, box 101; Clarendon to R.B. Lyons, 19, 26 July 1869, box 177; Elliot to R.B. Lyons, 31 August, 14 September 1869, 18 May 1870, box 131; R.B. Lyons to Clarendon, 9 July, 9 September 1869, 6 January, 3 February, 13, 31 May, 1 July 1870, box 102; Elliot to R.B. Lyons, 10 August 1869; Otway to R.B. Lyons, 19 August 1869, box 131.

9   Clarendon to R.B. Lyons, 31 August 1869, box 177; R.B. Lyons to Clarendon, 19, 20 August, 3 September 1869, box 108; 31 May 1870, box 109.

10   R.B. Lyons to Clarendon, 20 August, 3 September, 30 November 1869, box 108; Elliot to R.B. Lyons, 14 September 1869; Otway to R.B. Lyons, 1 December 1869, box 131; Clarendon to R.B. Lyons, 7, 31 August, 4, 9 December 1869, 5 January 1870, box 177; R.B. Lyons to Clarendon, 26 May 1870, box 109; Clarendon to R.B. Lyons, 28, 30 May, 1 June 1870, box 177; Hawkins and Powell, *Journal of John Wodehouse*, 249–50.

11   R.B. Lyons to Clarendon, 3, 21 December 1869, box 109; 2 January 1870, box 101; Clarendon to R.B. Lyons, 15 December 1869, box 177; Sudhir Hazareesingh, *From Subject to Citizen: The Second Empire and the Emergence of Modern French Democracy* (Princeton, NJ, 1998), 175; Milza, *Napoléon III*, 561, 564–6; Christiansen, *Paris Babylon*, 127–8; R.B. Lyons to Clarendon, 4 January 1870, box 109; Clarendon to R.B. Lyons, 8 January 1870, box 177.

12   R.B. Lyons to Odo Russell, 11 January 1870, FO 918/52, Odo Russell Papers; Milza, *Napoléon III*, 567–9; Gildea, *Children of the Revolution*, 192; King, *Judgment of Paris*, 258–9; Lady Layard's Journal, 11 January 1870; Malet to mother, 14 January 1870, Malet Papers; R.B. Lyons to Paget, 8 February 1870, BL Add. Ms. 51231, Paget Papers; Newton, *Lyons*, 1:245.

13   Clarendon to R.B. Lyons, 3 August, 18, 29 December 1869, 19 January, 19 February 1870, box 177; R.B. Lyons to Clarendon, 14 January 1870, box 101.

14 R.B. Lyons to Clarendon, 18 January, 25, 27 February 1870, box 101; 22, 24 March 1870, box 109; 29 March, 1, 5 April 1870, box 102.

15 R.B. Lyons to Clarendon, 29 March 1870, box 102.

16 R.B. Lyons to Clarendon, 5 April 1870, box 102; Clarendon to R.B. Lyons, 18 May, 13 April 1870, box 177; Newton, *Lyons*, 1:283.

17 King, *Judgment of Paris*, 269; R.B. Lyons to Clarendon, 5, 22, 28 April, 3 May 1870, box 109; 3 May 1870, box 102; Clarendon to R.B. Lyons, 24 January 1870, FO 27/1789; R.B. Lyons to Clarendon, 29 March, 8, 19 April 1870, box 102; Odo Russell to R.B. Lyons, 9 June 1870, box 197.

18 R.B. Lyons to Clarendon, 10 May 1870, box 102; Newton, *Lyons*, 1:286, 289; Clarendon to R.B. Lyons, 11 May 1870, box 177; R.B. Lyons to Clarendon, 13, 17, 21, 24, 27 May 1870, box 109; Desmond Seward, *Eugénie: The Empress and Her Empire* (Stroud, 2005), 195; R.B. Lyons to Clarendon, 25 February 1870, box 109; Alistair Horne, *The Fall of Paris: The Siege and the Commune, 1870–71* (London, 2002), 36; David Wetzel, *A Duel of Giants: Bismarck, Napoleon III, and the Origins of the Franco-Prussian War* (Madison, WI, 2001), 31–5; Clarendon to R.B. Lyons, 11 May 1870, box 177; E. Malcolm Carroll, *French Public Opinion and Foreign Affairs, 1870–1914* (Hamden, CT, 1964), 24.

19 Crampton to R.B. Lyons, 24 March [1869], box 130; Lady Layard's Journal, 14 October 1869 [Naples]; Vincent, *Derby Diaries*, 38; Vincent, *Derby Diaries*, 196–7, 213; Malet to mother, 25 October 1869, Malet Papers.

20 Lady Layard's Journal, 22 November 1869; Layard to R.B. Lyons, 28, 31 December 1869, 7, 28 January, 11 February 1870, box 190; R.B. Lyons to Layard, 21 December 1869, box 108; Lady Layard's Journal, 7 March 1870; Wetzel, *Duel of Giants*, 40–1; Layard to R.B. Lyons, 13 March 1870, box 190; Clarendon to R.B. Lyons, 11, 20 May 1870, box 177; Lady Layard's Journal, 12, 14 March, 11 June, 4 July 1870.

21 Clarendon to R.B. Lyons, 10 January 1870, box 177; R.B. Lyons to Clarendon, 25 January 1870, box 101; 30 January 1870, box 108; Otte, *Foreign Office Mind*, 56–7.

22 Clarendon to R.B. Lyons, 29 January, 2, 3 February 1870, box 177; R.B. Lyons to Clarendon, 1 February 1870, box 101; R.B. Lyons to Clarendon, 30 January, 1 February, 8 March 1870, box 109; Clarendon to R.B. Lyons, 12 March 1870, box 177.

23 Clarendon to R.B. Lyons, 26, 29 January, 9 February 1870; Loftus to Clarendon, 5 February 1870, box 177; R.B. Lyons to Clarendon, 15 February 1870, box 109; Christopher Clark, *The Iron Kingdom: The Rise and Downfall of Prussia, 1600–1947*, pb ed. (London, 2007), 513–14; Daru to R.B. Lyons, n.d.

[February] 1870, box 131; R.B. Lyons to Clarendon, 11 February 1870, box 109; Clarendon to R.B. Lyons, 15 February, 12, 15 March 1870; Clarendon to Loftus, 9 March 1870; Loftus to Clarendon, 12 March 1870; Clarendon to R.B. Lyons, 23 March, 9, 20 April 1870, box 177.

24 Clarendon to R.B. Lyons, 7 September 1869, box 177; Malet to mother, 5 September 1869, Malet Papers; Clarendon to R.B. Lyons, 26 March 1870, box 177; Hawkins and Powell, *Journal of John Wodehouse*, 250; Vincent, *Derby Diaries*, 63; H.C G. Matthew, *The Gladstone Diaries*, 14 vols (Oxford, 1982), 7:315–16; R.B. Lyons to Hammond, 27 June 1870, box 109.

25 Vincent, *Derby Diaries*, 66; Agatha Ramm, ed., *The Political Correspondence of Mr. Gladstone and Lord Granville, 1876–1886*, 2 vols (Oxford, 1962), 1:xiv; Hawkins and Powell, *Journal of John Wodehouse*, 268; Kenneth Bourne, ed., *The Foreign Policy of Victorian England, 1830–1902* (Oxford, 1970), 120; Granville to R.B. Lyons, 11 July, 1 August 1870, box 182; Dowager Duchess of Argyll, ed., *George Douglas Eighth Duke of Argyll (1823–1900) Autobiography and Memoirs*, 2 vols (London, 1906), 1:347; Layard to R.B. Lyons, 29 June 1870, box 190; Karina Urbach, *Bismarck's Favorite Englishman: Lord Odo Russell's Mission to Berlin* (New York, 2001), 43; G.R. Seale, *Entrepreneurial Politics in Mid-Victorian Britain* (Oxford, 1993), 172.

26 Anderson to R.B. Lyons, 9 July 1870, box 131; Hammond to R.B. Lyons, 6 July 1870, box 188; Hertslet, *Recollections*, 98, 124–5; Bullen, ed., *Foreign Office*, 47; Urbach, *Bismarck's Favorite Englishman*, 128.

27 Matthew, *Gladstone Diaries*, 7:315; Lady Layard's Journal, 5, 8 July; Jonathan Steinberg, *Bismarck: A Life* (Oxford, 2011), 281; Gordon Craig, *Germany 1866–1945* (Oxford, 1978), 24–5; Milza, *Napoléon III*, 577–8.

28 Milza, *Napoléon III*, 579; Malet to mother, 9 July 1870, Malet Papers; Granville to R.B. Lyons, 6 July 1870, box 182; Hammond to R.B. Lyons, 6 July 1870, box 188; Granville to R.B. Lyons, 7 July 1870, FO 27/1791.

29 R.B. Lyons to Granville, 7, 8, 10, 12 July 1870; R.B. Lyons to Layard, 10 July 1870, box 109; Malet to mother, 13 July 1870, Malet Papers; Granville to R.B. Lyons, 13 July 1870, box 182.

30 Milza, *Napoléon III*, 580–1; Hammond to R.B. Lyons, 12, 13 July 1870, box 188.

31 R.B. Lyons to Granville, 13 July 1870, box 109; Granville to R.B. Lyons, 13 July 1870, FO 27/1791; Granville to Lyons, 13 July 1870, box 182; Wetzel, *Duel of Giants*, 159–60; Pakula, *An Uncommon Woman*, 268; R.B. Lyons to Granville, 14 July 1870, box 109; Michael Knox Beran, *Forge of Empires, 1861–1871: Three Revolutionary Statesmen and the World They Made* (New York, 2007), 309; Steinberg, *Bismarck: A Life*, 285–7; Brown, *For the Soul of France*, 22; Newton, *Lyons*, 1:299.

32 Hammond to R.B. Lyons, 15, 16 July 1870, box 188; Granville to R.B. Lyons, 15 July 1870, box 182; Urbach, *Bismarck's Favorite Englishman*, 50; Pakula, *An Uncommon Woman*, 271; R.B. Lyons to Granville, 15, 16, 17 July 1870, box 109.

33 Granville to R.B. Lyons, 12, 13 July 1870, box 182; Bertrand and Patricia Russell, eds, *The Amberley Papers: The Letters and Diaries of Lord and Lady Amberley*, 2 vols (London, 1937), 2:363; R.B. Lyons to Granville, 17 July 1870, box 109; Matthew, *Gladstone Diaries*, 7:333; Malet to mother, 13 July 1870, Malet Papers; R.B. Lyons to Granville, 15 July 1870, box 109; Russells, *Amberley Papers*, 2:369.

34 Granville to R.B. Lyons, 1, 4, 6, 9 August 1870, box 182; R.B. Lyons to Granville, 19, 31 July, 3 August 1870, box 109; 1, 3, 5, 6, August 1870, box 102; Howard, *Britain and the Casus Belli*, 10.

35 R.B. Lyons to Granville, 16, 17, 19, 26, 31 July, 3, 5 August 1870, box 109; Malet to mother, 17 July 1870, Malet Papers.

36 Beran, *Forge of Empires*, 310, 321; Christiansen, *Paris Babylon*, 142; David Baguly, *Napoleon III and His Regime: An Extravaganza* (Baton Rouge, LA, 2000), 151; Milza, *Napoléon III*, 587; Stig Forster and Jorg Nagler, *On the Road to Total War: The American Civil War and the German Wars of Unification, 1861–1871* (Washington, DC, 1997), 283–9; Karine Varley, *Under the Shadow of Defeat: The War of 1870–71 in French Memory* (New York, 2008), 39; R.B. Lyons to Granville, 8 August 1870, box 109; Malet to mother, 7 August 1870, Malet Papers.

37 R.B. Lyons to Granville, 8, 11, 12 August 1870, box 102; 9, 10, 11, 12 August 1870, box 109; Malet to mother, 12 August 1870, Malet Papers; Seward, *Eugénie*, 218–19.

38 Seward, *Eugénie*, 220; R.B. Lyons to Granville, 10, 9 August 1870, box 109; 16 August 1870, box 102.

39 R.B. Lyons to Granville, 16, 17, 23 August 1870, box 109; 23 August 1870, box 102; Vincent, *Derby Diaries*, 67.

40 R.B. Lyons to Granville, 23 August; R.B. Lyons to Hammond, 23 August 1870, box 109; Granville to R.B. Lyons, 27 August, 2 September 1870, box 182; R.B. Lyons to Granville, 28 August, 1 September 1870, box 109; R.B. Lyons to Paget, 2 September 1870, BL Add. Ms. 51231, Paget Papers.

41 Paget to R.B. Lyons, 9 September 1870, box 132; Pakula, *An Uncommon Woman*, 277; Malet to mother, 4 September 1870, Malet Papers; Henry Wodehouse, *Letters from the Hon. Henry Wodehouse 1870–1871* (London, 1874), 4, 5, 9; R.B. Lyons to Granville, 7 September 1870, box 102; Lord

Randolph Sutherland Gower, *Records and Reminiscences: Selected from "My Reminiscences" and "Old Diaries"* (London, 1903), 182, 183.

1 R.B. Lyons to Granville, 26 August; R.B. Lyons to Hammond, 26 August, box 109; R.B. Lyons to Granville, 28 August 1870, box 102; Granville to R.B. Lyons, 28 August 1870, FO 27/1793; R.B. Lyons to Hammond, 26, 29 August, 1 September 1870, box 109.

2 Granville to R.B. Lyons, 5 September 1870, box 182; Gerald Carson, "The Dentist and the Empress," *American Heritage* 31 (1980): 65–80; Seward, *Eugénie*, 237–9; Malet to mother, 6 September 1870, Malet Papers; Seward, *Eugénie*, 232; R.B. Lyons to Granville, 5, 6 September 1870, box 109; Cobden to Chevalier, 2 June 1863, Cobden 44, WSRO; Jérôme Grévy, *La République des opportunistes, 1870–1885* (Paris, 1998), 11–12.

3 R.B. Lyons to Granville, 5, 6 September, box 109; R.B. Lyons to Granville, "very confidential," 8 September 1870, box 102; Hawkins and Powell, *Journal of John Wodehouse*, 252; Odo Russell to R.B. Lyons, 29 August 1870, box 197; Newton, *Lyons*, 1:323.

4 Odo Russell to R.B. Lyons, 29 August 1870, box 197; Hammond to R.B. Lyons, 6 September 1870, box 188; Granville to R.B. Lyons, 6, 7, 8 September 1870, box 182; Hawkins and Powell, *Journal of John Wodehouse*, 253; R.B. Lyons to Granville, 8 September 1870, box 102; Richard Congreve, *Paris* (10 September 1870); Malet to mother, 8 September; Sheffield to Lady Malet, 15 September 1870, Malet Papers; R.B. Lyons to Granville, 6, 7, 8, 19, 12 September, box 109; 7, 8, 12 September 1870, box 102.

5 R.B. Lyons to Granville, 8, 13 September 1870, box 102; 13 September 1870, box 109; Malet to R.B. Lyons, 16 September; Malet to Henry Malet, 20 September; Malet to mother, 19 September (and notes); Malet to R.B. Lyons, 16, 17, 19 September 1870, Malet Papers; Marvin L. Brown, Jr, *The Comte de Chambord: The Third Republic's Uncompromising King* (Durham, NC, 1967), 139–40; R.B. Lyons to Granville, 19 September 1870, box 109; 16, 25 September 1870, box 102.

6 Hammond to R.B. Lyons, 10 September 1870, box 188; Peter Thorold, *The British in France: Visitors and Residents since the Revolution* (New York, 2008), 144; Henry Wodehouse, *Letters from the Hon. Henry Wodehouse, 1870–1871* (London, 1874), 10, 12; R.B. Lyons to Granville, 19, 21 September 1870, box 102; R.B. Lyons to Granville, 19 September 1870, box 109; Wodehouse, *Letters*, 15, 26–27, 29, 60; Alistair Horne, *The Fall of Paris: The Siege*

and the Commune, 1870–71 (London, 1965), 96; Wodehouse to R.B. Lyons, 4 October 1870, box 133.

7 Graham Robb, *The Discovery of France* (New York, 2007), 117, 138; R.B. Lyons to Granville, 19 September 1870, box 109; Malet to mother, 6, 13, 24, 27, 10 October, 1 December 1870, Malet Papers; R.B. Lyons to Hammond, 25, 27 September, box 109; Granville to R.B. Lyons, 13, 14, 16 September, 4 October 1870, box 182; 1, 4, 11 October 1870, FO 27/1794; Hammond to R.B. Lyons, 1 October 1870, box 188.

8 R.B. Lyons to Granville, 25, 27 September, 6, 9, 16 October 1870, box 102; Geoffrey Wawro, *The Franco-Prussian War: The German Conquest of France in 1870–1871* (Cambridge, 2003), 244–5; R.B. Lyons to Granville, 17 October 1870, box 109.

9 R.B. Lyons to Granville, 13 October 1870, box 102; 7 October, box 109; Hammond to R.B. Lyons, 5, 15 October 1870, box 188; Beran, *Forge of Empires*, 353–4; R.B. Lyons to Granville, 20 October 1870, box 109.

10 Granville to R.B. Lyons, 20 October 1870, FO 27/1794; Malet to mother, 24, 27 October 1870, Malet Papers; R.B. Lyons to Granville, 22 October 1870, box 102; 24 October, 5 November 1870, box 109; Hammond to R.B. Lyons, 26 October 1870, box 188.

11 Wodehouse, *Letters*, 40; King, *Judgment of Paris*, 286; Wodehouse to R.B. Lyons, 13 October, 1, 8, 16 November 1870, box 133; Robert Baldick, *The Siege of Paris* (London, 1964), 83, 98; R.B. Lyons to Granville, 10 November 1870, box 102; 7, 11, 14 November 1870, box 109; R.B. Lyons to Layard, 9 November 1870, box 190.

12 R.B. Lyons to Granville, 14, 17, 21 November, 2 December 1870, box 109; 14, 21, 28 November 1870, box 102; Grévy, *République des opportunistes*, 16; Malet to mother, 6, 10 December 1870, Malet Papers; R.B. Lyons to Granville, 10 December 1870, box 102; R.B. Lyons to Hammond, 12 December 1870, box 109; Malet to mother, 1 January 1871, Malet Papers; Hammond to R.B. Lyons, 10, 12, 16, 20 December 1870, 21 January 1871, box 188.

13 R.B. Lyons to Granville, 17 November, 22 December 1870, box 109; 14 November, box 102; Otte, *Foreign Office Mind*, 66; Urbach, *Bismarck's Favorite Englishman*, 54–7; Steinberg, *Bismarck*, 299; Malet to mother, 29 December 1870, Malet Papers; R.B. Lyons to Granville, 26 December 1870, box 102; Granville to R.B. Lyons, 28 November 1870, box 182; R.B. Lyons to Granville, 29 November 1870, box 109; Granville to R.B. Lyons, 30 November 1870, box 182.

14 R.B. Lyons to Granville, 15, 21 December 1870, box 102; Granville to R.B. Lyons, 20 December 1870, 7 January 1871, box 182; Otte, *Foreign Office Mind*,

69; Forster and Nagler, *On the Road to Total War*, 545, 549; Hammond to R.B. Lyons, 28 December 1870, 21, 11 January 1871, box 188; Baldick, *Siege of Paris*, 128–9; R.B. Lyons to Granville, 27 December 1870, box 102.

15 R.B. Lyons to Granville, 12, 24, 26 January 1871, 22 December 1870, 7 January 1871, box 109; King, *Judgment of Paris*, 289; Bickerton Lyons, pocket book, 1871, box 221; Christiansen, *Paris Babylon*, 248, 256; Hammond to R.B. Lyons, 26 January 1871, box 188; R.B. Lyons to Granville, 26 January 1871, box 102; Steinberg, *Bismarck*, 305–7.

16 *Lancaster Gazette*, 7 December 1887; Hammond to R.B. Lyons, 4, 10 February 1871, box 188; Robert and Isabelle Tombs, *That Sweet Enemy: The French and the British from the Sun King to the Present* (London, 2006), 382; Horne, *Fall of Paris*, 167; Christiansen, *Paris Babylon*, 266; R.B. Lyons to Granville, 30, 31 January 1871, box 102; 1 February 1871, box 109; Malet to mother, 7 February 1871, Malet Papers; R.B. Lyons to Granville, 10 February 1871, box 109; Malet to mother, 10 February 1871; Horne, *Fall of Paris*, 254–5; Steven D. Kale, *Legitimism and the Reconstruction of French Society 1852–1883* (Baton Rouge, LA, 1992), 263–4, 10.

17 R.B. Lyons to Granville, 10 February 1871, box 109; Vincent, *Derby Diaries*, 67, 69; Pakula, *Uncommon Woman*, 288–9; R.B. Lyons to Granville, 16 February 1871, box 109; also "confidential," 10 February 1871, box 103; Bickerton Lyons, pocket book, 1871, box 221; Malet to mother, 16 February 1871, Malet Papers; R.B. Lyons to Granville, 16 February 1871, box 109; Granville to R.B. Lyons, 16 February 1871, box 182; Charles de Rémusat, *Mémoires de ma vie*, 5 vols (Paris, 1967), 5:324; Hawkins and Powell, *Journal of John Wodehouse*, 256; R.B. Lyons to Granville, 16 February 1871, box 103.

18 R.B. Lyons to Granville, 16 February 1871, box 109; Allen Mitchell, *The German Influence in France after 1870: The Formation of the French Republic* (Chapel Hill, NC, 1979), 8; R.B. Lyons to Granville, 2, 6 March 1871, box 103; see also 2, 6 March, box 109; Malet to mother, 2 March 1871, Malet Papers; Bickerton Lyons, pocket book, 1871, box 221; Wodehouse to R.B. Lyons, 15 February 1871; Tanfield to R.B. Lyons, 16 February, 3 March 1871; Claremont to R.B. Lyons, 3, 5 March 1871; Sackville-West to R.B. Lyons, 19, 10 March 1871, box 133; Malet to mother, 11 March 1871, Malet Papers.

19 *Parl. Deb.*, 3rd ser., vol. 204 (1871), 398, 450, 573, 577, 579–80, 1296; *Morning Post*, 6 March 1871; Granville to R.B. Lyons, 1 March 1871, box 182; Hawkins and Powell, *Journal of John Wodehouse*, 131, 180; Jenkins, *Fenian Problem*, 35; Sheffield to R.B. Lyons, 21 June 1871, box 199; Malet to mother, 19, 21 March 1871, Malet Papers; R.B. Lyons to Granville, 15 March 1871, box 109; Brown, *For the Soul of France*, 25; King, *Judgment of Paris*, 307; Stewart Edwards,

The Paris Commune, 1871 (Newton Abbot, 1971), 117–19, 133, 135, 145; Robert Tombs, *The War against Paris 1871* (Cambridge, 1981), 40–3; R.B. Lyons to Granville, 21 March 1871, box 103; M.A. Titmarch (William Makepeace Thackeray), *The Paris Sketch Book* (New York, 1840), 396–7; Edwards, *Paris Commune*, 167; R.B. Lyons to Granville, 18, 23, 24 March 1871, box 109.

20 Malet to mother, 18, 29 March 1871; Sheffield to Malet, 27 March, 16 April 1871, Malet Papers; Williams, "The Career of Sir Edward Malet," 30–3, 43; Malet to R.B. Lyons, 26 March 1871, box 191; Malet to father, 26 March; Malet to mother, 31 March 1871, Malet Papers; Malet to Granville, 30 March 1871, FO 27/1878; R.B. Lyons to Malet, 12 April 1871, Malet Papers; Granville to Queen, 12 April; Granville to Ponsonby, 14 April; Queen to Granville, 14 April; Ponsonby to Granville, 14, 15 April 1871, PRO 30/29/33, Granville Papers; Brown, *For the Soul of France*, 27–8; R.B. Lyons to Malet, 15 April 1871, Malet Papers; Dasent, *Delane*, 2:283.

21 R.B. Lyons to Granville, 14 April 1871, box 109; 14, 19, 21 April, box 103; Malet to R.B. Lyons, 21 April 1871, box 103; Malet to mother, 18 April 1871, Malet Papers; Malet to R.B. Lyons, 28 April, 1, 3, 10 May 1871, box 191; R.B. Lyons to Granville, 5, 9 May 1871, box 103.

22 R.B. Lyons to Granville, 16 May 1871, box 103; 16, 24, 26 May 1871, box 109; Brown, *For the Soul of France*, 29–31; Caroline Moorehead, *Dunant's Dream: War, Switzerland and the History of the Red Cross* (London, 1999), 81; R.B. Lyons to Granville, 30 May, 2 June 1871, box 109; Hammond to R.B. Lyons, 7 June 1871, box 188; Tombs and Tombs, *That Sweet Enemy*, 385–6; Hawkins and Powell, *Journal of John Wodehouse*, 260.

23 R.B. Lyons to Paget, 24 June 1871, BL Add. Ms. 51231, Paget Papers; for wine purchases see May 1871, box 134; Alan Albright, "Thomas W. Evans. A Philadelphian 'Yankee' at the Court of Napoleon III," Internet, 1, 2, 5; Bickerton Lyons, pocket book, 1871, 12 June, 10, 12 July, box 221; Lady Layard's Journal, 20, 21, 22 June 1871.

24 Sheffield to R.B. Lyons, 21 June 1871, box 199; Tombs and Tombs, *That Sweet Enemy*, 386–7; R.B. Lyons to Granville, 15, 30 June, 16, 14 July, 15 August 1871, box 109; 18 July 1871, box 103; Mitchell, *German Influence on France*, 23, 35; Grévy, *République des opportunistes*, 24; R.B. Lyons to Granville, 4 September 1871, box 103; Sanford Elwitt, *The Making of the Third Republic: Class and Politics in France, 1868–1884* (Baton Rouge, LA, 1975), 13; Granville to R.B. Lyons, 17 June 1871, box 182; R.B. Lyons to Granville, 23 June, 4, 7, 21, 25 July, 15 August 1871, box 109.

25 Kale, *Legitimism and Reconstruction*, 34, 183, 263–4, 268, 275; Harris, *Dreyfus*, 176; Brown, *Chambord*, 91–3, 115.

26   R.B. Lyons to Granville, 13 June, 4 July 1871, box 109; Gildea, *Children of the Revolution*, 247; Brown, *For the Soul of France*, 42; Elwitt, *Third Republic*, 60, 82; Seward, *Eugénie*, 258; R.B. Lyons to Granville, 11 July 1871, box 109; Grévy, *République des opportunistes*, 24; Theodore Zeldin, *France 1848–1945*, vol. 1: *Ambition, Love and Politics* (Oxford, 1973), 394–7; Jean-Marie Mayeur and Madeleine Rebérioux, *The Third Republic from Its Origins to the Great War, 1871–1914*, trans. J.R. Foster (Cambridge, 1984), 13; R.B. Lyons to Granville, 5 September 1871, box 109; also 29 August, 1 September 1871, box 103.

27   R.B. Lyons to Granville, 8 August, 4 July 1871, box 109; Zeldin, *France 1848–1945*, 1:101; Rémusat, *Mémoires*, 5: 385; Duke de Broglie, *An Ambassador of the Vanquished* (New York, 1896), 207; Newton, *Lyons*, 2:22.

28   Bickerton Lyons, pocket book, 1871, 26 August, 11, 14, 18 September, 7 October 1871, box 221; R.B. Lyons to Hammond, 10, 11, 18 September 1871, box 109; Whitehurst to Sheffield, 20 August 1871; Anderson to R.B. Lyons, 17 July, 14 October 1871, box 134; Bickerton Lyons pocket book, 1871, 16, 20, 23, 25, 27 October, 7 November, box 221; Gladstone to R.B. Lyons, 2 November 1871, box 134; R.B. Lyons to Gladstone, 1, 5 November 1871; R.B. Lyons to Granville, 17 October 1871, box 109.

29   Bickerton Lyons, pocket book, 1871, 17, 17, 29 November, 4, 5, 6, 7, 8, 11 December, box 221; Malet to R.B. Lyons, 28 December 1871, box 191; R.B. Lyons to Granville, 8 December 1871, box 109; Gregor Dallas, *At the Heart of the Tiger: Clemenceau and His World, 1841–1929* (New York, 1993), 198; R.B. Lyons to Granville, 12, 19, 21, 26 December 1871, box 109; also 29 December 1871, box 103; Whitehurst to Sheffield, 20 August 1871, box 134.

30   Brown, *For the Soul of France*, 93; Conolly to R.B. Lyons, 2 January 1872, box 134; Mayeur and Rebérioux, *Third Republic from Its Origins*, 15; Conolly to R.B. Lyons, 9 August 1872; Claremont to R.B. Lyons, 8 September 1872, box 136; Odo Russell to R.B. Lyons, 27 April 1872, box 197; Otte, *Foreign Office Mind*, 71; R.B. Lyons to Odo Russell, 9 April, 7 May, 18 June 1872, FO 918/52; Odo Russell Papers.

31   R.B. Lyons to Granville, 12, 25 January, 9 February, 14 March, 6 April, 18 June 1872, box 109; Peter T. Marsh, *Bargaining on Europe: Britain and the First Common Market, 1860–1892* (New Haven, CT, 1999), 83, 59; R.B. Lyons to Granville, 12 April, 21, 25 June, 5 March, 16 August 1872, box 109.

32   R.B. Lyons to Granville, 6 August 1872, box 109; Vincent, *Derby Diaries*, 97; Hawkins and Powell, *Journal of John Wodehouse*, 269; R.B. Lyons to Granville, 13, 15, 16 February, 31 May 1872, box 109; Richard Shannon, *Gladstone*, vol. 2: *1865–1898* (Chapel Hill, NC, 1999), 113; Vincent, *Derby Diaries*, 87;

Paul Kennedy, *The Realities behind Diplomacy: Background Influences on British External Policy, 1865–1914* (Hamden, CT, 1964), 79.

33 Bickerton Lyons, pocket book, 1872, 20, 29 August, 11 September, 4, 10, 14 October, box 221; Granville to R.B. Lyons, 20 June 1872, box 182; R.B. Lyons to Long, 20 August 1872; R.B. Lyons to Hammond, 23, 24 August, 5 September 1872; R.B. Lyons to Granville, 9, 29 September, 3, 28 October 1872; R.B. Lyons to Kennedy, 11, 14 October, 5 November 1872, box 109; Kennedy to R.B. Lyons 4 November 1872; Kennedy memorandum, 4 February 1873, box 136.

34 Kennedy memorandum, 4 February 1873; H.A. Lee memorandum, 4 February 187[3], box 136; Mitchell, *German Influence on France after 1870*, 43; Marsh, *Bargaining on Europe*, 85.

35 Bickerton Lyons, pocket book, 1872, November and December; pocket book, 1873, January, February, March, box 221; *British Medical Journal*, 20 May 1882; R.B. Lyons to Granville, 3, 10 December 1872, 14 January 1873, box 103; also 31 January 1873, box 110; R.B. Lyons to Odo Russell, 25 February 1873, FO 918/52; Zeldin, *France*, 1:563; R.B. Lyons to Granville, 3 December 1872, 23 February, 4 March 1873, box 110.

36 R.B. Lyons to Odo Russell, 8 April, 14 March 1873, FO 918/52, Odo Russell Papers; Odo Russell to R.B. Lyons, 18 January 1873, box 197; Otte, *Foreign Office Mind*, 81; R.B. Lyons to Granville, 25 February 1873, box 103; also 18 March, box 110; also 4, 25, 29 March 1873, box 103.

37 R.B. Lyons to Odo Russell, 8 April 1873; Odo Russell to R.B. Lyons 5 May, FO 918/52, Odo Russell Papers; E. Neill Raymond, *Victorian Viceroy: The Life of Robert, the First Earl of Lytton* (London, 1980), 103; Otte, *Foreign Office Mind*, 73; R.B. Lyons to Granville, 25 February 1873, box 103; also 18 March, box 110; also 14, 25, 29 March, box 103; Lady Layard's Journal, 26 September 1873; Bickerton Lyons, pocket book, 1873, 11, 14 April, box 221; R.B. Lyons to Granville, 11 April 1873, box 103; also 8 April, FO 519/52; also 31 March, box 110; Bickerton Lyons, pocket book, 1873, April and May, box 221.

38 Grévy, *République des opportunistes*, 26–7; Lytton to R.B. Lyons, 17 May 1873, box 136; R.B. Lyons to Granville, 23, 25 May 1873, box 110; Brown, *For the Soul of France*, 43; Mayeur and Rebérioux, *Third Republic from Its Origins*, 18; Gildea, *Children of the Revolution*, 248; R.B. Lyons to Granville, 14 January, 27 May 1873, box 110; Lord Randolph Sutherland Gower, *Records and Reminiscences* (London, 1903), 238–40.

39 Zeldin, *France*, 1:563; Lister to R.B. Lyons, 30 May 1873, box 137; Brown, *For the Soul of France*, 44; R.B. Lyons to Granville, 26, 27 30 May, 17, 20,

24 June, 24, 25, 29 July 1873, box 110; Granville, to R.B. Lyons, 30 July 1873, box 182.

40   R.B. Lyons to Granville, 3 June 1873, box 103; Mayeur and Rebérioux, *Third Republic from Its Origins*, 19; R.B. Lyons to Granville, 28 November 1873, box 110; Conolly to R.B. Lyons, 24 August 1873, box 137; R.B. Lyons to Elliot, 13 June 1873, box 110; Lytton to R.B. Lyons, 24, 29 August 1873, box 137; Grévy, *République des opportunistes*, 27; R.B. Lyons to Granville, 17 June 1873, box 110.

41   R.B. Lyons to Granville, 8 August 1873, box 103; also 8, 26 August, box 110; R.B. Lyons to Lytton, 26 September 1873, box 110; Lytton to R.B. Lyons, 9 October 1873, box 138; Sheffield to R.B. Lyons, 18 October 1873, box 199; Granville to R.B. Lyons, 20 October 1873, box 182.

42   Mayeur and Rebérioux, *Third Republic from Its Origins*, 20–1; R.B. Lyons to Granville, 27, 28, 31 October, 3, 4, 11, 14, 21 November 1873, box 110; Brown, *Chambord*, 133–6, 148; Conolly to R.B. Lyons, 30 October 1873, box 138; Vincent, *Derby Diaries*, 148.

43   R.B. Lyons to Granville, 28 November, 30 August, 2 December 1873, box 110; Broglie, *Ambassador of the Vanquished*, 137–8; Vincent, *Derby Diaries*, 148–9; Bickerton Lyons, pocket book, 1873, 7 November, box 221; Wolfgang Schivelbusch, *The Culture of Defeat: On National Trauma, Mourning and Recovery*, trans. Jefferson Chase (New York, 2001), 118–19; Varley, *Under the Shadow of Defeat*, 25–6.

44   Granville to R.B. Lyons, 23 January 1874, box 182; R.B. Lyons to Granville, 30 December 1873, 6, 16, 22, 24 January 1874, box 104; Helmut Walser Smith, *German Nationalism and Religious Conflict: Culture, Ideology, Politics, 1870–1914* (Princeton, NJ, 1995), 20, 28, 40–3; Pakula, *Uncommon Woman*, 304–5; Kennedy to R.B. Lyons, "very confidential," 22 January 1874, box 139; Otte, *Foreign Office Mind*, 94; R.B. Lyons to Granville, 2, 11, 13, 17, 23, 32 January, 3, 6, 10 February 1874, box 110; Pakula, *Uncommon Woman*, 315.

CHAPTER FIFTEEN

1   Bickerton Lyons, pocket book, 1874, box 221; Ralph G. Martin, *Jennie: The Life of Lady Randolph Churchill*, 2 vols (Englewood Cliffs, NJ, 1969/1971), 1:90–1; Hoffman to R.B. Lyons, 17 April 1874, box 139; R.B. Lyons to Duke of Edinburgh, 27 December 1875, box 110; R.B. Lyons to Minna, 25 February, 11 March 1874, box 301; Liebreich to R.B. Lyons, 26 February 1874, box 139.

2   Odo Russell to R.B. Lyons, 20 February 1874, box 197; Steinberg, *Bismarck*, 327; Conolly to R.B. Lyons, 17 January 1874, box 130; Burrowes to R.B.

Lyons, 29 December 1873, box 138; R.B. Lyons to Minna, 7 January, 1 February, 11 March, 19 May 1874, box 301; R.B. Lyons to Odo Russell, 3, 24 February 1874, FO 918/52; Odo Russell to R.B. Lyons, 11 March 1874, box 197.

3 Robert Blake, *Disraeli* (New York, 1967), 543, 570–1, 574; Marvin Swartz, *The Politics of British Foreign Policy in the Era of Disraeli and Gladstone* (New York, 1985), 28–9; Derby to R.B. Lyons, 23, 27 February, 4 March 1874, box 180.

4 R.B. Lyons to Derby, 24 February 1874; 6 May [March], 27 March 1874, box 110.

5 Odo Russell to R.B. Lyons, 17 March 1874, box 197; R.B. Lyons to Derby, 3, 10, 17, 24 March 1874, box 110; R.B. Lyons to Derby, 3 April 1874, box 104.

6 Derby to R.B. Lyons, 25, 28 March, 7, 20 April 1874, box 180; R.B. Lyons to Derby, 17, 19, 22, 26 May 1874, box 110; 29 May 1874, box 104.

7 R.B. Lyons to Derby, 17, 21, 25 July, 18, 23 August 1874, box 110; Derby to R.B. Lyons, 27 August 1874, box 180.

8 R.B. Lyons to Lytton, 1, 9 October 1874, box 110; Bickerton Lyons, pocket book, 1874, box 221; R.B. Lyons to Minna, 7, 12, 17, 25, 27 29 November 1874, box 301; R.B. Lyons to Lytton, 16 November 1874, box 110; Duchess of Cleveland to R.B. Lyons, 11 March 1875, box 141; Sheffield to R.B. Lyons, 20 September, 15 October, 15 November 1874, box 199; Lytton to R.B. Lyons, 27 November 1874, box 140; Otte, *Foreign Office Mind*, 24, 123.

9 Bickerton Lyons, pocket book, 1874, box 221; R.B. Lyons to Derby, 4 December 1874, box 110; R.B. Lyons to Minna, 2, 6, 23 December 1874, 2, 7, 24 January 1875, box 301; R.B. Lyons to Elliot, 22 January 1875; R.B. Lyons to Layard, 8 December 1874; R.B. Lyons to Derby, 8, 26 January, 2, 5 February 1875, box 110; R.B. Lyons to Derby, 9 February 1875, box 104; Derby to R.B. Lyons, 30, 20 January 1875, box 180.

10 R.B. Lyons to Derby, 5 February 1875, box 110; Mitchell, *German Influence in France after 1870*, 111–12; Mayeur and Rebérioux, *Third Republic from Its Origins*, 23–5; R.B. Lyons to Derby, 19, 26 February, 9, 12, 14 March 1875, box 110; 26 February 1875, box 104; Zeldin, *France 1848–1945*, 1:572, 484; Derby to R.B. Lyons, 20 February 1875, box 180.

11 R.B. Lyons to Derby, 9 March 1875, box 110; 12 March 1875, box 104; 15 March 1875, box 110; Steinberg, *Bismarck*, 351; Mitchell, *German Influence in France after 1870*, 124–5; Vincent, *Derby Diaries*, 207, 200–1; R.B. Lyons to Derby, 16, 30 March 1875, box 110; Conolly to R.B. Lyons, 4 April 1875, box 141.

12 R.B. Lyons to Minna, 19, 24 March 1875, box 301; Peter Thorold, *The British in France: Visitors and Residents since the Revolution* (New York, 2008), 125; Newton, *Lyons*, 2:72–3; Vincent, *Derby Diaries*, 206; R.B. Lyons to Adams,

5 May 1875, box 110; Knollys to R.B. Lyons, 9 April 1875, box 141; R.B. Lyons to Adams, 21 April 1875, box 110; Cairns to R.B. Lyons, 19 April 1875, box 141; Pakula, *Uncommon Woman*, 310–11; R.B. Lyons to Adams, 8 May 1875, box 110; Adams to R.B. Lyons, 6 May 1875, box 173.

13   Vincent, *Derby Diaries*, 216–17; Urbach, *Bismarck's Favourite Englishman*, 139; Steinberg, *Bismarck*, 352; Newton, *Lyons*, 2:81; Marquis of Zetland, ed., *The Letters of Disraeli to Lady Chesterfield and Lady Bradford*, vol. 1: *1873–1875* (New York, 1939): 311; R.B. Lyons to Derby, 18, 4 May 1875, box 110; R.B. Lyons to Derby, 18 May 1875, box 104; Vincent, *Derby Diaries*, 218.

14   Otte, *Foreign Office Mind*, 153; R.B. Lyons to Carnarvon, 3, 28 September; R.B. Lyons to Sanderson, 18 September; R.B. Lyons to Adams, 3, 4, 27 August 1875, box 110; Blake, *Disraeli*, 571, 577–8; Kennedy, *Realities behind Diplomacy*, 80; Derby to R.B. Lyons, 13 March 1875, box 180; Vincent, *Derby Diaries*, 211; Howard, *Britain and the Casus Belli*, 101.

15   Vincent, *Derby Diaries*, 230, 234, 241; Derby to R.B. Lyons, 15, 22 August, 24 October 1875, box 180; Vincent, *Derby Diaries*, 246–7; R.B. Lyons to Elliot, 15 October; R.B. Lyons to Derby, 15 October 1875, box 110; Sheffield to R.B. Lyons, 6 November 1875, box 199.

16   Stanley Weintraub, *Disraeli: A Biography* (New York, 1997), 541–2; Vincent, *Derby Diaries*, 252–3; Derby to R.B. Lyons, 17, 19, 20 November 1875, box 180; R.B. Lyons to Derby, 19, 23, November 1875; R.B. Lyons to Elliot, 26 November 1875, box 110; Weintraub, *Disraeli*, 544; Vincent, *Derby Diaries*, 256–7.

17   R.B. Lyons to Derby, 30, 25 November 1875, box 104; R.B. Lyons to Derby 30 November; R.B. Lyons to Layard, 2 December 1875, box 110; Derby to R.B. Lyons, 1 December 1875, box 180; Newton, *Lyons*, 2:92–3.

18   Tenterden to R.B. Lyons, 25 November 1875, box 202; R.B. Lyons to Prince of Wales, 7, 17 December 1875, box 110; R.B. Lyons to Derby, 29 October 1875, box 104; R.B. Lyons to Derby, 11, 17, 19 December 1875, box 110.

19   R.B. Lyons to Derby, 1 February; R.B. Lyons to Layard, 2 February; R.B. Lyons to Derby, 22, 29 February, 7 March; R.B. Lyons to Prince of Wales, 7 March 1876, box 110; Mayeur and Rebérioux, *Third Republic from Its Origins*, 27; Brown, *For the Soul of France*, 50.

20   R.B. Lyons, confidential memorandum, 6 March; R.B. Lyons to Derby, 7, 10, 14, 17, 21 March 1875, box 110; Zeldin, *France 1848–1945*, 1:612–15, 621–3; Mayeur and Rebérioux, *Third Republic from Its Origins*, 27; Vincent, *Derby Diaries*, 280.

21   Vincent, *Derby Diaries*, 260, 263, 265–7, 269.

22   Derby to R.B. Lyons, 12, 7 January 1876, box 180; R.B. Lyons to Derby, 14

January 1876, box 110; Derby to R.B. Lyons, 15, 22 January 1876, box 180; Vincent, *Derby Diaries*, 265n4.

23 R.B. to Derby, 14 January 1876, box 110; Vincent, *Derby Diaries*, 266–8, 276; Pakula, *An Uncommon Woman*, 344; Derby to R.B. Lyons, 7 January 1876, box 180; Howard, *Britain and the Casus Belli*, 101.

24 Bickerton Lyons, pocket book, 1876, box 221; R.B. Lyons to Tenterden, 14 April; to Derby, 22, 24 April 1876, box 110; Adams to R.B. Lyons, 14 May 1876, box 173; Lady Malet to R.B. Lyons, 14 May 1876, box 144; R.B. Lyons to Prince of Wales, 7 July 1876, box 110.

25 Sheffield to R.B. Lyons, 2 February 1876, box 199; Vincent, *Derby Diaries*, 279, 284, 293, 296, 299–301; Swartz, *Politics of British Foreign Policy*, 5, 20; Derby to R.B. Lyons, 7 June, 16 August 1876, box 180; Zetland, *Letters of Disraeli*, 2:65, 91, 94; Lady Layard's Journal, 15 May 1877; Andrew Roberts, *Salisbury: Victorian Titan* (London, 2000), 160.

26 Blake, *Disraeli*, 592–5; H.C.G. Matthew, *Gladstone 1875–1898* (Oxford, 1995), 18–21, 31; Steinberg, *Bismarck*, 353; Derby to R.B. Lyons, 6, 9 September 1876, box 180; Otte, *Foreign Office Mind*, 108; R.B. Lyons to Elliot, 4 August, 1 September 1876, box 110.

27 Bickerton Lyons, pocket book, 1876, box 221; R.B. Lyons to Derby, 30 June, 4, 9 August, 26 September, 3, 31 October 1876, box 110; Vincent, *Derby Diaries*, 332.

28 R.B. Lyons to Derby, 12, 15 December 1876, box 110; Vincent, *Derby Diaries*, 339–40; Zetland, *Letters of Disraeli*, 2:108–11; Roberts, *Salisbury*, 155, 152–3, 157; R.B. Lyons to Layard, 1 November, 1 December 1876; R.B. Lyons to Salisbury, 16 November; R.B. Lyons to Derby, 21 November 1876, 9 January 1877, box 110.

29 Vincent, *Derby Diaries*, 348, 365; R.B. Lyons to Derby, 12 October, 17 November, 8 December 1876, 25 January, 26 April, 7 May 1877, box 110; 8, 9, 13 May, 26 June, 6 July 1877, box 104.

30 R.B. Lyons to Derby, 7 May 1877; R.B. Lyons to Faner, 12 May 1877, box 110; Mayer and Rebérioux, *Third Republic from Its Origins*, 28–9; Broglie, *Ambassador of the Vanquished*, 269; R.B. Lyons to Derby, 16, 19, 25 May; R.B. Lyons to Layard, 18 May 1877, box 110.

31 Vincent, *Derby Diaries*, 401; R.B. Lyons to Derby, 18, 19, 24, 25 May, 8, 29 June 1877, box 110; Newton, *Lyons*, 2:109–11, 113.

32 Vincent, *Derby Diaries*, 428; R.B. Lyons to Adams, 22 July, 5 August; R.B. Lyons to Derby, 27 July 1877, box 110; 26 June, 6 July, "very confidential," 10 July, "secret," box 104; R.B. Lyons to Layard, 29 June, 6, 13, 15 July 1877, BL Add. 39013, Layard Papers.

33 Bickerton Lyons, pocket book, 1877, box 221; R.B. Lyons to Adams, 27 August, 17 September 1877, box 146; Sheffield to R.B. Lyons, 19 August 1877, box 199; R.B. Lyons to Derby, 12 September 1877, box 110; Zetland, *Letters of Disraeli*, 2: 177, 182; Steinberg, *Bismarck*, 174; Vincent, *Derby Diaries*, 440.

34 Adams to R.B. Lyons, 29 August, 25, 27, 28 September, 9, 17 October 1877, box 173; R.B. Lyons to Derby, 23,26 October, 15, 16, 20, 27, 29 November, 4, 7, 12, 18 December 1877, R.B. Lyons to Layard, 7, 14 December 1877, box 110; Mayer and Rebérioux, *Third Republic from Its Origins*, 30–1.

35 R.B. Lyons to Layard, 7 December, R.B. Lyons to Carnarvon, 29 November 1877, box 110; Bickerton Lyons, pocket book, 1877, box 221; R.B. Lyons to Mitford, 13 December 1877, 28 January 1878; R.B. Lyons to Derby, 14 December 1877, box 110; 12 February 1878, "secret," box 104; Agatha Ramm, ed., *The Political Correspondence of Mr Gladstone and Lord Granville, 1876–1886*, 2 vols (Oxford, 1962), 1:663; Beckles Wilson, *The Paris Embassy: A Narrative of Franco-British Diplomatic Relations, 1814–1920* (New York, 1927), 246.

36 R.B. Lyons to Layard 21 December 1877, 11 January 1878; R.B. Lyons to Derby, 24 December 1877, 23 January 1878, box 110; 27 December 1877, 1 January, 12 February 1878, box 104; R.B. Lyons to Layard, 18 January1878, BL Add. Ms. 39017, Layard Papers; 8 February, 1878, box 104; Adams to R.B.Lyons, 19, 21, 28 December 1877, box 173; Vincent, *Derby Diaries*, 474–5; Derby to R.B. Lyons, 21 December 1877, box 180; Zetland, *Letters of Disraeli*, 2: 201–4.

37 Blake, *Disraeli*, 638–9; Vincent, *Derby Diaries*, 499, 501, 512; Derby to R, B, Lyons, 2, 6 February 1878, box 180; Layard to R.B. Lyons, 15 February 1878, box 149; R.B. Lyons to Derby, 8, 22, 23, 26 February 1878, box 110.

38 Conolly to R.B. Lyons, 5 March; Feilding to R.B. Lyons, 5 March; Elliot to R.B. Lyons, 8, 19 March 1878; R.B. Lyons to Tenterden, 27 February, 1 March 1878, box 110; Lyons memorandum, box 151; Nancy E. Johnson, ed., *The Diary of Gathorne Hardy later Lord Cranbrook, 1866–1892: Political Selections* (Oxford, 1981), 360; Cowell to R.B. Lyons, 12 March 1878, box 149; Vincent, *Derby Diaries*, 530–1; R.A.J. Walling, ed., *The Diaries of John Bright* (London, 1930), 407; Blake, *Disraeli*, 640; Vincent, *Derby Diaries*, 532, 534.

39 Roberts, *Salisbury*, 187,190; Vincent, *Derby Diaries*, 522–3; Salisbury to R.B. Lyons, 6 March 1879, box 198; Swartz, *Politics of Foreign Policy*, 86–7; Newton, *Lyons*, 2:144; Salisbury to R.B. Lyons, 5 June 1878, box 198; R.B. Lyons to Russell, 16 March 1878, box 110; Roberts, *Salisbury*, 192–3; Otte, *Foreign Office Mind*, 122, 124; Salisbury to R.B. Lyons, 29 May 1878, box 198.

40 R.B. Lyons to Salisbury, "secret," 6 August 1878, box 104; 16 July 1878, box 111; Blaze de Bury to R.B. Lyons, 15 May 1878, box 149; Layard to R.B. Lyons, 18 October 1878, box 190; R.B. Lyons to Salisbury, 21 July 1878, box 111; Adams to R.B. Lyons, 18 September 1878, box 173; R.B. Lyons to Salisbury, 16 July, 4 June, 6 October 1878, box 111.

41 R.B. Lyons to Salisbury, 21 July 1878, box 111; Weintraub, *Edward the Caresser*, 252; R.B. Lyons to Salisbury, 9 August; R.B. Lyons to Adams, 21 August, 4, 12, 15, 17, 20 September 1878; R.B. Lyons to Salisbury, 1 October 1878, box 111; Swartz, *Politics of Foreign Policy*, 127; Salisbury to R.B. Lyons, 5 October 1878, box 198; R.B. Lyons to Salisbury, 11, 26 October, 22 November 1878, 3 January 1879, box 111.

42 Mayeur and Rebérioux, *Third Republic from Its Origins*, 34, 36; Brown, *For the Soul of France*, 54; R.B. Lyons to Salisbury, 7, 14, 16, 19, 28, 30, 31 January, 4, 5, 18 February, 4, 14, 11 March, 17 June 1879, box 111.

43 Salisbury to R.B. Lyons, 4, 13 January; R.B. Lyons to Salisbury, 7, 11 February; Salisbury to R.B. Lyons, 12 February, 1, 6 March 1879, box 198; R.B. Lyons to Layard, 20 June, 4 July; R.B. Lyons to Salisbury, 20 June 1879, box 111; Salisbury to R.B. Lyons, 10 July 1879, box 198.

44 Salisbury to R.B. Lyons, 10, 24 April, 6 June 1879, box 198; C.J. Lowe, *The Reluctant Imperialists: British Foreign Policy, 1878–1902*, 2 vols (London, 1967), 1:40–2; Roberts, *Salisbury*, 228–9; Salisbury to R.B. Lyons, 7, 15 July 1879, box 198.

45 R.B. Lyons to Salisbury, 20, 29 May, 10 June, 30 July, 1 August 1879, box 111.

46 Knollys to R.B. Lyons, 29 January, 21 March 1879; Ponsonby to R.B. Lyons, 10 February, 21, 24, 31 March, 31 May, box 165; Mitford to R.B. Lyons, 1 March 1879, box 151; R.B. Lyons to Salisbury, 25 February; R.B. Lyons to Tenterden, 2 May 1879, box 111; Salisbury to R.B. Lyons, 7 May 1879, box 198; Haia Shpayer-Makov, *The Ascent of the Detective: Police Sleuths in Victorian and Edwardian England* (Oxford, 2011), 65.

CHAPTER SIXTEEN

1 Ramm, *Political Correspondence of Gladstone and Granville 1876–1886*, 2:236, 33–4; R.B. Lyons to Rumbold, 18 January 1880, box 153; R.B. Lyons to Currie, 16 August 1880; Paget to R.B. Lyons, 29 September 1881, box 154; Minna to R.B. Lyons, 26 November 1879, box 296; Sarah Eron, "Coventry Patmore's Marriage to Marianne Caroline Byles, 1864–1880, and the Heron's Ghyll Estate," *The Victorian Web: Literature, History and Culture in the Age of Victoria*, www.victorianweb.org.; R.B. Lyons to

Granville, 10 September 1880, box 154; Sheffield to R.B. Lyons, 27 August 1879, box 199.

2 Weintraub, *Disraeli*, 599; K. Theodore Hoppen, *The Mid-Victorian Generation, 1846–1886* (Oxford, 1998), 630–1; Howard, *Britain and the Casus Belli*, 120; Matthew, *Gladstone 1875–1898*, 123, 23; Hawkins and Powell, *Journal of John Wodehouse*, 315; Shannon, *Gladstone: God and Politics*, 317.

3 Lister to R.B. Lyons, 13 April; Malet to R.B. Lyons, 19 April; Granville to R.B. Lyons, 1 May; R.B. Lyons to Adams, 8 May 1880, box 153.

4 David Nicholls, *The Lost Prime Minister: A Life of Sir Charles Dilke* (London, 1995), 95–6; Granville to R.B. Lyons, 2, 3, 9 June 1880, box 153.

5 Otte, *Foreign Office Mind*, 136; R.B. Lyons to Granville, 23 January 1883, "secret," box 104; 17 June 1881, 20 January 1885, box 112; Rosebery to R.B. Lyons, 19 May 1886, box 168; Granville to R.B. Lyons, 22 June 1881, box 156; 2 May 1883, box 160; Brackenbury to R.B. Lyons, 25 August 1886, box 168.

6 R.B. Lyons to Granville, 22 March, 8, 13 May 1881; 12 June, 13 April 1883, box 112; Granville to R.B. Lyons, 3 July 1883, box 160; Malet to R.B. Lyons 17 August 1880, box 154; Granville to R.B. Lyons, 30 September 1882, box 160; R.B. Lyons to Granville, 24 October, 23 November 1882, box 112.

7 Gladstone to Dilke, 11 May 1881, box 153; Dilke to R.B. Lyons, 26 January 1882, box 158; Ramm, *Political Correspondence of Gladstone and Granville 1876–1886*, 1:132; Marsh, *Bargaining on Europe*, 132; R.B. Lyons to Dilke, 8, 10 May, 14, 24, 26 June; Dilke to R.B. Lyons, 24 June 1881, BL Add. Ms. 43,883, Dilke Papers; R.B. Lyons to Dilke, 29 January 1882, box 112.

8 Marsh, *Bargaining on Europe*, 121, 129, 141–2, 144–6; see also Nicholls, *Lost Prime Minister*, 95–8; R.B. Lyons to Granville, 3 January 1882, box 104; R.B. Lyons to Dilke, 1 March, 21 February 1882, BL Add. Ms. 43,883; Dilke Papers, Dilke to R.B. Lyons, 2, 9 March 1882, box 158; R.B. Lyons to Dilke, 3 March 1882, BL Add. Ms. 43,883.

9 Ramm, *Political Correspondence of Gladstone and Granville 1876–1886*, 1:30; Adams to R.B. Lyons, 12 October; Malet to R.B. Lyons, 11, 14 November 1881, box 157; Granville to R.B. Lyons, 17 January; Sheffield to R.B. Lyons, 21 January 1882, box 158.

10 R.B. Lyons to Granville, 1 November 1881, 19 January 1882, box 112; Ramm, *Political Correspondence of Gladstone and Granville 1876–1886*, 1:334–5; Otte, *Foreign Office Mind*, 137; R.B. Lyons to Granville, 21, 30 April, 2 May 1882, box 112.

11 Granville to R.B. Lyons, 22 June 1882, box 159; Hawkins and Powell, *Journal of John Wodehouse*, 328; Colvin to R.B. Lyons, 26 June 1882, box 159; Nicholls, *Lost Prime Minister*, 101–2; Granville to R.B. Lyons, 28 June; R.B.

Lyons to Hervey, 24 July 1882, box 159; R.B. Lyons to Granville, 7 July 1882, box 112; Swartz, *Politics of British Foreign Policy*, 135–40; R.B. Lyons to Granville, 1 August 1882, box 104.

12 R.B. Lyons to Granville, 7, 14 November 1882, box 112; Nicholls, *Lost Prime Minister*, 103–4; R.B. Lyons to Granville, 23 January, 5 June 1883, box 104; R.B. Lyons to Plunket, 27 July 1883, box 112; Matthew, *Gladstone 1875–1898*, 139–40; Hawkins and Powell, *Journal of John Wodehouse*, 344.

13 R.B. Lyons to Granville, 20 January 1885, box 112; Matthew, *Gladstone 1875–1898*, 141; Nicholls, *Lost Prime Minister*, 163; R.B. Lyons to Granville, 20 March 1885, box 112; Salisbury to R.B. Lyons, 20 July 1887, box 171.

14 Shannon, *Gladstone*, 2:260–1; Tenterden to R.B. Lyons, 19 November 1880, box 154; R.B. Lyons to Granville, 12, 13, 15 February; Granville to R.B. Lyons, 18 February; R.B. Lyons to Granville, 19 February; Dilke to R.B. Lyons 21 February 1881, box 155; Nicholls, *Lost Prime Minister*, 107.

15 Shannon, *Gladstone*, 2:294–98; Brackenbury to R.B. Lyons, 7, 19 May 1882, box 159.

16 R.B. Lyons to Prince of Wales, 5 February 1883, box 161; Lee to R.B. Lyons, 21 May; Pauncefote to R.B. Lyons, 22 May 1884, box 163; Knollys to R.B. Lyons, 13 February 1885, box 165; R.B. Lyons to Knollys, 19 February 1886, box 112; R.B. Lyons to Granville, 25 December 1883, box 162; Walsham to R.B. Lyons, 18, 21 August 1885, box 166; Granville to R.B. Lyons, 28 December 1883, box 162; Ramm, *Political Correspondence of Gladstone and Granville 1876–1886*, 2:140.

17 *Freeman's Journal*, 1 January 1884; R.B. Lyons to Queen, 4 June 1885, box 112; Ponsonby to R.B. Lyons, 22 March; R.B. Lyons to Ponsonby, 16 April 1883, box 161; Ponsonby to R.B. Lyons, 29 February; R.B. Lyons to Ponsonby, 4 March 1884, box 163.

18 R.B. Lyons to Granville, 3 November, 1 December 1882, 20 March, 16 November 1883, 29 January 1884, box 112; Brown, *For the Soul of France*, 61, 71; Mayeur and Rebérioux, *Third Republic from Its Origins*, 46, 62.

19 R.B. Lyons to Granville, 23 January 1883, "secret," box 104; Newton, *Lyons*, 2:305; Mayeur and Rebérioux, *Third Republic from Its Origins*, 80, 84; Brown, *For the Soul of France*, 54–5.

20 R.B. Lyons to Granville, 22 January 1882, box 112; Adams to R.B. Lyons, 21 August 1880, box 154; R.B. Lyons to Granville, 25 May 1880, box 112; 3 January 1882, box 104; 15 November 1881, 27 January, 28 July, 2 October 1882, 29, 30, 31 January, 2, 6, 13, 16 February 1883, 31 March 1885, box 104; Ramm, *Political Correspondence of Gladstone and Granville 1876–1886*, 2:354; R.B. Lyons to Iddesleigh, 10, 14, 21 December 1886, box 112; R.B. Lyons to Salisbury 31 May 1887, box 104.

21 Granville to R.B. Lyons, 8 November 1882, box 160; 12 March 1884, box 183; H.C.G. Matthew and Brian Harrison, *Oxford Dictionary of National Biography* (Oxford, 2004), 23:114; Diamond, *Victorian Sensation*, 129–31; Gordon Martel, *Imperial Diplomacy: Rosebery and the Failure of Foreign Policy* (London, 1986), 22; Granville to R.B. Lyons, 12 March 1884, box 183; Rosebery to R.B. Lyons, 27 February 1886, box 167; Salisbury to R.B. Lyons, 5 February 1887, box 170; Bryce to R.B. Lyons, 15 July 1886, box 169; R.B. Lyons to Granville, 11 May 1883, box 112; Ramm, *Political Correspondence of Gladstone and Granville, 1876–1886*, 1:19.

22 Mayeur and Rebérioux, *Third Republic from Its Origins*, 126–7; Brown, *For the Soul of France*, 82–95; R.B. Lyons to Rosebery, 6 April, 28 May, 2, 16 July 1886, box 112.

23 R.B. Lyons to Iddesleigh, 28 December 1886, box 104; Brown, *For the Soul of France*, 96–102; Steinberg, *Bismarck*, 420–3; R.B. Lyons to Salisbury, 14 January, 15 February, 19 April 1887, box 104; 16, 21, 24 January, 4, 8, 22 February, 17, 20, 31 May 1887, box 112; Lyons memorandum, 23 January 1887, box 170; John Fisher and Antony Best, eds, *On the Fringes of Diplomacy: Influences on British Foreign Policy, 1800–1945* (Burlington, VT, 2011), 53–80; Roberts, *Salisbury*, 438–9; Varley, *Under the Shadow of Defeat*, 49.

24 R.B. Lyons to Granville, 27 January, 3 February 1885, box 181; Egerton to R.B. Lyons, 18 November 1887, box 171; Ramm, *Political Correspondence of Gladstone and Granville, 1876–1886*, 2:238, 240, 314; Newton, *Lyons*, 2:359; Brown, *For the Soul of France*, 99, 104; Granville to R.B. Lyons, 9 October 1881; Varley, *Under the Shadow of Defeat*, 48.

25 Gladstone to R.B. Lyons, 22 October 1881, box 157; Lytton to Paget, 2 March 1883, BL Add. Ms. 51,231, Paget Papers; Granville to R.B. Lyons, 18 October 1884; R.B. Lyons to Granville, 21 October, 12, 17 November 1884, box 181.

26 Salisbury to R.B. Lyons, 26 July; Trower to R.B. Lyons, 27 July 1886, box 168.

27 R.B. Lyons to Salisbury, 27 July 1886, box 112; Rosebery to R.B. Lyons, 10 August 1886, box 168; Barton Smith to R.B. Lyons, 8, 9, 10 April 1886, box 167; Minna to R.B. Lyons, 22, 23, 31 October, 5 November 1885, 17 February 1886, box 297; R.B. Lyons to Walsham, 4 January; to Salisbury, 14 January 1886, box 112; R.B. Lyons to Rosebery, 23 March, 6 April 1886, box 167; Egerton to R.B. Lyons, n.d. [18 August 1886], box 168.

28 Trower to R.B. Lyons, 24 April 1886, box 167; Herbert to R.B. Lyons, 15 September 1887, box 181; Hankey to R.B. Lyons, 4, 13 May 1886; Sheffield to R.B. Lyons, 2, 19 July, 29 August 1886, box 168; 2 November 1886, box 169; Hankey to R.B. Lyons, 2, 21 February 1887, box 170.

29 R.B. Lyons to Salisbury, 22, 29 March; Salisbury to R.B. Lyons, 26 March,

19 October 1887, box 172; R.B. Lyons to Salisbury, 1 November; to Atlee, 17 November 1887; Egerton to R.B. Lyons, 20 November 1887, box 112.

30 See the report of the Press Cutting Agency, box 172; *Lloyd's Weekly Newspaper*, 12 December 1887; *The Times*, 6 December 1887; Jones, *British Diplomatic Service*, 117, 126.

31 Otte, *Foreign Office Mind*, 12.

32 Otte, *Foreign Office Mind*, 25; Douglas Busk, *The Craft of Diplomacy: Mechanics and Development of National Representation Overseas* (London, 1967), 38; Lord Strang, *The Foreign Office* (London, 1955), 187.

33 Jones, *British Diplomatic Service*, 31; Strang, *Foreign Office*, 91.

34 Otte, *Foreign Office Mind*, 155–6; *London Standard*, 6 December 1887.

35 *Daily News*, 6 December 1887.

36 Otte, *Foreign Office Mind*, 26.

37 Jones, *British Diplomatic Service*, 127.

38 *Lloyd's Weekly Newspaper*, 12 December 1887.

39 *Derby Mercury*, 7 December 1887; *Huddersfield Chronicle*, 12 December 1887; *Pall Mall Gazette*, 15 December 1887; *Morning Post*, 19 December 1887; *Manchester Courier and Lancashire General Advertiser*, 21 December 1887; *Belfast News-Letter*, 8 January 1888.

40 Cairns, "Lord Lyons and Anglo-American Diplomacy," 380; Diamond, *Victorian Sensation*, 83; Hammond to R.B. Lyons, 11 November 1887, box 189; *Lancaster Gazette*, 7 December 1887; *Daily News*, 6 December 1887; *Sheffield Independent*, 6 December 1887; *Liverpool Mercury*, 6 December 1887; *Manchester Evening News*, 9 December 1887; *Morning Post*, 11 December 1887; *Parl. Deb., 3rd series*, vol. 322 (London, 1888), 24.

Index

Confederacy or mediation, 207;
on dealing with Americans, 92–3;
distrust of France, 79; doubts
Union acceptance of armistice,
214; as foreign secretary, 46–7,
68, 70–1, 80, 84, 254; and non-intervention, 74; return to Foreign
Office opposed by Disraeli, 272
Malta, 21, 23–6, 37
Mason, James Murray, 121, 229; as
chairman of Senate Foreign Relations Committee, 89, 121; as Confederate commissioner to Britain,
175, 178, 180, 183, 188, 205
Mazzini, Giuseppe, 49, 54, 65, 70–1
Mehemet Ali, viceroy of Egypt, 20,
25, 422
Mercier, Henri, 48, 111, 168, 178, 183;
as ambassador to Spain, 309;
angers Lyons, 193–4; and Anglo-
French mediation, 207, 209, 219;
as French minister to United
States, 123, 144, 148, 160, 165,
235; impulsiveness, 152, 159, 195;
Southern sympathies of, 159, 166,
194; visit to Richmond, 193–4
Mexico, 93, 100, 112–13, 116, 145; British policy towards, 116–18, 171;
European intervention in, 171–2
Milne, Sir Alexander, 152, 156,
162, 166, 180, 182, 184; anger at
conduct of American captains,
226–7; visit to Washington, 233–4
Monck, Lord, 234, 236–7; entertains Lyons, 232, 240, 242; as
governor general of Canada, 178;
welcomes no change in British
policy, 214
Monson, Edmund, 108, 163, 299;

in Britain, 121; desires to enter
Parliament, 230; as private secretary to Lyons, 13, 91; searches for
French cook, 110; takes post in
Foreign Office, 373; urges Lyons
to marry, 286; takes post in the
Foreign Office, 373; visits Confederacy, 139–40
Montgomery (AL), 132, 135
Montpensier, Duc de, 309, 310, 337;
candidate for Spanish throne, 337
Moore, George: consul at Ancona,
65; consul at Richmond, VA, 119,
129, 132, 138, 147, 228
Moustier, Léonel Marquis de, 277,
284, 307; disliked by diplomats,
262; as foreign minister, 299–301,
303, 309; dismissed, 311; as French
ambassador to Sublime Porte,
262–3, 266–8; 274; Lyons's success
in working with, 262, 277; suspicion of Bismarck, 309

Napier, Lord, 92, 135, 140, 215, 240;
advice to Lyons, 92–3; conduct
criticized, 86–7, 92; early career
of, 85; as minister to United
States, 85–6; removal of, 88–9
Naples, 72, 74–5, 79–80; British hostility to government of, 70
Napoleon III, 112, 274–5; adopts
more liberal regime, 291, 305, 308,
323–4, 326–7; and American Civil
War, 160; attempted assassination of, 69; attempted purchase of
Luxembourg, 282–3; and Belgian
railways, 315, 317–19; British
suspicion of, 97, 165, 193, 211;
collapse of regime, 344–5, 348–9;